Human Rights and Personal Self-Defense in International Law

Human Rights and Personal Self-Defense in International Law

Jan Arno Hessbruegge

OXFORD
UNIVERSITY PRESS

OXFORD
UNIVERSITY PRESS

Oxford University Press is a department of the University of Oxford. It furthers the University's objective of excellence in research, scholarship, and education by publishing worldwide. Oxford is a registered trademark of Oxford University Press in the UK and certain other countries.

Published in the United States of America by Oxford University Press
198 Madison Avenue, New York, NY 10016, United States of America.

First Edition published in 2017

Library of Congress Cataloging-in-Publication Data

Names: Hessbruegge, Jan Arno, author.
Title: Human rights and personal self-defense in international law / Jan Arno Hessbruegge.
Description: First edition | New York, NY : Oxford University Press, 2017. | Based on author's thesis (doctoral—European University Viadrina in Frankfurt (Oder), Germany, 2016) issued under title: The right to personal self-defence as a general principle of law and its general application in international human rights law. | Includes bibliographical references and index.
Identifiers: LCCN 2016026173 | ISBN 9780190655020 ((hardback) : alk. paper)
Subjects: LCSH: Self-defense (Law) | International law and human rights.
Classification: LCC K5087.S4 H47 2017 | DDC 345/.04—dc23 LC record available at https://lccn.loc.gov/2016026173

Note to Readers
This publication is designed to provide accurate and authoritative information in regard to the subject matter covered. It is based upon sources believed to be accurate and reliable and is intended to be current as of the time it was written. It is sold with the understanding that the publisher is not engaged in rendering legal, accounting, or other professional services. If legal advice or other expert assistance is required, the services of a competent professional person should be sought. Also, to confirm that the information has not been affected or changed by recent developments, traditional legal research techniques should be used, including checking primary sources where appropriate.

(Based on the Declaration of Principles jointly adopted by a Committee of the American Bar Association and a Committee of Publishers and Associations.)

to Angie

CONTENTS

ACKNOWLEDGMENTS

This book is based on my doctoral dissertation on "The right to personal self-defence as a general principle of law and its general application in international human rights law," which was accepted by the Law Faculty of European University Viadrina in Frankfurt (Oder), Germany. I am deeply grateful to my thesis advisor, Professor Wolff Heintschel von Heinegg. I was persuaded that it was a good idea to start a doctorate and a family at the same time by his advice that "one is never too old to write a doctoral dissertation." His wise guidance throughout the process, along with the swift second review by Professor Carmen Thiele, ensured that I completed my doctorate before actually becoming old.

I am also thankful to Mona Rishmawi, Nathalie Prouvez and Francesca Marotta at the Office of the United Nations High Commissioner for Human Rights (OHCHR), who always encouraged me to maintain an academic outlook to complement my work. This book was written during a leave of absence from OHCHR, which I spent at the wonderful U.N.-mandated University for Peace in Costa Rica. I am indebted to Rector Francisco Rojas and Dean Juan Carlos Sainz-Borgo for hosting me as a visiting scholar and professor at UPEACE. All views expressed in this book remain solely my own and do not necessarily reflect those of the United Nations.

Ideas and critical reflection on human rights and self-defense were inspired by exchanges I had with my UPEACE colleagues Jessica Lawrence, Mihir Kanade, Juan Amaya Castro, Swee-Hin Toh, Natacha John and Ross Ryan, with Paul Oertly at the U.N., with David Hemenway of Harvard University, and with Stuart Casey-Maslen of the University of Pretoria. My "reader-in-chief," Naresh Perinpanayagam, infused common sense and perspective into my thinking. At Oxford University Press, the sound advice of Blake Ratcliff and Alden Domizio ensured that what started as a humble thesis became the best book it could be.

I cannot end without thanking Monica Fronius and Rolf Heßbrügge for always encouraging me to write the doctoral dissertation that my late father Bernd Heßbrügge could never finish. In their own ways, my toddlers Amaya and William Hessbruegge also contributed. Their interactions gave me ample opportunity to reflect on why the natural instinct to defend oneself, and one's treasured toys, must be subject to reasonable restraint; otherwise mayhem will prevail.

Finally, and most importantly, I am immensely grateful to my universally gifted wife and best friend, Angie Brice Hessbruegge. Her boundless optimism that anything can be done convinced me to write this book. Her unwavering support ensured that I finished it.

1

Introduction

Self-defense is rooted in the instinct of self-preservation. The great Roman orator and jurist Cicero made the case thus:

> This, therefore, is a law, O judges, not written, but born with us,—which we have not learnt or received by tradition, or read, but which we have taken and sucked in and imbibed from nature herself; a law which we were not taught but to which we were made,—which we were not trained in, but which is ingrained in us,—namely, that if our life be in danger from plots, or from open violence, or from the weapons of robbers or enemies, every means of securing our safety is honorable.
>
> For laws are silent when arms are raised, and do not expect themselves to be waited for, when he who waits will have to suffer an undeserved penalty before he can exact a merited punishment.[1]

This potent, primordial and pre-legal instinct is a legacy from the Hobbesian anarchical state of nature when human beings lived in "continual fear, and danger of violent death" and life was "solitary, poor, nasty, brutish, and short."[2] Contrary to Cicero's assertion, however, the laws have never been silent on the exercise of self-defense. Legislators everywhere and at all times have used the law to address the conundrum of recognizing the legitimate human instinct to repel violence with violence while containing the potentially anarchical forces of violent self-help that are anathema to a centralized monopoly on the use of force and the rule of law grounded therein.

1. Marcus Tullius Cicero, For T.A. Milo, in: C.D. Yonge (trans.), The Orations of Marcus Tullius Cicero, vol. 3, Henry G. Bohn: London (1852), 390–437, at p. 394 [Mil. IV]. This segment of Cicero's defense of his client Milo against murder charges has been described as the "fountainhead of this whole tradition of self-defence as a natural right." See Peter Haggenmacher, Self-defence as a general principle of law and its relation to war, in: Arthur Eyffinger, Alan Stephens & Sam Muller (eds.), Self-Defence as a Fundamental Principle, T.M.C. Asser Press: The Hague (2009), pp. 3–38, at p. 5.

2. Thomas Hobbes, Leviathan [1651] (ed. J.C.A. Gaskin), Oxford University Press: Oxford/ New York (1998), p. 84 [Ch. XIII.9].

Human Rights and Personal Self-Defense in International Law. Jan Arno Hessbruegge

In relations among states, international law seeks to resolve this conundrum by recognizing the inherent right of states to defend themselves against armed external aggression, while imposing tight limits on the exercise of this right. Article 51 of the Charter of the United Nations (U.N. Charter) recognizes the inherent right of individual or collective self-defense in the event of such an attack and until the Security Council has taken measures to maintain international peace and security. This marks the sole explicit exception to the prohibition of the unilateral use of force in international relations established by Article 2(4) of the U.N. Charter.

As they sought to impose limits on states' prerogative to wage war, the early writers on international law readily conceived states' right to defend their sovereignty and territory against external aggression (interstate self-defense) as one instance of just war. They supported this position by drawing an analogy to individuals' right to defend their life and physical integrity against unlawful attacks (personal self-defense).[3] For instance, the eminent international law scholar Alberico Gentili (1552–1608) reasoned in his treatise, *De Jure Belli*:

> For to kill in self-defense is just, even though the one who kills may flee without danger and so save himself; and regardless of the question whether the one who slays in self-defense is in such a condition that it would be disgraceful for him to flee, or not disgraceful. These views have been admitted for private individuals and I consider them still more valid with regard to states.[4]

These early writers on international law had no difficulty in reasoning by analogy since they regarded "private war" (violence between individuals) and "public war" (violence between sovereigns) as forming a continuum, rather than as separate categories. Accordingly, they also wrote extensively on the nature and scope of personal self-defense. However, as the notion of "private war" faded away and war became the exclusive domain of sovereigns, international lawyers focused

3. Yoram Dinstein, War, Aggression and Self-Defence, Cambridge University Press: New York (5th ed., 2011), p. 88 [para. 497]. See also Haggenmacher, *supra* note 1, p. 15.

4. Alberico Gentili, De Iure Belli Tres Libri, Vol. II: The Translation of the Edition of 1612 (John C. Rolfe, trans.) Clarendon Press: Oxford (1933), p. 58 [Book I Ch. XIII.94]. Later writers also employed such reasoning. In the famous exchanges on the Caroline self-defense incidents, Lord Aberdeen, the British Secretary of State for Foreign Affairs, professed that he could not determine to what extent a plea to self-defense "may find a place in the Law of Nations." However, Aberdeen reasoned, self-defense "is the first Law of our nature; and it must be recognized by every Code which professes to govern the condition and relations of Man." See Note of Lord Aberdeen, British Secretary of State for Foreign Affairs, to Lord Ashburton, British Special Envoy to the United States, 9 February 1842, as cited in: Lord McNair (ed.), International Law Opinions, Vol. 2: Peace, Cambridge University Press: Cambridge (1956), at p. 222.

on interstate self-defense. Personal self-defense seemingly became relegated to a matter of domestic criminal law only.[5]

A closer look reveals, however, that the right of personal self-defense never vanished from the realm of international law. It has remained there as a general principle of law recognized by nations, hidden in the shadows of the more prominent right of interstate self-defense.

This book is about that right to personal self-defense: how it shapes international human rights law, and how it is shaped by human rights.

A. SUMMARY OF THE ARGUMENT

The analysis proceeds from the thesis that the right to personal self-defense constitutes a general principle recognized by nations under international law. It is a general principle because it can be found in the natural law concepts of the world's major religious, philosophical, and cultural traditions and is consequently shared by all the world's major legal systems (see Second Chapter).

The right to personal self-defense operates in different areas of international law. However, it has its deepest impact in the area of international law most concerned with the status of individual human beings: international human rights law. This is not to say that the right to personal self-defense is actually a human right in and of itself. It is not a human right, but an individual right sui generis, since it distinguishes itself from human rights in its social and political functions (see Third Chapter). Yet, the right to personal self-defense interacts with international human rights law on three levels:

- the state-to-individual level (top-down relationship);
- the individual-to-individual level (horizontal relationship); and
- the individual-to-state level (bottom-up relationship).

Within tightly delineated boundaries, the right to defend oneself and others from unlawful violence justifies a state's infringement of the most basic human rights. Notably, it marks the sole case where law enforcement agents may, intentionally and without judicial sentence, kill in times of peace. Although international humanitarian law usually prevails in situations of armed conflict, use of lethal force by the military may exceptionally also come to be assessed by the more exacting standards of the right to personal self-defense (top-down dimension, Fourth and Fifth Chapters).

At the same time, international human rights law establishes boundaries on how broadly or narrowly domestic laws on personal self-defense between private persons may be drawn (horizontal dimension, Sixth Chapter). In exceptional circumstances, the right to personal self-defense also sharpens the rights of individuals and peoples, allowing them to forcibly resist certain types of human

5. Haggenmacher, *supra* note 1, p. 34.

rights violations committed by or on behalf of the state (bottom-up dimension, Seventh Chapter).

At all three levels, the legal criteria of legality, immediacy, necessity and proportionality are in play. These criteria strike a balance between the individual's legitimate self-preservation instincts and the state's monopoly on the use of force, the rule of law, and the human rights of others (see Eighth Chapter).

B. DELINEATION OF THE TOPIC: WHAT IS PERSONAL SELF-DEFENSE?

Self-defense can be defined as conduct that is immediate, necessary and proportional to ward off an (imminent) unlawful attack. Common law jurisdictions distinguish between self-defense in the narrow, literal sense (defense of oneself), defense of others, and defense of property. For want of a more precise term in English, all three concepts are usually discussed together under the general heading of "self-defense" understood in a wider sense.[6] This wider notion is largely congruous with what is referred to as *légitime défense* or *legítima defensa* in the French and Spanish legal traditions, *nödvärn* in Scandinavian countries, or the composite of *Notwehr* (defense of oneself, including one's property) and *Nothilfe* (defense of others, including their property) in German-speaking countries.[7]

This wider notion of self-defense defines the scope of this book. It thus covers both *individual* self-defense (defending oneself or one's property) and *collective* self-defense (persons joining together to defend themselves or persons coming to the defense of others).[8]

I. Self-defense distinguished from other concepts of self-help

Self-defense must be distinguished from other uses of force employed for self-help and self-preservation: necessity, duress, and retaliatory reprisals.

6. Sometimes self-defense, defense of others and defense of property are also grouped together under the term "private defence." See R.D. Yadav, Law of Crime and Self-Defence, Mittal Publications: New Delhi (1993), p. 18; Boaz Sangero, Self-Defence in Criminal Law, Hart: Oxford (2006), p. 1. However, the use of that term here would lead to confusion, since under international human rights law, law enforcement agents may exercise self-defense and defense of others in the name of the state and not only in their private capacity.

7. See also Jens David Ohlin, The Doctrine of Legitimate Defense, International Law Studies vol. 91 (2015), 119–154, at pp. 138–139. For a discussion of the commonalities between the major legal systems see Second Chapter: E.II (pp. 63–67).

8. This use of terminology is congruent with the distinction that international law establishes for self-defense at the interstate level, where it distinguishes between individual self-defense (a state defending itself) and collective self-defense (a state coming to the defense of another state or two states collectively defending themselves against an attack on both). See U.N. Charter, art. 51. See also Dinstein, *supra* note 3, at pp. 278–280 [paras. 734–746].

The principle of necessity, which most legal orders recognize to some extent, allows actions that would otherwise be unlawful if the actor has no other way to safeguard an essential interest or good against harm and the harm prevented is disproportionally greater than the harm caused to the interests and goods of third parties[9]—for, example, a man who, to escape being struck and killed by a speeding car, violently pushes a woman out of his way, bruising her. Whereas self-defense may justify action only against the author(s) of a present or imminent unlawful attack, necessity can justify injuring an innocent party who did not cause the threat of harm and who broke no laws. In other words, "self-defense excuses the repulse of a wrong, whereas the rule of necessity justifies the invasion of a right."[10]

"Duress" refers to situations in which a person resorts to unlawful violence in response to a threat to himself or someone close to him, and in effect acts without free will.[11] Duress would arise, for instance, where prisoners are forced by their captors to kill other prisoners or be killed themselves. Like necessity, duress is distinguished from self-defense in that the harm may be directed against an innocent third party. Unlike necessity, however, the harm avoided does not have to outweigh the harm caused. For this reason, duress is mostly regarded as a mere excuse from culpability, unlike self-defense, which constitutes a full justification.[12]

Retaliatory reprisals are similar to self-defense in that they respond to attacks or other unlawful acts. However, they do not require an imminent or present attack. Instead, retaliatory reprisals are committed in response to past unlawful acts of others and are usually carried out with the intention to gain compensation or vengeance, to deter further unlawful acts, and to preserve the legal order.[13] A farmer who responds to a neighbor burning his crops by stealing the neighbor's cows carries out a retaliatory reprisal. Contemporary domestic legal orders generally do not allow for violent reprisals, in order to preserve the state's

9. See Jean Pradel, Droit Pénal Comparé, Dalloz: Paris (3rd ed., 2008), p. 140 [para. 103]. See also Article 25 of the ILC Draft Articles on Responsibility for Internationally Wrongful Acts [ILC Articles on State Responsibility], as contained in Ch. IV.E.1 of the Report of the International Law Commission, U.N. Doc. A/56/10.

10. United States v. Krupp et al., [United States Military Tribunal, Nuremberg], Law Reports of Trials of War Criminals, vol. X (1949), p. 148.

11. See Pradel, *supra* note 9, p. 155 [para. 114]. See also Rome Statute, Article 31 (1)(d).

12. See Second Chapter: E.I (pp. 59–63).

13. The German Enlightenment philosopher Samuel Pufendorf distinguished between self-defense ("defensive wars") and reprisals ("offensive (just) wars") as follows: "there is need of force for a twofold purpose, either to defend myself and my property against him who is attempting to harm them; or else to compel another person to restore the damages already done by him to me and to give a guarantee that he will not offend in the future; and from all this arises the distinction between defensive wars and offensive (just) wars." See Samuel Pufendorf, Two Books of the Elements of Universal Jurisprudence [1660] (trans.

monopoly to use force. The same applies for international law governing the relations of states in peacetime.[14]

II. Personal self-defense versus interstate self-defense

This book distinguishes between personal and interstate self-defense.[15] It addresses only the relationship between self-defense at the interpersonal level (personal self-defense) and international human rights law. It does not address the relationship between international human rights law and states' right to self-defense under Article 51 of the U.N. Charter (interstate self-defense), which allows for a forcible response to attacks by another state or from another state's territory without breaching the prohibition on the use of force under Article 2(4) of the U.N. Charter.[16]

William Abbott Oldfather; ed. Thomas Behme), Liberty Fund: Indianapolis (2009), p. 338 [Bk. II, Observation IV.12]. On the distinction between self-defense and reprisals, see also Stephen C. Neff, War and the Law of Nations: A General History, Cambridge University Press: Cambridge (2005), p. 129.

14. See ILC Articles on State Responsibility, *supra* note 9, art. 50 (1)(a).

15. In order to make substantively the same distinction between interstate self-defense and personal self-defense, different terminology has been proposed. Some use the term "individual self-defense" to describe personal self-defense, while referring to interstate self-defense as "collective self-defense." See Kai Ambos, Defences in international criminal law, in: Bartram S. Brown (ed.), Research handbook on international criminal law, Elgar: Cheltenham et al. (2011), 299–329, at p. 309; Hannah Tonkin, Defensive Force under the Rome Statute, Melbourne Journal of International Law, vol. 6 (2005), 86–117, at p. 89. However, such usage only adds to the confusion between interstate and personal self-defense in light of the distinct meanings that individual and collective self-defense are given under Article 51 of the U.N. Charter. See also Albin Eser, Article 31: Grounds for Excluding Criminal Responsibility, in: Otto Triffterer (ed.), Commentary on the Rome Statute of the International Criminal Court, C.H.Beck-Hart-Nomos: München/Oxford/Baden-Baden (2nd ed., 2008), 863–893, at pp. 879–880 [article 31, para. 39].

Eser (id.) distinguishes between *private* self-defense (i.e., personal self-defense) and *operational* self-defense (i.e., interstate self-defense). However, the reference to private self-defense fails to capture that state agents exercise the right to personal self-defense regularly in their official capacity to protect themselves and others.

Cassese makes a terminological distinction between self-defense under international criminal law (i.e., personal self-defense) and self-defense under public international law (interstate self-defense). See Antonio Cassese et al., International Criminal Law: Cases and Commentary, Oxford University Press: Oxford (2011), p. 461. However, terminology linking personal and interstate self-defense to particular disciplines of international law is misleading. Personal self-defense also operates outside the context of international criminal law and affects state obligations, notably under international humanitarian law (see Second Chapter, F.I, pp. 68–70) and human rights law (see Fourth to Seventh Chapters, pp. 91–345). Furthermore, the exercise of interstate self-defense in line with Article 51 has a direct bearing on international criminal law in that it excludes individual criminal responsibility for the crime of aggression.

16. Issues not discussed here include, for instance, the question to what extent the emerging human right to peace is limited by Article 51 of the U.N. Charter. For some reason, no explicit reference to Article 51 was included in the United Nations' Draft Declaration on the Right to

Personal and interstate self-defense have common characteristics. They both serve to protect the integrity and autonomy of the rights holder against unlawful aggression (with the terms "integrity" and "autonomy" translating into territorial integrity and sovereignty at the international level). In both cases, self-defense marks one exception to a monopoly on the use of force, which is claimed respectively by the state vis-à-vis its citizens and by the United Nations (acting through the Security Council) vis-à-vis its Member States.[17] Defensive action at the personal and interstate levels is also subject to the same basic requirements of immediacy, necessity and proportionality, although the precise meaning of these requirements differs between the two types of self-defense.[18]

Perhaps owing to these similarities, personal and interstate self-defense are easily confounded.[19] Different proposals have been made to distinguish the right

Peace as contained in the Report of the Human Rights Council Advisory Committee on the right of peoples to peace, U.N. Doc. A/HRC/20/31 (2012), Annex.

A second, more interesting question is whether international human rights law limits a state's right to defend itself against an imminent attack by a militarily superior adversary if resistance is clearly futile and will lead to disastrous casualties. Dinstein, *supra* note 3, p. 190 [para. 503] considers forgoing self-defense in such a situation to be a question of political prudence, since interstate self-defense is a right but not a duty. However, it may well be that state leaders who accept mass killing to achieve an "honorable," yet inevitable, defeat not only act imprudently but also violate the state's obligation to protect its population. Cf. Human Rights Committee, General Comment 6: Article 6 ICCPR (1982), para. 2, as restated in: U.N. Doc. HRI/GEN/1/Rev.1 at 6 (1994) (considering that states have the "supreme duty to prevent wars" and that "[e]very effort they make to avert the danger of war . . . would constitute the most important condition and guarantee for the safeguarding of the right to life"). For a discussion of some of the pertinent considerations see also Ben Saul, Defending 'Terrorism': Justifications and Excuses for Terrorism, in: International Criminal Law, Australian Year Book of International Law, vol. 25 (2006), 177–226, at p. 189.

17. See also Kjell Anderson, The Universality of War: Jus ad Bellum and the Right to Peace in Non-International Armed Conflicts, in: David Keane; Yvonne McDermott (eds.), The Challenge of Human Rights: Past, Present and Future, Edward Elgar: Cheltenham/ Northampton (2012), 52–73, at p. 52; Shana Wallace, Beyond Imminence: Evolving International Law and Battered Women's Right to Self-Defense, University of Chicago Law Review, vol. 71 (2004), 1749–1781, at pp. 1766–1767.

Self-defense is not necessarily the only exception to the monopoly on the use of force. Many domestic legal orders allow citizens to use force to arrest persons caught in the act of committing a crime of some severity. In international law, states have claimed a right to use force unilaterally and without Security Council mandate, inter alia, for purposes of protecting their nationals in other countries, although this is at times framed as a subcategory of Art. 51 of the U.N. Charter. See Dinstein, *supra* note 3, pp. 217–219 [paras. 575–577].

18. See First Chapter: C.II.3 (pp. 12–14).

19. Eser, *supra* note 15, pp. 879–880 [art. 31, para 39]. Examples of legal arguments that confound both concepts are the claim that interstate self-defense can justify extraterritorial targeted killings outside armed conflict (discussed in the Fifth Chapter: C, pp. 230–233) and the claim that the right to the personal defense of others can justify humanitarian interventions (discussed in the Seventh Chapter: E.V, pp. 341–343).

to interstate self-defense under Article 51 of the U.N. Charter from the right to personal self-defense, which is a general principle of law recognized by nations.[20] Such proposals have been advanced in particular in relation to the ambit of Article 31 (1)(c) of the Rome Statute of the International Criminal Court (Rome Statute), which reaffirms the right to personal self-defense as a circumstance precluding responsibility under international criminal law, while explicitly excluding interstate self-defense from its ambit (see Art. 31 (1)(c), second sentence, Rome Statute).

It has been suggested that the distinction lies in interstate self-defense relating to defensive action by states, whereas personal self-defense is about defensive action by individuals against other individuals.[21] Thus, interstate self-defense is said to justify a collective or state reaction, whereas personal self-defense refers to the justification of individual acts.[22] However, this approach omits that the right to personal self-defense regularly justifies state use of defensive force, where law enforcement officials act in the line of duty to defend themselves and others.[23] Equally, interstate self-defense may occasionally justify individual conduct: state officials who order the use of force against other states may be justified based on interstate self-defense and thereby evade liability for the international crime of aggression.

Another approach bases the distinction on the type of attack. In this view, interstate self-defense refers to the right of a state to use force to repulse an armed attack by one or several other states, while personal self-defense is defined as an individual's right to use force in the face of a violent attack by one or several other persons.[24] This distinction fails to take into account that, at least according to an increasingly accepted view, interstate self-defense can be exercised, not only against armed attacks launched by another state, but also against attacks by nonstate actors striking from another state's territory.[25] The proposed distinction

20. See Second Chapter (pp. 17–74).

21. Cassese et al., *supra* note 15, p. 461.

22. Kai Ambos, Other Grounds for Excluding Criminal Responsibility, in: Antonio Cassese, Paola Gaeta & John R.W.D. Jones (eds.), The Rome Statute of the International Criminal Court: A Commentary, Vol. I, Oxford University Press: Oxford (2002), 984–1029, at p. 997.

23. See Fourth Chapter (pp. 91–216).

24. Eric David, Self-Defence and State of Necessity in the Statute of the ICC, in: José Doria, Hans-Peter Gasser, & M. Cherif Bassiouni (eds.), The Legal Regime of the International Criminal Court, Martinus Nijhoff: Leiden/Boston (2009), 757–777, at pp. 757–758.

25. See Dinstein, *supra* note 3, pp. 227–230 [paras. 601–606]; Natalino Ronzitti, The Expanding Law of Self-Defence, Journal of Conflict & Security Law, vol. 11:3 (2006), 343–359, at p. 348; Michael N. Schmitt, Counter-Terrorism and the Use of Force in International Law, Israel Yearbook of Human Rights, vol. 32 (2002), 53–116, p. 82; Jean-Marc Thouvenin, Circumstances Precluding Wrongfulness in the ILC Articles on State Responsibility: Self-Defence, in: James Crawford et al. (eds.), The Law of International Responsibility, Oxford University Press: Oxford (2010), 455–467, at pp. 463–464. But cf. Legal Consequences of

also misses that personal self-defense may be exercised not only against attacks by particular individuals, but can be directed against the state itself, against human rights violations that pose a real risk of serious and irreparable harm.[26]

The real difference between state and personal self-defense lies in their distinct justificatory purposes. Interstate self-defense justifies the infringement of the sovereignty and/or territorial integrity of states that attack other states or fail to prevent such attacks being launched from their territory. It therefore excludes state responsibility for the infringement of the prohibition of the use of force under Article 2(4) of the U.N. Charter as well as individual criminal responsibility for the crime of aggression. Personal self-defense justifies the infringement of other persons' integrity and autonomy. States using force in justified exercise of the right to personal self-defense do not violate the targeted person's right to life, physical security, or liberty. By the same token, an individual (whether state agent or private individual) exercising such personal self-defense will not incur criminal responsibility under national or international criminal law.[27]

C. METHODOLOGY AND SOURCES

International bodies and scholars have analyzed many of the legal issues relating to the right to personal self-defense in international human rights law, albeit often not framing them in relation to that right. Other aspects remain underexplored. To fill those voids, this book relies on both universal and regional human rights jurisprudence. Furthermore, it considers the operation of the right to personal self-defense in other disciplines of international law, and also draws on self-defense jurisprudence from domestic law.

I. Reliance on universal and regional jurisprudence

There is, by and large, a sufficiently uniform body of law that can be referred to as international human rights law. This body comprises both global and regional human rights law, since the jurisprudence of universal and regional human rights bodies converges overall towards common standards.[28] While there are

the Construction of a Wall in the Occupied Palestinian Territory (Advisory Opinion), ICJ Reports 2004, 136, at p. 194 [para 139].

26. See Seventh Chapter: B (pp. 301–312).

27. See also Massimo Scalliotti, Defences before the international criminal court: Substantive grounds for excluding criminal responsibility—Part 1, International Criminal Law Review vol. 1, (2001), 111–172, at p. 159; Ambos, *supra* note 15, p. 309 (noting that Art. 51 of the U.N. Charter is "sovereignty orientated," unlike Art. 31 (1)(c) (Rome Statute). For further discussion, see also Fifth Chapter: C (pp. 230–233).

28. This convergence results notably from the principle that a treaty norm must be interpreted in light of any relevant rules of international law applicable in the relations between the parties (see Art. 31 (3)(c) Vienna Convention on the Law of Treaties). Human rights courts and

genuine concerns that certain sub-regional human rights declarations could undermine the universal character and content of human rights,[29] the jurisprudence of the established regional human rights systems "breathe[s] life into the notion of universality," rather than fragmenting international human rights law.[30] In particular, the jurisprudence of the European and Inter-American regional human rights courts converges with that of the universal human rights mechanisms regarding the use of force in law enforcement, which is at the heart of the topic.[31]

With a view to ascertaining general standards under international human rights law, the subsequent analysis relies on universal and regional human rights instruments, the pronouncements of the courts and independent expert bodies assigned to monitor their implementation, and the relevant academic literature. The discussion will note instances of significant divergence between different instruments or their interpretation by oversight bodies.

oversight bodies have given effect to this provision by taking into account universal human rights treaties, pronouncements of other oversight bodies and human rights soft-law instruments. For relevant examples from the jurisprudence of the European and Inter-American Human Rights Systems, see Magnus Killander, Interpreting Regional Human Rights Treaties, Sur International Journal on Human Rights, vol. 13 (2000), 145–170, at pp. 152–162; Gerald L. Neuman, Import, Export, and Regional Consent in the Inter-American Court of Human Rights, European Journal of International Law, vol. 19 (2008), pp. 101–123, at pp. 109–111. Article 61 of the African Charter on Human and Peoples' Rights specifically requires the African Commission to draw from the Universal Declaration of Human Rights and other instruments adopted by the United Nations, while Article 7 of the Protocol establishing the African Court on Human and Peoples' Rights requires the court to directly apply other relevant human rights instruments ratified by the states concerned. See also African Commission on Human and Peoples' Rights, Purohit et al. v. The Gambia (2003), para. 48, noting that the African Commission is "more than willing to accept legal arguments with the support of appropriate and relevant international and regional human rights instruments, principles, norms and standards taking into account the well-recognised principle of universality [of human rights]."

29. See, e.g., the criticism of the Declaration of Human Rights of the Association of Southeast Asian Nations (ASEAN) expressed by the U.N. High Commissioner for Human Rights (OHCHR) in: UN rights chief welcomes focus on human rights and democracy, calls for review of ASEAN draft human rights declaration, 8 November 2012, http://www.ohchr.org/RU/NewsEvents/Pages/DisplayNews.aspx?NewsID=12753&LangID=E.

30. Chaloka Bayani, Reconstituting the universal: human rights as a regional idea, in: Conor Gearty/Costas Douzinas (eds.), The Cambridge Companion to Human Rights Law, Cambridge University Press: Cambridge (2012), 173–190, at p. 178.

31. See Raúl Canosa Usera, Héctor Fix Zamudio, Edgar Corzo Sosa, El Derecho a la Integridad Personal, in: Javier García Roca et al. (eds.), El Diálogo entre los sistemas Europeo y Americano de Derechos Humanos, Civitas/Thomson Reuters: Cizur Menor (2012), 138–185; Paul Tavernier, Le recours à la force par la pólice, in: Christian Tomuschat, Evelyne Lagrange & Stefan Oeter (eds.), The Right to Life, Brill: Leiden (2010), 41–64, at pp. 58–63.

II. Transposition of jurisprudence from other disciplines of international law

International law constitutes a single, coherent legal order. Its norms act in relation to one another and, in accordance with the principle of systemic integration, they should be interpreted against the background of other applicable rules and principles of international law.[32] Studying other areas of international law, on which the right of personal self-defense has a bearing, may thus yield insights on how the right shapes international human rights law.

1. International Humanitarian Law

Valuable insights can be gained from international humanitarian law (IHL) jurisprudence, where the right to personal self-defense becomes relevant in two respects. First, IHL incorporates the right in assessing the legality of force employed by combatants against protected persons who use violence without directly participating in hostilities (e.g., violent prisoners of war, rioting protesters, or bandits).[33] In such situations, international humanitarian law applies law enforcement standards derived from international human rights law so that relevant jurisprudence can be easily transposed from one discipline to the other.

Second, the right to personal self-defense limits the scope of the IHL principle that civilians may not participate in armed conflict. and that they lose their protected status for such time as they directly participate in hostilities. Accordingly, self-defense is not considered direct participation in hostilities, and civilians may defend themselves against unlawful attacks without losing their protected status.[34] The degree to which this exception legitimizes violence by individuals against the state can help discern the extent to which international human rights law gives individuals a right to defend themselves by force against human rights violations, including outside the context of armed conflict.

2. International Criminal Law

Personal self-defense is also relevant to international criminal law, where it can preclude individual responsibility.[35] However, international criminal law jurisprudence should be relied upon only cautiously in interpreting international human rights law, since the former forms a basis to establish individual criminal responsibility and the latter addresses obligations to states and gives rise to state

32. Difficulties arising from the Diversification and Expansion of International Law: Report of the Study Group of the International Law Commission, U.N. Doc. A/CN.4/L.702 (2006), para. 14(1). The principle of systemic integration finds express recognition in Art. 31 (3) (c) of the Vienna Convention on the Law of Treaties. On the principle of systemic integration, see also Carmen Thiele, Fragmentierung des Völkerrechts als Herausforderung für die Staatengemeinschaft, Archiv des Völkerrechts, vol. 46 (2008), 1–41, at pp. 24–28.

33. See Second Chapter: F.I (pp. 68–70) for references.

34. See Second Chapter: F.I (pp. 68–70) and Seventh Chapter: C (312–316) for details and references.

35. See Second Chapter: F.II (pp. 70–71).

responsibility in the case of violations.[36] Their standards and outcomes do not necessarily coincide. For instance, a state agent using lethal force may not incur criminal responsibility if the agent killed in self-defense. Yet, the state on whose behalf he acted may still be held responsible due to organizational shortcomings that put the agent in a situation where he had to kill in order not to be killed.[37]

Furthermore, human rights norms are to be interpreted dynamically (as "living instruments"), whereas the criminal law principle of legality requires a more guarded approach to the evolutive interpretation of norms of international criminal law.[38]

Finally, international criminal law provides limited guidance because there are few, if any, precedents where personal self-defense has been successfully invoked. The absolute immorality of crimes such as genocide and crimes against humanity generally precludes a plea of self-defense.[39] Self-defense has also little practical relevance in relation to war crimes. As noted,[40] the right to personal self-defense is already incorporated into international humanitarian law, which has to be breached for war crimes to be charged in the first place.

3. Article 51 of the U.N. Charter

Few issues in contemporary international law have inspired as much legal commentary as the inherent right to interstate self-defense, reaffirmed in Article 51 of the U.N. Charter. At first sight, it may thus be tempting to apply the rich body of jurisprudence on Article 51 by analogy to personal self-defense. The early international jurists developed the principles of interstate self-defense by drawing on the concept of personal self-defense,[41] so it instinctively seems logical to reverse the process. Some writers have gone as far as to suggest that the requirements of state and personal self-defense are the same.[42] However, this view does not withstand scrutiny. While both types of self-defense rely on very similar

36. Gloria Gaggioli, The Relevance of International Criminal Law for Interpreting and Applying Human Rights Treaties: A Study of the Case Law of the European Court of Human Rights, in: Robert Kolb & Damian Scalia (eds.), Droit international penal: Précis, Helbing: Lichtenhahn (2nd ed., 2012), pp. 397–422, at p. 407; Ambos, *supra* note 15, p. 310.

37. See Fourth Chapter: C.IV (pp. 164–170).

38. Gaggioli, *supra* note 36, p. 408.

39. George P. Fletcher & Jens David Ohlin, Defending Humanity: When Force Is Justified and Why, Oxford University Press: New York (2008), p. 124; David, *supra* note 24, p. 767; Tonkin, *supra* note 15, pp. 110–113.

40. See this Chapter 1: C.II.1 (p. 11) and also Chapter 2: F.I (pp. 68–70).

41. See *supra* note 3 and accompanying text.

42. Wallace, *supra* note 17, p. 1767; Wayne McCormack, Targeted Killing at a Distance: Robotics and Self-Defense, Pacific McGeorge Global Business & Development Journal, vol. 25 (2012), 361–379, at p. 374. Cf. Geoffrey S. Corn, Self-Defense Targeting: Blurring the line between the Jus ad Bellum and the Ius in Bello, in: Kenneth Watkin/Andrew J. Norris (eds.), Non-International Armed Conflict in the Twenty-First Century, Naval War College: Newport, Rhode Island (2012), 53–92, at p. 67.

basic concepts—notably the existence of an unlawful attack and the immediacy, necessity, and proportionality of the response—these concepts mean very different things for interstate self-defense and personal self-defense.

Differences result notably from the fact that the international system remains a decentralized order.[43] Regrettably perhaps, there are no United Nations bailiffs or police officers with a global mandate to enforce international law and order. For the most part, states must rely on themselves or their allies to defend themselves. Even in the few instances where the Security Council has authorized action in the face of aggression, it has had to rely on individual states willing to enforce its decisions. Due to the lack of central enforcement, interstate self-defense may allow states greater latitude to take defensive action than individuals, who may eventually obtain help from the police and other state institutions, would have[44] To the extent that its power allows, a state exercising self-defense in practice will usually also calibrate its action so as to restore the status quo ante and deter the aggressor from resuming the attack.[45]

A state also, unlike a person, cannot avoid attack by retreating, at least in the archetypical case of aggression where its territory is attacked.[46] It has no choice but to "stand its ground" if it does not want to submit.

Perhaps most importantly, interstate self-defense employs different concepts of time. An individual may counter an attacker's blow by striking a split-second more quickly than his adversary. Conversely, a state may intercept an incoming attack hours before it can have an effect on that state's territory or installations.[47] At the other end of the time range, a state under attack will often need time to verify the circumstances of the armed attack, exhaust diplomatic avenues in response, and organize its forces for the counterstrike. It may, therefore, still take defensive action weeks or months after the attack.[48] In contrast, the time window for personal self-defense closes as soon as the attack is concluded, and

43. Anderson, *supra* note 17, p. 53; John Cerone, Is there a Human Right of Self-Defense?, in; Journal of Law, Economics and Policy, vol. 2 (2006), 319–329, at p. 321.

44. Fletcher & Ohlin, *supra* note 39, p. 40, offer the hypothetical example of an attacked state subjecting the vanquished aggressor to temporary defensive occupation to illustrate how interstate and personal self-defense differ in their temporal scope.

45. Fletcher & Ohlin, *id.* at 95; Julian Fernandez & Xavier Pacreau, Statut de Rome de la Cour pénale international: Commentaire article par article, vol.1, Pedone: Paris (2012), p. 918.

46. Cf. Anderson, *supra* note 17, p. 62.

47. Such *interceptive* interstate self-defense is generally accepted as legal under the U.N. Charter. There is even considerable support for the position that a state may exercise *pre-emptive* self-defense against an imminent attack. However, the position that a non-imminent threat may be countered with *preventive* self-defense is widely rejected. For an overview of the academic debate and relevant state practice, see Tom Ruys, "Armed Attack" and Article 51 of the UN Charter, Cambridge University Press: Cambridge (2010) pp. 250–367; Dinstein, *supra* note 3, pp. 194–207 [paras. 514–549].

48. Nigel D. White, Defending Humanity: When Force is Justified and Why [Book Review], Melbourne Journal of International Law, vol. 10 (2009), 379–393, at p. 387. See also Dinstein,

the victim then needs to turn to the authorities instead. As the great scholar of international law Hugo Grotius (1583–1645) observed, personal self-defense distinguishes itself from interstate self-defense because it is "only momentary, it ceases as soon as one can apply to a judge."[49]

In light of these fundamental differences, one cannot import jurisprudence pertaining to Article 51 of the U.N. Charter wholesale and apply it to interpret the right to personal self-defense. Jurisprudence on interstate self-defense can be drawn on only for "inspiration but not for determination."[50]

III. Consideration of arguments from domestic jurisprudence

Although international law constitutes an autonomous and complete legal order, standards remain to be discovered or clarified in several areas. Comparative law arguments, carefully derived from the review of different domestic legal orders, can help fill the remaining jurisprudential voids.

Applying domestic jurisprudence on self-defense to the international realm has obvious limits. The right to personal self-defense in international law is an autonomous principle; although rooted in domestic systems, it does not necessarily have the exact same requirements and rules.[51] Some domestic legal orders may impose stricter limits on self-defense than the minimum standards established by international human rights law; others may be more permissive and fall short of international standards. There is also a general risk of relativizing universal norms when drawing only on jurisprudence relating to particular domestic legal orders, given that each legal order is shaped by the specific political, social and cultural context in which it is set.

These risks noted, there is still room for what has been referred to as "cross fertilization ... between the national and international legal spaces (*espaces juridiques*)"[52] No study of personal self-defense can ignore the decades, or

supra note 3, p. 233 [para. 615]. For instance, the United States–led military responses to the invasion of Kuwait in 1991 and against the Taliban in 2001, which are generally regarded as justified exercises of self-defense under Article 51 of the U.N. Charter, took place only months or weeks after the initial attack.

49. Hugo Grotius, The Rights of War and Peace [1625], Book II (ed. Richard Tuck/Jean Barbeyrac, trans. John Morrice), Liberty Fund: Indianapolis (2005), p. 416 [Bk. 2, Ch.1.XVI].

50. Cf. White, *supra* note 48, p. 388 (on the inverse question whether insights for Art. 51 can be derived from personal self-defense jurisprudence). For a cautious approach, see also Fletcher & Ohlin, *supra* note 39, p. 12.

51. Cf. Second Chapter: C.I (p. 24).

52. Mireille Delmas-Marty, The Contribution of Comparative Law to a Pluralist Conception of International Criminal Law, Journal of International Criminal Justice, vol. 1 (1) (2003), 13–25, at p. 15. See also Javier Garcia Roca, El Diálogo entre el Tribunal Europea de Derechos Humanos y los Tribunales Constitutionales en la Construcción de un Orden Público Europea, Teoría y Realidad Constitucional, vol. 30 (2012), 183–224, at pp. 206 ff.

even centuries, of rich debate in domestic legal systems. International criminal law often borrows from national jurisprudence, a process that has been aptly described as "the gradual decanting of national criminal concepts and rules into the international receptacle."[53] There is no reason why a similarly careful approach cannot also be applied to fill genuine jurisprudential gaps in international human rights law. After all, international human rights law, like international criminal law, considers individuals as its subjects and thus ends up occupying the same regulatory space as domestic law.[54]

A methodology that includes comparative analysis is particularly appropriate for this subject. As will be shown in the next chapter, this right to personal self-defense forms part of international law because it is a general principle of law recognized by nations in the sense of Article 38 (1)(c) of the ICJ Statute. Its ubiquity in the world's domestic legal systems compels and justifies its recognition in international law. Analyzing the right to personal self-defense and its interplay with human rights without considering relevant jurisprudential debates in national legal systems would neglect the domestic foundations to which the right owes its very existence.

53. Prosecutor v. Erdemovic [ICTY Appeals Chamber], Case No. IT-96-22-A, Judgment of 7 October 1997, Sep. and Diss. Op. of Judge Cassese, para. 4.

54. See also Jaye Ellis, General Principles and Comparative Law, European Journal of International Law, vol. 22(4) (2011), 949–971, at pp. 950–952.

2

The Right to Personal Self-Defense as a General Principle of Law

It is often claimed that the right to self-defense constitutes a feature of any legal order and hence also international law. Sir Hersch Lauterpacht observed that the right to self-defense "is an absolute right, in as much as no law can disregard it."[1] Along the same lines, the International Military Tribunal for the Far East at Tokyo pronounced that "[a]ny law, international or municipal, which prohibits recourse to force, is necessarily limited by the right of self-defense."[2]

For the right to personal self-defense to constitute a norm of international law, it must derive from one of the three primary sources of that law. These sources are listed in Article 38(1) of the Statute of the International Court of Justice (ICJ Statute): treaty law, customary law, and "the general principles of law recognized by civilized nations."

While some aspects of treaty and customary law suggest the existence of an underlying right to personal self-defense, this chapter establishes that the right can best be conceived as a general principle of law recognized by nations.

A. NO TREATY PROVISIONS ESTABLISH A RIGHT TO PERSONAL SELF-DEFENSE

It has been suggested that there are "affirmative statements" of the right to personal self-defense in treaty law,[3] but this overstates what can be discerned from relevant treaty provisions. No international treaties explicitly recognize a general right to personal self-defense. In particular, Article 51 of the U.N. Charter does not

1. Hersch Lauterpacht, The Function of Law in the International Community, Oxford University Press: Oxford (2011) [re-issue of the first edition from 1933], at p. 188.

2. In re Hirota and Others [International Military Tribunal for the Far East], Judgment of 12 November 1948, as reproduced in John Pritchard and Sonia M. Zaide (eds.), The Tokyo War Crimes Trial, vol. 22, Garland: New York/London (1981), at p. 48, 494.

3. David B. Kopel, Paul Gallant, & Joanne D. Eisen, The Human Right of Self-Defense, BYU Journal of Public Law, vol. 22 (2008), 43–178, at p. 152.

Human Rights and Personal Self-Defense in International Law. Jan Arno Hessbruegge

establish such a right, since the "inherent right of individual and collective self-defence" referenced in the first sentence is explicitly framed in the second sentence as a right exercised by U.N. member states rather than by individuals. At most, the reference to an "inherent right" (*droit naturel* in the French translation) hints at a preexisting broader right that could also extend to the interpersonal level.

Certain other treaty provisions, while not establishing the right to personal self-defense, still suggest its existence. Article 31(1)(3) of the Rome Statute recognizes reasonable self-defense "against an imminent and unlawful use of force in a manner proportionate to the degree of danger" as a ground for excluding criminal responsibility. According to Article 2(2)(a) of the European Convention on Human Rights, no violation of the right to life occurs where "[d]eprivation of life . . . results from the use of force, which is no more than absolutely necessary . . . in defense of any person from unlawful violence." Without explicitly recognizing a right, both provisions presuppose that such a right exists and hence justify conduct that would be otherwise a violation of international law.

The closest to a specific recognition of the right to personal self-defense can be found in two regional human rights treaty provisions on peoples' right to self-determination. Article 2(4) of the Arab Charter on Human Rights recognizes that "[a]ll peoples have the right to resist foreign occupation." With more ornate wording, but essentially the same meaning, Article 20(2) of the African Charter on Human and Peoples' Rights stipulates that "[c]olonized or oppressed peoples shall have the right to free themselves from the bonds of domination." These provisions refer to a right in response to a forcible wrong. However, this right belongs to peoples, not to persons—not specific individuals, but to entire groups that often represent a state *in nascendi*. The provisions therefore incorporate a right to self-defense *sui generis* with elements drawn from both the right to interstate self-defense and the right to personal self-defense.[4] Moreover, these rights are applicable only to very specific denials of the right to self-determination.[5] Their existence does not establish a general right to personal self-defense held by individuals.

B. NO RECOGNITION UNDER CUSTOMARY INTERNATIONAL LAW

Although this has been asserted,[6] the right to personal self-defense does not constitute a rule of customary international law. According to Article 38(1)(b) of the ICJ Statute, customary international law requires "a general practice accepted as law." It is therefore formed from two elements: "actual practice and *opinio juris* of

4. See also Seventh Chapter: D.I (pp. 318–320).

5. See also Seventh Chapter: D, introduction (pp. 316–318).

6. See Geert-Jan Knoops, Defenses in Contemporary International Criminal Law, Transnational Publishers: Ardsley, New York (2nd ed., 2008), pp. 73–74. Cf. Prosecutor v. Kordić & Čerkez [ICTY Trial Chamber], Case No. IT-95-14/2, Judgment of 26 February 2001, para. 451 (finding that the "principle of self-defence enshrined in [Art. 31(1)(c) Rome

states."[7] The requisite state practice does not have to rigorously conform to the proclaimed norm of customary law, but it must be at least substantially uniform.[8] State practice derives from a variety of types of state conduct. It may also manifest itself in domestic laws and the decisions of national courts that relate to international law.[9] In principle, the general recognition of self-defense in domestic criminal law statutes and judicial decisions can therefore constitute relevant state practice.

However, state practice alone is not enough. To distinguish norms of customary international law from non-binding international usages, the state practice must be carried by the belief that it is required by international law (*opinio juris sive necessitatis*).[10] In a number of cases, the International Court of Justice has inferred the existence of the requisite *opinio juris* from sufficiently uniform state practice; in others, however, it applied greater rigor in establishing it.[11] In any case, the relevant *opinio juris* cannot be inferred from the existence of a uniform state practice of domestic laws and court decisions recognizing self-defense.[12] There is nothing indicating that national legislators and judges recognized a right to self-defense based on a belief that that they are legally compelled under international law to do so.[13] On the contrary, the self-defense norms found in most domestic legal orders harken all the way back to an era, when criminal matters (much as the relationship between a state and its subjects in general) were considered "internal affairs" and thus not subject to the scrutiny of international law. In many cases, legal recognition of the right to self-defense even predates the existence of the states applying them.[14] It would therefore amount

Statute] reflects provisions found in most national criminal codes and may be regarded as constituting a rule of customary international law.").

7. Continental Shelf (Libyan Arab Jamahiriya v. Malta), I.C.J. Reports 1985, 13, at p. 29.

8. Military and Paramilitary Activities (Nicaragua v. U.S.) (Merits), I.C.J. Reports 1986, 14, at p. 98 [para. 186]; James Crawford, Brownlie's Principles of Public International Law, Oxford University Press: Oxford (8th ed., 2012), p. 25.

9. Certain German Interests in Polish Upper Silesia (Germ. v. Pol.), 1926 P.C.I.J. (ser. A) No. 7 (May 25), at p. 19; Wolff Heintschel von Heinegg, Die weiteren Quellen des Völkerrechts, in: Knut Ipsen (ed.),Völkerrecht, C.H.Beck: München (6th ed., 2014), 470–510, at p. 478 [§ 17.18].

10. North Sea Continental Shelf (Ger.v. Denmark/Ger. v. Netherlands), I.C.J. Reports 1969, 3, at p. 44 [para. 77]; Crawford, *supra* note 8, p. 25; Heintschel von Heinegg, *id.*, p 477 [§ 17.14].

11. Crawford, *supra* note 8, p. 26.

12. But see Knoops, *supra* note 6, p. 74.

13. John Cerone, Is there a Human Right of Self-Defense?, Journal of Law, Economics and Policy, vol. 2 (2006), 319–329, at p. 327. See also Prevention of human rights violations committed with small arms and light weapons: Final report submitted by Barbara Frey, Special Rapporteur in accordance with Sub-Commission resolution 2002/25, U.N. Doc. A/HRC/Sub.1/58/27 (2006), para 22.

14. See this Second Chapter: D.I (pp. 30–47).

to pure fiction to presume that states have recognized the right to personal self-defense in their domestic legal orders out of a sense of being required to do so by international law.

The sole instance where international law probably already recognizes personal self-defense as a customary norm is where it constitutes a ground for excluding criminal responsibility for international crimes.[15] This position is buttressed by the fact that a majority of states have now ratified the Rome Statute. They have therefore accepted as a matter of international law that self-defense, as laid down in Article 31(1)(c) of the Rome Statute, can be pleaded with regard to international crimes and that in thus far self-defense must also be reflected in the domestic criminal laws implementing the Rome Statute. Yet even that position remains, to some degree, contested. Eric David, in particular, has argued that international crimes, owing to their peremptory nature (*ius cogens*), cannot possibly be subject to self-defense pleas, and has criticized the very existence of Article 31(1)(c) of the Rome Statute on that ground.[16] Similar concerns were expressed by a number of eminent members of the International Law Commission (ILC) when the ILC discussed the Draft Code of Crimes against the Peace and Security of Mankind.[17]

In any case, even if customary international law accepts self-defense as a ground excluding criminal responsibility for a narrow range of international crimes, this cannot support a claim that states consider themselves bound under international law to recognize a general right of self-defense that also applies to other uses of force.[18]

The absence of the requisite *opinio juris* thus excludes recognition of a general right to self-defense under customary international law. Yet, the fact that

15. Prosecutor v. Kordić & Čerkez [ICTY Trial Chamber], *supra* note 6, para. 451; Wilhelm Mundo and Erich Weiss [United States General Military Government Court at Ludwigsburg, Germany, 9–10 November 1945], Law Reports of Trials of War Criminals, vol XIII (1949), 149–150, at p. 150; Willi Tessmann [British Military Court, Hamburg, 1-24 September 1947], Law Reports of Trials of War Criminals, vol. XV (1949), at p. 177; Antonio Cassese et al., International Criminal Law: Cases and Commentary, Oxford University Press: Oxford (2011), p. 461; Georg Werle, Principles of International Criminal Law, TMC Asser Press: The Hague (2nd ed., 2009), p. 203 [para. 552]; Albin Eser, Article 31: Grounds for Excluding Criminal Responsibility, in: Otto Triffterer (ed.), Commentary on the Rome Statute of the International Criminal Court, C.H.Beck-Hart-Nomos: München/Oxford/Baden-Baden (2nd ed., 2008), 863–893, p. 878 [Art. 31, para. 37]; Knoops, *supra* note 6, p. 74.

16. Eric David, Self-Defence and State of Necessity in the Statute of the ICC, in: José Doria, Hans-Peter Gasser & M. Cherif Bassiouni (eds.), The Legal Regime of the International Criminal Court, Martinus Nijhoff: Leiden/Boston (2009), 757–777, at pp. 758–772 & 776. See also Julian Fernandez & Xavier Pacreau, Statut de Rome de la Cour pénale international: Commentaire article par article, vol.1, Pedone: Paris (2012), pp. 920–921. On the Rome Statute's recognizing defense of property, see Fourth Chapter: C.V.2.b (pp. 178–180).

17. Relevant statements by ILC members cited in David, *id.*, pp. 759–760.

18. Cerone, *supra* note 13, pp. 327–328.

self-defense is a shared feature of domestic legal orders is still legally relevant. It points to the existence of another type of international legal norm. As will be shown, the right to personal self-defense constitutes a general principle of law recognized by nations under Article 38 (1)(c) of the ICJ Statute.

C. GENERAL PRINCIPLES ACCORDING TO ARTICLE 38(1)(c) OF THE ICJ STATUTE

Article 38(1)(c) of the ICJ Statute recognizes "the general principles of law recognized by civilized nations" as the third primary source of international law. Such general principles constitute an autonomous source of international law.[19]

While the question has not yet received much attention, some scholars have described the right to personal self-defense as a general principle of law under Article 38(1)(c) of the ICJ Statute.[20] However, this view is not unopposed. Notably, the U.N. Special Rapporteur on Small Arms, Barbara Frey, has argued that there is no general principle recognizing an international human right to self-defense, because no such right "is expressly set forth."[21] More attuned to how general principles are actually formed, Cerone argues that no right to personal self-defense can be recognized under Article 38(1)(c) of the ICJ Statute since self-defense is not universally recognized as a right in different domestic legal orders.[22]

Following a brief overview on how general principles are formed and operate, the remainder of this chapter will set out why the right to self-defense is indeed a general principle of law under Article 38 (1)(c) of the ICJ Statute.

19. Therefore, they must not be confused with the general principles of international law, which are principles of universal application that can derive from universally ratified treaties, customary law or general principles recognized by nations. See Crawford, *supra* note 8, p. 37; Heintschel von Heinegg, *supra* note 9, p. 488 [§ 18.1]. But see Peter Malanczuk, Akehurst's Introduction to International Law, Routledge: London/New York (7th ed., 1997), p. 48.

20. See Werle, *supra* note 15, p. 200 [para. 541]; Kopel, Gallant & Eisen, *supra* note 3, p. 58; Karl Doehring, Die humanitäre Intervention: Überlegungen zu ihrer Rechtfertigung, in: Antônio Augusto Cancado Trindade (ed.), The Modern World of Human Rights: Essays in Honour of Thomas Buergenthal, Inter-American Institute of Human Rights: San Jose (1996), 549–565, at pp. 561–563; Peter Haggenmacher, Self-defence as a general principle of law and its relation to war, in: Arthur Eyffinger, Alan Stephens & Sam Muller (eds.), Self-Defence as a Fundamental Principle, T.M.C. Asser Press: The Hague (2009), 3–38, at p. 3; Bodo Missling, Widerstand und Menschenrechte: Das völkerrecht begründete Individualwiderstandsrecht gegen Menschenrechtsverletzungen, Medien Verlag Köhler: Tübingen (1999), p. 145; Andrew Murdoch, Recent Legal Issues and Problems Relating to Acts of Piracy off Somalia, in: Clive R. Symmons (ed.), Selected Contemporary Issues in the Law of the Sea, Martinus Nijhoff: Leiden (2011), 139–168, at p. 148.

21. U.N. Special Rapporteur on Small Arms, Barbara Frey, Final Report, *supra* note 13, para. 21.

22. Cerone, *supra* note 13, p. 327.

I. Formation of general principles

References to general principles as sources of international law already appeared in *compromis* establishing arbitrary tribunals in the 19th century.[23] The current wording of Article 38(1)(c) of the ICJ Statute dates back to the Statute of the Permanent International Court of Justice. Within the drafting committee for that statute, a fundamental difference in opinion arose as to the origin and nature of general principles. Some members considered general principles to be rooted in natural law, while others espoused a positivist approach and wanted to recognize only sources grounded in state consent.

The president of the drafting committee, Baron Descamps (Belgium), favored the natural law approach. His initial draft referred to the "the rules of international law recognized by the legal conscience of civilized peoples."[24] The representative of the United States, Elihu Root, opposed this proposal, fearing that a Permanent International Court of Justice would prove unacceptable to governments if it was allowed to rely on such unpredictable, subjective norms. At the same time, there was general agreement in the drafting committee that an additional source of law was needed to fill gaps in the incomplete patchwork of international treaty and customary norms. This led to the current wording, which is based on a compromise formula put forward by Lord Phillimore (United Kingdom) and Elihu Root.[25] General principles are thus neither derived from peoples' conscience, nor expressly based on the consent of states. Their existence is based on the recognition by *nations*—a term that can variably refer to the world's peoples or its states.

Owing to this deliberately ambiguous wording, the debate over the formation and nature of general principles has carried on.[26] One school of opinion has maintained that general principles are fundamentally norms of natural law.[27]

23. Paul Guggenheim, Contribution à l'histoire des sources du droit des gens, Recueil des cours de l'Académie de la Haye, vol. 94 (1958), 1–84, at pp. 74–76; Crawford, *supra* note 8, p. 34.

24. Guggenheim, *id.*, p. 76; Crawford, *supra* note 8, p. 34.

25. Crawford, *id.*

26. The only matter undisputed today is that the jarring reference to "civilized" nations in Article 38 (1)(c) of the ICJ Statute, a painful relic of the Eurocentric colonial era of international law, no longer has an independent meaning. See Heintschel von Heinegg, *supra* note 9, p. 489 [§ 18.2]; J.-Maurice Arbour & Geneviève Parent, Droit International Public, Editions Yvons Blais: Montreal (6th ed., 2012), p. 144; Malanczuk, *supra* note 19, p. 48. It is therefore more appropriate to refer to "general principles of law recognized by nations."

27. Alexander Orakhelashvili, Natural Law and Customary Law, Zeitschrift für ausländisches öffentliches Recht und Völkerrecht, vol. 68 (2008), 69–110, p. 77; Stephen Hall, The Persistent Spectre: Natural Law, International Order and the Limits of Legal Positivism, European Journal of International Law, vol. 12(2) (2001), 269–307, at pp. 292–298; Hersch Lauterpacht, An International Bill of Rights of Man, Columbia University Press: New York (1945), p. 42; Jean Spiropoulos, Die allgemeinen Rechtsgrundsätze im Völkerrecht, Verlag des Instituts für

Article 38(1)(c) of the ICJ Statute thus provides a portal through which natural law can enter the realm of international law.

Some of the proponents of this view consider that judges may discern general principles directly from natural law.[28] However, in light of the wording of Article 38 (1)(c) of the ICJ Statute, which requires general principles to be "recognized by nations," the more coherent view within this school of opinion is that general principles, although rooted in natural law, must have found some form of positive recognition by the international community.[29] Such recognition can take the shape of the principle being a common feature of domestic legal orders. However, other expressions of universal recognition of a particular principle may also suffice, such as consensual United Nations resolutions in the area of human rights.[30]

The prevailing view today considers that general principles derive directly from the shared features of domestic legal orders.[31] Lord Phillimore himself succinctly defined general principles as those "accepted by all nations in *foro domestico*."[32] Similarly, Article 21 of the Rome Statute allows the ICC to apply "general principles of law derived by the court from national laws of legal systems of the world." While it would generally be unrealistic to require positive proof that every single state recognizes a certain principle, it has to be at least established that the principle is common to the major legal systems of the world.[33] The

Internationales Recht an der Universität Kiel: Kiel (1928), p. 26. See also Bin Cheng, General Principles of Law as Applied by International Courts and Tribunals, Cambridge University Press: Cambridge (1953), p. 24 (noting that general principles "express the essential qualities of juridical truth itself").

28. South West Africa (Ethiopia & Liberia v. South Africa) (diss. op. Judge Tanaka), ICJ Reports 1966, p. 4, at p. 298.

29. See Spiropoulous, *supra* note 27, p. 26.

30. See Bruno Simma & Philip Alston, The Sources of Human Rights Law: Custom, Jus Cogens and General Principles, Australian Yearbook of International Law, vol. 12 (1988–1989), 82–108, at pp. 102–106.

See also Reservations to the Convention Genocide (Advisory Opinion), ICJ Reports 1951, 15, at p. 23, where the ICJ observed, without a detailed comparative analysis of relevant domestic laws, that the "principles underlying the [Genocide] Convention are principles which are recognized by civilized nations as binding on states, without any conventional obligation."

31. Guggenheim, *supra* note 23, p. 78; Louis Henkin, International law: politics, values and functions, Recueil des cours de l'Académie de la Haye, vol. 216 (1989), 9–400, at p. 61; Heintschel von Heinegg, *supra* note 9, pp. 488–489 [§ 18.1].

32. Lord Phillimore, as cited in Bin Cheng, *supra* note 27, p. 25.

33. Henkin, *supra* note 31, p. 61; Wolfgang Friedmann, The Uses of "General Principles" in the Development of International Law, American Journal of International Law, vol. 57(2) (1963), 279–299, at p. 284; Heintschel von Heinegg, *supra* note 9, p. 489 [§ 18.2]; Malanczuk, *supra* note 19, p. 49.

commonality only has to extend to the basic principle. The specific rules emanating from the principle do not have to be exactly identical in every legal system.[34]

Once a norm has been identified as a universal feature of domestic laws, it is not automatically considered to form part of international law. The transposition of general principles from the domestic arena into international law is not a mechanical process whereby international law imports "private law institutions 'lock, stock and barrel,' ready-made and fully equipped with a set of rules."[35] Only the underlying general principle is transposed, but not the concrete rules that are based on it. Instead, the general principle is adapted and fitted to the specific context of international law and the necessities of the subject matter under regulation. Careful reflection is required as to whether a common feature of municipal systems actually suits the international environment. In some cases, it may prove entirely inappropriate to transpose a principle to the international arena notwithstanding its being a common feature of the major domestic legal systems of the world.[36]

Both the positivist and the natural law approaches to general principles suffer from conceptual weaknesses. Invoking natural law will always raise the question how, and by whom, it can be determined that a norm constitutes universally applicable natural law, rather than just a firmly held belief peculiar to particular cultural, religious, or philosophical traditions.[37] Rousseau, certainly no ardent critic of natural law, observed that there are rarely two important writers who are of the same mind about the contents of natural law and even jested that philosophers "seem to have done their best purposely to contradict one another on [its] most fundamental principles."[38] In order to address the subjectivity problem, natural law proponents therefore regularly have to show that a norm enjoys universal recognition to justify its natural law status.

Meanwhile, strict positivists, who require international law to be based on state consent, are hard pressed to explain why the mere fact that domestic legal orders share certain legal principles, should establish states' consent that such principles also apply in international law.[39] The role of states in the formation of general principles is further diminished by the fact that judges, not states,

34. Friedmann, *id.*, p. 284; Michael Akehurst, Equity and General Principles of Law, International and Comparative Law Quarterly, vol. 25 (1976), 801–825, p. 814.

35. International Status of South West Africa (Advisory Opinion) I.C.J. Reports 1950, 128 (Sep. Op. Lord McNair), at 148. See also Crawford, *supra* note 8, p. 35; Heintschel von Heinegg, *supra* note 9, p. 489 [§ 18.3]; Malanczuk, *supra* note 19, p. 50.

36. Akehurst, *supra* note 34, p. 816; Arbour/Parent, *supra* note 26, p. 146. See also International Status of South West Africa, *id.*, p. 132; Dujay v. United Mexican States (Mex.-U.S. General Claims Commission), Report on International Arbitral Awards, vol. 4 (1929), 449, at p. 456.

37. See Akehurst, *supra* note 34, p. 812.

38. Jean Jacques Rousseau, What is the origin of inequality among men? And is it authorized by natural law? [1754], in: Jean Jacques Rousseau, The Social Contract and Discourses (trans. G.D.H.Cole), J.M. Dent: London/Toronto (1923), p. 170.

39. Cf. Henkin, *supra* note 31, p. 61.

establish whether a general principle is suitable for transposition to international law and how it is to be adapted to befit the needs of international law. If one does not want to venture down the path of natural law, one is therefore left only with pragmatically declaring that general principles are a "triumph of good sense and practical needs over the limitations of concepts and other abstractions."[40]

In practice, both approaches to the formation of general principles will often lead to very similar outcomes anyhow, because the universal recognition of the natural law character of a norm will usually find reflection in a universally shared norm of positive law and vice versa. The right to personal self-defense is a case in point, which makes further deliberation of how general principles are formed unnecessary regarding the issue at hand. As will be set out below,[41] the existence of the general principle of the right to personal self-defense can be deduced from the existence of this right in the natural law concepts of the world's major cultural and religious traditions. In light of these universally shared concepts, it is no wonder that the right to self-defense is also a common feature of domestic legal systems across the world.

II. Functions of general principles

General principles of law are a source of international law that is separate and distinguishable from treaty and customary law. While they often relate to matters of interpretation and procedural fairness, they are not limited to these categories and can also set out substantive principles.[42]

Some scholars have taken the view that general principles are only a "subsidiary" or "secondary" source of international law, pointing to the fact that they were historically meant to fill gaps in treaty and customary law and that they are only mentioned after treaty and custom in Article 38 of the ICJ Statute.[43] Support for this view can also be derived from Article 21 of the Rome Statute according to which general principles of law are only to be applied where no other norms of international law can be found.

Yet the preferable view holds that there is no hierarchy between the three primary sources of international law that would relegate general principles to a mere subsidiary role.[44] For one, the wording of Article 38 of the ICJ Statute

40. *Id.*, p. 62.

41. See this Second Chapter: D–F (pp. 27–73).

42. Friedmann, *supra* note 33, p. 287.

43. See Heintschel von Heinegg, *supra* note 9, p. 490 [§ 18.6]; Henkin, *supra* note 31, p. 61; Arbour/Parent, *supra* note 26, pp. 143 & 147.

44. Difficulties arising from the Diversification and Expansion of International Law: Report of the Study Group of the International Law Commission [ILC Fragmentation Study], U.N. Doc. A/CN.4/L.702 (2006), para. 14(31); Crawford, *supra* note 8, p. 34; Giorgio Gaja, General Principles of Law, in: Rüdiger Wolfrum (ed.), Max Planck Encyclopedia of Public International Law (online ed., updated May 2013), para. 21, http://opil.ouplaw.com/home/EPIL.

suggests no such hierarchy. Only judicial decisions and the teachings of the most highly qualified publicists of the various nations are designated as subsidiary means for the determination of the law (see Article 38 (1)(d) of the ICJ Statute). This indicates in turn (*argumentum a contrario*) that the first three sources all operate on the same hierarchical level.[45] Furthermore, during the drafting of the Statute an initial reference to "in the order following" in the introductory phrase of the draft article was deleted so as to remove any notion of hierarchy.[46] Instead, the current order of sources within Article 38 of the ICJ Statute merely serves to "indicate the [logical] order in which they would normally present themselves to the mind of an international judge when called upon to decide a dispute in accordance with international law."[47]

Most importantly, an assumption of general subsidiarity fails to take into account the diverse functions that general principles fulfil in international law. In some cases, they fill gaps in the incomplete puzzle of treaty and customary law. In this, they can of course be relevant only to the extent that treaty and customary have left such gaps. However, general principles remain relevant even where specific rules of treaty or customary law can be found, because they set out broader principles that have an impact on the formulation and interpretation of rules under treaty and customary law.[48] This follows not least from the interpretive principle of harmonization in international law. According to this principle, relevant general norms (as the name implies, general principles often fall into this category of *lex generale*) continue to give direction for interpretation and application of the relevant *lex specialis*.[49] In this regard, general principles may be compared to subatomic particles whose mere presence will have an impact on the configuration of other subatomic particles on the plane of international law. The principle of good faith, for instance, has found entry into international law as a general principle of law.[50] Yet it does not fill gaps and, owing to its general nature, could not do so. Instead, it serves to give direction to more detailed rules of treaty and customary law. The right to personal self-defense operates in a similar fashion. It shapes the formation and interpretation of treaty and customary rules in a diverse set of areas of international law. These areas include, as will be explored, international human rights law.

45. See also Crawford, *id.*, p. 34.

46. Bin Cheng, *supra* note 27, p. 20.

47. *Id.*

48. See also Gaja, *supra* note 44, para. 22.

49. ILC Fragmentation Study, *supra* note 44, para 14(9).

50. Bin Cheng, *supra* note 27, pp. 121 ff., Heintschel von Heinegg, *supra* note 9, p. 489-490 [§ 18.4]; Malanczuk, *supra* note 19, p. 49. Today, the good faith principle has been incorporated into international treaty law, e.g., under Article 2 (2) of the U.N. Charter and Articles 26 and 31 of the Vienna Convention on the Law of Treaties. It also forms part of customary international law. See Oil Platforms (Iran v. USA) [Preliminary Objections], 1996 I.C.J. Reports 803 (Dec. 12), at 812 [para. 23].

However, before turning to this matter, it remains to be shown that the right to personal self-defense indeed constitutes a general principle of law. The following sections will establish that this right is both a universally shared feature of the major legal systems of the world and of the natural law traditions underlying them. Furthermore, this right is suitable for transposition into the realm of international law—as evidenced by the fact that it can already be discerned in a number of core disciplines of international law. It is therefore immaterial whether one considers general principles of law to be based on natural law or shared domestic practice. Both schools of opinion must come to the conclusion that there is a general principle of law establishing the right to personal self-defense.

D. THE RIGHT TO SELF-DEFENSE AS A PRINCIPLE OF NATURAL LAW

Natural law can be defined in contrast to positive law. While positive law derives from any source of legal authority established by human beings, natural law claims universal and permanent validity independent of any human action providing it with authority. Aristotle already distinguished a "particular law … which each community lays down and applies to its own members" from a "universal law" being the "law of nature," which is grounded in a "natural justice and injustice that is binding on all men, even on those who have no association or covenant with each other."[51] Similarly, Cicero took the view that there is a "true law", which he indicated to be "right reason conformable to nature, universal, unchangeable, eternal … ."[52]

International law scholars adhering to the natural law tradition have variably considered natural law to be rooted in nature, reason, inherently valid concepts of justice, or divine command. Hugo Grotius considered natural law to be rooted in "human nature," famously declaring that it would exist if "there is no god, or that he takes no care of human affairs."[53] Meanwhile, the German philosopher and international law scholar Samuel von Pufendorf (1632–1694) considered it "certain that the same must be the author of all the laws of nature, who was the Creator of the universe."[54] Following the more secular strand of natural law theory, the eminent Swiss international lawyer Emer de Vattel (1714–1767) defined

51. Aristotle, Rhetoric (ed. W.D. Ross, transl. W. Rhys Roberts), Cosimo: New York (2010), p. 48 [Book I.13].

52. Marcus Tullius Cicero, The Republic and The Laws (trans. C.D. Yonge), Digireads: Lawrence (2009), p. 51 [The Republic, Bk. III, 22].

53. Hugo Grotius, The Rights of War and Peace: Book I (trans. John Morrice, ed. Richard Tuck/Jean Barbeyrac), Liberty Fund: Indianapolis (2005), pp. 88–89 [Bk. I, Preliminary Discourse, IX & XI].

54. Samuel von Pufendorf, The Whole Duty of Man According to the Law of Nature (trans. Andrew Tooke, ed. Ian Hunter/David Saunders), Liberty Fund: Indianapolis (2003), p. 45.

natural laws as "those that we derive from nature, or whose rationale is found in the essence and nature of man, and of things in general."[55]

Many contemporary legal scholars consider the right to personal self-defense to be rooted in natural law, often even affording it the character of a natural right.[56] Others have called this characterization in question arguing that a right to self-defense can logically exist only within an instituted legal order and thus cannot constitute a pre-social right of nature.[57] However, this critique confounds the practical relevance of a norm with its very existence. In the anarchical, pre-societal state of nature, the right to self-defense did not have a particular function because everyone was free to employ any degree of violence. It became relevant only when juxtaposed with the state's monopoly on the use of force. However, in the lawless state of nature, no legal norms carried any relevance. Yet norms of natural law, including the right to self-defense, still existed—unless one denies the existence of natural law altogether.

The concern about the subjectivity of natural law weighs more heavily: Any assertion that a particular norm constitutes natural law is open to the criticism that determinations of natural law are inherently subjective and depend on the importance the interpreter of the law gives to particular values underlying the law. Representative of many other positivists, Hans Kelsen objected that the "norms allegedly deduced from nature are—in truth—tacitly presupposed, and are based on subjective values, which are presented as the intentions of nature as a legislator."[58]

55. Emer de Vattel, Essay on the Foundation of Natural Law and on the First Principle of the Obligation Men Find Themselves Under to Observe Laws, in: Béla Kapossy & Richard Whatmore (trans. & eds.), Emer de Vattel: The Law of Nations, Or, Principles of the Law of Nature, Applied to the Conduct and Affairs of Nations and Sovereigns, with Three Early Essays on the Origin and Nature of Natural Law and on Luxury, Liberty Fund: Indianapolis (2008), 747–771, at p. 747.

56. See Shabtai Rosenne, Self-Defence and the Non-use of Force: Some Random Thoughts, in: Eyffinger/Stephens/Sam Muller, *supra* note 20, 49–65, at p. 55; George P. Fletcher & Jens David Ohlin, Defending Humanity: When Force is Justified and Why, Oxford University Press: New York (2008), p. 145; Reinhard Merkel, Folter und Notwehr, in: Michael Pawlik/Rainer Zaczyk (eds.), Festschrift für Günther Jakobs zum 70. Geburtstag, C. Heymanns: Berlin (2007), 375–403, at p. 386; Knoops, *supra* note 6, p. 76; R.D. Yadav, Law of Crime and Self-Defence, Mittal Publications: New Delhi (1993), pp. 19–20; Volker Erb, Notwehr als Menschenrecht—Zugleich eine Kritik der Entscheidung des LG Frankfurt am Main im "Fall Daschner," Neue Zeitschrift für Strafrecht (NStZ) 2005, 593–602, at p. 595; Volker Krey, Deutsches Strafrecht Allgemeiner Teil, vol. 1, Kohlhammer Verlag: Stuttgart (2008), p. 158; Kopel, Gallant & Eisen, *supra* note 3, pp. 136 & 170; Thomas Rönnau/Kristian Hohn, § 32: Notwehr, in: Heinrich Wilhelm Laufhütte; Ruth Rissing-van Saan & Klaus Tiedemann (eds.), Strafgesetzbuch. Leipziger Kommentar, vol. 2: §§ 32–55, De Gruyter: Berlin (12th ed., 2010), at p. 399 [§ 32, para. 63]; Doehring, *supra* note 20, p. 561; Jens David Ohlin, The Doctrine of Legitimate Defense, International Law Studies, vol. 91 (2015), 119–154, at p. 124.

57. Nikolaos Bitzilekis, Die neue Tendenz zur Einschränkung des Notwehrrechts, Duncker & Humblot: Berlin (1984), p. 28; Haggenmacher, *supra* note 20, at p. 7.

58. Hans Kelsen, The Natural Law Doctrine before the Tribunal of Science, Western Political Quarterly, vol. 2 (4) (1949), 481–513, at p. 485. See also Rousseau, *supra* note 38.

In order to address the concern regarding subjectivity, the following sections will establish an objective case for why the right to personal self-defense forms part of natural law and constitutes a natural right. In this regard, two arguments will be made. Firstly, the moral validity of the right to personal self-defense has been recognized across different cultural, philosophical, and religious traditions, which indicates that it is not based on subjective values but embodies a universal truth (comparative argument). Secondly, it is reasonable and morally justified to recognize the right to personal self-defense, while it would be unreasonable and morally unjustifiable not to do so (rationalist argument).

In making this case, two interrelated counterarguments will be refuted that have been raised against the proposition that the right to self-defense constitutes part of natural law.

Firstly, it has been argued that if the right to personal self-defense derived from reason or human nature it would have to be the same for all times and all peoples, based on the same principles and applied in the same way.[59] However, the argument goes, this is not the case, as self-defense has reflected and will always reflect the values and structures of the specific society whose legal system it serves to protect.[60]

A second, related argument against a natural law–based right to self-defense is its supposed lack of determinacy. Eyffinger goes so far as to characterize the right to self-defense as "eminently protean" since it "has been prone to endless reinterpretation and has been tossed around infinitely."[61] He suggests that

> the principle of self-defense, while nimbly taking the hurdles separating the private and public spheres and debonairly skipping the barriers of national and international domains, has presented itself as the perfect chameleon to serve man's ever varying needs.[62]

If this were indeed the case, the right to self-defense would be nothing but a convenient label, rather than an actual principle with a determinable content.

Neither argument is convincing. As will be shown, there is a general agreement about the core features of self-defense across the world's major cultural, philosophical, and religious traditions. This is not to say that approaches to self-defense have not varied to some degree between different times and places. However, no natural law principle is so determinate that it can be implemented in only one particular way. What characterizes natural law is that it forms a sufficiently defined anchor of principle around which the positive law can elaborate more detailed rules taking into account local needs and realities.

59. Bitzilekis, *supra* note 57, pp. 27–28.

60. *Id.*

61. Arthur Eyffinger, Self-Defence or the Meanderings of a Protean Principle, in: Eyffinger/Stephens/Sam Muller, *supra* note 20, 103–138, at p. 103.

62. *Id.*, 108.

I. Personal self-defense: a shared principle across cultural and religious traditions

The English dramatist and writer Douglas William Jerrold once quipped that "self-defense is the clearest of all laws, and for this reason: lawyers didn't make it."[63] A survey of the world's major philosophical and religious traditions shows that there is indeed a general conviction that the right to self-defense was not drafted by lawyers but stems from concepts of natural law that go deeper than positive law. These concepts are not limited to the Western world, but can be found across human civilization. These traditions all have in common that they generally consider the person acting in self-defense to be morally right and justified, even though of course not all construe self-defense in the language of rights and obligations, which is a rather modern construct associated with Western legal thought.

At the same time, none of these traditions considers the right to self-defense to be a boundless license to violence. Instead, concepts such as imminence of attack, necessity and proportionality of the defense, and defensive intent are invoked across very different traditions to circumscribe the parameters of legitimate self-defense.

1. Greco-Roman Legal thought and Practice

Legal and moral thought in the Western world is rooted in an amalgamation of the Greco-Roman and Judeo-Christian traditions. Both espouse a carefully circumscribed right to personal self-defense. The Greek orator Demosthenes (384-322 BCE) considered attempts to curtail the right to self-defense in ancient Athens, as contrary to natural law:

> Is it not monstrous, is it not manifestly contrary to law,—I do not mean merely to the statute law but *to the unwritten law of our common humanity*,—that I should not be permitted to defend myself against one who violently seizes my goods as though I were an enemy ?[64]

Demosthenes specifically characterized killing in self-defense as righteous and lawful,[65] thus recognizing the character of self-defense as a right, rather than a mere excuse. Ancient Attic law's recognition of a right to self-defense also follows from the writings of Antiphon and Plato as well as surviving fragments of the law on homicide enacted by Draco, the (in)famous 7th century BCE Athenian

63. Blanchard Jerrold (ed.), The Wit and Opinions of Douglas Jerrold, W. Kent: London (1859), p. 9.

64. Demosthenes, Oratio 23 against Aristocrates, in: James Herbert Vince (trans.), Demosthenes against Meidias, Androtion, Aristocrates, Timocrates, Aristogeiton, Harvard University Press: Cambridge (1935), 212–367, at pp. 253–255 [§ 61 of the Oratio, emphasis added].

65. *Id.*, p. 253 [§ 60].

legislator.[66] In that respect at least, Draco's laws were not "draconian." However, self-defense was not automatically accepted wherever a person was a victim of unlawful attack. At trial, persons relying on self-defense had to convince the jury that their defensive action was reasonable and guided by defensive intent.[67]

Roman law also recognized a right to self-defense, restricted by considerations of necessity and proportionality, especially regarding the defense of property.[68] Roman jurists considered self-defense to be a natural right. Cicero's famous defense in the murder trial of his client Milone described it as a right "imbibed from nature herself . . . and ingrained in us."[69]

In accordance with its natural law character, the right to self-defense under Roman law did not find recognition solely in the *ius civile*, the positive law that applied to Roman citizens only. It also formed part of the *ius gentium*, a legal order that the Romans considered to be rooted in natural law and thus universally binding for both Romans and non-Romans. The *Litterra Florentinus*, one of the major surviving digests of Roman law, notes that the universal *jus gentium* included "the *right* of repelling violence and wrong; it is in fact by virtue of this law whatever a man does in defense of his own person he is held to do *lawfully*."[70] Also assuming universal application of self-defense, the digests of Paulus, one of the most influential Roman jurists of the 2nd or 3rd century CE. indicate that "all statutes and all rules of law allow people to repel force by force."[71] At the same time, Paulus recognized clear limits of self-defense, namely that the force may only be directed against the aggressor and must have the object of self-defense and not revenge.[72]

2. Judeo-Christian Tradition

In the Judeo-Christian tradition, the right to self-defense finds its roots in the book of Exodus, which recognizes the right of a homeowner to kill a thief breaking into

66. For references see Michael Gagarin, Self-Defence in Athenian Homicide Law, Greek, Roman, and Byzantine Studies, vol. 19 (1978), 111–120.

67. *Id.*, at p. 118.

68. Rules subjecting self-defense to limitations of necessity and proportionality can notably be found in the Twelve Tables, a set of laws from the early Roman Republic, and in the Codex Iustianianus gathered at the behest of Emperor Justinian. For references, see Kopel, *supra* note 3, pp. 109 & 115.

69. Marcus Tullius Cicero, For T.A. Milo, in: C.D. Yonge (trans.), The Orations of Marcus Tullius Cicero, vol. 3, Henry G. Bohn: London (1852), 390–437, at p. 394 [Mil. IV].

70. Digest. 1.1.3 (Florentinus, Institutes 1), as translated in Charles Henry Monro, The Digest of Justinian, vol. 1, Cambridge University Press: Cambridge (1904), p. 4 (emphasis added). See also Haggenmacher, *supra* note 20, at pp. 19–20 with further references to Roman law sources.

71. Digest 9.2.45 (Paulus), as translated in Charles Henry Monro, The Digest of Justinian, vol. 2, Cambridge University Press: Cambridge (1909), p. 139.

72. Digest 9.2.45 (Paulus), *id.*

his house.[73] The Mishnah in the Sanhedrin tractate (around 200 CE), which sets out fundamental principles of Jewish Law, clarifies that the right to use lethal force is not justified by the danger for the homeowner's property, but based on the expectation that the thief is likely to use deadly force against the homeowner trying to defend his property.[74] Jewish Law also permits the defense of others against attack. The exhortation in the Book of Leviticus not to stand in the blood of one's neighbor[75] has even been interpreted by the Mishnah as a *duty* to defend others.[76] However, the use of lethal force is allowed only to prevent killings or rape, but does not extend to a defense against attacks that merely affect public order, such as idolatry.[77]

The Jewish religious and legal tradition thus pronounces itself very clearly in favor of a right to self-defense that extends even to the taking of life, setting out an exception to the commandment that one should not kill. The major schools of interpretation of Jewish Law concur that lethal self-defense is justified, because the life of the victim is considered preferable to that of the aggressor.[78] Concepts central to self-defense as understood today, such as immediacy, necessity, and proportionality, can also be discerned in ancient Jewish Law.[79]

Christian scholars initially struggled much harder to justify personal self-defense, in particular if it involved lethal force.[80] The New Testament of the Christian Bible had introduced notions of pacifism and nonviolence into the sacred scripture. According to the Gospel of Matthew, Jesus exhorted his followers not to resist evil, but to turn the other cheek if slapped on one cheek.[81] Similarly, his disciple Paul advised the early Christians not to defend themselves, but to leave vengeance to the Lord.[82] The early Christian thinkers found it difficult to reconcile self-defense, especially were it involved the taking of life, with these commands. Augustine (354–430 CE) described his dilemma as follows:

> But as for those [who kill in self-defense], I do not see how they can be excused, even if the law itself is just. For the law does not force them to kill; it merely leaves that in their power. They are free not to kill anyone for those

73. See Exodus 22:2.

74. Babylonian Talmud Sanhedrin 72a.

75. See Leviticus 19:16.

76. Babylonian Talmud Sanhedrin 73a. See also Fletcher & Ohlin, *supra* note 56, p. 49; Boaz Sangero, Self-Defence in Criminal Law, Hart: Oxford (2006), pp. 31–32.

77. Fletcher & Ohlin, *supra* note 56, p. 51.

78. Sangero, *supra* note 76, p. 31 (citing a comprehensive study in Hebrew by Arnold Enker of the Rashi (Rabbi Shlomo Itzhaki), Maimonides and Rabbi Mairi schools of thoughts).

79. Sangero, *supra* note 76, p. 33.

80. Stephen C. Neff, War and the Law of Nations: A General History, Cambridge University Press: Cambridge (2005), p. 60; Eyffinger, *supra* note 61, p. 114.

81. Matthew 5:39.

82. Romans 12:19.

> things which can be lost against their will, and which they should therefore not love .... Idon't blame the law that allows such people to be killed, but I can't think of any way to defend those who do the killing.[83]

Later Christian scholars tried to step back from a doctrine of pacifism in light of acute social demands.[84] They reverted to natural law, which they construed as a category separate from divine law. Isidore of Seville, Archbishop of Seville and eminent scholar of the late 6th and early 7th centuries, considered that there is a natural law "common to all nations" that "exists everywhere by the instinct of nature."[85] In his view, natural law extended to the repulsion of violence by force, which "is never considered unjust, but is held to be natural and fair."[86]

The same line of reasoning was also pursued by the Canon scholars who developed the Law of the Roman Catholic Church in the 12th and 13th centuries by building on the ancient Roman law texts. Gratian, the most influential among the early Canonists, took the view that natural law considered self-defense never as unjust, but as "natural and equitable."[87] According to Gratian, both clerics and lay persons were permitted to defend themselves against attack against their bodies and their property. However, self-defense had to be proportionate and not take place after the attack had already concluded.[88]

It was left to the greatest philosopher and theologian among the scholastics, Thomas Aquinas (1224–1275), to put forward a theory reconciling the apparent pacifism of the Christian Gospel with the Roman law–inspired teachings of the Canon Law scholars. Aquinas reasoned that any "[lethal] act of self-defense may have two effects, one is the saving of one's life, the other is the slaying of the aggressor."[89] Since the defender's intention is not to slay, but to save his own life and every being naturally seeks to survive, self-defense is lawful. However, the defender must "not exceed the limits of blameless violence," but use "only necessary violence" and repel force "with moderation."[90]

83. See Augustine, On Free Choice of the Will (trans. Thomas Williams), Hackett: Indianapolis (1993), p. 9 [De Libero Arbitrio I.5].

84. Eyffinger, *supra* note 61, p. 111.

85. Stephen A. Barney et al. (eds. & trans.), The Etymologies of Isidore of Seville, Cambridge University Press: New York (2006), p. 117 [Bk.V.4.1].

86. *Id.*, p. 117 [Bk. V.4.2].

87. Gratian, The Treatise on Laws (Decretum DD. 1-20) (trans. Augustine Thompson), Catholic University of America Press: USA (1993), pp. 6-7 [Decretum, Distinction 1, C. 7 § 3]. For further references to the Canonists work on self-defense, see Haggenmacher, *supra* note 20, pp. 21–23.

88. See Haggenmacher, *supra* note 20, pp. 22–23, citing from Gratian's Causa 23.

89. Thomas Aquinas, Summa theologiae, vol. II (transl. by fathers of the English Dominican Province), Benziger Bros: New York (1947), p. 67 [Summa theologiae II-II, Q 64, art 7].

90. *Id.*

To this day, Aquinas's double effects theory guides the moral and legal doctrine of the Roman Catholic Church. Citing Aquinas, its Catechism advises that persons using lethal force to defend their own life are not murderers, because their intent is to protect their own life and it is legitimate to insist on respect for one's own right to life. At the same time, the Catholic Church recognizes self-defense as legitimate only to the extent that force is necessary and used with moderation. Within these bounds, the Catholic Church explicitly recognizes self-defense as a right, rather than merely an instance of excusable violence.[91]

3. European Judicial Practice in the Middle Ages and the Early Modern Period

The Germanic tribes of the early Middle Ages recognized that persons who killed others in self-defense would not have to atone for their deed if they could prove, in a formal legal suit brought against the victim's dead body, that the person killed was an aggressor and thus unworthy of legal protection. Not all tribes agreed that this entailed absolution from the parallel duty to make a compensatory payment to the victim's family, which is why there is still some debate about whether Germanic law truly recognized self-defense or not.[92]

As Europe's tribal societies gradually became more centralized entities and sovereign rulers consolidated their power, forms of violent self-help by private individuals, including self-defense, were initially suppressed. To some extent, this may have reflected the debate among the early Christians on the permissibility of taking life for purposes of self-defense.[93] However, pragmatic policy considerations were probably more relevant. Fledgling sovereigns considered the suppression of private force necessary to enforce their authority and impose their monopoly on the use of power on societies that traditionally relied on self-help (blood revenge) and compensatory justice (blood money) to contain violence.[94]

However, assertions of self-defense could not be suppressed for long and the principle of self-defense re-emerged. Legal texts from the Germany of the late medieval ages, such as the *Sachsenspiegel* (13th century) and the *Mainzer Landfrieden* (1235), recognize self-defense.[95] In 1532, German Emperor Charles V promulgated the *Constitutio Criminalis Carolina*, the first codification of

91. Catholic Church, Catechism of the Catholic Church; Burns & Oates: London (2nd ed., 2002), p. 487 [§§ 2263–2265].

92. Eberhard Schmidt, Einführung in die Geschichte der deutschen Strafrechtspflege, Vandenhoek & Ruprecht: Göttingen (3rd ed., 1995), p. 36 [§ 24]; Frank Wittemann, Grundlinien und Grenzen der Notwehr in Europa, Peter Lang: Frankfurt a.M. (1997), p. 3.

93. Bernard Bouloc, Droit pénal général, Dalloz: Paris (21st ed., 2009), p. 340 [para. 388].

94. Sangero, *supra* note 76, pp. 30–31; Carthryn Jo Rosen, The Excuse of Self-Defence: Correcting a Historical Accident on Behalf of Battered Women Who Kill, American University Law Review, vol. 36 (1986) 11–56, at pp. 25–26.

95. Wittemann, *supra* note 92, pp. 3–4.

criminal law claiming application to all of the German empire. It established "rightful self-defense" (*rechte Notweer*) as a justification even for killing. However, such defensive killings were only permitted against imminent or ongoing attacks, where retreat was not an option.[96]

The same year, 1532, the English Parliament passed a law that classified the killing of robbers and other assailants on highways as justifiable homicide.[97] Before then, English common law had not recognized self-defense as a justification, especially not for lethal force. Instead, it relied on the principle of *se defendendo*, according to which a person who retreated from attack as far as he could before resorting to deadly force would receive a pardon from the King and not be executed. However, the defendant still forfeited his goods to the English Crown as a sanction for the taking of life.[98]

In the wake of the 1532 Statute, this doctrine gradually gave way to the general recognition of self-defense as a full criminal defense under the common law, which was well established by the late 16th or early 17th century.[99] When Blackstone published his famous Commentaries on the Laws of England in 1769, he accordingly considered lethal self-defense to be a case of justifiable homicide, limiting the scope of the medieval *se defendendo* pardon only to brawls where all involved would usually bear some fault in starting the fight.[100] Underlying this shift was Blackstone's recognition that self-defense "is justly called the primary law of nature, for it is not, neither can it be in fact, taken away be the law of society."[101]

Notwithstanding the legal changes in neighboring states, absolutist France clung to a legal doctrine that refused to recognize self-defense as a right and justification all the way up to the French Revolution. A person who killed in self-defense was not considered to be free of guilt, but had to plead for the King's pardon.[102] Self-defense as a justification was only introduced into French law by the revolutionary Penal Code of 1791. That statute was drafted under the influence

96. Constitutio Criminalis Carolina (1532), §§ 139–140, http://www.smixx.de/ra/Links_F-R/Constitutio_Criminalis_Carolina_1532.pdf. See also Wittemann, *supra* note 92, pp. 5–6; Friedrich-Christian Schroeder, Die Notwehr als Indikator politischer Grundanschauungen in: Friedrich-Christian Schroeder/Heinz Zipf (eds.), Festschrift für Reinhart Maurach zum 70. Geburtstag, C.F. Müller: Karlsruhe (1972), 127–142, at p. 128.

97. Sangero, *supra* note 76, at p. 35; George P. Fletcher, A Crime of Self-Defense: Bernhard Goetz and the Law on Trial, Free Press: New York (1988), p. 32.

98. Fletcher, *id.*, p. 30; Sangero, *supra* note 76, pp. 33–34.

99. Wittemann, *supra* note 92, p. 121.

100. Sir William Blackstone, Commentaries on the Laws of England, vol. 4, Clarendon Press: Oxford (1769), p. 184.

101. Sir William Blackstone, Commentaries on the Laws of England, vol. 3, Clarendon Press: Oxford (1769), p. 4.

102. Bouloc, *supra* note 93, p. 340 [para. 388]; Wittemann, *supra* note 92, p. 75.

of enlightened reformers, such as Montesquieu and Rousseau, whose writings pointed to a natural right of self-defense.[103]

4. The Classic Writers on International Law

Parallel to these developments in Europe's judicial practice, European legal scholars shaped a new body of law: international law. In the absence of state-approved rules, they heavily relied on natural law, drawing on the Greek and Roman classics as well as on Christian scripture.

Since "private war" (violence between individuals) and "public war" (war between sovereigns) were still considered part of a continuum in the early modern period, the early scholars of international law discussed questions of personal self-defense extensively in order to extrapolate rules applicable to relations between sovereigns. Generally unperturbed by the concerns of the early Christian scholars or the domestic judicial practice prevailing at the time, these writers largely considered that natural law established a right to personal self-defense, albeit circumscribed by clear boundaries of immediacy, necessity and proportionality.

Giovanni da Legnano, the eminent Milanese international law scholar of the 14th century, took the view that "self-defense proceeds from natural law, and not from positive law, civil or canon."[104] He considered the right to self-defense to be an inalienable part of human nature, so much so that not even a master could forbid his slave from exercising that right.[105] Recognizing that the right also extended to the defense of others and of property, he insisted that justifiable defense had clear limits, both regarding the time window of defense and the means used for defense.[106] In particular, preemptive action was only permissible once the assailant was "bold and ready to strike."[107]

Among the early Spanish scholars of international law, Francisco de Vitoria (1486–1546), founder of the Salamanca school of theology that applied new insights to the Scholastic school of thought, declared that "[a]nyone, even a private person, can accept and wage a defensive war," because "there would be no condition of happiness for the world, nay, its condition would be one of utter misery, if oppressors and robbers and plunderers could with impunity commit their crimes and oppress the good and innocent, and these latter could not in turn retaliate on them."[108] Private persons had a right to self-defense but not to

103. See *infra*, notes 126–128 and accompanying text.

104. Giovanni Da Legnano, De Bello, de Represaliis et de Duello (ed. Thomas Erskine Holland, trans. J.K. Brierly), Carnegie Institution: Washington D.C. (1917), p. 278.

105. *Id.*, p. 287.

106. *Id.*, pp. 300–302.

107. *Id.*, p. 304.

108. Francisco de Vitoria, De Indis et de Ivre Belli Relectiones (ed. Ernest Nys.; trans. John Pawley Bate), Carnegie Institution: Washington, D.C. (1917), pp. 163 & 167. See also *id.*, pp. 168 & 178.

vengeance, since self-defense "must be a response to immediate danger, made in the heat of the moment."[109] Francisco Suárez (1548–1617), another eminent international jurist of the Salamanca School, wrote that it would be impossible "to do away with the right of self-defense—springing from the law of nature—against a criminal charge . . . . for it would not be permissible that the Emperor should abolish those things which proceed from the natural law."[110] The Italian legal scholar Alberico Gentili, who taught about the same time at Oxford University, recognized individual persons' right to defend themselves and others since "[e]ven the brutes are given the right of defense by nature, and we are persuaded and convinced of this right, not by argument, but by some innate power."[111]

Hugo Grotius also considered it inherent to "the law of nature, for anyone to repel injuries by force."[112] According to Grotius, the establishment of state authorities did not eclipse the self-defense option, since individuals would still find themselves in situations where they could not avail themselves of state help.[113] Grotius struggled with reconciling the pacifist teachings of the Christian Gospel with the Roman law precedents known to him. On the one hand, he consistently described self-defense as a right. On the other, he refused to concede that the person who kills in self-defense should be free from all rebuke when taking life. Killing in self-defense "may be understood to take off the punishment, but not to give him a real right to the act itself."[114]

With the latter, Grotius stood alone among the classic writers of international law. Notably, Emer de Vattel, who followed in his footsteps, does not pick up this position. Instead, he reaffirms the status of self-defense as a natural right and full justification for both individuals and for states. Since nature requires both nations and individuals to preserve themselves, every nation and every human being has a right not to suffer any assault on its survival.[115]

5. Enlightenment Philosophy

The Enlightenment transformed the concept of natural law. Its proponents sought to derive empirical arguments from the state of nature that they

109. Francisco de Vitoria, On the Law of War, in: Anthony Pagdan & Jeremy Lawrance, Vitoria: Political Writings, Cambridge University Press: Cambridge (1991), p. 300 [§ 5].

110. Francisco Suárez, A Treatise on Laws and God the Lawgiver, in: Gwladys L. Williams et al. (eds.), Selections from Three Works of Francisco Suárez, S. J., Clarendon Press: Oxford (1944), at p. 273.

111. Alberico Gentili, De Iure Belli Tres Libri, Vol. II: The Translation of the Edition of 1612 (John C. Rolfe, trans.) Clarendon Press: Oxford (1933), pp. 58–59 [Book I Ch. XIII.94].

112. Grotius, *supra* note 53, p. 240 [Book I, Ch. 3.I.2].

113. *Id.*, p. 241 [Bk. I, Ch. 3.II.1].

114. Hugo Grotius, The Rights of War and Peace [1625], Book II (ed. Richard Tuck/Jean Barbeyrac, trans. John Morrice), Liberty Fund: Indianapolis (2005), p. 415 [Bk. II Ch. 1.XIV].

115. Vattel, The Law of Nations, *supra* note 55, p. 288 [Bk. II, Ch.IV, § 49].

presumed to have existed prior to the social contract, the basis of human societies and eventually of states. Based on this premise, they established that human beings enjoy natural rights that predate the formation of the state and are thus inalienable. They generally considered the right to personal self-defense to be among these natural rights, which also comprised many of the rights known as human rights today.

Thomas Hobbes (1588–1679), the first major figure of the English Enlightenment movement, considered that in the original state of nature, individual human beings have the right to do everything necessary to preserve their life, including to "one another's body."[116] On their own, however, human beings are exposed to "continual fear and danger of violent death" and a life that is "solitary, poor, nasty, brutish, and short."[117] For their own good, human beings have therefore voluntarily divested themselves of many self-preservation rights to form societies and states for their mutual protection. Yet the right to self-defense marks an exception. Human beings retain it as a remnant of the state of nature, even under the social contract, because "a man cannot lay down the right of resisting them that assault him by force to take away his life, because he cannot be understood to aim thereby at any good to himself."[118]

Reaffirming that self-defense amounts to a natural right, John Locke (1632–1704) offered a stronger moral basis for that right than did Hobbes. Locke argued that the attacker puts himself "in a state of war" with the victim and "so has exposed his life to the other's power to be taken away by him, or any one that joins with him in his defense, and espouses his quarrel; it being reasonable and just, I should have a right to destroy that which threatens me with destruction."[119] Locke's further reasoning implies the requirement of necessity, since he wrote that "by the fundamental law of nature, man being to be preserved as much as possible, *when all cannot be preserved*, the safety of the innocent is to be preferred."[120]

Locke's German contemporary Samuel von Pufendorf (1632–1694), puts forward a two-pronged justification for self-defense. Similar to Locke, he considers self-defense "lawful and altogether blameless," since the attacker who is "hurt or slain must impute [that result to] his own wickedness which set me under a necessity of doing what I did [to defend myself]."[121] Pufendorf offers an additional

116. Thomas Hobbes, Leviathan [1651] (ed. J.C.A. Gaskin), Oxford University Press: Oxford/New York (1998), p. 87 [Ch. XIV.4].

117. *Id.*, at p. 84 [Ch. XIII.9].

118. *Id.*, p. 88 [Ch. XIV.8].

119. John Locke, Two treatises of government [1689], Whitmore, Fenn and C. Brown: London (1821), p. 200 [Bk. II, Ch. 2 § 16].

120. *Id.* [emphasis added].

121. Pufendorf, *supra* note 54, p. 82 [Bk. I, Ch.V.XII–XIII].

argument for self-defense that looks more at the negative impact a denial of self-defense would have on society as a whole, in that

> honest men would be but a ready prey for villains, if they were not allowed to make use of force in defense of themselves . . . it would tend to the destruction of mankind, if self-defense even with force were prohibited to us.[122]

According to Pufendorf, the right to self-defense must be limited to what is necessary and proportional. Before having recourse to extreme measure, Pufendorf contends,

> we must first try the more harmless remedies; for instance, we must endeavor to keep out the invader by cutting off his access to us; to withdraw into strong places; and to admonish him to desist from his outrageous fury. And it is also the duty of a prudent man to put up a slight wrong, if it may conveniently be done, and to remit somewhat of his right, . . . especially if that thing or concern of ours upon which the attempt is made, be such as may easily be made amends for or repaired."[123]

Immanuel Kant (1724–1804) also considers that to prohibit self-defense would violate natural law in light of the impact on the individual. He writes that authorities that unduly limit self-defense are taking away the human being's most sacred right.[124] Yet Kant appears to be alone among the great Enlightenment philosophers in contending that proportionality in self-defense is not a legal requirement, only an ethical one.[125]

Key figures of the French Enlightenment endorsed self-defense as a natural right as well. Montesquieu (1689–1755) recognized in *De l'Esprit des lois* that all citizens have the right to natural self-defense. Self-defense may even entail a right to kill "because my life is in respect to me is what the life of my antagonist is to him."[126] However, they may exercise this right only against sudden attacks, where they would be killed if they waited for the assistance of the law.[127]

Jean Jacques Rousseau (1712–1778) considered that all norms of natural law are derived from two principles that are rooted in natural impulses that exist prior to

122. Pufendorf, *id.*, pp. 82–83 [Bk. I, Ch. V.XIII].

123. *Id.*, p. 83 [Bk. I, Ch. V.XIV].

124. See Immanuel Kant, Reflexion Nr.7195, in: Werner Busch, Die Entstehung der kritischen Rechtsphilosophie Kants, De Gruyter: Berlin/New York (1979), p. 154.

125. Immanuel Kant, Metaphysik der Sitten (1797), in: Immanuel Kant, Gesammelte Schriften, vol. VI, Preußische Akademie: Berlin (1907/1914), p. 235.

126. Baron de Montesquieu, Spirit of the Laws, vol. 1 (ed. and trans. not identified), Ebenezer Wilson Bookfeller in Dumfries: Edinburgh (3rd ed., 1762), p. 147 [Bk.10, Ch.2].

127. *Id.*

reason—"one of them deeply interesting us in our own welfare and preservation, and the other exciting a natural repugnance at seeing any other sensible being, and particularly any of our own species, suffer pain or death."[128] The latter impulse of compassion prevents human beings from hurting other sensible beings, "except on those lawful occasions on which his own preservation is concerned and he is obliged to give himself the preference."[129] Rousseau thus sees the right to self-defense as resulting from a forced choice between countervailing impulses, which the individual may lawfully resolve in favor of his own preservation.

The 19th century saw the raise of positivist theories at the expense of natural law thinking. However, even utilitarian thinker Jeremy Bentham, the ardent positivist who famously dismissed the very idea of natural rights as "nonsense on stilts," could not help but recognize the intrinsic value of the right to self-defense:

> This right of [self-]defense is absolutely necessary. The vigilance of magistrates can never make up for the vigilance of each individual on his own behalf. The fear of the law can never restrain bad men so effectually as the fear of the sum total of individual resistance. Take away this right, and you become, in so doing, the accomplice of all bad men.[130]

6. Islam and the Sharia

Recognition of self-defense as morally and legally justified within clear boundaries extends beyond the West to the other major cultures and religions of human civilization. Islamic law, the *Sharia*, is a natural law order, which bases itself on the divine commands that are laid down in the verses of the Quran (*Sura*) and emerge from the life and example set by the Prophet Muhammad (*Sunnah*). Islamic law recognizes self-defense as the natural right of every human being.[131] This right is considered to find its base notably in the following Quranic verses:

> Fight in Allah's cause those who fight you, but do not transgress limits; for Allah loves not transgressors. . . . and make not your own hands contribute to (your) destruction.[132]

128. Rousseau, *supra* note 38, p. 172.

129. *Id.*

130. Jeremy Bentham, Theory of Legislation, Vol. II, (ed. Richard Hildreth), Weeks, Jordan & Company: Boston (1840), p. 38.

131. Matthew Lippman, Sean McConville & Mordechai Yerushalmi, Islamic Criminal Law and Procedure: An Introduction, Praeger: New York (1988), p. 56; Abdul Ghafur Hamid & Khin Maung Sein, Islamic International Law and the Right of Self-Defense of States, Journal of East Asia and International Law, vol. 2 (2009), 67–101, at p. 88; Azhar Javed, Intoxication & Self-defence: A Comparative Study of Principles of English Law and Shari'ah, (2004), http://etheses.whiterose.ac.uk/526/1/uk_bl_ethos_416550.pdf, pp. 286.

132. The Holy Quran (trans. Abdullah Yusuf Ali), Islamic Book Trust: Kuala Lumpur (2007), at 2:190 & 2:195.

> And those who, when an oppressive wrong is inflicted on them, (are not cowed but) help and defend themselves. . . . But indeed if any do help and defend themselves after a wrong (done) to them, against such there is no cause of blame.[133]

Further support for the moral justification of self-defense can be gained from a *Sunnah* attributed to the Prophet:

> Whoever fights in defense of his person and is killed, he is a martyr; whoever is killed in defense of his property, is a martyr; whoever fights in defense of his family and is killed, is a martyr . . . .[134]

Based on the Quranic exhortation cited above not to contribute to one's own destruction, almost all schools of interpretation in Islamic law consider it even a duty to defend one's own life from attack, even if means killing the assailant.[135] At the same time, the Quran prohibits "transgress[ing] limits." Self-defense must be exercised only against an imminent or ongoing attack, must not exceed the level of violence necessary to ward off the aggressor and be proportional to the acts of the attacker.[136] Within these limits, self-defense, including killing an attacker, is considered lawful and the defender will face no criminal or financial liability, because the aggressor is considered to have lost his legal protection.[137]

7. African Customary or "Traditional" Legal Systems

There is no uniform body of African legal customs, even if many ethnic groups in sub-Saharan Africa share commonalities in their legal thinking. Discerning substantive legal principles in African customary laws is further complicated by the fact that the customary authorities applying such laws tend to prioritize flexible, interest-based conflict resolution methods over adjudication based on fixed legal norms. Furthermore, the original content of customary laws that remain in existence was often altered by the encounter with colonial law and authority, which is why anthropologists generally avoid describing such legal systems as "traditional."[138]

These caveats noted, some scholars still underscore that African customary legal systems generally recognize self-defense and that such that recognition

133. *Id.*, at 42:39 & 42:41.

134. As translated in Hamid & Maung Sein, *supra* note 131, p. 77.

135. Rudolph Peters, Crime and Punishment in Islamic Law, Cambridge University Press: Cambridge (2005), p. 25.

136. Peters, *id.*; Lippman et al., *supra* note 131, p. 56.

137. Peters, *id.*; Yadav, *supra* note 56, p. 97.

138. See Martin Chanock, Law Custom and Social Order: The Colonial Experience in Malawi and Zambia, Cambridge University Press: Cambridge (1985), at p. 4; Mahmood Mamdani, Citizen and Subject, Princeton University Press: Princeton (1996), p. 110.

predates colonial rule.[139] Even killings may be justified by self-defense. For instance, there are documented cases of customary law courts in Malawi that acquitted persons of murder charges on self-defense grounds. In these cases, killing in self-defense was considered a justification, because the perpetrator provoked the confrontation and thus brought his death on himself: In one case, the aggressor was equated to a person who puts his hands into a hole where there is a snake and gets bitten as a result; in another the assailant was compared to someone disturbing bees in their hive.[140] Likewise, a 1904 codification by French colonial administrators that claims to summarize pre-existing law in French-controlled Africa indicates that no punishment or compensation attaches to homicide in self-defense.[141]

It should be noted, though, that some ethnic groups, while recognizing self-defense in principle, consider that it does not fully preclude compensatory claims in cases of loss of life, and some form of payment to the clan or family of a killed aggressor may still be required.[142] This is at times explained with the particular respect held by African custom for the sanctity of life.[143] However, more pragmatic policy considerations that aim to preclude cycles of retributive revenge also play a part when demanding compensation regardless of circumstances.[144]

8. Confucianism, Taoism and at Traditional Chinese Law

Taoism and, even more so, Confucianism are key foundations of contemporary Chinese philosophy and legal thought. Both are believed to have developed from the 6th century BCE. They share the primary objective of attaining harmony in the world but differ on how to achieve this.

Taoism takes the view that superior persons should conduct themselves with compassion, moderation, and humility to establish harmony with nature. Violence generally indicates failure to accommodate oneself to the natural way, the *Tao*. Its principal text, the Tao Te Ching, finds that "arms, however beautiful,

139. Taslim Olawale Elias, The Nature of African Customary Law, Manchester University Press: Manchester (1972), p. 283; Peter Kasenene, Religious Ethics in Africa, Fountain: Kampala (1998), pp. 41ff.

140. Paul Brietzke, Murder and Manslaughter in Malawi's Traditional Courts, Journal of African Law, vol. 18(1) (1974), 37–56, pp. 45–46.

141. Roger Villamur & Maurice Delafosse, Les Coutumnes Agni, rédigées et codifies d'après les documents officiels les plus récents, Challamel: Paris (1904), pp. 98–99 [Articles 326 & 327].

142. A.L. Epstein, Injury and Liability in African Customary Law in Zambia, in: Max Gluckman (ed.), Ideas and Procedures in African Customary Law, Oxford University Press: London (1969), 292–304, at p. 297; Claude Durand, Les Anciennes Coutumes Penales Du Tchad, Harnattan: Paris/Budapest/Turin (2002), p. 18; Mohammed Hassan Fadlalla, Customary Laws in Southern Sudan: Customary Laws of Dinka and Nuer, iUniverse: Bloomington (2009), p. 95.

143. Epstein, *id.*

144. Durand, *supra* note 142, p. 18.

are instruments of evil omen and . . . they who have the Tao do not like to employ them." Yet the Tao Te Ching does not condemn all violence, counseling that the superior person uses arms "only on the compulsion of necessity" and with "calm and repose."[145] Self-defense within these limits does not constitute violence in contradiction to the *Tao* as long as one's heart is free from anger.[146] Taoism thus recognizes the concepts of necessity and defensive intent that limit self-defense.

The recognition of self-defense as a virtue also finds reflection in Wen-Tzu's *Understanding the Mysteries*, one of the Taoist classics. Wen-Tzu warns that military action based on anger, greed, and pride will result respectively in death, defeat, and extinction. However, acting in self-defense accords with the *Tao* and will lead to positive results as long as necessity and defensive intent are established:

> To execute the violent so as to rescue the weak is called justice. To mobilize only when it becomes unavoidable because of aggression of enemies is called response . . . and results in victory.[147]

Confucianism prescribes a life founded on key virtues and lived in firmly established hierarchical relationships. Although supportive of violent state punishments and not opposed to just warfare, Confucianism abhors interpersonal violence to the extent that it upsets social harmony and order. Violence generally also runs counter to Confucius' "Golden Rule" that one should treat others as benevolently as one wishes to be treated oneself.[148] Yet self-defense, whether exercised by sovereigns or by individuals, is considered a permissible exception.[149] When asked for advice by a prince facing attack from powerful neighbors, Confucius' primary follower, Mencius (371–289 BCE), counseled that preparing to exercise self-defense was the "proper course."[150] Mencius went as far as suggesting that people have a right to defend themselves against tyrannical rulers

145. Lao Tse, Tao Te Ching (trans. James Legge), Arc Manor: Rockville, Maryland (2008), p. 47 [Ch. 31.2].

146. George W. Wolfe, The Spiritual Power of Nonviolence, JOMAR Press: Austin (2012), pp. 104–105.

147. Wen-Tzu, Understanding the Mysteries, No. 80, as translated in: Thomas Cleary, The Taoist Classics, Shambhala Publications: Boston (1999), p. 209.

148. See Confucius, Analects (ca. 5th–3rd century B.C.), Book XV, Ch. XXIII, as translated in James Legge, The Chinese Classics, vol. 1: Confucian analects, the Great Learning and the Doctrine of the Mean, Trübner & Co.: London (1861), p. 165.

149. Daniel Thürer, Religion and International Humanitarian Law: Support and Tension, Recueil des cours de l'Academie de la Haye, vol. 338 (2008), 165–195, at p. 170; Frederick Tse-shyang Chen, The Confucian View of World Order, Indiana International and Comparative Law Review, vol. 1 (1991), 45–69, at p. 58.

150. As cited in Chen, *id.*, p. 58.

(and may even depose them) given that such rulers fail to live up to the Mandate of the Heavens on which their rule is built.[151]

At the interpersonal level, neither the ancient Confucian texts nor the ancient Chinese Imperial legal codes that built on them set out a full-fledged right to self-defense. However, elements of a self-defense doctrine can already be discerned in ancient Chinese legal thought.[152] Among the earliest surviving documents that suggest recognition of the right to self-defense is an advisory opinion prepared for the Court of Emperor Han Wudi (156–87 BCE). It highlighted that people must be able to defend themselves against the attacks of criminals in order to justify why there should be no restrictions on the private possession of bows and crossbows.[153]

The Rites of Zhou, one of the classic Confucian ritual texts dating back at least to the middle of the 2nd century BCE, consider that it is not a crime to kill persons in defense of one's own home or community from robbers.[154] This principle was also integrated into the legal code of the Tang Dynasty (618–907 CE), the oldest of the imperial legal codes that has survived in its entirety. The Tang Code establishes that the master of the house incurs no punishment if he kills a nocturnal intruder, unless he knows that the intruder means no harm. Only immediate defense was allowed; self-defense could no longer be exercised after the intruder was seized.[155]

9. Hinduism

Hinduism centers on the reincarnation of souls (*jives*), which transmigrate from increasingly complex animals until they inhabit a human body. Within humans, the soul can attain more and more awareness and moral virtue with each reincarnation, ideally reaching a supreme and eternal condition (*moksha*). The morality of one's action (*karma*) determines to what extent the soul may advance in its next reincarnation. Conducting oneself without physical or mental violence (*ahimsa*) is considered a source of positive karma and necessary to reach the most exalted levels.

However, mainstream Hinduism does not command a life of nonviolence. In particular, self-defense is considered righteous and justified. The Books of

151. Tom Ginsburg, Daniel Lansberg-Rodriguez & Mila Versteeg, When to Overthrow your Government: The Right to Resist in the World's Constitutions, UCLA Law Review, vol. 60 (2013), 1184–1260, at pp. 1197–1198.

152. Daniel Sprick, Die Grenzen der Notwehr im Strafrecht der Volksrepublik China, Nomos: Baden-Baden (2015), pp. 25–88.

153. Charles Sanft, Bow Control in Han China: Yuqiu Shouwang on Self-Defense, Journal of Asian History, vol. 42 (2008), 143–164, at p. 158.

154. See Edouard Biot [ed. & trans.], Le Tcheou-Li ou Rites des Tchéou, vol. 2, Imprimerie nationale: Paris (1851), at p. 352 [Book XXXVI].

155. Wallace Johnson [ed. & trans.], The T'Ang Code, Volume II: Specific Articles, Princeton University Press: Princeton (2012), pp. 276–277 [Article 269 Tang Code].

Manu, a comprehensive set of Hindu norms of conduct from ca. 500 BCE, stipulate that a person who kills in self-defense or defense of others "kills in the cause of right [and] commits no sin."[156] This applies even if the attacker, who himself has to approach with murderous intent, is a "teacher, a child or an aged man, or a Brahmana deeply versed in the Vedas."[157]

The *Dharma-Shastra*, the ancient body of Hindu jurisprudence on the right course of personal conduct, even establishes a duty to defend one's life against present or imminent threats:

> When an aggressor is attacking a man with an upraised weapon, if the latter kills him, even if he be a Brahmin, the slayer does not incur the sin of killing a Brahmin. In fact he would incur such sin if he does not so kill.[158]

Along the same lines is the exhortation to defend oneself so as to thwart the joy of one's enemies, which can be found in the Thirrikurral, an influential code of conduct in rhyme form ascribed to the revered Tamil poet-sage Thiruvalluvar (ca. 1st century CE).[159]

10. Buddhism

Buddhism is based on the teachings of Siddhartha Gautama Buddha (ca. 4th–6th century CE), which are seen as an exposition of natural law. Buddhism shares with Hinduism basic concepts such as rebirth and *karma*. However, it differs from Hinduism notably in its belief in a supreme state of nonbeing (*nirvana*) that breaks the cycle of suffering in life and rebirth. The *nirvana* can only be reached by renouncing one's desires and self and living a moral life.

Nonviolence (*ahimsa*) is one of five moral precepts (*pancha shila*) that every Buddhist has to live by. Violent actions or mere thoughts of violence are generally considered negative karma, and various passages in Buddhist scripture extol examples of nonviolent submission to aggression. The *Abhidharmakosabhasyam* treatise, for instance, exalts the deed of a group of Buddha's kinsmen who allowed themselves to be massacred by an enemy king rather than defend themselves.[160]

156. Georg Bühler (ed.), The Laws of Manu, Library of Alexandria: Los Angeles (1964), p. 118 [Ch. VIII, verse 349].

157. *Id.* [Ch. VIII, verse 350].

158. As cited in Yadav, *supra* note 56, p. 81.

159. Thiravilluvar, Tirrikular (trans. G.U. Pope et al.), Project Madurai: Lausanne (2002), at p. 106 [Ch. 2.3.15, verse 878]: "Know thou the way, then do thy part, thyself defend; Thus shall the pride of those that hate thee have an end."

160. See Lambert Schmithausen, Aspects of the Buddhist Attitude Towards War, in: Jan E.M. Houben & Karel R. Van Kooij (eds.), Violence Denied: Violence, Non-Violence and the Rationalization of Violence in South Asian Cultural History, Brill: Boston (1999), 45–68, at p. 49. See also Eyffinger, *supra* note 61, p. 107, reciting the story of the Buddha calmly awaiting the attack of an intoxicated elephant, instead of preparing to defend himself.

However, the ideal of nonviolence does not translate into a complete prohibition of violence. Buddhist practice still recognizes exceptions to the concept of nonviolence, including on the basis of self-defense.[161] The *I Ching*, a Buddhist text from the 7th century CE, already stipulates that it is "beneficial to defend against enemies, harmoniously protecting one another."[162] Among contemporary Buddhist authorities, the Dalai Lama, the highest dignitary in Tibetan Buddhism, has characterized self-defense, including by lethal means, as permissible if absolutely necessary and proportional.[163] The *Pattimokkha*, the basic monastery code of discipline in Theravada Buddhism, recognizes that even monks have a right to self-defense. The code considers it a grave offense leading to expulsion from the monastic order to hit or threaten to hit another monk when impelled by anger. However, an exception applies when such deed is done in self-defense with purely defensive intent.[164]

Like Thomas Aquinas's double effect theory, Buddhist scripture invokes considerations of motive to reconcile the seemingly irreconcilable concepts of nonviolence and self-defense. Where absolutely necessary, even a killing in self-defense can be justified if it is driven by compassion rather than anger. In this respect, not only is defensive killing an act of compassion towards the victim of the aggression, but self-defense is understood as an act of compassion towards the aggressor who is stopped from committing an act of bad karma.[165] The contention advanced by Eyffinger that "from the Buddhist perspective compassion, not self-defense . . . has always been the paramount yardstick"[166] therefore misses the point that Buddhism does not understand the two as antonyms, but links them.

The justification of compassionate killings in self-defense finds a basis in the tale of the compassionate captain, which is described in the *Upaya-Kausalya*, an

161. Michael Jerryson, Buddhist Traditions and Violence, in: Mark Juergensmeyer; Marco Kitts; & Michael Jerryson (eds.), Oxford Handbook of Religion and Violence, Oxford University Press: New York (2013), 41–66, at p. 44, Thürer, *supra* note 149, p. 175; Bernard Faure, Buddhism and Symbolic Violence, in: Andrew R. Murphy (ed.), The Blackwell Companion to Religion and Violence, Blackwell Publishing: Chichester (2011), 211–226, pp. 218–219 (recalling also the story of the referred 13th century Buddhist Master U Rgyan Pa, who used potent magic formulas to kill bandits who attacked him).

162. Thomas Cleary (ed.), Classics of Buddhism and Zen, vol. 5, Shambhala Publications: Boston (2002), at p. 336.

163. Statements of the Dalai Lama, as cited in Jens Schlieter, Compassionate Killing or Conflict Resolution? The Murder of King Langdarma according to Tibetan Buddhist Sources, in: Michael Zimmermann (ed.), Buddhism and Violence, Lumbini International Research Institute: Bhairahawa, Nepal (2006), 131–158, at p. 147; David B. Kopel, Self-defence in Asian Religions, Liberty University Law Review, vol. 2 (2007), 79–164, at p. 146.

164. Thanissaro Bhikkhu, The Buddhist Monastic Code I: The Pattimokkha Rules, Metta Forest Monastery: Valley Center, California (3rd ed., 2013), p. 398.

165. Schlieter, *supra* note 163, p. 152; Schmithausen, *supra* note 160, p. 59.

166. Eyffinger, *supra* note 61, p. 107.

important Buddhist treatise of the Mahayana School. In one of his many previous births, the Buddha is a captain of a ship. When told that a robber wants to kill five hundred passengers and the captain, he realizes that killing the robber is the only way to prevent him from slaying the passengers and going to hell for that mass murder. He further rationalizes that the passengers, if told about the robber, would kill the robber with angry thoughts and therefore go to hell themselves. The captain therefore compassionately kills the robber, receiving good karma for saving both robber and passengers from incurring bad karma.[167]

Similarly, Tibetan Buddhism signals approval of compassionate self-defense through the glorification and ritualization of the killing of King Langdarma by the monk Palgyi Dorie. Tibetan Buddhist mythology depicts Langdarma as a tyrannical king whose killing constituted an act of liberation. Even though his killer Palgyi Dorie is a monk, he nevertheless receives good karma for the killing because he acted from compassionate motives, to protect the community and free the consciousness of the evil king.[168]

Despite its ideal of absolute nonviolence, Buddhism can therefore conceive of forcible self-defense as a morally justifiable act (although nonviolent resistance or submission to aggression may be even more virtuous). It thereby falls into line with the world's other major religious, cultural, and philosophical traditions, which all morally approve of self-defense if exercised within limits of immediacy, necessity, and moderation and carried out with defensive intent.

II. Inherent moral justification of self-defense

The universal support for self-defense shown in the previous section is not coincidental. Instinctively, most people would consider that the exercise of self-defense is morally justified even if they may not be able to explain why. "He hit me first" is a justification that even brawling toddlers are quick to pick up.

Legal philosophers have advanced various theories to provide a rational explanation underpinning this moral instinct. Some theories focus on facts about the attacker, others on facts about the victim; yet others focus on considerations beyond the immediate conflict.

This section provides an overview of theories, beginning with less convincing accounts, then moving to more coherent theories. Particular attention will be paid to whether and how a theory reconciles a natural right to self-defense with other natural rights in play, especially the human rights of the attacker, defender, and third parties. The inherent moral justification of self-defense not only lends further support to the thesis that the right to self-defense forms part of natural law, it also explains why the law must carefully limit self-defense. It thus provides the conceptual basis for the analysis on the extent to which the

167. Jerryson, *supra* note 161, p. 51; Schmithausen, *id.*, p. 59; Schlieter, *supra* note 163, p. 146.

168. On the historical and ritualized personas of King Langdarma and the Monk Palgyi Dorie, see Schlieter, *id.*

right to self-defense must be recognized, yet limited as a matter of international human rights law.

1. Self-defense as Punishment

Emotionally, self-defense may often be perceived as punishment—"the vengeful response of a private citizen against those who deserve to suffer."[169] In jury-based judicial systems, seasoned trial lawyers will regularly play on this emotional undercurrent by portraying the attacker as someone who merited punishment. Popular culture further reinforces it, often building revenge fantasies around scenarios that are, in legal terms, self-defense situations.

The punishment account of self-defense reverberates in the works of Cicero[170] and also of John Locke, who stated that man has "by nature a power, not only to preserve his property, that is, his life, liberty and estate, against the injuries and attempts of other men; but to *judge of, and punish* the breaches of that law in others."[171]

Yet, the punishment theory neglects that punishment is a state prerogative[172] that must be exercised only within the procedural and substantive limits established by international human rights law. De Vitoria already recognized that the fundamental difference between state and private person lies in the fact that "the private person has . . . the right to defend himself and his property, but does not have the right to avenge injury."[173]

Furthermore, self-defense and punishment have very different limits. In some respects, self-defense may go beyond what would be allowed as punishment; in others, the limits of defensive force are drawn more narrowly. Thus, self-defense permits the infliction of harm that would constitute disproportionate punishment.[174] For instance, most would agree that one may use lethal force to defend against assaults threatening grave bodily harm. Yet, even death penalty supporters would generally agree that it would be disproportionate to punish such assault with the death penalty. It is also generally accepted that non-culpable attackers, such as mentally disabled persons, may be harmed in self-defense, even though they may not be punished for their actions. Conversely, self-defense is narrower than punishment in that it allows only the measure of defense necessary to ward

169. Fletcher, *supra* note 97, p. 19.

170. See Cicero, *supra* note 69, p. 394 [Mil. IV].

171. Locke, *supra* note 119, pp. 259–260 [Bk. II, Ch. VII, § 87] (emphasis added).

172. See Andrew J. Ashworth, Self-Defence and the Human Right to Life, Cambridge Law Journal, vol. 34 (1975), 282–307, at p. 288; Judith Jarvis Thomson, Self-Defense, Philosophy and Public Affairs, vol. 20 (1991), 283–310, at p. 285.

173. De Vitoria, *supra* note 109, p. 300 [§ 5].

174. Whitley Kaufman, Is there a "right" to self-defense?, Criminal Justice Ethics, vol. 23(1) (2004), 20–32, at p. 24; Kimberly Kessler Ferzan, Self-Defense and the State, Ohio State Journal of Criminal Law, vol. 5 (2007–2008), 449–478, at pp. 463–464; Fletcher, *supra* note 97, p. 29.

off the attack. If the justification for self-defense included punishment, one would have to question why it should be limited to necessary defensive action, rather than allowing a degree of force that befits the gravity of the criminal attack.[175]

2. Self-defense as Self-preservation

Writers such as Cicero, Hobbes, and de Vattel build their case for self-defense on human nature and the natural instinct of self-preservation.[176] This instinct indeed drives self-defense. However, legal recognition of an instinct can only incompletely make a case for self-defense. Firstly, not every conduct emanating from human instinct constitutes legally and morally acceptable behavior. Much of legal and moral rule-setting is concerned with regulating and confining our base human instincts such as greed or lust. An explanation of self-defense that sees it merely as the inevitable consequence of human instinct would, at best, set forth a case for excuse from culpability, but not a justification or right.

Furthermore, the self-preservation account fails to morally distinguish self-defense from other actions of self-preservation. It cannot explain, for instance, why self-defense has more extensive boundaries than necessity, which also aims at self-preservation. Nor can such theories justify the defense of strangers with whom we have no emotional ties, since the human instinct of self-preservation does not come into play in those cases. Instead, the defender may act out of a sense of solidarity or justice. This is psychologically far less compelling than the survival instinct, evidenced by the sad fact that in public spaces, people often fail to come to the aid of strangers under attack.

3. Intent-based Theories

Thomas Aquinas's double effect doctrine justifies self-defense on the basis that defenders are not motivated by an intent to harm, but by an intent to protect themselves or others.[177] Buddhist scripture also espouses an intent-based theory by depicting the defender as someone who acts out of compassion for the attacker, rather than anger.[178] One of the strengths of theories based on the motive of the defender is that they more easily explain why self-defense may also be exercised against non-culpable attackers (e.g., mentally disturbed aggressors) because the focus is only on the intended protective impact.[179]

However, such theories build on an entirely assumed account of the mental state of the defender, who will be fully aware that the objective—to

175. Cf. Thomson, *supra* note 172, p. 285.

176. See *supra* First Chapter (p. 1, note 1) and, in this Second Chapter, notes 115 & 116 ff. and accompanying text on pp. 37–38. See also Yadav, *supra* note 56, pp. 15 & 114–117.

177. See *supra* notes 89–90 and accompanying text.

178. See *supra* notes 161–168 and accompanying text.

179. Kaufman, *supra* note 174, p. 29.

protect—necessarily involves harming or even killing the attacker.[180] It also fails to explain why the negation of the intent to harm achieved by the intent to protect should morally justify the actual harm done. If thought all the way through, intent-based theories open the way for very extensive self-defense doctrines. As long as the defender acts with good faith defensive intent, all action should be justifiable self-defense, even action that is objectively not necessary or grossly disproportional.[181] Indeed, an intent-based account might also extend to the killing of a non-attacking innocent bystander, as long as this was done with protective intent—for example, by grabbing a bystander to use that person as a human shield against a third person's lethal attack.[182]

4. Self-defense as a Vindication of Individual Autonomy and Freedom

Some scholars justify self-defense as a right to defend one's autonomy or freedom against unjust interference.[183] Immanuel Kant's work points in that direction. According to Kant, any unjust infringement of one's freedom may be forcibly resisted, because it is just to remove obstacles to the exercise of one's freedoms.[184]

This approach has been criticized for being too vague because it relies on the very broad and diffuse notion of autonomy or freedom.[185] While relying on human rights to define the space circumscribed by the general concepts of freedom or autonomy may provide some clarity, the individualist theory has further weaknesses. It is unclear whether any interference with someone else's autonomy is inherently unjust and thus gives grounds for self-defense, or whether some interferences are justified and do not justify self-defense. The first account, providing absolute protection to autonomy, ignores that spheres of autonomy might overlap; it "treats every person as an island [and] ignores our interdependence, both in shaping our sense of self and in cooperating in society for mutual advantage."[186] The second account, qualified protection of autonomy, fails to provide

180. Sanford H. Kadish, Respect for Life and Regard for Rights in Criminal Law, California Law Review, vol. 64 (1976), 871–901, at p. 880.

181. George P. Fletcher, The Right and the Reasonable, Harvard Law Review, vol. 98 (1985) 949–982, at p. 975.

182. Jeff McMahan, Self-Defense and the Problem of the Innocent Attacker, Ethics, vol. 104 (1994), 252–290, at p. 273.

183. Robert F. Schopp, Self-defence, in: Jules L. Coleman & Allen Buchanan (eds.), In Harm's Way: Essays in Honor of Joel Feinberg, Cambridge University Press: New York (1994), 255–290, at pp. 266–273; George P. Fletcher, Proportionality and the Psychotic Aggressor, A Vignette in Comparative Criminal Theory, Israel Law Review, vol. 8 (1973), 367–390, at p. 378. See also Ximenes-Lopes v. Brazil, Judgment of 4 July 2006, IACtHR Ser. C No. 149, Reasoned Opinion of Judge Sergio García Ramírez, para. 10.

184. Kant, *supra* note 125, p. 232.

185. Kaufman, *supra* note 174, p. 22.

186. Fletcher & Ohlin, *supra* note 56, p. 60.

criteria for assessing which interferences with autonomy are unjust and which are not. So the autonomy theory in itself is not a sufficient rationale to justify self-defense.

Undeniably, self-defense derives much of its inherent justification from the fact that it serves to protect rights—to life, physical security, property, and so on. To that extent, theories emphasizing the autonomy or rights of the victim provide one element of the justification. However, taken in themselves they are unconvincing, because they fail to assign any value to the human rights of the aggressor who ventures into our sphere of autonomy.[187] Applied with rigor, they suggest that one could also defend one's autonomy by all necessary means against even trivial interferences, without regard to whether the aggressor will suffer grossly disproportional harm.[188] Furthermore, one may never have to retreat (and thus lose autonomy) to avoid a lethal confrontation.[189] This approach thus completely neglects the right to life or physical security of the attacker, without offering a moral reason why the rights of the attackers (including those of non-culpable attackers) should always and at any price be trumped by the victims' autonomy and freedom.

5. Rights Forfeiture Theory

In order to explain why the rights of the attacker can be neglected, another theory suggests that the attacker who threatens others temporarily forfeits his rights (including his right to life, where relevant).[190] Attempting to justify a legislative proposal to extend self-defense rights to apply to such circumstances as home invasions, former British Prime Minister David Cameron argued that burglars "give up their rights" when they invade homes and threaten the inhabitants.[191]

But this argument is circular; it fails to set out the underlying moral principle based on which these rights are forfeited.[192] It is also difficult to understand how

187. See also Mordechai Kremnitzer, Proportionality and the Psychotic Aggressor: Another View, Israeli Law Review, vol. 18 (1983), 178–214, at p. 189.

188. Sangero, *supra* note 76, p. 62. Immanuel Kant, as cited *supra* note 125, indeed suggests that self-defense may be exercised without any proportionality restraint since moderation is only a matter of (personal) ethics but not law.

189. Cf. Kaufman, *supra* note 174, p. 22.

190. Suzanne Uniacke, Self-Defense and Natural Law, American Journal of Jurisprudence, vol. 36 (1991), 73–101, at p. 101; Fiona Leverick, Defending Self-Defence, Oxford Journal of Legal Studies, vol. 27(3) (2007), 563–579, at pp. 571–573; Ashworth, *supra* note 172, p. 288. According to Peters, *supra* note 136, p. 25, Islamic law justifies self-defense on the basis of the rights forfeiture theory.

191. As cited in Stuart Casey-Maslen, The use of weapons in law enforcement, in: Stuart Casey-Maslen (ed.), Weapons under International Human Rights Law, Cambridge University Press: Cambridge (2014), 3–31, at p. 27.

192. McMahan, *supra* note 182, p. 278.

the rights that are supposedly forfeited are then regained as soon as the attack ends and the aggressor is therefore protected from revenge.[193]

Most importantly, the supposedly forfeited rights are human rights, which are considered inalienable.[194] The forfeiture theory considers the aggressor as a kind of temporary outlaw who no longer enjoys the right to physical security or even life. If this is the case, it would appear that self-defense would not need to have any restrictions, given that the aggressor's countervailing human rights that morally justify such restrictions are no longer put into the balance.[195]

Finally, even if the right to life were construed as being forfeitable due to culpable action, it would not explain why self-defense can also be exercised against non-culpable attackers such as young children or mentally disabled persons.[196]

6. Self-defense as a Right against the State

Another theory construes the right to self-defense as a right to resist aggression.[197] This right is considered to derive from the right of citizens to be protected by the state against the violence of others. Where the state cannot provide such protection, it must afford victims, and third parties disposed to help them, the right to take action themselves to resist aggression. Since the relevant relationship is between state and defender, it is claimed, the aggressor's rights are irrelevant and no account why the aggressor's rights are overridden is given.

The starting point of this theory deserves support. The right to self-defense would be practically meaningless if it only applied vis-à-vis the attacker, who does not respect the defender's rights anyhow. Logically, it must also entail the defender's right vis-à-vis the state not to be punished or otherwise be held liable for actions taken in self-defense. This also follows from the Hobbesian idea of the social contract and the formation of the state.[198] If the right to self-defense marks an agreed exception from the state's monopoly on the use of force, it must necessarily entail the state's commitment not to punish self-defense.

However, the conclusion drawn from recognizing a relationship of right and obligation between defender and state is incorrect. The right to self-defense cannot be depicted as solely a relationship between defender and state. It remains also a legal relationship between defender and aggressor. Otherwise, it could not be explained why the aggressor may not defend himself against the defender's counterforce. Furthermore, the state also has a legal relationship with the aggressor, because the state has a duty, based on the right to life and physical security,

193. Schopp, *supra* note 183, p. 268; Kadish, *supra* note 180, p. 884.

194. Kaufman, *supra* note 174, p. 23; Shlomit Wallerstein, Justifying Self-Defense: A Theory of Forced Consequences, Virginia Law Review, vol. 91 (2005), 999–1035, at p. 1016.

195. Rönnau/Hohn, *supra* note 56, p. 407 [§ 32, para. 72].

196. Kadish, *supra* note 180, p. 884; McMahan, *supra* note 182, p. 258.

197. Kadish, *id.*, pp. 884–886.

198. See Hobbes, *supra* note 118 and accompanying text.

to protect the aggressor from the victim's excessive force used in self-defense. In this triangle of legal relations, the state has to balance the defender's right to resist against the aggressor's right to be protected from excessive measures of resistance. The aggressor thus remains in the picture and the question remains why the rights of the defender morally trump those of the aggressor.

7. Balance of Harms Theory

Some argue that allowing the defender to kill the aggressor in order to protect innocent life is, on balance, the less harmful outcome and thus justified.[199] The balance of harms theory marks a step forward in comparison with the individualist and rights forfeiture theories, because it does not completely neglect the human rights of the attacker. However, it raises the question why it is morally justified to exercise self-defense even where the harm done to the aggressor is quantitatively and/or qualitatively greater than the harm prevented by the defender (e.g., if one has to kill five attackers to save oneself from grave bodily harm).[200] Why should one be allowed to place a finger on the defender's side of the scale when establishing the balance of harms?

Applied to the case of lethal self-defense, the balance of harm theory suggests that the life of the innocent defender is worth more than that of the aggressor due to the latter's culpability.[201] But this runs counter to the human rights principle that everyone enjoys human rights and that all human lives are of equal value regardless of a person's moral worth.[202] It is also unclear why a balancing test should only take into account the presumed moral worth of the person as it transpires in the moment of the attack. Why should the defender's contribution to the conflict not be thrown in the balance?[203] Why should one not take into account the relative moral worth of the aggressor and defender to the community in general?[204]

Most importantly, theories attaching more weight to the life of the innocent victim than to that of the aggressor break down where the attacker is incapable of incurring culpability, such as a small child or an individual suffering from a severe psychotic disorder.[205] In such cases both sides are morally innocent.

199. Sangero, *supra* note 76, pp. 93–106. See also Fletcher, *supra* note 183, p. 377.

200. Cf. McMahan, *supra* note 182, p. 261; David Wasserman, Justifying Self-Defense, Philosophy & Public Affairs, vol. 16 (1987), 356–378, at p. 359.

201. According to Sangero, *supra* note 76, p. 31, Jewish religious law justifies killing in self-defense on this basis.

202. Leverick, *supra* note 190, p. 566; Kadish, *supra* note 180, p. 882; Wallerstein, *supra* note 194, p. 1003.

203. Leverick, *id.*, p. 566.

204. Wasserman, *supra* note 200, p. 359; Wallerstein, *supra* note 194, p. 1003 (both constructing the example of an aggressor who is on the brink of discovering a cure for a serious disease).

205. Kadish, *supra* note 180, p. 882; Schopp, *supra* note 183, p. 260; Leverick, *supra* note 190, p. 569.

8. Self-defense as Defense of the Social-legal Order

The argument has been made that the scale tips in favor of the defenders, because they not only defend their own rights (or those of others they defend) but also protect the wider social and legal order against unlawful attack.[206] Self-defense thus positively reaffirms the social-legal order and deters future aggression. In German legal philosophy, the adage that "Right [i.e., the legal order] never has to yield to wrong"[207] is often cited to explain why the balance of interests weighs heavily in favor of the defenders and self-defense has thus a much wider ambit than other self-preservation justifications such as necessity.[208]

The theory has some merit, because it helps to distinguish the peculiar moral value of self-defense from other self-help situations such as necessity or duress. However, it also has inherent weaknesses. For one, the underlying idea of self-help to vindicate the legal order sits uneasily with the state's monopoly to enforce the law and inflict punishment.[209] Relying on the legal order as the ultimate trump card, may also lead to an undue discount of the aggressor's rights,[210] especially since it is impossible to measure what weight should be attached to the defense of the socio-legal order.[211] Furthermore, it raises the question why the defender should not be allowed to go beyond the limits of necessary defense if doing so would better vindicate the legal order by deterring future attacks.[212] Neither does it provide a strong justification for self-defense against non-culpable aggressors, since their conduct does not call the legal order into question the same way as that of culpable aggressors does.

Most importantly, this theory could not explain why self-defense constitutes a natural right. If the right to self-defense predates the human-made legal order, it cannot derive its justification from that legal order. Instead, it would have to be necessarily conceived as forming part of positive law only.[213] One could modify the understanding of the theory in that self-defense is justified because it reaffirms abstract natural law notions of right/justice and wrong/injustice. But this modified argument then begs the question of why it is indeed right and justified under natural law to kill in self-defense.

206. See George P. Fletcher, Punishment and Self-Defence, Law and Philosophy, vol. 8 (1989), 201–215, at p. 21; Sangero, *supra* note 76, pp. 68–73; Kremnitzer, *supra* note 187, p. 190.

207. "*Das Recht braucht dem Unrecht nicht zu weichen,*" as first referenced in Albrecht Friedrich Berner, Die Notwehrtheorie, Archiv des Criminalrechts, vol. 29 (1848), 547–598, at p. 562.

208. Rönnau/Hohn, *supra* note 56, p. 401 [§ 32, para. 66].

209. See also Georg Freund, Strafrecht Allgemeiner Teil, Springer: Berlin/Heidelberg (2nd ed., 2009), pp. 103–104.

210. Leverick, *supra* note 190, p. 567.

211. Rönnau/Hohn, *supra* note 56, p. 402 [§ 32, para. 66].

212. Cf. Wallerstein, *supra* note 194, p. 1004; Wasserman, *supra* note 200, p. 360.

213. Bitzilekis, *supra* note 57, pp. 27–28.

9. Self-defense as a Forced Choice between Negative Consequences

The most coherent theory, which already reverberates in Rousseau's and Locke's thinking,[214] sees self-defense as a forced choice between negative consequences for competing rights.[215] In the extreme case of lethal self-defense, this is the choice between one's own life and the life of the aggressor. Since the aggressor caused the forced choice dilemma, he must be the one who pays the price. Applying this approach, the South African Constitutional Court has justified lethal self-defense as follows:

> Where a choice has to be made between the lives of two or more people, the life of the innocent is given preference over the life of the aggressor.[216]

Overcoming a central weakness of the balance of harm theory, the forced choice theory does not have to construe a different moral worth of the defender and aggressor's human rights. Instead, it builds on the principle of fairness that the person who is morally responsible for a situation ought to bear the burdens of that situation.[217] In addition, it is entirely in the hands of the aggressor to end the forced choice dilemma at any point, because the aggressor can cease the attack and withdraw from the engagement.[218]

To the extent that it builds on the aggressor's guilt, however, the forced choice theory still does not easily explain why self-defense should be applied against non-culpable attackers.[219] Culpability provides the moral element on which the forced choice is based. When this element is missing, various arguments have been suggested to explain why the choice may still be made at the expense of the non-culpable attacker.

According to the personal partiality argument, defenders may resolve the forced choice dilemma in his favor because they understandably value their own rights more than those of the attackers.[220] Montesquieu's point on self-defense that "my life is in respect to me is what the life of my antagonist is to him" essentially espouses this argument.[221] However, the personal partiality argument is

214. See *supra* notes 120 and 128ff. and accompanying text.

215. Phillip Montague, Self-Defense and Choosing among Lives, Philosophical Studies, vol. 40 (1981), 207–219; Wallerstein, *supra* note 194, p. 1035; Freund, *supra* note 209, p. 105.

216. S v Makwanyane 1995 (3) SA 391 (CC), para 138.

217. Wallerstein, *supra* note 194, p. 1028. See also Freund, *supra* note 209, p. 105.

218. Sangero, *supra* note 76, p. 46; Wasserman, *supra* note 200, p. 371; Erb, *supra* note 56, p. 595.

219. Sangero, *id.*, 47.

220. McMahan, *supra* note 182, pp. 268–269.

221. See Montesquieu, *supra* note 126.

really a variant of the self-preservation theory referenced above and thus subject to the same criticism. Choosing one's own life over that of another person is psychologically understandable and may provide the ground for an excuse of culpability. However, it does not provide an objective moral justification. Otherwise, persons who kill innocent bystanders to preserve their own life could also claim to be justified due to their understandable personal partiality.[222] Furthermore, it could not explain why anyone should have the right to defend a stranger, since they have no claim of personal partiality to justify saving the stranger at the expense of the attacker.

Another approach justifies self-defense against non-culpable attackers based on the social utility of this rule. In the spur of the moment of the attack, it is often uncertain whether the attacker is culpable or not. When raising a knife, a mentally deranged person and a coldblooded criminal look very similar. Therefore, social utility may be best served if there is agreement that self-defense is always justified against objectively unlawful attacks, regardless of the culpability of the attacker.[223] The approach makes a significant practical argument. Nevertheless, it cannot sustain what is being investigated here, namely whether there is a rule of natural law that self-defense is justified. The argument relies on a supposed social convention that is itself rooted in a utility argument. Conventionalism and utilitarianism are anathema to natural law and natural rights. More importantly, the social convention argument also finds inherent limits when applied to the most extreme case of killing in self-defense. The fundamental importance of the right to life requires that a rule that may ultimately justify killing provide a strong moral justification that flows from the circumstances of the individual case. Abstract considerations of social utility and agreed convention should not suffice to justify deliberate killings; otherwise one finds oneself quickly on a very slippery slope.

A more principled moral argument lies in invoking causality for an objectively unlawful attack as the guiding ethical principle. Where a forced choice of harm must be made between two persons, neither of whom is culpable, the harm should fall with the person whose action produced the forced choice. Since someone has to pay the price of the confrontation, it is only fair that it falls upon the attacker, because there is a strong moral presumption against shifting harm from the person who caused it to another person.[224] Put more simply: If a non-culpable person is attacking me and one of us will lose his life, that consequence ought to be the attacker's misfortune, not mine.[225]

The moral validity of the causation principle is reaffirmed by the fact that it adequately distinguishes situations of self-defense from necessity and duress—a

222. McMahan, *supra* note 182, p. 270.

223. *Id.*, pp. 288–289.

224. *Id.*, p. 252.

225. Wallerstein, *supra* note 194, p. 1035.

point other self-defense theories regularly struggle with.[226] Suppose a person grabs an innocent bystander to use the bystander as a human shield that catches the attacker's bullet. If that person thereby saves his own life at the expense of the innocent bystander, this may be excusable based on duress, but not justified. Otherwise, the bystander would have no right to defend himself against being abused as a human shield. Not providing a full justification is morally justified because the forced choice between the life of victim and bystander was caused by the victim's action, even if that choice was ultimately forced on the victim by the aggressor.

From a human rights perspective, a forced choice approach—based on guilt and, failing that, causation of an objectively unlawful attack—has the advantage that it minimizes harm for defender and aggressor by recognizing the full moral value of the human rights of both victim and aggressor. In the case of lethal self-defense, one person's right to life is given preference over another only because a choice has to be made (sometimes a very tragic one), not because they are of different worth.

10. Implications of the Forced Choice Justification for the Ambit of Self-defense

The review of self-defense theories provides several valid interlinking arguments why self-defense is justified. Self-defense serves to protect autonomy, related individual rights, and the socio-legal order. However, this alone cannot explain why it should justify the taking of life, especially if self-defense is exercised against non-culpable aggressors. According to the view taken here, this drastic consequence only gains its justification from the fact that self-defense provides a response to a forced choice between conflicting rights that is caused by the aggressor. This finding has important implications for the ambit of the right to self-defense, because it can be relied upon only if there is truly a forced choice and that forced choice has been caused by the aggressor.

Firstly, it means that self-defense must be strictly necessary to escape the forced choice. If there is a possible way to resolve the forced choice without harm to the aggressor, the defender, or a third party, this must be pursued. This means, notably, that the defender must use opportunities to retreat, unless retreat would cause him harm that is significant in proportion to the harm avoided.[227] This duty to retreat becomes even more morally compelling where the forced choice is not produced by the attacker's fault, but is only caused by the non-culpable attacker's bad luck of causing a confrontation. Duties to retreat are therefore particularly called for vis-à-vis small children, persons with mental disabilities, and others who cannot be held fully accountable for their actions.[228]

226. McMahan, *supra* note 182, p. 282.

227. Ashworth, *supra* note 172, p. 289, links this conclusion to a "human rights approach to self-defence." See also Sixth Chapter: C.III.2 (pp. 258–264).

228. See also Fourth Chapter: C.I.4 (129–131).

Even where the forced choice cannot be resolved without harm, the fact remains that both defender and aggressor retain fully valid human rights interests. While the aggressor's (culpable) causation of an unlawful attack indicates that the forced choice of harm inherent in the self-defense situation should generally fall at the aggressor's expense, his human rights interests cannot be totally disregarded. For this reason, self-defense cannot be justified if the harm caused to the aggressor is disproportionately greater than the harm prevented.[229] The case for proportionality becomes particularly compelling in cases involving non-culpable attackers who incur the consequences of the forced choice due only to their misfortune of having caused the self-defense situation.

Furthermore, the moral preference for resolving the forced choice in favor of the victim may be diminished or eclipsed where the victim caused the forced choice by culpably provoking the attack.[230]

This section's review of self-defense theories thus reaffirms the findings from the previous section's review of self-defense conceptions in different cultural and religious traditions of the world. Self-defense is inherently justified and therefore also a right. However, from its inherent justification it also follows that it may be exercised only within carefully delineated boundaries.

A strong case can therefore be made that both the right to self-defense and its limits form part of natural law. It is not surprising that this natural law also finds reflection in domestic legal practice across the world, as will be shown in the next section.

E. THE RIGHT TO SELF-DEFENSE AS A GENERAL PRINCIPLE DERIVED FROM DOMESTIC LAW

The prevailing understanding of general principles of law recognized by nations under Article 38(1)(c) of the ICJ Statute derives from domestic law by studying whether they are a common feature of different national legal systems. The right to personal self-defense is such a common feature.

Self-defense is recognized in all of the world's major legal systems.[231] Comparative law studies analyzing contemporary domestic law provisions in different regions of the world do not identify a single domestic legal order that

229. See also Fourth Chapter: C.V (pp. 170–189) and Sixth Chapter: C.III.3 (pp. 264–268).

230. Freund, *supra* note 209, p. 113. See also Fourth Chapter: C.III.2.a (pp. 146–148).

231. Werle, *supra* note 15, p. 200 [para. 541]; Don B. Kates, Genocide, Murder and the Fundamental Human Right to Defend One's Life, Journal of Law, Economics and Policy, vol. 2 (2006), 309–317, at p. 311; Kai Ambos, Other Grounds for Excluding Criminal Responsibility, in: Antonio Cassese, Paola Gaeta & John R.W.D. Jones (eds.), The Rome Statute of the International Criminal Court: A Commentary, Vol. I, Oxford University Press: Oxford (2002), 984–1029, at p. 1004; Massimo Scalliotti, Defences before the international criminal court: Substantive grounds for excluding criminal responsibility—Part 1, International Criminal Law Review vol. 1, (2001), 111–172, at p. 160; Doehring, *supra* note 20, p. 561; S v Makwanyane [Constitutional Court South Africa], 1995 (3) SA 391 (CC), para. 138.

does not recognize self-defense.[232] However, the inquiry cannot end there. Self-defense provisions vary between countries. At the root of these variations are divergent political views on how different values are to be accommodated: individualism and social responsibility; state power and individual freedom; and the human rights of victim and aggressor.[233] The question therefore arises whether the commonalities are nevertheless so strong that one can speak of a principle common to all major domestic legal systems, even if the specific rules emanating from this principle differ to some degree between different legal orders.

The following section will first examine the commonalities regarding the *legal consequences* of self-defense, namely whether it is generally construed as a right and justification. The subsequent section will then examine whether the *legal requirements* giving rise to a claim of self-defense are comparable between the major legal systems of the world.

I. Common classification as a right and justification

Interstate self-defense amounts to a right, given that Article 51 of the U.N. Charter expressly refers to the "inherent right to self-defense."[234] Since the right to interstate self-defense was historically derived from an analogy to personal self-defense in domestic law, one could suppose that self-defense also constitutes a right at the interpersonal level.[235] Empirical evidence bears out this supposition. On the basis of comparative analysis of domestic law, a number of scholars

232. Jean Pradel, Droit Pénal Comparé, Dalloz: Paris (3rd ed., 2008), p. 138 [para. 102]; Wittemann, *supra* note 92, p. 220; Eduardo José Pintore, Das präventive Selbsverteidigungsrecht im Lichte allgemeiner Rechtsgrundsätze, Peter Lang: Frankfurt a.M (2011), pp. 113–172 (comparing self-defense provisions in Latin America, Asia and Europe); Stanley Yeo, Anglo-African Perspectives on Self-Defence, African Journal of International and Comparative Law, vol. 17 (2009), 118–135; Sangero, *supra* note 76, pp. 107 ff.; Peters, *supra* note 135, p. 25.

233. See also Schroeder, *supra* note 96, p. 127.

234. See also Jean-Marc Thouvenin, Circumstances Precluding Wrongfulness in the ILC Articles on State Responsibility: Self-Defence, in: James Crawford et al. (eds.), The Law of International Responsibility, Oxford University Press: Oxford (2010), pp. 459–460; Yoram Dinstein, War, Aggression and Self-Defence, Cambridge University Press: New York (5th ed., 2011), pp. 189–190 [para. 501]. Despite the explicit language of the U.N. Charter, this is not uncontested. In particular, Roberto Ago, then the International Law Commission's Rapporteur on State Responsibility, took the view that self-defense connotes "a de facto condition, not a subjective right." Addendum—Eighth report on State responsibility by Mr. Roberto Ago, Special Rapporteur - the internationally wrongful act of the State, source of international responsibility, U.N. Doc. A/CN.4/318/Add.5–7, para. 87, in: Yearbook of the International Law Commission, vol. II(1) (1980), 13, at p. 53. Article 21 of the final version of the ILC Draft Articles on Responsibility for Internationally Wrongful Acts, as contained in Ch. IV.E.1 of the Report of the International Law Commission, U.N. Doc. A/56/10, also avoids describing self-defense as a right, but uses instead the compromise formula of characterizing it as a circumstance precluding wrongfulness.

235. See also Kopel, Gallant & Eisen, *supra* note 3, p. 136; Kates, *supra* note 231, p. 311.

concur that self-defense is commonly recognized as a right in domestic legal orders.[236]

However, others maintain that self-defense is not really a right in many domestic legal orders. The claim is made that many states recognize self-defense only as a ground for excluding criminal responsibility[237] or a legal permission to break rules that prohibit killing and the infliction of bodily harm.[238] In countries following the common law tradition in particular, self-defense mostly features as a defense that may be pleaded in criminal proceedings, rather than being commonly framed as a right. Common law jurists therefore sometimes find it hard to conceive of self-defense as a right. However, both the Appellate Committee of the House of Lords and the U.S. Supreme Court have acknowledged the character of self-defense as a right.[239] They therefore fall in line with what civil law jurists quite readily conceive of as a *Notwehrrecht* or a *droit à la légitime défense* and what in Sharia law systems is also considered the lawful exercise of a natural and legal right.[240]

The doctrinal underpinnings of self-defense, which are universally followed, lend further support to its character as a right. The main characteristic of a right lies in the fact that another person or entity has a corresponding duty to the rights-holder. Conversely, a liberty is simply a freedom for the liberty-holder to do something, and there are no obligations on other parties to do or not do anything.[241] In the criminal law context, in which self-defense usually becomes relevant, rights and liberties articulate themselves respectively as justifications and excuses. A justification legitimizes certain conduct as right and lawful. This also

236. See Ambos, *supra* note 231, p. 1004; Kates, *supra* note 231, p. 311; Yadav, *supra* note 56, p. 19; Doehring, *supra* note 20, p. 561. See also Haggenmacher, *supra* note 20, p. 15 (indicating that "most jurisdictions" recognize self-defense as a right, without offering any example to the contrary).

237. Cerone, *supra* note 13, p. 327; David Robertson, A Dictionary of Human Rights, Europa Publications: London/New York (2nd ed., 2004), p. 208; Rosen, *supra* note 94, p. 17.

238. Lindsey Cameron & Vincent Chetail, Privatizing War: Private Military and Security Companies under Public International Law, Cambridge University Press: Cambridge et al. (2013), p. 459.

239. For the U.K., see the Appellate Committee of the House of Lords in R v Jones, [2006] UKHL 16, at para. 79. See also Beckford v R (1988) 1 AC 130, where the Judicial Committee indicated that the defendant is "entitled" to use self-defense.

For the U.S., see the Supreme Court judgment in District of Columbia v. Heller 554 U.S. 570, 128 S. Ct. 2783 (2008), at 2817. See also *id.*, at p. 2822 (diss. op. Stevens J), who refers to the "common-law right of self-defense". See also People v. McManus [New York Court of Appeal], 67 N.Y.2d 541 (1986), at 546.

240. On Islamic law, see Hamid & Maung Sein, *supra* note 131, p. 88; Peters, *supra* note 135, p. 25; Javed, *supra* note 131, p. 296; Lippman et al., *supra* note 131, p. 56.

241. Wesley Newcomb Hohfeld, Some Fundamental Legal Conceptions as Applied in Judicial Reasoning, Yale Law Journal, vol. 23 (1913) 16–59, pp. 28ff.

entails a duty on the part of others to tolerate such conduct. An excuse maintains that the conduct is wrong, unlawful, and opposable, but accepts that the defendant cannot be personally blamed for the conduct.[242]

Duress, for instance, is generally understood as an excuse. Illegal use of force under duress does not become lawful, but the perpetrator is considered to be under such constraint that he cannot be blamed for using it. However, the target of the force is under no duty to tolerate the force just because the person attacking him is under duress. Someone blackmailed into committing a robbery by threats to the blackmail victim's life or the lives of close family members might be excused based on duress, but this does not mean that the victim of the robbery must tolerate the robbery and not resist it.

Conversely, self-defense is generally recognized as a justification.[243] Its justificatory character implies a right to self-defense.[244] The corresponding duty of the aggressor is to endure the defensive force until the aggressor ceases the attack. If self-defense were instead an excuse or liberty, the aggressor would have no such duty and could fight back against the defender.[245] However, all legal orders, domestic and international, prohibit the exercise of "self-defense against self-defense."[246] Thus, "[t]he assassin who is being repulsed by his intended victim may not slay him and then, in turn, plead self-defense."[247]

The character of self-defense as a right and justification, rather than merely an excuse, becomes even more obvious when one considers the position of third parties. Where a person is in a situation of duress, a third party cannot claim the other person's duress as an excuse for getting involved in the

242. Kadish, *supra* note 180, p. 873; Fletcher, *supra* note 181, p. 958; Leverick, *supra* note 190, p. 570; Rosen, *supra* note 94, p. 18.

243. See Pradel, *supra* note 232, p. 138 [para. 102]; Kates, *supra* note 231, p. 311; Yadav, *supra* note 56, p. 19; Eser, *supra* note 15, p. 878 [article 31, para. 37]; Cassese et al., *supra* note 15, p. 461. For the contrary view, *de lege ferenda*, see Claire O. Finkelstein, Self-Defense as a Rational Excuse, University of Pittsburgh Law Review, vol. 57 (1996), 621–649; Rosen, *id.*, p. 17.

244. Bouloc, *supra* note 93, pp. 340–341 [para. 389]; Guido den Dekker & Eric P.J. Myjer, The Right to Life and Self-Defence of Private Military and Security Contractors in Armed Conflict, in: Francesco Francioni and Natalino Ronzitti (eds.), War by Contract: Human Rights, Humanitarian Law and Private Contractors, Oxford University Press: Oxford (2011), 171–193, at p. 182. See also Supreme Court of Spain, Case No. STS 2148/1995, Judgment of 11 April 1995, http://www.poderjudicial.es/search/. But cf. Cameron & Chetail, *supra* note 238, p. 457.

245. See also Fletcher, *supra* note 183, p. 375; Kopel, Gallant & Eisen, *supra* note 3, p. 154.

246. See Weizsaecker et al. ["The Ministries Case"], Trials of War Criminals before the Nurernberg Military Tribunals, vol. XIV (1946–1949), 308, at p. 329 (considering it a "long-established principle of criminal law" that also applies to the context of interstate self-defense). See also Den Dekker/Myjer, *supra* note 244, p. 180.

247. United States v. Ohlendorf ["the "Einsatzgruppen Case"], Trials of War Criminals before the Nurernberg Military Tribunals, vol. 4 (1949), 411, at p. 494.

situation. That third person must show to be under duress personally (e.g., as a close relative of the person directly under duress). No such restrictions apply with regard to the right to self-defense. Since the conduct emanating from the exercise of that right is lawful and right, domestic laws generally allow a third party to defend the victim even if there is no personal connection between victim and defender. Because the third party is justified, the aggressor has a duty to endure that defensive action as well and must not fight the intervening defender.[248] By the same token, it is generally accepted that no third party may intervene on behalf of the aggressor, even though that should be the case if self-defense was merely an unlawful, yet excused exercise of force on the part of the defender.[249]

A second conceptual argument against recognizing self-defense as a right holds that self-defense merely gives a limited legal recognition to an inevitable human reaction that is driven by the self-preservation instinct.[250] However, as noted above, self-defense has an inherent justification. The victim is morally and legally justified in choosing self-preservation at the expense of the aggressor's rights, because it was the aggressor, through his culpable or at least objectively unlawful action, who forced the choice on the victim. The fact that the permissibility of making this choice accords with the natural self-preservation instinct does not weaken the case, but only sharpens the common sense intuition that self-defense is justified. The weakness of the argument becomes even more apparent when applied to the defense of others. As noted, it is unfortunately not uncommon that people lack the courage to come to the defense of strangers under attack. The defense of others can therefore not be characterized as an inevitable, instinctive human reaction. Nevertheless, it is something that laws everywhere encourage and consider to be lawful and right.

A third conceptual argument raised against a right to self-defense considers that self-defense is unworthy of being qualified as a right and justification, because it is primarily self-regarding and does not benefit others.[251] Instead, it is claimed, such violent self-help is contrary to the interests of modern society, since it diminishes respect for the rule of law and increases the overall quantum of violence.[252] A rights account is said to distort our perception towards an "uncompromising absolutism" that abandons considerations of proportionality at the expense of the aggressor.[253]

248. Fletcher, *supra* note 183, p. 375; Sangero, *supra* note 76, p. 38; Kopel, Gallant & Eisen, *supra* note 3, p. 154.

249. See Fletcher, *id.*

250. Robertson, *supra* note 237, p. 208; Finkelstein, *supra* note 243, p. 631.

251. Finkelstein, *id.*, p. 644.

252. Rosen, *supra* note 94, p. 52.

253. Kaufman, *supra* note 174, p. 26.

This line of argument neglects that self-defense also has a social benefit because it reaffirms the validity of the social legal order and deters attacks.[254] It is hard to imagine that a society where third parties were no longer justified in coming to the defense of others—an implication of not seeing self-defense as a right—would see less unlawful violence. To prevent the right to self-defense from escalating confrontations and to balance the countervailing rights of victim and aggressor, its boundaries have to be carefully limited. However, characterizing self-defense as generally unlawful and socially unwanted sends a wrong signal to both law-abiding citizens and would-be criminals. This is why domestic legal orders everywhere construe it as a justification and hence acknowledge its character as a right.

II. Comparable requirements of application

Across domestic legal orders, the requirements of a self-defense claim rest on the same basic tenets.[255] The response to (1) an unlawful human attack against a protected interest must be (2) immediate, (3) necessary, and (4) proportional. Many jurisdictions also require (5) a subjective element, i.e., the defenders must at least know that they act in self-defense.

The rules structured around these basic tenets differ somewhat between the major legal traditions. However, even where these differences are based on divergent doctrinal approaches, the legal outcomes are comparable overall.

1. Unlawful Attack against a Protected Interest

Some legal systems allow self-defense against any private interest protected under the legal order or establish catalogues of defensible interests that include items such as privacy or honor. Socialist states (past and present) have generally allowed also for the defense of the state and public interests.[256] Other states opt for narrowly drawn lists of interests that may be protected through self-defense. However, all major legal systems converge on a core of interests that may be protected: life, physical integrity, physical liberty, and property.[257]

To justify invoking self-defense, the circumstances must involve a threat to these interests from an unlawful attack by another human being, directed

254. See this Second Chapter: D.II.8 (p. 54).

255. See also Fletcher & Ohlin, *supra* note 56, pp. 86–87; Ambos, *supra* note 231, p. 1004; Pradel, *supra* note 232, p. 138 [para. 102]; Cameron & Chetail, *supra* note 238, pp. 461–462.

256. Sangero, *supra* note 76, at pp. 124–125. For a discussion of the human rights compatibility of this approach, see Fourth Chapter: C.I.1 (pp. 125–126).

257. See also Pradel, *supra* note 232, pp. 138–139 [para. 102]; Walter Perron, Rechtsvergleichende Betrachtungen zur Notwehr, in: Jörg Arnold et al. (eds.), Menschengerechtes Strafrecht: Festschrift für Albin Eser zum 70. Geburtstag, C.H. Beck: München 2005), 1019–1039, at pp. 1025 & 1032; Sangero, *supra* note 76, p. 123; Peters, *supra* note 135, p. 25; Javed, *supra* note 131, p. 290.

against the defender or a third person.[258] There is acceptance across domestic legal orders that the aggressor does not necessarily have to act with personal culpability, although the assessment of defensive action against attacks by, for example, children or mentally disabled persons will usually lead to special considerations at the levels of necessity and proportionality.[259]

Legal systems diverge in their doctrinal approach to cases of putative self-defense, where the attack exists only in the mind of the defender, not in objective reality. A successful self-defense plea under English law requires only that the defendant believed in good faith the attack was real.[260] However, to the extent that English law criminalizes negligence (as it does with regard to killings), a person unreasonably presuming to act in self-defense may still incur responsibility on that basis.[261] U.S. criminal law is also based on the perception of the defender, rather than the actual situation. However, the legislation in force in many U.S. states requires that belief in the attack was also objectively reasonable under the circumstances prevailing at the time.[262] The reasonable belief approach is also followed by Islamic law.[263]

In principle, civil law countries allow self-defense only against an attack that actually takes place. However, criminal practice tends to produce very similar results since putative self-defense is considered to negate criminal intent or culpability, thereby precluding conviction for an intentional crime.[264] A conviction for negligence remains possible in such cases if the defender unreasonably assumed the existence of a situation requiring self-defense. Overall, the major legal systems therefore produce more or less the same results even for putative self-defense.

2. Immediate Response

Domestic legal systems generally require a close temporal connection between attack and defensive action, so as to safeguard the state's monopoly on the use of

258. Sangero, *supra* note 76, pp. 128–129; Wittemann, *supra* note 92, p. 235; Yeo, *supra* note 232, pp. 125–126; Pintore, *supra* note 232, p. 343.

259. Wittemann, *supra* note 92, pp. 224 & 237; Sangero, *supra* note 76, p. 129 (fn. 561); Yeo, *supra* note 232, p. 126; Javed, *supra* note 131, pp. 291–293.

260. For a discussion of the precedents in English law, see Fiona Leverick, Is English Self-Defence Law incompatible with art 2 of the ECHR?, Criminal Law Review (May 2002), 347–362, at p. 348; Sangero, *supra* note 76, p. 288. The subjective standard also applies in some Anglophone African countries. See Yeo, *supra* note 232, p. 124.

261. John C. Smith, The use of force in public or private defence and Article 2 ECHR, Criminal Law Review 2002, 958–962, at p. 961.

262. Knoops, *supra* note 6, pp. 67–69.

263. Mohammad M. Hedayati-Kakhhiki, Islamic Law, in: Alan Reed & Michael Bohlander (eds.), General Defences in Criminal Law: Domestic and Comparative Perspectives, Ashgate: Dorchester (2014), 241–254, p. 244; Javed, *supra* note 131, pp. 312 & 324. See also section 61(a) of the Sharia-based Sudanese Penal Code, as cited in Yeo, *supra* note 232, p. 124.

264. Perron, *supra* note 257, p. 1037; Pradel, *supra* note 232, pp. 139–140 [para. 102].

force in other situations. Thus, "when a citizen uses force too soon or too late, the citizen steps on the sovereign's toes."[265]

A violent response after the attack has terminated is therefore universally condemned as illegal self-help or revenge. On the other end of the time spectrum, it is generally required that self-defense does not anticipate action long before it takes place, but is exercised only against an ongoing or immediately imminent attack.[266] Exceptions from the imminence requirement have been proposed for cases of recurrent attacks to which the victim cannot effectively respond at the time of the attack. Such cases usually involve domestic violence, for example a woman killing her habitually and severely abusive partner in his sleep. Legal practice tends to resolve such cases on the basis of the exculpatory excuses or through sentencing considerations, rather than expanding the scope of self-defense.[267]

Almost no domestic criminal law system accepts the argument that self-defense may also be exercised against threats that will materialize only later but require a defensive reaction right away. There is a virtually uniform approach permitting self-defense only against immediately antecedent or ongoing attacks.[268] The current Israeli Criminal Code, drafted against the peculiar backdrop of frequent suicide bombings that may require pre-emptive action, marks an exception. It allows preventive self-defense where force is immediately required to ward off unlawful attacks that will create a real risk of harm to life, body, liberty, and/or property.[269] In other words, self-defense is allowed before the actual attack commences, if that is the only way to effectively prevent a future attack.

3. Necessity

Domestic legal systems everywhere limit self-defense to the least harmful means necessary to safely ward off the attack.[270] Necessity is generally to be determined based on how the circumstances would have appeared to a reasonable person

265. Kessler Ferzan, *supra* note 174, p. 459.

266. See also Pradel, *supra* note 232, p. 138 [para. 102]; Wittemann, *supra* note 92, pp. 227–228; Sangero, *supra* note 76, pp. 153–154.

267. For a more detailed discussion of these types of intra-family abuse cases and boundaries set by international human rights law, see Sixth Chapter: C.II (pp. 247–255).

268. Sangero, *supra* note 76, pp. 151 & 153; Yeo, *supra* note 232, pp. 126–127; Wittemann, *supra* note 92, pp. 227–228; Fletcher & Ohlin, *supra* note 56, p. 90; Pintore, *supra* note 232, pp. 336–338; Pradel, *supra* note 232, p. 138 [para. 102]; Javed, *supra* note 131, p. 312; Cameron & Chetail, *supra* note 238, p. 477.

269. Israel Penal Law (as amended by Law No. 626/1996), s. 34J. On the background to the enactment of the law, see Sangero, *supra* note 76, p. 159.

270. Sangero, *supra* note 76, p. 143; Perron, *supra* note 257, p. 1036. On Islamic law, see Peters, *supra* note 135, p. 25; Javed, *supra* note 131, p. 293.

in the situation of the defender at the moment of the attack (*ex ante* perspective). Objectively understandable miscalculations do not negate necessity—a point illustrated by the well-known quote of U.S. Supreme Court Justice Oliver Wendell Holmes that "[d]etached reflection cannot be demanded in the presence of an uplifted knife."[271]

Some differences exist between legal systems on the question whether the defender has to use safe options to retreat from the confrontation, especially so as to avoid the use of lethal force. According to a view prevalent in German-speaking countries and an increasing number of U.S. states, persons may stand their ground if attacked and do not have to retreat from places where they are lawfully present.[272] Other countries impose a duty to retreat from confrontations in the public space. However, most countries do not impose a duty to retreat in situations where defenders would have to flee their own homes.[273]

4. Proportionality

Virtually all states require self-defense to be proportional.[274] However, this does not mean that the harm to the aggressor must be equal to or less than the harm prevented. It only prohibits a balance of harm that is grossly disproportional.

Doctrinally, Germany marks an exception since it knows no proportionality requirement as such.[275] In judicial practice, however, German law produces similar outcomes. Self-defense will not be recognized where it causes disproportionate harm. Such disproportional self-defense is considered as abusing the right to self-defense or as exceeding boundaries derived from social-ethical considerations.[276]

5. Subjective Element

Beyond the objective requirements of self-defense, there is widespread consensus that self-defense also requires a particular mindset on the part of the

271. Brown v. United States [U.S. Supreme Court], 256 U.S. 335 (1921), 343 (per Holmes, J).

272. Wittemann, *id.*; Knoops, *supra* note 6, pp. 69–71. For a detailed discussion of the human rights implications, see Sixth Chapter: C.III.2 (pp. 258–264).

273. Wittemann, *supra* note 92, p. 234.

274. Pradel, *supra* note 232, p. 138 [para. 102]; Perron, *supra* note 270, p. 1036; Wittemann, *id.*, pp. 231–233; Yadav, *supra* note 56, pp. 121–123; Javed, *supra* note 131, pp. 316–317. In common law systems, necessity and proportionality considerations tend to be grouped together under the umbrella of reasonableness.

275. Bundesgerichtshof [Federal Supreme Court of Germany], Judgment of 12 February 2003, Neue Juristische Wochenschrift: NJW 2003, 1955, at p. 1957; Fletcher & Ohlin, *supra* note 56, p. 97; Erb, *supra* note 56, p. 593.

276. Perron, *supra* note 257, p. 1021; Sangero, *supra* note 76, pp. 171–172; Fletcher & Ohlin, *supra* note 56, pp. 118–119; Ambos, *supra* note 231, p. 1015. Textually, such limits are usually tied to language in § 32 of the German Criminal Code, which accepts only self-defense that is "called for" (*geboten*).

person exercising it.[277] In the United Kingdom and Austria, for instance, the defender must at least know about the circumstances that entitle him to exercise self-defense.[278] Many other states even require that he act with the purpose of exercising self-defense.[279] The requirement of a subjective element serves as an additional safeguard to prevent abusive reliance on the right.

It has been shown that the law on self-defense is sufficiently similar in outcomes between legal systems, even if doctrinal approaches differ to some extent. There are only isolated points, where there are significant differences in both doctrine and outcome. However, these differences are not so marked that one can no longer discern a shared principle of a right to exercise immediate, necessary, and proportional defense to protect oneself or others against an unlawful attack.

However, congruence between domestic legal systems does not yet establish a general principle of law recognized by nations. It also must be established that the shared principle is apt for transposition and use in international law, a question that will be addressed in the next section.

F. TRANSPOSITION OF THE PERSONAL SELF-DEFENSE PRINCIPLE INTO INTERNATIONAL LAW

Not every legal principle common to domestic legal orders gains automatic entry into the realm of international law. In a second step of the inquiry, it must be affirmed that the principle is also appropriate for usage in the peculiar context of international law.[280] In a more distant past, this may have been less obvious for the right to personal self-defense since international law was mainly concerned with regulating the relationships between states and had less impact on the interaction of persons within a state, where the right to personal self-defense unfolds its relevance. However, even then there were occasional cases where it was deemed appropriate to apply the right to personal self-defense in international law. In the well-known 1928 *Naulilaa* arbitration, Germany's reprisals against Portugal, which were at the center of that case, were triggered by a fatal encounter between German and Portuguese soldiers. The altercation commenced when a Portuguese soldier shot and killed one of the Germans. The arbitrators considered that the shooting occurred, because the Portuguese soldier had reason to believe that the German was about to shoot him and therefore found himself "*en état de légitime défense*."[281] Accordingly, the arbitrators ruled that the killing of

277. Fletcher & Ohlin, *supra* note 56, p. 103; Sangero, *supra* note 76, p. 229; Ambos, *supra* note 231, p. 1016.

278. Sangero, *supra* note 76, p. 227; Rönnau/Hohn, *supra* note 56, p. 371 [§ 31, para. 9).

279. Sangero, *supra* note 76, pp. 229–230; Rönnau/Hohn, *supra* note 56, p. 371 [§ 32, 13 & 34]; Javed, *supra* note 131, p. 318.

280. See *supra* note 36 and accompanying text.

281. Naulilaa (Portugal v. Germany), 2 Reports of International Arbitral Awards, vol. 2, 1012 (1928), at p. 1025.

the German was not a violation of international law and could hence not give rise to a reprisal.[282] In other words, they saw it appropriate to apply the right to personal self-defense under international law. This approach is not exceptional, but rather represents the norm. International law has shown its willingness to adopt the right to personal self-defense in many contexts. Apart from human rights law (see Fourth to Seventh Chapters), the right to personal self-defense can also be discerned as a legal principle in international humanitarian law, international criminal law, the law of the sea, and the law of diplomatic relations.[283] Its recognition in such core disciplines of international law demonstrates a consensus that it is appropriate to transpose it into international law as a general principle of law recognized by nations.

I. International humanitarian law

During armed conflict, international humanitarian law (IHL) prohibits attack against civilians unless and for such time as they take a direct part in hostilities.[284] However, military personnel maintain a right to personal self-defense in armed conflict and in peacetime.[285] When they or third parties face unlawful attacks by civilians or other protected persons, they may therefore defend themselves with immediate, necessary, and proportionate force even where the attackers do not cross the threshold of direct participation in hostilities.[286] Examples

282. *Id.*, p. 1027.

283. The examples provided in this section do not seek to provide an exhaustive list of the applications of the right to personal self-defense in international law. It may also find application in other areas. The right to unit self-defense, for instance, allows military units to respond with force when fired upon, even if the attack against them falls below the threshold of an armed attack as defined by Article 51 of the U.N. Charter. To that extent, the right to unit self-defense may therefore emerge from the right to personal self-defense. See also Dale Stephens, Rules of Engagement and the Concept of Unit Self Defence, Naval Law Review, vol. 45 (1998), 126–151, at p. 128; Charles P. Trumbull, The Basis of Unit Self-Defense and Implications for the Use of Force, Duke Journal of Comparative and International Law, vol. 23 (2012) 121–148, at pp. 146–147; Rosenne, *supra* note 56, pp. 63–64. But see Dinstein, *supra* note 234, p. 243 [para. 641] (considering that unit self-defense is merely a subset of Article 51 of the U.N. Charter).

284. Protocol Additional to the Geneva Conventions of 12 August 1949, and relating to the Protection of Victims of International Armed Conflicts [Geneva Protocol I], art. 51(3); Protocol Additional to the Geneva Conventions of 12 August 1949, and relating to the Protection of Victims of Non-International Armed Conflicts [Geneva Protocol II], article 13(3); Jean-Marie Henckaerts & Louise Doswald-Beck, Customary International Humanitarian Law vol. I: Rules, International Committee of the Red Cross and Cambridge University Press: Cambridge (2005), p. 19 [rule 6].

285. See Report (Part One) of The Public Commission to Examine the Maritime Incident of 31 May 2010 (Turkel Commission), January 2011, http://www.turkel-committee.gov.il/files/wordocs//8707200211english.pdf, at para. 185.

286. *Id.*, para. 188. See also Nils Melzer, Interpretive Guidance on the Notion of Direct Participation in Hostilities under International Humanitarian Law [ICRC Interpretive

of such violence by protected persons include violence directed against soldiers during civilian demonstrations or riots, as well as attacks by prisoners of war against guards.[287]

The right to personal self-defense also shapes the determination of what constitutes direct participation in hostilities under IHL. Where civilians merely exercise self-defense against attacks that are unlawful under international law, this does not amount to direct participation and thus does not remove their protected status.[288] Civilian self-defense against looting, rape, or murder by marauding soldiers therefore does not amount to direct participation in hostilities.

This self-defense exception, which is well entrenched in contemporary IHL, already found reflection in Francisco De Vitoria's seminal treatise *De Indis et De Iure Belli Reflectiones* (1539). Insisting that the innocent must not be targeted in war, de Vitoria also stressed that it was "certain that innocent folk may defend themselves against any who try to kill them."[289] It has been confirmed in judgments of the International Criminal Tribunal for Yugoslavia (ICTY).[290] Likewise, in *Bagosora*, the International Criminal Tribunal for Rwanda (ICTR) considered that Tutsi civilians did not lose their protected status for defending themselves against repeated illegal attacks by the genocidal *Interahamwe* militia.[291]

The right to personal self-defense can also be claimed by other categories of persons who enjoy the protection of international humanitarian law. It resonates, for instance, in the principle that civilian medical units do not lose their

Guidance on Direct Participation in Hostilities], ICRC: Geneva (2009), p. 76; Trumbull, *supra* note 283, p. 122 [n. 7].

287. See Gloria Gaggioli, Expert meeting on the use of force in armed conflict: Interplay between the conduct of hostilities and law enforcement paradigms, ICRC: Geneva (2013), pp. 59–60. For a more detailed discussion, see Fifth Chapter: A (pp. 218–225).

288. ICRC Interpretive Guidance on Direct Participation in Hostilities, *supra* note 286, p. 61; Final Report of the Commission of Experts Established Pursuant to Security Council Resolution 780 (1992), U.N. Doc. S/1994/674 (1994), para. 78; Michael N. Schmitt, Direct Participation in Hostilities and 21st Century Armed Conflict, in: Horst Fischer et al. (eds.), Crisis Management and Humanitarian Protection: Festschrift für Dieter Fleck, Berliner Wissenschafts-Verlag: Berlin (2004), 505–529, at pp. 519–520; Chia Lehnhardt, Private military companies, in: Nigel D. White & Christian Henderson (eds.), Research Handbook on International Conflict and Security Law (Cheltenham: Edward Elgar, 2013), 421–443, at p. 429; Alexander Zahar & Göran Sluiter, International Criminal Law: A Critical Introduction, Oxford University Press: Oxford (2008), p. 434; Den Dekker/Myjer, *supra* note 244, pp. 172, 176, 181 & 187; Cameron & Chetail, *supra* note 238, p. 462; Corinna Seiberth, Private Military and Security Companies in International Law, Intersentia: Cambridge/Antwerp/Portland (2014), pp. 171–172.

289. De Vitoria, *supra* note 108, pp. 178–179.

290. See Prosecutor v. Tadic [ICTY Trial Chamber], Case No. IT-94-I-T, Judgment of 7 May 1997, para. 640; Prosecutor v. Blaskic [ICTY Trial Chamber], Case No. IT-95-14-I-T, Judgment of 3 March 2000, paras. 407–410.

291. Prosecutor v. Bagosora et al. [ICTR Trial Chamber], Case No. ICTR-98-41-T, Judgment of 18 December 2008, para. 2238.

protected status where they are equipped with light individual weapons to defend themselves or the wounded and sick in their charge.[292]

Due to their impartial mandate, peacekeeping forces deployed under Chapter VI or VII of the U.N. Charter are also considered protected under international law. They do not lose their protected status when they use force to defend themselves or civilians from imminent attack.[293] In the *Revolutionary United Front (RUF)* case, the Special Court for Sierra Leone upheld the protection of peacekeepers who had defended their base and a nearby civilian installation against an attack by the RUF militia.[294] The court held that the protection of peacekeeping personnel does not cease "if the personnel use armed force only in exercising their right to individual [i.e., personal] self-defense."[295] The same principle was also upheld by the ICC in a pre-trial decision concerning a militia attack on an African Union peacekeepers base in Darfur (Sudan) against which some of the peacekeepers defended themselves.[296]

One of the open questions relating to the self-defense exception is whether it covers any defensive force exercised by civilians and other protected persons against unlawful attack or whether self-defense will transform into active participation once it reaches a certain degree of organization and intensity. This issue will be examined in the Seventh Chapter, since it is central to the question whether massive human rights violations may be resisted by means of militarily organized self-defense.

II. International criminal law

International criminal law recognizes self-defense as a ground for excluding criminal responsibility. Article 31 (1)(c), first sentence, of the Rome Statute

292. See Geneva Convention (I) for the Amelioration of the Condition of the Wounded and Sick in Armed Forces in the Field, art. 22(1); Geneva Convention (II) for the Amelioration of the Condition of Wounded, Sick and Shipwrecked Members of Armed Forces at Sea, art. 35 (1); Geneva Protocol I, *supra* note 284, art. 13(2)(c). A similar provision was also contained in Article 8(1) of the Convention for the Amelioration of the Condition of the Wounded and Sick in Armies in the Field, 11 L.N.T.S. 440, entered into force August 9, 1907. On the right to self-defense of medical personnel see also United States v. Hagendorf [United States Intermediate Military Government Court at Dachau, Germany], Judgment of 9 August 1946, Law Reports of Trials of War Criminals, vol. XIII, at pp. 147–148.

293. Prosecutor v. Bagosora et al. [ICTR Trial Chamber], *supra* note 291, para. 2239; Marten Zwanenburg, Accountability of Peace Support Operations Martijnus Nijhoff: Leiden/Boston (2005), p. 190. Cf. Convention on the Safety of United Nations and Associated Personnel, art. 21.

294. Prosecutor v. Sesay et al. [SCSL Trial Chamber], Case No. SCSL-04-15-T, Judgment of 2 March 2009, para. 1928. See also Prosecutor v. Sesay et al. [SCSL Appeals Chamber], Case No. SCSL-04-15-A, Judgment of 26 October 2009, para. 529.

295. Prosecutor v. Sesay et al. [SCSL Trial Chamber], *id.*, at para. 233.

296. Prosecutor v Abu Garda [ICC Pre-trial chamber I], Case No. ICC-02/05-02/09, Decision on the Confirmation of Charges of 8 February 2010, para. 83.

stipulates that a person is not criminally liable for conduct if "[t]he person] acts reasonably to defend himself or herself or another person . . . against an imminent and unlawful use of force in a manner proportionate to the degree of danger to the person or the other person." The second sentence of this provision clarifies that it refers only to the right to personal self-defense. It is legally immaterial that the criminal acts in question may have been carried out in the course of a defensive operation that complies with the right to interstate self-defense under Article 51 of the U.N. Charter.[297]

In order to avoid debates on the character of self-defense, the drafters of Article 31 (1)(c) of the Rome Statute did not specifically characterize the provision as a right or justification. However, there can be no doubt that it constitutes a justification.[298] This follows from the principle that international law considers that "there can be no self-defense against self-defense."[299]

There is considerable support for the position that customary international criminal law also recognizes self-defense.[300] However, hardly any cases are known where a plea of self-defense was actually upheld against charges of international crimes. In the case of *Mundo and Weiss*, a U.S. Military Court acquitted two German police offers who had shot and killed an American prisoner of war who they had reason to believe tried to shoot them. While the court upheld a plea of self-defense,[301] the doctrinally correct holding would have been to consider that this marked one of the exceptions where IHL allows killing protected persons in self-defense (see above) and a war crime was thus out of the question on that ground already.

III. The law of the sea

The law of the sea incorporates the right to personal self-defense. An example under treaty law can be found in Article 8bis of the 2005 Protocol amending the Rome Convention for the Suppression of Unlawful Acts against the Safety of Maritime. It authorizes states to use force during the boarding of a vessel flying the flag of another state. inter alia, "when necessary to ensure the safety of its officials and persons on board."

This provision reflects a broader right under customary international law to use necessary and proportional force on the high seas in self-defense and in defense of others.[302] Such defensive force may be used, for instance, by both state

297. For a discussion on this distinction in particular in ICTY jurisprudence, see Zahar & Sluiter, *supra* note 288, at pp. 433–437.

298. David, *supra* note 16, p. 758.

299. See also Second Chapter: E.I (p. 61) and the references there in notes 246 and 247.

300. See the references *supra* note 15.

301. Wilhelm Mundo and Erich Weiss [United States General Military Government Court at Ludwigsburg, Germany], *supra* note 15, at p. 150.

302. Alice Priddy, The use of weapons in counterpiracy operations, in: Casey-Maslen (ed.), *supra* note 191, 122–160, at pp. 130 & 134; Wolff Heintschel von Heinegg, Repressing Piracy

and private vessels against pirates.[303] The example of self-defense by private vessels against pirates goes to show that such self-defense cannot constitute a case of interstate self-defense according to Article 51 of the U.N. Charter because it is neither exercised by a state nor affects another state's sovereignty, national vessels, or territory (since pirate ships generally fly no flag and carry out their attacks on the high seas, outside any state's territory).

IV. The law of diplomatic relations

The law of diplomatic relations stipulates that ambassadors and other diplomatic agents are inviolable.[304] Accordingly, they are generally not subject to arrest or any other force. An exception applies, however, when force is used against the diplomatic agent in self-defense.[305]

Grotius had recognized already that "if an ambassador makes an assault with arms, it is lawful to kill him, not indeed by way of punishment, but in our own defense."[306] Likewise, a U.S judgment from 1830 found, in relation to a fight involving a private U.S. citizen and a Danish diplomat, that, although a diplomat is inviolable, he is not exempted from the law of self-defense, so if he attacks someone the attack may be repelled by force.[307] In 1927, the Costa Rican Supreme Court found that a man who had insulted and assaulted the Peruvian chargé d'affaires had acted in justified self-defense because the diplomat had insulted and threatened the man.[308] In 1984, following the shooting of a British police officer from the premises of the Libyan embassy, the United Kingdom

and Armed Robbery at Sea—Towards a New International Regime?, Israel Yearbook on Human Rights, vol. 40 (2010), 219–241, at p. 228; Murdoch, *supra* note 20, p. 148; Laurie R. Blank, The use of force against pirates, in: Michael P. Scharf, Michael A. Newton & Milena Sterio (eds.), Prosecuting Maritime Piracy: Domestic Solutions to International Crimes, Cambridge University Press: New York (2015), 103–118, at p. 108.

303. Priddy, *id.*, p. 134, noting that this position was also taken in 2008 by the Indian Navy when its warship *Tabar* sunk a pirate vessel on the high seas after the pirate threatened to attack the warship.

304. See Article 29 of the Vienna Convention on Diplomatic Relations.

305. See ILC Commentary to Vienna Convention on Diplomatic Relations [1957], Yearbook of the International Law Commission, U.N. Doc. A/CN.4/SER.A/1957/Add.1 (1957), Vol. II, Pt. 2, at 138; John S. Beaumont, Self-Defence as a Justification for Disregarding Diplomatic Immunity, Canadian Yearbook of International Law, vol. 29 (1991), 391–402, at p. 391; Eilleen Denza, Diplomatic Law, Oxford University Press: Oxford (3rd ed. 2008) p. 257; Jean Salmon, Manuel de Droit Diplomatique, Bruylant: Brussels (1994), p. 292 [para. 394].

306. Grotius, *supra* note 114, p. 914 [Bk. II, Ch. XVIII.IV.7].

307. United States v. Benner (Case No. 14,568) 24 Fed. Cas. 1084 (1830), at 1085, also available at: http://press-pubs.uchicago.edu/founders/documents/a2_2_2-3s33.html.

308. Salmon, *supra* note 305, p. 294 [para. 395].

asserted its right to search Libyan diplomats as they left the Embassy as justified by self-defense.[309]

In the U.K. case, self-defense was not exercised in response to violence of a gravity that would amount to an armed attack and thus trigger the right to interstate self-defense under Article 51 of the U.N. Charter. In the U.S. and Costa Rican cases, the defensive action did not even emanate from the state itself and could thus not be covered by pre–U.N. Charter conceptions of interstate self-defense. The underlying principle is therefore not interstate self-defense, but the right to personal self-defense. This fact also finds recognition in an 1895 resolution of the *Institut de Droit International*, which found that diplomatic inviolability could not be invoked in the face of "*légitime défense de la part des particuliers*."[310]

G. CONCLUSION: A UNIVERSALLY RECOGNIZED RIGHT, BUT NO UNLIMITED LICENSE FOR VIOLENCE

Regardless of whether general principles of law under Article 38 (1)(c) of the ICJ Statute derive from natural law or from universally shared features of domestic legal orders, the right to personal self-defense forms part of the corpus of these general principles.

Personal self-defense is recognized across different cultural, philosophical. and religious traditions. Its character as a natural right was already established in the Greco-Roman period. While this characterization was temporarily called into question by early Christian doctrine and medieval European judicial practice, the rights approach prevailed in the Western tradition and was further reinforced by the natural rights thinking of the Enlightenment.

Non-Western natural law traditions also recognize self-defense. They typically do not recognize the concept of individual rights and thus do not construe self-defense as such. However, they still overwhelmingly consider self-defense as morally justified and righteous, rather than merely being excusable or pardonable. They thereby afford it a character akin to what constitutes a right in contemporary legal thought.

The conclusion that the right to self-defense forms part of natural law is buttressed by the fact that self-defense rests on a strong inherent moral justification. This justification chiefly derives from the moral principle that the negative consequences of a self-defense situation should fall with the attacker whose culpable or at least objectively unlawful action causes the situation.

In light of the broad support that the right to personal self-defense enjoys across different cultural, philosophical, and religious traditions, it is no wonder that it also constitutes a universal principle shared by all major legal systems in

309. Beaumont, *supra* note 305, p. 396; Denza, *supra* note 305, p. 268.

310. See Institut de Droit International, Annuaire de l'Institut, Vol. 14 : 1895–1896 (session de Cambridge—août 1895), A.Pedone: Paris (1895), 204–205, http://gallica.bnf.fr/ark:/12148/bpt6k5721782t/f223.image. See also Salmon, *supra* note 305, p. 293 [para. 395].

the world today. No country in the world can be identified where self-defense is not legally recognized.

However, it was also established that the right to self-defense is nowhere seen as a license to use unlimited violence in the face of an attack. While there exists no entirely uniform set of rules across different traditions and legal orders, basic requirements of the right to self-defense such as imminence of the attack, necessity and proportionality of the response, and defensive intent are transcendent features. These limits are morally underpinned by the need to balance the countervailing legitimate interests of the victim and the aggressor (with a degree of preference given to the former since the latter created the clash of rights).

Finally, it was shown that it is appropriate to transpose the right of personal self-defense into international law, evidenced by the fact that it is already present in core disciplines such as international humanitarian law, international criminal law, the law of the sea and the law of diplomatic relations.

The following chapters will examine how the general principle of a right to personal self-defense shapes international human rights law, beginning with the basic question whether the right to personal self-defense, recognized in natural and international law, might not actually be a human right in and of itself.

3

A Human Right to Self-Defense?

Since personal self-defense articulates itself as an individual right—a right rooted in natural law, at that—it is reasonable to consider whether the right to self-defense might not actually be a human right. In international law, this human right might flow from the general principle of law recognized by nations that was identified in the previous chapter. Although human rights under international law are commonly considered to be based in treaties and/or customary international law, there is no principled reason why they might not find their source in a general principle of law recognized by nations. Notably, Alston and Simma have taken the position that the relatively rapid recognition of core human rights as general international law can be better explained by considering them to be general principles of law, rather than trying to prove the consistent state practice and *opinio juris* necessary for the formation of customary international law.[1] Human rights also tend to be formulated in open and general terms, rendering them structurally similar to general principles that do not consist in "specific rules formulated for practical purposes, but in general propositions underlying the various rules of law which express the essential qualities of juridical truth itself."[2]

It is contested in the academic literature whether self-defense is a human right. A closer look at state practice and a comparison of the historical, social, and political functions of the right to self-defense on the one hand and human rights on the other show that it is not. Human rights may mandate the recognition of self-defense. However, as will be shown, the right to personal self-defense is not a human right in and of itself, but constitutes an individual right sui generis under international law.

1. Bruno Simma & Philip Alston, The Sources of Human Rights Law: Custom, Jus Cogens and General Principles, Australian Yearbook of International Law, vol. 12 (1988–1989), 82–108, at p. 105. Olivier De Schutter, International Human Rights Law: Cases, Materials, Commentary, Cambridge University Press: Cambridge (2014), pp. 66–67; Michael O'Boyle & Michelle Lafferty, General Principles and Constitutions as Sources of Human Rights Law, in: Dinah Shelton (ed.), Oxford Handbook for International Law, Oxford University Press: Oxford (2013), 194–221, at p. 221. See also South West Africa (Ethiopia & Liberia v. South Africa) (diss. op. Judge Tanaka) I.C.J. Reports 1966, 4, at p. 298.

2. Bin Cheng, General Principles of Law as Applied by International Courts and Tribunals, Cambridge University Press: Cambridge (1953), p. 24.

Human Rights and Personal Self-Defense in International Law. Jan Arno Hessbruegge

A. POSITIONS IN THE ACADEMIC LITERATURE

Recognizing self-defense as a human right or another type of individual right recognized under international law may not make much of a difference in strictly legal terms. As the Fourth to Seventh Chapters will elaborate, the right to personal self-defense has in any case a strong influence on human rights law by informing the interpretation of established human rights such as the rights to life, physical integrity, and effective remedy. Recognizing self-defense as a human right would still have important repercussions beyond the law itself. Symbolically, a human right to self-defense would carry greater moral weight. At the political level, human rights tend to trump conflicting interests not framed as a human right. In the particular case of self-defense, the claim that it amounts to a human right has been used to chip away at the state monopoly on the use of force in favor of more individualist positions on issues such as broader domestic self-defense laws, more permissive gun laws, and comprehensive rights of resistance against state authorities. It therefore comes as no surprise that the divergent positions writers take on the human rights status of the right to self-defense tend to be colored by their leanings on aforementioned issues.

At one end of the spectrum of opinion, there are writers who assert that there is an independent human right to personal self-defense, which is variably described as a "*véritable droit de l'homme*,"[3] a "fundamental human right,"[4] a "well-established human right under international law,"[5] an "international human right,"[6] or even as "a non-derogable human right."[7] Some of these writers advocate for the recognition of a human right as a stepping stone towards an argument that international human rights law requires states to permit the

3. Axel Delannay, Les homicides et lésions corporelles volontaires, in: Henri-D. Bosly & Christian De Valkeneer (eds.), Les Infractions, vol. 2, Larcier: Bruxelles (2007), 85–420, at p. 370.

4. Don B. Kates, Genocide, Murder and the Fundamental Human Right to Defend One's Life, Journal of Law, Economics and Policy, vol. 2 (2006), 309–317, at p. 312. See also Volker Krey, Deutsches Strafrecht Allgemeiner Teil, vol. 1, Kohlhammer Verlag: Stuttgart (2008), p. 158; Madison Fair, Dare Defend: Standing for Stand Your Ground, Law and Psychology Review vol. 38 (2014), 153–176, at p. 162; Mary Zeiss Stange, From Domestic Terrorism to Armed Revolution: Women's Right to Self-Defense as an Essential Human Right, Journal of Law, Economics and Policy, vol. 2 (2006), 385–411.

5. David B. Kopel, Paul Gallant & Joanne D. Eisen, The Human Right of Self-Defense, BYU Journal of Public Law, vol. 22 (2008), 43–178, at p. 44.

6. Christopher Schmidt, An International Human Right to Keep and Bear Arms, William & Mary Bill of Rights Journal, vol. 15 (2007), 983–1017, at p. 1003.

7. Dale Stephens, Rules of Engagement and the Concept of Unit Self Defence, Naval Law Review, vol. 45 (1998), 126–151, at p. 128; Mark David Maxwell, Individual Self-Defence and the Rules of Engagement: Are the Two Mutually Exclusive?, The Military Law and the Law of War Review, vol. 41(1–2) 2002, 39–53, at p. 46. See also Volker Erb, Notwehr als Menschenrecht—Zugleich eine Kritik der Entscheidung des LG Frankfurt am Main im "Fall Daschner", Neue Zeitschrift für Strafrecht (NStZ) 2005, 593–602.

possession of arms for purposes of self-defense in certain circumstances[8] or even recognizes a general human right to bear arms.[9]

Other scholars consider the right to personal self-defense to be a derivative right that flows from established human rights, without characterizing it as a human right itself. Some of them consider it to derive from the right to life and the pertaining state obligation to protect life against attacks by third parties.[10] If a state were to prohibit or otherwise obstruct an individual from exercising self-defense against a lethal attack, it is argued, this would amount to a failure to adequately protect the right to life.[11] Erb even contends that to prohibit self-defense may be considered actively aiding and abetting attacks on the right to life, because if the state outlaws the victim's potential exercise of self-defense, it removes an obstacle to an aggressor's attack, making it more likely to succeed.[12]

A variation of the derivative rights view suggests that the right to personal self-defense flows from the human right to an effective remedy for human rights violations.[13] This builds on the consideration that the first available remedy against an aggression targeting one's rights is to use force to counter the aggression.[14]

8. Kopel, Gallant & Eisen, *supra* note 5, pp. 174–177.

9. Schmidt, *supra* note 6. For a discussion why international human rights law provides no right to firearms or other means of self-defense, see Sixth Chapter: E (pp. 268–279).

10. B. A. Wortley, Some jurisprudential reflections on human rights and self-defense, in: Heinrich Kipp (ed.), Um Recht und Freiheit: Festschrift für Friedrich August Freiherr von der Heydte zur Vollendung des 70. Lebensjahres, Duncker and Humblot: Berlin (1977), 751–758, at p. 754; Shlomit Wallerstein, Justifying Self-Defense: A Theory of Forced Consequences, Virginia Law Review, vol. 91 (2005), 999–1035, at pp. 1027–1028; Guido den Dekker & Eric P.J. Myjer, The Right to Life and Self-Defence of Private Military and Security Contractors in Armed Conflict, in: Francesco Francioni and Natalino Ronzitti (eds.), War by Contract: Human Rights, Humanitarian Law and Private Contractors, Oxford University Press: Oxford (2011), 171–193, at pp. 172 & 179; Sanford H. Kadish, Respect for Life and Regard for Rights in Criminal Law, California Law Review, vol. 64 (1976), 871–901, at p. 884; Erb, *supra* note 7, p. 594; Reinhard Merkel, Folter und Notwehr, in: Michael Pawlik/Rainer Zaczyk (eds.), Festschrift für Günther Jakobs zum 70. Geburtstag, C. Heymanns: Berlin (2007), 375–403, at 386. Cf. Kopel, Gallant & Eisen, *supra* note 5, p. 133 (as a fallback position to their claim that self-defense is an independent human right).

Michael Gorr, Private Defense, Law and Philosophy, vol. 9 (1990), 241–268, p. 252, at p. 268, turns the derivative rights argument on its head. Rather than considering the right to self-defense to be a consequence of the right to life, he suggests that the right to life is really a compendium of independent rights; i.e., "a person has a right to life in virtue of her possessing such rights as (say) the right not to be killed, the right to be provided with assistance necessary to sustain life, and the right to defend herself." This view would logically consider the right to self-defense to be an independent human right.

11. Kadish, *supra* note 10, pp. 884–885.

12. Erb, *supra* note 7, p. 594. See also Kates, *supra* note 4, p. 311.

13. Specifically with regard to a right to defend against genocide: David B. Kopel, Paul Gallant & Joanne D. Eisen, Is Resisting Genocide a Human Right?, Notre Dame Law Review, vol. 81(4) (2006), 1275–1346, at p. 1277.

14. Cf. George P. Fletcher & Jens David Ohlin, Defending Humanity: When Force is Justified and Why, Oxford University Press: New York (2008), p. 28.

A third school of opinion insists that self-defense is not even a right under international law, but constitutes only a recognized exemption from criminal responsibility.[15] In the absence of a right, there can also be no human right to personal self-defense. This view would essentially relegate personal self-defense to be relevant only for international criminal law. Cerone even calls into question whether established human rights such as the right to life require the recognition of a right to personal self-defense, arguing that states have a margin of discretion on how to implement their obligation to uphold the right to life and do not necessarily have to protect it through the recognition of self-defense.[16]

B. LACK OF STATE RECOGNITION OF A HUMAN RIGHT TO SELF-DEFENSE

If the right to personal self-defense, in and of itself, were a human right under international law, one would expect it to be recognized as such by states in their international or national practice. However, this is not the case.

I. No recognition of a human right in international treaties or resolutions

None of the nine major international human rights treaties makes any direct reference to a human right to self-defense. There are also no references to a general human right to self-defense in United Nations resolutions. Proponents of an independent human right to self-defense argue that the existence of the human rights to life and physical security logically imply that there is also a human right to self-defense.[17] As will be further discussed in the Sixth Chapter, the rights to life and physical security indeed imply that states must recognize a right to personal self-defense under domestic law, since states themselves will never be able to effectively defend individuals from all attacks and must therefore allow

15. Prevention of human rights violations committed with small arms and light weapons: Final report submitted by Barbara Frey, Special Rapporteur in accordance with Sub-Commission resolution 2002/25, U.N. Doc. A/HRC/Sub.1/58/27 (2006), para. 20; John Cerone, Is there a Human Right of Self-Defense?, Journal of Law, Economics and Policy, vol. 2 (2006), 319–329, at pp. 319 & 327; Stuart Casey-Maslen, The use of weapons in law enforcement, in: Stuart Casey-Maslen (ed.), Weapons under International Human Rights Law, Cambridge University Press: Cambridge (2014), 3–31, at p. 28; Antonio Cassese, The Various Aspects of the Right to Self-Defence, in: Graduate Institute of International Studies (Geneva), Small Arms Survey 2004: Rights at Risk, Oxford University Press: Oxford (2004), 181; Lindsey Cameron & Vincent Chetail, Privatizing War: Private Military and Security Companies under Public International Law, Cambridge University Press: Cambridge et al. (2013), p. 458.

16. Cerone, *id.*, pp. 325–325. See also J.F.R. Boddens Hosang, Self-Defence in Military Operations: The Interaction between the Legal Bases for Military Self-Defence and Rules of Engagement, The Military Law and the Law of War Review, vol. 47 (2008), 25–96, at p. 57.

17. Schmidt, *supra* note 6, p. 1004. Cf. Kopel, Gallant & Eisen, *supra* note 5, p. 133.

people to defend themselves. However, the fact that a human right calls for the lawfulness of certain actions does not mean that these actions become human rights. For instance, there is a human right to gain one's living by work that one freely chooses or accepts.[18] Individuals who want to effectively exercise this right in a market economy must have the right to conclude employment or other transactional contracts. However, it does not follow from there that the right to conclude contracts is a human right. The particular rights and entitlements flowing from a human right are not the same as the human right itself. The recognition of the rights to life, physical integrity, liberty, or effective remedy therefore provides no evidence for the existence of a human right to personal self-defense.

While conceding that Article 51 of the U.N. Charter only pertains to states, proponents of the independent human rights thesis also argue that the right to interstate self-defense was historically derived from the right to self-defense at the interpersonal level. Therefore, it is argued, its "parent right"—the right to personal self-defense—must be a human right.[19] However, arguments based on analogies with Article 51 are inherently problematic because interstate and personal self-defense operate in different environments.[20] In any case, the Article 51 analogy falls short of establishing support for a *human* right to personal self-defense. The fact that personal self-defense indeed constitutes a right under international law (taking the shape of a general principle of law recognized by nations) does not mean there is a *human* right to self-defense. Individuals can have rights under international law without every such right amounting to a human right. For instance, the ICJ held that the right to consular assistance under Article 36 of the Vienna Convention on Consular Relations constitutes an individual right, but left it explicitly open whether it is also a human right.[21] This logically implies that the ICJ considers it in principle possible that there are individual rights that are not human rights. Bilateral investment treaties concluded between states, for instance, will regularly afford individuals (and corporations) substantive and procedural rights under international law that allow them to protect their investment through arbitration proceedings against the state of investment.[22] However, this does not mean that such treaties establish new human rights. Neither the reaffirmation of an inherent right to self-defense by Article 51 of the U.N. Charter nor cross-references to that provision in other

18. See Article 6(1) IESCR.

19. Kopel, Gallant & Eisen, *supra* note 5, p. 136, Kates, *supra* note 4, pp. 310–311.

20. See First Chapter: C.II, pp. 12–14.

21. See Avena and Other Mexican Nationals (Mexico v. United States of America), ICJ Rep. 2004, 12, at pp. 60–61 [para 124].

22. Martins Paparinskis, Investment Treaty Arbitration and the (New) Law of State Responsibility, European Journal of International Law, vol. 24(2) (2013), 617–647, at pp. 622–624.

multilateral treaties[23] therefore provide any argument for or against the existence of a human right to self-defense.[24]

With the same reasoning, the self-defense exemption from criminal responsibility for international crimes established under Article 31(1)(c) of the Rome Statute does not support the existence of a human right to self-defense.[25] Even though the provision should be understood as a justification and thus grounded in a right,[26] this does not mean that the underlying right must necessarily be a *human* right.

Among actual human rights treaties only three regional treaties contain more or less specific references to self-defense. Article 2(2)(a) European Convention on Human Rights justifies infringement of the right to life where absolutely necessary to defend any person from unlawful violence. However, this provision does not establish a human right. It establishes a human rights limitation that aims to balance the right to life of the aggressor on the one hand and the rights to life or physical security of police and third parties defended by them on the other.[27] It thus reflects the typical case of a general principle of law, namely the right to personal self-defense, that has been integrated into a treaty provision and providing guidance on how to reconcile conflicting legal interests.

Very specific collective rights of resistance are recognized in the African and the Arab regional human rights conventions. Article 20(2) of the African Charter on Human and Peoples' Rights gives "[c]olonized or oppressed peoples . . . the right to free themselves from the bonds of domination by resorting to any means recognized by the international community." Article 2(4) of the Arab Charter on Human Rights states that "[a]ll peoples have the right to resist foreign occupation." The same right is also contemplated by a number of General Assembly resolutions that seek to provide an authoritative interpretation of the (human) right to self-determination that exists under customary international law and common Article 1 of the two human rights covenants.[28]

23. A reference to the "inherent right to individual or collective self-defense recognized in Article 51 of the Charter of the United Nations" can be found inter alia in the Arms Trade Treaty, last preambular paragraph and the Protocol against the Illicit Manufacturing of and Trafficking in Firearms, Their Parts and Components and Ammunition, supplementing the United Nations Convention against Transnational Organized Crime, last preambular paragraph. Kopel, Gallant & Eisen, *supra* note 13, pp. 1278–1279, erroneously understand the reference to Art. 51, U.N. Charter, in the Firearms Protocol as reaffirming a right to personal self-defense.

24. See also Cerone, *supra* note 15, p. 320.

25. But see Kopel, Gallant & Eisen, *supra* note 5, pp. 149–150.

26. See Second Chapter: E.I (pp. 59–63).

27. See also U.N. Special Rapporteur on Small Arms, Barbara Frey, Final Report, *supra* note 15, para. 21; Cerone, *supra* note 15, p. 324. But see Delannay, *supra* note 3, p. 370 [para. 370]; Kopel, Gallant & Eisen, *supra* note 5, p. 149.

28. See Seventh Chapter: D.I (pp. 318–320) for details and references.

As will be discussed in the Seventh Chapter,[29] these treaties and resolutions reflect a right of peoples to defend their right to self-determination using organized armed resistance as a last resort. However, this defensive right has a narrow ambit. It is limited to peoples, is directed against states, and may be exercised only in very particular contexts, chiefly de-colonialization situations. Furthermore, the right to resist colonialization and occupation is a derivative of the human right to self-determination, rather than being a stand-alone human right. One can therefore not conclude from the existence of this narrow and derivative collective right that there exists a much broader individual human right to self-defense.[30]

Only the Universal Declaration of Human Rights alludes to the existence of a narrow right to self-defense against the state that extends beyond the colonial self-determination contexts. Its preamble states "it is essential, if man is not to be compelled to have recourse, as a last resort, to rebellion against tyranny and oppression, that human rights should be protected by the rule of law." As the drafters could not agree whether there is a human right to rebel against severe human rights violations, the text is deliberately ambiguous as to whether there is a right to rebellion against tyranny and oppression or whether rebellion is merely a natural consequence of a complete denial of the rule of law.[31] And following the first interpretation still leaves one with a narrowly tailored human right that is directed primarily against serious state human rights violations. Such a narrow right cannot sustain the purported existence of a general human right to self-defense.[32]

II. Insufficient national practice supporting a human right

The Second Chapter established that recognition of personal self-defense as a right constitutes a common feature of the major legal systems of the world, thus giving rise to a general principle of law recognized by nations. However, recognition of this right in ordinary statutes or the common law does not indicate that states consider this right to have the status of a human right. Evidence to that effect could be adduced, if states commonly considered the right to self-defense to be so fundamental that it is afforded constitutional protection, notably in a constitutional bill of rights.[33]

29. Seventh Chapter: D (pp. 316–320).

30. But see Kopel, Gallant & Eisen, *supra* note 5, p. 135.

31. See Seventh Chapter: E.I (pp. 326–329) for more details and references.

32. But see Kopel, Gallant & Eisen, *supra* note 5, p. 134; *id.*, *supra* note 13, p. 1277.

33. On the relevance of comparative constitutional law for discerning human rights and their content, see also O'Boyle & Flattery, *supra* note 1, p. 197.

Yet, the national constitutions of only four out of 193 UN member states expressly consider self-defense to be a fundamental right: Haiti, Mexico, Peru, and Timor Leste.[34] The Haitian Constitution guarantees citizens the right to armed self-defense within the bounds of one's domicile.[35] Mexico grants a constitutional right to have arms for purposes of protection and self-defense.[36] The Constitutions of Peru and Timor Leste both recognize the right to self-defense, without explicitly extending such right to armed self-defense.[37]

The constitutions of several states of the United States of America explicitly recognize a right to defend life and liberty.[38] In addition, the Second Amendment to the U.S. Constitution recognizes a "right of the people to bear arms," which recent U.S. Supreme Court jurisprudence considers to be grounded in an (unstated) right to self-defense. In a 2008 decision, the Supreme Court held by the narrowest of margins (5–4) that the Second Amendment provided for an individual right to bear arms for purposes of self-defense, adopting the argument that "the inherent right of self-defense has been central to the Second Amendment right."[39]

Twenty-seven countries explicitly recognize a more narrow constitutional right of citizens to forcibly defend themselves against state violations of basic rights or attempts to overthrow the constitutional order.[40] This represents less

34. Kopel, Gallant & Eisen, *supra* note 5, p. 141, erroneously list Honduras as also constitutionally recognizing a right to self-defense, even though the reference to defense in article 82 of the Constitution of Honduras refers to the right to defend oneself in court against criminal charges.

35. Constitution of the Republic of Haiti, article 268-1.

36. Political Constitution of the United States of Mexico, art. 10.

37. Political Constitution of Peru, art. 23; Constitution of the Democratic Republic of Timor Leste, section 28.

38. For references, see Kopel, Gallant & Eisen, *supra* note 5, p. 102 [n. 314].

39. District of Columbia v. Heller 128 S. Ct. 2783 (2008), at 2817. See also *id.*, at 2801, where the majority takes the view that self-defense was not a subsidiary interest, but the "central component" of the right to bear arms. The U.S. Supreme Court reaffirmed its position in McDonald v. Chicago, 561 U.S. 742 (2010).

40. Constitution of the Democratic People's Republic of Algeria, art. 33; Constitution of the Argentine Nation, § 36; Constitution of the Republic of Azerbaijan, art. 54(2); Constitution of the Republic of Benin, art. 66; Constitution of the Republic of Cape Verde, art. 18; Constitution of the Republic of Chad, preamble; Constitution of the Democratic Republic of Congo, art. 64; Constitution of the Republic of Cuba, art. 3; Constitution of Ecuador, art. 98; Constitution of the Republic of El Salvador, art. 87; Constitution of the Republic of Estonia, § 54(2); Constitution of the French Republic, preamble (read in conjunction with article II of the 1789 Déclaration des Droits de l'Homme et Du Citoyen); Basic Law of the Federal Republic of Germany, art. 20(4); Constitution of the Republic of Ghana, arts. 1(4) and 1(5); Constitution of Greece (Syntagma), art. 120(4); Political Constitution of the Republic

than one in six of the world's states. In any case, one cannot conclude from the constitutional recognition of such a narrow right of resistance, which may be exercised only against state authorities or those trying to usurp state authority, that these twenty-seven states consider that the right to self-defense generally enjoys the character of a fundamental right.

Occasionally, domestic norms other than constitutional provisions will use formulations that point to the right to personal self-defense having an inalienable or fundamental character akin to a human right. Examples can notably be found in norms guiding the military. The Australian Defense Force interprets self-defense exercised on an individual or unit level by its soldiers as a "non-derogable right."[41] Similarly, the 2000 version of the U.S. military's Standing Rules of Engagement described individual self-defense exercised by soldiers to defend themselves or U.S. forces in their vicinity as an "inherent right."[42] However, this characterization was deliberately excluded from the present version of the U.S. Standing Rules of Engagement. At present, only unit commanders retain "the inherent right and obligation of unit self-defense," while the exercise of individual self-defense by soldiers may be limited by their unit commanders.[43] Canada applies the same doctrine, allowing commanders to order individuals under their command not to respond to an imminent threat.[44] Both the U.S. and Canadian doctrines therefore do not attribute to the right to personal self-defense a human rights–like, inalienable character, but explicitly leave it to the disposition of the unit commander.[45]

of Guatemala, art. 45; Constitution of Guinea, art. 21; Constitution of Honduras, art. 3; Constitution of the Republic of Lithuania, art. 3(2), Constitution of the Republic of Paraguay, art. 138; Political Constitution of Peru, art. 46(2); Constitution of the Portuguese Republic, art. 21; Constitution of the Slovak Republic, art. 32; Constitution of the Democratic Republic of Timor Leste, art. 28; Constitution of Togo, arts. 45 and 150; Constitution of the Republic of Uganda, art. 3(4).

See also Tom Ginsburg, Daniel Lansberg-Rodriguez & Mila Versteeg, When to Overthrow your Government: The Right to Resist in the World's Constitutions, UCLA Law Review, vol. 60 (2013), 1184–1260, at pp. 1242–1259 (listing also constitutions that provide only for a right to peaceful civil disobedience or defiance of unconstitutional laws and orders).

41. Australian Defence Force Publication 3 (1st ed.), as cited in Stephens, *supra* note 7, p. 144.

42. Chairman of the Joint Chiefs of Staff, Instruction 3121.01A: Standing Rules of Engagement for US Forces, CJSCI (2000), at A-4.

43. Chairman of the Joint Chiefs of Staff, Instruction 3121.01B: Standing Rules of Engagement for US Forces, CJSCI (2005), at A-3.

44. Canadian Forces Use of Force Manual, as cited in Zoltan Hegedüs & Sherrod Lewis Bumgardner (eds.), NATO Legal Deskbook, NATO Office of the Legal Advisor: Mons/Norfolk (2nd ed., 2010), p. 257.

45. On the question to what extent limiting a soldier's right to self-defense can be reconciled with the rights to life and physical security, see Fourth Chapter: A.II (pp. 101–102).

C. CONCEPTUAL DIFFERENCES BETWEEN THE RIGHT TO SELF-DEFENSE AND HUMAN RIGHTS

Proponents of a human right to self-defense put forward the additional argument that a human right does not necessarily have to find reflection in the views and practice of states because human rights ultimately flow from natural law.[46] This view could be squared with the list of sources of international law enumerated in Article 38(1) of the ICJ Statute if one adopts the contested view that general principles of law are directly rooted in natural law and can enter international law even if they have not yet found state recognition.[47]

The Second Chapter found strong support for the idea that the right to personal self-defense constitutes a right under natural law. The Enlightenment philosophers who laid the basis for contemporary thinking on human rights even considered that the right to self-defense amounts to a natural right and thus gave it the same status as the rights to life, equality, liberty, and so forth. They argued that human beings retained all these rights when entering the social contract that formed human societies and, eventually, states.

However, even accepting that self-defense constitutes a natural right, this does not mean that the right to self-defense must automatically be considered to constitute a human right. Other rights have been considered to constitute natural rights without being recognized as human rights. For instance, some prominent philosophers, such as Rousseau, have taken the view that animals enjoy some natural rights.[48] Yet, by definition, any natural rights that animals may possess would not be human rights. Incidentally, the right to self-defense might actually be an individual right that we may instinctively attribute to animals as well, e.g., when considering that a dog justifiably bit the person who unlawfully tormented it.

Natural rights specifically attributed to human beings are also not necessarily human rights. Apparently drawing on work of the eminent Swiss natural lawyer Jean-Jacques Burlamaqui (1694–1748), the U.S. Declaration of Independence of 1776 states that the pursuit of happiness is among the unalienable rights that all human beings have been endowed with by their Creator.[49] However, this natural

46. Kopel, Gallant & Eisen, *supra* note 5, p. 99. See also Krey, *supra* note 4, p. 158.

47. Taking this minority view: South West Africa (Ethiopia & Liberia v. South Africa) (diss. op. Judge Tanaka), ICJ Reports 1966, p. 4, at p. 298.

48. Jean Jacques Rousseau, What is the origin of inequality among men? And is it authorized by natural law? [1754], in: Jean Jacques Rousseau, The Social Contract and Discourses (trans. G.D.H. Cole), J.M. Dent: London/Toronto (1923), p. 172.

49. See U.S. Declaration of Independence of July 4, 1776, para. 2.

While recognizing a natural right to pursue happiness, Burlamaqui explicitly affords this right only to states. See Jean Jacques Burlamaqui, Principes du Droit politique: ou second volume du droit naturel, Geneva (1754) [no identified publisher], p. 180 [Part II.iv.1 § 5] However, he derives this right from the consideration that the pursuit of happiness is an essential feature of individual human nature. See *id.*, Principes du droit naturel, Barrillot & Fils: Geneva (1747), pp. 55–56 [Part I Ch. 5 § VII–VIII].

right has found no explicit reflection in international human rights law (or the U.S. Constitution, for that matter).

In the case of right of self-defense, there are good reasons not to equate it with established human rights and instead regard it as an individual right sui generis. Although the right to self-defense shares some of the characteristics of a human right, it differs in critical aspects from established human rights.

I. Inalienable nature as a commonality

Neither the 1948 Universal Declaration of Human Rights, nor the 1993 Vienna Declaration and Programme of Action on Human Rights, nor any of the universal human rights treaties offer a comprehensive definition of human rights.[50] However, the Universal Declaration and the Vienna Declaration point to a few particular characteristics of human rights. One central characteristic of human rights is that that they are "inalienable rights" that are the "birth right of all human beings."[51]

To this extent, the right to self-defense is similar to human rights. All states assert a general monopoly on the use of force. This monopoly is grounded in the idea of a social contract between state and citizen through which the latter submits to state authority. Just like human rights, the right to self-defense has been left untouched by that contract. Hobbes even took the position that human beings could not even voluntarily divest themselves of their right to self-defense upon concluding the social contract.[52] Self-defense is thus inalienable.

However, there are a number of other characteristics of human rights to which the right to self-defense does not conform.

II. Auxiliary and relational nature of the right to self-defense

The Vienna Declaration clarifies that human rights derive "from the dignity and worth inherent in the human person."[53] As such, human rights generally protect

50. An attempt to put forward a comprehensive definition has been made by the U.N. Committee for Economic, Social and Cultural Rights, which has defined human rights as "fundamental, inalienable and universal entitlements belonging to individuals and, under certain circumstances, groups of individuals and communities" with their fundamental character deriving from the fact that they are inherent to the human person. See Committee on Economic, Social and Cultural Rights, General Comment No. 17, U.N. Doc. E/C.12/GC/17 (2006), para. 1.

51. See Universal Declaration of Human Rights, first preambular paragraph; Vienna Declaration and Programme of Action adopted at the World Conference on Human Rights, U.N. Doc. A/CONF.157/24 (Part I) at 20 (1993) [Vienna Declarartion], para. 1.

52. See Thomas Hobbes, Leviathan [1651] (ed. J.C.A. Gaskin), Oxford University Press: Oxford/New York (1998), p. 88 [Ch. XIV.8].

53. Vienna Declaration, *supra* note 51, preambular paragraph 2.

objective values rooted in dignity and humanity: life, equality, physical integrity, and so on. Human beings have these rights by virtue of their humanity: they do not derive from a special legal relationship with another person or entity.[54] By contrast, the right to self-defense does not protect a specific objective value. Instead, it serves to protect the objective values contained in those human rights against unlawful attack. In some cases, it also acts as a guide to balance two human rights in conflict when only one can prevail, notably the right to life of the aggressor versus that of the victim. The right to self-defense is thus auxiliary in nature. It is a second-order right that serves to maximize protection for other rights that protect inherent objective values. Furthermore, it arises only on the basis of a legal relationship with other persons that ensues when such persons carry out an unlawful attack.

This factor alone, though, would not rule out that the right to self-defense may constitute a human right. There are genuine human rights that are auxiliary or relational in character. The right to a fair trial and the right to an effective remedy for human rights violations are, without question, human rights.[55] Like self-defense, however, they are more auxiliary in character, because they serve to protect other human rights such as the rights to life, physical security, and liberty and derive their inherent value chiefly from that relation. They are also relational in the sense that they come into play only where persons are involved in a trial against the state or another person or have suffered a violation of their rights. Perhaps not coincidentally, the right to self-defense links in many ways to those two rights. A criminal trial could not be considered fair if well-founded self-defense claims of the defendant would not be considered.[56] In some constellations, allowing victims of human rights violations to defend themselves against ongoing violations may amount to the only available effective remedy to prevent serious and irreparable harm.[57] However, this is not to say that the right to self-defense is a subset of the right to an effective remedy, as it may be exercised against any unlawful attack, including ordinary crime, not just human violations by states and other human rights duty-bearers.

III. No specific aim of curbing state power and abuses

What distinguishes human rights far more decisively from the right to self-defense is their historical, social, and political function. Historically, human

54. Cf. H.L.A. Hart, Are There Any Natural Rights?, The Philosophical Review vol. 64.2 (1955), 175–191. Hart distinguishes natural rights, which he calls "general rights," from other types of "special rights" by the fact that the latter only arise out of special transactions between individuals or out of some special relationship in which they stand to each other (*id.*, p. 183).

55. See Universal Declaration, arts. 8 & 10.

56. See Sixth Chapter: B (pp. 239–242) for references to the jurisprudence of international human rights mechanisms.

57. See also Seventh Chapter: B (pp. 301–312).

rights have primarily been used to protect individuals from previously unchecked state power. They first appeared as an ideology to curb the power of European monarchs who either reigned as absolute sovereigns (in the case of the *ancien régime* preceding the French Revolution of 1789) or were perceived as colonial oppressors (to the framers of the 1776 U.S. Declaration of Independence). Human rights became recognized as an international concern against the backdrop of the oppression and atrocities committed by totalitarian states in the first half of the 20th century, notably National Socialist Germany. The 1948 Universal Declaration picks up on this context when finding that "disregard and contempt for human rights have resulted in barbarous acts which have outraged the conscience of mankind."[58]

Politically, states are singled out as subject to human rights obligations because of the absolute socioeconomic and legal power they wield over the individual in the absence of legal restraints.[59] As power has shifted to nonstate actors, international human rights law has to some extent responded by also creating obligations or at least non-binding responsibilities for specific types of powerful nonstate actors such as non-state armed groups or multinational companies.[60] Yet the primary focus on countering vast differences in power has remained the same. Even today, human rights remain rights that are primarily directed against the state. The major human rights treaties all address states as duty bearers.[61] Similarly, the Vienna Declaration reaffirms that human rights are primarily directed at the state, noting in its very first paragraph that their protection is "the first responsibility of Governments."

The right to self-defense lacks that orientation. It is not primarily directed at preventing abuses by the state (or other powerful actors, for that matter) but directed against any unlawful attacker. Occasionally self-defense may be directed against the state and its agents, but these cases are the exception, not the rule. In most instances, self-defense is exercised against attacks by private individuals. It is true that the right to self-defense, even if directed against private persons, also places obligations on the state, namely a duty not to prosecute or otherwise

58. Universal Declaration, preambular paragraph 2.

59. Frances Raday, Privatising Human Rights and the Abuse of Power, Canadian Journal of Law and Jurisprudence, vol. 13 (2000), 103–134, at pp. 108–110 (2000).

60. See Jean-Marie Henckaerts & Cornelius Wiesener, Human Rights Obligations of Non-state Armed Groups: A Possible Contribution from Customary International Law?, in: Robert Kolb and Gloria Gaggioli (eds.), Research Handbook On Human Rights And Humanitarian Law, Edward Elgar: Cheltenham (2013), 146–169; Jan Arno Hessbruegge, Human Rights Violations Arising from Conduct of Non-State Actors, Buffalo Human Rights Law Review, vol. 11, (2005), 21–88, at pp. 28–46. See also Principles 11–24 of the United Nations Guiding Principles on Business and Human Rights (U.N. Doc., A/HRC/17/13), as endorsed by consensual Human Rights Council Resolution 17/4, U.N. Doc. A/HRC/RES/17/4 (2011).

61. For a rare exception, see Article 4(1) of the Protocol to the Convention on the Rights of the Child on Children in Armed Conflict.

hold liable those who legitimately exercise self-defense.[62] In this regard, it is also directed against the state. However, this is a secondary function. Its primary thrust is directed against any potential aggressors—whoever they may be. And there is often no vast power differential placing the average victim at a disadvantage vis-à-vis the average aggressor. Indeed, the right to self-defense is probably more likely to be exercised where the victim feels stronger, better trained, or in other ways more powerful than the aggressor and thus expects to prevail in the confrontation.

The one specific case where the right to self-defense obtains a human rights–like function of checking state power is where it articulates itself as a right to resist serious human rights violations by the state. There, it serves to counterbalance state power. And even in that specific case, it does not necessarily have to be understood as an independent human right. As will be discussed in the Seventh Chapter, it can rather be seen as shaping the right to an effective remedy for violations of the right to life, freedom from torture, and other fundamental rights, because self-defense is the remedy of last resort where no other remedy can be effective.[63] In any case, even if one were to accept that there is a human right to defend oneself against attacks by the state, this would not support the general conclusion that the right to personal self-defense as a whole must be considered a human right.

IV. Neutrality of the right to self-defense on the nature of the state

A closer look at the concept of the social contract, the basis on which Enlightenment philosophers recognized both self-defense and many of today's human rights as natural rights, reveals another difference. The social contract, and the state monopoly on the use of force embedded therein, necessarily had to carve out an exception for the right to self-defense because no state could expect to perfectly live up to the original reason for its existence, namely offering protection from violence. On this basis, Hobbes recognized in his theory of the state that the pre-societal right to self-defense was carried over into society and the state.[64]

However, the Enlightenment philosophers who followed Hobbes did not stop there. They also used the idea of the social contract to introduce a new type of rights—a set of natural rights that were ultimately aimed at reshaping the overbearing, unequal, and absolutist *anciens régimes* into an entirely new type of state based on *liberté, égalité et fraternité*. International human rights, as formulated today, embody this vision. Even if they do not explicitly prescribe a particular social or economic order, they envision a state where respect for human

62. See Second Chapter: D.II.76 (p. 52).

63. See Seventh Chapter: B (pp. 301–312).

64. See Hobbes, *supra* note 52, p. 88 [Ch. XIV.8].

dignity, democratic participation, the rule of law, equality, justice, and accountability prevail.[65]

In comparison, the right to self-defense is neutral with regard to these overarching values. It embodies no transformative vision. It can therefore be upheld in any type of state, and all states recognize self-defense. Even the most totalitarian regimes that have systematically suppressed human rights have not called the right to self-defense into question (at least as long as such defense was not directed against their abuses of power).[66]

D. CONCLUSION: RIGHT SUI GENERIS, NOT HUMAN RIGHT

Even though international law recognizes an individual right to self-defense as a general principle of law, this right does not amount to a human right in and of itself. The right to self-defense and human rights may share roots in natural law, but they are ultimately of a different nature and have different functions. The right to self-defense is a genuinely pre-societal right that evolved in the *absence* of the state. It survived the formation of the state because no state will ever have *enough power* to perfectly protect individuals. Conversely, human rights evolved in response to the overbearing *presence* of the state and serve primarily to ensure that states do not accumulate *too much power*. Unlike human rights, self-defense does not additionally incorporate a vision to transform the state. It can accommodate any type of state, including authoritarian states that fail to respect human rights. For these reasons, the right to personal self-defense can best be described as an individual right sui generis under international law.

Even if it does not constitute a human right in its own right, the right to personal self-defense still links closely to international human rights law. Human rights shape the right to self-defense because they prohibit denying or unduly curtailing the right to personal self-defense. In this sense, the right to personal self-defense is a derivative of human rights, even if it is not a human right itself.

As the next chapter will discuss, human rights considerations also explain why law enforcement officials are allowed to use very high levels of force in self-defense and defense of others. They may even deliberately kill where necessary to save lives. This extraordinary power is to some extent explained by the fact that even on active duty, law enforcement agents retain their human rights vis-à-vis

65. The Vienna Declaration, *supra* note 51, eighth preambular paragraph, even projects the transformative vision of human rights to the international plane, calling for an international order based on principles such as "democracy, justice, equality, rule of law and pluralism."

66. On the recognition of self-defense in the law and judicial practice of National-Socialist Germany and Stalin's Soviet Union, see Friedrich-Christian Schroeder, Die Notwehr als Indikator politischer Grundanschauungen in: Friedrich-Christian Schroeder/Heinz Zipf (eds.), Festschrift für Reinhart Maurach zum 70. Geburtstag, C.F. Müller: Karlsruhe (1972), 127–142, at pp. 131–134. See also the self-defense provision in Article 15 of the Criminal Code of the Democratic People's Republic of Korea (as amended in 2009), unofficial translation available at: http://eng.nkhumanrights.or.kr/board/download.php?fileno=1103&no=4&board_table=bbs_literature.

the state employing them and must therefore be allowed to exercise their right to self-defense where necessary to effectively protect their rights to life and physical security. But the relationship between the right to self-defense and human rights is not a one-way street. Human rights also define and limit the right to self-defense. As the next chapter will explore, human rights impose tight procedural and substantive restrictions on the use of defensive force by law enforcement agents. These aim to maximize respect for the right to life and other human rights affected by the use of force.

4

Defensive Force by Law Enforcement Agents

On November 24, 2014, large-scale protests erupted across the United States of America in response to the controversial decision of a grand jury in St. Louis, Missouri, not to indict a white police officer, Darren Wilson for shooting and killing Michael Brown, an unarmed black man. According to the highly contentious factual findings of the grand jury, Wilson and Brown had an altercation during which the police officer fired an initial two shots, wounding Brown. Brown ran away and Officer Wilson gave chase. When Brown turned around and moved towards Wilson, the police officer shot him a further ten times, hitting him in the chest and head. The jury decided not to indict Wilson, ruling that he used necessary and proportional deadly force in self-defense.[1]

Claims of self-defense are often at the center of controversies involving police killings. This is no coincidence. The police may use force to maintain law and order in a variety of situations.[2] However, self-defense and defense of others are the only instances in which international human rights law allows police to shoot with the intent to kill. Accordingly, this chapter will focus mainly on lethal defensive force by law enforcement agents, because here the right to personal self-defense reveals its greatest relevance in the absence of other justifications.

1. Grand jury determination as reflected in Statement of St. Louis Prosecuting Attorney Robert P. McCulloch, Nov. 24, 2014, full transcript available at: http://www.stltoday.com/news/local/crime-and-courts/statement-of-st-louis-prosecuting-attorney-robert-p-mcculloch/article_2becfef3-9b4b-5e1e-9043-f586f389ef91.html.

2. Finca "La Exacta" v. Guatemala [IACommHR], Case 11.382, Report No. 57/02 (2002), para. 39; Corumbiara Massacre v. Brazil [IACommHR], Case 11.556, Report No. 32/04 (2004), para. 170; Neira Alegria et al. v. Peru, Judgment of 19 January 1995, IACtHR Ser. C No. 21, para. 61.

Although there is no definition under international human rights law, use of force can be defined as "any physical constraint imposed on a person in order to obtain compliance" and would include physically arresting a person, hitting the person or using other violence, and ultimately the use of firearms. See Cees de Rover & Anja Bienert, To Serve and to Protect: Human Rights and Humanitarian Law for Police and Security Forces, ICRC: Geneva (2nd ed., 2014) [ICRC, Human Rights and Humanitarian Law for Police and Security Forces], p. 247.

A. SELF-DEFENSE AS A JUSTIFIED LIMITATION OF THE RIGHTS TO LIFE AND PHYSICAL SECURITY

When assessing the legality of the use of force by law enforcement agents, four different degrees of force (i.e., physical means deployed against a person) should be distinguished:

- *Deliberately lethal force* refers to a level of force that is often also labeled as "shooting to kill" in common parlance. It comprises three subcategories: deadly force used (i) with the intention to kill, (ii) with knowledge that the force will kill in the ordinary course of events or (iii) acceptance of a high degree of probability of that outcome, regardless of whether death actually ensues.[3] Targeted head shots and repeated firing at the chest or back would surely be categorized as deliberately lethal force.[4]
- *Potentially lethal force* means force that carries a very significant risk of death for the targeted person, even though such death is not intended. The use of firearms where the weapon is trained only on the legs or other non-vital organs would generally still have to be considered potentially lethal force. With a low-velocity small-caliber weapon, a single shot aimed at the lower torso may also still be considered potentially lethal force, provided that effective emergency trauma care is accessible at the location of the shooting.[5]

3. The three subcategories correspond to the distinction used in the criminal law of many civil law jurisdictions between (i) *dolus directus* (intent to kill), (ii) *dolus indirectus* or *dolus directus* of the second degree (knowledge that death will ensue), and (iii) *dolus eventualis* (accepted very high probability of death). In common law jurisdictions, *dolus eventualis* is often also referred to as advertent recklessness.

The present author avoids use of the alternative term "intentional lethal use of force," employed in, e.g., Amnesty International, Use of Force: Guidelines for the Implementation of the UN Basic Principles on the Use of Force of Force and Firearms by Law Enforcement Officials, Amnesty International Dutch Section: Amsterdam (2015), at p. 23. The term "intentional lethal use of force," just like the colloquial expression of "shooting to kill" may invite confusion, as it may be understood as meaning that only killings with purposive intent are subject to the strict requirements attached to the use of deliberately lethal force. In fact, even in self-defense situations, killing must never be the purposive intent of law enforcement action, but always the incidental, if unavoidable consequence of stopping attackers from carrying out their attack.

4. According to U.S. data, head shots have a fatality rate of around 90%, shots at the heart area around 80%, whereas abdominal gunshot wounds have fatality rates of 50% or lower. See Paul Murphy, Shootings: What EMS Providers Need to Know (2010), http://www.emsworld.com/article/10319706/gunshot-wounds. However, fatality rates would presumably increase in countries and areas where effective emergency trauma care is harder to access.

5. Amnesty International, Use of Force Guidelines, *supra* note 3, pp. 23 & 116–117 seems to regard only head shots or repeated shots into the body mass (i.e., the torso) as amounting to

- *Less lethal force* using means such as batons, water cannons, or tear gas usually does not carry any significant risk of death. However, death may occasionally still result from the improper use of such less lethal weapons or in plainly unfortunate circumstances. For this reason, the term "non-lethal weapons," which was more commonly used in the past for these weapons, is inappropriate.[6]
- *Non-lethal bodily force* involves police grabbing, kicking, or hitting a person without using any weapons and with almost no risk of causing death.[7]

International human rights law recognizes that self-defense or defense of others may entitle law enforcement agents to use any of these types of force. The right to personal self-defense serves to justify the underlying infringements of the rights to life and physical security.

I. Recognition in universal and regional human rights law

Self-defense and defense of others as a justification for state agents' use of force finds express recognition only in the European Convention for Human Rights (ECHR). However, the self-defense justification is also recognized by the jurisprudence of the relevant United Nations, Inter-American, and African human rights bodies. Across regional and universal bodies, it is established that, in exceptional circumstances, law enforcement agents may even intentionally kill for defensive purposes.

1. European Convention on Human Rights

Protecting the right to life, Article 2 ECHR provides an exhaustive list of instances where the extrajudicial taking of life may be justified. Deprivation of

intentional lethal use of force. The present author considers that even a single shot aimed at the chest or upper back would generally qualify as deliberately lethal force, considering also that criminal law practice would generally assume homicidal intent where a defendant killed a victim with one targeted shot to the chest or back.

6. See ICRC, Human Rights and Humanitarian Law for Police and Security Forces, *supra* note 2, p. 253; Report (Part One) of The Public Commission to Examine the Maritime Incident of 31 May 2010 (The Turkel Commission), January 2011 [First Turkel Commission Report], http://www.turkel-committee.gov.il/files/wordocs//8707200211english.pdf, at para. 226. Even the term "less-lethal" has been criticized by Abi Dymond-Bass & Neil Corney, The use of "less lethal" weapons in law enforcement, in: Stuart Casey-Maslen, The use of weapons in law enforcement, in: Stuart Casey-Maslen (ed.), Weapons under International Human Rights Law, Cambridge University Press: Cambridge (2014), 32–52, at p. 32 (n.2). See also this Fourth Chapter: C.III.3.a (pp. 156–157).

7. Not all bodily force is non-lethal force. Some particular types of bodily force (e.g., choke-holds or high-impact martial arts moves targeting vital body parts) carry a significant risk of death and may thus have to be classified as potentially lethal force.

life constitutes no violation, inter alia, "when it results from the use of force which is no more than absolutely necessary . . . in defense of any person from unlawful violence." The European Convention thus allows law enforcement agents to use lethal force in self-defense and defense of others. It is firmly established that law enforcement agents may shoot with the intent to kill where absolutely necessary to defend their lives or that of others.[8] The European Court of Human Rights (ECtHR) has held, for instance, that police may shoot to kill hostage takers who place the life of their hostages at imminent risk, terrorists who are about to detonate a bomb, or suspects who try to kill a police officer.[9]

The specific reference to depriving life "intentionally" in Article 2(1) of the ECHR might suggest that the exhaustive list of exceptions in Article 2(2) applies only to intentional killings, providing greater leeway for other killings.[10] However, this narrow interpretation would exclude from the protective ambit of Article 2 the much more common cases of unintentional killings and killings where intent to kill cannot be positively established. As noted by the ECtHR, this "would hardly be consistent with the object and purpose of the Convention or with a strict interpretation of the general obligation to protect the right to life."[11] For this reason, the list of exceptions in Article 2(2) does not apply only

8. Jacques Velu & Rusen Ergec, La Convention européenne des droits de l'homme, Brussels: Bruylant (2nd ed., 2014), para 232; Robert Esser, EMRK; IPBPR, in: Erb, Volker et al. (eds.), Löwe-Rosenberg: Die Strafprozessordnung und das Gerichtsverfassungsgesetz: Grosskommentar, vol. 11, De Gruyter: Berlin (26th ed., 2012), p. 120 [Art. 2. EMRK/Art. 6 IPBBR, para. 48]; Jens Meyer-Ladewig, EMRK : Europäische Menschenrechtskonvention, Nomos: Baden-Baden (3rd ed., 2011) p. 61 [art. 2, para. 41]; Hans-Ullrich Paeffgen, Art. 2 EMRK, in: Jürgen Wolter (ed.), SK-StPO: Systematischer Kommentar zur Strafprozessordnung, Band X: EMRK, Carl Heymanns: Köln (4th ed., 2012), p. 387 [Art 2., para. 59]; Walter Gollwitzer, Menschenrechte im Strafverfahren: MRK und IPBPR, De Gruyter: Berlin (2005), pp. 163–164 [MRK Art. 2, para. 17], Jochen A. Frowein & Wolfgang Peukert, Europäische Menschenrechtskonvention: EMRK-Kommentar, N.P. Engel Verlag: Kehl (3d. ed., 2009), p. 36 [Artikel 2, paras. 11–12].

9. Ramsahai et al. v. The Netherlands [ECtHR Grand Chamber], Appl. No. 52391/99, Judgment of 15 May 2007, para. 289 (suspect killed with shot in neck after drawing a gun and pointing it at officers). Bubbins v. United Kingdom, Appl. No. 50196/99, Judgment of 17 March 2005, para. 140 (suspect killed with shot to chest after training a real-looking replica gun at police officer); Andronicou and Constantinou v. Cyprus, Appl. No. 25052/94, Judgment of 9 October 1997, para. 193 (hostage taker who threatened to kill the hostage, shot and killed by special forces team after first shooting at and injuring an officer); McCann et al. v. United Kingdom [ECtHR Grand Chamber], Appl. No. 18984/91, Judgment of 29 September 1995, para. 200 (SAS soldiers intentionally killed three IRA members who they had good reason to believe were about to detonate a deadly car bomb). In *McCann*, the court still found a violation owing to deficient planning of the operation (see this Fourth Chapter: C.IV, p. 164).

10. Cf. Claus Roxin, Strafrecht: Allgemeiner Teil, vol. I, Ch.Beck: Munich (4th ed., 2006), pp. 698–699.

11. Stewart v. United Kingdom [ECommHR], Appl. No. 10044/82, Decision of 10 July 1984, para. 15.

to intentional killings, but also to cases of less lethal or potentially lethal force that results, as an unintended outcome, in death.[12] In *Stewart*, for instance, the European Commission of Human Rights ruled that the accidental killing of a teenager by a stray rubber bullet could be justified only if it conformed to one of the three justifications set out in Article 2(2) of the ECHR.[13] In *Huohvanainen*, the ECtHR evaluated the Finnish police killing a mentally disturbed man who had confronted police officers with a gun in his hand on the basis of the deprivation of life standard of Article 2(2). It did so even though the police officers at the scene intended only to immobilize the man and did not want to kill him.[14]

Exceptionally, Article 2 of the ECHR also covers cases in which the police's use of force greatly endangers the life of a person, but does not actually kill the victim. These can include cases where the force used is not even meant to kill. In *Makaratzis*, the ECtHR found a violation of the right to life where police chaotically, but without intent to kill, shot numerous times at the vehicle of a suspected terrorist. The court found a violation of the right to life even though the victim was merely injured and survived.[15] In *Trevalec*, it found a violation of the right to life where the victim was shot twice at close range but survived.[16]

The right to self-defense also applies to physical force below the threshold of Article 2 of the ECHR. The right not to be subjected to ill-treatment under Article 3 and the right to physical security under Article 5 do not explicitly recognize self-defense as a justification. However, it would defy common sense if police could not defend themselves or others against attack by using force below the threshold of potentially lethal force.[17] In fact, such an interpretation could not be reconciled with the requirement of necessity, according to which the least

12. Ogur v. Turkey [ECtHR Grand Chamber], Appl. No. 21594/93, Judgment of 20 May 1999, para. 78; McCann et al. v. United Kingdom, *supra* note 9, para. 148; Andronicou and Constantinou v. Cyprus, *supra* note 9, para. 171; Ramsahai v. The Netherlands, *supra* note 9, para. 286. See also Roland Otto, Targeted Killings and International Law, Springer: Berlin (2010), p. 153; Frowein & Peukert, *supra* note 8, p. 36 [art. 2, para. 11]; Pieter van Dijk et al., Theory and Practice of the European Convention on Human Rights, Intersentia: Antwerpen (4th ed., 2006), p. 395. Critical of this approach: Dirk Diehm, Die Menschenrechte der EMRK und ihr Einfluss auf das deutsche Strafgesetzbuch, Logos Verlag: Berlin (2006), pp. 339–341.

13. Stewart v. United Kingdom, *supra* note 11, para. 15.

14. Huohvanainen v. Finland, Appl. No. 57389/00, Judgment of 13 March 2007, para. 97.

15. Makaratzis v. Greece [ECtHR Grand Chamber], Appl. No. 50385/99, Judgment of 20 December 2004, paras. 51–55. See also Ilhan v. Turkey, Appl. No. 22277/93 Judgment of 27 June 2000, para. 76.

16. Trevalec v. Belgium, Case No. 30812/07, Judgment (Merits) of 14 June 2011, paras. 60–61 & 87.

17. Andrew Ashworth, The European Convention and the Criminal Law, in: Jack Beatson & Tony Smith (eds.), The Human Rights Act and the Criminal Justice and Regulatory Process, Hart Publishing: Oxford (1999), 37–44, at p. 42. See this Fourth Chapter: C.VI (pp. 189–197), for a discussion of the special case of a suspect being subjected to torture or inhumane treatment in order to extract information to save the life of a third person.

harmful level of force must be used when exercising self-defense.[18] The ECtHR gives effect to the right to self-defense by considering that cases involving physical force applied in self-defense fall below the threshold of ill-treatment under Article 3 of the ECHR. In *Rivas v. France*, it therefore did not call into question France's basic contention that a police officer may be justified in defending himself against a suspect who attacks him.[19] Likewise, the European Commission of Human Rights found no violation of Article 3 in *Antonio Joaquim Laginha de Matos*, where a game warden shot a poacher in the legs in order to protect a colleague whom the poacher was about to shoot.[20]

2. International Covenant on Civil and Political Rights

In protecting the right to life, Article 6 of the ICCPR requires that "[n]o one shall be arbitrarily deprived of his life." As an open term, the word "arbitrary" must be construed in light of other applicable principles of international law. These include the right to personal self-defense as a general principle of law recognized by nations. Law enforcement agents that act within the bounds of this right cannot be said to act arbitrarily.

International jurisprudence supports this proposition. The drafters of Article 6 of the ICCPR considered including a more detailed list of instances where lethal force is allowed and one delegation put forward language similar to Article 2(2) of the ECHR. However, the proposal was ultimately rejected, out of fear that a detailed list of exceptions could give more weight to the limitations than to the right itself and that such a list could be incomplete.[21] Nevertheless, it is widely considered today that the word "arbitrary" in Article 6 of the ICCPR must be construed as considering as arbitrary all killings that do not fall within essentially the same exceptions that are also included in Article 2(2).[22] In particular, the jurisprudence

18. See this Fourth Chapter: C.III.3 (pp. 154–164).

19. Rivas v. France, Appl. No. 59584/00, Judgment of 1 April 2004, para. 41. Cf. Caloc v. France, Appl. No. 33951/96, Judgment of 20 July 2000, paras. 100–101 (justifying force against man who fought the police officers trying to arrest him).

20. Laginha de Matos v. Portugal, Appl. No. 28955/95, Decision of 7 April 1997.

21. Daniel D. Nsereko, Arbitrary Deprivation of Life: Controls on Permissible Deprivations, in: Bertrand Ramcharan (ed.), The Right to Life in International Law, Martinus Nijhoff: Dordrecht (1985), 245–283, at p. 248; Manfred Nowak, UN Covenant on Civil and Political Rights: CCPR Commentary, N.P. Engel: Kehl/Strasbourg/Arlington (2nd ed., 2005), p. 128 [Art. 6 CCPR, para. 13]; Otto, *supra* note 12, pp. 78–79.

22. Report of the Special Rapporteur on extrajudicial, summary or arbitrary executions, Christof Heyns U.N. Doc. A/HRC/17/28 (2011), para. 50; Nigel Rodley & Matt Pollard, The Treatment of Prisoners under International Law, Oxford University Press: Oxford (3rd ed., 2009), p. 253; Nowak, *id.*, p. 128 [Art. 6 CCPR, para .14]; Nils Melzer, Targeted Killing in International Law, Oxford University Press: Oxford (2008), p. 118; Stefanie Schmahl, Targeted Killings—A Challenge for International Law?, in: Christian Tomuschat, Evelyne Lagrange & Stefan Oeter (eds.), The Right to Life, Brill: Leiden (2010), 233–266, at p. 239; David Kretzmer, Targeted Killing of Suspected Terrorists: Extra-Judicial Executions or Legitimate Means of Defence?, European Journal of International Law, vol. 16 (2005), 171–212, at p. 177.

of the Human Rights Committee establishes that law enforcement agents can take life for defensive purposes. In *Suarez de Guerrero*, the Human Rights Committee judged the intentional killing of alleged kidnappers by police to be a violation of the right to life, inter alia, because there was "no evidence that action of the police was necessary in their own defense or that of others."[23] In *Rickly Burrell*, which concerned prison wardens intentionally killing an inmate, it also considered what was essentially a self-defense justification for the use of lethal force but ultimately found that the requirements were not complied with in that case.[24]

This interpretation of the ICCPR is also supported by subsequently adopted soft-law instruments, in particular by the United Nations Basic Principles on the Use of Force and Firearms by Law Enforcement Officials (U.N. Basic Principles on the Use of Force and Firearms) and the United Nations Code of Conduct for Law Enforcement Officials.[25] The development and adoption of both documents involved a very large number of states providing an indication of the near universal consensus on their content.[26] Although they are not legally binding, human rights courts and other international human rights mechanisms regularly cite them as part of the normative framework and rely on them in their interpretation of human rights treaty law.

Principle 9 of the Basic Principles limits the use of lethal force to an exhaustive list of circumstances that includes self-defense:

> Law enforcement officials shall not use firearms against persons except in self-defense or defense of others against the imminent threat of death or serious injury, to prevent the perpetration of a particularly serious crime involving grave threat to life, to arrest a person presenting such a danger and resisting their authority, or to prevent his or her escape, and only when less extreme means are insufficient to achieve these objectives. In any event, intentional lethal use of firearms may only be made when strictly unavoidable in order to protect life.

In the same vein, Article 3(c) of the Code of Conduct for Law Enforcement Officials stipulates:

> In general, firearms should not be used except when a suspected offender offers armed resistance or otherwise jeopardizes the lives of others and less extreme measures are not sufficient to restrain or apprehend the suspected offender.

23. Suarez de Guerrero v. Colombia, Comm. R.11/45 (1982), para. 13.2.

24. Rickly Burrell v. Jamaica, Comm. 546/1993 (1996), para. 9.5.

25. Basic Principles on the Use of Force and Firearms by Law Enforcement Officials, adopted at the Eighth United Nations Congress on the Prevention of Crime and the Treatment of Offenders, Havana, 27 August to 7 September 1990, U.N. Doc. A/CONF.144/28/Rev.1 at 112 (1990); Code of Conduct for Law Enforcement Officials, adopted by U.N. General Assembly Resolution 34/169, 34 U.N. GAOR Supp. (No. 46) at 186, U.N. Doc. A/34/46 (1979).

26. Interim report of the Special Rapporteur on extrajudicial, summary or arbitrary executions, Philip Alston, U.N. Doc. A/61/311 (2006) [2006 Report to General Assembly], para. 35.

Self-defense also constitutes a justification for use of force below the threshold of lethal force. In terms of legal logic, the same arguments apply as were discussed with regard to the ECHR. Evidence of this can be seen in the revised United Nations Standard Minimum Rules for the Treatment of Prisoners, which state that prison wardens "shall not, in their relations with the prisoners, use force *except in self-defense* or in cases of attempted escape, or active or passive physical resistance to an order based on law or regulations."[27] The Human Rights Committee also accepted the principle that self-defense could justify a prison guard beating an inmate and thus preclude a violation of the prohibition of inhuman treatment under Article 7 of the ICCPR.[28]

3. American Convention on Human Rights

Like the ICCPR, Article 4 of the American Convention on Human Rights (ACHR) prohibits the arbitrary deprivation of life. In interpreting what is and is not arbitrary, the Inter-American human rights bodies rely on the U.N. Basic Principles on the Use of Force and Firearms as well. Accordingly, they accept that state agents may use force, including deliberately lethal force, in self-defense and defense of others.[29]

In *Corumbiara Massacre,* which concerned a police operation against peasant workers occupying a farm in rural Brazil, the Inter-American Commission on Human Rights (Inter-American Commission) partially accepted Brazil's claim that the police used lethal force in self-defense. In the initial stage of that police operation the workers offered such strong armed resistance that the police forces had well-founded reasons to believe that their lives were in danger.[30] Conversely, in *Zambrano Vélez*, the Inter-American Court on Human Rights (Inter-American Court) found that three suspected criminals were summarily executed during a crackdown on crime in Ecuador, dismissing as not credible the state's factual assertion that the suspects were shot in self-defense.[31] On the basis of the United Nations Standard Minimum Rules for the Treatment of

27. Rule 82 (1) of the United Nations Standard Minimum Rules for the Treatment of Prisoners (the Nelson Mandela Rules), adopted by General Assembly Resolution 70/175 (2016) (emphasis added).

28. Allan Henry v. Trinidad and Tobago, Comm. 752/1997 (1999), para. 7.1.

29. Montero-Aranguren et al. (Detention Center of Catia) v. Venezuela, Judgment of 5 July 2005, IACtHR Ser. C No. 150, paras. 68–69; Zambrano Vélez et al. v. Ecuador, Judgment of 4 July 2007, IACtHR Ser. C No. 166, para. 84; Barrios Family v. Venezuela, IACtHR Ser. C No. 237, Judgment of 24 November 2011, IACtHR Ser. C No. 237, para. 67; Brothers Landaeta Mejias v. Venezuela, Case 12.606, Report No. 58/12 (2012), para. 187; Corumbiara Massacre v. Brazil [IACommHR], *supra* note 2, para. 173; Inter-American Commission on Human Rights, Report on Terrorism and Human Rights, OEA/Ser.L/V/II.116 Doc. 5 rev.1 corr. (2002), para. 87.

30. Corumbiara Massacre v. Brazil, *supra* note 2, para. 180.

31. Zambrano Vélez et al. v. Ecuador, *supra* note 29, paras. 105–110.

Prisoners, the Inter-American bodies also accept that prison officers may use defensive force against prisoners.[32]

4. African Charter on Human and Peoples' Rights

Article 4 of the ACHPR entitles every human being to respect for his life and the integrity of his person, while prohibiting any arbitrary deprivation of this two-pronged right. The African Commission on Human and Peoples' Rights (African Commission) takes the position that arbitrariness is to be interpreted with reference to considerations such as appropriateness, justice, predictability, reasonableness, necessity, and proportionality.[33] It has established that state force infringing on life or physical integrity, including lethal force, may be based on self-defense or the defense of others.[34] In this regard, the African Commission takes the view that the U.N. Basic Principles on the Use of Firearms and the U.N. Code of Conduct for Law Enforcement Officials constitute authoritative statements of international law.[35]

The African Commission's jurisprudence accepts that law enforcement agents may deliberately kill where absolutely necessary to protect life against an imminent threat.[36] The Commissioner representing the African Commission on a 1998 visit to Cameroon made no objection when the government informed him that gendarmes were entitled to shoot highway robbers in self-defense, given that many gendarmes had apparently lost their lives at the hand of such robbers.[37] In *Kazingachire*, the African Commission assessed several intentional killings by Zimbabwean security forces in light of the right to self-defense, although it

32. Penitentiary Center of the Central Occidental Region (Uribana Prison), Order of 2 February 2007 on Provisional Measures, IACtHR Ser. E No. 1, considerations para. 11; Urso Branco Prisons, Order of the Court of 29 August 2002, IACtHR Ser. E (2002), considerations—para. 10; Inter-American Commission on Human Rights, Report on the Human Rights of Persons Deprived of Liberty in the Americas, OEA/Ser.L/B/II.Doc.64 (2001), para. 222 & pertaining n.260.

33. African Commission on Human and Peoples' Rights, General Comment No. 3 on The African Charter on Human And Peoples' Rights: The Right To Life (Article 4), adopted at the 57th session (2015), para. 12.

34. *Id.*, para. 27; Kazingachire et al. v. Zimbabwe, Comm. 295/04, Decision of 12 October 2013, paras. 108–115. See also Otto, *supra* note 12, p. 141. The African Court on Human and Peoples' Rights had not yet had an opportunity to make a pronouncement on the inherent limitations to the right to life and physical integrity in Art. 4 of the ACHPR.

35. Kazingachire, *id.*, para. 110. Cf. African Commission on Human and Peoples' Rights, Principles and Guidelines on the Implementation of Economic, Social and Cultural Rights in the African Charter on Human and Peoples' Rights, November 2010, http://www.achpr.org/files/instruments/economic-social-cultural/achpr_instr_guide_draft_esc_rights_eng.pdf, para. 79 (z) (bb).

36. African Commission on Human and Peoples' Rights, General Comment on the Right to Life, *supra* note 33, para. 27.

37. African Commission on Human and Peoples‘ Rights, Report of Promotional Visit to Cameroon by Prof. E.V.O. Dankwa—September 13–19, 1998 (undated), http://www.achpr.

ultimately found that the requirements of self-defense were not fulfilled in any of these cases.[38]

II. Defensive force as a state obligation

Whenever the state uses force in law enforcement, it needs to balance three competing concerns: the ability of law enforcement officers to act effectively in the public interest where their intervention is called for; the officers' safety; and the concern that state force does not unnecessarily or disproportionately limit the rights of those targeted by it.[39] In some areas, the state enjoys a certain margin of discretion on how to balance these concerns. For instance, it may calculate whether or not to react with (moderate) force against unlawful acts of civil disobedience. However, in the face of an imminent or ongoing violent unlawful attack threatening significant physical harm, the state no longer enjoys the same level of discretion, but must allow its officers to defend themselves and must instruct them to defend others threatened by such harm.

1. The State's Duty to Allow its agents to Defend Themselves

In light of the right to personal self-defense, the state must allow its police officers to defend themselves with force, including lethal self-defense where absolutely necessary and proportionate. This also follows from the fact that, even on active duty, law enforcement agents remain human beings entitled to the rights to life and physical security. In their relationship vis-à-vis citizens they represent the state and are therefore human rights duty-bearers. However, in their internal relationship with their state employer, they are human rights-holders who can expect that the state put in place rules and measures to protect, as far as the nature of their work reasonably permits, their human rights to life, physical integrity, and safe working conditions.[40] Respect for these rights means that the state must not unduly curb its police officers' right to defend themselves when attacked on duty.

The state may circumscribe to some extent how aggressively its law enforcement agents may interpret their right to self-defense. For instance, it would be legitimate if a police commander requires police officers in full riot gear to

org/files/sessions/24th/mission-reports/cameroon/achpr24_misrep_promo_cameroon_1998_eng.pdf, at p. 5.

38. Kazingachire et al. v. Zimbabwe, *supra* note 34, paras. 116–121.

39. Cf. David Bruce, Beyond Section 49: Control of the use of lethal force, South African Crime Quarterly, vol. 36 (2011), 3–12, at p. 4.

40. See also United Nations Office on Drugs and Crime (UNODC), Handbook on police accountability, oversight and integrity, United Nations: New York (2011), p. 86. Cf. Mosendz v. Ukraine [ECtHR], Appl. No. 52013/08, Judgment of 17 January 2013, para. 91 (requiring states to protect military conscripts from risks to life or limb that may result from the nature of military activities and operations).

stoically endure being pelted with bottles or other smaller objects rather than charging the rioters in self-defense and thus further escalating the confrontation. This holds true even if some officers will sustain light injuries. However, police officers must not be prohibited from exercising self-defense where an attack threatens the officers with death or serious injury and can be averted only through defensive force. In such situations, law enforcement agents' right to personal self-defense translates into a duty to permit self-defense from the perspective of the state as a whole.

The issue has also been discussed with regard to the exercise of self-defense by soldiers, even though in armed conflict they technically do not come under the type of unlawful attack that the right to personal self-defense generally requires.[41] The United States and Canada have established in their military doctrines that an individual soldier's right to personal self-defense may be limited by the soldier's unit commander.[42] Conversely, other states provide no option to limit an individual soldier's right to personal self-defense. For instance, the rules of engagement for German troops in Afghanistan place no restrictions on the right of soldiers to protect themselves (although the defense of others may be restricted by commanders if required by the military situation).[43] Australia views the soldier's right to personal self-defense as non-derogable and thus not at the disposition of the soldier's military hierarchy.[44] Building on the Australian position, Dale Stephens has argued that the government cannot compel soldiers from not exercising their right to personal self-defense.[45] Similarly, Amore criticizes that

41. As long as no prohibited means and methods of warfare are employed, international humanitarian law does not prohibit soldiers from killing each other in armed conflict and even protects state combatants from being penalized for such killings under domestic law. Soldiers defending themselves in armed conflict, therefore technically do not exercise their right to personal self-defense against unlawful attack. Instead, a right to use necessary defensive force even contrary to military orders might best be understood as deriving directly from their human rights to life and physical integrity and the state obligation not to create unreasonable obstacles to the protection of life.

By contrast, the right to personal self-defense becomes directly relevant where soldiers use force against unlawful attacks by violent civilians that do not directly participate in hostilities as it explains why such civilians may be targeted even though they otherwise remain protected persons under international humanitarian law. See Fifth Chapter: A & B (pp. 218–230) for details.

42. See Chairman of the Joint Chiefs of Staff, Instruction 3121.01B: Standing Rules of Engagement for US Forces, CJSCI (2005), at A-3; Canadian Forces Use of Force Manual, as cited in Zoltan Hegedüs & Sherrod Lewis Bumgardner (eds.), NATO Legal Deskbook, NATO Office of the Legal Advisor: Mons/Norfolk (2nd ed., 2010), p. 257.

43. Rules of Engagement for German troops deployed in the International Security Assistance Force (ISAF) in Afghanistan, as reissued in 2009 and cited in Stefan Löwenstein, Zur Durchsetzung des Auftrags, Frankfurter Allgemeine Blog, 27 July 2009, http://blogs.faz.net/sicherheit/2009/07/27/auftrag-39/.

44. Australian Defence Force Publication 3 (1st ed.), as cited in Dale Stephens, Rules of Engagement and the Concept of Unit Self Defence, Naval Law Review, vol. 45 (1998), 126–151, at 144.

45. Stephens, *id.*, pp. 147–148.

the commanders' privileges to limit the right to personal self-defense of their soldiers constitutes "a dramatic departure . . . from the foundational principles of law recognizing an inherent right to self-defense."[46] The present author considers that a balance has to be struck between legitimate interests regarding the command and control of military operations and soldiers' rights to life and physical security that underpin their right to personal self-defense. It may sometimes be permissible that commanders prohibit their soldiers from responding to force in self-defense. In some situations, commanders may order soldiers to temporarily hold their fire and not yet engage an attacking enemy in order to gain a tactical advantage (e.g., to conceal the exact positions of their troops or the type of weapons available to them) and thus better protect the lives of the unit members.[47] Or the commanders may order soldiers to take safe cover or pursue safe retreat options, rather than take a stand and fight back against an attacking enemy or violent civilians as soldiers would normally be entitled to do. Like police officers, soldiers may also be ordered to endure an attack by violent civilians and not escalate the confrontation if they are only at risk of light injuries. However, soldiers may not be prohibited from defending themselves if refraining from the use of force would expose them to serious risk of death or serious injury. This would be tantamount to expecting them to commit suicide or self-mutilation.[48] Even if they enlisted for an inherently dangerous mission, soldiers retain their human rights to life and physical security on duty and these rights must be interpreted in light of the right to personal self-defense as a general principle of law.

2. The Duty of Law Enforcement Agents to Defend Others

In the case of law enforcement agents, their individual right to defend others even translates into a duty to defend private persons against imminent attack. Grotius had already taken the view that those "whose particular office and duty it is to defend others, such as those who are engaged to guard travelers; or the governors of the state," may even have a duty to kill where necessary to protect others.[49] Similarly, contemporary international human rights law places a duty on the state to exercise due diligence in protecting the lives of individuals against imminent attack by criminals and others. This duty to protect requires the state and its law enforcement agents to use necessary and proportionate force in defense of others, including lethal force where such force is strictly unavoidable to prevent

46. Christopher D. Amore, Rules of Engagement: Balancing the (Inherent) Right and Obligation of Self-defence with the Prevention of Civilian Casualties, National Security Law Journal, vol. 1 (2013), 39–76, at p. 50.

47. See also Blaise Cathcart, Application of Force and Rules of Engagement in Self-Defence Operations, in: Terry D. Gill & Dieter Fleck (eds.), Handbook of International Law of Military Operations, Oxford University Press: New York (2010), 201–210, at p. 209 [para. 10.3/21].

48. See also Stephens, *supra* note 45, p. 148.

49. Hugo Grotius, The Rights of War and Peace [1625], Book II (ed. Richard Tuck/Jean Barbeyrac, trans. John Morrice), Liberty Fund: Indianapolis (2005), p. 403 [Bk II, Ch. I.VIII].

the loss of innocent life.[50] Emphasizing the legal duty of law enforcement agents to perform their functions, the African Commission has underlined that "[n]ot giving the police the proper scope to protect the public and themselves could compromise the safety of the public as well as members of the police force."[51]

The duty to defend others is not absolute. In deciding how best to defend others, the state and its agents may factor in whether a particular defensive measure would cause unreasonable risks for the intervening police officers. However, where the life of a private person is under threat, police officers in the line of duty can be expected to incur a certain level of risk to save that life.

The state must give practical meaning to this right and duty of self-defense by ensuring that it is reflected it in relevant laws, regulations, orders, and training materials guiding the use of force by state agents. Police and others authorized to use force on behalf of the state must know that they may defend themselves and that they must defend others against imminent or ongoing unlawful attack targeting life or physical security.

The fact that the right to personal self-defense translates into a duty to defend from the perspective of the state helps explain why state agents may resort to particularly drastic levels of force for defensive purposes. As will be shown in the next section, self-defense and defense of others are the only reasons international human rights law recognizes as justifying law enforcement agents shooting to kill. Such grave levels of force are permitted because otherwise the state could find itself entrapped between contradictory duties: its duty to protect the life of police officers and members of the general public versus its duty to respect the right to life of everyone, including dangerous criminals. The right to personal self-defense thus serves as the deciding criterion to resolve a conflict of human rights duties.

III. Self-defense as the sole peacetime justification of deliberately lethal force

The right to life has been characterized as "the fulcrum of all other rights . . . the fountain through which other rights flow" or even the "supreme right."[52]

50. Report of the Special Rapporteur on extrajudicial, summary or arbitrary executions, Philip Alston, U.N. Doc. E/CN.4/2006/53 (2006) [2006 Annual Report], para. 47; Inter-American Commission on Human Rights, *supra* note 29, para. 87; Neira Alegria et al. v. Peru [IACtHR], *supra* note 2, para. 61. Jiménez Vaca v. Colombia [HRCttee], Comm. 859/1999, U.N. Doc. CCPR/C/74/D/859/1999 (2002), para. 7.3; Nowak, *supra* note 21, pp. 126–127 [Art. 6, paras. 3–6] Otto, *supra* note 12, p. 80; Dymond-Bass/Corney, *supra* note 6, p. 33; House of Lords/House of Commons Joint Committee on Human Rights, The Government's policy on the use of drones for targeted killing Second Report of Session 2015–16, paras. 3.70–3.72, http://www.publications.parliament.uk/pa/jt201516/jtselect/jtrights/574/574.pdf.

51. Kazingachire et al. v. Zimbabwe [ACommHPR], *supra* note 34, para. 109.

52. Forum of Conscience v. Sierra Leone [ACommHPR], Comm. No. 223/98 (2000), para. 19; Human Rights Committee, General Comment 6: Article 6 ICCPR (1982), para. 1, as restated in: U.N. Doc. HRI/GEN/1/Rev.1 at 6 (1994).

Despite its fundamental nature, the right to life is not absolute. The state may still use deliberately lethal force in extraordinary circumstances. In armed conflict, state forces may, in general, intentionally kill active combatants and civilians directly participating in hostilities. Human rights generally and the right to life in particular continue to apply in such situations. However, vis-à-vis killings that occur in the course of armed conflict hostilities, the right to life must be chiefly interpreted in light of the applicable rules of international humanitarian law, even if those are to some extent influenced by the general norms of human rights law.[53] Furthermore, Article 6 (2) of the ICCPR seemingly allows those states that have not yet abolished the death penalty to impose and execute it for the most serious crimes, although this is increasingly challenged in light of the prohibition of inhuman treatment and punishment under Article 7 of the ICCPR.[54]

53. Legality of the Threat or Use of Nuclear Weapons (Advisory Opinion), ICJ Rep. 1996, 226, at p. 240 [para. 25]; Report of the Special Rapporteur on extrajudicial, summary or arbitrary executions, Christof Heyns, U.N. Doc. A/68/382 (2013) [Report on Armed Drones], para. 40; African Commission on Human and Peoples' Rights, General Comment on the Right to Life, *supra* note 33, para. 12; Dieter Fleck, Law Enforcement and the Conduct of Hostilities: Two Supplementing or Mutually Excluding Legal Paradigms?, in: Andreas Fischer-Lescano et al. (eds.), Frieden in Freiheit. Peace in Liberty. Paix En Liberté. Festschrift für Michael Bothe zum 70 Geburtstag, Nomos/DIKE: Baden-Baden/Zürich (2008), 391–407, at p. 395. See also Fifth Chapter: A (pp. 218–221).

Even with regard to killings in conflict, human rights law as the *lex generalis* can still influence the interpretation of international humanitarian law (see notably the debate as to whether fighters in an armed group may be killed where their safe capture is possible, reflected below in the Fifth Chapter: A (pp. 220–221, notes 11 & 12 and accompanying text)). For more detailed discussions of the complex relationship between international human rights law and international humanitarian law generally, see Office of the United Nations High Commissioner for Human Rights, International Legal Protection of Human Rights in Armed Conflict, OHCHR: New York/Geneva (2011), pp. 32–68; Matthew Happold, International humanitarian law and human rights law, in: Nigel White & Christian Henderson (ed.), Research Handbook on International Conflict and Security Law, Elgar: Cheltenham (2013), pp. 444–466; Marco Sassoli & Laura M. Olson, The Relationship between international humanitarian and human rights law where it matters: admissible killing and internment of fighters in non-international armed conflicts, International Review of the Red Cross, vol. 90 (2008), 599–627.

54. There are no execution methods not involving cruel, inhuman, or degrading punishment. Furthermore, the inevitable waiting period, during which the condemned person will attempt to invoke any available rights of appeal and consideration of pardon, keeps the victim in a terrifying limbo tantamount to inhuman treatment. See, e.g., United Nations High Commissioner for Human Rights Navanethem Pillay, Statement at the United Nations General Assembly Ministerial-level Event on "The Death Penalty: From Moratorium to Abolition," 27 September 2012, http://humanrightsdoctorate.blogspot.com/2012/09/high-commissioner-speech-to-united.html; Report of the Special Rapporteur on torture and cruel, inhuman or degrading treatment or punishment Manfred Nowak, U.N. Doc. A/HRC/10/44 (2009), paras. 38–47; Interim report of the Special Rapporteur on torture and other cruel, inhuman or degrading treatment or punishment, Juan E. Méndez, U.N. Doc. A/67/279 (2012).

The extent to which state agents may use force outside the specific contexts of armed conflict and the death penalty is subject to debate. Some insist that deliberately lethal force may be used not only for self-defense and defense of others, but also for other purposes, such as to prevent future crimes involving a grave threat to life or serious injury, to arrest or to prevent the escape of persons presenting such threats,[55] or even to quell riots.[56] In the same vein, the highest courts of South Africa and the United States have considered it compatible with fundamental rights under their respective constitutions to shoot dead, as a last resort, escaping suspects whose alleged crimes involve the infliction or threatened infliction of death or seriously bodily harm.[57]

However, the prevailing and more persuasive view with regard to international human rights law is that law enforcement agents may only employ deliberately lethal force where absolute necessary and proportionate to defend against imminent attacks that may result in loss of life.[58] No other ground than self-defense and defense of others can provide a valid reason for police to shoot to kill. As will be shown below, the jurisprudence of universal and regional human rights bodies has evolved towards that position.

55. Michael Ramsden, Targeted Killings and International Human Rights Law: The Case of Anwar Al-Awlaki, Journal of Conflict & Security Law, vol. 16 (2011), 385–406, at p. 395; Clemens Arzt, Europäische Menschenrechtskonvention und polizeilicher Todesschuss, Deutsche öffentliche Verwaltung (DöV) (2007), 230–237, at p. 233; Bruce, *supra* note 39, p. 5. For the prevention of escape of dangerous criminals only: Isabel Schübel-Pfister, Art. 2 EMRK, in: Ulrich Karpenstein & Franz Mayer, EMRK: Konvention zum Schutz der Menschenrechte und Grundfreiheiten, C.H.Beck: München (2012), p. 62 [Art. 2, para. 26]; Otto, *supra* note 12, p. 537.

56. Arzt, *id.*, 233; Adam Bodnar & Irmina Pacho, Targeted Killings (Drone Strikes) and the European Convention on Human Rights, Polish Yearbook of International Law, vol. 32 (2012), 189–208, at p. 201.

57. Tennessee v. Garner [U.S. Supreme Court], 471 U.S. 1 (1985), at pp. 11–12; Ex Parte Minister of Safety and Security and Others: In Re S v Walters and Another [South African Constitutional Court] (CCT28/01) [2002] ZACC 6; 2002 (4) SA 613; 2002 (7) BCLR 663 (21 May 2002), at para. 52.

58. Walter Kälin & Jörg Künzli, The Law of International Human Rights Protection, Oxford University Press: Oxford (2009), pp. 276–277; Melzer, *supra* note 22, p. 235; Nsereko, *supra* note 21, pp. 254–255; Rob McLaughlin, The Legal Regime Applicable to Use of Lethal Force When Operating under a United Nations Security Council Chapter VII Mandate Authorising "All Necessary Means,", Journal of Conflict & Security Law, vol. 12 (2007), 389–417, at p. 417; Meagan S. Wong, Targeted Killings and the International Legal Framework: With Particular Reference to the US Operation against Osama Bin Laden, Chinese Journal of International Law, vol. 11(1) (2012), 127–163, at pp. 130–131; Schmahl, *supra* note 22, p. 240; Amnesty International, Use of Force Guidelines, *supra* note 3, pp. 31 & 34. See also Sarah Joseph, Denouement of the Deaths on the Rock: The Right to Life of Terrorists, Netherlands Quarterly of Human Rights, vol. 14 (1996), 5–23, at p. 10. Too far-reaching: Ralph Crawshaw, Stuart Cullen & Tom Williamson, Human Rights and Policing, Martinus Nijhoff: Leiden/Boston (2nd ed., 2007), p. 157 (considering that any use of firearms may be employed only in self-defense).

1. Jurisprudence of the European Court of Human Rights

Article 2(2) of the ECHR allows for three instances in which deprivation of life may be justified outside the context of armed conflict:

(a) Defense of any person from unlawful violence
(b) In order to effect a lawful arrest or to prevent the escape of a person lawfully detained;
(c) In action lawfully taken for the purpose of quelling a riot.[59]

However, the provision does not specify whether all of these instances allow deliberately lethal force or whether some of them only allow deprivation of life unintentionally resulting from the use of potentially lethal force or less lethal force. Some take the view that deliberately lethal force is allowed under all three alternatives set out in Article 2(2) of the ECHR.[60] More persuasive is the counterview that self-defense and defense of others pursuant to Article 2(2)(a) are the sole instances where the ECHR allows for the use of deliberately lethal force in times of peace.[61]

Early case law of the European Commission on Human Rights suggests that deliberately lethal force is also justified to prevent the escape of dangerous criminals and thereby prevent future violent crimes. In *Kelly*, a British soldier in Northern Ireland shot and killed a 17-year-old boy joyriding in a stolen car because he mistook the boy and his friends for IRA terrorists. According to the findings of the U.K. courts, the shots were designed to kill or at least seriously injure the boy. Even though the car was speeding away from the soldier and posed no immediate threat to him or others, the European Commission still found no violation of Article 2 of the ECHR because it found that the soldier had good reason to believe, under the circumstances prevailing at the time, that the boys were escaping IRA terrorists. The court noted that although "the risk of harm to the occupants of the car was high, the kind of harm to be averted (as the soldiers reasonably thought) by preventing their escape was even greater, namely

59. Article 2(2)(c), the second alternative of the ECHR, allows deprivation of life for the purpose of quelling an insurrection. That exception relates to the state's use of force against insurgents in non-international armed conflict, where persons directly participating in the hostilities emerging from the insurrection may be targeted and killed. Louise Doswald-Beck, The right to life in armed conflict: Does international humanitarian law provide all the answers?, International Review of the Red Cross, vol. 88 (2006), 881–904, at p. 883. The European Court approaches such cases by either tacitly or expressly applying IHL standards on the use of force. See, e.g., Ergi v. Turkey, Appl. No. 23818/94, Judgment of 28 July 1998, para 81; Benzer et al. v. Turkey, Appl. No. 23502/06, Judgment of 12 November 2013, para 184. See also Fleck, *supra* note 53, p. 400.

60. See Ladewig, *supra* note 8, p. 61 [Artikel 2, paras. 42 & 44]; Arzt, *supra* note 55, p. 233 (conceding only that intentional killings to carry out an arrest would be inappropriate); Schübel-Pfister *supra* note 55, p. 62 [Art. 2, para. 26] (for Art. 2(2)(b) ECHR).

61. Kälin & Künzli, *supra* note 58, pp. 276–277.

the freedom of terrorists to resume their dealing in death and destruction."[62] In *Wolfgram*, a group of bank robbers resisted arrest by exploding a hand grenade. In response, police opened fire and killed two of the robbers. The Commission held that the police killings were absolutely necessary both for purposes of self-defense and for effecting the robbers' arrest.[63]

The ECtHR has distanced itself from this jurisprudence in line with its emphasis on narrowly interpreting the exceptions in Article 2(2) of the ECHR.[64] It has consistently stressed that Article 2(2) "does not primarily define instances where it is permitted intentionally to kill an individual, but describes the situations where it is permitted to 'use force' which may result, as an unintended outcome, in the deprivation of life."[65]

In respect of Article 2(2)(b) of the ECHR, the court takes the position that not even potentially deadly force can be lawful under the ECHR, where it is known that a person evading arrest or escaping from lawful detention poses no threat to life or limb and is not suspected of having committed a violent offense. This applies even if failing to use lethal force results in the fugitive's escape.[66] It would follow in turn (*argumentum e contrario*) that the ECtHR's jurisprudence allows *potentially* lethal force, in particular the use of firearms aimed at non-vital organs, where absolutely necessary and proportionate to secure the arrest or prevent the escape of seriously violent criminals or criminal suspects.[67]

However, *deliberately* lethal force ("shooting to kill") for purposes of effecting an arrest or preventing escape remains prohibited under the ECHR even if the target is suspected of very serious crimes.[68] This emerges from *Wasilewska and*

62. Kelly v. United Kingdom, Appl. No. 17579/90, Decision of 13 January 1993.

63. Wolfgram v. Germany, Appl. No. 11257/84, Decision of 6 October 1986.

64. Aydan v. Turkey, Appl. No. 16281/10, Judgment of 12 March 2013, para. 66; Salman v Turkey, Appl. No. 21986/93, Judgment of 27 June 2000, para. 97.

65. McCann et al. v. United Kingdom [ECtHR Grand Chamber], *supra* note 9, para. 148; Giuliani and Gaggio v. Italy [ECtHR Grand Chamber], Appl. No. 23458/02, Judgment of 24 March 2011, para. 175.

66. Nachova et al. v. Bulgaria [ECtHR Grand Chamber], Appl. No. 43577/98 & 43579/98, Judgment of 6 July 2005, para. 95; Putintseva v Russia, Appl. No. 33498/04, Judgment of 10 May 2012, para. 69; Wasilewska and Kalucka v. Poland, Appl. No. 28975/04 & 33406/04, Judgment of 23 February 2010, para. 43. See also Kälin & Künzli, *supra* note 58, p. 276 (n.12). But cf. Esser, *supra* note 8, p. 123 [EMRK art. 2, para. 57].

67. See also D.J. Harris et al., Law of the European Convention on Human Rights, Oxford University Press: Oxford (3rd ed., 2014), p. 232; Doswald-Beck, *supra* note 59, p. 886; Velu/Ergec, *supra* note 8, para. 233. See also M.D. v. Turkey [ECommHR], Appl. No. 28518/95, Decision of 30 June 1997.

68. Frowein/Peukert, *supra* note 8, p. 37 [Art.2, para. 13]; Gollwitzer, *supra* note 8, pp. 164–165 [Art. 2 MRK, para. 20]; Velu/Ergec, *supra* note 8, para. 233; William Schabas, The European Convention on Human Rights: A Commentary, Oxford University Press: Oxford (2015), p. 151.

Kalucka, which concerned members of a violent armed gang in Poland who were fleeing in a car and nearly ran over a police officer who tried to block their path. Throughout the whole incident, police shot at the car with automatic assault rifles that they apparently aimed at the passengers' heads and torsos. One gang member was killed, another seriously wounded. The ECtHR accepted that the use of weapons was absolutely necessary while the car was charging at the police officer because he was exposed to a clear and immediate danger. However, it considered the gunfire no longer lawful once the vehicle had passed the officer and the officers' only intention was to prevent the suspects' escape.[69] In *Juozaitiene and Bikulcius*, police had also fired at a car fleeing the scene in a way that posed a "very high risk of killing the passengers," and two passengers had indeed been killed. The court held that such use of lethal force could be justified only as a last resort to avert a "very clear and *imminent* danger" posed by the suspect's continued escape.[70] The ECtHR has thus reversed the approach taken by the European Commission of Human Rights in *Kelly*. It thereby established that deliberately lethal force may be used for purposes of self-defense or defense of others against clear and imminent threats, but not to effect arrests or prevent escapes, even where the target are armed and violent criminals.

The ECtHR's approach is sensible. The very idea of intentionally killing in order to effect an arrest (see Article 2(2)(b), first alternative) is nonsensical since it is impossible to arrest a corpse.[71] There is no good reason to assume that a different standard should apply for the second alternative of Article 2(2)(b) ECHR—preventing the escape of a person lawfully detained. The objective of Article 2(2)(b) ECHR is to allow law enforcement agents to ensure that a person can be brought to trial and serves his punishment if convicted. Potentially lethal force can still be reconciled with that objective; deliberately lethal force makes achieving it impossible.[72]

The case for allowing deliberately lethal force to quell riots (Article 2(2)(c) of the ECHR) is even less convincing. Where the violent crowd or individuals within

69. Wasilewska and Kalucka v. Poland, *supra* note 66, paras. 52–53.

70. Juozaitiene and Bikulcius v. Lithuania, Appl. No. 70659/01 & 74371/01, Judgment of 24 April 2008, paras. 77–78.

71. Joseph, *supra* note 58, p. 9. See also Harris et al., *supra* note 67, p. 232; Ashworth, *supra* note 17, p. 42; Otto, *supra* note 12, p. 95; Diehm, *supra* note 12, p. 338. While the European Court has not explicitly adopted this argument, it acknowledged the inherent inappropriateness of deliberately lethal force to affect arrests in Esmukhambetov et al. v. Russia, Appl. No. 23445/03, Judgment of 29 March 2011. In that case Russia had claimed that it shot air-to-surface missiles at a village to effect the arrest of Chechen armed fighters. The court [*id.*, para 146) considered such heavy weapons grossly disproportionate for the said purpose, noting wryly that no Chechen armed fighters were arrested based on the bombardment.

72. Paeffgen, *supra* note 8, p. 395 [Art. 2 EMRK, para. 68]; Christoph Grabenwarter & Katharina Pabel, Europäische Menschenrechtskonvention, C.H.Beck: München (5th ed., 2012), p. 153; Harris et al., *supra* note 67, p. 232 (also noting that shooting to kill escapees ignores the possibility of a later arrest).

the crowd pose an imminent and concrete danger to the life of law enforcement officers or others, deliberately lethal force may be used as a last resort against the individuals posing such danger. However, this is already established by the self-defense justification under Article 2(2)(a) of the ECHR. In *Giuliani and Gaggio*, for instance, rioting protesters at the G-8 Summit in Genoa attacked a group of gendarmes with various objects so that "the possibility of lynching could not be excluded."[73] One of the gendarmes under attack shot one of the assailants dead. The court considered the killing to amount to justified self-defense under Article 2(2)(a) of the ECHR and saw no need to revert to the "quelling riots" justification under Article 2(2)(c).[74]

Deliberately lethal force may not be used only for purposes of quelling the riot as such and restoring law and order.[75] In the absence of any concrete and imminent threats to anyone's life or limb in such cases, force using less lethal means is generally the most that may be used for this purpose. This also follows from the comparison with Article 2(2)(a) of the ECHR, which the drafters consciously extended only to the defense of "any person from unlawful violence," thereby excluding lethal force for purposes of defense of property or abstract values such as the public order.[76] If lethal force were permissible under Article 2(2)(c) for quelling riots as such and curbing the risk riots pose to such lesser values, this would undercut the principled decision taken in respect of the ambit of Article 2(2)(a).

In *Gülec*, the ECtHR recognized the limited reach of the "quelling riots" justification under Article 2(2)(c) of the ECHR, noting that "a balance must be struck between the aim pursued [of quelling a riot] and the means employed to achieve it."[77] Although the law enforcement authorities were faced with a very violent demonstration, the court considered it a violation of the right to life that the authorities had used lethal force in the form of a tank-mounted machine gun to disperse the demonstrators. Instead, the police should have been equipped with less lethal means such as truncheons, riot shields, water cannons, rubber bullets, or tear gas in order to contain the violent crowd.[78]

The court took the same line in *Simsek*, where demonstrators were throwing stones and fire bombs and causing damage to buildings. The court found

73. Giuliani and Gaggio v. Italy, *supra* note 65, para. 188.

74. *Id.*, paras. 191 & 196.

75. See also Otto, *supra* note 12, p. 178; Louise Doswald-Beck, Assessing "incapacitating chemical agents" under human rights law, in: ICRC, Expert Meeting: "Incapacitating Chemical Agents"—Law Enforcement, Human Rights Law and Policy, ICRC: Geneva (2013), 39–45, at p. 41. But see Velu/Ergec, *supra* note 8, para. 232; Grabenwarter/Pabel, *supra* note 72, p. 153.

76. See this Fourth Chapter: C.I.1 (p. 126) and C.V.2.a (pp. 175–178).

77. Gülec v. Turkey, Appl. No. 21593/93, Judgment of 27 July 1998, para. 71.

78. *Id.*

a violation because the Turkish authorities fired live ammunition at the rioters rather than having recourse to less lethal means.[79]

2. United Nations Jurisprudence

Older jurisprudence of the U.N. Human Rights Committee does not rule out the use of deliberately lethal force for purposes of carrying out arrests or preventing escapes of dangerous suspects. In *Suarez de Guerrero*, the Committee found Colombia responsible for intentional killings, noting, inter alia, that the police action had not been "necessary to effect the arrest or prevent the escape of the persons concerned."[80] In *Baboeram-Adhin*, which concerned the summary execution of 15 people, the Committee found it pertinent to note that the "State party has failed to submit any evidence proving that these persons were shot while trying to escape."[81] In *Carlton Linton*, the complainant was shot and seriously injured while trying to escape from death row. The wardens were apparently shooting to kill, given that a second escapee was killed with a shot to the head. Nevertheless, the Committee made no finding against Jamaica for using deliberately lethal force to stop the two escapees.[82]

The Committee no longer seems to follow this permissive interpretation of Article 6 of the ICCPR. In its recent Draft General Comment on the Right to Life, the Committee takes the view that lethal force may be used in self-defense, but not to deliberately kill an escaping convict who poses no serious and imminent threat to the lives or bodily integrity of others.[83] This shift in approach may reflect the impact of the adoption in 1990 of the U.N. Basic Principles on the Use of Force and Firearms. Principle 9 introduces a clear distinction between the use of firearms generally (i.e., potentially lethal force) and deliberately lethal force. According to Principle 9, the use of firearms is allowed only where necessary for the objectives of

> self-defense or defense of others against the imminent threat of death or serious injury, to prevent the perpetration of a particularly serious crime involving grave threat to life, to arrest a person presenting such a danger and resisting their authority, or to prevent his or her escape.

Conversely, "intentional lethal use of firearms may only be made when strictly unavoidable in order to protect life" (Principle 9, second sentence). Therefore,

79. Simsek et al. v. Turkey, Appl. No. 35072/97 & 37194/97, Judgment of 26 July 2005, paras 107–108.

80. Suarez de Guerrero v. Colombia, *supra* note 23, para. 13.2.

81. Baboeram-Adhin v. Suriname, Comm. No. 146/1983 and 148–154/1983, U.N. Doc. Supp. No. 40 (A/40/40) at 187 (1985), para. 14.3.

82. Carlton Linton v. Jamaica, Comm. No. 255/1987, U.N. Doc. CCPR/C/46/D/255/1987 (1992), paras. 2.6 & 8.5.

83. Human Rights Committee, Draft general comment No. 36—Article 6: Right to life, U.N. Doc. CCPR/C/GC/R.36/Rev.2 (2015), para. 18.

preventing serious crimes, arresting their perpetrators, or preventing their escape are not, as such, objectives that justify deliberately lethal force.[84] It could be argued that such acts also protect life, because they may prevent life-threatening situations from developing. However, such an interpretation would render the restriction imposed by the second sentence of Principle 9 largely meaningless. The contextually more persuasive reading is therefore that the second sentence of Principle 9 restricts deliberately lethal force to situations where it is strictly unavoidable to protect life against imminent or present threats. This also aligns the Basic Principles with the position under the 1979 U.N. Code of Conduct for Law Enforcement Officials, which allows lethal force only when a "suspected offender offers armed resistance or otherwise jeopardizes the lives of others,"[85] that is, in a situation of self-defense or defense of others against an imminent threat.

This reading of the U.N. Principles finds support in the jurisprudence of the U.N. Special Rapporteur on Extrajudicial, Summary or Arbitrary Executions. Special Rapporteur Philip Alston (2004–2010) took the view that "[f]or [deliberate] lethal force to be considered to be lawful it must be used in a situation in which it is necessary for self-defense or the defense of another's life."[86] On this basis he has criticized government policies authorizing police to shoot alleged terrorists and criminals as "dangerous official rhetoric that displaces the clear legal standards on the use of lethal force which stipulate that the police may shoot to kill only when it is clear that an individual is *about to kill* someone (making lethal force proportionate) and there is no other available means of detaining the suspect (making lethal force necessary)."[87]

The Special Rapporteur specifically found that the possible escape of an alleged violent criminal "who presents no *direct* threat to the lives of others, cannot justify shooting to kill."[88] Following the same approach, the United Nations Sub-Committee on the Prevention of Torture criticized orders given to wardens in a Honduran high-security prison to shoot any inmate who ventures into a "dead zone" near the prison perimeter as a means to prevent escapes of the dangerous criminals detained in the prison.[89]

84. See also Report of the Special Rapporteur on extrajudicial, summary or arbitrary executions, Christof Heyns, U.N. Doc. A/HRC/26/36 (2014) [2014 Annual Report], para. 72.

85. See U.N. Code of Conduct for Law Enforcement Officials, *supra* note 25, Art. 3(c).

86. U.N. Special Rapporteur on extrajudicial, summary or arbitrary executions Philip Alston, 2006 Annual Report, *supra* note 50, para. 48. See also *id.*, Study on targeted killings, U.N. Doc. A/HRC/14/24/Add.6 (2010) [Targeted Killings Study], para. 33.

87. Report of the Special Rapporteur on extrajudicial, summary or arbitrary executions, Philip Alston, U.N. Doc. A/HRC/14/24 (2010) [2010 Annual Report] para. 35 (emphasis added).

88. Report of the Special Rapporteur Extrajudicial, summary or arbitrary executions, Philip Alston: Mission to Nigeria, U.N. Doc. E/CN.4/2006/53/Add.4 (2006), para. 47 (emphasis added).

89. Report on the visit of the Subcommittee on Prevention of Torture and Other Cruel, Inhuman or Degrading Treatment or Punishment to Honduras, U.N. Doc. CAT/OP/HND/1 (2010) Paras. 254–255.

Alston's successor, Special Rapporteur Christof Heyns (2010–2016) has followed the same restrictive interpretation of the law, taking the position that intentional lethal force is permissible only against a person who presents an imminent threat to life.[90] Deliberately lethal force therefore may not be employed to contain violent demonstrations and riots. Such force "may only be targeted at the person or persons constituting the threat of death or serious injury."[91]

During his 2014 visit to the Gambia, the Special Rapporteur criticized that the Gambian Constitution "does not require the existence of an imminent threat of death or serious injury for the use of lethal force, as prescribed by international law." Instead, it allows the use of lethal force for the defense of property, to effect a lawful arrest or prevent the escape of a lawfully detained person, to prevent criminal offenses, or in the cases of riots, insurrection, or mutiny. The Special Rapporteur determined that this sets "the standards for the use of force too low and is incompatible with international law norms."[92]

The United Nations High Commissioner for Human Rights also considers that, in peacetime, deliberately lethal force may be employed only in situations of self-defense and defense of others. In relation to the use of lethal drone strikes outside the context of armed conflict, High Commissioner Navi Pillay set out her Office's legal position as follows:

> In any situation other than active hostilities in an armed conflict, the prohibition of the arbitrary deprivation of life means that the intentional use of lethal force would be lawful only in a law enforcement context, when an individual poses an imminent threat to the life of another, and where the use of lethal force is strictly unavoidable to protect life.[93]

90. U.N. Special Rapporteur on extrajudicial, summary or arbitrary executions Christof Heyns, Report on Armed Drones, *supra* note 53, paras. 33 & 35; *id.*, Annual Report 2014, *supra* note 84, para. 60.

91. U.N. Special Rapporteur on extrajudicial, summary or arbitrary executions, Christof Heyns, 2011 Annual Report, *supra* note 22, paras. 60–61 (cit. at para. 61). See also *id.*, 2014 Annual Report, *supra* note 84, para. 73; U.N. Basic Principles on the Use of Force and Firearms, *supra* note 25, Principle 14 read in conjunction Principle 9, second sentence; Crawshaw/Cullen/Williamson, *supra* note 58, p. 151; ICRC, Human Rights and Humanitarian Law for Police and Security Forces, *supra* note 2, p. 263.

92. Special Rapporteur on extrajudicial, summary or arbitrary executions, Christof Heyns & Special Rapporteur on torture and other cruel, inhuman and degrading treatment or punishment, Juan Mendez, The Gambia: End of visit statement of the Special Rapporteur, 7 November 2014, http://www.ohchr.org/en/NewsEvents/Pages/DisplayNews.aspx?NewsID=15265&LangID=E.

93. See High Commissioner for Human Rights Navi Pillay, Opening Statement at the Human Rights Council's interactive panel discussion on the use of remotely piloted aircraft or armed drones in compliance with international law , 22 September 2014, http://www.ohchr.org/AR/NewsEvents/Pages/DisplayNews.aspx?NewsID=15113&LangID=A. Endorsing the same position also Report of the detailed findings of the commission of inquiry on human rights

Consistent with this standard, successive High Commissioners have also criticized the use of lethal force for the mere purpose of quelling riots, noting that such force is only permissible when strictly unavoidable to protect life.[94] The United Nations Human Rights Council has endorsed the same position. In successive resolutions on the freedom of assembly, it recalled "that lethal force may only be used to protect against an imminent threat to life and that it may not be used merely to disperse a gathering."[95]

3. Jurisprudence of the Inter-American Human Rights System

The Inter-American Commission and Court have cited with approval the standards on the use of lethal force set out in the U.N. Code of Conduct and U.N. Basic Principles.[96] Accordingly, neither body recognizes the legality of using deliberately lethal force in peacetime for any other purposes than self-defense or defense of others, in particular not for purposes of carrying out arrests or preventing escapes. Notably, the Inter-American Commission has established that prison wardens may shoot to kill escaping prisoners only "in cases of imminent danger in which prisoners attempting to escape react against prison guards or third parties with violent means that threaten their lives."[97] In *Finca "La Exacta"* it also found that the police's use of deliberately lethal force in an operation to execute arrest warrants violated the right to life, as the state had offered no evidence to

in the Democratic People's Republic of Korea, U.N. Doc. A/HRC/25/CRP.1 (2014), para. 403; Comment by the Spokesperson for the UN High Commissioner for Human Rights, Rupert Colville, on the killing of a Palestinian man in Hebron, 30 March 2016, http://www.ohchr.org/EN/NewsEvents/Pages/DisplayNews.aspx?NewsID=18540&LangID=.

94. UN human rights chief alarmed by high loss of life in China's Xinjiang región, 7 July 2009, http://www.ohchr.org/en/NewsEvents/Pages/DisplayNews.aspx?NewsID=9051&LangID=E. See also United Nations Office of the High Commissioner for Human Rights in Nepal, The April Protests: Democratic Rights and the Excessive Use of Force, September 2006, http://nepal.ohchr.org/en/resources/Documents/English/reports/IR/Year2006/2006_09_21_OHCHR-Nepal.Report%20on%20The%20April%20Protests.pdf, at p. 12 & 16; Office of the United Nations High Commissioner for Human Rights, Press Briefing on Venezuela, 10 February 2015, http://www.ohchr.org/EN/NewsEvents/Pages/DisplayNews.aspx?NewsID=15559&LangID=E.

95. HRC Res. 22/10.The promotion and protection of human rights in the context of peaceful protests U.N. Doc. A/HRC/RES/22/10 (2013), para. 8; HRC Res. 25/38. The promotion and protection of human rights in the context of peaceful protests, U.N. Doc. A/HRC/RES/25/38 (2014), para. 10. Resolution 22/10 was adopted without a vote. Resolution 25/38 was passed by vote for reasons unrelated to the cited paragraph.

See also Joint report of the Special Rapporteur on the rights to freedom of peaceful assembly and of association and the Special Rapporteur on extrajudicial, summary or arbitrary executions on the proper management of assemblies, U.N. Doc. A/31/36 (2016), para. 60.

96. Zambrano Vélez et al. v. Ecuador, *supra* note 29, para. 101; Montero-Aranguren et al. (Detention Center of Catia) v. Venezuela, *supra* note 29, para. 69; Finca "La Exacta" v. Guatemala [IACommHR], *supra* note 2, para. 42.

97. Inter-American Commission, *supra* note 32, para. 237.

show that the police agents had reason to believe that their lives or the lives of third parties were in danger.[98]

The Inter-American's court jurisprudence follows the same line. In *Barrios Family*, one of the victims physically tried to stop police from arresting his brother. The police shot him dead. The court found a violation considering that the man did not pose an immediate threat of death or injury.[99] In *Nadege Dorzema*, Dominican security forces had fired indiscriminately at a truck full of Haitian migrants that had failed to stop at a checkpoint, killing several passengers. The court held that "even when abstaining from the use of force would have allowed the individuals that were the subject of the state's action to escape, the agents should not have used lethal force against people who did not represent a threat or a real or imminent danger to the agents or third parties."[100]

In *Montero-Aranguren (Detention Center of Catia)*, the court established that deliberately lethal force was not permissible to put down a riot in a Venezuelan prison through which armed and dangerous convicts were trying to achieve a mass prison break.[101] Incidentally, the case also goes to show that the ACHR does not permit the use of deliberately lethal force for the sole purpose of quelling a riot.[102]

4. Jurisprudence under the African Human Rights System

The African Commission also takes the position that the use of deliberately lethal force can only be justified by self-defense or defense of others against an imminent threat.[103] As long as the suspect of a crime does not pose such an immediate danger, deliberately lethal force cannot be employed in order to secure an arrest and prevent escape because "the sanctity of life requires that lives not be taken in the interest of the common good."[104] In this context, the African Commission has noted, with reference to counterterrorism operations, that international human rights law prohibits targeted killings.[105]

98. Finca "La Exacta" v. Guatemala [IACommHR], *supra* note 2, paras. 41–43.

99. Barrios Family v. Venezuela, *supra* note 29, para. 67.

100. Nadege Dorzema et al. v. Dominican Republic [IACtHR], Judgment of 24 October 2012, Ser. C No. 251, para. 85.

101. Montero-Aranguren et al. (Detention Center of Catia) v. Venezuela, *supra* note 29, paras. 70–73.

102. On the impermissibility of quelling riots by deliberately lethal force, see also Neira Alegria, *supra* note 2, paras. 74-76.

103. African Commission on Human and Peoples' Rights, General Comment on the Right to Life, *supra* note 33, para. 27; Kazingachire et al. v. Zimbabwe [ACommHPR], *supra* note 34, para. 120. Cf. Mouvement Burkinabé des Droits de l'Homme et des Peuples v. Burkina Faso [ACommHPR], Comm. No. 204/97, Decision of 7 May 2001, para. 43.

104. Kazingachire v. Zimbabwe, *id.*, paras. 117 and 120.

105. African Commission on Human and Peoples' Rights, Principles and Guidelines on Human and Peoples' Rights while Countering Terrorism in Africa, adopted by its 56th

In the same vein, the African Commission's Working Group on the Death Penalty and Extrajudicial Killings has underscored that lethal force "may only be used to protect life." On this basis, it noted that police may not use lethal force in dispersing illegal demonstrations unless lives are threatened.[106] The African Commission's General Comment on the Right to Life further specifies that no use of firearms is lawful for the sole reason of dispersing an assembly, even where acts of violence occur during such events.[107]

5. Why only Self-defense Justifies Deliberately Lethal Force

Defensive force is in a category of its own, because it protects against concrete and immediate threats of unlawful and violent attack. Self-defense scenarios require a reaction on the spot to prevent irreparable harm. In particular, innocent lives will be lost if the police are not allowed, as a last resort, to shoot to kill to defend themselves and others.

The other grounds that some claim to justify deliberately lethal force are different. The interests that they protect, or the threats that they protect against, are more abstract: to see that arrest warrants are executed; that criminals do not escape justice; that they cannot commit future crimes; and, in the case of riots, that public order is restored. There are sound policy reasons why international human rights law prohibits the use of deliberately lethal force in these other situations. In the case of riots, the state can equip itself with the trained personnel and less lethal means necessary to contain riots. After all, riots, by definition, involve a level of violence that remains below the threshold of armed conflict.[108] The state should therefore not be allowed to militarize the confrontation by "going to war" with the rioters and shooting at them as if they were an enemy force. This approach does not unduly neglect the safety of the law enforcement agents dealing with the riot. In the isolated instances, where state agents find themselves overpowered by particularly violent elements and their life is at risk, they retain of course the right to shoot and kill in self-defense as a last resort.

On self-defence grounds, police are also allowed to shoot and kill, as a last resort, where violent criminals use or threaten deadly force to resist arrest or

Ordinary Session (2015), p. 17 [Part 2: B]. The document does not specify whether targeted killings are also prohibited in armed conflict.

106. African Commission on Human and Peoples' Rights Working Group on the Death Penalty and Extra-Judicial, Summary or Arbitrary Killings in Africa, Intersession Activity Report (November 2013–April 2014), May 2014, para. 50, http://www.achpr.org/sessions/55th/intersession-activity-reports/death-penalty.

107. African Commission on Human and Peoples' Rights, General Comment on the Right to Life, *supra* note 33, para. 28.

108. See Protocol Additional II to the Geneva Conventions of 12 August 1949, and relating to the Protection of Victims of Non-International Armed Conflicts, art. 1(2).

force their escape. The same applies where police officers pursue a perpetrator of serious violence (for instance, a terrorist who just attacked members of the public) if the officers have good reason to believe that the target person continues to pose an imminent threat to the lives of others and shooting dead the person is the only way to neutralize that imminent threat.

However, there will also be cases where suspects or convicts of serious violence manage to stage non-violent escapes and do not pose a risk of imminent violence. Should international human rights law really allow the escape of dangerous individuals such as convicted murderers even at the risk that they may commit further crimes at an uncertain point in the future before they are recaptured? In response to this question, it should be kept in mind that potentially lethal force remains an option. Well trained and equipped prison guards or law enforcement agents will usually be able to stop an escaping highly dangerous suspect with a shot targeting the legs or the lower torso. In the rare cases, where this cannot be achieved, such as when the suspect is already at a distance, they should probably not be shooting anyhow, in light of the high risk of accidentally killing an innocent bystander.

Allowing the police to pursue the policy that a dead criminal is better than one on the loose creates a serious risk of deadly errors. In self-defense situations, police officers are required to assess an imminent and concrete threat based on a situation that unfolds before their eyes. This is already a very difficult task and examples of tragic mistakes abound in the jurisprudence of domestic and international courts.[109] However, where domestic laws entitle police to shoot to kill suspects of violent crime to prevent their escape, officers are asked to make, in a split second and without the suspect having any chance to be heard, a life-or-death decision based on a far more difficult assessment. As if they were a court, they have to pass judgment on past events (whether the suspect really committed a violent crime). Even more problematically, they have to predict uncertain future behavior (whether the suspect will carry out further violent crime if allowed to escape). As the tragic killing of the 17-year-old boy in the abovementioned case of *Kelly*[110] shows, such complex assessments carry a great risk of deadly errors. Law enforcement personnel should therefore not be endowed with "the authority of judge and executioner in [escape] situations where the likelihood of a reasonable, yet fatal, mistake by those law enforcers is high."[111] Such fatal errors made on the basis of policies to shooting to kill escapees can also be highly counterproductive, because they undermine public confidence in the police and make members of the targeted community reluctant to cooperate with them.[112]

109. See e.g. McCann et al. v. United Kingdom, *supra* note 9.

110. See *supra* note 62 and accompanying text.

111. Joseph, *supra* note 58, p. 10. See also Nsereko, *supra* note 21, p. 255; Report of the Special Rapporteur on extrajudicial, summary or arbitrary executions, Christof Heyns, U.N. Doc. A/66/330 (2011), para. 14 (considering that police officers should not make "godlike decisions without godlike wisdom").

112. U.N. Special Rapporteur on extrajudicial, summary or arbitrary executions Philip Alston, [2006 Annual Report] *supra* note 50, para. 52.

If deliberately lethal force to prevent escapes were legal, this could also be abused by unscrupulous states or individual rogue police officers to cover up summary executions of unarmed suspects with the terse explanation "shot while trying to escape." Human rights practice shows that is a real concern. For example, Chile's military dictatorship was notorious for invoking the "*ley de fuga*" to disguise summary executions of political dissidents as thwarted escape attempts.[113] In a more contemporary context, the Special Rapporteur on Summary Executions found that Nigerian legislation, which allows the police to use lethal force against fleeing robbers, has resulted in one robber being killed for every six reported armed robberies. Many such cases are in reality clandestine summary executions.[114]

Admittedly, self-defense can also serve to cover up illegal police violence. Because self-defense is the only justification for police shooting to kill, security forces may present summary executions of suspects as self-defense. In a 2015 report on Brazil, for instance, Amnesty International alleged that suspicious police killings were routinely classified as "resistance followed by death" cases and officers could therefore easily obtain impunity for summary executions by claiming self-defense.[115] Human Rights Watch came to similar conclusions in relation to police operations in Mexico.[116] This shows the need to effectively regulate self-defense. As the next two sections will show, international human rights law imposes very clear formal and substantive requirements in that respect.

B. FORMAL REQUIREMENT: SUFFICIENT BASIS FOR THE USE OF FORCE IN DOMESTIC LAW

According to international human rights law, any use of force by state agents requires a sufficient legal basis under domestic law.[117] For the use of firearms and other lethal force, this also follows directly from the right to life provisions

113. The Chilean Truth and Reconciliation Commission documented 101 cases of summary executions that were covered up as "shot while trying to escape." See Informe de la Comisión nacional de Verdad y Conciliación, vol. I.2, Andros Impresores: Santiago de Chile (1996), p. 1311.

114. U.N. Special Rapporteur on extrajudicial, summary or arbitrary executions, Philip Alston, 2006 Report to General Assembly, *supra* note 26, paras. 33–34.

115. Amnesty International, You killed my son: Homicides by military police in the city of Rio de Janeiro, Amnesty International: Rio de Janeiro/London, 3 August 2015, p. 7, https://www.amnesty.org/en/documents/amr19/2068/2015/en/.

116. Human Rights Watch, Mexico: Police Killings in Michoacán, 28 October 2015, https://www.hrw.org/news/2015/10/28/mexico-police-killings-michoacan.

117. Finogenov et al. v. Russia [ECtHR], Appl. No. 18299/03 & 27311/03, Judgment of 20 December 2011, para. 207; Bakan v. Turkey, Appl. No. 50939/99, Judgment of 12 June 2007, para. 49; Nadege Dorzema v. Dominican Republic [IACtHR], *supra* note 100, para. 80; Barrios Family v. Venezuela, *supra* note 29, para. 49; African Commission on Human and Peoples' Rights, General Comment on the Right to Life, *supra* note 33, para. 27; U.N. Basic Principles

in universal and regional human rights conventions, which require the state to protect the right to life "by law." [118] No exception applies where police officers use defensive force. The right to personal self-defense exercised in such cases may be grounded in a general principle of law recognized by nations, but the general principle is in and of itself not a sufficient legal basis, given that, even when exercising personal self-defense, the police still act under color of the law and with all the power that this position gives them.

The requirement of a sufficient legal basis is a separate formal requirement that seeks to strengthen the protection of human rights by extending the rule of law to the state's use of force, facilitating public scrutiny and providing legal certainty to the individual confronting state authorities. Any exercise of state force without sufficient legal basis is therefore arbitrary. It is not necessary that the lack of a sufficient legal basis caused the force used in the concrete case to be excessive or otherwise substantively unlawful.[119] Otherwise, the requirement of a sufficient legal basis would not serve a real purpose. It would come into play only when a violation can be established on other grounds anyway.

I. Minimum specifications

Not just any law will do as a justification for police use of force. The domestic legal framework regulating police use of force must itself be compatible with international standards.[120] However, this does not mean that it needs to mirror

on the Use of Force and Firearms, *supra* note 25, Principles 1 &11; Kälin & Künzli, *supra* note 58, p. 277; Fleck, *supra* note 53, p. 393; ICRC, Human Rights and Humanitarian Law for Police and Security Forces, *supra* note 2, p. 248; Amnesty International, Use of Force Guidelines, *supra* note 3, p. 17.

118. See Art. 6 ICCPR, Art. 2(1) ECHR, Art. 4 ACHR and Art. 5(2) Arab Charter on Human Rights. See also Human Rights Committee, General Comment 6: Article 6 ICCPR, *supra* note 52, para. 3; Montero-Aranguren et al. (Detention Center of Catia) v. Venezuela, *supra* note 29, para. 66; Zambrano Vélez et al. v. Ecuador, *supra* note 29, para. 86; Kazingachire et al. v. Zimbabwe [ACommHPR], *supra* note 34, para. 108; Makaratzis v. Greece [ECtHR], *supra* note 15, paras. 57–59; U.N. Special Rapporteur on extrajudicial, summary or arbitrary executions, Christof Heyns [2014 Annual Report], *supra* note 84, para. 26; Melzer, *supra* note 22, p. 100; Ramsden, *supra* note 55, p. 396.

119. In *Makaratzis*, a minority of judges argued that deficiencies in Greek law on police use of force were immaterial, because they did not cause the police's operational failures in that case. However, the majority refused to follow the argument that such causality has to be shown. See Makaratzis v. Greece, *supra* note 15, para. 62 & Joint Concurring Opinion of Judges Costa, Sir Nicolas Bratza, Lorenzen and Vajic. See also C.K. Boyle, The concept of arbitrary deprivation of life, in: Bertrand Ramcharan (ed.), The Right to Life in International Law, Martinus Nijhoff: Dordrecht (1985), 221–244, at p. 239.

120. Human Rights Committee, General Comment 31: Nature of the General Legal Obligation on States Parties to the Covenant, U.N. Doc. CCPR/C/21/Rev.1/Add.13 (2004), para 13. See also Suarez de Guerrero v. Colombia, *supra* note 23, para. 13.3; Streletz, Kessler and Krenz v. Germany [ECtHR Grand Chamber], Appl. No. 34044/96, 35532/97 & 44801/98, Judgment

the wording of relevant international provisions.[121] On the contrary, domestic legislation that merely replicates the terse terms of international human rights treaties is not sufficient. National law has to regulate the police use of force, especially lethal force, with far more precision so as to prevent abuses and provide legal certainty to citizens in their engagement with police officers.[122]

The Inter-American Court assesses legislation against the criteria established by Principle 11 of the U.N. Basic Principles on the Use of Force and Firearms, [123] which stipulates that rules and regulations on the use of firearms by law enforcement officials should:

(a) Specify the circumstances under which law enforcement officials are authorized to carry firearms and prescribe the types of firearms and ammunition permitted;
(b) Ensure that firearms are used only in appropriate circumstances and in a manner likely to decrease the risk of unnecessary harm;
(c) Prohibit the use of those firearms and ammunition that cause unwarranted injury or present an unwarranted risk;
(d) Regulate the control, storage and issuing of firearms, including procedures for ensuring that law enforcement officials are accountable for the firearms and ammunition issued to them;
(e) Provide for warnings to be given, if appropriate, when firearms are to be discharged;
(f) Provide for a system of reporting whenever law enforcement officials use firearms in the performance of their duty.

of 22 March 2001, para. 87; Makaratzis v. Greece [ECtHR], *supra* note 15, para. 59; Kälin & Künzli, *supra* note 58, p. 277; Nsereko, *supra* note 21, pp. 249 & 257; Amnesty International, Use of Force Guidelines, *supra* note 3, p. 17.

121. In *McCann*, for instance, the European Court considered domestic legislation sufficient that authorized lethal force where "reasonably justifiable" (as opposed to "absolutely necessary" according to Art. 2(2)(c) ECHR) given that domestic judicial practice interpreted that term along similarly strict lines. McCann et al. v. United Kingdom [ECtHR Grand Chamber], *supra* note 9, para. 154. See also Bakan v. Turkey, *supra* note 117, para. 51; Giuliani and Gaggio v. Italy, *supra* note 65, para. 214.

122. See also Rodley/Pollard, *supra* note 22, p. 253; Harris et al., *supra* note 67, p. 229; Arzt, *supra* note 55, p. 237; Schübel-Pfister, *supra* note 55, p. 62 [Art. 2, para. 26]; Francisco De Sanctis, What duties do states have with regard to the rules of engagement and the training of security forces under article 2 of the European Convention on Human Rights?, International Journal of Human Rights, vol. 10 (2006), 31–44, at p. 33; Human Rights Committee, Concluding Observations on the Initial Report of Liechtenstein, U.N. Doc. CCPR/C O/81/ LIE 12 (2004), para. 10.

123. Montero-Aranguren et al. (Detention Center of Catia) v. Venezuela, *supra* note 29, paras. 75–76.

The ECtHR also considers that Principle 11 forms part of the relevant framework of international law.[124] It has further elaborated that the "national legal framework must make recourse to firearms dependent on a careful assessment of the situation . . . and secure a system of adequate and effective safeguards against arbitrariness and abuse of force and even against avoidable accident."[125] However, the court's case law does not provide a consistent and clear line in implementing these principles.

In *Erdogan*, the ECtHR found there was no sufficient legal basis for the use of lethal force, as Turkey sought to rely on a 1934 law that permitted the police to use firearms, subject to necessity and graduation of force, in nine broad areas.[126] However, in *Perk*, adjudicated by another chamber two months before the *Erdogan* decision, the court upheld the very same legislation,[127] and in *Bakan*, the court upheld subsequent Turkish legislation although it was rather similar in substance.[128]

If a statute was enacted by an authoritarian regime of the past, the ECtHR tends to scrutinize it more carefully. In *Makaratzis*, the court held that there was no sufficient legal basis in Greek law for shooting a suspected terrorist. The court stressed that Greece sought to rely on a 1943 statute (enacted under German occupation, as the court emphasized), complemented by a more recent presidential decree. That legislative framework had been considered as "defective" and "vague" by Greek law enforcement authorities themselves.[129]

However, in *Giuliani and Gaggio*, the court saw a sufficient legal basis for the shooting of a violent demonstrator in a combination of the general self-defense provision of the Italian Criminal Code and a second, vaguely worded provision of the Italian Criminal Code that authorizes state agents to use force "to repel an act of violence."[130] Whereas *Makaratzis* considered the authoritarian pedigree of the Greek legislation to be a relevant factor, the *Giuliani and Gaggio* judgment entirely passed over the applicant's argument that the said provisions of the Italian Criminal Code dated back to the 1930s and thus reflected the authoritarian approach of the Fascist dictatorship at the time.[131]

124. Giuliani and Gaggio v. Italy, *supra* note 65, para. 154.

125. Guiliani and Gaggio, *id.*, para. 209.

126. Erdogan et al. v. Turkey, Appl. No. 19807/92, Judgment of 25 April 2006, paras. 58 & 77.

127. Perk et al. v. Turkey, Appl. No. 50739/99, Judgment of 28 March 2006, para. 60.

128. Bakan v. Turkey, *supra* note 117, paras. 33 & 50–51.

129. Makaratzis v. Greece, *supra* note 15, paras. 25 & 62.

130. Giuliani and Gaggio v. Italy, *supra* note 65, paras. 213–214.

131. *Id.*, para 202. Critical on this aspect of the judgment, Stephen Skinner, The Right to Life, Democracy and State Responsibility in "Urban Guerrilla" Conflict: The European Court of Human Rights Grand Chamber Judgment in Giuliani and Gaggio v. Italy, Human Rights Law Review, vol. 11(3) (2011), 567–577, at p. 569 (n.12).

Of even greater concern is the fact that the *Giuliani and Gaggio* judgment accepts an ordinary criminal code provisions as the legal basis for lethal force by law enforcement agents. This is problematic since self-defense provisions between private persons may in some respects be more permissive than what ought to be expected from state agents. Moreover, provisions in the criminal code regarding self-defense usually lack the detail necessary to effectively regulate life-and-death decisions by law enforcement officials.[132]

In *Soare*, the court considered the legal basis insufficient, even though Romanian legislation identified the grounds on which police could make use of firearms and specified that such use was absolutely necessary and no other means of restraint or immobilization were possible. However, there were no other provisions governing the use of weapons during police operations, apart from a requirement to give a warning, nor had there been any guidelines on the planning and management of such operations.[133] Yet, in *Finogenov* the court took no issue with the fact that the use of a knockout gas to end a standoff in a Moscow theatre, in which Chechen extremists took 202 hostages, rested on no specific legal basis but was an ad hoc solution, not described in the regulations and manuals for law enforcement officials. The court reasoned that the situation faced by the authorities was "totally unpredictable, exceptional and requiring a tailor-made response," and thus distinguishable from situations where even routine police operations lacked a proper legal basis.[134] This approach is not convincing (and not only because of the questionable factual premise that a mass hostage-taking by Chechen extremists was "totally unpredictable" three years into the Second Chechen War). Especially exceptional situations that necessitate force of a type and level that exceed the ordinary require a legal basis so as to guide, control, and reassure the law enforcement agents placed in such extreme situations.

The jurisprudence of the ECtHR on the legal basis for use of firearms and lethal force leaves much to be desired. At times, it appears as if the court's findings on the adequacy of the legal basis under domestic law depend on the court's assessment of whether a particular operation also failed to comply with the convention on other grounds or not.

II. Publicity

Laws on the use of force must be officially published and they must also be, in practice, accessible to the public.[135] Otherwise neither the legitimacy of the laws

132. Arzt, *supra* note 55, pp. 234 & 236; Esser, *supra* note 8, p. 121 [art. 2, para. 49].

133. Soare et al. v. Romania, Appl. No. 24329/02, Judgment of 22 February 2011, para. 132.

134. Finogenov et al. v. Russia, *supra* note 117, para. 230.

135. U.N. Special Rapporteur on extrajudicial, summary or arbitrary executions, Christof Heyns, [2014 Annual Report], *supra* note 84, para. 57; Nachova et al. v. Bulgaria, *supra* note 66, para. 99. Melzer, *supra* note 22, pp. 116 & 225.

themselves nor the legality of action based on them can be subject to public scrutiny and effective democratic control.

For purposes of public scrutiny, law enforcement agencies should, as much as possible, publicize their operational doctrines and instructions on the use of force, especially lethal force.[136] This also ensures that individuals know what kind of behavior may trigger force and avoids tragic errors. For instance, motorists who are pulled over by the police should know what kind of behavior may be considered life-threatening—for example, suddenly reaching into the glove compartment—and hence prompt police to open fire in self-defense.

Police doctrines may remain internal to the extent that their publication would undermine legitimate law enforcement aims and an overall minimum of transparency is still ensured. In hostage situations, for example, a police force may follow the operational policy to move from negotiating surrender to a shoot-to-kill approach as soon as the hostage-taker kills the first victim. Tactical guidelines of this nature do not have to be publicized so as not to put future hostage-takers on alert and increase the risk for their victims.

III. Parliamentary prerogative to regulate lethal force

Providing state agents with the authority to take life, especially the authority to kill intentionally, has such a profound impact on human rights that it should be regulated by primary legislation, that is, by parliamentary statute.[137] Reserving the prerogative to regulate lethal force to the legislature ensures checks and balances necessary to protective the right to life against executive arbitrariness. It also gives effect to human rights, ensuring democratic participation (see notably Article 25 of the ICCPR).[138]

With these considerations in mind, the German Constitutional Court has recognized a parliamentary prerogative (*Parlamentsvorbehalt*) for regulating matters that greatly affect fundamental rights, in particular infringements on the

136. Cf. U.N. Special Rapporteur on extrajudicial, summary or arbitrary executions, Philip Alston, Targeted Killings Study, *supra* note 86, para. 74; U.N. Special Rapporteur on extrajudicial, summary or arbitrary executions Christof Heyns, Report on Armed Drones, *supra* note 53, para. 98; Human Rights Committee, Concluding observations on the fourth periodic report of the United States of America, U.N. Doc. CCPR/C/USA/CO/4 (2014), para. 9.b (all calling for transparency of laws, policies and criteria on targeted killings).

137. Mordechai Kremnitzer, Präventives Töten, in: Dieter Fleck (ed.), Rechtsfragen der Terrorismusbekämpfung durch Streitkräfte, Nomos: Baden-Baden (2004), 201–222, at p. 202. See also A. Redelbach, Protection of the Right to Life by Law and by Other Means, in: Bertrand Ramcharan (ed.), The Right to Life in International Law, Martinus Nijhoff: Dordrecht (1985), 182–221, at pp. 208–209.

138. See also Jochen Frowein, Der europäische Grundrechtsschutz und die nationale Gerichtsbarkeit, De Gruyter: Berlin/New York (1983), at pp. 14–15, who finds support for a parliamentary prerogative to legislate on profound infringements of ECHR rights in the reference to an effective political democracy structure contained in the ECHR's preamble.

right to life.[139] Similarly, the Inter-American Court takes the view that requirements in the American Convention for Human Rights, according to which human rights can be restricted only "by law," require a formal law. By this term, the court means "a legal norm passed by the legislature and promulgated by the Executive Branch, pursuant to the procedure set out in the domestic law."[140] The Inter-American Court reasons as follows:

> In order to guarantee human rights, it is therefore essential that state actions affecting basic rights not be left to the discretion of the government but, rather, that they be surrounded by a set of guarantees designed to ensure that the inviolable attributes of the individual not be impaired. Perhaps the most important of these guarantees is that restrictions to basic rights only be established by a law passed by the Legislature in accordance with the Constitution. Such a procedure not only clothes these acts with the assent of the people through its representatives, but also allows minority groups to express their disagreement, propose different initiatives, participate in the shaping of the political will, or influence public opinion so as to prevent the majority from acting arbitrarily.[141]

Since Article 4 of the ACHR requires the protection of the right to life "by law," the basic tenets of police using defensive lethal force and other infringements on the right to life must therefore be regulated by parliamentary laws.[142]

Regrettably, other international human rights bodies do not yet apply a parliamentary prerogative doctrine.[143] This applies even to the regulation of lethal force, despite the fundamental nature of the right to life. For instance, the Special Rapporteur on Summary, Arbitrary and Extrajudicial Executions accepted that rules allowing the use of lethal force may be contained in an executive police

139. German Constitutional Court, Decision of 15 February 2006, Entscheidungen des Bunderverfassungsgerichts (BVerfGE) 115, 118, official translation available at: http://www.bundesverfassungsgericht.de/SharedDocs/Entscheidungen/EN/2006/02/rs20060215_1bvr035705en.html, at p. 139 [para. 85 of the official translation]. See also *id.*, Decision of 18 July 1967, BVerfGE 22, 180, 219 (para. 141).

140. The Word "Laws" in Article 30 of the American Convention on Human Rights, IACtHR Ser. A No. 6, Advisory Opinion of 9 May 1986, paras. 17, 27 & 35. Reaffirmed in Suárez-Rosero v. Ecuador, IACtHR Ser. C No. 35, Judgment of 12 November 1997, para 89; Claude-Reyes et al. v. Chile Judgment of 19 September 2006, IACtHR Ser. C No. 151, para 89; Escher et al. v. Brazil, IACtHR Ser.C. No. 200, Judgment of July 6, 2009, para 130.

141. *Id.*, para. 22.

142. See Inter-American Commission on Human Rights, Report on Citizen Security and Human Rights, OEA/Ser.L/V/II.Doc. 57 (2009), para. 232.13 (b). Cf. Artavia Murillo et al. v. Costa Rica, Judgment of 28 November 2012, IACtHR Ser. C No. 257, para. 273.

143. See Bardo Fassbender, Der Gesetzesvorbehalt in europäischen und internationalen Menschenrechtsverträgen in: Eckart Klein (ed.), Gewaltenteilung und Menschenrechte, Berliner Wissenschaftsverlag: Berlin (2nd ed., 2010), 83–137, at p. 88.

order.[144] Likewise, the Human Rights Committee has not called into question that deadly drone strikes outside areas of active hostilities can be based on a mere presidential policy guidance.[145] In *Makaratzis*, the ECtHR rejected as overly "slender" Greece's legislative framework on the use of lethal force, which consisted of a presidential decree and a law adopted in 1943 during Germany's occupation of Greece. However, the court took issue only with the historical pedigree of the 1943 law and the substantive deficits of the legislation, but did not specifically call into question that key tenets of the regulation were based on a mere presidential decree.[146]

Burying fundamental decisions on lethal force in executive regulations is problematic, not least because it limits public scrutiny and debate on whether the regulation fulfills the substantive requirements that international human rights law imposes on police use of defensive force. These requirements will be discussed in the following section.

C. SUBSTANTIVE REQUIREMENTS FOR SELF-DEFENSE AS A GROUND OF JUSTIFICATION

The basic tenets for law enforcement agents' use of defensive force appear to be essentially the same as those found in domestic self-defense provisions across the world: (i) unlawful attack, (ii) immediacy, (iii) necessity, and (iv) proportionality of the defensive response; and, in many jurisdictions, (v) knowledge of the defense situation. In some respects, however, international human rights law regulating the use of defensive force by law enforcement agents assigns particular features to each of these requirements.

I. Unlawful attack against protected individual interests

As with any other invocation of the right to self-defense, law enforcement agents can claim to use defensive force in accordance with international human rights law only in response to an unlawful human attack on protected interests.

1. Violent Attack on Tangible, Individual Interests

State agents may undoubtedly defend themselves and others against attacks on life and physical integrity. This follows directly from Article 2(2)(a) of the ECHR and Principle 9 of the U.N. Basic Principles on the Use of Force and Firearms,

144. See U.N. Special Rapporteur Extrajudicial, summary or arbitrary executions, Mr. Philip Alston, Mission to Nigeria, *supra* note 88, paras. 46–47 & 105(c) (calling for the amendment of the executive police order authorizing lethal force, rather than its replacement by a parliamentary statute).

145. Human Rights Committee, Concluding observations on the fourth periodic report of the United States of America, *supra* note 136, para. 9.

146. Makaratzis v. Greece, *supra* note 15, paras. 25 & 62.

which allow the use of defensive force against "violence" and "threat of death or serious injury." Threats of such violence against persons can also be countered with defensive force, but the threats must appear credible and create an immediately coercive situation.[147] Thus, police officers can use necessary and proportionate defensive force to overpower or neutralize a person threatening the police or private persons with a gun. Conversely, no self-defense situation arises where a person threatens others with a replicate gun that the victim and law enforcement officers involved recognize as not dangerous.

State agents may also defend property with force, although proportionality considerations will always rule out the use of firearms and other lethal force solely for such purposes.[148] In cases of attacks on property, the right to use force will already follow from the police's general right and duty to use necessary force to prevent property-related crimes. However, even where a person is incapable of incurring criminal responsibility (e.g., a person with serious mental disabilities or a child below the age of criminal responsibility), police could still use necessary and proportionate non-lethal or less lethal force to defend the targeted property.

A more difficult question is whether state agents may use force to defend themselves or others against attacks on intangible interests. These include attacks on honor. Some countries recognize self-defense in respect of one's honor under their criminal law. This already raises problems from the perspective of international human rights law with regard to self-defense by private persons where definitions of honor are not compatible with human rights values.[149] In any case, state agents should never be allowed to defend themselves even against a barrage of serious insults by using force, because the state and its representatives have a particular duty to promote the rule of law and must resolve such matters through civil lawsuits or, where necessary and appropriate, criminal proceedings.[150] When police officers beat suspects who insult them, they offer no defense against humiliation, but humiliate the state they represent.

147. See also Esser, *supra* note 8, p. 120 [Art 2 EMRK, para. 48]. With regard to personal self-defense under international criminal law also Georg Werle, Principles of International Criminal Law, TMC Asser Press: The Hague (2nd ed., 2009), p. 201 [para. 544]; Paul de Hert et al., Code of International Criminal Law and Procedure, Larcier: Brussels (2013), p. 176; Kai Ambos, Defences in international criminal law, in: Bartram S. Brown (ed.), Research handbook on international criminal law, Elgar: Cheltenham et al. (2011), 299–329, at p. 307.

148. See this Fourth Chapter: C.V.2 (pp. 174–180).

149. See Sixth Chapter: C.I.1 (pp. 245–246).

150. The question has not yet been considered by human rights bodies. As a matter of (internationalized) criminal law, the Special Panels for Grave Crimes in Timor Leste have held that even a grave insult cannot constitute a ground for forcible self-defense. See Prosecutor v. Carlos Soares also known as Carman [Dili District Court, Grave Crimes Section], Case No. 9/2002, Judgment of 8 December 2003, p. 6, also available at: http://www.worldcourts.com/un_etta/eng/decisions/2003.12.08_Prosecutor_v_Soares.pdf#search=%22carman%22.

Authoritarian socialist states have extended self-defense provisions in their criminal law to cover the defense of public interests and the abstract entity of the state itself. The present criminal code of the Democratic People's Republic of Korea, for instance, exempts from punishment any reasonable defensive measures "to prevent an offence against the interests of the state" or "public interests."[151] Occasionally, similar thinking also appears in the academic literature. Boyle, for instance, has contemplated that soldiers may use firearms against pacifist activists who seek to gain access to a nuclear missile because they exercise a defense of "national security."[152] Leaving aside serious concerns about necessity and proportionality that such cases will regularly raise, the defense of public interests can never be justified under the self-defense exemption as a matter of international human rights law. As discussed above,[153] international human rights law recognizes state agents' use of force, even lethal force, for purposes of self-defense and defense of others in order to give effect to the state's duty to protect human rights from attacks by others. Defensive force must therefore be limited to the protection of individual interests.[154] Opening the self-defense justification to public interests would invite abuse and excessive force,[155] not least because such abstract interests are vague and amorphous. If such interests could be made the subject of defensive force, it would be extremely difficult to determine what level of force would still be proportionate. Especially authoritarian states might set the proportionality bar for defending the dignity of the state and its leaders too low.

2. Unlawfulness under National and International Law

To be justified as self-defense, an action must be in response to unlawful violence, as is also explicitly required under Article 2(2)(a) of the ECHR. First and foremost, the relevant domestic law determines whether the attack is unlawful. However, the domestic law must itself be compatible with international law.[156] For example, a domestic law categorizing a peaceful demonstration expressing dissatisfaction with government officials as an unlawful attack on such officials would not entitle the state to use force on grounds of "defending" the concerned officials.

151. Criminal Code of the Democratic People's Republic of Korea (as amended in 2009), art. 15, unofficial translation available at: http://eng.nkhumanrights.or.kr/board/download.php?fileno=1103&no=4&board_table=bbs_literature.

152. Boyle, *supra* note 119, p. 222.

153. See this Fourth Chapter: A.II (p. 103).

154. See also Ralf Krüger, Die Bedeutung der Menschenrechtskonvention für das deutsche Notwehrrecht, Neue Juristische Wochenschrift 1970, 1483–1485, at p. 1484; Melzer, *supra* note 22, p. 101.

155. Cf. Nsereko, *supra* note 21, p. 258.

156. For references, see *supra* note 120.

Furthermore, state agents cannot claim to exercise self-defense against an "attack" by private persons that is really an act of lawful self-defense against state violence. There can be no lawful self-defense against lawful acts of self-defense.[157] The lawfulness of the private person's self-defense may emerge from domestic law, which may recognize a right of forcible resistance against certain types of unlawful police action. Or it may flow directly from international law and the general principle of the right to personal self-defense embodied therein, as this right can also be invoked against the state.[158] In *Miguel Castro-Castro Prison*, which concerned large-scale use of force by Peruvian security forces against prisoners affiliated with the *Sendero Luminoso* armed group, the Inter-American Court made essentially this point. Its factual findings established that the Peruvian state initiated the violence by carrying out an illegal large-scale attack on the life and physical integrity of the prisoners. Predictably, the inmates used violence to defend themselves against the first wave of attack. The court qualified this resistance "as a normal reaction to the offensive of the police officials, as the result of a natural instinct of defense of their life and physical integrity."[159] Consequently, the court also considered unlawful the state authorities' subsequent use of force that then aimed at breaking this violent resistance. Instead of considering the matter to involve justified self-defense by law enforcement agents, the court stressed that it was the inmates who were "looking for ways to survive the multiple and constant actions of the state that could lead to their death."[160]

However, the attack need only be objectively unlawful. It is not necessary that the attacker also incurs criminal accountability, which is why law enforcement officers may in principle also exercise self-defense against innocent aggressors such as mentally disabled persons.[161]

3. No targeting of Innocent Bystanders

When using defensive force, state agents must distinguish between persons who, by their actions, constitute an imminent threat (aggressors) and persons who

157. In the Nuremberg trials, this principle was also recognized as a principle existing in international law. See Weizsaecker et al. ["The Ministries Case"], Trials of War Criminals before the Nurernberg Military Tribunals, vol. XIV (1946–1949), 308, at p. 329 (considering it a "long-established principle of criminal law" that also applies to the context of interstate self-defense); United States v. Ohlendorf ["the "Einsatzgruppen Case"], Trials of War Criminals before the Nurernberg Military Tribunals, vol. 4 (1949), 411, at p. 494. See also Douglas Guilfoyle, International Criminal Law, Oxford University Press: Oxford (2016), p. 370.

158. On the latter, see Seventh Chapter: B (p. 303).

159. Miguel Castro-Castro Prison v. Peru, Judgment of 25 November 2006, IACtHR Ser. C No. 160, para. 241.

160. *Id.*, para. 242.

161. See also Guilfoyle, *supra* note 157, p. 370 and this Fourth Chapter: C.I.4 (pp. 129–131).

do not present such a threat (innocent bystanders). Force may be directed only against aggressors.[162]

The principle appears self-evident. In practice, however, law enforcement agents are often confronted with violence emanating from heterogeneous crowds. One and the same demonstration may include extremists who actively target police with lethal force, rioters who destroy property, and peaceful demonstrators. In such situations, the police cannot treat the entire demonstration and all of its participants as a single violent collective entity. Instead, they must make individual decisions on the use of force appropriate to the threat posed by each individual participant.[163]

In *Olmedo*, which concerned such a heterogeneous demonstration, the Human Rights Committee therefore held that even if some demonstrators may have shot at the police, the police were not entitled to shoot and kill a demonstrator who had himself not been involved in the violence and visibly submitted to arrest without resistance.[164]

In *Güler and Öngel*, a small group of participants in a demonstration attacked the police with sticks and stones. The ECtHR found a human rights violation because the police responded with force against all demonstrators, including the applicants who had no part in the attack on the police.[165]

The foregoing observations are not to say that force used in self-defense must never place innocent bystanders at risk or that any harm suffered by innocent bystanders automatically entails a human rights violation. In policing contexts, self-defense situations regularly arise in crowded spaces. Where the police uses force to defend others, these others are invariably innocent bystanders for whom the police's use of force will typically also entail a certain risk of getting caught in crossfire. In light of these implications, it would be unrealistic, and irreconcilable with the right to personal self-defense, to expect state agents not to exercise defensive force because it might affect innocent bystanders. As discussed below,

162. Zambrano Vélez et al. v. Ecuador [IACtHR], *supra* note 29, para. 85; Inter-American Commission on Human Rights, *supra* note 29, para. 111; Solomou v. Turkey [ECtHR], Appl. No. 36832/97, Judgment of 24 June 2008, para. 78; U.N. Human Rights Committee, *supra* note 83, para. 18; Joint U.N. special rapporteurs report on assembly management, *supra* note 95, para. 57. See also Crawshaw, Cullen & Williamson, *supra* note 58, p. 149.

163. U.N. Special Rapporteur on extrajudicial, summary or arbitrary executions, Christof Heyns, Annual Report 2011, *supra* note 22, para. 61; Solomou v. Turkey [ECtHR], *supra* note 162, para. 78; Eleventh periodic report of the United Nations High Commissioner for Human Rights on the situation of human rights in the Sudan: Killing and injuring of civilians on 25 August 2008 by government security forces: Kalma IDP camp, South Darfur, Sudan, 23 January 2009, p. 11, http://www.ohchr.org/Documents/Countries/11thOHCHR22jan09.pdf; Amnesty International, Use of Force Guidelines, *supra* note 3, p. 36.

164. Olmedo v. Paraguay, Comm. No. 1828/2008, U.N. Doc. CCPR/C/104/D/1828/2008 (2012), para. 3.2.

165. Güler and Öngel v. Turkey, Appl. No. 29612/05 30668/05, Judgment of 4 October 2011, para. 29.

international human rights law permits that action in self-defense and defense of others may carry a reasonable amount of risk for bystanders.[166] Where a bright line is drawn, however, is that innocent bystanders may not be the intentional target of force exercised in self-defense. Law enforcement agents must therefore distinguish between aggressors and innocent bystanders at all times.

4. Self-defense against Non-culpable Aggressors

Non-culpable aggressors are persons such as young children or persons with mental disabilities whose actions may constitute objectively unlawful attacks but who cannot be held criminally responsible. International law allows state agents to defend themselves and others against attacks by non-culpable aggressors. Grotius already observed that self-defense may be exercised even against mentally disabled persons or others who are in "no ways to blame," because "self-defense arises directly and immediately from the care of our own preservation, which nature recommends to everyone, and not from the injustice or crime of the aggressor."[167]

International human rights bodies have followed the same approach. They even allow the killing of non-culpable aggressors as a last resort where their actions pose an imminent threat to life. In *Huohvanainen*, for instance, the ECtHR considered police justified in killing a man who threatened them with imminent lethal force, notwithstanding the fact that the man was suffering from a serious paranoid personality disorder and was undergoing psychiatric treatment.[168] In *Bubbins*, the court found no human rights violations when police officers, in self-defense, killed an extremely drunk man who they had good reason to believe was about to shoot at them.[169]

Both the European and the Inter-American human rights courts have also accepted that, subject to proper medical protocol and tight necessity and proportionality restrictions, medical staff in psychiatric hospitals may use force to restrain patients who attack staff or other patients.[170]

Some criminal law scholars have suggested that self-defense should not be permissible against non-culpable aggressors, especially persons with mental disabilities. Yadav and Kremnitzer have argued that such persons are not capable of violating the law.[171] Otsuka considers that they are no different from innocent

166. See this Fourth Chapter: C.V.3.a (pp. 180–183).

167. Grotius, *supra* note 49, 397 [Bk. II Ch. I.III].

168. Huohvanainen v. Finland, *supra* note 14, paras. 14 & 59.

169. Bubbins v. United Kingdom, *supra* note 9, para. 67.

170. Ximenes-Lopes v. Brazil, Judgment of 4 July 2006, IACtHR Ser. C No. 149, para. 134; Herczegfalvy v. Austria [ECtHR], Appl. No. 10533/83, Judgment of 24 September 1992, para. 81. See also General Assembly Resolution 46/119. The protection of persons with mental illness and the improvement of mental health care, U.N. Doc. A/RES/46/119 (1992), Principle 11(11).

171. R.D. Yadav, Law of Crime and Self-Defence, Mittal Publications: New Delhi (1993), p. 6; Mordechai Kremnitzer, Proportionality and the Psychotic Aggressor: Another View, Israeli

bystanders since the innocent human person persists in the body of the non-culpable aggressor.[172] Some of these scholars suggest that cases involving non-culpable aggressors should be resolved by applying the justification of necessity.[173]

This approach is unpersuasive. It is true that cases in which the police must use defensive force against non-culpable aggressors are often tragic, especially if the non-culpable aggressor is killed. For this reason, self-defense exercised against younger children, persons with mental disabilities, and others who cannot incur criminal culpability must be assessed against particularly stringent considerations of necessity and proportionality.[174] In particular, the police have to consider whether they can retreat from the confrontation without risk to themselves or others, and thus avoid having to harm a non-culpable aggressor in self-defense. In *Shchiborshch*, for instance, police officers were attacked with a knife by a man suffering from a severe mental disorder when they tried to apprehend and hospitalize him against his will. In the ensuing confrontation, the man was killed. The ECtHR found that the operation violated the man's life because, inter alia, police should have pulled back and discontinued their efforts to apprehend the man until professional psychiatric assistance was available.[175]

However, in other situations retreat is not an option. If a police officer faces the inevitable choice of either saving his own life or sparing that of the non-culpable aggressor, it is morally and legally justified that the harm be suffered by the aggressor whose objectively unlawful action caused this tragic choice.[176] Also, the proposed alternative of resolving cases involving force against non-culpable aggressors on the basis of the justificatory defense of necessity is inappropriate. Necessity can be invoked only where the harm prevented outweighs

Law Review, vol. 18 (1983), 178–214, at pp. 186–187. See also Klaus Marxen, Die "sozialethischen" Grenzen der Notwehr, Alfred Metzner Verlag: Frankfurt a.M. (1979), pp. 61–62.

172. Michael Otsuka, Killing the Innocent in Self-Defense, Philosophy & Public Affairs, vol. 23 (1994), 74–94, at p. 93.

173. Boaz Sangero, Self-Defence in Criminal Law, Hart: Oxford (2006), pp. 16, 53 & 91; Marxen, *supra* note 171, p. 62; Kremnitzer, *supra* note 171, p. 209; Georg Freund, Strafrecht Allgemeiner Teil, Springer: Berlin/Heidelberg (2nd ed., 2009), p. 107.

174. On persons with mental disabilities, see Shchiborshch and Kuzima v. Russia [ECHR], Appl. 5269/08, Judgment of 16 January 2014; para. 236; Herczegfalvy v. Austria [ECtHR], *supra* note 170, para. 82; Ximenes-Lopes v. Brazil [IACtHR], *supra* note 170, para. 134. For self-defense against children, see Rivas v. France, *supra* note 19, para. 40; Finca "La Exacta" v. Guatemala [IACommHR], *supra* note 2, paras. 56, 65 & 81; Garcia Ibarra v. Ecuador, Judgment of 17 November 2015, IACtHR Ser. C No. 306, para. 117; Committee against Torture, Concluding Observations on the third to fifth periodic reports of the United States of America, U.N. Doc. CAT/C/USA/CO/3-5 (2014), para 27 (recommending the prohibition of the use of Tasers against children). See also Manfred Nowak, Article 6: The Right to Life, Survival and Development, Martinus Nijhoff: Leiden/Boston (2005), p. 24; Amnesty International, Use of Force Guidelines, *supra* note 3, pp. 100–101.

175. Shchiborshch and Kuzima v. Russia, *id.*, para. 236.

176. See Second Chapter: D.II.9 (p. 56).

the harm done.[177] This is not the case where life is on both sides of the balance and the defender saves his life at the expense of the non-culpable aggressor's life.

5. No Self-defense against Human Threats that Lack Agency

Altogether different cases are non-agent threats, i.e., persons from whose body a threat emanates without them having any agency; for example, if a raucous crowd of demonstrators pushes forward the peaceful demonstrators in the first row so that they threaten to crush police officers in a cordon holding back the crowd. May the police officers use their batons and beat back the first row of demonstrators in self-defense even though those demonstrators pose a threat only for reasons not related to any action of their own?

The legal issues related to non-agent threats have been discussed in more detail outside the context of law enforcement, namely with regard to the issue of abortion. A dilemma is faced by opponents of abortion who consider that the unborn embryo is fully entitled to the right to life, but want to make an exception allowing abortions when continuing the pregnancy places the life of the mother at risk. The dilemma becomes particularly apparent where the embryo is viable and could survive without the mother at the time the abortion is performed. Why should the life of the mother be given preference over the viable embryo if both lives are considered to be of equal value? In response, some argue that the abortion is an act of self-defense against the embryo whose presence and growth within the womb places the mother's life at risk.[178] On the basis of this argument, doctors in a state hospital performing the abortion would not violate the nascent being's right to life because they defend the mother from an attack by the embryo.[179]

A similar argument, but relating to born life, was sustained by the Court of Appeals of England and Wales in a case concerning twins who were born conjoined at the pelvis. According to the medical evidence, Mary, one of the twins, survived only by drawing oxygenated blood from Jodie, the stronger twin. Jodie was weakening in consequence of Mary taking her blood so that both were expected to die within six months if left together. If surgically separated, however, Jodie would survive and Mary would die (a medical prognosis that proved correct for both twins). The Court of Appeals ruled that the doctors were justified in going ahead with the surgery to separate the twins. The presiding judge

177. See, e.g., Art. 25 of the ILC Draft Articles on Responsibility for Internationally Wrongful Acts, as contained in Ch. IV.E.1 of the Report of the International Law Commission, U.N. Doc. A/56/10.

178. See L.W. Sumner, Abortion and Moral Theory, Princeton University Press: Princeton (1981) 111–115; Donald H. Regan, Rewriting Roe v. Wade, Michigan Law Review vol. 77 (1979), 1569–1646, at pp. 1611–1618. See also Eugene Volokh, Medical Self-Defense: Prohibited Experimental Therapies and Payment for Organs, Harvard Law Review, vol. 120 (2007), 1813–1846, pp. 1824–1826.

179. See also Sumner, *id.*, p. 112.

found that the surgery amounted to a case of "quasi self-defense," as the doctors would be "coming to Jodie's defense and removing the threat of fatal harm to her presented by Mary's draining her lifeblood."[180]

The resolution of non-agent threat cases is controversial. Some see no distinction between non-culpable aggressors and non-agent threats, as both invade the legally protected space of the defender without the latter having caused that invasion.[181]

However, this position is not convincing as far as international human rights law is concerned. Self-defense responds to unlawful violence (see also Article 2(2)(c) of the ECHR). However, only conscious human conduct can be lawful or unlawful. Non-agent threats are therefore more akin to innocent bystanders. Neither of them actively creates a threat and no unlawful conduct emanates from them that would call the legal order into question.[182] Therefore, neither may be the target of self-defense.

Cases involving non-agent threats can also be better solved on the basis of the doctrines of necessity or, failing that, duress. If the police officers in the initial example have to beat back and injure the non-agent threat demonstrators to save their own life, this would amount to a case of necessity, since they prevent considerably more harm than they cause. However, if they only protect themselves from injury at the expense of comparable injuries being incurred by the innocent demonstrators, they may at best be excused from criminal responsibility due to duress. But their conduct cannot be justified as it would be in a case of self-defense. Otherwise, the innocent first-row demonstrators would have a duty to sacrifice their own health to prevent injury to the police. This would also mean that the demonstrators could not lawfully defend themselves against the police beating them.[183]

180. Re A (Children) (Conjoined Twins: Surgical Separation) [2000] 4 All England Law Reports 961, at p. 1017 (per Ward LJ).

181. See Judith Jarvis Thomson, Self-Defense, Philosophy and Public Affairs, vol. 20 (1991), 283–310, at pp. 289–291.

182. See also Otsuka, *supra* note 172, p. 84; George P. Fletcher, Punishment and Self-Defence, Law and Philosophy, vol. 8 (1989), 201–215, at p. 210; Felix Herzog, § 32, in: Urs Kindhäuser et al., Strafgesetzbuch: Band 1, Nomos: Baden-Baden (2nd ed., 2010), at pp. 1146–1147 [§ 32, para. 6].

183. Similarly, necessity, rather than self-defense is the much more appropriate paradigm to answer the extremely complex question when abortion is compatible with the right to life. See also Fletcher, *id.*, pp. 209–210. How the balance of harms calculation, which is at the heart of the necessity justification, is made depends on medically, ethically, and legally difficult determinations: if and when the embryo constitutes life; whether the embryo's right to life carries the same weight as that of a born person; and how any rights it has are to be balanced against those of the mother. Providing answers to these complex questions cannot be evaded by building a contrived argument according to which the embryo's natural growth constitutes an unlawful attack on the mother.

6. Mistaken Belief in an Unlawful Attack (Putative Self-defense)

State agents often have to decide whether to exercise self-defense on the spur of the moment and with limited understanding of the situation. As a result, tragic errors may arise where the agent believed an unlawful attack was imminent, but no such attack actually took place (putative self-defense). The question arises to what extent police force used in putative self-defense is still justified.

a) The prevailing hybrid subjective/objective standard of assessment

How to address a situation of putative personal self-defense under international law was already considered in the 1928 *Naulilaa* arbitration on German armed reprisals against Portugal. The altercation between German and Portuguese soldiers that gave rise to the reprisals commenced when one of the Portuguese soldiers shot dead a German official who appeared to have reached for his gun. The arbitrators considered that the German's imprudent action could have led the Portuguese soldier to believe that he was under threat and therefore in a situation of justified self-defense.[184] Thus, the arbitration panel did not consider it relevant whether the German was actually about to initiate a lethal attack. It sufficed that the objective circumstances could lead the Portuguese soldier to believe an attack was imminent, so that personal self-defense was a legitimate response.

The prevailing approach under contemporary international human rights law follows essentially the same approach as *Naulilaa* regarding cases of putative self-defense by state agents. In what has been long the approach of the ECtHR (at least prior to the Court's *Armani Da Silva* decision, discussed below), the court has considered that even where no actual attack takes place, the state can still claim self-defense under Article 2(2)(a) of the ECHR if its agents acted had an "honest belief" in the attack which "is perceived, for good reasons, to be valid at the time but which subsequently turns out to be mistaken."[185] The standard thus combines a subjective element (honest belief) with an objective one (good reasons for that belief). The existence of good reasons must be assessed from an *ex ante* perspective. It has to be assessed whether a reasonable law enforcement officer, placed in the same position as the officer involved in the incident, would have also believed in the existence of an unlawful attack.

In *McCann*, the leading case on this issue, the Grand Chamber of the ECtHR considered that British special forces soldiers were justified in shooting dead three Irish Republican Army (IRA) members because they had good reason to believe the IRA members were about to detonate a deadly car bomb. The soldiers had been briefed that the IRA members could trigger the bomb with a remote-control button concealed on one of their bodies. Shortly before the deadly

184. Naulilaa (Portugal v. Germany), 2 Reports of International Arbitral Awards 1012 (1928), at p. 1025.

185. McCann et al. v. United Kingdom, *supra* note 9, para. 200; Bubbins v. United Kingdom, *supra* note 9, para. 138.

shooting, they received further information that one of the IRA members had parked a car with a suspicious-looking antenna close to the target. When confronted by the soldiers, the IRA members moved in such a way that it appeared they might be pushing the trigger button. After the fatal shooting, however, it was discovered that none of the IRA members actually carried any bomb-triggering remote control.[186]

In *Bubbins*, a British police officer shot dead a man who had aimed what appeared to be a real gun at him. The man had ignored previous warnings to give himself up and instead conveyed on several occasions a clear impression that he would shoot at the police. It was later discovered that the gun was only a replica and the officer was therefore never under any actual threat.[187]

In *Makaratzis*, Greek police officers wrongly thought they were pursuing an armed and dangerous terrorist during a high-speed car chase through Athens. Furthermore, they wrongly believed that the suspect was about to shoot at them when they brought his car to a halt. In light of the circumstances of the chase and the general terrorist threat prevailing in Greece at the time, the officers had good reason to consider it necessary to use firearms even though it later turned out that the suspect was not an armed terrorist.[188]

Conversely, in *Gül*, the ECtHR found no good reasons to believe in an attack. In that case, Turkish police officers went to the apartment of a suspected member of the Kurdish Workers Party (PKK) and rang the doorbell. Perhaps because the officers mistook the sound of the door bolt being drawn back for the suspect uncocking his gun, they immediately and without warning opened fire, shooting more than 50 times at the closed door and killing the suspect, who was standing behind it.[189] In *Ogur*, Turkey claimed that its security forces came under fire during an anti-PKK operation conducted under conditions of bad visibility and therefore mistook an innocent bystander for one of the alleged shooters. Once again, the court rejected the putative self-defense claim, because it found insufficient evidence that the security forces actually came under attack from anyone.[190]

The Inter-American Commission also follows the hybrid subjective/objective approach requiring "well-founded reasons to believe" in the existence of an unlawful attack.[191] The jurisprudence of the African Commission points in the same direction since it considers that the situation must be assessed "in an

186. McCann, *id.*, paras. 196–200.

187. *Id.*, paras. 138–139.

188. Makaratzis v. Greece, *supra* note 15, paras. 64–67. Although the court found that, in principle, there were good reasons to use firearms, it still found a violation due to the chaotic manner in which the officers employed their guns.

189. Gül v. Turkey, Appl. No. 22676/93, Judgment of 14 December 2000, para. 82.

190. Ogur v. Turkey, *supra* note 12, para. 81.

191. Corumbiara Massacre v. Brazil [IACommHR], *supra* note 2, para. 180; Finca "La Exacta" v. Guatemala [IACommHR], *supra* note 2, para. 43; Jurisprudence of the Inter-American

objective way, in in the light of *the prevailing circumstances at the time* when the final decision on the use of lethal force is made."[192] Among academics and practitioners, the hybrid subjective/objective approach has also met with general approval.[193]

b) Inappropriateness of a purely objective standard

Occasionally, the hybrid subjective/objective standard has been contested. Apparently espousing a purely objective standard with regard to the ECHR, Paeffgen suggests that, in the absence of an actual attack, self-defense is not necessary and hence is unlawful. He bases his position mainly on the text of Article 2(2)(a) of the ECHR, which refers to force "in defense of any person from unlawful violence," rather than defense from reasonably perceived violence.[194] A dissenting minority of judges in the ECtHR's judgment in *Armani Da Silva* (discussed further below), seem to take the same view in considering that "[f]orce used in putative self-defense is never absolutely necessary" as the text of Article 2 of the ECHR would require.[195]

This view is unconvincing regarding the ECHR and regarding international human rights law generally. Regarding the arguments based on the ECHR text, the words "in defense of" contained in Article 2(2)(a) can also be understood as referring to force employed with the intent to defend against unlawful violence. Similarly, putative self-defense can also be "absolutely necessary," if the ex ante view point of a reasonable observer in the position of the officer is the benchmark of necessity.

On a policy level, an approach that requires an actual attack "would impose an unrealistic burden on the state and its law enforcement personnel in the

Court seems to suggest that there always has to be an actual attack. See Nadege Dorzema v. Dominican Republic, *supra* note 100, para. 91; Zambrano Vélez et al. v. Ecuador, *supra* note 29, para. 108. However, the Inter-American has not yet had to rule on a situation where putative self-defense was at issue.

192. Kazingachire et al. v. Zimbabwe [ACommHPR], *supra* note 34, para. 116 [emphasis added].

193. Nsereko, *supra* note 21, p. 254; Melzer, *supra* note 22, p. 236; Joseph, *supra* note 58, p. 16; Skinner, *supra* note 131, p. 568; Ladewig, *supra* note 8, p. 61 [Artikel 2, para. 44]; Fiona Leverick, Is English Self-Defence Law incompatible with art 2 of the ECHR?, Criminal Law Review (May 2002), 347–362, at p. 362; Harris et al., *supra* note 67, p. 228; Schabas, *supra* note 68, p. 147; International Association of Police Chiefs, Model Policy on the Use of Force, IACP: Alexandria (2006), IV.A.1.a; First Turkel Commission Report, *supra* note 6, para. 224.

194. See Paeffgen, *supra* note 8, p. 388 [art. 2, para. 60].

195. Armani Da Silva v. United Kingdom, Appl. 5878/08, Judgment of 30 March 2016, Joint Dissenting Opinion of Judges Karakas, Wojtyczek and Dedov, para. 5. It should be noted though that the dissent (*id.*) endorsed the hybrid subjective/objective test for purposes of determining whether the state must prosecute the individual officers involved.

execution of their duty, perhaps to the detriment of their lives and those of others."[196] If police officers could take defensive action only after they are absolutely certain of an attack, their defensive response would often come too late. They or others may already have been killed or injured by the aggressors. Furthermore, police officers who have good reason to believe that persons are at risk of violence have a human rights duty to defend these victims.[197] Therefore they should not be held responsible for a human rights violation if it turns out in hindsight that they misjudged the situation.[198] International law must not establish inherently contradictory duties of conduct.

Finally, even hindsight often cannot determine whether a lethal threat truly existed. Was the attacker actually willing to pull the trigger or only bluffing when he was shot? If the attacker is dead or invokes his right to remain silent, one will never know.

c) Inappropriateness of a purely subjective standard

A third possible approach would be to adopt an entirely subjective standard, under which it would be sufficient that the law enforcement agents in question honestly believed the situation called for self-defense, regardless of the reasonableness of that belief. In international human rights law, this approach had not gained any support. However, the 2016 judgment of the ECHR Grand Chamber in *Armani Da Silva* is moving towards a subjective standard, even though the court claims to follow the jurisprudence emerging from *McCann*.

The case concerns the intentional killing of Brazilian electrician Jean Charles de Menezes by British police, who mistook him for a suicide bomber due to what British authorities themselves recognized to have been a series of serious operational errors.[199] According to the court, the "principal question to be addressed is whether the person had an honest and genuine belief that the use of force was necessary." However, in addressing this question, it must be considered "whether the belief was subjectively reasonable" and in the absence of "subjective good reasons . . . it is likely that the court would have difficulty accepting that it was honestly and genuinely held."[200] Thus, reasonableness, approached from an

196. McCann et al. v. United Kingdom, *supra* note 9, para. 200.

197. See this Fourth Chapter: A.II (pp. 102–103).

198. Cf. Volker Erb, Notwehr gegen rechtswidriges Verhalten von Amtsträgern, in: Dieter Dölling & Volker Erb (eds.), Festschrift für Karl Heinz Gössel zum 70. Geburtstag, C.F. Müller: Heidelberg (2002), 217–233, at p. 219.

199. For a summary of the relevant decisions of British authorities, see Armani da Silva v. United Kingdom, *supra* note 195, paras. 39–101. On the Menezes case, see also Casey-Maslen, *supra* note 6, pp. 16–19.

200. Armani da Silva v. United Kingdom, *supra* note 195, para 248. For a critical discussion of the case, see Jan Arno Hessbruegge, ECtHR Armani Da Silva v UK: Unreasonable on Police Killings in Putative Self-Defence?, 14 April 2016, EJIL Talk, http://www.ejiltalk.org/ecthr-armani-da-silva-v-uk-unreasonable-police-killings-in-putative-self-defence/.

ex ante perspective of someone placed in the law enforcement agent's situation, is seen not "as a separate requirement but rather as a relevant factor in determining whether a belief was honestly and genuinely held."[201] Due to the applicant's framing of the case, *Armani Da Silva* concerned only the question whether the United Kingdom was under a duty to prosecute any of the individual officers involved in the killing and not the separate question to what extent the state bore responsibility for the killing itself. It therefore remains to be seen whether the court will also apply a subjective test (with reasonableness as an indicator only) where a case directly focuses on holding the state responsible for unreasonable actions of its law enforcement agents.

Both dimensions (responsibility for failing to prosecute versus responsibility for the killing itself) have to be carefully distinguished and may well have different standards. In fact, a purely subjective standard prevails in international criminal law with regard to putative self-defense. There, the prevailing view is that individual perpetrators will face no criminal responsibility if they honestly believed in the existence of an attack, regardless of whether they had good reasons for such belieft.[202] This standard may suit international criminal law, given that only intentional crimes can justify the grave sanctions attached to them. A perpetrator who honestly believes to act in self-defense has no intent to commit a crime.

However, a purely subjective approach is inappropriate for purposes of human rights law, because this approach would allow the state to escape responsibility, even where its agents used defensive force with negligence or even gross negligence, without any good reason to believe an attack was imminent or underway. In practice, it would place victims trying to hold states responsible for human rights violations at an unfair disadvantage. They would have to show that the state agents involved did not have a particular state of mind (honest belief in an

201. *Id.*, para. 246.

202. United States v. Krupp et al. [United States Military Tribunal, Nuremberg], Law Reports of Trials of War Criminals, vol. X (1949), p. 148. While the self-defense provision in Art. 31(1)(c) of the Rome Statute requires the existence of an actual attack, criminal responsibility for perpetrators who act in putative self-defense can be excluded based on their mistake of fact, either in direct or analogous application of Art. 32(1) of the Rome Statute). See Kai Ambos, Other Grounds for Excluding Criminal Responsibility, in: Antonio Cassese, Paola Gaeta & John R.W.D. Jones (eds.), The Rome Statute of the International Criminal Court: A Commentary, Vol. I, Oxford University Press: Oxford (2002), 984–1029, at p. 1013; Albin Eser, Article 31: Grounds for Excluding Criminal Responsibility, in: Otto Triffterer (ed.), Commentary on the Rome Statute of the International Criminal Court, C.H.Beck-Hart-Nomos: München/Oxford/Baden-Baden (2nd ed., 2008), 863–893, at p. 882 [art.31, para. 45]; Julian Fernandez & Xavier Pacreau, Statut de Rome de la Cour pénale international: Commentaire article par article, vol.1, Pedone: Paris (2012), pp. 919; Guilfoyle, *supra* note 157, pp. 377–378.

But see de Hert et al., *supra* note 147, p. 177; Antonio Cassese, Under What Conditions May Belligerents Be Acquitted of the Crime of Attacking an Ambulance?, Journal of International Criminal Justice, vol. 6 (2) (2008), 385–397, at p. 394 (both favoring the hybrid subjective/objective standard also for putative self-defense under international criminal law).

attack), rather than having to show only that the objective circumstances rendered their belief unreasonable.

The present author therefore takes the view that the state can be held responsible to provide reparation if its agents infringed on the right to life or physical security based on an unreasonable and wrong belief in a self-defense situation. It is a different question to what extent this also translates into a duty to prosecute and criminally sanction the officers responsible for the individual belief. As will be discussed below, the state must only prosecute where individual officers form an honest but mistaken belief in an attack due to gross negligence or recklessness, causing death or serious injury as a result.[203]

d) Strict scrutiny of "good reasons" under the hybrid approach

The hybrid subjective-objective standard represents a reasonable compromise between the legitimate interests of states and rights-holders. However, any assessment of whether a state agent really had "good reasons" to believe in an attack must be subject to strict scrutiny. State law enforcement agents can be held to a higher standard than the average private person. Their extensive training and professional experience puts them in a better position to distinguish real from imaginary attacks.[204] In particular, when using deliberately lethal force, they may only act based on clear and convincing indications pointing to a lethal and imminent threat, rather than acting based on mere conjecture.[205]

Furthermore, the assessment of "good reasons" must duly take into account other applicable human rights norms, in particular the prohibition of discrimination. State agents are prohibited from drawing any inferences from a person's race or ethnicity as to their propensity to launch an attack. In this regard, the state as a whole also has a duty to ensure, as far as possible, that neither overt racism within the police nor subconscious bias affects decisions to use force. This requires particular diligence in investigating police use of force, where reasonable belief in a nonexistent attack by a member of a racial or ethnic minority is claimed.[206] Furthermore, the state must not stigmatize particular population groups as inherently dangerous and has to take proactive training measures to

203. See this Fourth Chapter: E.III.1 (p. 211).

204. Cf. Otto, *supra* note 12, pp. 85-86; Kremnitzer, *supra* note 137, p. 202; Aydan v. Turkey [ECtHR], *supra* note 64, paras. 97–99.

205. See also U.N. Special Rapporteur on extrajudicial, summary or arbitrary executions Philip Alston, [2006 Annual Report], *supra* note 50, para. 50; Schmahl, *supra* note 22, p. 241; Melzer, *supra* note 22, p. 236; Fleck, *supra* note 53, p. 394.

206. This also follows from the general duty of states to investigate violent incidents that may have a racist background with particular vigour. See Soare et al. v. Romania, *supra* note 133, para. 206; Wallace de Almeida v. Brazil [IACommHR], Case 12.440, Report No 26/09, Decision of 20 March 2009, paras. 139–140.

sensitize officers about implicit racial biases so as to diminish their impact on the rapid assessment of potential threats.[207]

II. Immediacy of defensive action

Fletcher's well-known adage that "self-defense must be neither too soon nor too late"[208] also applies to the assessment of self-defense under international human rights law. State agents may use defensive force only against violence that is imminent, that is, immediately antecedent, presently exercised or ongoing. Self-defense may not be invoked in relation to attacks that took place in the past or will occur in a more distant future.

1. Prohibition of Self-defense against Concluded Attacks

In accordance with Article 10 of the Universal Declaration and Article 14 (1) of the ICCPR, international human rights law reserves the right to impose punishment for criminal conduct to courts of law. Where violent crimes have taken place, law enforcement officers have the right and duty to use force to arrest suspects and "bring them to justice"—in a very literal sense. However, they may not "defend" themselves or others by taking vengeance. The time window to use defensive force, including deliberately lethal force, therefore closes as soon as there is no longer an ongoing attack. In *Zambrano Vélez*, the Inter-American Court determined that lethal force against suspected violent criminals who were already in the custody of the authorities and thus no longer presented a threat amounted to a flagrant violation of the right to life.[209] In *Brothers Landaeta Mejias*, the Inter-American Commission found a killing by police to be unlawful even though the suspect might have shot at the police, because police shot him dead when he was lying wounded on the ground and begged not to be killed.[210] In *Rickly Burrell*, the Human Rights Committee considered it a violation that Jamaican prison wardens shot dead an inmate during a hostage crisis in the prison, because the killing occurred after the hostages had already been rescued.[211] In *Kitanovski*, the European Court considered that a police officer who had fired at the driver of a car that crashed through a roadblock the officer was manning was not justified by self-defense, because he kept firing after the car passed the roadblock and no longer posed a physical threat to him.[212]

207. Cf. Wallace de Almeida, *id.*, para. 168.4; Garcia Ibarra v. Ecuador, Judgment of 17 November 2015, IACtHR (Ser. C) No. 306, para. 117.

208. George P. Fletcher, A Crime of Self-Defense: Bernhard Goetz and the Law on Trial, Free Press: New York (1988), p. 20.

209. Zambrano Vélez et al. v. Ecuador, *supra* note 29, para. 108. See also Inter-American Commission on Human Rights, *supra* note 29, para. 91.

210. Landaeta Mejias v. Venezuela [IACommHR], *supra* note 29, para. 197.

211. Rickly Burrell v. Jamaica, *supra* note 24, para. 9.5.

212. Kitanovski v. Former Yugislav Republic of Macedonia, Judgment of 22 January 2015, Appl. 15191/12, para. 69.

Further support for the temporary restriction of self-defense can also be derived from international criminal law cases. In *Josef Hangobl*, self-defense was ruled out since the victim had turned his back towards the perpetrator and was running away when he was shot and killed.[213] In *Yamamoto Chusaburo*, a self-defense plea failed because the civilian victim was killed while already in the custody of the soldier who shot him dead.[214]

2. Prohibition of "Preventive Self-Defense"

The contours of the other end of the time window (self-defense exercised "too soon") are far more contested. According to the prevailing view endorsed by United Nations human rights bodies, the European and Inter-American human rights courts and scholars, self-defense can be exercised only against an immediately antecedent attack; for example, the police officer shooting the criminal suspect as he reaches for his gun.[215] Apart from temporal proximity between the defensive action and the thwarted attack, immediately antecedent attacks

213. Josef Hangobl [General Military Court, Dachau, Germany, 17–18 October 1945], Law Reports of Trials of War Criminals, vol. XIV (1949), 86, at p. 87.

214. Yamamoto Chusaburo [British Military Court, Kuala Lumpur, 30 January–1 February 1946], Law Reports of Trials of War Criminals, vol. III (1948), 76–80, p. 78.

215. U.N. Human Rights Council, Resolutions 22/10, para. 8 & 25/38, para. 10, *supra* note 95; U.N. Basic Principles on the Use of Force and Firearms, *supra* note 25, Principle 9; High Commissioner for Human Rights Navi Pillay, *supra* note 93; *id.*, Opening Statemenet at the Human Rights Council 24th Session, 9 September 2013, http://www.ohchr.org/RU/NewsEvents/Pages/DisplayNews.aspx?NewsID=13687&LangID=E; U.N. Special Rapporteur on extrajudicial, summary or arbitrary executions, Philip Alston, 2010 Annual Report, *supra* note 87, para. 35; U.N. Special Rapporteur on extrajudicial, summary or arbitrary executions, Christof Heyns, Report on Armed Drones, *supra* note 53, paras. 33 & 35; Human Rights Committee, *supra* note 93, para. 403; Human Rights Committee, Concluding Observations on the Second Report of Israel, U.N. Doc. CCPR/CO/78/ISR (2003), para. 15 (calling for a restriction of targeted killings to "persons being in the process of commiting acts of terror"); Kakoulli v. Turkey [ECHR], Appl. No. 38595/97, Judgment of 22 November 2005, para. 120; Zambrano Vélez et al. v. Ecuador [IACtHR], *supra* note 29, paras. 85 & 101; Barrios Family v. Venezuela, *supra* note 29, para. 67; Inter-American Commission, *supra* note 32, para. 237; Kazingachire et al. v. Zimbabwe [ACommHPR], *supra* note 34, para. 117; ICRC, Human Rights and Humanitarian Law for Police and Security Forces, *supra* note 2, p. 257; Report of the international fact-finding mission to investigate violations of international law, including international humanitarian and human rights law, resulting from the Israeli attacks on the flotilla of ships carrying humanitarian assistance, U.N. Doc. A/HRC/15/21 (2010), paras. 165 & 167; Amnesty International, Use of Force Guidelines, *supra* note 3, p. 60; Rodley/Pollard, *supra* note 22, p. 256; Georg Nolte, Preventive Use of Force and Preventive Killings: Moves into a Different Legal Order, Theoretical Inquiries in Law, vol. 5 (2004) 111–129, at p. 117; Nsereko, *supra* note 21, p. 254; Onder Bakircioglu, The Right to Self-Defence in National and International Law: The Role of the Imminence Requirement, Indiana International & Comparative Law Review, vol. 19 (2009), 1–48, at p. 9; Schmahl, *supra* note 22, p. 264; Wong, *supra* note 58, pp. 130–131; Boyle, *supra* note 119, p. 241; Velu/Ergec, *supra* note 8, para. 232; Otto, *supra* note 12, pp. 86–92; Casey-Maslen, *supra* note 6, p. 15; Guido den Dekker & Eric P.J. Myjer, The Right to Life and Self-Defence of Private Military and Security

are generally also characterized by a geographic proximity of the attacker to the target and the fact that the attacker has to take no more preparatory steps to implement the threat.

Preventive force, that is force used in anticipation of a future attack, cannot be justified by invoking the right to personal self-defense. This view accords with the understanding of personal self-defense in classic international law, where it was limited in time to instances that Giovanni da Legnano described as the aggressor being "bold and ready to strike."[216] In the same vein, Grotius noted that where an aggressor only plans a deadly attack and "we have nothing to fear for the present, on the part of that person . . . we cannot lawfully kill him."[217]

Scholars such as Kremnitzer and Kretzmer promote a wider understanding of immediacy, according to which self-defense can also be exercised against attacks that are not immediately antecedent when the nature of the threat is such that there is a need to use force immediately to prevent a violent attack later.[218] This rationale is frequently invoked to justify extraterritorial targeted killings of terrorist suspects outside the context of armed conflict, such as by means of armed drones. A targeted killing is said to be justified where the suspected terrorist cannot be captured and the authorities have a last window of opportunity to kill the suspect and thereby prevent him from staging a future deadly attack.[219]

Article 2(2)(a) of the ECHR does not explicitly limit itself to defense against *imminent* unlawful violence. Similarly, the Basic Principles on the Use of Force and Firearms only refer to "the imminent threat of death or serious injury," rather than to a threat of imminent death or serious injury. On the basis of the text alone, both would leave room for the "last window of opportunity" approach.

However, a broad reading of the self-defense justification, especially in relation to deliberately lethal force, would fail to pay due respect to the fundamental value of the right to life.[220] It would also mark a notable departure from the

Contractors in Armed Conflict, in: Francesco Francioni and Natalino Ronzitti (eds.), War by Contract: Human Rights, Humanitarian Law and Private Contractors, Oxford University Press: Oxford (2011), 171–193, at p. 182. For personal self-defense under international criminal law, also Eser, *supra* note 202, pp. 880–881 [art. 31, para. 41], Werle, *supra* note 147, p. 201 [para. 544]; Ambos, *supra* note 147, p. 307; de Hert et al., *supra* note 147, pp. 176–177; Fernandez & Pacreau, *supra* note 202, pp. 919–920; Hannah Tonkin, Defensive Force under the Rome Statute, Melbourne Journal of International Law, vol. 6 (2005), 86–117, at p. 97.

216. Giovanni Da Legnano, De Bello, de Represaliis et de Duello (ed. Thomas Erskine Holland, trans. J.K. Brierly), Carnegie Institution: Washington D.C. (1917), p. 304.

217. Grotius, *supra* note 49, p. 401 [Bk. II, Ch.I.V.2].

218. Kretzmer, *supra* note 22, pp. 182 & 203; Kremnitzer, *supra* note 137, p. 218.

219. Kretzmer, *id.*; Ramsden, *supra* note 55, pp. 403–405; Kevin Jon Heller, "One Hell of a Killing Machine": Signature Strikes and International Law, Journal of International Criminal Justice, vol. 11 (2013), 89–119, at pp. 116–117; Michael N. Schmitt, Counter-Terrorism and the Use of Force in International Law, Israel Yearbook of Human Rights, vol. 32 (2002), 53–116, at p. 110.

220. Nolte, *supra* note 215, p. 118; Schmahl, *supra* note 22, p. 264.

virtually universal understanding of immediacy of self-defense in domestic laws, where an immediately antecedent attack is generally required.[221] There are sound policy reasons to insist on immediacy, because it limits self-defense to situations where there is a concrete and visible threat. Not only does this limit the potential for unintended fatal errors, it also curbs the tendency to abuse the self-defense justification, particularly where the real motive in using lethal force is to exact vengeance or extrajudicial punishment.[222] If international human rights law were to move away from the requirement of immediacy, legal uncertainty would prevail.[223] National and international courts would be hard pressed to effectively review executive assertions that the victim of a supposed pre-emptive killing really intended to carry out a deadly attack in the future and that the killing truly marked the last and only opportunity to neutralize the would-be killer.

As noted, the "last window of opportunity" rationale is usually discussed against the backdrop of the extraterritorial targeted killing of terrorists. However, it is not obvious why this particular context should require an expansion of the right to kill in law enforcement. Where the terrorist violence that is supposed to justify the pre-emptive killing is really as grave as claimed, states will generally be engaged in a non-international armed conflict with the terrorist group in question. They will therefore be entitled to respond with force under the paradigm of armed conflict, where deliberate killing is not limited to self-defense and more permissive rules of international humanitarian law apply.[224]

An exception carved out in the counterterrorism context easily becomes the rule for any law enforcement action targeting serious crime. At least one author has contemplated already that the "last window of opportunity" approach should also allow the killing of drug cartel leaders whom the authorities cannot arrest, given that the drug cartels have been responsible for thousands of deaths.[225] And herein lies the problem. Any state with inefficient law enforcement and justice systems, and correspondingly high levels of violent crime, could easily use the pre-emptive self-defense exception as an argument for setting up death squads that pursue violent criminals who pose an abstract threat to life but manage to escape the authorities. The potential for abusing such a broad definition of self-defense for purposes of extrajudicial punishment or even political oppression is obvious and serious. It is for good reason that international human rights law, as laid down, for instance, in Article 14 of the ICCPR, presumes the innocence of

221. See Second Chapter: E.II.2 (pp. 64–65).

222. Bakircioglu, *supra* note 215, p. 26.

223. Nolte, *supra* note 215, p. 118, Schmahl, *supra* note 22, p. 264.

224. See Fifth Chapter: A (pp. 218–221). See also Geoffrey S. Corn, Self-Defense Targeting: Blurring the line between the Jus ad Bellum and the Ius in Bello, in Kenneth Watkin/Andrew J. Norris (eds.), Non-International Armed Conflict in the Twenty-First Century, Naval War College: Newport, Rhode Island (2012), 53–92, at 73.

225. Wayne Wayne McCormack, Targeted Killing at a Distance: Robotics and Self-Defense, Pacific McGeorge Global Business & Development Journal, vol. 25 (2012), 361–379, at p. 369.

suspects and leaves the determination of their guilt to independent and impartial courts, where the suspect can be heard prior to the sentence and guilt must be proven by the state. An understanding of self-defense that is no longer limited to a response to concrete and visible threats undercuts these fundamental due process guarantees and values. It therefore has no place in international human rights law on peacetime law enforcement.

III. Necessity of defensive action

The rationale of self-defense is not to punish wrongdoing, but to prevent or minimize harm. For this reason, state agents can use defensive force only to the extent necessary to avert the unlawful attack. Defensive state force is not necessary where non-forcible means are available to counter the attack with equal certainty and effectiveness (qualitative dimension of necessity). Even where the use of force is unavoidable, law enforcement agents must use only the minimum of force necessary to safely and effectively defend against the attack (quantitative dimension).

A particularly rigorous necessity standard applies in relation to lethal force. Article 2(2)(a) of the ECHR only allows for deprivation of life in defense against unlawful violence where "absolutely necessary." Elaborating on this term, the ECtHR has held that a "stricter and more compelling test of necessity" applies to the use of lethal defensive force, which calls for "the most careful scrutiny."[226] Similarly, the Inter-American Court noted that lethal force may only be used under "exceptional circumstances ... to the minimum extent possible"[227] and in a recent judgment explicitly adopted the standard of absolute necessity.[228] The high threshold to justify lethal force also follows from the U.N. Basic Principles on the Use of Force and Firearms, which only allows for the intentional lethal use of firearms where "*strictly unavoidable* to protect life."[229]

1. Assessment from the Perspective of a Reasonable Officer Placed in that Situation

Effective self-defense against an unlawful attack often requires determined action in the absence of a nuanced understanding of the situation that may be gained only in hindsight. The necessity of defensive force must therefore be determined from the *ex ante* perspective of a reasonable law enforcement officer placed in

226. Giuliani and Gaggio v. Italy, *supra* note 65, para. 176; Andronicou and Constantinou v. Cyprus, *supra* note 9, para. 171. See also Harris et al., *supra* note 67, pp. 227–228; Frowein & Peukert, *supra* note 8, p. 36 [Art. 2, para. 11]; Velu/Ergec, *supra* note 8, para. 231; Gollwitzer, *supra* note 8, pp. 163 [Art. 6 IPBPR, para 17].

227. Zambrano Vélez et al. v. Ecuador, *supra* note 29, para. 84.

228. Landaeta Mejias v. Venezuela [IACommHR], *supra* note 29, para. 134.

229. U.N. Basic Principles on the Use of Force and Firearms, *supra* note 25, Principle 9 (emphasis added).

the same situation as the officer(s) in question.[230] If the officer honestly believed that the level of force was necessary and there were good objective reasons for that belief, the state incurs no responsibility even if it turns out later that the situation could have been resolved with less force. Thus, the same hybrid subjective/objective standard applies as in the case of an unlawful attack. With regard to the requirement of necessity, the reasons for applying a subjective/objective approach are even more compelling. There is, after all, an actual aggression and the officer only assesses wrongly what it takes to effectively defend against it.

Furthermore, an objective post facto approach relying on the "true level" of necessity would be unworkable, because often it cannot be discerned even in hindsight whether the aggressors truly intended to shoot or not, for example, if they are dead or exercise their right to remain silent and not incriminate themselves. In *Huohvanainen*, for instance, the ECtHR found that a police officer had good reason to shoot a mentally disturbed man who confronted the police with two guns in his hand, although even hindsight could not clarify whether the man had actually wanted to shoot the officers. In establishing that there were good objective reasons to believe it was necessary to shoot the man, the court took into account that the man had already shot at the police on several occasions during the preceding two-day siege and that he had not heeded any previous warnings to give himself up.[231]

In the *Andronicou* hostage drama, the hostage-taker no longer had a loaded weapon in his hands when he was shot dead. The police officer who fired the fatal shots could not see that. The ECtHR held that the officer had good reason to believe that it was necessary to shoot and kill the suspect. The court took into account that the suspect had shot another police officer moments earlier, that the hostage was still in his grip, and that he made what appeared to be a threatening move just before the police officer fired his weapon.[232]

In *Corumbiara Massacre*, which concerned a large-scale police operation against peasants occupying a farm, the Inter-American Commission accepted that, at least during the initial stages of the operation, police officers could reasonably conclude from the armed resistance put up by the peasants that the officers' lives were in danger and lethal force thus was necessary to defend themselves.[233] Conversely, in *Finca "La Exacta."* which also concerned a farm occupation, it found that police had no good reason to believe that it was necessary to use lethal force. The Inter-American Commission stressed in particular that there was no credible evidence that the farm occupiers were in possession of lethal arms such as firearms or bombs.[234]

230. Esser, *supra* note 8, p. 120 [Art 2 EMRK, para 48], Gollwitzer, *supra* note 8, p. 163 [MRK Art.2, para 17]; Paeffgen, *supra* note 8, p. 386 [Art 2, para 58]. Cf. Cassese, *supra* note 202, p. 392. For international criminal law, see also Guilfoyle, *supra* note 157, p. 371.

231. Huohvanainen v. Finland, *supra* note 14, paras. 97–98.

232. Andronicou and Constantinou v. Cyprus, *supra* note 9, para. 191–193.

233. *Id.*

234. Finca "La Exacta" v. Guatemala [IACommHR], *supra* note 2, paras. 43–46.

In determining whether there are good reasons to believe in the necessity of the defensive action taken, international human rights bodies will take into account that psychological factors such as stress and anxiety can blur even the best police officer's assessment when placed in a critical self-defense situation. The ECtHR regularly emphasizes in this regard that it "cannot with detached reflection substitute its own assessment of the [self-defense] situation for that of the officers who were required to react in the *heat of the moment* in what was for them a unique and unprecedented operation to save life."[235] The relevance of psychological factors emerges, for instance, in *Giuliani and Gaggio*, a case concerning an attack of violent demonstrators on a group of gendarmes in a non-armored jeep. The jeep was surrounded by violent demonstrators "who launched an unrelenting onslaught on the vehicle and its occupants, tilting it sideways and throwing stones and other hard objects."[236] In this situation, one of the police officer shot and fatally wounded one of the assailants. The court acknowledged that other gendarmes who were positioned nearby could have intervened to assist the jeep's occupants had the situation degenerated further. However, "this fact could not have been known to M.P., who, injured and *panic-stricken*, was lying in the rear of the vehicle surrounded by a large number of demonstrators."[237]

When taking into account psychological factors, the "reasonable officer" who has the appropriate training, experience and steadfastness of character for law enforcement work, remains the benchmark of assessment.[238] Therefore, it has to be assessed whether the stress and anxiety of the situation would have clouded even the judgment of a reasonable law enforcement agent in the same situation, or whether the officer in question panicked unduly. The ECtHR made this admittedly fine distinction in *Aydan*. Incidentally, the case also involved an attack by angry demonstrators on a group of gendarmes in a jeep. One of the gendarmes fired a burst of seven bullets from his automatic gun at the crowd, killing an innocent bystander. The Turkish courts did not convict him, finding that the man had exceeded the limits of necessary self-defense while in the grip of excusable fear or panic. On the contrary, the ECtHR found a human rights violation, holding that such a case was distinguishable from a case where an agent used lethal force in an honest belief that can be considered reasonable under the circumstances. The attack had not been so violent that the gendarme could have

235. Andronicou and Constantinou v. Cyprus, *supra* note 9, para. 192 (emphasis added). See also Huohvanainen v. Finland, *supra* note 14, para. 97; Giuliani and Gaggio v. Italy, *supra* note 65, para. 178.

236. Giuliani and Gaggio, *id.*, para. 179.

237. *Id.*, para. 188 (emphasis added).

238. Cf. Simsek et al. v. Turkey [ECtHR], *supra* note 79, para. 109; Aydan v. Turkey [ECtHR], *supra* note 64, paras. 97–99.

reasonably feared that his life was in danger and that opening fire with an automatic weapon was necessary.[239]

2. Duty to Minimize the Need for the Use of Force

Necessity requires law enforcement officials to apply nonviolent means as far as possible and only resort to the use of force where unavoidable.[240] The duty to minimize the need to use force has both a negative and a positive dimension: Law enforcement agents must not illegitimately provoke a self-defense situation. Furthermore, they must also take all reasonable measures to de-escalate a situation that might otherwise require defensive force on their part, especially if they may otherwise have to resort to lethal defensive force.[241] However, this does not translate into a general duty to retreat to avoid lethal confrontations, since such a duty would be incompatible with the police's professional duty to uphold law and order.

a) Provocation of self-defense

Self-defense derives its inherent justification from the fact that the aggressor unlawfully causes a situation of forced choice where the victim's rights cannot be protected without harming the aggressor's rights.[242] However, the basis for this justification falls away where the claimant of self-defense produced this forced choice by illegitimately provoking the aggression. For this reason, the state cannot claim the necessity of self-defense where its own agents provoked the attack through conduct that falls short of national or international standards.[243]

239. Aydan, *id.*, paras. 81–85. See also Simsek, *id.*, para. 109, where the European Court also rejected the argument that police used excessive lethal force due to great stress and psychological pressure. Similar reasoning might underlie the U.N. Human Rights Committee's decision in *Rickly Burrell,* although the Committee did not elaborate on its decision. In that case, prison wardens panicked during a highly dangerous hostage-taking situation and kept shooting at the prisoners even after they released their hostages. The Committee found Jamaica's responsibility established, thus apparently not attributing any weight to the panicked state of the individual perpetrators. See Rickly Burrell v. Jamaica, *supra* note 24, para. 9.5. The related question to what extent international human rights law allows states to excuse individual officers from criminal responsibility if they exceed the boundaries of necessary self-defense due to fear or panic is discussed in this Fourth Chapter: E.III.2 (pp. 211–212).

240. U.N. Basic Principles on the Use of Force and Firearms, *supra* note 25, Principle 4; U.N. Special Rapporteur on extrajudicial, summary or arbitrary executions, Christof Heyns [2014 Annual Report], *supra* note 84, para. 61; Zambrano Vélez et al. v. Ecuador [IACtHR], *supra* note 29, para. 83; Montero-Aranguren et al. (Detention Center of Catia) v. Venezuela, *supra* note 29, para 67; Kazingachire et al. v. Zimbabwe [ACommHPR], *supra* note 34, para. 113.

241. Cf. ICRC, Human Rights and Humanitarian Law for Police and Security Forces, *supra* note 2, p. 252; Skinner, *supra* note 131, p. 574.

242. See Second Chapter: D.II.9 (pp. 56–57).

243. See also Interim report of the Independent Expert on the promotion of a democratic and equitable international order, Alfred-Maurice de Zayas, U.N. Doc. A/69/272 (2014), para. 74;

The most obvious case, discussed above, is that of a state agent unlawfully attacking someone and the victim responding with justified self-defense. Law enforcement agents cannot claim self-defense since there is no unlawful attack against them—in line with the principle that there can be no self-defense against self-defense.[244]

However, state agents may not avail themselves of self-defense if they engaged in unlawful, provocative conduct, even where the victim would not be entitled to exercise force in self-defense. In *Shchiborshch and Kuzima*, for instance, ordinary police officers tried to arrest a man with a psychiatric disorder in order to place him in a psychiatric hospital. Relevant domestic procedures would have required that such involuntary hospitalization be carried out only by qualified psychiatric emergency services personnel. During the operation, the man resisted arrest and injured several police officers with a knife before police killed him. The ECtHR refused to classify the killing as justified self-defense under Article 2(2)(a) of the ECHR. It considered that the need to use force was "caused by the police's own actions," because they were not supposed to proceed with the involuntary hospitalization in the absence of qualified medical personnel and should have waited until psychiatric assistance arrived.[245]

In *Diaz Ruano*, a suspect under interrogation seized the gun of one of the interrogators and tried to shoot him. The other interrogator shot the suspect dead. By majority vote, the European Commission on Human Rights considered this a simple case of justified self-defense and hence not a violation of the right to life.[246] However, the minority, led by the Commission's president, considered that the killing was not absolutely necessary since the interrogators' prior illegal actions heightened the risk of an altercation to which they then had to respond with lethal force. In particular, the suspect had been illegally interrogated at night without his lawyer present. The interrogators also drank alcohol prior to the interrogation and had brought loaded guns into the interrogation chamber.[247]

In some situations, more systemic state failures may provoke large-scale violence, during which law enforcement officers are then placed in a situation where they need to defend themselves or others. However, it will often be hard to establish a sufficiently clear causal connection between the systemic failure

Otto, *supra* note 12, p. 94; J.F.R. Boddens Hosang, Self-Defence in Military Operations: The Interaction between the Legal Bases for Military Self-Defence and Rules of Engagement, The Military Law and the Law of War Review, vol. 47 (2008), 25–96, at pp. 59–60; Lindsey Cameron & Vincent Chetail, Privatizing War: Private Military and Security Companies under Public International Law, Cambridge University Press: Cambridge et al. (2013), p. 482; Antonio Cassese et al., International Criminal Law: Cases and Commentary, Oxford University Press: Oxford (2011), p. 461.

244. See this Fourth Chapter: C.I.2 (p. 127).

245. Shchiborshch and Kuzima v. Russia, *supra* note 174, para. 236.

246. Diaz Ruano v. Spain, Appl. No. 16988/90, Report of 31 August 1993, paras. 48–50.

247. *Id.*, Dissenting Opinion of Trechsel, joined by Soyer, Thune, Rozakis and Gözübüyük.

and the specific self-defense situation. In *Giuliani and Gaggio*, for instance, the applicants argued that the violent attack on gendarmes at the G-8 Summit, during which one of the gendarmes under attack killed an assailant in self-defense, occurred only because the gendarmes had enraged the demonstrators by charging one of their authorized marches. The ECtHR's Grand Chamber rejected the argument, finding that in light of the general violence surrounding the entire G-8 demonstrations, there were no objective grounds for believing that the attack on the gendarmes would not have occurred if the police had not charged that particular march.[248]

The Inter-American Court entertained what was essentially a systemic provocation argument in *Montero-Aranguren (Detention Centre of Catia)*. It found that systematic human rights violations and the state's lack of control of its prisons increased arms and drug trafficking, the formation of gangs, and a subculture of violence in the penitentiaries. When armed and desperate prisoners subsequently launched a concerted attack on the prison guards, the state could not base the need to use lethal force to put down this revolt only on the basis of the armed, large-scale threat created by its own failures. "Otherwise," the court reasoned, "it would imply to release the state from its duty to take preventive measures and also from its responsibility for the creation of such conditions."[249]

b) Retreat only in exceptional cases

Many domestic legal orders require private individuals to use available options of safe retreat from a confrontation to avoid being placed in a situation where they have to use force in self-defense. At least to the extent that the private person's retreat avoids the need to use lethal force, this duty also corresponds with a requirement imposed by international human rights law.[250]

However, law enforcement agents are under no general duty to retreat to avoid having to use force. In upholding the state's monopoly on the use of force, they may stand their ground and uphold the law against unlawful attack.[251] Where retreat would place the human rights of third parties at an imminent risk of

248. Giuliani and Gaggio v. Italy, *supra* note 65, paras. 253–254.

249. Montero-Aranguren et al. (Detention Center of Catia) v. Venezuela, *supra* note 29, para. 70. See also Inter-American Commission, *supra* note 32, paras. 233–234.

250. See Sixth Chapter: C.III.2 (pp. 258–264).

251. See Stewart v. United Kingdom [ECommHR], *supra* note 11, para. 27; Kremnitzer, *supra* note 137, p. 203; Dekker & Myjer, *supra* note 215, p. 182; Sangero, *supra* note 173, pp. 202–203.

The validity of this position under international law also follows from a comparison with the defensive force that peacekeepers may use without losing their protected status as noncombatants. Peacekeepers may hold their positions in exercise of their duties and may exercise self-defense against attempts to forcibly dislodge them from such positions, without being under a duty to retreat. See Katherine E. Cox, Beyond Self-Defense: United Nations Peacekeeping Operations & The Use of Force, Denver Journal of International Law and Policy, vol. 27 (1999), 239–273, p. 250; McLaughlin, *supra* note 58, p. 410.

attack, they even have a human rights duty to remain in place and confront the aggressors.

If police officers face criminals who use force to compel the police not to block their escape route, the police may therefore respond with force to defend themselves and their position and secure the arrest. They do not have to retreat and allow the criminals to flee. Where absolutely necessary to protect against death or serious injury, they may even resort to lethal force.

The International Association of Police Chiefs (IAPC) has suggested that an exception applies in situations where a suspect uses moving vehicles to threaten officers blocking their path. In such situations, the IAPC argues, the officers must move out of the path of the vehicle instead of discharging their firearms at the vehicle or any of its occupants.[252] The ECtHR takes the contrary position on this point and even allows police to shoot to kill the driver of a vehicle charging at an officer trying to block its escape route.[253] The IAPC position is the more reasonable one here. At first glance, it might appear an aberration that officers should be required to retreat from their positions and let a suspect escape just because the deadly weapon used to secure the escape is a vehicle. On closer inspection, however, special reasons make this a sound exception to the no-retreat principle. The careful set-up of police checkpoints, using such means as barricades or tire puncturing devices, will often make it unnecessary for police officers to place themselves in the way of a moving vehicle.[254] Furthermore, even in unforeseeable circumstances where officers suddenly find themselves in front of a vehicle charging at them, the use of firearms is inappropriate. Firstly, shooting at rapidly moving vehicles regularly places innocent bystanders inside and outside of the vehicle at risk, not least since the bullet has to traverse metal or glass and may therefore be deflected or ricochet. Second, and more importantly, firearms may neutralize the driver but will not bring the vehicle to an immediate halt. Therefore, such force is not effective against the deadly threat faced by the officer. It might even increase the danger for innocent bystanders if the vehicle goes out of control.[255]

The situation is different if the driver or passengers of the vehicle threaten the officer with deadly force by means other than the moving vehicle itself. For instance, the driver or passengers may shoot from the vehicle, or use the vehicle in a suicide bomb attack. In such situations, officers may open fire at the vehicle's occupants, since getting out of the way of the vehicle will not remove the threat to their lives or that of others.[256]

252. International Association of Police Chiefs, *supra* note 193, IV.B.3.

253. Wasilewska and Kalucka v. Poland, *supra* note 66, paras. 52–53.

254. Cf. Nadege Dorzema v. Dominican Republic, *supra* note 100, para. 88.

255. Bruce, *supra* note 39, p. 7.

256. See International Association of Police Chiefs, *supra* note 193, Section IV.B.3.

A second type of situation that requires officers to retreat to avoid having to resort to deadly force is that of siege situations, where armed suspects barricade themselves in a house or other confined space and threaten to use deadly force if approached. In such cases, law enforcement officers may not immediately move in to arrest the suspect and then respond with deadly force if fired upon. Instead, they will usually have to stage a temporary tactical retreat from the immediate vicinity of the suspects' hideout and cordon off the area to prevent their escape. This approach is obvious in hostage situations, where precipitate action may endanger the lives of the hostages. However, it also applies where the suspects are alone and the main risk is that they will die during the raid. In *Erdogan* and in *Mansuroglu*, two ECtHR cases which concerned the killing of alleged terrorists during government raids on their hideouts, the court found a violation of the right to life because, inter alia, the police had proceeded immediately to storm their hideouts without first trying to negotiate a peaceful surrender.[257] Similarly, in *Shchiborshch and Kuzima*, the court found that the police should have retreated from the kitchen where the mentally disturbed perpetrator had barricaded himself after stabbing a police officer. The ECtHR found that "the only appropriate recourse was to discontinue any efforts to apprehend him until the arrival of psychiatric assistance."[258]

In siege situations, it is reasonable to demand a temporary retreat, because it does not mean the suspect is allowed to escape. Arrest is merely deferred. The high risk of having to use deadly force that is associated with an immediate operation against a spatially contained suspect is therefore not necessary for carrying out the police's duty to enforce law and order.

c) Negotiation of surrender in hostage and other siege situations

As also emerges from the abovementioned cases of *Erdogan* and *Mansuruglo*, temporary retreat in siege situations is not enough. Law enforcement officers have a duty to proactively de-escalate the situation. In particular, they must make reasonable efforts to broker in good faith a peaceful surrender where this can be done without increasing the risk for hostages, suspects or the officers involved.

In *Suarez de Guerrero*, the Human Rights Committee therefore found a violation because, inter alia, alleged kidnappers who were killed by the police were given no opportunity to surrender.[259] In *Vachkovi*, police chased after a heavily armed suspect who had fled into a building and shot him dead. The European Court considered that even though the whole area was sealed off and the police were in complete control of the situation, the police failed to employ "any strategy aimed at minimizing to the greatest extent possible recourse to lethal

257. Erdogan et al. v. Turkey, *supra* note 126, para. 79; Mansuroglu v. Turkey, Appl. 43443/98, Judgment of 26 February 2008, para. 87.

258. Shchiborshch and Kuzima v. Russia, *supra* note 174, para. 236.

259. Suarez de Guerrero v. Colombia, *supra* note 23, para. 13.2.

force" such as negotiating with the man to put down his weapon.[260] In *Finca "La Exacta,"* the police negotiated with the occupiers of a farm for only an hour or two, demanding that they surrender those occupiers against whom an arrest warrant was pending. The police then raided the farm with the stated objective of carrying out the arrests. The Inter-American Commission found that the police could have waited longer to see whether the persons named in the arrest warrants would surrender or leave the estate so that they could be arrested.[261]

Negotiations should be handled by professionals according to best practices, especially where hostages are involved. However, in the heat of the moment it cannot be expected that every police operation will be perfectly executed. Police have a certain leeway to commit mistakes in the handling of negotiations as long as an overall reasonable effort to negotiate a peaceful surrender in good faith can be shown.

In *Andronicou*, where a man took his girlfriend hostage, the ECtHR held in favor of the Cypriot police that they tried to resolve the situation through persuasion and dialogue right up to the last possible moment. It found no violation based on the unprofessional handling of the negotiations. Notably, the police had negligently left the hostage-taker's regular telephone line open so that different relatives ended up contacting the hostage-taker with conflicting messages. Meanwhile, the police's own negotiator did not have a separate line and could not reach him at crucial moments of the hostage crisis.[262]

In *Bubbins*, the court noted with approval that it was the uppermost concern of the police that the stand-off with the armed man barricaded in his apartment be resolved by persuasion. Although the court considered it regrettable that no trained negotiator was available to convince the man to surrender, it did not find a violation mainly because "it would appear that the police were at all times unwilling to take precipitate action, but tried to defuse the situation without recourse to lethal force or to tactics which might provoke a violent response from the man inside the flat."[263]

In the *Huohvanainen* siege, the court did not consider it a shortcoming that the police did not give the victim's brother a chance to negotiate a surrender, since a trained negotiator and a psychologist were available to conduct negotiations with the mentally disturbed man.[264] Conversely, in *Shchiborshch and Kuzima*, the court factored into its finding of a violation that the negotiations with the mentally disturbed victim were conducted by a police sniper who had neither training nor experience in handling mentally disturbed individuals.[265]

260. Vachkovi v. Bulgaria, Appl. No. 2747/02, Judgment of 8 July 2010, para. 74.

261. Finca "La Exacta" v. Guatemala [IACommHR], *supra* note 2, para. 52–54.

262. Andronicou and Constantinou v. Cyprus, *supra* note 9, para. 183. But see *id.*, Diss. Op. Judge Pekannen, para. 3, finding an organizational failure relating to the negotiations.

263. Bubbins v. United Kingdom, *supra* note 9, paras. 146–148 (cit. at para. 148).

264. Huohvanainen v. Finland, *supra* note 14, paras. 103–104.

265. Shchiborshch and Kuzima v. Russia, *supra* note 174, para. 237.

There is only a duty to try and broker a peaceful surrender, but no duty to offer substantive concessions. The ECtHR was very clear on this point in *Finogenov*, where the Moscow theatre hostage-takers sought to achieve political concessions on Chechnya's territorial status. The court underscored that it is left up to states "whether to negotiate with terrorists and make concessions or to remain firm and require unconditional surrender."[266] It was therefore sufficient that some form of negotiations were conducted that gave the terrorists an opportunity to formulate their demands, to reflect on the situation and to cool down.[267] Similarly, in *Finca "La Exacta,"* which involved peasant workers occupying a farm, the Inter-American Commission did not suggest that the authorities should have made any substantive concessions to the occupiers, but rather emphasized the lack of effort to negotiate their peaceful surrender.[268]

The window for negotiations closes once a longer wait puts lives at risk. In making that assessment, the authorities have a certain degree of flexibility as long as they do not act unreasonably. In the *Andronicou* hostage crisis, the ECtHR considered reasonable the police's decision to storm the apartment and overpower the hostage-taker by lethal force shortly before midnight, considering that the hostage-taker had credibly threatened to kill his girlfriend and himself precisely at that hour.[269] In *Finogenov*, the court regarded it as justified that Russia broke off negotiations with the Chechen hostage-takers and stormed the Moscow theatre with force, as the terrorists had already executed several hostages and the remaining hostages' physical and psychological condition was worsening.[270]

d) De-escalation measures in the handling of demonstrations

The duty to proactively de-escalate also becomes highly relevant in the policing of demonstrations. Police must take measures to prevent demonstrations from degenerating into riots that may then necessitate police to use force, including lethal force in self-defense. Such de-escalation measures have to comply with other human rights. In particular, they must not unduly restrict freedom of assembly, expression, and movement. This would be the case, for instance, if the state were to pre-emptively ban a peaceful demonstration just because there is a possibility that some elements with violent intentions outside the control of the organizing association use the opportunity to mingle among the peaceful demonstrators.[271]

266. Finogenov et al. v. Russia, *supra* note 117, para. 223.

267. *Id.*, para. 224.

268. Finca "La Exacta" v. Guatemala [IACommHR], *supra* note 2, para. 54.

269. Andronicou and Constantinou v. Cyprus, *supra* note 9, para. 184.

270. Finogenov et al. v. Russia, *supra* note 117, para. 226.

271. Primov v Russia [ECtHR], Appl. No. 17391/06, Judgment of 12 June 2014, para. 155; United Nations High Commissioner for Human Rights, Effective measures and best practices to ensure the promotion and protection of human rights in the context of peaceful protests, U.N. Doc. A/HRC/22/28 (2013), para. 10. Cf. Joint U.N. special rapporteurs report on assembly management, *supra* note 95, para. 45.

In implementing a strategy of de-escalation, the state must pay special attention to understanding crowd behavior and employing methods of persuasion, negotiation, and mediation to lessen the need to use force.[272] In this regard, it is problematic that a number of states still employ demonstration management doctrines that rely heavily on the massive show of force and rapid escalation of coercive measures. This approach is premised on the assumption that large crowds are irrational and hence inherently prone to violence. In light of empirical research disproving this assumption, many police forces in Europe and North America have moved to a "negotiated management" philosophy, where police seek to facilitate peaceful demonstrations through contact with the organizers and resist the use of force even in the face of unlawful, yet non-violent, acts of civil disobedience. However, in order to quell anticipated violent protests at high-level political gatherings such as the World Trade Organization and G-8 Summits, some European and North American police forces have reverted to a coercion-focused approach that relies on show of force, excessive control of space to isolate and contain potentially disruptive protest, pre-emptive arrests, and surveillance.[273]

The ECtHR has shown a certain willingness to accept coercive crowd control approaches where the demonstrator's predisposition to use violence could be shown. In *Austin*, it upheld the U.K. police's practice of "kettling," which involves pre-emptively confining crowds that are potentially violent in a tight space surrounded by menacing riot police.[274] In *Giuliani and Gaggio*, the court's majority refused to entertain arguments from the applicants on the overall handling of the G-8 protests in Genoa.[275] Conversely, the court found violations in a series of cases concerning the violent dispersion of unauthorized but nonviolent demonstrations in Turkey, because the police failed to show the necessary degree

272. U.N. Basic Principles on the Use of Force and Firearms, *supra* note 25, Principle 20; U.N. Special Rapporteur on extrajudicial, summary or arbitrary executions, Christof Heyns, 2011 Annual Report, *supra* note 22, para. 105; Joint U.N. special rapporteurs report on assembly management, *supra* note 95, paras. 53–54 & 67(b); Amnesty International, Use of Force Guidelines, *supra* note 3, p. 151.

273. For a discusson of the different approaches, see U.N. Special Rapporteur on extrajudicial, summary or arbitrary executions, Christof Heyns, *id.*, paras. 106–118; Clifford Stott, Martin Scothern & Hugo Gorringe, Advances in Liaison Based Public Order Policing in England: Human Rights and Negotiating the Management of Protest?, Policing, vol. 7(2) (2013), 212–226, at pp. 213-214. On more recent heavy-handed approaches, see Amnesty International, Policing Demonstrations in the European Union, October 2012, http://www.amnesty.org.uk/sites/default/files/eu-police.pdf.

274. Austin v. UK [ECtHR Grand Chamber], Appl. No. 39692/09, 40712/09 & 41008/09, Judgment of 15 March 2012, para. 56. Critical of kettling: Stuart Casey-Maslen, Crowd management, crowd control, and riot control, in: Casey-Maslen (ed.), *supra* note 6, 53–70, at pp. 77–78; Amnesty International, Use of Force Guidelines, *supra* note 3, pp. 155–156.

275. Giuliani and Gaggio v. Italy, *supra* note 65, para. 253. But cf. *id.*, Joint Partly Dissenting Opinion of Judges Rozakis, Tulkens Zupancic, Gyulumyan, Ziemele, Kalaydjieva and Karakasuliani, para. 2.

of tolerance and restraint towards the demonstrations and thus escalated the situation to large-scale violence.[276]

Heavy-handed crowd control measures are not only problematic due to their impact on political freedoms; they are also prone to be counterproductive from a security perspective. Coercion may infuriate the more restrained participants and exacerbate the crowd's overall propensity to violence. As noted by the U.N. Special Rapporteur on Summary Executions, "if a crowd is treated like an irrational group of criminals who only understand the language of force, that is how they will behave."[277] Demonstrated shows of force may also unleash powerful group dynamics and exacerbate tensions. The repeated use of police dogs to contain African-American demonstrators in the United States, for instance, has evoked highly provocative parallels with the violent suppression of civil rights protests against racial segregation in the 1960s.[278]

More promising approaches emphasize communication with organizers and demonstrators. For example, Sweden overhauled its crowd control approach after Swedish police had to use live ammunition in self-defense during violent protests at the G-8 Summit in Gothenburg in 2001. Sweden has moved away from crowd policing that relies on large formations of armored police officers and mass charges against violent protests. The new approach seeks to establish relationships of trust and understanding through specially trained liaison officers. Other useful de-escalation measures include keeping menacing riot police out of sight, making individual officers identifiable by name, involving both male and female officers in policing protests, properly communicating and explaining orders to disperse and giving participants in illegal demonstrations sufficient time to disperse.[279]

3. Duty to Minimize and Graduate the Level of Force

Even where the use of force becomes inevitable, the *level* of force employed still must be as minimal as possible.[280] International human rights law establishes a graduated scale on the use of force. When faced with an unlawful attack, law enforcement agents have to consider the following means, in the order indicated:

(1) Identification as police and verbal warning to cease the attack;
(2) Use of non-lethal bodily force;

276. Iczi v. Turkey, Appl. No. 42606/05, 23 July 2013, para 67; Bicici v. Turkey, Appl. No. 30357/05, Judgment of 27 May 2010, para. 35. Nurettin Aldemir and Others v. Turkey, Appl. No. 32124/02, 32126/02, 32129/02, 32132/02, 32133/02, 32137/02 and 32138/02, Judgment of 18 December 2007, para. 46; DISK and KESK v. Turkey, Appl. No. 38676/08, Judgment of 27 November 2012, para 36; Akgöl and Gol v. Turkey, Appl. No. 28495/06 & 28516/06, Judgment of 17 May 2011, para 43.

277. U.N. Special Rapporteur on extrajudicial, summary or arbitrary executions, Christof Heyns, 2011 Annual Report, *supra* note 22, para. 111.

278. Casey-Maslen, *supra* note 274, p. 74.

279. *Id.*, paras. 115 & 119; Amnesty International, *supra* note 273, p. 7.

280. Mouvementet des Peuples v. Burkina Faso [ACommHPR], *supra* note 103, para. 43; Rodley/Pollard, *supra* note 22, p. 254; United Nations Department of Peacekeeping

(3) Use of less lethal force;
(4) Use of "moderately lethal" force (defined in subsection c, below);
(5) Verbal warning that police may use firearms or other potentially lethal force;
(6) Warning shots (where reasonable);
(7) Use of firearms so as to incapacitate the aggressor;
(8) Use of firearms so as to kill the aggressor.[281]

Among these means, a police officer has to choose the least harmful that can still be expected to effectively counter the attack. The officer does not have to try less harmful means first if their effectiveness is uncertain and delay in resorting to more serious measures increases the risk for the officer or others.[282] There is also no duty to maintain an "equality of arms" in confronting the aggressor.[283] For example, police officers facing physical assaults by unarmed suspects do not have to engage in hand-to-hand combat if it would entail a significant risk of being overpowered and injured. They may use their truncheons in self-defense.

Models that establish a graduated scale of force based on the means deployed by the police, like the model suggested above, have been criticized as placing too much emphasis on the officer and too little on the threat faced. A proposed alternative is the Dynamic-Resistance-Response Model that matches broad categories of suspect resistance with suitable conduct on the part of law enforcement agents. It distinguishes three levels of resistance:

(1) passively resistant (fails to follow officer's commands and may be verbally abusive): firm grip, control holds, or the use of pressure points is recommended;
(2) aggressively resistant (attempts to control the officer or another person through physical attacks/restraints): a stun gun, pepper spray, baton, or tactical physical maneuvers are recommended;

Operations: Policy (Revised): Formed Police Units in United Nations Peacekeeping Operations, Doc. Ref. 2009.32, 1 March 2010, para. 36.

281. See also U.S. National Institute of Justice, The Use of Force Continuum (2009), http://www.nij.gov/topics/law-enforcement/officer-safety/use-of-force/Pages/continuum.aspx; Dymond-Bass/Corney, *supra* note 6, p. 43. For the addition of the proposed additional category of moderately lethal force, see the discussion on tasers below, this Fourth Chapter: C.III.3.b (pp. 161–162).

282. Otto, *supra* note 12, pp. 83–84. Cf. U.N. Special Rapporteur on extrajudicial, summary or arbitrary executions Philip Alston, 2006 Annual Report, *supra* note 50, para. 48; Dymond-Bass/Corney, *supra* note 6, p. 44 (n.32); Charles Joyner & Chad Basile, Dynamic Resistance Response Model: A Modern Approach to the Use of Force, FBI Law Enforcement Bulletin, vol. 76(9) (2007), 15–20, at p. 17.

283. See also Guilfoyle, *supra* note 157, p. 372.

(3) deadly resistant (suspect attempts to seriously injure or kill the officer or another person if immediate action is not taken to stop the threat): firearms and any other tool sufficient to counter the threat are recommended.[284]

From the perspective of international human rights law, such a model can provide useful guidance to ensure that no disproportional force is used.[285] However, its rigid matching of threat and means makes it entirely unsuitable for making necessity determinations in line with the requirements of international human rights law.[286] Even against a suspect using lethal force, only the force necessary to counter the threat may be used. If under the specific circumstances, the suspect's attack can be safely and effectively defended against by a less harmful means than firearms, such means must be chosen. An attack with lethal force does not always necessitate a lethal defensive response.

a) Less lethal means

Modern law enforcement agencies have a number of weapons and other means at their disposal to subdue aggressors without killing them. These include:

- Direct kinetic impact weapons (batons, truncheons, etc.)
- Chemical irritant agents (tear gas or pepper spray)
- Audible and optical distraction devices (stun grenades, flash bangs, or smoke munitions)
- Less lethal kinetic impact munitions (rubber bullets, plastic baton rounds, or water cannons).[287]

These means are best described as less lethal means, rather than "non-lethal," because they still carry a certain risk of killing, especially if used inappropriately. For instance, tear gas may asphyxiate if it is used against persons trapped in a closed room or persons suffering from certain respiratory diseases. Rubber bullets shot from close range or truncheon blows to the head may cause fatal injuries.[288]

284. Joyner/Basile, *id.*, pp. 17–18. See also Dymond-Bass/Corney, *id.*, p. 43. A similar model also guides United Nations–formed police units in peacekeeping missions, which are authorized to use force. See United Nations Department of Peacekeeping Operations, *supra* note 280, para. 38.

285. On proportionality, see this Fourth Chapter: C.V (pp. 170–189).

286. ICRC, Human Rights and Humanitarian Law for Police and Security Forces, *supra* note 2, p. 261; Amnesty International, Use of Force Guidelines, *supra* note 3, p. 103.

287. Cf. Otto, *supra* note 12, p. 83; Dymond-Bass/Corney, *supra* note 6, pp. 36–37.

288. For an example of death resulting from rubber bullets, see Stewart v. United Kingdom, *supra* note 11. On deaths related to tear gas use, see Report of the Special Rapporteur on

States must therefore take sufficient precautions to minimize the lethal potential of such weapons. A less lethal weapon must be assessed prior to its first use and periodically reassessed. Based on the assessment, protocols on their non-lethal use have to be adopted and law enforcement agents trained accordingly.[289] A violation ensues if such protocols are not followed. In *Perisan*, prison wardens used truncheons to defend themselves against assault, causing the death of several prisoners from head and internal injuries. The ECtHR considered the wardens' actions violated the right to life because they had evidently failed to respect instructions to aim the truncheon blows only at the legs and arms.[290] In *Abdullah Yasa*, police used tear gas grenade launchers against youths throwing stones at them. While not questioning the use of tear gas as such, the court found a violation because police did not launch the tear gas grenades at a high angle, but aimed them directly at the demonstrators, so that one victim was hit in the head and seriously injured by a tear gas canister.[291] In *DISK and KESK*, a violation ensued because tear gas was used around a hospital, placing patients at risk.[292]

Even where properly used, less lethal means still infringe on the physical security of the aggressor. A residual risk of death always remains. Therefore, the police still must consider whether the use of less lethal means is truly necessary or if the threat can be safely addressed by verbal warning or non-lethal bodily force.

b) Use of firearms

The use of firearms—weapons with projectiles designed to kill—is considered an extreme measure that state agents may only employ for defensive purposes where less harmful means, such as verbal warnings, bodily force, less lethal, or moderately lethal means, will not safely protect against the attack.[293] In *Erdogan*, the state authorities raided the hideouts of suspected terrorists using live ammunition guns and hand grenades, without having tear gas bombs or other non-lethal means at their disposal. The ECtHR found that the lack of less lethal means significantly jeopardized the lives of the suspects, ten of whom were indeed shot and

extrajudicial, summary or arbitrary executions, Christof Heyns—Addendum: Mission to Turkey, U.N. Doc. A/HRC/23/47/Add.2, para. 19.

289. See also U.N. Basic Principles on the Use of Force and Firearms, *supra* note 25, Principle 3; African Commission on Human and Peoples' Rights, General Comment on the Right to Life, *supra* note 33, para. 30. Cf. Dymond-Bass/Corney, *supra* note 6, pp. 45 & 48–49.

290. Perisan et al. v. Turkey, Appl. No. 12336/03, Judgment of 20 May 2010, paras. 81–82.

291. Abdullah Yasa et al. v. Turkey, Appl. No. 44827/08, Judgment of 16 July 2013, paras. 42–49.

292. DISK and KESK v. Turkey, *supra* note 276, para. 34.

293. See also U.N. Code of Conduct for Law Enforcement Officials, *supra* note 25, art. 3(c); Garcia Ibarra v. Ecuador, Judgment of 17 November 2015, IACtHR (Ser. C) No. 306, para. 112.

killed.[294] Yet, in *Perk*, where the police also raided terrorists' hideouts, the court found the police's use of live ammunition, without first using tear gas or other less lethal means, to be absolutely necessary for purposes of self-defense, because the suspects started firing at the police, placing the officers' lives at risk.[295]

Even where the use of firearms becomes absolutely necessary, it still has to be calibrated to the threat so as to decrease the risk of unnecessary harm.[296] In *Makaratzis*, the ECtHR accepted that police could use firearms to neutralize a driver since they had good reason to believe he was a dangerous terrorist who was about to shoot at them. However, it took issue with the intensity and chaotic way in which guns were used, which the court described as "a hail of shots at the applicant's car with revolvers, pistols and submachine guns."[297]

Calibrated use of firearms also requires police officers to shoot at the legs or lower torso of a suspect who charges with a knife or other close-combat weapon, to immobilize him. Provided the suspect is still at a sufficient distance, they may not fire kill-shots to the head or repeatedly at the chest.[298] In *Kakoulli*, for instance, Turkish security forces deployed in Cyprus shot dead a man running towards the ceasefire line in Cyprus. Although the man carried a garrote and a bayonet, the ECtHR refused to justify the killing as self-defense because he was still about 30 meters away when shot, and thus posed no threat.[299] The Michael Brown case in the United States, described at the outset of this chapter, raises similar concerns, especially considering that Brown was visibly unarmed when he was running towards the police officer who repeatedly shot him in the chest and neck.

Law enforcement agents generally must not use automatic weapons in a constant fire mode, considering the principle of calibrated force and the particular risks for innocent bystanders due to the inaccuracy of automatic fire. Such weapons may be deployed only in high-intensity operations, such as storming the hideout of heavily armed terrorists, where law enforcement agents can expect to be engaged in a sustained firefight and risks to innocent bystanders can be controlled. Even then, they should preferably be used in a more controllable "burst mode" fire setting.[300]

294. Erdogan et al. v. Turkey, *supra* note 126, para. 79. See also Gülec v. Turkey, *supra* note 77, para. 71; Hamiyet Kaplan et al. v. Turkey [ECtHR], Appl. No. 36749/97, Judgment of 13 September 2005, para. 51.

295. Perk et al. v. Turkey, *supra* note 127, para. 72.

296. U.N. Basic Principles on the Use of Force and Firearms, *supra* note 25, Principle 11(b); Fleck, *supra* note 53, p. 394.

297. Makaratzis v. Greece, *supra* note 15, para. 67.

298. See also Guilfoyle, *supra* note 157, p. 371.

299. Kakoulli v. Turkey, *supra* note 215, paras. 118–121.

300. Amnesty International, Use of Force Guidelines, *supra* note 3, pp. 34 & 121. See also Joint U.N. special rapporteurs report on assembly management, *supra* note 95, para. 67(e), indicating that automatic firearms must not be used in the policing of assemblies.

Firearms set to discharge autonomously, that is without being controlled by a human being, must never be used in law enforcement because the highly context-specific decisions on whether and what degree of force is necessary and proportional can only be taken by human beings.[301] For this reason, automatic discharge firearms deployed to control borders (e.g., along the East German/West German border during the Cold War), as well as armed and fully autonomous robotic law enforcement systems, are per se irreconcilable with international human rights law.

As an additional safeguard, law enforcement officials may use firearms only after identifying themselves as such and giving a clear warning of their intent, with sufficient time for the warnings to be heeded.[302] In *Suarez de Guerrero*, the Human Rights Committee therefore found a violation, inter alia, because police shot at the alleged kidnappers without warning.[303] In *Ogur*, the ECtHR criticized the authorities for not warning the victim by a loud announcement of the intent to use firearms, as would have been required under official instructions.[304] In *Giuliani and Gaggio*, where a gendarme was already under attack, it constituted sufficient warning that the officer waved his gun and shouted at the aggressors to leave unless they wanted to be killed.[305]

It is disputed whether verbal warnings have to be followed by a warning shot. The International Association of Chiefs of Police recommends that warning shots generally should not be fired.[306] Many national police agencies forbid the use of warning shots in light of the danger that they pose to innocent bystanders.[307] In some circumstances, a warning shot may also be mistaken for an actual attack and escalate the confrontation rather than subdue the aggressor.[308]

301. African Commission on Human and Peoples' Rights, General Comment on the Right to Life, *supra* note 33, para. 31; Joint U.N. special rapporteurs report on assembly management, *supra* note 95, para. 67(f); Amnesty International, Use of Force Guidelines, *supra* note 3, p. 34.

302. U.N. Basic Principles on the Use of Force and Firearms, *supra* note 25, Principle 10. See also Bubbins v. United Kingdom [ECtHR], *supra* note 9, para. 139; Gül; Ramsahai v. The Netherlands, *supra* note 9, para. 281; Erdogan et al. v. Turkey, *supra* note 126, para. 79; Montero-Aranguren et al. (Detention Center of Catia) v. Venezuela, *supra* note 29, para. 75; Inter-American Commission on Human Rights, *supra* note 142, para. 118. See also Nsereko, *supra* note 21, p. 254, Melzer, *supra* note 22, pp. 103–104 & 235–236; Kremnitzer, *supra* note 137, p. 202; First Turkel Commission Report, *supra* note 6, para. 189; Bruce, *supra* note 39, p. 6.

303. Suarez de Guerrero v. Colombia, *supra* note 23, para. 13.2.

304. Ogur v. Turkey, *supra* note 12, para. 82.

305. Giuliani and Gaggio v. Italy, *supra* note 65, paras. 190–191.

306. International Association of Police Chiefs, *supra* note 193, part IV.B.2. See also Amnesty International, Use of Force Guidelines, *supra* note 3, p. 34.

307. Bruce, *supra* note 39, p. 6. See also ICRC, Human Rights and Humanitarian Law for Police and Security Forces, *supra* note 2, p. 258.

308. ICRC, *id.*

However, in other situations, the psychological effect of hearing an actual shot may intimidate the aggressor enough to cease the attack, which makes a subsequent targeted shot resulting in actual injury or death unnecessary. Perhaps with this consideration in mind, the ECtHR has taken the position that opening fire must, whenever possible, be preceded by warnings shots.[309] Accordingly, it found no violation in *Golubeva*, where an attacker was killed by the ricochet of a warning shot, or in *Bakan*, where a warning shot accidentally killed an innocent bystander.[310]

Considering the different impacts that a warning shot may have depending on the circumstances, the present author takes the view that international human rights law neither categorically requires nor prohibits warning shots. Instead, police officers must follow the requisite national regulations and apply them reasonably. A violation may therefore ensue where under the circumstances it appears wholly unreasonable either to use a warning shot, such as in a particularly crowded setting where there is no clear trajectory for the bullet, or not to use one (e.g., because it is very likely that the attacker may heed the warning and innocent bystanders are obviously not put at risk).

No warning of any kind needs to be given where this would place the law enforcement officials or others at risk or would be clearly inappropriate or pointless in the circumstances.[311] Where the perpetrator has already used his own firearm or has raised it to shoot, there is usually no time to give a warning without undue risk to the officer.[312] Nor need a warning be given to stop a perpetrator who is about to detonate a bomb, such as a suicide bomber. State agents can graduate directly to deliberately lethal force and instantly fire to kill so that the perpetrator is given no chance to set off the bomb.[313] However, law enforcement agents must act with a high degree of certainty that the suspect is indeed about to detonate a bomb. This certainty must be based on reliable information evaluated by persons with appropriate expertise and experience. Orders to shoot to

309. Kitanovski v. Former Yugislav Republic of Macedonia, Appl. No. 15191/12, Judgment of 22 January 2015, para 72; Kallis and Androulla Panayi v. Turkey, Appl. No. 45388/99, Judgment of 27 October 2009, para. 62; Giuliani and Gaggio v. Italy, *supra* note 65, paras. 177. Cf. Solomou v. Turkey, *supra* note 162, para. 75; Olah, Appl. No. 56558/00, Decision of 14 September 2004. See also Harris et al., *supra* note 67, p. 228; Velu/Ergec, *supra* note 8, para. 231.

310. Golubeva v. Russia, Appl. No. 1062/03, Judgment of 17 December 2009, para. 101; Bakan v. Turkey, *supra* note 117, para. 55. See also Giuliani and Gaggio, *supra* note 65, para 192.

311. U.N. Basic Principles on the Use of Force and Firearms, *supra* note 25, Principle 10.

312. See also Diaz Ruano v. Spain [ECommHR], *supra* note 246, para. 49; Huohvanainen v. Finland, *supra* note 14, para. 97.

313. See McCann et al. v. United Kingdom, *supra* note 9, para. 196-200; U.N. Special Rapporteur on extrajudicial,summary or arbitrary executions Philip Alston, 2006 Annual Report, *supra* note 50, para. 49.

kill a potential bomber based on the person's "suspicious" profile or other vague assumptions are not reconcilable with international human rights law.[314]

The killing of Brazilian electrician Jean-Charles de Menezes by British police marks a tragic case in point. Shortly after the London Public Transport Bombings of July 7, 2005, police mistook de Menezes for a member of the terrorist group that perpetrated the bombings due to a series of unsubstantiated assumptions and communication failures that the United Kingdom's Independent Police Complaints Commission qualified as avoidable, "very serious mistakes."[315] Police arrested him as he entered a subway carriage. Wrongly assuming that he carried a suicide bomb, they shot him repeatedly in the head although he was already under the physical control of the arresting officer.[316]

c) Other means of instant incapacitation: Tasers and knockout gases

Modern technology offers the promise of new means that can instantly incapacitate an aggressor while still non-lethal. However, at least based on the current state of technology, such devices and their classification raise significant human rights concerns.

Electromuscular incapacitation devices—commonly known as Tasers—deliver a high-voltage, low-amperage electrical shock that disrupts the suspect's control of his muscles. The shock is supposed to be calibrated to be non-lethal. In the great majority of cases this seems to be the case, making the Taser overall a less harmful weapon than firearms. However, Tasers can still kill by causing ventricular fibrillation and subsequent heart attack.[317] The risk of death is particularly high for persons with a heart condition or whose cardiac systems have been weakened by drug and alcohol abuse or the chase and struggle before they are tased. In addition, Taser victims may suffer fatal injuries during their uncontrolled fall.[318] Although no comprehensive global or national statistics exist, hundreds of deaths in the United States alone have been attributed to the use of Tasers.[319]

314. U.N. Special Rapporteur on extrajudicial, summary or arbitrary executions, *supra* note 50, para. 50; McCann, *supra* note 9, para. 211.

315. See Independent Police Complains Commission, Publication of the Stockwell One Report, 8 November 2008, https://www.ipcc.gov.uk/news/publication-stockwell-one-report.

316. See Armani da Silva v. United Kingdom, *supra* note 195, paras. 39–101. For details of the Menezes case, see also Casey-Maslen, *supra* note 6, pp. 16–19.

317. Douglas P. Zipes, Sudden Cardiac Arrest and Death Associated with Application of Shocks from a TASER Electronic Control Device, Circulation [American Heart Association], vol. 125 (2012), 2417–2422; Braidwood Commission on Conducted Energy Weapon Use, Restoring Public Confidence: Restricting the Use of Conducted Energy Weapons in British Columbia (2009), http://www.braidwoodinquiry.ca/report/P1Report.php, Executive Summary, Part B: Medical Risks.

318. Dymond-Bass/Corney, *supra* note 6, pp. 47–48.

319. Amnesty International counted 670 Taser-related deaths in the period between 2001 and 2015. See Amnesty International, Report 2015/16: United States of America,

Against this backdrop, the U.N. Committee against Torture takes the position that Tasers should be used only by trained law enforcement personnel in extreme and limited situations, where there is a real and immediate threat to life or risk of serious injury, as a substitute for lethal weapons.[320] The present author agrees with classifying Tasers above the less lethal means category and limiting their use to countering immediate threats of deaths or serious injury. However, the suggestion that Tasers and firearms are interchangeable is problematic and counterproductive. In many situations the use of Tasers, even though not a less lethal weapon, still constitutes a less harmful alternative to firearms. In August 2012, for instance, New York City police officers shot dead a mentally disturbed man near Times Square after he attacked them with a kitchen knife. Warnings and repeated applications of pepper spray had failed to stop him. The incident has met with justified criticism, not least since the officers had no Tasers available that could have been used to incapacitate the man with much less risk of death.[321]

In line with these considerations, and in light of the current state of technology, Tasers should be classified in a separate intermediate category between less lethal means and firearms. This category could be referred to as "moderately lethal means."

Toxic chemical agents that incapacitate instantly by acting on the central nervous system (so-called knockout gases) are even more problematic than Tasers. Knockout gas of an unknown composition was used by the Russian Security Forces to end the 2002 Moscow theatre hostage crisis during which a group of armed Chechens took 850 hostages and threatened to blow up the entire building. About 130 hostages died from adverse reactions to the gas and delay in providing them with necessary medical care. In its *Finogenov* judgment, the ECtHR nevertheless considered the use of knockout gas to be compatible with human rights, since it was not intended to be lethal, but rather was intended to prevent the hostage-takers from detonating their suicide vests so the authorities could free the hostages.[322]

Others have questioned the legality of incapacitating chemical agents. In particular, the International Committee of the Red Cross (ICRC) has taken the position that international law leaves little, if any, room for the legitimate use

https://www.amnesty.org/en/countries/americas/united-states-of-america/report-united-states-of-america/.

320. Committee against Torture, *supra* note 174, para. 27. See also ICRC, Human Rights and Humanitarian Law for Police and Security Forces, *supra* note 2, p. 253; Braidwood Commission on Conducted Energy Weapon Use, *supra* note 317, Executive Summary, Part A, at para. 2; Crawshaw, Cullen & Williamson, *supra* note 58, p. 147. But cf. First Turkel Commission Report, *supra* note 6, para. 231.

321. Casey-Maslen, *supra* note 6, pp. 7–8.

322. Finogenov et al. v. Russia, *supra* note 117, para. 232–236. For violations related to the Russian authorities' rescue and evacuation operation, see this Fourth Chapter: E.I (p. 203).

of toxic chemicals as weapons for law enforcement, other than the use of classic riot control agents such as tear gas. The ICRC fears that incapacitating chemical agent present serious risks to life and health, risk undermining international law prohibiting chemical weapons, and may create a "slippery slope" towards the reintroduction of chemical weapons into armed conflict.[323]

It is highly desirable that international weapons law maintains a bright line on the prohibition of chemical weapons. However, the Chemical Weapons Convention (CWC), as it stands, expressly does not extend to "the use of toxic chemicals for purposes of law enforcement including domestic riot control purposes."[324] Although his provision was meant to preserve the legality of using tear gas in law enforcement, the exception is broad enough to also cover knockout gases. At the last CWC review conference, state parties have unfortunately not followed suggestions by the ICRC and others to clarify that incapacitating chemical agents do not fall under the CWC's law enforcement exception.[325] As currently interpreted, the CWC therefore apparently does not ban such weapons.

However, the use of incapacitating chemical agents is hard to square with international human rights law. The difference between an incapacitating dosage and a lethal one varies greatly, depending on the target person's age, body size, health history including pre-existing conditions, and potentially other unknown factors. It is therefore impossible to safely gauge in a law enforcement operation what dose will be non-lethal. Therefore, a certain percentage of persons in a targeted group of people can be expected to die as a measure of statistical certainty.[326] In *Finogenov*, the ECtHR may have still generously assumed in Russia's favor that its state agents had good reasons to believe the knockout gas would be non-lethal. However, the harrowing experience of the Moscow theatre hostage crisis does not permit states to make the same erroneous assumption in future situations.[327]

At the current stage of research and technology, the use of incapacitating chemical agents must therefore be considered deliberately lethal force. This rules out its use in hostage situations, where both hostage-takers and hostages will be exposed. As will be discussed below, the hostages are innocent bystanders who may not be

323. ICRC position on the use of toxic chemicals as weapons for law enforcement, 2 June 2013, https://www.icrc.org/eng/resources/documents/legal-fact-sheet/2013-02-06-toxic-chemicals-weapons-law-enforcement.htm.

324. Chemical Weapons Convention, art. II(9)(d).

325. Cf. Report of the Third Special Session of the Conference of the States Parties to Review the Operation of the Chemical Weapons Convention, OPCW Doc. No. RC-3/3 (2013).

326. Peter Blain, Scientific and medical assessment of new weapons for law enforcement: Issues that would be raised by "incapacitating chemical agents,", in: ICRC, Expert Meeting: "Incapacitating Chemical Agents"—Law Enforcement, Human Rights Law and Policy, ICRC: Geneva (2013), 30–33, at p. 33; Doswald-Beck, *supra* note 75, p. 40 (noting studies that point to an averge death rate among target persons of 10%).

327. Doswald-Beck, *id.*, p. 42.

subjected to deliberately lethal force that is sure to kill at least some who might otherwise survive.[328] This leaves incapacitating chemical agents as a potential means of deliberately lethal force for the far less likely siege situations in which armed perpetrators pose an immediate threat to life without holding hostages.

If incapacitating chemical agents are someday to become a viable less lethal weapon for law enforcement, it would require not only further technological progress but also careful evaluation to minimize the risk of endangering innocent bystanders.[329] In light of their potentially fatal nature, however, it seems impossible to field-test them in conditions resembling actual use in law enforcement without seriously breaching medical ethics and the human rights of test subjects.

IV. Organizational or precautionary duties

Human rights entail obligations of the entire state. Therefore, the inquiry into whether the use of defensive force is necessary must extend beyond the actions taken by the individual law enforcement officers at the scene. It must also be assessed to what extent the state as a whole organized itself adequately, taking precautions to ensure that force will be used only where it is necessary and unavoidable.[330]

Accordingly, there can be situations where the individual officers on the scene exercised justified self-defense and accordingly incur no criminal responsibility, while there were organizational failures at the command level so that the state as a whole nevertheless bears responsibility for a human rights violation. The *McCann* case is an illustrative example. The ECtHR considered that the individual SAS soldiers who intentionally shot and killed three IRA members had good reason to (erroneously) believe that the killings were necessary to prevent the victims from triggering a fatal car bomb.[331] However, the court still considered the United Kingdom responsible for a human rights violation due to organizational failures. Firstly, the U.K. authorities could have arrested the IRA members when they crossed the border into Gibraltar, which made the subsequent use of lethal force unnecessary. Second, the situational briefing, based on which the SAS soldiers at the scene were led to believe that they needed to shoot to kill to prevent the triggering of the car bomb, was based on a series of erroneous assumptions that made insufficient allowances for alternative explanations.[332]

328. See this Fourth Chapter: C.V.3.b (pp. 183–189).

329. U.N. Basic Principles on the Use of Force and Firearms, *supra* note 25, Principle 3.

330. Relevant duties have therefore also been summarized under a "requirement of precaution" (see, e.g., Melzer, *supra* note 22, p. 101). However, it should be emphasized that this requirement has a different content from the requirement of precaution existing under international humanitarian law.

331. See McCann et al. v. United Kingdom, *supra* note 9, paras. 196–200.

332. *Id.*, paras. 203–210. Both findings met with the vigorous dissent of nine out of the 19 judges sitting in the Grand Chamber. See *id.*, Joint Dissenting Opinion of Judges Ryssdal et al.

Organizational failures seized upon by international human rights bodies generally center on operational planning, command and control, the selection and training of personnel, and the provision of adequate equipment. Shortcomings in any of these areas may give rise to human rights violations if they create a situation where more defensive force has to be used than would otherwise be necessary. Thus, a causal connection between the organizational failure and the use of force must be shown.

1. Planning, Command and Control of Operations

Law enforcement operations have to be planned, commanded and controlled so as to minimize the use of force, including force in self-defense.[333] International human rights bodies generally hold states to a stricter standard where there was time to plan the operation.[334] In *Finca "La Exacta,"* the Inter-American Commission thus found a violation not only because the police on the scene used excessive force to subdue peasant workers who were occupying a farm and resisting their eviction; it also found that these violations were predetermined by the operational plan, based on which the police acted. The plan vilified the peasants as an "enemy force" and "subversive groups" and made exaggerated and unsubstantiated assertions about the type of weaponry possessed by them. It also foresaw the involvement of heavily armed police and failed to emphasize requirements to minimize force, especially vis-à-vis children at the scene. The Commission established causality in finding that "the type of force to be used [according to the plan], together with the failure to clearly indicate to the police units that they should limit the use of the force applied, made it inevitable that excessive force would be used."[335]

In *Zambrano Vélez*, the Inter-American Court criticized that the Ecuadorian military's large-scale crackdown on crime, during which the victims were executed in purported self-defense, had such a broad and vague scope ("to arrest criminals, drug dealers and terrorists") that it was practically impossible to carry out an appropriate control and verification of the legality of the use of force.[336]

In *Trevalec*, Belgian police allowed a journalist to be embedded within a police anti-gang unit. During a nighttime operation to arrest two armed and dangerous criminals, police officers mistook the journalist for an armed gang member

333. Kälin & Künzli, *supra* note 58, p. 277; Ashworth, *supra* note 17, p. 40; Gollwitzer, *supra* note 8, p. 163 [MRK Art. 2, para. 17]; Arzt, *supra* note 55, p. 234; Crawshaw/Cullen/Williamson, *supra* note 58, pp. 132–134; Ramsden, *supra* note 55, p. 400. See also African Commission on Human and Peoples' Rights, General Comment on the Right to Life, *supra* note 33, para. 27; Joint U.N. special rapporteurs report on assembly management, *supra* note 95, para. 65.

334. See also Paul Tavernier, Le recours à la force par la pólice, in: Christian Tomuschat, Evelyne Lagrange & Stefan Oeter (eds.), The Right to Life, Brill: Leiden (2010), 41–64, at p. 51.

335. Finca "La Exacta" v. Guatemala [IACommHR], *supra* note 2, paras. 57–65 (cited passage in para. 65).

336. Zambrano Vélez et al. v. Ecuador, *supra* note 29, para. 94.

who was about to fire at them and shot him twice. The ECtHR found a violation even though the journalist had received a detailed pre-deployment briefing with warnings and had been provided with a bulletproof vest, because the Belgian police had failed to inform all of the officers of the anti-gang unit before the operation that the journalist would be participating.[337]

More leeway for organizational errors is allowed where the state is suddenly confronted with a crisis situation that requires quick decisions without much time to plan and deliberate. To the extent possible, however, the police must still anticipate such scenarios and put in place command and control arrangements that effectively guide and oversee the use of force and minimize the risks for officers, suspects and innocent bystanders.

In *Makaratzis*, the ECtHR acknowledged that the police shot and injured the victim during an unplanned counterterrorism operation where the police were called upon to react without prior preparation.[338] However, it still found a violation due to the lack of an overall control of the operation, the absence of a clear chain of command, and the lack of clear guidance on the use of force. Under these conditions, the court considered it "unavoidable that the police officers who chased and eventually arrested the applicant should have enjoyed a greater autonomy of action and have been left with more opportunities to take unconsidered initiatives."[339]

In contrast, the ECtHR noted with approval in its assessment of the *Bubbins* siege that the operation to contain an armed man threatening police with a gun was at all times under the control of senior officers and that the deployment of armed officers was reviewed and approved by tactical firearms advisers summoned to the scene. Given the sudden onset of the crisis, the court did not fault the operational command and control center for failing to appropriately assess and pass on information based on which the officers on the scene may have concluded that the suspect was not actually a dangerous armed burglar but the tenant of the flat, who was drunk and only threatened police with a replica gun. In this regard, the court appreciated that the incident was "fraught with risk . . . and operational decisions had to be made as the situation evolved and more information became available."[340]

2. Training and Selection of Personnel

Unnecessary or disproportionate use of force may also result from inadequate selection and training of personnel. The U.N. Basic Principles on the Use of Force and Firearms sum up the relevant requirements as follows:

> Governments and law enforcement agencies shall ensure that all law enforcement officials are selected by proper screening procedures, have appropriate

337. Trevalec v. Belgium, *supra* note 16, paras. 80–87.

338. Makaratzis v. Greece, *supra* note 15, para. 69.

339. *Id.*, para 70.

340. Bubbins v. United Kingdom, *supra* note 9, paras. 143–149.

> moral, psychological and physical qualities for the effective exercise of their functions and receive continuous and thorough professional training. Their continued fitness to perform these functions should be subject to periodic review.
>
> Governments and law enforcement agencies shall ensure that all law enforcement officials are provided with training and are tested in accordance with appropriate proficiency standards in the use of force. Those law enforcement officials who are required to carry firearms should be authorized to do so only upon completion of special training in their use.[341]

Firearms training in this respect requires not only that officers know how to aim and shoot accurately, but that their training includes simulations of actual shooting situations and conditions to enhance the officers' judgment when using force, including in self-defense.[342] Moreover, officers must be trained in techniques to de-escalate potentially dangerous situations so as to avoid having to resort to defensive force.[343]

In selecting personnel for particular operations, states enjoy a considerable margin of discretion as long as the selection is overall reasonable and experienced senior officers are deployed at the command and control level.[344]

Regarding the *Andronicou and Constantinou* hostage-taking, the European Commission on Human Rights took the view that recourse to a police special forces unit was inappropriate because the hostage-situation was essentially a domestic quarrel, and involving the special forces inevitably led to a use of force which was not absolutely necessary in the circumstances.[345] The ECtHR rejected this view and considered it natural that the Cypriot authorities reverted to highly professionally trained police special forces to resolve a hostage situation. Furthermore, the court took no issue with the fact that the officers of the

341. U.N. Basic Principles on the Use of Force and Firearms, *supra* note 25, Principles 18 & 19. See also Nadege Dorzema v. Dominican Republic, *supra* note 100, para. 81; Montero-Aranguren et al. (Detention Center of Catia) v. Venezuela [IACtHR], *supra* note 29, para. 78; Zambrano Vélez et al. v. Ecuador [IACtHR], *supra* note 29, para. 87; Nachova et al. v. Bulgaria [ECtHR Grand Chamber], *supra* note 66, para. 97; Giuliani and Gaggio v. Italy [ECtHR Grand Chamber], *supra* note 65, para. 250; African Commission on Human and Peoples' Rights, General Comment on the Right to Life, *supra* note 33, para. 27.

342. International Association of Police Chiefs, *supra* note 193, IV.D; Casey-Maslen, *supra* note 6, pp. 24–25; Sanctis, *supra* note 122, p. 34.

343. Inter-American Commission on Human Rights, *supra* note 142, para. 117; Joint U.N. special rapporteurs report on assembly management, *supra* note 95, para. 67(b); Kremnitzer, *supra* note 137, pp. 202–203; Nsereko, *supra* note 21, p. 263; Amnesty International, Use of Force Guidelines, *supra* note 3, p. 35. See also this Fourth Chapter: C.III.2 (pp. 150–155).

344. On the latter, see Bubbins v. United Kingdom, *supra* note 9, para. 143, Huohvanainen v. Finland, *supra* note 14, para.107.

345. Andronicou and Constantinou v. Cyprus, *supra* note 9, para. 170.

special forces unit were trained to shoot to kill, since they were issued with clear instructions as to when to use their weapons in the particular situation.[346]

In *Giuliani and Gaggio*, a minority of seven judges found an organizational failure since the officer who shot and killed the demonstrator at the G-8 Summit in Genoa, like many other law enforcement agents deployed to police the Summit, was a very young man serving his military conscription with the *Carabinieri* gendarmerie. These new recruits had not received any specific training concerning public order operations or how to act in the event of disturbances during demonstrations.[347] However, the majority in the Grand Chamber stressed that the government had to deploy a total of 18,000 officers, all of whom received at least some ad hoc training on maintaining order during mass gatherings. Requiring every single officer deployed at such a large event to have lengthy experience and/or to have been trained over several months or years, the court held, would impose a disproportionate and unrealistic obligation on the state.[348]

3. Adequate Equipment

States have an obligation to provide their police with the weaponry and equipment they need to carry out their functions with the minimum of force necessary.[349] In particular, police must be equipped with less lethal means of force such as truncheons or tear gas. The U.N. Basic Principles on the Use of Force and Firearms also emphasize the need to equip police with protective "self-defensive equipment such as shields, helmets, bullet-proof vests and bullet-proof means of transportation, in order to decrease the need to use weapons of any kind."[350] Similarly, the United Nations Department of Peacekeeping Operations prescribes that U.N. Formed Police Units, which are deployed in peacekeeping missions and authorized to use force in anti-riot and other law enforcement operations, must be equipped with adequate protective equipment (full body armor, helmets, and shields) and a range of weapons, including less lethal weapons, in order to be able to escalate the level of force gradually.[351]

346. *Id.*, para 185.

347. Giuliani and Gaggio v. Italy, *supra* note 65, Joint Partly Dissenting Opinion of Judges Rozakis, Tulkens Zupancic, Gyulumyan, Ziemele, Kalaydjieva and Karakas, para. 8.

348. *Id.*, para. 255.

349. U.N. Basic Principles on the Use of Force and Firearms, *supra* note 25, Principle 2; U.N. Special Rapporteur on extrajudicial, summary or arbitrary executions, Christof Heyns 2014 Annual Report, *supra* note 84, para. 62; Joint U.N. special rapporteurs report on assembly management, *supra* note 95, paras. 53-55; Landaeta Mejias v. Venezuela [IACtHR], *supra* note 29, para. 126; Inter-American Commission on Human Rights, *supra* note 142, para. 115; African Commission on Human and Peoples' Rights, General Comment on the Right to Life, *supra* note 33, paras. 27 & 30.

350. U.N. Basic Principles on the Use of Force and Firearms, *supra* note 25, Principle 2.

351. United Nations Department of Peacekeeping Operations, *supra* note 280, para. 44.

If state agents have to defend themselves with lethal force because the state failed to provide them with less lethal weapons or protective equipment, such force is not absolutely necessary and hence unlawful. However, the need for such equipment must be foreseeable and a causal link must be established between the lack of adequate equipment and the use of lethal force.

In *Mouvement Burkinabé*, the African Commission found a violation, because police lacked the less lethal equipment to disperse an unlawful demonstration and instead shot two demonstrators dead.[352] In *Gülec*, the ECtHR held that gendarmes unnecessarily had to use a tank-mounted machine gun because they were not provided with truncheons, riot shields, water cannon, rubber bullets, or tear gas even though it was foreseeable that they would encounter violent demonstrators.[353]

In *Giuliani and Gaggio*, a minority of judges in the ECtHR's Grand Chamber considered that a lethal self-defense situation developed at the G-8 Summit in Genoa because the gendarmes deployed were not provided with rubber-bullet guns and their vehicles were not fitted with protective grilles on the rear and side windows, even though it was foreseeable that they might come under attack.[354] However, the majority found that the use of non-armored jeeps for the particular purpose of transporting injured officers from the scene was reasonable. The majority also ruled that there was no causal connection between the killing of the demonstrator and the general failure to provide the gendarmes with rubber-bullet guns, since such guns would have been used only to disperse demonstrations, not in the sudden and violent attack sustained by the gendarmes in question.[355]

Even where a situation warrants the use of lethal force, the weaponry provided still has to be calibrated to fit the threat. In *Andronicou and Constantinou*, the ECtHR considered it appropriate that the special police team assigned to overpower the hostage-taker and rescue his girlfriend was equipped with machine guns. It noted that the guns bore the advantage of being fitted with flashlights that could illuminate the dark room where the hostage-taker and his victim were located and that they were to be used subject to the same instructions as standard-issue police pistols.[356]

In *Ugarte and Durand* and *Neira Alegria*, imprisoned members of the *Sendero Luminoso* armed group in Peru staged a riot, during which they took several wardens hostage and used the wardens' guns to kill security forces that entered

352. Mouvement Burkinabé des Droits de l'Homme et des Peuples v. Burkina Faso, *supra* note 103, para. 43.

353. Gülec v. Turkey, *supra* note 77, para. 71.

354. Giuliani and Gaggio v. Italy, *supra* note 65, Joint Partly Dissenting Opinion of Judges Rozakis, Tulkens Zupancic, Gyulumyan, Ziemele, Kalaydjieva and Karakas, paras. 5–6 & 11.

355. *Id.*, paras. 216 & 258.

356. Andronicou and Constantinou v. Cyprus, *supra* note 9, para. 185.

to crush the riot. Called in to handle the situation, the Peruvian Navy placed plastic explosives on the walls of the building where the rioting prisoners were held, so that the entire building collapsed on the prisoners. Despite recognizing the lethal threat posed by the prisoners, the Inter-American Court considered that the use of explosives constituted a violation of the right to life.[357]

V. Proportionality of defensive action

State agents may only use defensive force that is not out of proportion. The proportionality requirement is established by the U.N. Basic Principles on the Use of Force and Firearms, the Code of Conduct for Law Enforcement Officials. and the jurisprudence of the United Nations, African, and Inter-American human rights bodies.[358] Article 2(2) of the ECHR demands that to be justifiable, lethal force must be "absolutely necessary," but lacks an explicit reference to proportionality.[359] However, the ECtHR has firmly established that the proportionality requirement is also inherent to the right to life under the ECHR.[360] This interpretation also gives full meaning to the requirement of self-defense having to be "*absolutely* necessary" under Article 2(2) of the ECHR, as it helps explain the otherwise tautological nature of the term (either something is necessary or it is not).

In the proportionality analysis, various elements have to be factored in:

- the intensity and extent of the harm inflicted versus that defended against;
- the probability of harm if the defensive measure is taken or not taken;

357. Durand and Ugarte, Judgment of 16 August 2000, IACtHR Ser. C No. 68, paras. 59, 71–72; Neira Alegria v. Peru [IACtHR], *supra* note 2, paras. 61 & 74.

358. U.N. Basic Principles on the Use of Force and Firearms, *supra* note 25, Principle 5; U.N. Code of Conduct for Law Enforcement Officials, *supra* note 25, art. 3(b); Human Rights Committee, Concluding Observations on Liechtenstein, *supra* note 122, para. 10; U.N. Special Rapporteur on extrajudicial, summary or arbitrary executions, Christof Heyns, 2014 Annual Report, *supra* note 84, paras. 65–73; Prevention of human rights violations committed with small arms and light weapons: Final report submitted by Barbara Frey, Special Rapporteur in accordance with Sub-Commission resolution 2002/25, U.N. Doc. A/HRC/Sub.1/58/27 (2006), para. 27; Zambrano Vélez et al. v. Ecuador [IACtHR], *supra* note 29, para. 108; Neira Alegria v. Peru, *supra* note 2, para. 72; Montero-Aranguren et al. (Detention Center of Catia) v. Venezuela, *supra* note 29, para. 74; Inter-American Commission on Human Rights, *supra* note 29, paras. 87 & 92; Corumbiara Massacre v. Brazil [IACommHR], *supra* note 2, para. 180, Finca "La Exacta" v. Guatemala [IACommHR], *supra* note 2, paras. 40, 43 & 56; Kazingachire et al. v. Zimbabwe [ACommHPR], *supra* note 34, paras. 111, 113 & 115–116. See also Kälin & Künzli, *supra* note 58, p. 277; Ramsden, *supra* note 55, p. 397; Doswald-Beck, *supra* note 59, p. 887.

359. Frank Zieschang, Tödliche Notwehr zur Verteidigung von Sachen und Art. 2 IIa EMRK, Goltdammer's Archiv für Strafrecht (GA) 2006, 415–419, at p. 418 therefore concludes that a justification under Art. 2(2) of the ECHR requires only necessity but not proportionality.

360. Giuliani and Gaggio v. Italy, *supra* note 65, para. 176; Ogur v. Turkey, *supra* note 12, para. 78; Huohvanainen v. Finland, *supra* note 14, para. 98; Rodley/Pollard, *supra* note 22, p. 257;

- the number of victims protected versus the number of aggressors harmed; and
- the culpability or non-culpability of the aggressor.[361]

Proportionality becomes relevant only where it is established that the amount of force used was necessary, i.e., the least harmful means to safely counter the unlawful attack. It essentially demands that law enforcement officers make a sacrifice for the benefit of the aggressor and not use the most effective measure of force necessitated by the situation even if that means that the officers incur some harm or a greater risk of serious harm. With this consideration in mind, the proportionality analysis cannot require a strict balancing, where the harm prevented has to outweigh that inflicted on the aggressor. All that is required is that the force used is not disproportionate in relation to its defensive objective.[362]

1. Lethal Force to Defend against Attack Threatening Death or Serious Injury

Proportionality becomes most relevant with regard to the most extreme use of force, namely lethal force. Under international human rights law, state agents may use firearms and potentially lethal force only to protect themselves and others against unlawful attacks that are likely to result in death or serious injury. Jurisprudence indicated that an even higher proportionality threshold applies for the use of deliberately lethal force, which may be used only to protect life from imminent threat. Police officers must assess the appropriate level of force

Ashworth, *supra* note 17, p. 41; van Dijk et al., *supra* note 12, p. 395; Kretzmer, *supra* note 22, p. 178.

Below the threshold of a violation of the right to life, disproportionate use of force may still amount to ill-treatment under art. 3 ECHR. See Caloc v. France, *supra* note 19, para. 101; Rivas v. France, *supra* note 19, para. 40.

361. Cf. Landaeta Mejias v. Venezuela [IACommHR], *supra* note 29, para. 136; Crawshaw/Cullen/Williamson, *supra* note 58, p. 156; van Dijk et al, *supra* note 12, p. 396. On the relevance of culpability, see already this Fourth Chapter: C.I.4 (pp. 129–131).

362. See also U.N. Code of Conduct for Law Enforcement Officials, *supra* note 25, Art. 3(b); Melzer, *supra* note 22, p. 232. For International Criminal Law, see Ambos, *supra* note 202, p. 1015; Reinhard Merkel, Gründe für den Ausschluss der Strafbarkeit im Völkerrecht, Zeitschrift für die gesamte Strafrechtswissenschaft (2002), 437–454, at p. 445. But cf. Fernandez/Pacreau, *supra* note 202, p. 918; Thomas Weigend, Notwehr im Völkerstrafrecht, in: Ulrich Sieber et al. (eds.), Strafrecht und Wirtschaftsstrafrecht – Dogmatik, Rechtsvergleich, Rechtstatsachen: Festschrift für Klaus Tiedemann zum 70. Geburtstag (2008), 1439–1451, at p. 1449; Guilfoyle, *supra* note 157, p. 371.

The "no disproportionality" approach also accords with the standards in most national orders. See Sangero, *supra* note 173, pp. 168 & 172–173; Walter Perron, Rechtsvergleichende Betrachtungen zur Notwehr, in: Jörg Arnold et al. (eds.), Menschengerechtes Strafrecht: Festschrift für Albin Eser zum 70. Geburtstag, C.H. Beck: München (2005), 1019–1039, at p. 1036; Jean Pradel, Droit Pénal Comparé, Dalloz: Paris (3rd ed., 2008), p. 139, para. 102.

to employ, based on an individualized case-by-case assessment and not based on abstract categories that classify certain groups of people—e.g., terrorism suspects—as inherent threats to life.

a) European Convention on Human Rights

Article 2(2)(a) of the ECHR restricts the use of both deliberately lethal force and potentially lethal force to defense against "unlawful *violence*," not just unlawful killings.[363] Law enforcement agents may therefore use firearms against attacks that threaten serious injury, including in defense against rape or kidnapping.[364]

However, less serious violence may not be countered with lethal force, since the latter must be strictly proportional to the aim pursued, according to the ECtHR.[365] An armored riot police officer shooting a demonstrator who beats him with a stick uses disproportional force and hence commits a human rights violation.[366] In such situations, officers must to resort to less lethal means to defend themselves even if that is less effective than the use of firearms.

More exacting proportionality standards apply when police officers shoot to kill (deliberately lethal force). The ECtHR has not formulated an explicit doctrine on the matter. However, in the instances where it found such deliberately lethal force to be proportional, it has consistently stressed the existence of a threat to life. In *McCann*, soldiers used intentionally lethal force to prevent IRA members "from detonating a bomb and causing serious loss of life."[367] In *Bubbins*, it found that the police officer who shot a man training a gun on him acted in response "to a real and immediate risk to his life and the lives of his colleagues."[368] In *Andronicou*, the court found that police were entitled to intentionally kill the hostage-taker to eliminate any risks to the hostage's life or to their own lives.[369] Conversely, in *Gül*, where police intentionally or at least recklessly killed the suspect, the court found that the force used was grossly disproportionate, stressing

363. See this Fourth Chapter: A.I.1 (p. 94).

364. Paul Bockelmann, Menschenrechtskonvention und Notwehrrecht, in: Paul Bockelmann, Arthur Kaufmann & Ulrich Klug (eds.), Festschrift für Karl Engisch zum 70. Geburtstag, Vittorio Kostermann: Frankfurt am Main (1969), 456–467, at p. 459; Helmut Frister, Zur Einschränkung des Notwehrrechts durch Art. 2 der Europäischen Menschenrechtskonvention, Goltdammer's Archiv für Strafrecht 1985, 553–565, at p. 563; Esser, *supra* note 8, p. 120 [Art 2, para 48]; Paeffgen, *supra* note 8, p. 387 [Art. 2, para 59]; Nikolaos Bitzilekis, Die neue Tendenz zur Einschränkung des Notwehrrechts, Duncker & Humblot: Berlin (1984), p. 133.

365. Cf. McCann et al. v. United Kingdom, *supra* note 9, para. 149; Bubbins v. United Kingdom, *supra* note 9, para. 135; Ogur v. Turkey, *supra* note 12, para. 78.

366. See X v. Belgium [ECommHR], Appl. No. 2758/66, Decision of 21 May 1969.

367. McCann et al. v. United Kingdom, *supra* note 9, para. 200.

368. Bubbins v. United Kingdom, *supra* note 9, para. 140.

369. Andronicou and Constantinou v. Cyprus, *supra* note 9, para. 192.

that there was no risk to the police officers' lives.[370] It therefore emerges from the case law that law enforcement agents may use deliberately lethal force under Article 2(2)(a) of the ECHR only to defend against serious threats to life.[371]

b) ICCPR, American Convention, and African Convention

The U.N. Basic Principles on the Use of Force and Firearms provide the yardstick for the interpretation of what constitutes arbitrary deprivation of life under Article 6 of the ICCPR and the similar provisions found in Article 4 of the ACHR and Article 4 of the ACHPR. Principle 9 sets out essentially the same standard that also emerges from the jurisprudence of the ECtHR. The use of firearms (i.e., potentially lethal force) is allowed "in self-defense or defense of others against the imminent threat of death or serious injury"; the intentional lethal use of firearms is permitted only "in order to protect life." This bifurcated standard on the use of lethal force has met with the general approval of universal and regional human rights mechanisms.[372]

Occasionally, it is argued that any use of firearms or other potentially lethal force is restricted to situations where it is necessary to protect life. Notably, the U.N. Special Rapporteur on the Use of Small Arms has argued that small arms and light weapons may be used "defensively only in the most extreme circumstances, expressly, where the right to life is already threatened or unjustifiably impinged" because "of the lethal nature of such weapons and the jus cogens human rights obligations imposed upon all states and individuals to respect the right to life."[373] However, this view is unreasonably restrictive because the degree of lethal risk varies greatly, depending on where the shooter aims and hits. It

370. Gül v. Turkey, *supra* note 189, para. 82.

371. See also Velu/Ergec, *supra* note 8, para. 232; Zieschang, *supra* note 359, p. 418.

372. Special Rapporteur on extrajudicial, summary or arbitrary executions, Christof Heyns, 2014 Annual Report, *supra* note 84, para. 70; U.N. Special Rapporteur on extrajudicial,summary or arbitrary executions Philip Alston, Targeted Killing Studys, *supra* note 86, para. 32; Joint U.N. special rapporteurs report on assembly management, *supra* note 95, para. 59; Human Rights Committee, Concluding Observations on Indonesia, U.N. Doc. CCPR/C/IDN/CO/1 (2013), para. 16; *id.*, Concluding Observations on Uzbekistan, U.N. Doc. CCPR/C/UZB/CO/3 (2010), para. 8; *id.*, Concluding Observations on Belize CCPR/C/BLZ/CO/1 (2013), para. 19; Office of the United Nations High Commissioner for Human Rights, Human rights standards and practice for the police, OHCHR: Geneva (2004), p. 24; Montero-Aranguren et al. (Detention Center of Catia) v. Venezuela [IACtHR], *supra* note 29, para. 69; Kazingachire et al. v. Zimbabwe [ACommHPR], *supra* note 34, paras. 114–120; African Commission on Human and Peoples' Rights, General Comment on the Right to Life, *supra* note 33, para. 13; Inter-American Commission on Human Rights, *supra* note 29, para. 87 (n.250). See also S v Makwanyane [Constitutional Court South Africa], 1995 (3) SA 391 (CC), para. 138; First Turkel Commission Report, *supra* note 6, para. 189; Heller, *supra* note 219, p. 113; Melzer, *supra* note 22, pp. 233 & 235; Ramsden, *supra* note 55, p. 396.

373. U.N. Special Rapporteur on Small Arms, Barbara Frey, Final Report, *supra* note 358, para. 27. See also Joseph, *supra* note 58, p. 20; Doswald-Beck, *supra* note 75, p. 40.

would also demand too much of a sacrifice from police officers if they could not even have recourse to their firearms to incapacitate an aggressor with a shot in the leg where absolutely necessary to ward off an attack threatening serious injury but not death, such as an attack by a physically superior assailant with a wooden club.

The question is rather whether the "protect life" standard set out in the U.N. Basic Principles on the Use of Force and Firearms is not too demanding and whether deliberately lethal force should not also be considered proportional if it serves to fend off serious injuries. On its face, it would seem that Principle 9 would allow police snipers to shoot and kill hostage-takers only once there is an immediate danger that they may start executing the hostages. Yet the sniper would have to stand by if the hostage-takers "merely" proceeded to chop off the hostages' fingers or ears in order to lend weight to their demands.[374] Similarly, a police officer who is being raped would have to endure the ordeal if the only means of defense is to draw a pistol and shoot the rapist dead at close range. However, this would be too narrow a reading of Principle 9, because in both situations police officers not only are entitled to take into account the present harm being inflicted, but may also consider whether there are good reasons to fear an imminent deadly outcome. The police sniper may therefore conclude that the hostage-taker who maims his victims might well proceed to murder those who resist. The police officer who is being raped has reason to fear being murdered after the rape or contracting HIV. The bifurcated proportionality standard for potentially and deliberately lethal force will therefore usually not make much of a practical difference, while signaling that the state's deliberate taking of life is qualitatively in a category of its own and must be the rare exception. As a matter of principle, it nevertheless is still unsatisfactory that the Basic Principles restrain a police officer from shooting to kill if that is the last resort to protect against a "mere" serious injury. Among human rights mechanisms and in the academic literature, one therefore finds increasing recognition that deliberately lethal force may also be proportional to protect against serious injury.[375]

2. No Lethal Force Solely to Protect Property

In line with the principles outlined above, police may use firearms to defend themselves or others against armed and violent robbers where absolutely necessary and proportionate.[376] In such cases, the defensive force is justified to counter the threat against the human person posed by the robber, even if it incidentally

374. Cf. Karl Doehring, Zum, "Recht auf Leben" aus nationaler und internationaler Sicht, in: Rudolf Bernhardt (ed.), Völkerrecht als Rechtsordnung, internationale Gerichtsbarkeit, Menschenrechte: Festschrift für Hermann Mosler, Springer: Berlin (1983), 145–157, at p. 152.

375. For this view U.N. Human Rights Committee, *supra* note 83, para. 18; Barrios Family v. Venezuela [IACtHR], *supra* note 29, para. 50 (contrary to the court's jurisprudence in other cases), Kremnitzer, *supra* note 137, p. 203; Ashworth, *supra* note 17, p. 42; Boyle, *supra* note 119, p. 241.

376. Ashworth, *supra* note 17, p. 42; Doehring, *supra* note 374, p. 151, Bockelmann, *supra* note 364, pp. 458–459; Diehm, *supra* note 12, p. 355.

also protects the property. As noted above, police may also use potentially lethal force (but not deliberately lethal force) to prevent violent robbers from escaping.[377] In addition, police may use firearms even against thieves who violently resist arrest in such a way that their resistance poses a threat of death or serious injury.[378]

What remains hotly contested is whether lethal force, whether deliberately or at least potentially lethal, may be used solely to defend property against an attack that does not involve violence. Put simply, the question is whether police may shoot at fleeing thieves in order to recover their loot.

a) European Convention on Human Rights

The ECtHR has not yet explicitly pronounced itself on the question whether law enforcement agents may use lethal force solely to defend property. In the academic literature the question remains in dispute. Some scholars maintain that police could use potentially lethal force that does not aim to kill in order to protect particularly valuable property, but must not employ deliberately lethal force.[379] In accordance with this view, the police could shoot a thief of precious jewelry in the legs if that was the only way to prevent the thief's escape. Other scholars go further and would even allow the police to defend very valuable property by shooting with *dolus eventualis*, that is, in acceptance of a high probability that the thief may be killed.[380] In the older literature, one even finds the view that intentional killings aimed at defending property can be legal under the ECHR.[381]

The contrary position, which appears to be the prevailing view today, holds that firearms and other types of lethal force may never be used to protect property, regardless of its value.[382] There are good reasons for this position to the extent that firearms use with a serious potential of killing is used to defend property. First and foremost, there is the text of Article 2(2)(a) of the

377. See this Fourth Chapter: A.III (p. 107).

378. Cf. Cameron & Chetail, *supra* note 243, p. 464. But cf. Bockelmann, *supra* note 364, p. 461, who rejects a right to use firearms against thieves violently resisting arrest with the unpersuasive argument that the initial crime has to establish what force is allowed and that a right to use lethal force cannot be claimed because the thief violently resists his arrest.

379. Krüger, *supra* note 154, p. 1484; Frister, *supra* note 364, p. 561; Paeffgen, *supra* note 8, p. 389 [art. 2, para. 61); Carl-Friedrich von Scherenberg, Die sozialethischen Einschränkungen der Notwehr, Peter Lang: Frankfurt a.M. (2009), p. 105.

380. Roxin, *supra* note 10, pp. 698–699; Zieschang, *supra* note 359, p. 419; Bitzilekis, *supra* note 364, p. 135; Herzog, *supra* note 182, p. 1174 [§ 32, para. 98].

381. Doehring, *supra* note 374, p. 151; Bockelmann, *supra* note 364, pp. 461–467.

382. Velu/Ergec, *supra* note 8, para. 232; Ashworth, *supra* note 17, p. 42; Fiona Leverick, Killing in Self-Defence, Oxford University Press: Oxford (2006), p. 181; Harris et al., *supra* note 67, p. 229 ; Esser, *supra* note 8, pp. 120–121 [Art 2, paras. 48 & 50–51]; Walter Perron, Notwehr, in: Albin Eser et al. (eds.), Schönke/Schröder: Strafgesetzbuch, C.H. Beck: Munich (28th ed., 2010), pp. 647–648 [§ 32, para. 62]; Gollwitzer, *supra* note 8, p. 164 [MRK Art. 2, para. 18], Helmut Satzger, Internationales und Europäisches Strafrecht, Baden Baden: Nomos

ECHR. It clearly speaks against a right to defend property with any type of lethal force, since it only allows "deprivation of life . . . in defense of a *person* against *violence*" (emphasis added). Theft is not violent and it targets property, not persons.[383]

Proponents of a right to defend property with lethal force try to get around the textual argument by asserting, firstly, that defense of a person is not necessarily limited to the person's body, but could also refer to all of the person's legitimate interests, including the person's property.[384] However, this is a rather contrived reading of the text and still cannot explain why theft or similar nonviolent property crimes would amount to violence as would be required by Article 2(2)(a).[385]

Secondly, the contextual argument is made that Article 2(2)(b) of the ECHR allows shooting thieves to arrest them. Therefore, it is argued, Article 2 of the ECHR must also allow shooting to defend property.[386] However, this argument no longer holds water in light of the ECtHR's established position that law enforcement agents may not use firearms to secure the arrest of nonviolent criminals.[387] The comparison with Article 2(2)(b) of the ECHR therefore rather supports a narrow reading of Article 2(2)(a). The ECtHR will unlikely undermine its fundamental value decision in favor of a narrow reading of Article 2(2)(b) by turning around and allowing police to rely on Article 2(2) to shoot nonviolent criminals in order to recover their loot.

A third argument proceeds from the premise that private citizens may shoot to protect their property. Police officers must therefore also be allowed to do so, because they are also private citizens and must therefore have at least the same self-defense rights as any other individual.[388] It is further argued that forbidding police to shoot to protect property may drive citizens into establishing armed

(4th ed., 2010), p. 201 (fn 69); Grabenwarter/Pabel, *supra* note 72, p. 153; George P. Fletcher & Jens David Ohlin, Defending Humanity: When Force is Justified and Why, Oxford University Press: New York (2008), p. 97; Kristian Kühl, Der Einfluss der Menschenrechte und Grundfreiheiten der Europäischen Menschenrechtskonvention auf das deutsche und europäische Strafrecht, in: Heinz Müller-Dietz (ed.), Festschrift für Heike Jung, Nomos: Baden-Baden (2007), 433–443, at p. 440.

383. See also Heinz Koriath, Einschränkung des deutschen Notwehrrechts (§ 32 STGB) durch art 2 II a EMRK?, in: Filippo Ranieri (ed.), Europäisierung der Rechtswissenschaft, Nomos: Baden-Baden (2002), 47–60, at p. 59; Velu/Ergec, *id.*, Diehm, *supra* note 12, p. 377.

384. Doehring, *supra* note 374, p. 151.

385. Esser, *supra* note 8, p. 121 [art. 2, para. 51]; Paeffgen, *supra* note 8, p. 390 [Art. 2, para. 61], Diehm, *supra* note 12, p. 355; von Scherenberg, *supra* note 379, p. 101; Koriath, *supra* note 383, p. 59.

386. Paeffgen, *supra* note 8, p. p. 390 [Art 2, para. 62); Doehring, *supra* note 374, p. 151; Herzog, *supra* note 182, p. 1174 [§ 32, para. 97].

387. See references *supra* note 66.

388. Bockelmann, *supra* note 364, pp. 466–467; Krüger, *supra* note 154, p. 1484.

vigilante organizations that will use the type of force denied to police.[389] The entire line of argument is unpersuasive. The premise is flawed because the state's obligation to protect human rights also requires the state to impose limits on self-defense by private persons.[390] In any case, police officers derive their authority and the means to use lethal force—their guns—from their official position and can therefore be held to stricter standards than private persons.

Fourthly, some proponents of a right to defend property with potentially lethal force stress that Article 2(1) of the ECHR only refers to *intentional* deprivation of life. Therefore, the entire article, including the exceptions in Article 2(2) should limit only intentional lethal force that aims to kill.[391] A variation of that argument acknowledges that Article 2(2) of the ECHR might also refer to non-intentional killings, but argues that justifications for such non-intentional killings can also be found outside the list of justifications in Article 2(2).[392] Neither argument can be reconciled with the jurisprudence of the ECtHR according to which Article 2(2) "does not primarily define instances where it is permitted intentionally to kill an individual, but describes the situations where it is permitted to 'use force' which may result, as an unintended outcome, in the deprivation of life."[393] The list of justifications in Article 2(2) thus covers killings resulting from deliberately lethal and also from potentially lethal force. It has also long been established that the list is exhaustive[394]—hence the court's observation that Article 2(2) of the ECHR describes "the situations" (rather than "situations" or "some situations") where deliberately or potentially lethal force may be used.

Occasionally, hypothetical examples are produced to demonstrate why a general prohibition of lethal force to defend property must be evidently wrong. Some of these examples seem rather removed from reality, such as that of a blackmailer who must be shot to prevent him from making good on his threat to blow up a TV tower in such a way that not a single person's life would be put at risk.[395] Other examples center on the use of lethal force to defend irreplaceable cultural objects.[396] This raises the question why such objects were not better

389. Bockelmann, *id.*, p. 466.

390. See Sixth Chapter: C (pp. 242–244).

391. Roxin, *supra* note 10, pp. 698–699; Krüger, *supra* note 154, p. 1484; Frister, *supra* note 364, p. 561; Herzog, *supra* note 182, p. 1174 [§ 32, para. 97].

392. Zieschang, *supra* note 359 pp. 418–419.

393. Giuliani and Gaggio v. Italy, *supra* note 65, para. 175; McCann et al. v. United Kingdom, *supra* note 9, para. 148.

394. See the European Commission on Human Rights' 1984 decision in Stewart v. United Kingdom, *supra* note 11, para. 13. See also Harris et al., *supra* note 67, p. 227; Velu/Ergec, *supra* note 8, para. 231; Arzt, *supra* note 55, p. 231; Otto, *supra* note 12, p. 165; Doehring, *supra* note 374, p. 146.

395. Paeffgen, *supra* note 8, pp. 390 & 392 [Art 2, para 62].

396. *Id.*, p. 392 [Art. 2, para. 62]; Koriath, *supra* note 383, p. 47.

protected in the first place and how shooting in such situations would not pose an equally grave risk for the integrity of the object. Such fictitious examples only distract attention from the practically relevant cases, namely whether fleeing cat-burglars and other nonviolent criminals may be shot to recover their loot. Once one moves away from a general prohibition to shoot them, the question arises: how much must the loot be worth to be worth forfeiting a life? However, the European Convention does not put a price tag on human life. Instead, its text embodies the explicit value decision to allow self-defense with lethal means only to defend a person against unlawful violence.

b) ICCPR, American Convention, and African Convention

The question arises: is the European Convention's prohibition on using lethal force to defend property reflective of general international human rights law, or does it amount to a regional peculiarity? With regard to the ICCPR, the position has been taken that Article 6 prohibits only the arbitrary deprivation of life, which does not necessarily imply that police killings to defend property are generally illegal.[397] The same position could also be taken with regard to the similarly worded prohibition of arbitrary deprivation of life under Article 4 of the ACHR and Article 4 of the ACHPR.

However, the prevailing view, endorsed by the relevant universal and regional human rights bodies, considers that the U.N. Basic Principles on the Use of Force and Firearms provide an authoritative interpretation of the right to life under the ICCPR, ACHR, and ACHPR.[398] Basic Principle 9 allows the use of firearms against persons only "in self-defense or defense of others against the imminent threat of death or serious injury, to prevent the perpetration of a particularly serious crime involving grave threat to life, to arrest a person presenting such a danger and resisting their authority, or to prevent his or her escape." Law enforcement agents may therefore not use firearms or other potentially lethal force for the sole purpose of protecting property.[399]

One may ask whether this position was changed by subsequent practice, namely the adoption of the Rome Statute, to which the great majority of states are now party. According to Article 31(1)(c) of the Rome Statute, criminal responsibility for war crimes may be excluded if a person defends "property which is essential for the survival of the person or another person or property which is essential for accomplishing a military mission."

397. Doehring, *supra* note 374, p. 154.

398. See the references *supra* note 372.

399. U.N. Special Rapporteur on extrajudicial, summary or arbitrary executions, Christof Heyns, 2011 Annual Report, *supra* note 22, para. 61; *id.*, 2014 Annual Report, *supra* note 84, para. 72; U.N. Human Rights Committee, *supra* note 83, para. 18; ACommHPR Working Group on on Death Penalty and Extra-Judicial, Summary or Arbitrary Killings in Africa, *supra* note 106, para. 51 (criticizing Kenya for allowing police to use lethal force in defense of property); Kremnitzer, *supra* note 137, p. 202; Casey-Maslen, *supra* note 6, p. 9.

This aspect of the Rome Statute reflects a drafting compromise between the demands of the United States and Israel, which proposed to include an even wider defense of property provision in the Rome Statute, and many other states that were highly critical of any proposal to allow defense of property as a ground for excluding criminal responsibility.[400]

The "property essential for survival" alternative falls in line with the exceptions in the U.N. Basic Principles on the Use of Force and Firearms, since it implies that force is used to defend against the risk of death. However, the reference to property "essential for accomplishing a military mission" seems to allow the use of lethal force to protect property for reasons unrelated to protecting life and physical security. Essentially, it introduces a new and vague military necessity defense into international criminal law, which unravels the careful balance between military necessity and humanity established through international humanitarian law.[401]

At first glance, Article 31(1)(c) of the Rome Statute may not appear directly relevant for the interpretation of international human rights law since it only concerns individual responsibility for war crimes. However, the provision can be expected to eventually reshape the obligations of states as well, by changing norms of international humanitarian law.[402] This is not least the case because serious violations of international humanitarian law could no longer be enforced through the punishment of individual war criminals, wherever the defense of property provision applies.[403] Furthermore, the impact would not necessarily be limited to international humanitarian law, but could radiate into international human rights law, because the provision can be expected to find greatest relevance where soldiers use force against civilians in a "law enforcement paradigm," i.e., subject to the same human rights standards that also apply in peacetime.[404] On its face, the text of the provision would appear to allow, for instance, the deliberate killing of opportunistic thieves not affiliated with any of the parties to the conflict who try to steal property that happens to be essential for accomplishing a military mission. Interpreted in this way, Article 31(1)(c) would therefore

400. Ambos, *supra* note 202, p. 1014; Fernandez/Pacreau, *supra* note 202, p. 921; Massimo Scalliotti, Defences before the international criminal court: Substantive grounds for excluding criminal responsibility—Part 1, International Criminal Law Review vol. 1, (2001), 111–172, at p. 169.

401. See Antonio Cassese, The Statute of the International Criminal Court: Some Preliminary Reflections, European Journal ofInternational Law vol. 10 (1999), 144–171, at pp. 154–155; Fernandez/Pacreau, *supra* note 202, p. 922. Cf. Geert-Jan Knoops, Defenses in Contemporary International Criminal Law, Transnational Publishers: Ardsley, New York (2nd ed., 2008), pp. 76–80.

402. Cassese, *id.*, p. 154; Weigend, *supra* note 362, p. 1444; Fernandez/Pacreau, *id.*, p. 922.

403. Cf. Weigend, *id.*, 1448

404. On soldiers acting within the law enforcement paradigm in armed conflict, see Fifth Chapter: A (pp. 218–225).

carve out an exception to the prohibition of killing in defense of property, which could call the entire prohibition into question.

Yet, rather than allowing the tail to wag the dog, the better approach to reconcile the seemingly contradictory normative positions is to interpret the controversial "defense of property" clause in Article 31(1)(c) of the Rome Statute consistent with international human rights standards, as expressly required by Article 21(3) of the Rome Statute. Interpreted in this way, Article 31(1)(c) should only provide a defense for the protection of property essential for accomplishing a mission through the use of less lethal means. Lethal defensive force should remain restricted to cases involving a real risk of death or seriously bodily harm.[405] This human rights–compliant interpretation would also assuage the abovementioned concern that the property "essential for accomplishing a military mission" would unhinge the careful balance between military necessity and humanity struck by international humanitarian law.

3. Strict Proportionality vis-à-vis Innocent Bystanders

In a defense situation involving persons other than the aggressor and defender, any harm or risk of harm that such innocent bystanders incur as the result of the defensive action requires its own proportionality analysis.

a) Endangering innocent bystanders

While defensive force against attackers need only be not disproportionate, a stricter standard applies vis-à-vis innocent bystanders. The risk of harm for the innocent bystanders must be outweighed by the harm the defensive force is expected to prevent. In other words, a true balancing standard is applied that is tantamount to the standard applicable for the justification of necessity.[406]

The ECtHR's *Finogenov* judgment provides an illustrative example. In that case, the court considered that there was an immediate risk that the Chechen hostage-takers in the Moscow theatre would start executing their hostages. This risk was aggravated by the fact that the aggressors were determined and heavily

405. Eser, *supra* note 202, pp. 881–883 [Art. 31, paras. 44 & 47]. Cf. Ambos, *supra* note 202, p. 1014; Tonkin, *supra* note 215, p. 102.

406. A doctrinally clean approach to analysing defense of others and other self-defense situations where innocent bystanders are present should actually assess the situation based on two different legal justifications. The harm caused to the aggressor should be assessed based against the right to self-defense. The risk the defensive situation carries for innocent bystanders is to be assessed against the justification of necessity as recognized, e.g., in Art. 25 of the Articles on State Responsibility (see *supra* note 177; on the difference between self-defense and necessity, see First Chapter: B.I, p. 5). However, in practice, human rights bodies tend to lump both issues together and consider risks for innocent bystanders as part of of the self-defense assessment. In *Garcia Ibarra*, for instance, the Inter-American Court considered that police shooting dead a teenager was not justified by self-defence, even based on the officer's own account that the fatal shot was accidentially fired at the teenager when the officer used his pistol butt to hit another person who supposedly attacked him. See Garcia Ibarra v. Ecuador, Judgment of 17 November 2015, IACtHR (Ser. C) No. 306, paras. 114–115.

armed extremists and that negotiations were unlikely to succeed. Furthermore, the hostages' physical and psychological condition was worsening. In light of these factors, the court considered that "there existed a real, serious and immediate risk of mass human losses and that the authorities had every reason to believe that a forced intervention was the '*lesser evil*' in the circumstances."[407] In other words, the foreseeable harm that the innocent hostages were likely to incur if the state had not acted outweighed the potential harm of storming the theatre in an attempt to rescue the hostages.

As indicated by the *Finogenov* judgment as well, an ex ante standard of assessment must be applied based on what the authorities had "reason to believe" in the situation. Not the actual balance of harms, as determined in hindsight, must be compared, but rather the likely balance of harms as it would have appeared under the circumstances to a reasonable law enforcement agent placed in the situation of the acting officer(s). Three factors must be considered in making that assessment:

- The intensity and extent of harm innocent bystanders may suffer as the result of the envisaged defensive action versus the expected harm for the defender or innocent bystanders resulting from non-action or other defensive action;
- The number of innocent bystanders endangered by the envisaged defensive action versus the number endangered by non-action or other defensive action;
- the probability of the harm risked by defensive action becoming reality versus the probability of such harm in case no action or other defensive action is taken.

The last point is particularly important since it implies that defensive force may still be justified even though in hindsight the intervention caused more harm to innocent bystanders than it actually prevented. The *Andronicou and Constantinou* judgment marks a case in point. In that case, the authorities decided to resolve a hostage situation by force, based on the honest and reasonable belief that the hostage-taker would make good on his threat to kill himself and his hostage. During the rescue operation, however, the security forces ended up shooting dead both hostage-taker and victim—that is, the defensive action caused the very harm it was supposed to prevent. Nevertheless, the ECtHR saw no violation, since under the circumstances prevailing at the time of the decision, the "authorities could reasonably consider . . . that an attempt had to be made to get into the flat, disarm and arrest [the hostage-taker,] and free [the hostage]."[408]

407. Finogenov et al. v. Russia, *supra* note 117, para. 226 {emphasis added).

408. Andronicou and Constantinou v. Cyprus, *supra* note 9, para. 184.

In *Stewart,* demonstrators were throwing dangerous objects at the police, who defended themselves with less lethal plastic baton rounds. An innocent bystander was hit in the head and killed. The European Commission on Human Rights found no violation, since the soldier firing the baton round was aiming at an actual rioter but lost his aim when he was hit in the shoulder by an object.[409] Thus, the Commission took no issue with the outcome of intervention (killing of an innocent bystander) being worse than if no action had been taken (continued throwing of objects at the police), because the probability of the actual outcome was low, whereas it was certain that more dangerous objects would have been thrown if the police had not used baton rounds.

The requirement to assess risks and benefits based on the ex ante perspective, rather than hindsight, also works in the other direction. A high risk of harm for innocent bystanders must also be factored into the proportionality analysis, even if the risk does not materialize. In *Gül,* for instance, the state authorities had fired 50 to 55 bullets at a door in an apartment block, killing the suspect standing behind the door. The ECtHR found a violation, inter alia, because "opening fire with automatic weapons on an unseen target in a residential block *inhabited by innocent civilians, women and children* was . . . grossly disproportionate." It made this finding even though no such innocent bystanders were actually harmed.[410] In *Finca "La Exacta,"* the Inter-American Commission based its findings of excessive force being used against workers occupying a farm, inter alia, on the authorities' failure to take precautions to protect children present on the farm, despite the fact that no children were actually killed or injured in the raid.[411]

The state has to take precautions so as to ensure as much as possible that innocent bystanders are not harmed by others, namely by counter-force used by the aggressors. In *Ergi,* Turkish authorities defended themselves with force against PKK members shooting at them to avoid arrest. An innocent bystander was killed, but it could not be established whether the bullet was fired by the Turkish security forces or the PKK. The ECtHR still found a violation, deciding that the Turkish authorities took insufficient protections to protect the lives of the population of the village where the shoot-out occurred.[412] In *Abdurashidova,* a six-year old girl was killed when special police forces stormed a house, in which

409. Stewart v. United Kingdom, *supra* note 11, para. 20. In *Bakan,* a police officer fired a warning shot in response to a fugitive shooting at the police. The bullet accidentally killed an innocent bystander. The ECtHR found that this constituted mere bad luck, rather than a violation. See Bakan v. Turkey, Appl. No. 50939/99, Judgment of 12 June 2007, para.55. Like in the Stewart case, the low probability of the outcome versus the anticipated benefit of the police action could justify the outcome of an innocent bystander being killed.

410. Gül v. Turkey, *supra* note 189, para. 82.

411. Finca "La Exacta" v. Guatemala [IACommHR], *supra* note 2, paras. 56, 65 & 80–81.

412. Ergi v. Turkey, *supra* note 59, para. 81. Cf. Hamiyet Kaplan v. Turkey, *supra* note 294, para. 52.

armed suspects were hiding. Even though hand grenades thrown by the suspects killed the girl, the authorities were held responsible for their failure to use a prior opportunity to evacuate her.[413] The opposite conclusion was drawn by the Inter-American Commission in *Corumbiara Massacre*, where a girl was killed when police fired back at workers who started shooting at them. The Commission determined that the state authorities failed to take any special measures to protect children, as would have been required under international human rights law. However, it saw no violation in the girl's death, since it could not be established that she was killed by a state agent.[414] The position of the Inter-American Commission is unconvincing, since the state has to factor in and take appropriate precautions covering all foreseeable risks of its defensive action, including the possibility that innocent bystanders will be harmed by the aggressors.

b) Killing innocent bystanders

The foregoing considerations all related to situations where innocent bystanders are endangered by force aimed at the aggressors but any harm they incur is unintentional. To some extent, law enforcement agents using force may also knowingly injure innocent bystanders. For instance, police officers may use tear gas to defend themselves against violent rioters even if they know that innocent peaceful demonstrators standing close by will also be harmed.[415]

The legal situation becomes far more complex where innocent bystanders are subjected to deliberately lethal force and consequently killed. Three situations should be distinguished:

1. Law enforcement agents use force with the intent to kill an innocent bystander. For instance, police might intentionally shoot and kill one hostage in order to scare the hostage-takers into giving up and releasing the other hostages unharmed.
2. Law enforcement agents use lethal force against the aggressor with the knowledge that an innocent bystander will be killed, so as to save the lives of other innocent bystanders. An example would be a hostage-taker who is keeping one hostage with him as a human shield. The other hostages are in a separate room, which the hostage-taker can blow up with a remote-controlled bomb. Since his demands are not being fulfilled, the hostage-taker is about to detonate the bomb. He plans to spare his human shield so as to use that hostage to escape. A police

413. Abdurashidova v. Russia, Appl. No. 32968/05, Judgment of 8 April 2010, para. 79.

414. Corumbiara Massacre v. Brazil [IACommHR], *supra* note 2, para. 206.

415. In *Finogenov*, the European Court even accepted the use of a toxic knockout gas in a Moscow theatre filled with aggressors (the Chechen hostage-takers) and innocent bystanders (their hostages). Although the Russian authorities did not intent or know that the gas would lead to mass fatalities among the hostages, they were still aware that the gas would damage the hostages' health. See Finogenov et al. v. Russia, *supra* note 117, para. 232.

sniper can take out the hostage-taker and prevent the detonation of the bomb with an instantly lethal head shot—but only at the expense of the bullet traversing and killing the human-shield hostage as well.

3. Law enforcement agents use lethal force against the aggressors with the knowledge that it will kill some innocent bystanders whom the aggressors would soon kill anyhow. For example, if domestic terrorists hijack a civilian plane with a very small number of crew and passengers and intend to fly it into a multi-story building, which will kill dozens of innocent people including everyone on the plane. Fighter jets can still shoot down the plane, killing the hostage-takers as well as the innocent crew and passengers.[416]

No one seriously suggests that law enforcement agents purposely killing innocent bystanders (case 1) can ever be justified even if it is supposed to serve wider protective purposes. Such a measure would not be allowed even under the far more permissive rules applicable in armed conflict, where innocent civilians may never be made the target of attack.[417]

However, different views are taken with regard to the assessment of cases 2 and 3. Some take the position that, under international human rights law, the deliberate killing of innocent bystanders can never be justified in peacetime.[418] In respect of fundamental rights protected under their respective constitutions, the German and Polish Constitutional Courts have taken this view. Accordingly, they struck down laws that would have allowed the shooting down of passenger planes in scenarios of the type described in Case 3. The German Constitutional Court argued that killing the innocent crew and passengers on the plane would violate not only their right to life, but also their right to human dignity since

416. Although the example draws on the 9/11 Attacks, it has been deliberately adapted to a purely domestic scenario of smaller proportions, so as not to raise the additional question whether this might not be an armed attack in the sense of Article 51 of the U.N. Charter so that the state authorities could respond within the far more permissive conduct of hostilities paradigm under IHL. On the differences between the hostilities and law enforcement paradigms, see Fifth Chapter: A (pp. 218–221).

417. Protocol Additional to the Geneva Conventions of 12 August 1949, and relating to the Protection of Victims of International Armed Conflicts [Geneva Protocol I], art. 51(2); Protocol Additional to the Geneva Conventions of 12 August 1949, and relating to the Protection of Victims of Non-International Armed Conflicts [Geneva Protocol II], article 13(2); Jean-Marie Henckaerts & Louise Doswald-Beck, Customary International Humanitarian Law vol. I: Rules, International Committee of the Red Cross and Cambridge University Press: Cambridge (2005), p. 3 [Rule 1].

418. Otto, *supra* note 12, p. 537; Schübel-Pfister *supra* note 55, p. 62 [art. 2, para. 26]. See also Amnesty International, Use of Force Guidelines, *supra* note 3, p. 34. Cf. (based on German constitutional law): Claus Roxin, Der Abschuss gekaperter Flugzeuge zur Rettung von Menschenleben, Zeitschrift für internationale Strafrechtsdogmatik, vol. 6 (2011), 552–563; Horst Dreier, Grenzen des Tötungsverbots—Teil 1, Juristen Zeitung (JZ), vol. 62 (2007), 261–270, at p. 265.

they would be used as a means to save others and thus as mere objects of state action. Although themselves victims in need of protection, they would be denied the value due to a human being for his or her own sake.[419] The Polish Court also found violations of the rights to life and human dignity, finding that it is "by no means permissible to expose to certain death passengers and crew members, who are not aggressors but rather the victims of the perpetrators."[420]

On the other end of the spectrum of opinion is a consequentialist view: Defensive action that is known to incidentally kill innocent bystanders may still be proportional and compatible with international human rights law if it can be expected to save many more innocent lives than it costs.[421] Accordingly, lethal force would be permissible in cases 2 and 3.

An intermediate view differentiates between killing one innocent bystander to save several others (case 2) and killing innocent bystanders whose life is doomed in any case (case 3).[422] In the latter case, it is argued, upholding the otherwise non-derogable principle that one may not kill one innocent person to save the life of other innocent persons serves no real purpose. Since the passengers on the hijacked plane face certain death, their life expectation has been factually reduced to such an insignificant level that the state can demand of them to give up the rest in solidarity with the many others whose life is saved by shooting down the plane.[423]

In support of the consequentialist view it could be argued that Article 2(2)(a) of the ECHR permits the use of lethal force "in defence of any person from unlawful violence," which does not require such force to be directed exclusively against aggressors.[424] A similar textual argument could be made with regard to

419. German Constitutional Court, BVerfGE 115, 118, *supra* note 139, p. 154 [para. 122 of the official translation]. Although the European Court has not yet had to rule on this question, the European Court appers to signal support for the German Constitutional Court's decision in Finogenov et al. v. Russia, *supra* note 117, paras. 231–232.

420. Polish Constitutional Court, K/44/07, Judgment of 30 September 2008, para. 14 of the official translation of excerpts available at: http://trybunal.gov.pl/fileadmin/content/omowienia/K_44_07_GB.pdf.

421. Leaning in that direction, Georg Nolte, The Bundesverfassungsgericht on the German Aerial Security Law: A Sonderweg from the perspective of international law?, in: Christian Tomuschat, Evelyne Lagrange & Stefan Oeter (eds.), The Right to Life, Brill: Leiden (2010), 83–94. For this view as a matter of legal philosophy: Tatjana Hörnle, Shooting Down a Hijacked Plane—The German Discussion and Beyond, Criminal Law and Philosophy, vol. 3 (2009), 111–131, p. 128; Michael Gorr, Private Defense, Law and Philosophy, vol. 9 (1990), 241–268, p. 263; Whitley Kaufman, Is there a "right" to self-defense?, Criminal Justice Ethics, vol. 23 (1) (2004), 20–32, at p. 24.

422. Merkel, *supra* note 362, pp. 452–453; Manuel Ladiges, Die notstandsbedingte Tötung von Unbeteiligten im Fall des § 14 Abs. 3 LuftSiG—ein Plädoyer für die Rechtfertigungslösung, Zeitschrift für internationale Strafrechtsdogmatik, vol. 3 (2008), 129–140, at p. 140.

423. Merkel, *id.*

424. See also Nolte, *supra* note 421, p. 89.

the U.N. Basic Principles on the Use of Force and Firearms, which require only that deliberately lethal force must "protect life," but do not expressly prohibit the state from killing some innocent bystanders for the purpose of protecting many other innocent lives.[425]

Furthermore, consequentialists argue that in armed conflict, international human rights law also permits security forces knowingly to kill innocent bystanders, because the right to life has to be interpreted in line with IHL, which allows to some extent for the foreseeable death of civilians as collateral damage.[426] However, analogies with armed conflict to justify the killing of innocent persons in peacetime must be treated with extreme caution. International humanitarian law accepts war, and the large-scale killing it involves, as an inevitable evil in order to at least mitigate the suffering of combatants and civilians. On this basis, it permits killings even for purposes other than saving life or preventing serious injuries. IHL may allow the incidental killing of innocent civilians to gain an abstract military advantage; for instance, by bombing a train station or a transport hub despite the presence of civilians. This may be done even if that prolongs the war and leads to more killing. However, such abstract advantages could never justify the foreseeable killing of innocent bystanders in peacetime.

The consideration of armed conflict situations shows, however, that the right to life is not absolute and that the state may deliberately kill the innocent in extreme circumstances. This is not limited to armed conflict situations. As noted above, international human rights law also allows the police to kill non-culpable aggressors even though they are legally and morally innocent.[427] If one accepts that the right to life applies from conception (as Article 4 of the ACHR expressly does), abortion is another case where the deliberate taking of innocent (unborn) life may be justified.[428] The right to life thereby differs from the right not to be tortured, which is absolute regardless of the circumstances or purpose of torture.[429]

425. The only pertinent reference can be found in Principle 3, which calls for the evaluation of less lethal weapons "in order to minimize the risk of endangering uninvolved persons."

426. Hörnle, *supra* note 421, p. 119; Nolte, *supra* note 421, pp. 85-86. Neither IHL, nor human rights law as applicable in armed conflict, prohibit the use of force in armed conflict where it will result in the unintended, yet foreseeable death of a innocent civilians, as long as such loss of life is not excessive in relation to the military advantage gained it and occurs despite all feasible precautions being taken.

427. See this Fourth Chapter: C.I.4 (pp. 129–131).

428. International human rights bodies have not taken the position that abortion constitutes a violation of the right to life. On the contrary, they have criticized states that continue to criminalize abortion in cases involving rape or incest. See, e.g., Human Rights Committee, Concluding Observations on the Dominican Republic, U.N. Doc. CCPR/C/DOM/CO/5 (2012), para. 15; Committee on Economic and Social Rights, Concluding Observations on Costa Rica, U.N. Doc. E/C.12/CRI/CO/4 (2008), para. 46.

429. See the discussion on life-saving torture below, this Fourth Chapter: C.VI (pp. 189–197).

These points noted, there are still good reasons not to allow the deliberate killing of one innocent bystander in order to save others, as contemplated in case 2. In such cases, the state essentially demands that an innocent bystander sacrifice his own life so that the state can save others. However, this sacrifice goes beyond what may be reasonably asked of a person.[430] Accepting that the state can trade off innocent lives against one another may also create a slippery slope and even open the door for abusive invocations of this doctrine. In hostage scenarios, the state may, for example, argue that it is necessary to kill hostage-takers and human shields because the alternative of a police raid would put the lives of too many police officers at risk.

The airplane scenario (case 3) is different. In these situations, the state can no longer protect the innocent passengers and crew. Their lives will be lost one way or another. The sole sacrifice that shooting down the plane demands of them is to give up the final few minutes of life, which are anyhow filled with panic and terror.[431]

Against this position it has been argued that the state can never determine with certainty whether an innocent bystander's life is really doomed.[432] In case 3, for instance, the passengers may overpower the hostage takers or the state may be mistaken in its assessment that the civilian plane was actually captured by hostage takers with the intent to crash it into a populated area. However, this argument only goes to show that decisions entailing deliberately lethal force for defensive purposes should be taken based on a high degree of certainty about the existence of a lethal threat.[433] A degree of uncertainty will always remain, but this is typical for any self-defense scenario where life-and-death difficult decisions have to be taken on the spot without the benefit of hindsight. It would be clearly allowed to shoot down the plane if there are only terrorists on board and they plan to crash it into a building or other populated area.[434] This principle holds true even though that scenario entails very similar uncertainties, notably uncertainty about whether the terrorists might not have brought innocent hostages on board.

It has also been suggested that the extreme case of a plane being used as a suicide bomb can be appropriately resolved by protecting the commanders and pilots involved from criminal responsibility, while maintaining that shooting down the plane remains illegal.[435] However, this solution would introduce a great deal of

430. Hörnle, *supra* note 421, p. 123; Roxin, *supra* note 418, p. 553.

431. Hörnle, *id.*, p. 121.

432. See Polish Constitutional Court, *supra* note 420, para. 14 of the official translation of excerpts; German Constitutional Court, *supra* note 139, p. 158 [para. 131 of the official translation]; Roxin, *supra* note 418, p. 561; Dreier, *supra* note 418, p. 266.

433. See also *supra* note 314 and accompanying text.

434. See also Polish Constitutional Court, *supra* note 420, para. 17 of the official translation of excerpts; German Constitutional Court, *supra* note 139, p. 161 [para. 139 of the official translation].

435. Dreier, *supra* note 418, p. 267; Roxin, *supra* note 418, p. 563.

legal and operational uncertainty. The pilot of the plane might refuse to obey the order to shoot down a civilian airliner—not least since many national jurisdictions allow soldiers to disobey manifestly illegal orders.[436] In situations, where action must be taken within minutes to be effective, a lack of legal clarity may lead to deadly delays. Recordings of exchanges between U.S. Air Force officials during the 9/11 attacks, for instance, showed that some within the military chain of command were reluctant to carry out a reported order to shoot down any remaining civilian planes in the airspace that appeared to be used for further attacks.[437]

A more principled counterargument holds that shooting down the airplane treats the passengers as objects, a mere means to an end.[438] However, this is not the case. The destruction of the plane, which the terrorists intend to use as a bomb, is the means to save the lives of other innocent persons on the ground. The death of the passengers and crew is only a tragic incidental loss. The situation thus differs from morally and legally unacceptable hypothetical scenarios of another kind, such as where terminally ill patients are killed as a means to harvest their organs and save the lives of others.

Proponents of a strict prohibition against knowingly killing innocent bystanders also argue that all lives are of equal worth and therefore the state may not make decisions based on a determination that a life doomed to imminent death carries little worth anymore.[439] For the German Constitutional Court this argument will carry special weight since it is taken against the historical experience of National-Socialist Germany murdering tens of thousands of persons with disabilities with the argument that their lives were not worth enough to be kept alive (so-called *lebensunwertes Leben*). However, this monstrous doctrine was based on supposed distinctions based on the *quality* of a human life. Shooting down the plane entails making distinctions based on a *quantitative* measure, the remainder of the lifespan. This does not entail an equally grave affront to human dignity. This is why, for instance, doctors are allowed to give terminally ill passengers strong painkillers even if such medication is known to further shorten their lives.[440]

436. Illegally shooting down an airliner in the knowledge that a very large number of persons will be killed may even amount to a crime against humanity, so that international criminal law would require a pilot to ignore such a manifestly unlawful order to shoot down the plane. Cf. Rome Statute, art. 33(2).

437. The 9/11 Tapes: The Story in the Air, New York Times, 7 September 2011 [recordings from 10:32 A.M.], also available at: http://www.nytimes.com/interactive/2011/09/08/nyregion/911-tapes.html.

438. See German Constitutional Court, *supra* note 139, at p. 154 [para. 122 of the official translation]. Cf. Polish Constitutional Court, *supra* note 420, para. 14 of the official translation of excerpts.

439. German Constitutional Court, *id.*, p. 158 [para 130 of the official translation]; Polish Constitutional Court, *id.*, para. 14 of the official translation of excerpts.

440. See also Ladiges, *supra* note 422, p. 138; Hörnle, *supra* note 421, p. 122.

The decision on whether to permit the killing of innocent bystanders who are doomed to an imminent death one way or another essentially comes down to the question whether the principle that the taking of innocent life is taboo must be upheld even at the price of actually failing to protect innocent life.[441] International law does not adhere to such a rigid principle. This is evidenced by the fact that innocent life may also be taken for other purposes, such as winning wars, preserving the life of a pregnant woman, and protecting against lethal threats posed by non-culpable aggressors. State agents may therefore use deliberately lethal force in self-defense or defense of others where it is known to kill innocent bystanders, but only if it can be determined with a high degree of certainty that the innocent bystander would be doomed to an imminent death even if the state did not use lethal force.

VI. Absolutely prohibited means of self-defense: torture and inhuman treatment

Torture as well as other types of cruel, inhuman and degrading treatment (inhuman treatment) are by their nature so abhorrent that they are per se disproportional—even if they are the only means to protect life against an unlawful attack.

1. The Absolute Prohibition of Torture and Inhuman Treatment

Whether torture may be carried out to reveal information to protect innocent life is a longstanding moral debate. True to his utilitarian philosophy, the English Enlightenment philosopher Jeremy Bentham contemplated that it would be legal to torture a criminal if this would reveal information that could rescue hundreds of innocent persons.[442] In more recent times, internal memorandums prepared by senior U.S. government lawyers in the wake of the 9/11 attacks (the infamous "torture memos") claimed that self-defense may justify the torture of suspected terrorists and would not violate human rights obligations, in particular not those under the Convention against Torture (CAT). John Yoo, then U.S. Deputy Assistant Attorney General, argued notably that

> if interrogation were inconsistent with the United States' obligations under CAT, but were justified by necessity or self-defense we would view these actions still as consistent ultimately with international law. Although these actions might violate CAT, they would still be in service of the more fundamental principle of self-defense that cannot be extinguished by CAT or any other treaty.[443]

441. Ladiges, *id.*, p. 140.

442. Jeremy Bentham Mss. Box 74.b. (27th May, 1804), as cited in: W.L. & P.E. Twinning, Bentham on Torture, Northern Ireland Law Quarterly, vol. 24 (1973), 305–356, at p. 347.

443. Memorandum by U.S. Deputy Assistant Attorney General John C. Yoo to William J. Haynes II, General Counsel of the Department of Defense (14 March 2003) [declassified on 31 March 2008], https://www.aclu.org/files/pdfs/safefree/yoo_army_torture_memo.pdf, p. 58.

As a matter of international law, this position is baseless and the United States has since formally dissociated itself from it.[444] International human rights law allows neither torture nor inhuman treatment even if it would serve to defend the lives of innocent persons against imminent death,[445] Neither the ICCPR nor any of the regional treaties foresee any limitations to the prohibition against torture and inhuman treatment, nor do they admit any derogation from these prohibitions even in times of armed conflict or other emergency.[446] Driving home the same point, Article 2(2) of the CAT unequivocally stipulates:

> No exceptional circumstances whatsoever, whether a state of war or a threat of war, internal political instability or any other public emergency, may be invoked as a justification of torture.[447]

See also Memorandum by U.S. Assistant Attorney General Jay Bybee to Attorney General Alberto R. Gonzales (1 August 2002), http://www2.gwu.edu/~nsarchiv/NSAEBB/NSAEBB127/02.08.01.pdf, pp. 42–46; Working Group Report on Detainee Interogations in the Global War on Terrorism: Assessment of Legal, Historical, Policy, and Operational Considerations (4 April 2003), http://www2.gwu.edu/~nsarchiv/NSAEBB/NSAEBB127/03.04.04.pdf, pp. 27–31.

444. See President of the United States of America, Executive Order 13491—Ensuring Lawful Interrogations, 22 January 2009,: http://www.whitehouse.gov/the_press_office/Ensuring_Lawful_Interrogations. Section 3(c) expressly prohibits U.S. government employees from relying on any of the legal interpretations in the said torture memos.

445. Alex J. Bellamy, No Pain, No Gain? Torture and. Ethics in the War on Terror, International Affairs, vol. 82 (2006), 121–148, at p. 126; Claus Roxin, Kann staatliche Folter in Ausnahmefällen zulässig oder wenigstens straflos sein?, in: Jörg Arnold et al. (eds.), Menschengerechtes Strafrecht: Festschrift für Albin Eser zum 70. Geburtstag, C.H. Beck: München 2005), 461–471, at pp. 462–463; Jamie Mayerfeld, In Defense of the Absolute Prohibition of Torture, Public Affairs Quarterly, vol. 22 (2008), 109–128, pp. 109–110; Günter Jerouschek & Ralf Kölbel, Folter von Staats wegen?, JuristenZeitung 2003, 613–620, at pp. 616–619; Harald Maihold, Folterknechte im Dienste des Rechtsstaats?—Zur Strafbarkeit der „Gefahrenabwehrfolter nach schweizerischem und deutschem Recht, in: Martino Mona & Kurt Seelmann (eds.), Grenzen des rechtfertigenden Notstands, Schulthess: Zurich (2006), 117–142, at p. 135; Diehm, *supra* note 12, p. 369; Satzger, *supra* note 382, p. 202; Kai Ambos, May a State Torture Suspects to Save the Life of Innocents?, Journal of International Criminal Justice, vol. 8 (2008), 261–287, at p. 266; Walter Perron, Foltern in Notwehr?, in: Bernd Heinrich et al. (eds.), Festschrift für Ulrich Weber zum 70. Geburtstag, Verlag Ernst und Werner Gieseking: Bielefeld (2004), 143–154, at p. 144; Florian Jessberger, Bad Torture—Good Torture?: What International Criminal Lawyers may Learn from the Recent Trial of Police Officers in Germany, Journal of International Criminal Justice, vol. 3 (2005), 1059–1073, at pp. 1068–1069; Paola Gaeta, May Necessity Be Available as a Defence for Torture in the Interrogation of Suspected Terrorists?, Journal of International Criminal Justice, vol. 2 (2004), 785–794, at p. 787; Yuval Shany, The Prohibition against Torture and Cruel, Inhuman, and Degrading Treatment and Punishment: Can the Absolute be Relativized under Existing International Law?, Catholic University Law Review, vol. 56 (2007), 837–869, at p. 861.

446. See Art. 4(2) & 7 ICCPR; Art. 3 and 15(2) ECHR; Art. 5 and 27(1) ACHR; Art. 5 ACHPR; Art. 4(1) and 8(1) Arab Charter on Human Rights. Cf. Common Article 3(1)(b) of the 1949 Geneva Conventions.

447. While the provision makes no specific reference to inhuman treatment, this should not be understood as excluding inhuman treatment from the absolute prohibition. Article 16(2)

The absolute prohibition of torture and inhuman treatment represents the longstanding consensus view of the state community. This consensus dates back at least to the 1975 U.N. Declaration against Torture, which unequivocally recognizes the prohibition of torture and cruel, inhuman and degrading treatment even under the most exceptional circumstances.[448] In the intergovernmental debate preceding the consensual adoption of the Declaration, not a single state defended the use of torture on any ground.[449]

Pursuant to the clear wording of human rights treaties and the underlying state consensus, the relevant universal and regional rights bodies all take the position that both torture and inhuman treatment are absolutely prohibited.[450]

CAT stipulates that the CAT provisions are without prejudice to the provisions prohibiting torture under other conventions. These other conventions, namely the ICCPR and the regional human rights treaties, extend the absolute prohibition to both torture and inhuman treatment. See also Ambos, *supra* note 445, p. 266; Shany, *supra* note 445, pp. 858–859.

448. Declaration on the Protection of All Persons from Being Subjected to Torture and Other Cruel, Inhuman or Degrading Treatment or Punishment, G.A. res. 3452 (XXX), annex, 30 U.N. GAOR Supp. (No. 34) at 91, U.N. Doc. A/10034 (1975), art. 3. See also U.N. Code of Conduct for Law Enforcement Officials, *supra* note 25, Art. 5.

449. Bellamy, *supra* note 445, p. 127.

450. Human Rights Committee, General Comment 20, Article 7 (1992), in: Compilation of General Comments and General Recommendations Adopted by Human Rights Treaty Bodies, U.N. Doc. HRI/GEN/1/Rev.1 at 30 (1994), para 3; Committee Against Torture, General Comment 2, Implementation of article 2 by States Parties, U.N. Doc. CAT/C/GC/2/CRP. 1/Rev.4 (2007), paras. 5–6; Report of the Special Rapporteur on torture and other cruel, inhuman or degrading treatment or punishment, Juan E. Méndez, U.N. Doc. A/HRC/22/53 (2013), para. 64; United Nations Secretary-General Ban-Ki Moon, Secretary General's Message for the International Day in support of Victims of Torture, 26 June 2004, http://www.un.org/en/events/torturevictimsday/2014/sgmessage.shtml; African Commission on Human and Peoples' Rights Measures for the Prohibition and Prevention of Torture, Cruel, Inhuman or Degrading Treatment or Punishment In Africa (Robben Island Guidelines), adopted at the 32nd ordinary session (2002), paras. 9 and 10; Ireland v. United Kingdom [ECtHR Plenary], Appl. No. 5310/71, Judgment of 18 January 1978, para. 163; Kashiyev and Akayeva v. Russia [ECtHR], Appl. No. 57942/00 57945/00, Judgment of 24 February 2005, para 170; Miguel Castro-Castro Prison v. Peru [IACtHR], *supra* note 159, para. 271; Zambrano Vélez et al. v. Ecuador, *supra* note 29, para. 96.

The one deviation from this bright line emerging from some European Court and Inter-American Court cases is that necessary and proportional force exercised by police officers to defend themselves will not meet the threshold of the right not to be subject to torture or inhuman treatment for the very reason that such force was exercised in self-defense. See Ruano Torres et al. v. El Salvador, Judgment of 5 October 2015, IACtHR Ser. C No. 303, para. 123, and the ECtHR case references *supra* notes 19 & 20. See also Leverick, *supra* note 193, p. 360; Ambos, *supra* note 445, p. 267. However, such cases are different from those discussed here, because they do not entail an attack on the core of human dignity. In such cases, cruelty and inhumanity are not used as the instrumental means to force the victims to speak turning mere objects deprived of any free will and autonomy. See also Christian Jäger, Folter und Flugzeugabschuss—rechtsstaatliche Tabubrüche oder rechtsguterhaltende Notwendigkeiten?, Juristische Ausbildung (JA) 2008, 678–684, at p. 680.

This leaves no room for the argument, advanced by some scholars,[451] that only torture is absolutely prohibited, whereas terrorists or other criminals may still be subjected to inhuman treatment in order to extract life-saving information from them. The absolute prohibition of torture would be quickly undermined if it were not complemented by an absolute ban on inhuman treatment. Since the line between torture and inhuman treatment is hard to draw, states could easily claim that their interrogation techniques may well be inhuman but remain just below the torture threshold. For this reason, international law draws a bright line and absolutely prohibits both torture and inhuman treatment.

Threats of torture are usually also impermissible even if they are meant to defend lives.[452] Criminal suspects will typically give up life-saving information (and thus incriminate themselves) only if the threat appears so serious that it causes them significant fear and mental anguish. However, threats of that seriousness will amount in and of themselves to torture or at least inhuman treatment. This was clearly established by the Grand Chamber of the ECtHR in *Gäfgen*. The case concerned police officers who threatened the kidnapper of a child with torture to get him to reveal the whereabouts of the child, because they had good reason to believe that the child would otherwise die soon.[453] The Grand Chamber considered that the real and immediate threat made during the interrogation caused the suspect considerable fear, anguish, and mental suffering on a level reaching inhuman treatment, but not torture.[454] Although the court expressly acknowledged that the officers "acted in an attempt to save a child's life" (i.e., in defense of the life of others), it nevertheless found a violation, since "[t]orture, inhuman or degrading treatment cannot be inflicted even in circumstances where the life of an individual is at risk."[455]

451. Rolf Dietrich Herzberg, Folter und Menschenwürde, Juristen Zeitung 2005, 321–328, at p. 326; Eric Hilgendorf, Folter im Rechtsstaat?, JuristenZeitung 2004, 331–339, at p. 338. Cf. Shany, *supra* note 445, p. 859 & 862–867, who acknowledges that international human rights law establishes an absolute prohibition of both torture and inhuman treatment, but argues that at least individual law enforcement agents who engage in inhuman treatment to save lives can be considered individually justified under criminal law and hence not held criminally responsible.

452. Roxin, *supra* note 445, p. 464; Satzger, *supra* note 382, p. 203; Diehm, *supra* note 12, p. 344; Jäger, *supra* note 450, p. 681; Perron, *supra* note 445, pp. 149–150; Hilgendorf, *id.*, p. 334; Maihold, *supra* note 445, pp. 135–136. But cf. Herzberg, *supra* note 451, pp. 325–326; Reinhard Merkel, Folter und Notwehr, in: Michael Pawlik/Rainer Zaczyk (eds.), Festschrift für Günther Jakobs zum 70. Geburtstag, C. Heymanns: Berlin (2007), 375–403, at pp. 401–402.

453. In hindsight, it turned out that this effort was in vain, because the child had already died. However, since the necessity of defensive force has to be based on an ex ante perspective (see this Fourth Chapter: C.I.6, pp. 133–139), this tragic fact had no bearing on the legal assessment under the European Convention.

454. Gäfgen v. Germany, Appl. No. 22978/05, Judgment of 1 June 2010, paras. 101–108.

455. *Id.*, para. 107.

2. Attempts to Circumvent the Absolute Prohibition

Some academics have tried to construct legal arguments to allow for torture or inhuman treatment, where it can lead to life-saving information. Neither these legal arguments nor the underlying moral and policy considerations are persuasive.

One approach suggests that the limitations to the right to life, namely the right to exercise lethal force in self-defense or defense of others, must also be read into the right not to be subjected to torture or inhuman treatment. Where it is even allowed to kill, the argument goes, it must also be allowed to commit the lesser harm of inflicting torture or inhuman treatment.[456] However, as noted above, the absence of limitations to the right not to be subjected to torture or cruel, inhuman, or degrading treatment is not an oversight but a deliberate value decision made by the international community. If anything, the fact that the right to life leaves room for exceptions, while the prohibition of torture and inhuman treatment does not, only reinforces that the latter prohibition is absolute.[457] Torture also cannot be equated on an ethical level with the use of deliberately lethal force against aggressors, because it entails a profound assault on the core of human dignity. The victim is powerless in the hands of the state and is reduced to a mere object that is forced to cooperate; a lump of pain deprived of any free will and autonomy.[458]

Another attempt to justify torture invokes the right to personal self-defense as an inherent limitation to the prohibition of torture and ill-treatment.[459] As established above, the right to personal self-defense forms part of international law since it constitutes a general principle of law recognized by nations. Nevertheless, it cannot trump the absolute prohibition of torture and inhuman treatment, because the latter constitutes a hierarchically superior norm of peremptory international law (*ius cogens*).[460] The right to self-defense does not limit the absolute

456. Winfried Brugger, Vom unbedingten Verbot der Folter zum bedingten Recht auf Folter?, JuristenZeitung 2000, 165–173, pp. 16–170; Ashworth, *supra* note 17, p. 42; Steven Greer, Should Police Threats to Torture Suspects Always be Severely Punished?: Reflections on the Gäfgen Case, Human Rights Law Review. vol. 11(1) (2011), 67–89, at pp. 82–84; Uwe Steinhoff, Defusing the Ticking Social Bomb Argument: The Right to Self-Defensive Torture, Global Dialogue, vol. 12(1) (2000), http://www.worlddialogue.org/print.php?id=457.

457. Satzger, *supra* note 382, p. 202; Nolte, *supra* note 421, p. 90; Roxin, *supra* note 445, p. 463.

458. Roxin, *supra* note 10, p. 707; Maihold, *supra* note 445, p. 136; Hilgendorf, *supra* note 451, p. 336; von Scherenberg, *supra* note 379, p. 243; Roxin, *supra* note 445, p. 464; Bellamy, *supra* note 445, p. 129; Nolte, *supra* note 421, p. 91.

459. See Volker Erb, Notwehr als Menschenrecht—Zugleich eine Kritik der Entscheidung des LG Frankfurt am Main im „Fall Daschner", Neue Zeitschrift für Strafrecht (NStZ) 2005, 593–602, p. 599. The right to self-defense is also invoked in the internal memorandums prepared by senior U.S. officials cited *supra*, note 443. See also Steinhoff, *supra* note 456.

460. Jessberger, *supra* note 445, p. 1072; Shany, *supra* note 445, p. 859. Cf. International Law Commission, Articles on State Responsibility, *supra* note 177, art. 26.

prohibition of torture and inhuman treatment; rather, the inverse is true. Self-defense can never be proportional to the extent that it is exercised through such monstrous means as torture or inhuman treatment. In questioning this conclusion, the point has been made that interrogational torture may at times be used to prevent terrorists from committing *ius cogens* violations, notably war crimes and crimes against humanity.[461] However, even in such extreme cases, one *ius cogens* violation may not justify another *ius cogens* violation. If such *tu quoque* arguments held water, the international legal order would quickly fall back on practices involving the most barbarous reprisals.

A third line of argument holds that the state is confronted with conflicting human rights duties of equal importance where torture may reveal information to ward off a deadly attack: the duty not to torture the perpetrators, versus the duty to protect their innocent victims who could be saved. On both sides of the equation, human dignity is said to be in play. In light of this dilemma, the state may choose the dignity of the victims over that of the perpetrator and resort to torture.[462] Brugger even suggests that the state has a duty to torture to save life.[463] The conflicting duties argument is flawed, because the state can have a duty to protect only using the lawful means at its disposal. The argument begs the question that it pretends to answer, namely whether torture may ever be legal.[464]

On the ius cogens character of the absolute prohibition of torture, see Committee against Torture, General Comment no. 2, *supra* note 450, para. 1; *id.*, Concluding Observations on Spain, U.N. Doc. CAT/C/ESP/CO/5 (2009), para. 21; Interim report of the Special Rapporteur on torture and other cruel, inhuman or degrading treatment or punishment, Manfred Nowak, U.N. Doc. A/65/273 (2010), para. 88; Report of the independent international commission of inquiry on the Syrian Arab Republic, U.N. Doc. A/HRC/19/69 (2012), para. 106; Prosecutor v. Furundzija [ICTY], IT-95-17/1-T, Judgment of 10 December 1998, para. 153; Ambos, *supra* note 445, p. 265; Bellamy, *supra* note 445, p. 126; Gaeta, *supra* note 445, p. 788.

Specifically recognizing also the prohibition of inhuman treatment as *ius cogens:* Ximenes-Lopes v. Brazil [IACtHR], *supra* note 170, para. 126; Barrios Family v. Venezuela, *supra* note 29, para. 50; Special Rapporteur on the promotion and protection of human rights and fundamental freedoms while countering terrorism, Ben Emerson, Follow-up report to country missions, U.N. Doc. A/HRC/20/14/Add.2 (2012), para. 24; Constitutional Court of Colombia, Constitutional Case No. C-281/07, Judgment of 25 April 2007, p. 11; Rodley/Pollard, *supra* note 22, pp. 65–66; Jordan J. Paust, The Absolute Prohibition of Torture and Necessary and Appropriate Sanctions, Valparaiso University Law Review, vol. 43 (2009), 1535–1575, at p. 1535.

461. Gaeta, *supra* note 445, p. 79 (making this point only in relation to international criminal law).

462. Fabian Wittreck, Menschenwürde und Folterverbot, Die öffentliche Verwaltung 2003, 873–882, at pp. 880–882; Ian Turner, Human Rights and Antiterrorism: A Positive Legal Duty to Infringe Freedom From Torture?, Studies in Conflict & Terrorism, vol. 35(11) (2012), 760–778, at pp. 765–777; Greer, *supra* note 456, pp. 80–82.

463. Brugger, *supra* note 456, p. 171. Cf. Greer, *id.*, 80–82 & 84.

464. See also Ambos, *supra* note 445, p. 278; Roxin, *supra* note 445, p. 466.

Even less cogent is the argument that the state becomes complicit in the terrorists' and criminals' denial of the human dignity of innocent victims if it prohibits its law enforcement agents to use all means at their disposal, including of torture and inhuman treatment, to protect the life and dignity of victims.[465] The criminal's assault on dignity cannot be imputed to the state just because the state fails to prevent the crime.[466] Furthermore, torture or inhuman treatment are not "at the disposal" of law enforcement agents if they are absolutely prohibited. Like the conflicting duties argument, the complicity argument works only by setting as a premise (torture and inhuman treatment may be exceptionally used to save life) the very point that is sought to be proved.

Furthermore, the conflicting duties and complicity arguments both rest on the flawed premise that terrorist acts or other serious crimes affect the human dignity as profoundly as the state torturing the perpetrators of such crimes. Torture constitutes a significantly greater assault on human dignity because it bears the imprimatur of the state. As such, it not only denies the dignity of the victim but also entails an assault on the collective dignity of the citizens in whose name the state acts.[467] One must only think through what it would take to operationalize "legal torture" in light of other human rights requirements. A law would have to lay down the police's basic right, and even duty, to torture and then specify the permissible means and methods of torture. Police officers and supervising doctors would have to be trained in non-lethal, yet highly effective—that is, painful—torture techniques. Judicial torture warrants, video recordings of the proceedings, and other effective means to curb abuse would have to be put in place.[468] None of this is imaginable in any state that maintains a semblance of the rule of law. Nor is it necessary. It seems far more sensible and less dangerous to the rule of law to resolve the rare case of a police officer who ill-treats a suspect to extract life-saving information (as in the abovementioned *Gäfgen* case) by considering the protective intent as a strongly mitigating factor in the officer's sentencing.[469] This takes into account the moral pressure that the perpetrator

465. Erb, *supra* note 459, p. 599; Merkel, *supra* note 452, pp. 393–394.

466. Ambos, *supra* note 445, p. 279.

467. Some authors make a similar point in arguing that torture undermines the dignity and moral superiority of the state itself. See Jäger, *supra* note 450, pp. 680–681; Roxin, *supra* note 445, p. 466; von Scherenberg, *supra* note 379, p. 245.

468. See also Perron, *supra* note 445, pp. 144–145; Hilgendorf, *supra* note 451, pp. 335–336; von Scherenberg, *supra* note 379, p. 246. Remarkably, Dershowitz seriously suggests legalizing torture to defend life and regulate its use by means of judicially approved torture warrants. See Alan Dershowitz, Why Terrorism Works, Yale University Press: New Haven (2002), pp. 158–163.

469. Cf. Gaeta, *supra* note 445, p. 793; Jessberger, *supra* note 445, p. 1066; Bellamy, *supra* note 445, pp. 145–147. In the Gäfgen kidnapping, for instance, a German Court found the police officer who ordered that the child kidnapper be threatened with torture to be guilty

may feel to save innocent life, while maintaining that torture is always wrong and those who engage in it will get their hands dirty.

In an age of significant terrorist threats, those sustaining the argument for life-saving torture almost invariably return to a hypothetical example that encapsulates Bentham's simple utilitarian logic. If torture can force a terrorist to give up the location and deactivation code of a ticking time-bomb and hundreds of lives can be saved, why should such torture not be carried out?[470] However, this well-known fictional case rarely finds its match in reality. For one, it will almost always be uncertain whether the victim is indeed a terrorist and whether he has the life-saving information sought.[471] Even if that is the case, torture is rarely an effective means to gain relevant and reliable information in a very short span of time and may distract the investigators' from pursuing other, more effective means to obtain life-saving information.[472]

The futility of torture to save lives is well illustrated by the euphemistically called "enhanced interrogation techniques" pursued by the United States: methods of torture and inhuman treatment through which Central Intelligence Agency (CIA) officers and private contractors sought to extract high-value information from suspected Al Qaeda terrorists. A detailed study by the U.S. Senate's Intelligence Committee of the enhanced interrogation program found that the CIA had falsely asserted that information gained from these brutal interrogations had actually thwarted specific terrorist plots and saved lives.[473] The CIA's own officers regularly called the effectiveness of these "enhanced interrogation

of incitement to coercion, but sentenced him only to a suspended monetary fine. In Gäfgen v. Germany, *supra* note 454, para. 124, the European Court acknowledged that mitigating circumstances existed in the case, although it found a mere suspended fine to be manifestly disproportionate to a breach of one of the core rights of the Convention. However, the Grand Chamber itself then turned around and awarded the kidnapper no compensation, so that its finding remains largely symbolic.

Some authors suggest that, in exceptional cases, the officer should be entirely excused from criminal responsibility. See Ambos, *supra* note 445, p. 285; Roxin, *supra* note 445, p. 469; Diehm, *supra* note 12, pp. 373–374. However, this goes too far and would fail to ensure the minimum of accountability necessary to effectively uphold the absolute prohibition of torture and inhuman treatment.

470. See, e.g., Dershowitz, *supra* note 468, p. 137; Brugger, *supra* note 456, p. 166; Herzberg, *supra* note 451, p. 322; Steinhoff, *supra* note 456.

471. Ambos, *supra* note 445, p. 271; Bellamy, *supra* note 445, p. 141; Mayerfeld, *supra* note 445, pp. 111 & 114; Turner, *supra* note 462, p. 770.

472. For a detailed review of empirical research and case studies demonstrating the futility of torture, especially where information has to be obtained quickly, see Darius Rejali, Torture and Democracy, Princeton University Press: Princeton (2009), pp. 446–479. See also Perron, *supra* note 445, p. 148; Bellamy, *supra* note 445, pp. 138–140; Mayerfeld, *id.*, pp. 121–122.

473. U.S. Senate Select Committee on Intelligence, Committeel, Study of the CIA's Detention and Interrogation Program: Findings and Conclusions (2012) [unclassified version, as published in December 2014], http://www.intelligence.senate.gov/study2014/sscistudy1.pdf, pp. 2–3.

techniques" into question, not least since victims ended up fabricating information on critical intelligence issues.[474]

Even in established democracies with an otherwise strong rule of law, any deviations from the bright line prohibition of torture and inhuman treatment may also pry open the floodgates for the uncontrolled use of torture.[475] In this respect, the U.S. Senate Report is once again instructive. It found that the CIA secretly detained 26 individuals for enhanced interrogation even though their detention was not allowed under the CIA program's own permissive standards.[476] At least 17 detainees were subjected to torture and/or inhuman treatment without the required authorization from CIA headquarters.[477] Throughout the program, the CIA lied to civilian oversight bodies about central tenets of the program and even actively impeded their oversight work.[478]

Finally, it should be noted that even if the prohibition to torture could be limited based on utilitarian considerations, the case for torture to defend life would remain weak. The ticking time-bomb scenario invokes sympathy for torture because it puts forward a grossly oversimplified cost-benefit analysis: torture one terrorist to save the lives of dozens or hundreds of innocents. However, this does not factor in the real costs generated by a departure from the rule of absolute prohibition. This is particularly apparent in the context of terrorism. Crucial international counterterrorism cooperation will break down, both in terms of exchange of information and extradition of suspects, where some partners cannot be trusted to respect the most elementary principles of international law. By resorting to torture, the state also gives up its moral superiority and affords terrorists a superb recruitment narrative.[479] Torturing suspected terrorists thus ensures that for every ticking time-bomb deactivated, more bombs are planted.

VII. Defensive intent

Most national domestic systems require a subjective element for claims of self-defense, namely that the defender must act with the intent to defend or at least be aware of the existence of the self-defense situation. Some authors suggest that a requirement of defensive intent also exists under international human rights

474. *Id.*, p. 2.

475. Roxin, *supra* note 445, pp. 467–468; Mayerfeld, *supra* note 445, p. 113; Jessberger, *supra* note 445, p. 1064; Turner, *supra* note 462, pp. 769–770. Bellamy, *supra* note 445, p. 124 also warns rightfully that torture creates a precedent that authoritarian regimes may use.

476. U.S. Senate Select Committee on Intelligence, *supra* note 473, p. 12.

477. *Id.*, p. 12.

478. *Id.*, pp. 2-8.

479. Mayerfeld, *supra* note 445, pp. 121–122.

law.[480] This means that a police officer who shoots at a fleeing thief for the sole purpose of arresting him would still commit the human rights violation of using excessive force, even if it turned out later that the thief, unbeknownst to the officer, had actually been shooting at the officer and the officer would have been allowed to fire back in self-defense.

Neither Article 2(2)(a) of the ECHR nor the U.N. Basic Principles on the Use of Force and Firearms expressly require that state agents act with defensive intent. At first glance, such a subjective requirement appears unsuitable in relation to the state obligations established by human rights law, because as an abstract entity the state cannot have subjective intent. In practice, a number of different state agents are involved in the command, control, and implementation of the use of force in self-defense or defense of others, and their motivations may differ.

However, in the inverse case of putative self-defense, where state agents honestly and reasonable belief in an attack, although no attack objectively exists, human rights bodies have been willing and able to make findings on subjective intent. If the honest and reasonable belief of state agents in a self-defense situation can exculpate the state, then the lack of such belief should also be able to inculpate it, because human rights entail not only duties of outcome, but also duties of action. Notably, it is possible for the state to violate the right to life where illegal actions of its agents endanger life but, by a fortunate coincidence, no one actually dies.[481] In the same vein, the state should be held responsible where its agents tried to kill illegally but, by coincidence, objective circumstances make the killing appear to be self-defense. In both cases, the outcome may be in line with human rights, but the motivation and actions of the agents show disrespect for human rights.

The present author therefore takes the view that the state can claim self-defense as a justification only if the state agents involved did not know of the existence of the objective circumstances providing a justification. Incidentally, this position is also congruent with the prevailing view under international criminal law, where self-defense can be claimed only if the perpetrator acted with a bona fide belief in the self-defense situation.[482]

International human rights bodies have not yet been confronted with a case that turned solely on the question of defensive intent and thus have not yet developed a position on this issue. However, the language of some decisions suggests support for the existence of a subjective requirement. In *Huohvanainen*, the ECtHR stressed, for instance, that the officers involved "honestly believed it was necessary to open fire,"[483] even though the objective circumstances clearly established such need and putative defense was out of question. In *Kazingachire*, the

480. Paeffgen, *supra* note 8, p. 387 [Art 2., para. 59]; Otto, *supra* note 12, p. 84.

481. See *supra* note 15 and accompanying text.

482. See the references *supra* note 202.

483. Huohvanainen v. Finland, *supra* note 14, para. 96.

African Commission stressed that police exercising lethal force must be "motivated" by a situation of self-defense or defense of others.[484] In *Alejandre v. Cuba*, the Inter-American Commission found that pilots committed a human rights violation in shooting down a civilian aircraft, inter alia, because the pilots used lethal force without "due motivation."[485]

D. BURDEN OF PROOF AND EVALUATION OF EVIDENCE

Cases in which the state asserts that its agents acted in self-defense or defense of others regularly turn on determinations of fact. In this regard, international human rights law requires a lower standard of proof than criminal proceedings.[486] In particular, proof may follow from the co-existence of sufficiently strong, clear, and concordant inferences, unrebutted presumptions of fact, and circumstantial evidence.[487] Having accepted the jurisdiction of international human rights bodies and concordant duties to cooperate with their proceedings, states also have no "right to remain silent." If the applicant establishes a plausible prima facie case establishing violations, the onus is on the Government to provide detailed and satisfactory explanations to refute the allegations and call their factual validity into question.[488]

In cases where the relevant information is entirely in the hands of the state, the burden of proof shifts fully to the state, which must adduce evidence fully disproving the allegation. This is notably the case where a person is killed or

484. Kazingachire et al. v. Zimbabwe [ACommHPR], *supra* note 34, para. 120.

485. Alejandre et al. v. Cuba, Case 11.589, Report No. 86/99, Report of 29 September 1999, para. 42.

486. See also Julia Kokott, The Burden of Proof in Comparative and International Human Rights Law, Kluwer Law International: The Hague (1998), p. 199; Ilias Bantekas & Lutz Oette, International Human Rights Law and Practice, Cambridge University Press: Cambridge (2013), p. 294. In particular, the Inter-American Court, applies a standard that is "capable of establishing the truth of the allegations in a convincing manner." See Velasquez Rodriguez v. Honduras, Judgment of 29 July 1988, IACtHR (Ser. C) No. 4, para. 129. The European Court professes to apply a standard of proof "beyond reasonable doubt." Salman v. Turkey, *supra* note 64, para. 100, Solomou v. Turkey, *supra* note 162, para. 66. However, this standard is more flexible than what the same terms imply in criminal proceedings. See also Erdogan et al. v. Turkey, *supra* note 126, para. 71; Aydan v. Turkey, *supra* note 64, para. 70.

487. Salman v. Turkey, *id.*; Simsek et al. v. Turkey [ECtHR], *supra* note 79, para. 101; Gangaram Panday v. Suriname, Judgment of 21 January 1994, IACtHR (Ser. C) No. 16, para. 49.

488. Bantekas/Oett, *supra* note 486, p. 294; Bousseloub v. Algeria, Comm. 1974/2010, U.N. doc. UCCPR/C/111/D/1974/2010 (2014), para. 7.3; Velasquez Rodriguez v. Honduras [IACtHR], *supra* note 486, paras. 79–80; Corumbiara Massacre v. Brazil [IACommHR], *supra* note 2, para. 129; Wallace de Almeida v. Brazil [IACommHR], *supra* note 206, para. 99; Amnesty International et al. v. Sudan [ACHPR], Comm. No. 48/90, 50/91, 52/91, 89/93 (1999), para. 52; African Commission on Human and Peoples' Rights, General Comment on the Right to Life, *supra* note 33, para. 37.

injured while in detention,[489] not least because the immediate witnesses in such cases are usually either prison employees or fellow detainees who remain under the state's control.

Several international human rights bodies also take the position that where it is unrefuted or proven that the state used force that killed or injured a person, the burden of proof shifts to the state to prove that the force used was justified and not excessive.[490] Where the state claims self-defense, it would therefore have to produce evidence proving that its agents knowingly exercised immediate, necessary and proportional action in response to an unlawful attack. Thus, in *Cosme Rosa Genoveva, Evandro de Oliveira and others*, the Inter-American Commission found violations in relation to police killing 26 suspects that had supposedly resisted arrest and engaged the police in a shoot-out, because the state did not prove, on the basis of credible investigations, that the victims were armed, that they had fired at the police, and that they had really posed a threat to the lives of police or third parties.[491]

A reversal of the burden of proof in such cases makes sense when establishing state responsibility for human rights violations. In criminal proceedings, the presumption of innocence may demand that the state disprove a plea of self-defense advanced by the defendant.[492] However, states appearing in human rights proceedings cannot be compared with individual criminal defendants, because human rights proceedings are not about punishing states but about protecting the victims and providing them with effective remedies.[493] Moreover, many crucial issues that determine whether the defensive force used was compatible with

489. Krasnova v. Kirgyzstan [HRComm], Comm. 1402/2005, U.N. Doc. CCPR/C/101/D/1402/2005 (2011), para. 8.3; Allen Henry v. Trinidad and Tobago, *supra* note 28, para. 7.1; Salman v. Turkey [ECtHR], *supra* note 64, para. 99–100; Selmouni v. France [ECtHR Grand Chamber], Appl. No. 25803/94, Judgment of 28 July 1999, para. 87; Neira Alegria v. Peru [IACtHR], *supra* note 2, para. 65; 334/06 Egyptian Initiative for Personal Rights and Interights v Arab Republic of Egypt [ACommHPR], Comm. 334/06, Decision of 1 March 2011, para. 169; Kokott, *supra* note 486, p. 198.

490. Mansuroglu v. Turkey [ECtHR], *supra* note 257, para. 76; Bicici v. Turkey, *supra* note 276, paras. 34 & 37; Zambrano Vélez et al. v. Ecuador [IACtHR], *supra* note 29, paras. 101 & 108; Montero-Aranguren et al. (Detention Center of Catia) v. Venezuela, *supra* note 29, para. 80; Nadege Dorzema v. Dominican Republic, *supra* note 100, para. 89; Miguel Castro-Castro Prison v. Peru, *supra* note 159, para. 273; Finca "La Exacta" v. Guatemala [IACommHR], *supra* note 2, para. 43; Mejias v. Venezuela [IACommHR], *supra* note 29, paras. 190 & 198. Cf. Kazingachire et al. v. Zimbabwe [ACommHPR], *supra* note 34, para. 121; Suarez de Guerrero v. Colombia [HRComm], *supra* note 23, para. 13.2; Allen Henry v. Trinidad and Tobago, *supra* note 28, para. 7.1. See also Harris et al., *supra* note 67, p. 227.

491. Cosme Rosa Genoveva, Evandro de Oliveira and others v. Brazil, Cases 11.566 & 11.694, Report No. 141/11 (2011), para. 140. See also Döndü Günel v. Turkey [ECtHR], Appl. 34673/07, Judgment of 16 September 2016, para. 35.

492. See also Perron, *supra* note 362, p. 1037.

493. Godínez Cruz v. Honduras, Judgment of 20 January 1989, IACtHR (Ser. C) No. 5 (1989), para. 140.

human rights tend to depend on information within the exclusive possession of the law enforcement authorities. Usually, only the state will usually know how the operations was planned, commanded, and controlled. In cases of putative self-defense, the applicant will also have a hard time showing that from the officer's perspective there were no good reasons to believe in the attack. Furthermore, the state controls the forensic evidence from which important information about the unlawful attack and the law enforcement agents' defensive action can be drawn. In cases involving police killing in alleged self-defense, it must also be borne in mind that the victims can no longer present their side of the story.

Shifting the burden of proof does not place states at an unfair disadvantage. States are obligated to investigate any cases of self-defense resulting in death or injury.[494] As long as the investigation lives up to basic requirements, international human rights bodies show considerable deference towards the state's investigative findings.[495] The findings of a properly conducted national investigation can exculpate the state.[496]

International bodies will draw adverse inferences of fact, however, if a state's fails to comply with its obligation to investigate or if the investigation undertaken suffers from significant deficiencies.[497] Such deficiencies often relate to the collection and appreciation of forensic evidence. Human rights bodies frequently reject state assertions that the victim brandished a weapon because standard evidence collection practices were not followed to ensure that law enforcement agents did not plant the weapon on the victim after the altercation.[498]

494. See this Fourth Chapter: E.II (204–209).

495. Agdas v. Turkey, Appl. No. 34592/97, Judgment of 27 July 2004, para. 91; Erdogan et al. v. Turkey, *supra* note 126, para. 71; Perk et al. v. Turkey, *supra* note 127, para. 57. See also Velu/Ergec, *supra* note 8, para. 231.

However, international human rights bodies will not necessarily appropriate the *legal* analysis; not least since domestic criminal proceedings have a much higher standard of proof than human rights proceedings. See Erdogan, *id.* On the requirements for a proper investigation, see this Fourth Chapter: E.II (pp. 204–209).

496. Occasionally, however, it may also provide decisive evidence establishing its responsibility. See, e.g., Neira Alegria v. Peru [IACtHR], *supra* note 2, para. 69; Allen Henry v. Trinidad and Tobago [HRComm], *supra* note 28, para. 7.1. Cf. Kazingachire et al. v. Zimbabwe [ACommHPR], *supra* note 34, para. 118.

497. See Baboeram-Adhin v. Suriname [HRCttee], *supra* note 81, para. 14.2; Olmedo v. Paraguay, *supra* note 164, para. 7.5; Zambrano Vélez et al. v. Ecuador [IACtHR], *supra* note 29, para. 110; Corumbiara Massacre v. Brazil [IACommHR], *supra* note 2, para. 182; Erdogan et al. v. Turkey [ECtHR], *supra* note 126, para. 72; Agdas v. Turkey, *supra* note 495, paras. 94–96; Cangöz v. Turkey, Judgment of 26 April 2016, Appl. No. 7469/06, para. 138.

498. See Gül v. Turkey, *supra* note 189, para. 81 (no proper recordings of the alleged findings of two guns a spent cartridge next to the victim); Agdas, *id.*, para. 93 (no fingerprinting of the gun allegedly carried by the victim); Soare et al. v. Romania, *supra* note 133, para. 146 (unprofessional collection and recording of the knife allegedly seized from victim); Cangöz v. Turkey, *supra* note 497, para. 135 (no fingerprinting of rifles found next to victims).

Adverse inferences can also be drawn from crime scene evidence, notably if the weapons allegedly used to attack the police are never found,[499] if the crime scene does not show any signs of the violent altercation that supposedly took place,[500] or if officers tampered with the evidence.[501] International human rights bodies will also closely study the forensic record of injuries. The fact that the police officers sustained no injuries or only light injuries may undermine the credibility of the state's claims that they came under serious attack.[502] Meanwhile, telling injuries sustained by the victims (shots in the back, head shots from close range) can indicate that the police did not actually kill in self-defense.[503]

E. POST-ACTION DUTIES OF CARE, ACCOUNTABILITY, AND REMEDY

Even where state agents use justified defensive force, the state still has certain post-action duties of care. Furthermore, it has to provide effective remedies and accountability where state force exceeds the bounds of justified self-defense.

499. Perisan et al. v. Turkey, 290, para. 83 (iron bars and other blunt objects supposedly used by rioting prisoners not found); Gülec v. Turkey, *supra* note 77, para. 72 (no guns found at crime scene); Zambrano Vélez et al. v. Ecuador, *supra* note 29, para. 107 (presence of arms mentioned only in military's own report); Aydan v. Turkey, *supra* note 64, para. 79 (no arms or bullet cartridges found at scene of attack).

500. Erdogan et al. v. Turkey, *supra* note 126, para. 83 (no evidence of an exchange of fire in the apartments where the gunfight supposedly took place) Ogur v. Turkey, *supra* note 12, para. 81 (no recently fired bullet cartridges found at scene of alleged sustained exchange of fire). See also Perk et al. v. Turkey, *supra* note 127, para. 69 (finding of 21 cartridges fired by the suspects provides evidence for the necessity of killing them in self-defense).

501. Mejias v. Venezuela [IACommHR], *supra* note 29, para. 200 (victim's body removed from the crime scene); Cosme Rosa Genoveva, Evandro de Oliveira and others v. Brazil, *supra* note 491, para. 139 (victims' bodies removed from the scene); Cangöz v. Turkey, *supra* note 497, para. 133 (victim's clothes destroyed before forensic investigation)

502. Gülec v. Turkey [ECtHR], *supra* note 77, para. 72; Erdogan v. Turkey, *supra* note 126, para. 81; Mansuroglu v. Turkey, *supra* note 257, para. 91; Perisan et al. v. Turkey, 290, para. 83; Zambrano Vélez et al. v. Ecuador [IACtHR], *supra* note 29, para. 107.

503. Suarez de Guerrero v. Colombia [HRComm], *supra* note 23, para. 11.5 (victims killed at point-blank range, some with shots in the back or in the head); Ogur v. Turkey [ECtHR], *supra* note 12, para. 83 (gunshot wound at the nape of the neck from supposed warning shot); Erdogan v. Turkey, *supra* note 126, paras. 83 & 85 (bullet holes indicating that victims were shot while already on the ground); Kakoulli v. Turkey, *supra* note 215, para. 120 (third shot fired several minutes after shots that already neutralized the victim); Corumbiara Massacre v. Brazil [IACommHR], *supra* note 2, para. 193 (shots in the neck from behind) and para. 198 (victim repeatedly shot from very close range); Cosme Rosa Genoveva, Evandro de Oliveira and others v. Brazil, *supra* note 491, para. 141 (head shots, including from the back). See also Perk et al. v. Turkey, *supra* note 127, para. 69 (forensic evidence showing that no suspect was killed from close range affirmed police's self-defense account). See also Keremedchiev v. Bulgaria [Committee against Torture], U.N. Doc. CAT/C/41/D/257/2004 (2008), para. 9.3 (serious injuries indicating that police used excessive force).

I. Medical care and psychosocial support

The state has to ensure that injured aggressors and innocent bystanders receive rapid and effective medical care irrespective of whether the police's use of force was justified.[504] Even the suspect who tried to shoot the police must not be left to die.

Where it is foreseeable that state agents may have to use force in self-defense or for other purposes, the authorities have to plan for this contingency and ensure that adequate medical care capacity is in place at the site of the operation.[505] In *Olmedo*, the Human Rights Committee therefore found a violation because the authorities had failed to ensure that public medical emergency teams were present at the site of the potentially violent demonstration. As a result, 12 hours elapsed between the shooting of the victim in purported self-defense and his admission to a hospital.[506] In *Wasilewska and Kalucka*, the ECtHR criticized that the authorities planned an elaborate ambush to capture an armed criminal gang but failed to make provisions for an ambulance, so the seriously injured victims had to wait about 20 minutes for one to arrive.[507] In *Finogenov*, the authorities knew that the knockout gas used in the Moscow theatre hostage situation was dangerous and that hundreds of exposed hostages would require immediate medical attention. However, the authorities still failed to sufficiently prepare for the medical rescue operation due to "inadequate information exchange between various services, the belated start of the evacuation, limited on-the-field coordination of various services, lack of appropriate medical treatment and equipment on the spot, and inadequate logistics."[508]

Care must also be extended to law enforcement agents who use force in self-defense. Where police have to resort to their firearms, especially if they have to kill in self-defense, this can have a serious impact on the psychological health of the officers involved and even augment their suicide risk.[509] If left untreated, post-traumatic stress disorder may also cloud the officer's judgment in future critical

504. U.N. Basic Principles on the Use of Force and Firearms, *supra* note 25, Principle 5(c); U.N. Code of Conduct for Law Enforcement Officials, *supra* note 25, art. 6; Nadege Dorzema v. Dominican Republic, *supra* note 100, para. 100. Wallace de Almeida v. Brazil [IACommHR], *supra* note 206, para. 107; Carlton Linton v. Jamaica [HRComm], *supra* note 82, para. 8.5.; African Commission on Human and Peoples' Rights, Principles and Guidelines on Human and Peoples' Rights while Countering Terrorism in Africa, *supra* note 105, p. 18 [Part 2: B(iii)]; Kälin & Künzli, *supra* note 58, p. 279; Melzer, *supra* note 22, p. 236.

505. Giuliani and Gaggio v. Italy, *supra* note 65, para. 251; Oya Ataman v. Turkey, Appl. No. 74552/01, 5 December 2006, para. 39.

506. Olmedo v. Paraguay, *supra* note 164, para. 3.3.

507. Wasilewska and Kalucka v. Poland, *supra* note 66, para. 55.

508. Finogenov et al. v. Russia, *supra* note 117, para. 266.

509. See, e.g., André Marin, "In the line of duty": Investigation into operational stress injuries affecting police officers, Ombudsman of Ontario: Ottawa (2012).

situations. For these reasons, officers must be provided with post-incident stress counselling and other psychosocial support.[510]

II. Duty to investigate incidents involving firearms and other force

In order to effectively protect the rights to life and physical integrity, the state has a duty to investigate cases involving the use of force by law enforcement officials, especially if they involve the discharge of firearms, significant injuries or deaths.[511] The authorities have to commence the investigation at their own initiative (*ex officio*), even if the victim or the victim's family fail to submit a complaint.[512] The investigation must be independent, impartial, effective, reasonably prompt, and transparent.[513] The more serious the incident under investigation, the more rigorously these criteria must be complied with. The utmost rigor is required for cases of police killings.

The duty to investigate is a separate legal duty. A failure to investigate with due diligence may therefore result in a violation of the right to life or physical security, even if it cannot be established that the use of force failed to comply with

510. U.N. Basic Principles on the Use of Force and Firearms, *supra* note 25, Principle 21. See also Crawshaw/Cullen/Williamson, *supra* note 58, pp. 152–153; ICRC, Human Rights and Humanitarian Law for Police and Security Forces, *supra* note 2, pp. 260–261; Amnesty International, Use of Force Guidelines, *supra* note 3, p. 39.

511. Human Rights Committee, General Comment 31, *supra* note 120, paras. 15 & 18; *id.*, Bousseloub v. Algeria, *supra* note 488, para. 73; U.N. Special Rapporteur on extrajudicial, summary or arbitrary executions, Christof Heyns [2014 Annual Report], *supra* note 84, para. 80; McCann et al. v. United Kingdom [ECtHR Grand Chamber], *supra* note 9, para. 161; Finogenov et al. v. Russia [ECtHR], *supra* note 117, para. 268; Velasquez Rodriguez v. Honduras [IACtHR], *supra* note 486, para. 177, Zambrano Vélez et al. v. Ecuador [IACtHR], *supra* note 29, para. 88; Corumbiara Massacre v. Brazil [IACommHR], *supra* note 2, para. 175; Amnesty International et al. v. Sudan [ACommHPR], *supra* note 488, para. 51; United Nations Department of Peacekeeping Operations, *supra* note 280, paras. 33 & 41.

512. Zambrano Vélez et al. v. Ecuador [IACtHR], *supra* note 29, paras. 119–120; Ilhan v. Turkey [ECtHR], *supra* note 15, para. 63; Jaloud v. The Netherlands, Appl. 47708/08, Judgment of 20 November 2014, para. 186. 143; Case of the Mapiripan Massacre. Judgment of 15 September 2005. Series C No. 134, paragraph 219.

513. Principles on the Effective Prevention and Investigation of Extra-Legal, Arbitrary and Summary Executions, ECOSOC Res. 1989/65, annex, 1989 U.N. ESCOR Supp. (No. 1) at 52, U.N. Doc. E/1989/89 (1989), para. 9; Human Rights Committee, General Comment 31, *supra* note 120, para. 15; Hugh Jordan v. United Kingdom [ECtHR], Appl. No. 24746/94, Judgment of 4 May 2001, paras. 105–109; Giuliani and Gaggio v. Italy, *supra* note 65, paras. 298–305; Ruano Torres et al. v. El Salvador, Judgment of 5 October 2015, IACtHR Ser. C No. 303, para. 124; Inter-American Commission on Human Rights, *supra* note 142, para. 45; Amnesty International et al. v. Sudan [ACommHPR], *supra* note 488, para. 51; African Commission on Human and Peoples' Rights, General Comment on the Right to Life, *supra* note 33, para. 17.

substantive requirements.[514] In the practice of international human rights bodies, self-defense cases regularly turn on compliance with the duty to investigate, because the actual facts surrounding the alleged use of defensive force can often not be fully established.

1. Independence and Impartiality of the Investigative Body

Investigations of police use of force must be carried out by hierarchically and institutionally separate oversight bodies that also enjoy independence in practice.[515] These need not necessarily be judicial or judicially supervised bodies, although international bodies tend to apply a stricter measure of scrutiny where only national executive authorities were involved in the investigation.[516] The investigation is not independent if it involves persons from units directly involved in the operation under review or if both investigators and involved officers are under the same chain of command.[517]

The investigative body must be provided with the "necessary powers, resources, independence, transparency and reporting, community and political support, and civil society involvement."[518] Where investigations by the ordinary independent oversight bodies appear inadequate, notably because of the importance of the matter or the apparent existence of a pattern of abuse, the government

514. U.N. Special Rapporteur on extrajudicial, summary or arbitrary executions, Christof Heyns [2014 Annual Report], *supra* note 84, para. 79; Montero-Aranguren et al. (Detention Center of Catia) v. Venezuela, *supra* note 29, para. 83.

515. Ramsahai v. The Netherlands [ECtHR Grand Chamber], *supra* note 9, para. 325; Jaloud v. The Netherlands, *supra* note 512, para. 186 Montero-Aranguren et al. (Detention Center of Catia) v. Venezuela [IACtHR], *supra* note 29, para. 81; Zambrano Vélez et al. v. Ecuador, *supra* note 29, para. 122; African Commission on Human and Peoples' Rights, General Comment on the Right to Life, *supra* note 33, para. 16.

516. Finogenov et al. v. Russia, *supra* note 117, para. 240. See also Agdas v. Turkey, *supra* note 495, paras. 101–102. Conversely, in Giuliani and Gaggio v. Italy, *supra* note 65, paras. 308–315, the court attached importance to the fact that the police killing of a G-8 Summit demonstrator was subject to a judicial investigation and, concerning the wider issues surrounding the G8 Summit, to a parliamentary inquiry and to internal disciplinary action.

517. Finogenov, *id.*, para. 281 (involvement of the FSB intelligence service in both rescue operation and the subsequent investigation); Corumbiara Massacre v. Brazil [IACommHR], *supra* note 2, para. 262; Wallace de Almeida v. Brazil [IACommHR], *supra* note 206, para. 82 (both concerning military police investigating itself); Amnesty International et al. v. Sudan [ACHPR], *supra* note 488, para. 51 (commission of inquiry consisting police and security officials from agencies involved in the massacres under investigation); Hugh Jordan v. United Kingdom, *supra* note 513, para. 120 (independent police monitoring authority and police unit under the authority of the same chief constable); Ogur v. Turkey, *supra* note 12, para. 91 (investigation committee chaired by governor who was administratively in charge of security forces); Cangöz v. Turkey, *supra* note 497, para. 126 (evidence collection left to soldiers under investigation).

518. U.N. Special Rapporteur on extrajudicial, summary or arbitrary executions, Christof Heyns [2014 Annual Report], *supra* note 84, para. 84.

needs to establish independent commissions of inquiry or similar special ad hoc procedures.[519]

Due to the particularly strong pressures that can be exercised through military chains of command, international bodies impose strict criteria of independence for investigations carried out within the military.[520] In particular, the investigators must be within a separate chain of command and not outranked by the persons under investigation.[521]

Investigators must not only act without bias but also be seen to be impartial. Yet not every premature public pronouncement on the potential outcome of the investigation necessarily compromises the impartiality of the investigators. For instance, the ECtHR accepted that investigators issued an interim press release indicating that there were grounds for investigating whether a suspect had committed suicide, even though it was later established that the suspect was killed by the police in self-defense.[522] The appointment of a ballistics expert who had previously characterized the case as self-defense in a specialist journal article was considered "delicate" but not grave enough to compromise the impartiality of the entire investigation.[523]

2. Effectiveness of the Investigation

An effective investigation "must be capable of leading to a determination of whether the force used was or was not justified in the circumstances."[524] In examining individual responsibility, it must not only investigate the officers who used force, but also seek to ascertain responsibility up the chain of command.[525] Effectiveness and impartiality are closely linked. Both are undermined where investigators attach undue weight to information provided by the state agents involved, while neglecting to pursue other obvious lines of investigations. In *Gülec*, for instance, the ECtHR found a violation of the duty to investigate because the investigating officer readily accepted the official account and failed to interview available eyewitnesses.[526] In *Cosme Rosa Genoveva, Evandro de*

519. U.N. Principles on effective investigation of arbitrary executions, *supra* note 513, para. 11.

520. U.N. Special Rapporteur on extrajudicial,summary or arbitrary executions Philip Alston, 2006 Annual Report, *supra* note 50, para. 37; Corumbiara Massacre v. Brazil [IACommHR], *supra* note 2, paras. 261–263; Soare et al. v. Romania, *supra* note 133, para. 169.

521. Soare, *id.*, para. 169; Ogur v. Turkey, *supra* note 12, para. 91.

522. Huohvanainen v. Finland, *supra* note 14, para. 110.

523. Giuliani and Gaggio v. Italy, *supra* note 65, para. 323.

524. Giuliani and Gaggio, *id.*, 301; Hugh Jordan v. United Kingdom, *supra* note 513, para, 107.

525. Erdogan et al. v. Turkey, *supra* note 126, para. 91; Iczi v Turkey, *supra* note 276, para. 68. See also U.N. Basic Principles on the Use of Force and Firearms, *supra* note 25, Principle 24.

526. Gülec v. Turkey, *supra* note 77, para. 79. See also Gül v. Turkey, *supra* note 189, para. 93 (court heard only evidence from officers involved, but not from the victim's family); Ergi v. Turkey, *supra* note 59, para. 83 (prosecutor heavily relied on incident report of involved

Oliveira and others, the Inter-American Commission criticized the practice of registering police killings by default as justified due to resistance offered by the victims.[527]

Cases of lethal self-defense raise particular challenges, because the victim is dead and often the only direct witnesses are the officers involved. Investigators must therefore prevent collusion between them by directly interrogating them separate from one another soon after the incident.[528] Furthermore, investigators must procure and safeguard all relevant and available objective sources of evidence, in particular forensic evidence.[529] The deliberate destruction or suppression of evidence will call the impartiality and effectiveness of the entire investigation into question.[530]

3. Prompt Initiation and Reasonable Expeditiousness

When law enforcement officials injure or kill someone, they must report the incident promptly to their superiors. From there, the independent body responsible

gendarmes and placed the onus on victim's relatives to show wrongdoing on the part of the security forces); Soare et al. v. Romania, *supra* note 133, para. 145 (reliance on statements of police officers while disregarding accounts of other eyewitnesses); Wasilewska and Kalucka v. Poland, *supra* note 66, para. 62 (authorities unconditionally embraced statement of police officers involved, despite forensic evidence to the contrary).

527. Cosme Rosa Genoveva, Evandro de Oliveira and others v. Brazil, *supra* note 491, para. 139.

528. Jaloud v. The Netherlands, *supra* note 512, para. 227 (no precautions to prevent collusion between officer who fired fatal shots and other witnesses); Ramsahai v. The Netherlands, *supra* note 9, paras. 330–331 (officers involved not kept separate from one another and only questioned three days after the fatal shooting); Jordan 127 (coroner received only written statements from involved officers); Erdogan et al. v. Turkey, *supra* note 126, para. 72 (lack of contemporary individual statements by police officers involved in lethal operation). But cf. Kerr v. United Kingdom, Appl. No. 28883/95, Judgment of 4 May 2001, para. 126 (delay of several days in interviewing officers involved does not prejudice investigation).

529. Ramsahai v. The Netherlands, *supra* note 9, para. 329 (no gunshot residue testing, no adequate pictorial record of the injuries, no weapons examination); Soare et al. v. Romania, *supra* note 133, para. 173 (forensic medical analysis only four months after the fatal shooting); Ogur v. Turkey, *supra* note 12, para. 90 (no post-mortem or ballistics examinations); Agdas v. Turkey, *supra* note 495, para. 93 (no fingerprint dusting of gun) & para. 103 (autopsy results disregarded); Erdogan, *id.*, paras. 92–93 (no crime scene photography or sketch and no fingerprint, ballistics, or other forensic analysis); Corumbiara Massacre v. Brazil [IACommHR], *supra* note 2, para. 282 (incomplete ballistics analysis). For details on forensic evidence gathering procedures to be carried out, see also United Nations Manual on the Effective Prevention and Investigation of Extra-Legal, Arbitrary and Summary Executions, U.N. Doc. E/ST/CSDHA/.12 (1991), Chapters III.C and IV.

530. See Finogenov et al. v. Russia [ECtHR], *supra* note 117, para. 279 (burning of the operational crisis cell's working papers); Corumbiara Massacre v. Brazil [IACommHR], *supra* note 2, para. 281 (deliberately setting fire to the crime scene); Olmedo v. Paraguay, *supra* note 164, para. 7.5 (bullet that killed the victim "misplaced"); Kerr v. United Kingdom, *supra* note 528, para. 127 (involved officers were instructed not to reveal to investigators their special branch affiliation and access to intelligence sources).

to investigate police use of force must be informed right away and start investigating promptly.[531] In *Ramsahai,* for instance, the ECtHR considered it insufficient that the responsible National Police Internal Investigations Department became involved only fifteen and a half hours after police killed the suspect in alleged self-defense.[532]

In carrying out their work, investigators have to draw a reasonable balance between moving the inquiry along with "reasonable expedition" without coming to "rely on hasty or ill-founded conclusions to close their investigation."[533] In *Giuliani and Gaggio*, the ECtHR accepted that the preliminary investigation into the police killing took one year and four months.[534] Conversely, in *Soare*, the investigation was considered not expeditious enough. A forensic autopsy was not ordered until four months after the incident and fourteen months elapsed before a prosecutor questioned one of the officers involved.[535] In *Hugh Jordan*, the ECtHR found a violation based on an inquest that had still not concluded eight years and four months after the police killing, even though repeated procedural challenges by the victim's family had contributed to the delays.[536] In *Olmedo*, the Human Rights Committee took issue with the state party failing to explain how the investigation could drag on for nine years with reaching any definitive conclusion.[537] The Inter-American Court characterized an investigative delay of 14 years in *Zambrano Vélez* even as a "blatant denial of justice."[538]

4. Transparency and Victim Involvement

Where the state is investigating itself, it is particularly important to keep investigations as transparent as possible, so as to reassure the victims and the general public about its impartiality and effectiveness.

The ECtHR has acknowledged that the degree of public scrutiny may vary from case to case.[539] While it has expressed appreciation where the state carried

531. U.N. Basic Principles on the Use of Force and Firearms, *supra* note 25, Principles 6, 11(f) & 22; U.N. Special Rapporteur on extrajudicial, summary or arbitrary executions, Christof Heyns, *supra* note 22, para. 63.

532. Ramsahai v. The Netherlands, *supra* note 9, para. 334.

533. Jaloud v. The Netherlands, *supra* note 512, para. 186; Finogenov et al. v. Russia, *supra* note 117, para. 271.

534. Giuliani and Gaggio v. Italy, *supra* note 65, para. 325.

535. Soare et al. v. Romania, *supra* note 133, paras. 172–173.

536. Hugh Jordan v. United Kingdom, *supra* note 513, para. 136.

537. Olmedo v. Paraguay, *supra* note 164, para. 7.5.

538. Zambrano Vélez et al. v. Ecuador, *supra* note 29, para. 126.

539. Giuliani and Gaggio v. Italy, *supra* note 65, para. 303.

out public inquests,[540] more confidential types of investigation are also permissible. Disclosure of materials may prejudice private individuals or the investigation itself. Therefore, the victims or their families do not necessarily have to be granted full access to the investigative materials as the investigation progresses.[541] However, they must be involved enough in the investigation to safeguard their essential interests, notably by having the right to submit pleadings at any state of the investigation, to request inclusion of relevant evidence, or to suggest additional lines of inquiry that are then also given good faith consideration.[542]

Furthermore, the results of the investigation must be shared with the victim and made public, including details on how and by whom the investigation was carried out and what the major findings are.[543] Where highly significant to the case, this will require disclosure of information considered sensitive on national security grounds.[544] In *Finogenov*, the ECtHR considered the investigation manifestly incomplete because the FSB never disclosed to the investigators the formula of the dangerous knockout gas that it deployed during its operation against the Moscow theatre hostage-takers.[545] In *McCann*, the court accepted that public security interests justified not disclosing information about the identity, training, chains of command, and prior operational activities of the Special Forces soldiers involved in the killing of IRA terrorists.[546] However, it then also held that the state had failed to show that the soldiers had the appropriate training to engage in law enforcement activities.[547]

540. McCann et al. v. United Kingdom, *supra* note 9, para. 162; Bubbins v. United Kingdom, *supra* note 9, para. 153.

541. Ramsahai, v. The Netherlands, *supra* note 9, para. 347; Bubbins v. United Kingdom, *supra* note 9, para. 161; Kerr v. United Kingdom, *supra* note 528, para. 129.

542. See also U.N. Principles on effective investigation of arbitrary executions, *supra* note 513, para. 16; Kalamiotis v. Greece [HRCommittee], Comm. 1486/2006, U.N. Doc. CCPR/C/93/D/1486/2006 (2008), para. 7.2; Giuliani and Gaggio v. Italy [ECtHR], *supra* note 65, para. 311; Huohvanainen v. Finland, *supra* note 14, para. 111; Soare et al. v. Romania, *supra* note 133, para. 174; Cangöz v. Turkey, *supra* note 497, para. 123.

543. U.N. Special Rapporteur on extrajudicial, summary or arbitrary executions Philip Alston, [2006 Annual Report], *supra* note 50, para. 25. See also U.N. Principles on effective investigation of arbitrary executions, *supra* note 513, para. 17; Hugh Jordan v. United Kingdom, *supra* note 513, paras. 122–123; Soare, *id.*, paras. 174–175

544. U.N. Special Rapporteur on extrajudicial, summary or arbitrary executions Philip Alston, *id.*, para. 54.

545. Finogenov et al. v. Russia, *supra* note 117, para. 277.

546. McCann v. United Kingdom, *supra* note 9, paras. 104, 157 & 164. Permitting the non-disclosure of the involved officers' identity on security grounds. See also Bubbins v. United Kingdom, *supra* note 9, paras. 155–157.

547. McCann v. United Kingdom, *id.*, para. 212.

III. Duty to prosecute perpetrators of excessive force

The protection of the rights to life and physical integrity would be ineffective if excessive use of force, especially lethal force, had no personal consequences for the law enforcement agents involved. Where the state's investigation establishes that excessive force was used, it must therefore be followed by the prosecution and adjudication of the responsible individual state agents at the operational and command level.[548] This raises the question to what extent police officers can rely on specific domestic defenses excluding criminal responsibility that go beyond the boundaries of justified self-defense established by international human rights law.

1. Unreasonable Putative Self-defense

In England and some Anglophone African jurisdictions, self-defense pleas are accepted where defendants can show that they honestly but mistakenly believed in a self-defense situation, even if this belief was not based on good reasons. In *Armani da Silva*, the ECtHR considered the subjective standard of English criminal law to be compatible with human rights, although it stressed that the absence of good reasons would be relevant for the factual determination of whether the mistaken belief was indeed honestly held.[549]

Conversely, some scholars have taken the view that England and other jurisdictions following the same approach have to amend their criminal laws, at least in relation to putative self-defense by law enforcement agents, to bring them in line with international human rights law, which requires both an honest belief in the need for self-defense and good reasons for that mistaken belief.[550] However, that view fails to appreciate the difference between state and individual responsibility. At the individual level, it is still appropriate that honest belief in self-defense alone excludes conviction for an intentional crime. After all, the perpetrators did not intend to do anything wrong, since they believed they were acting in

548. Human Rights Committee, General Comment 31, *supra* note 120, para. 18; Gäfgen v. Germany [ECtHR], *supra* note 454, para. 119; Gutiérrez Soler v. Colombia, Judgment of 12 September 2005, IACtHR (Ser. C) No. 132, paras. 96-07; Kazingachire et al. v. Zimbabwe [ACommHPR], *supra* note 34, para. 113; ACommHPR Working Group on the Death Penalty and Extra-Judicial, Summary or Arbitrary Killings in Africa, *supra* note 106, para. 59; ICRC, Human Rights and Humanitarian Law for Police and Security Forces, *supra* note 2, p. 250.

549. See also Armani Da Silva v. United Kingdom, *supra* note 195, para. 251.

550. Ashworth, *supra* note 17, p. 42; Richard Buxton, The Human Rights Act and the Substantive Criminal Law, Criminal Law Review 2000, 331–340, at pp. 337–338; Leverick, *supra* note 193, p. 361.

Leverick therefore proposes that unreasonable belief in self-defense should only be considered a partial injury that mitigates punishment. See Fiona Leverick, The use of force in public or private defence and Article 2: A reply to Professor Sir John Smith, Criminal Law Review 2002, 963–967, at p. 966. See also Armani Da Silva v. United Kingdom [ECtHR], *supra* note 195, Joint Dissenting Opinion of Judges Karakas, Wojtyczek and Dedov, para. 5.

self-defense. Incidentally, the criminal law of many civil law countries and international criminal law would also lead to that outcome.[551]

Nonetheless, in the most serious cases, excessive force based on an unreasonable belief in self-defense must not result in complete impunity for the law enforcement agents involved. International human rights law requires the prosecution of officials who cause death due to recklessness or gross negligence.[552] In line with this requirement, the state has be able to prosecute officials at least for involuntary manslaughter where they mistakenly believe in a self-defense situation requiring lethal force and such belief is grossly unreasonable.[553]

2. Excessive Defense Due to Fear or Panic

Under the criminal codes of a number of civil law countries, persons do not incur criminal responsibility if they knowingly exceed the boundaries of necessary self-defense out of fear, anxiety, panic or similar asthenic effects.[554] It has been suggested that this is irreconcilable with the human rights obligation to prosecute excessive use of force by law enforcement agents.[555] The ECtHR has taken this position to the extent that law enforcement agents would escape criminal responsibility for a killing, in *Aydan*.[556] The ECtHR reasoned that the effective protection of the right to life would be a dead letter if state agents enjoyed impunity even if they exceeded the bounds of absolutely necessary self-defense.[557]

551. Perron *supra* note 362, p. 1037. For international criminal law, see the references *supra* note 202.

552. Öneryildiz v. Turkey [ECtHR Grand Chamber], Appl. No. 48939/99, Judgment of 30 November 2004, para. 93. See also Amnesty International, Use of Force Guidelines, *supra* note 3, p. 32 (emphasizing also a duty to prosecute commanding officers fail to prevent excessive force of their officers that they ought to have known about). But cf. Calvelli and Ciglio v. Italy, Appl. No. 32967/97, Judgment of 17 January 2002, para. 51; Vo v. France, Appl. No. 53924/00, Judgment of 8 July 2004, para. 90 (holding that a killing involving simple negligence does not necessarily have to result in a criminal prosecution). Schabas, *supra* note 68, p. 128 takes the view that according to the ECHR, only intentional homicide must be criminalized.

553. At least in England, this appears to be already the case. See John C. Smith, The use of force in public or private defence and Article 2 ECHR, Criminal Law Review 2002, 958–962, at p. 961.

554. A comparative legal analysis carried out by the European Court of Human Rights indicates that 19 out of 25 European states reviewed would not punish a person who exceeds the boundaries of self-defense due to fear or related factors. Aydan v. Turkey, *supra* note 64, paras. 48–51.

555. Diehm, *supra* note 12, pp. 401 & 404; Stephen Skinner, Populist politics and shooting burglars: comparative comments on the Lega Nord's proposal to reform Italian self-defense law, Criminal Law Review 2005, 275–284, at p. 282. For the contrary position, based on the outdated view that human rights generally entail no duty to prosecute, see Rudolf Echterhölter, Die Europäische Menschenrechtskonvention in der juristischen Praxis, JuristenZeitung 1958, 142–148, p. 144.

556. Aydan v. Turkey, *supra* note 64, paras. 101.

557. *Id.*

In *Rickly Burrell*, the U.N. Human Rights Committee seemed to endorse the opposite view. In that case, prison wardens shot and killed a prisoner in a hostage crisis, exceeding the bounds of necessary self-defense because they panicked when they saw some of their colleagues being threatened by the inmates. The Committee considered that the state had to pay compensation to the victim's family. Contrary to its jurisprudence in other cases involving excessive state force, however, it did not insist on the prosecution of the individual perpetrators.[558]

Many jurisdictions do not consider excessive self-defense due to fear or panic worthy of punishment because these are uncontrollable emotions that understandably arise in situations of self-defense.[559] However, one needs to bear in mind that law enforcement agents must have the appropriate moral, psychological, and physical qualities for the effective exercise of their functions.[560] They should therefore be particularly resistant to letting fear determine their actions. Although in extreme circumstances psychological pressure and emotions can still affect the judgment of appropriately selected and trained police officers, this is already factored into the standard of assessment under international human rights law, which takes into account that officers have to make decisions under pressure and "in the heat of the moment." Where the situation was objectively so threatening that even a reasonable officer would have exceeded the bounds of necessary out of fear, then there is no human rights violation[561] and accordingly also no duty to prosecute. However, allowing for an individual exculpatory ground that extends impunity even further goes too far. In practice, states may easily abuse such an exculpatory ground to shield their agents from accountability. Perhaps with this consideration in mind, the drafters of the Rome Statute did not excuse fear-related excessive self-defense, even though such an excuse was foreseen, for instance, in preparatory work of the International Law Association.[562] The present author therefore takes the view that unreasonable fear that leads to the state agent knowingly exceeding the boundaries of self-defense should be considered only as a factor mitigating punishment.[563] However, it should not be a ground for full impunity, especially in cases involving killings by the police.

558. Rickly Burrell v. Jamaica, *supra* note 24, paras. 9.5 & 11.

559. Roxin, *supra* note 418, p. 562.

560. Aydan v. Turkey, *supra* note 64, para 99, making reference to the U.N. Basic Principles on the Use of Force and Firearms (*supra* note 25), Principle 18.

561. See *supra* notes 235 & 236 and accompanying text.

562. See International Law Association, Protocol II to the Statute for an International Criminal Court and to the Statute for an International Commission of Criminal Inquiry containing defenses, as cited in Ambos, *supra* note 202, p. 999. Merkel, *supra* note 362, pp. 447–448 has critizicized the Rome Statute for failing to recognize fear-driven excesses of self-defense as an excuse.

563. See also Skinner, *supra* note 555, p. 282; Sangero, *supra* note 173, p. 92.

IV. Duties to provide compensation and make amends

Human rights violations give rise to an obligation to provide full, effective and prompt reparation for the wrong suffered. In particular, compensation has to be provided for irreplaceable harm suffered, including moral damages for pain and suffering.[564]

There is a duty to provide full compensation where the victim has been intentionally subjected to summary execution or inhuman treatment and self-defense was only invoked as a pretext to try and justify such serious violations. In such cases, it is immaterial whether the victims were actually dangerous and a lesser degree of force would have been justified under the circumstances.[565]

However, where the state only exceeds the bounds of necessary self-defense due to negligence or inadvertent recklessness, mitigating factors such as the culpability of the victim in provoking the situation may reduce the moral damages awarded to the victim. In *Makaratzis*, for instance, the ECtHR awarded far less damages for non-pecuniary harm than the applicant requested. In so doing, the court took into account that the applicant's own dangerous behavior, namely his attempt to escape the police in a high-speed car chase, had put the lives of innocent people at risk.[566] In *McCann*, where negligent planning led to the unjustifiable killing of IRA terrorists, it considered it appropriate to award no damages at all since the victims had actually intended to plant a bomb in Gibraltar.[567] Mitigating circumstances can also be taken into account, where death resulted from negligence in providing follow-up medical care. Thus, in *Finogenov*, where the rescue operation to provide medical assistance to the Moscow theatre hostages affected by the knockout gas was badly planned and implemented, the ECtHR lowered the amount of moral damages awarded to the victims and their families considering that "the authorities used the gas while trying to help the hostages and that the lethal force was, in principle, directed against the terrorists, not the hostages."[568]

564. United Nations General Assembly, Basic Principles and Guidelines on the Right to a Remedy and Reparation for Victims of Gross Violations of International Human Rights Law and Serious Violations of International Humanitarian Law, U.N. Doc. A/RES/60/147 (2005), paras. 15 & 20; Human Rights Committee, General Comment 31, *supra* note 120, para. 15; Caracazo v. Venezuela, Judgment of 29 August 2002, IACtHR Ser. C No. 95, paras. 76-77; Kazingachire et al. v. Zimbabwe [ACommHPR], *supra* note 34, paras. 127 & 131.

565. Cf. Montero-Aranguren et al. (Detention Center of Catia) v. Venezuela, *supra* note 29, paras. 130–132; Zambrano Vélez et al. v. Ecuador [IACtHR], *supra* note 29, paras. 141–145; Neira Alegria v. Peru [IACtHR], *supra* note 2, para. 91 (3); Soare et al. v. Romania, *supra* note 133, paras. 248–251. In Gäfgen v. Germany, *supra* note 454 (paras. 190–191) no compensation was awarded despite the intentional infliction of cruel, inhuman, and degrading treatment, but only because the applicant had explicitly not pleaded for such compensation.

566. Makaratzis v. Greece, *supra* note 15, paras. 92–93.

567. McCann et al. v. United Kingdom, *supra* note 9, para. 219.

568. Finogenov et al. v. Russia, *supra* note 117, para. 289.

Where state agents exercised justified self-defense, there is no wrongful act that would give rise to a duty to provide reparation. However, even where self-defense precludes wrongfulness and reparation under the law of state responsibility, international law may still recognize a duty to provide a payment to make good for material loss, which arises directly from the primary law. The International Law Commission's Articles on State Responsibility contain a clause to that effect.[569] At least *de lege ferenda*, there are two case constellations where the state ought to make amends for harm resulting from the lawful exercise of self-defense by state agents, not merely *ex gratia* but on the basis of its obligations under international human rights law.[570]

The first constellation concerns cases of justified self-defense based on the honest and reasonable, yet mistaken, belief in the existence of an unlawful attack. Where the victim's own unlawful behavior led to the erroneous belief in an attack, it is entirely appropriate not to award any compensation.[571] However, there will be other cases where plainly unfortunate circumstances lead the police to honestly and reasonably, though wrongly, believe in the existence of an attack and kill or seriously injure the presumed attacker. In such cases, the state ought to compensate the victim or the bereaved family.[572] International human rights law affords law enforcement agents the privilege to err when exercising defensive force so that they can effectively protect the general public and themselves in the line of duty. It is therefore equitable to place the financial burden for the harm done on the general public and not on the unfortunate individual victims (or their bereaved families), who already suffer the physical and psychological harm caused by the error.

A second constellation concerns innocent third parties affected by defensive use of force. Two scenarios must be distinguished. Where the state endangers an innocent third person in an attempt to save that person and the danger unfortunately materializes, it is justified not to make amends. An example is *Andronicou*, where police accidentally shot and killed the hostage during the

569. ILC Articles on State Responsibility, *supra* note 177, art. 27(b). See also Mathias Forteau, Reparation in the Event of a Circumstances Precluding Wrongfulness, in: James Crawford et al. (eds.), The Law of International Responsibility, Oxford University Press: Oxford (2010), 887–893, at p. 891.

570. The concept of making amends has been so far mainly raised in relation to harm caused by lawful acts of armed conflict. See Andrew Childers & Anna Lamut, Legal Foundations for "Making Amends" to Civilians Harmed by Armed Conflict, International Human Rights Clinic, Harvard Law School, February 2012, http://hrp.law.harvard.edu/wp-content/uploads/2012/02/making-amends-foundations-paper-feb-2012-final.pdf.

571. See, e.g., Bubbins v. United Kingdom, *supra* note 9, where the victim of lethal force threatened police with a fake gun, thus creating the false appearance of a lethal attack.

572. Cassese has suggested a payment of indemnity for the comparable case of soldiers who, in honest belief and with good reasons, mistake civilians for armed group fighters and open fire on them, even though the error was not caused by the civilians in question. See Cassese, *supra* note 202, p. 396.

attempt to liberate her and save her life.[573] In that case, the state acted in the victim's best interests, so that it is also equitable that if the defensive action goes wrong, the burden remains with the victim. The situation is different where defensive action harms an innocent person who is only a bystander in the true sense of the word. For instance, in *Bakan,* a warning shot fired by police in self-defense killed an innocent bystander who was not at all involved in the situation. In such a case, it would be equitable to make amends to the victim's family. The innocent bystander sacrificed his life as a result of lawful action aimed at protecting state agents, so the further financial burden caused by the loss should rest with the state for whose benefit the action was undertaken.

The jurisprudence of international human rights bodies does not yet recognize a duty to make amends for harm lawfully inflicted in the said constellations. However, doctrinally, it would not be completely alien to international human rights law to recognize a post-action duty that applies even though the state did not violate the right to life or physical integrity in the first place. After all, the duties to provide medical care to victims of police use of force and to investigate the use of force also do not depend on whether the state used unlawful force or not.[574] Morally, compensation would be justified, because the victims are made to sacrifice their physical integrity or even life without any fault of their own.[575]

F. CONCLUSION: A DEEP, BUT NARROW, JUSTIFICATION FOR THE USE OF FORCE IN LAW ENFORCEMENT

The right to personal self-defense shapes international human rights law by establishing a deep but narrow justification for the use of force in law enforcement. It is "deep" because the defense of life against imminent threat constitutes the sole ground on which law enforcement agents may deliberately deprive individuals of their right to life. In some constellations, the police may even have a duty to take an aggressor's life where this is absolutely necessary to protect innocent life.

At the same time, the self-defense justification is "narrow," since it is subject to strict formal and substantive requirements. Police cannot simply assume a right to use force in self-defense, but such a right has to be established and regulated in publicly available laws. There are even good reasons to take the view, as the Inter-American human rights bodies do, that the police's right to kill in self-defense must be established by parliamentary statute.

The substantive requirements for law enforcement agents' use of defensive force established by international human rights law seemingly mirror those generally found in domestic criminal laws. Self-defense may only be exercised against an unlawful (but not necessarily culpable) human attack targeting protected

573. See, e.g., Andronicou and Constantinou v. Cyprus [ECtHR], *supra* note 9, where police accidentally shot and killed the hostage in an attempt to free her and save her life.

574. See this Fourth Chapter: E.I and E.II (pp. 202–209).

575. Cf. Forteau, *supra* note 569, p. 893.

individual interests. Law enforcement agents can claim to defend themselves or others only in the face of immediately antecedent, present, or ongoing threats. Retribution for past attacks or pre-emptive force cannot be justified as self-defense. Furthermore, the defensive action must be necessary, proportional, and driven by subjective awareness of the defense situation.

These requirements have particular features where law enforcement agents use defensive force. This is notably the case because law enforcement officers, unlike private individuals, represent the state and its values, and have a proclaimed monopoly on the use of force. State agents therefore have no general duty to retreat to avoid lethal force. But they must proactively de-escalate potentially violent situations where force in self-defense might become otherwise necessary. As state representatives, law enforcement agents are also prohibited from defending property with lethal force. They may not engage in torture or inhuman treatment even where information extracted from such acts can defend innocent lives against an imminent threat.

As each officer's individual defensive action is embedded in the authorities' wider collective response, both have to be assessed to determine whether the use of force constituted necessary and proportional self-defense. Human rights violations may ensue if the authorities place individual agents in situations where they unnecessarily use force, either because the authorities did not appropriately plan, command, and control operations or because they failed to adequately select, train, and equip its law enforcement agents.

The duties of the state do not end as soon as the defensive action is concluded. The state has a duty to provide medical care to anyone injured during law enforcement operations. Furthermore, it must ensure that the use of force is duly investigated so as to ensure that perpetrators of intentional or grossly negligent excessive force are held accountable and the victims duly compensated.

5

Personal Self-Defense in Military-Led Operations

In 2008, Sudanese army units and other security forces tried to force their way into the Kalma Camp for Internally Displaced Persons (IDPs) in Darfur. Confronted by a hostile crowd of IDPs, they opened fire, killing 32 persons and injuring at least 108 more. The government claimed that its forces defended themselves against IDPs attacking them with spears and knives, while fighters armed with guns and positioned behind the IDPs were firing at them. A U.N. investigation could not ascertain the presence of fighters, but confirmed that some of the IDPs were armed with sticks and knives. Applying self-defense standards applicable to law enforcement operations, the U.N. further determined that the Sudanese forces violated human rights, because they shot to kill even though they did not face a legitimate threat to life.[1]

Following his 2013 visit to Mexico, the U.N. Special Rapporteur on Summary Executions called for an end to the use of military forces in fighting organized criminal cartels, warning about a "a military approach to public security risks creating a situation where a civilian population is vulnerable to a wide range of abuses."[2] The Special Rapporteur found one particular incident of two college students who, after they were shot and killed by soldiers, were wrongly identified as members of organized criminal groups. Subsequently, the crime scene was altered to make it appear that they had died in a shoot-out and weapons were planted on the victims to try to show that the military had acted in self-defense.[3]

1. Eleventh periodic report of the United Nations High Commissioner for Human Rights on the situation of human rights in the Sudan Killing and injuring of civilians on 25 August 2008 by government security forces: Kalma IDP camp, South Darfur, Sudan, 23 January 2009, pp. 2, 6 & 11, http://www.ohchr.org/Documents/Countries/11thOHCHR22jan09.pdf.

2. Special Rapporteur on Summary, Extrajudicial and Arbitrary Executions, Mission to Mexico, U.N. Doc. A/26/36/add.1 (2014), paras. 21 & 103.

3. *Id.*, para. 45.

Human Rights and Personal Self-Defense in International Law. Jan Arno Hessbruegge

While the Darfur incident occurred in the context of a non-international armed conflict, the Mexican situation is usually not framed as an armed conflict in a legal sense (even if the local popular discourse often refers to a war against narcotraffickers).[4] Nevertheless, the two cases share common features representative of larger trends. Armed non-state actors increasingly have the capacity and will to challenge state authority, and the lines between conflict participants and civilian bystanders have become exceedingly blurry. In turn, states show an increasing propensity to deal with armed nonstate threats by resorting to their military forces. Both trends are exacerbated as extremist groups across the globe carry out more terrorist attacks and states increasingly respond with their military.

Against this backdrop, this chapter will examine to what extent the right to personal self-defense is also relevant for military-led operations. In principle, the right of state agents to use defensive force is relevant primarily for civilian law enforcement agents operating in peacetime. In times of armed conflict, military use of force has to follow primarily the far more permissive conduct of hostilities rules under IHL, which are based on a very different paradigm. However, as will be discussed in the next section, law enforcement standards find application even in armed conflict in exceptional constellations. In those exceptional cases, soldiers may kill with intent only where absolutely necessary to defend life against an immediate threat.

The chapter's second section looks at situations where military forces are exceptionally tasked to carry out law enforcement functions in peacetime. In such cases, they are bound by the same rules as civilian law enforcement agents, in particular by the limitations on the use of defensive force. These rules apply in domestic and in extraterritorial law enforcement operations.

Counterterrorism operations, including targeted killings of suspects, often occur at the cusp between armed conflict and law enforcement. As will be discussed in the final section of this chapter, states increasingly invoke self-defense only, without any reference to international humanitarian law or human rights, to justify extraterritorial targeted killings of suspected terrorists. This blurs the distinction between the right to personal self-defense and the right to interstate self-defense in a dangerous and legally impermissible way.

A. EXCEPTIONAL RELEVANCE OF THE PERSONAL SELF-DEFENSE PRINCIPLE IN ARMED CONFLICT

The right to life and the right to physical security continue to apply to the use of force during armed conflict hostilities, but their content is chiefly defined by the *lex specialis* rules of international humanitarian law (IHL) on the conduct of

4. See, e.g., Mexico: Challenges to international humanitarian law and humanitarian action - Speech given by Mr Peter Maurer, President of the ICRC, Mexico City, 7 April 2015, pp. 2 & 8, https://www.icrc.org/en/document/mexico-challenges-international-humanitarian-law-and-humanitarian-action.

hostilities.[5] Although similarities are sometimes claimed,[6] these rules are based on principles very different from the right to personal self-defense that shapes the use of lethal force in time of peace. Rather than differentiating between aggressors and defenders, IHL regulates the conduct of hostilities based on a distinction between civilians and other protected persons not directly participating in the hostilities on the one hand, and combatants and persons who directly participate in the hostilities on the other. Thus, IHL does not prohibit combatants and direct participants in hostilities from intentionally killing one other and no distinctions are made based on who attacked first.[7]

Unlike in the case of self-defense, the principle of (military) necessity underlying IHL rules on the conduct of hostilities does not restrict the belligerent parties to employing graduated force and the least harmful means to neutralize enemy combatants.[8] Lethal force may be the measure of "first resort": every active participant is per se considered a legitimate target and may be immediately

5. See the references in the Fourth Chapter: A.III (p. 104, note 53) on the complex relationship between IHL and international human rights law. See also below, notes 11 & 12 and the accompanying text.

International humanitarian law knows only two types of armed conflicts, namely international armed conflicts, involving armed force between two or more states, and non-international armed conflicts, characterized by protracted armed violence between governmental forces and non-governmental armed groups or between such groups within the territory of a state. See Prosecutor v. Tadić [ICTY Appeals Chamber], IT-94-1, Decision on Jurisdiction of 2 October 1995, at para. 70; ICRC, How is the Term "Armed Conflict" Defined in International Law?, March 2008, https://www.icrc.org/eng/assets/files/other/opinion-paper-armed-conflict.pdf. While there is no third category of transnational armed conflict, it is widely accepted that non-international armed conflicts can sometimes also spill over and extend beyond the territory of a state. However, it is contested whether there can be purely transnational non-international armed conflicts that have no nexus to a particular territory. Cf. Marko Milanovic and Vidan Hadzi-Vidanovic, A taxonomy of armed conflict, in: Nigel White & Christian Henderson (ed.), Research Handbook on International Conflict and Security Law, Elgar: Cheltenham (2013), 256–314, pp. 289ff.

6. See Wayne McCormack, Targeted Killing at a Distance: Robotics and Self-Defense, Pacific McGeorge Global Business & Development Journal, vol. 25 (2012), 361–379, at p. 363.

7. State combatants are even provided with positive legal authority to intentionally kill other combatants, which also protects them against prosecution. Conversely, rebel fighters and other civilians who directly participate in hostilities can still be prosecuted under domestic law. See also Seventh Chapter: E.IV (p. 339), discussing to what extent international law ought to give the latter type of persons privileged combatant status and protection from prosecution where they defend themselves against massive human rights violations.

8. In order to maintain a bright line prohibition against chemical weapons, IHL even prohibits the employment of tear gas as a less lethal means. This constitutes one of the rare instances where the law enforcement paradigm is more permissive than the armed conflict paradigm. See Dieter Fleck, Law Enforcement and the Conduct of Hostilities: Two Supplementing or Mutually Excluding Legal Paradigms?, in: Andreas Fischer-Lescano et al. (eds.), Frieden in Freiheit. Peace in Liberty. Paix En Libertè. Festschrift für Michael Bothe zum 70 Geburtstag, Nomos/DIKE: Baden-Baden/Zürich (2008), 391–407, at p. 394.

engaged with lethal force.[9] Exceptions apply only where an enemy combatant clearly communicates an intention to surrender that it is feasible to accept or is already *hors de combat,* notably due to an injury.[10] Furthermore, there is increasing support for the view that the government may not directly target and kill nonstate fighters who do not pose a significant threat to government forces and can be safely arrested, especially fighters who find themselves unarmed in territory under firm government control.[11] This view approximates the understanding of necessity under IHL as somewhat similar to that under the self-defense/law enforcement paradigm, except that fighters who cannot be safely captured

9. Geoffrey S. Corn, Self-Defense Targeting: Blurring the line between the Jus ad Bellum and the Ius in Bello, in Kenneth Watkin/Andrew J. Norris (eds.), Non-International Armed Conflict in the Twenty-First Century, Naval War College: Newport, Rhode Island (2012), 53–92, at p. 68; I Gloria Gaggioli, Expert meeting on the use of force in armed conflict: Interplay between the conduct of hostilities and law enforcement paradigms [ICRC Expert Meeting on Use of Force in Hostilities and Law Enforcement], ICRC: Geneva (2013), p. 12.

10. Jean-Marie Henckaerts & Louise Doswald-Beck, Customary International Humanitarian Law vol. I: Rules, International Committee of the Red Cross and Cambridge University Press: Cambridge (2005), p. 164 [Rule 47].

11. Nils Melzer, Interpretive Guidance on the Notion of Direct Participation in Hostilities under International Humanitarian Law [ICRC Interpretive Guidance on Direct Participation in Hostilities], ICRC: Geneva (2009), pp. 81–82; Office of the United Nations High Commissioner for Human Rights, International Legal Protection of Human Rights in Armed Conflict, OHCHR: New York/Geneva (2011), pp. 67–68; U.N. Special Rapporteur on extrajudicial, summary or arbitrary executions Philip Alston: Study on targeted killings, U.N. Doc. A/HRC/14/24/Add.6 (2010), para. 77; African Commission on Human and Peoples' Rights, General Comment No. 3 on the African Charter on Human and Peoples' Rights: The Right To Life (Article 4), adopted at the 57th session (2015), para. 34; Marco Sassoli & Laura M. Olson, The Relationship between international humanitarian and human rights law where it matters: admissible killing and internment of fighters in non-international armed conflicts, International Review of the Red Cross, vol. 90 (2008), 599–627, p. 614; Stuart Casey-Maslen, The use of weapons in armed conflict, in: Stuart Casey-Maslen (ed.), Weapons under International Human Rights Law, Cambridge University Press: Cambridge (2014), 240–281, at p. 278; Louise Doswald-Beck, The right to life in armed conflict: Does international humanitarian law provide all the answers?, International Review of the Red Cross, vol. 88 (2006), 881–904, at pp. 890–891; Stefanie Schmahl, Targeted Killings—A Challenge for International Law?, in: Christian Tomuschat, Evelyne Lagrange & Stefan Oeter (eds.), The Right to Life, Brill: Leiden (2010), 233–266, at p. 264; Fleck, *supra* note 8, p. 395 (taking this position for armed conflicts generally). Pointing in the same direction, albeit without explicitly invoking the armed group fighter status of the victims, Hamiyet Kaplan et al. v. Turkey [ECtHR], Appl. No. 36749/97, Judgment of 13 September 2005, para. 51; Mansuroglu v. Turkey, Appl. 43443/98, Judgment of 26 February 2008, 85–89; Suarez de Guerrero v. Colombia [HRCttee], Comm. R.11/45 (1982), para. 13.2. See also Public Committee against Torture in Israel and the Palestinian Society for the Protection of Human Rights and the Environment v. Government of Israel et al. [Supreme Court of Israel, sitting as the High Court of Justice], Case HCJ 769/02, Judgment of 11 December 2005, para. 40. However, it is not clear to what extent the High Court derives this requirement from international law or only from Israeli constitutional law.

may still be deliberately killed, even where they pose no imminent threat to life. Precisely because it departs from the clear-cut distinction between lawfully targetable conflict participants and protected civilians that is central to IHL, this view remains contested.[12]

IHL also recognizes a requirement of proportionality, but this requirement is less onerous than the proportionality requirement applicable to personal self-defense. Firstly, proportionality restrictions under IHL relate only to civilians not participating in hostilities, that is, "innocent bystanders," not to the targeted combatant.[13] Self-defense also must be proportional vis-à-vis the aggressor. Secondly, IHL accepts the foreseeable yet incidental killing of civilians if it constitutes unavoidable "collateral damage" that is not excessive in light of the military objectives pursued. In contrast, self-defense cannot justify the use of deliberately lethal force against innocent bystanders whose death would not necessarily occur if no force was used.[14]

The IHL rules cater to the special needs of an armed conflict situation, where the conflict parties engage in intense violence. However, even in armed conflict, soldiers may sometimes have to obey the more restrictive law enforcement standards that are informed by international human rights law. This is specifically the case when faced with violence from persons that remain protected under international humanitarian law because they do not participate directly in hostilities. In these situations, the right to personal self-defense becomes particularly relevant, because it is the sole ground that can justify deliberately lethal force against such protected persons.

I. Riots, violent demonstrations, and opportunistic banditry

Situations of armed conflict and military occupation are often characterized by high political tensions and unstable general security. As a result, soldiers may also confront riots, violent demonstrations, opportunistic banditry, and other types of civilian violence. While such civilians do not use violence in direct support of a party to an armed conflict at a level of organization and intensity that qualifies them as participants in the armed conflict, soldiers and other security forces may still take measures against them, but only within the law enforcement

12. Michael N. Schmitt, The Interpretive Guidance on the Notion of Direct Participation in Hostilities: a critical analysis, Harvard National Security Journal, vol. 1 (2010), 5-55, at pp. 41–42; W. Hays Parks, Part IX of the ICRC's "Direct Participation in Hostilities" Study: No Mandate, No Expertise, and Legally Incorrect, New York University Journal of International Law and Politics, vol. 42 (2010), 767–830.

13. Fleck, *supra* note 8, pp. 403–404; Corn, *supra* note 9, p. 72. At most, IHL protects combatants by outlawing certain cruel means of warfare that might hence be seen as per se disproportional.

14. Kevin Jon Heller, "One Hell of a Killing Machine": Signature Strikes and International Law, Journal of International Criminal Justice, vol. 11 (2013), 89–119, p. 114. See also this Fourth Chapter: C.V.3.b (pp. 183–189).

paradigm.[15] Even if such civilians are armed and dangerous, they may not be killed as if they were civilians directly participating in hostilities.

Soldiers may not use deliberately lethal force against them unless absolutely necessary to defend their life or that of others against imminent threat. For instance, in the case of *Gülec*, set against the non-international armed conflict between the Turkish government and the Kurdish Workers Party (PKK), the Turkish authorities faced a violent protest by Kurdish demonstrators who shouted pro-PKK slogans and attacked the police with sticks and stones. Applying law enforcement standards, the ECtHR ruled that shooting at the demonstrators with a machine gun amounted to excessive use of force.[16]

The same approach was taken by the U.N. High Commissioner for Human Rights when reporting on an incident during the non-international armed conflict in Darfur, where Sudanese security forces opened fire on a hostile crowd of internally displaced persons armed with sticks and knives. Assessing the situation solely on the basis of the law enforcement paradigm, the High Commissioner found a human rights violation because the security forces shot to kill even though they did not face a legitimate threat to life.[17]

In both cases, the government's assertions that armed members of the combatant group had sheltered within the crowd and fired from there at the state security forces were rejected as factually not credible. Neither the ECtHR nor the High Commissioner therefore had to address the contested question what paradigm applies where a violent crowd consists of both rioting civilians and armed combatants.

Some suggest that the more protective law enforcement paradigm should govern such a situation in its entirety, at least where the security forces firmly control the situation and the level of violence is low, or where it is materially impossible to distinguish clearly between fighters and violent civilians.[18] However, the prevailing view is that a mixed paradigm applies, where the authorities should confront the fighters according to the rules applying to the conduct of hostilities, and the rioting civilians according to those of the law enforcement paradigm.[19] The latter

15. ICRC Expert Meeting on the Use of Force in Hostilities and Law Enforcement, *supra* note 9, pp. 24–25; ICRC Interpretive Guidance on Direct Participation in Hostilities, *supra* note 11, p. 63; Douglas Guilfoyle, The *Mavi Marmara* Incident and Blockade in Armed Conflict, British Yearbook of International Law, vol. 81 (2011), 171–223, p. 210; Doswald-Beck, *supra* note 11, p. 893. For situations of occupation, that is already indicated by Art. 27 of Geneva Convention (IV) relative to the Protection of Civilian Persons in Time of War, which refers to "measures of control and security in regard to protected persons."

16. Gülec v. Turkey, Appl. No. 21593/93, Judgment of 27 July 1998, paras. 17 & 72–73.

17. Eleventh periodic report of the United Nations High Commissioner for Human Rights on the situation of human rights in the Sudan, *supra* note 1, p. 11.

18. ICRC Expert Meeting on the Use of Force in Hostilities and Law Enforcement, *supra* note 9, p. 25.

19. *Id.*

view deserves support since security forces would be put at a grave disadvantage if they could not respond within the same force paradigm as the armed group members attacking them. In this sense, mixed crowd scenarios are no different from other situations where armed group members launch attacks from behind human shields. This is not to say that there is a license to fire at will at a crowd that includes enemy fighters who are attacking. State forces remain bound under IHL to strictly distinguish between fighters and civilians not participating in hostilities. They must take all feasible precautions to protect such civilians and refrain from force to the extent that it would lead to excessive civilian loss.

II. Violent prisoners of war and interned fighters

Prisoners of war enjoy protected status since they are no longer actively participating in conflict. If they riot, try to stage a violent escape, or engage in other types of violence, this does not turn them again into active combatants who may be countered immediately with deliberately lethal force. Instead, law enforcement standards apply. The camp guards must first use less lethal means to contain the violence. They may resort to the use of firearms only after due warning, to defend against an imminent threat of death or serious injury.[20] This also follows from of the Third Geneva Convention, according to which the use of weapons against prisoners of war constitutes "an extreme measure, which shall always be preceded by warnings appropriate to the circumstances."[21] Shooting to kill is allowed only to defend life against an immediate threat. In applying this principle, the War Crimes Section of the Court of Bosnia and Herzegovina accepted that a soldier guarding prisoners of war exercised justified self-defense in killing a prisoner who had managed to grab a rifle and had shot another guard dead.[22]

20. Thomas Weigend, Notwehr im Völkerstrafrecht, in: Ulrich Sieber et al. (eds.), Strafrecht und Wirtschaftsstrafrecht—Dogmatik, Rechtsvergleich, Rechtstatsachen: Festschrift für Klaus Tiedemann zum 70. Geburtstag (2008), 1439–1451, at p. 1444; Julian Fernandez & Xavier Pacreau, Statut de Rome de la Cour pénale international: Commentaire article par article, vol.1, Pedone: Paris (2012), p. 922; ICRC Expert Meeting on the Use of Force in Hostilities and Law Enforcement, *supra* note 9, p. 33. It is contested at what point escaping prisoners of war can be targeted like combatants again. In light of Art. 91 of the Third Geneva Convention, the preferable view is to consider prisoners of war subject to force under the law enforcement paradigm until they manage to rejoin their armed forces. See ICRC Expert Meeting on the Use of Force in Hostilities and Law Enforcement, *supra* note 9, p. 36.

21. See Geneva Convention III relative to the Treatment of Prisoners of War, art. 42.

22. See Prosecutor v. Radomir Vukovic et al. [Court of Bosnia and Herzegovina, Section I for War Crimes], Case. No. X-KR-06/180-2, Judgment of 22 April 2010, http://www.worldcourts.com/wcsbih/eng/decisions/2010.04.22_Prosecutor_v_Vukovic_Radomir.pdf, para. 435. See also Petar Mitrović, a.k.a. Pera [Court of Bosnia and Herzegovina, Appellate Division of Section I for War Crimes], Case. X-KRŽ-05/24-1, Judgment of 7 September 2009, http://www.worldcourts.com/wcsbih/eng/decisions/2009.09.07_Prosecutor_v_Mitrovic.pdf, para. 164.

The same principles apply to interned or imprisoned armed group fighters.[23] Even if they attack their guards with lethal means, they cannot be considered direct participants in armed conflict and thus lawful military targets. Only force within the self-defense paradigm may be applied against them. In 1986, for instance, imprisoned members of the Sendero Luminoso a armed group staged a coordinated riot, which was crushed by Peruvian military units using military means, including explosives and heavy weapons. In several judgments relating to these events, the Inter-American Court found that Peru's actions violated the right to life. The court centered its criticism on Peru having seen the incident as a "confrontation" between the government and Sendero Luminoso and having approached it with a "war logic," rather than limiting itself to necessary and proportional force under law enforcement standards.[24]

III. Enforcement of naval blockades and ceasefire lines

The enforcement of naval blockades marks one of the rare instances where IHL allows making unarmed civilian vessels a legitimate target of military operations if such vessels are used to breach the blockade. However, in such situations only force compatible with law enforcement standards may be applied unless the vessel or civilians on board directly participate in the hostilities.[25] Not every act of violent resistance put up by the civilian crew and passengers of a blockade-running vessel against an attempt by the blockading state to board can be considered direct participation in hostilities.[26] Instead, this must be carefully established on a case-by-case basis based on the general criteria of direct participation established by IHL.[27]

In May 2010, a flotilla of six ships sailed from Turkey towards the Gaza Strip with the stated aim of breaching the Israeli naval blockade and bringing

23. ICRC Expert Meeting on the Use of Force in Hostilities and Law Enforcement, *supra* note 9, p. 34.

24. Neira Alegria et al. v. Peru, Judgment of 19 January 1995, IACtHR Ser. C No. 21, para. 74; Durand and Ugarte, Judgment of 16 August 2000, IACtHR Ser. C No. 68, para. 70; Miguel Castro-Castro Prison v. Peru, Judgment of 25 November 2006, IACtHR Ser. C No. 160, para. 235.

25. Guilfoyle, *supra* note 15, pp. 210–211.

26. But cf. Alan Dershowitz, Israel obeyed international law: Legally, the Gaza flotilla conflict is an open-and-shut case, 1 June 2010, http://www.nydailynews.com/opinion/israel-obeyed-international-law-legally-gaza-flotilla-conflict-open-and-shut-case-article-1.180324.

27. James Farrant, The Gaza Flotilla Incident and the Modern Law of Blockade, Naval War College Review, vol. 66 (2013), 81–98, at p. 91; Office of the Prosecutor of the International Criminal Court, Situation on Registered Vessels of Comoros, Greece and Cambodia: Article 53(1) Report (6 November 2014), paras. 43–53. For views on the criteria for direct participation in hostilities see ICRC Interpretive Guidance on Direct Participation in Hostilities, *supra* note 11, p. 46; Israeli Supreme Court of Israel sitting as the High Court, *supra* note 11, paras. 30–40.

humanitarian supplies to that territory. Israeli naval commandos forcibly boarded and brought the ships under their control in order to enforce the blockade. The civilian passengers on one ship violently resisted. Nine passengers were killed in the ensuing struggle and many more wounded. A total of four inquiries set up to investigate the "Flotilla" incident (two from the United Nations, one Israeli, and one Turkish) came to different views on the human rights violations involved, in particular due to different views on the legality of the blockade itself, the question whether violently resisting passengers could be qualified as direct participants in hostilities, and divergences on findings of fact. However, as a matter of law, all inquiries assessed the force employed by the Israeli soldiers against those persons it found to be genuine civilians on board by applying the international standards on law enforcement and the right to personal self-defense embodied therein.[28]

A similar case is that of soldiers guarding ceasefire lines where armed hostilities may occasionally flare up. Where civilians (who are discernible as such) try to illegally cross a ceasefire line, they may only be targeted using force under law enforcement standards. Accordingly, the security forces may resort to deliberately lethal force against them only in self-defense or defense of others. In *Kakoulli* and *Solomou*, the ECtHR therefore found violations in Turkish soldiers killing Greek-Cypriot civilians who crossed the ceasefire line in Cyprus, because the killings had not been absolutely necessary or proportional to defend any person from unlawful violence.[29]

B. MILITARY INVOLVEMENT IN PEACETIME LAW ENFORCEMENT

From a policy perspective, the deployment of military personnel to carry out civilian law enforcement functions raises serious concerns, because the military

28. Report of the international fact-finding mission to investigate violations of international law, including international humanitarian and human rights law, resulting from the Israeli attacks on the flotilla of ships carrying humanitarian assistance, U.N. Doc. A/HRC/15/21 (2010), paras. 66 & 163–167; Report of the Secretary-General's Panel of Inquiry on the 31 May 2010 Flotilla Incident (July 2011), http://www.un.org/News/dh/infocus/middle_east/Gaza_Flotilla_Panel_Report.pdf, para 164; Report (Part One) of The Public Commission to Examine the Maritime Incident of 31 May 2010 (The Turkel Commission), January 2011,: http://www.turkel-committee.gov.il/files/wordocs//8707200211english.pdf , at, paras. 188–189, although the Turkel Commission made some legal and factual findings on the basis of which it considered some of the passengers to be civilians directly taking part in hostilities (*id.*, paras. 192–201). For a summary in English of the relevant sections of the Turkish-language report of the Turkish Commission, see the Report of the Secretary-General's Panel of Inquiry, *id.*, para 33 & 37(e). The Turkish inquiry did not invoke self-defense on the part of the Israeli forces, consistent with its finding that the Israeli boarding operation was illegal so that it was the passengers who used force in self-defense. See *id.*, para. 32.

29. Solomou v. Turkey, Appl. No. 36832/97, Judgment of 24 June 2008, para. 75; Kakoulli v. Turkey, Appl. No. 38595/97, Judgment of 22 November 2005, para. 121.

is trained and equipped to subdue the enemy in a shoot-to-kill paradigm.[30] The Inter-American Commission has on some occasions gone as far as suggesting that policing must always remain the exclusive domain of the civilian police.[31] While this view reflects understandable concerns rooted in the deplorable history of military dictatorships in Latin America, it neglects that in some extraordinary situations the state must be able to call upon the special capabilities of the military to effectively protect its population against certain threats. International human rights law therefore permits the use of the military for law enforcement purposes, but only in exceptional circumstances, where strictly necessary, and subject to tight civilian control and a clearly delineated mandate specified by law.[32] Consequently, the Inter-American Court found a planning violation where a general crime-fighting mission with the broad and vague mandate "to arrest

30. Report of the Special Rapporteur on extrajudicial, summary or arbitrary executions, Christof Heyns: Mission to Mexico, U.N. Doc. A/HRC/26/36/Add.1, para. 21; Daniel D. Nsereko, Arbitrary Deprivation of Life: Controls on Permissible Deprivations, in: Bertrand Ramcharan (ed.), The Right to Life in International Law, Martinus Nijhoff: Dordrecht (1985), 245-283, at p. 263.

31. Inter-American Commission on Human Rights, Report on Citizen Security and Human Rights, OEA/Ser.L/V/II.Doc. 57 (2009), paras. 103-105. See also *id.*, Report on the Situation of Human Rights in Mexico, Doc. OEA/Ser.L/V/11.100.Doc7.rev.1 (1998), para 403. But cf. *id.*, Report on the Situation of Human Rights in Mexico, OEA/Ser.L/V/II.Doc. 44/15 (2015), para. 203.

32. Montero-Aranguren et al. (Detention Center of Catia) v. Venezuela, Judgment of 5 July 2005, IACtHR Ser. C No. 150, para. 78; Committee against Torture, Concluding Observations on Venezuela, U.N. Doc. CAT/C/VEN/CO/3-4, para. 12 (c); African Commission on Human and Peoples' Rights, General Comment on the Right to Life, *supra* note 11, para. 29; Tenth periodic report of the United Nations High Commissioner for Human Rights on the situation of human rights in the Sudan: Arbitrary arrest and detention committed by national security, military and police (2008), p. 22, http://www.ohchr.org/Documents/Countries/10thOHCHR28nov08.pdf; President of the Inter-American Court, Diego Garcia-Sayan, Opening Remarks at the 48th Extraordinary Session of the Inter-American Court, as reported in Charles Parkinson, Human Rights Judge Backs Use of Military to Fight Crime, 8 October 2013, http://www.insightcrime.org/news-briefs/military-street-deployment-legal-hr-court; Office of the United Nations High Commissioner for Human Rights, Press Briefing on Venezuela, 10 February 2015, http://www.ohchr.org/EN/NewsEvents/Pages/DisplayNews.aspx?NewsID=15559&LangID=E; Joint report of the Special Rapporteur on the rights to freedom of peaceful assembly and of association and the Special Rapporteur on extrajudicial, summary or arbitrary executions on the proper management of assemblies, U.N. Doc. A/31/36 (2016), para. 66.

See also ICRC Expert Meeting on the Use of Force in Hostilities and Law Enforcement, *supra* note 9, p. 12. That international law does not fully exclude the use of military in law enforcement also follows from the Basic Principles on the Use of Force and Firearms by Law Enforcement Officials, adopted at the Eighth United Nations Congress on the Prevention of Crime and the Treatment of Offenders, Havana, 27 August to 7 September 1990, U.N. Doc. A/CONF.144/28/Rev.1 at 112 (1990), footnote; Code of Conduct for Law Enforcement Officials, adopted by U.N. General Assembly Resolution 34/169, 34 U.N. GAOR Supp. (No. 46) at 186, U.N. Doc. A/34/46 (1979), art. 1.

criminals, drug dealers and terrorists" was assigned to the military.[33] On the contrary, the U.N. High Commissioner for Human Rights has taken the view that, exceptionally and for a limited time, Mexican armed forces may be temporarily deployed in law enforcement operations against drug cartels and other organized criminal groups while the state builds up the policing capacity to deal with such threats.[34] In *McCann*, the ECtHR upheld the deployment of SAS special forces to impede a bomb attack by suspected IRA terrorists, given that the SAS had the skill and experience to deal with this specific type of threat in the safest and most knowledgeable manner.[35] In allowing for the exceptional use of military personnel in law enforcement where strictly necessary, the African Commission as well as United Nations special rapporteurs have emphasized that such personnel must receive appropriate instructions, equipment, and training suitable to the law enforcement context.[36]

Especially for law enforcement operations requiring extraterritorial action, the military is often the only body with the means to carry out such operations. For instance, only navy ships are generally equipped for the type of long-term deployment on the high seas necessary to effectively curb piracy targeting maritime trade routes off the coasts of Somalia and Nigeria. However, the involvement of navy soldiers and warships does not automatically trigger the applicability of the armed conflict paradigm since, at least so far, these pirates are not directly connected to any party to an armed conflict and lack the organization or intent to engage naval forces in military hostilities.[37] By the same token, the use of military assets such as armed drones does not automatically make an extraterritorial

33. Zambrano Vélez et al. v. Ecuador, Judgment of 4 July 2007, IACtHR Ser. C No. 166, para. 94.

34. United Nations High Commissioner for Human Rights, Navi Pillay, Defending Rights in Mexico, 16 July 2011, http://www.ohchr.org/EN/NewsEvents/Pages/DisplayNews.aspx?NewsID=11251&LangID=E. More guarded, U.N. Special Rapporteur on extrajudicial, summary or arbitrary executions, Christof Heyns, Mission to Mexico, *supra* note 30, paras. 20–26; Statement by United Nations High Commissioner Louise Arbour at the end of her mission to Mexico, 8 February 2008, http://www.cinu.org.mx/prensa/comunicados/2008/08016discursoarbouringles.htm .

35. McCann et al. v. United Kingdom, Appl. No. 18984/91, Judgment of 29 September 1995, para. 183.

36. African Commission on Human and Peoples' Rights, General Comment on the Right to Life, *supra* note 11, para. 29; Joint report of the Special Rapporteur on the rights to freedom of peaceful assembly and of association and the Special Rapporteur on extrajudicial, summary or arbitrary executions on the proper management of assemblies, *supra* note 33, para. 66.

37. See also Caroline Laly-Chevalier, Lutte contre la piraterie maritime et droits de l'homme, Revue Belge de Droit International 2009, 5–51, at p. 23; Alice Priddy, The use of weapons in counterpiracy operations, in: Casey-Maslen (ed.), *supra* note 11, 122-160, at p. 135; Douglas Guilfoyle, The Laws of War and the Fight against Somali Piracy: Combatants or Criminals?, Melbourne Journal of International Law, vol. 11 (2010), 1–13, at pp. 3–7; Andrew Murdoch, Recent Legal Issues and Problems Relating to Acts of Piracy off Somalia, in: Clive R. Symmons (ed.), Selected Contemporary Issues in the Law of the Sea, Martinus

counterterrorism operation subject to the IHL rules governing conduct of hostilities. Instead, it must be determined whether the target is a participant in an armed conflict.[38] If not, it remains a law enforcement operation.

Soldiers involved in law enforcement operations outside armed conflict must comply with the same strict international legal standards that limit the use of force and firearms by civilian police, including the duty to investigate incidents involving the use of force.[39] Thus, in *McCann*, the ECtHR assessed the intentional killing of IRA terrorists by British soldiers in Gibraltar on the same strict standards that it applies to the use of deliberately lethal force by police.[40] In *Zambrano-Vélez*, the Inter-American Court followed the same approach with regard to a major operation by Ecuadorian military to crack down on ordinary crime.[41] The African Commission also takes the view that the human rights framework fully applies even where soldiers are involved in law enforcement work.[42]

Nothing else applies with regard to extraterritorial law enforcement operations.[43] This is sometimes met with the contention that human rights never apply

Nijhoff: Leiden (2011), 139–168, at p. 145; Wolff Heintschel von Heinegg, Repressing Piracy and Armed Robbery at Sea—Towards a New International Regime?, Israel Yearbook on Human Rights, vol. 40 (2010), 219–241, at p. 228 (also noting that the law of non-international armed conflict cannot apply because piracy takes place on the high seas and thus not on the territory of a state).

38. See also Michael Ramsden, Targeted Killings and International Human Rights Law: The Case of Anwar Al-Awlaki, Journal of Conflict & Security Law, vol. 16 (2011), 385–406, at p. 391; Meagan S. Wong, Targeted Killings and the International Legal Framework: With Particular Reference to the US Operation against Osama Bin Laden, Chinese Journal of International Law, vol. 11(1) (2012), 127–163, at p. 142.

39. Fleck, *supra* note 8, pp. 393 & 396. See also Office of the United Nations High Commissioner for Human Rights, *supra* note 11, p. 64; Joint U.N. Special Rapporteurs report on assembly management, *supra* note 33, para. 66; Murdoch, *supra* note 37, p. 148

40. McCann et al. v. United Kingdom, *supra* note 35.

41. Zambrano Vélez et al. v. Ecuador [IACtHR], *supra* note 33, paras. 82–90.

42. African Commission on Human and Peoples' Rights, General Comment on the Right to Life, *supra* note 11, para. 29.

43. See also U.N. Special Rapporteur on extrajudicial, summary or arbitrary executions, *supra* note 11, paras. 31–33; Paul Tavernier, Le recours à la force par la pólice, in: Christian Tomuschat, Evelyne Lagrange & Stefan Oeter (eds.), The Right to Life, Brill: Leiden (2010), 41–64, at p. 44; African Commission on Human and Peoples' Rights, Principles and Guidelines on Human and Peoples' Rights while Countering Terrorism in Africa, adopted by its 56th Ordinary Session (2015), p. 15 [Part 1:L]; House of Lords/House of Commons Joint Committee on Human Rights, The Government's policy on the use of drones for targeted killing Second Report of Session 2015–16, para. 3.58, http://www.publications.parliament.uk/pa/jt201516/jtselect/jtrights/574/574.pdf; Noam Lubell, Extraterritorial Use of Force against Non-State Actors, Oxford University Press: Oxford (2010), pp. 224–226; Wong, *supra* note 38, p. 157.

outside a state's territory[44] or that they apply only where the state has effective control of the person concerned or of the territory in which the person is present.[45] In the absence of an armed conflict and the IHL obligations pertaining to such conflict, this view would imply that the state had no obligations that protect the person targeted by an extraterritorial killing, provided that the state never establishes effective control over the person. This is unconscionable.[46] Denying the extraterritorial applicability of the right to life, the most fundamental of rights, is also irreconcilable with the basic principle that human rights are universal.[47] Pirates do not lose their human rights protection because they venture from territorial waters onto the high seas. Likewise, a state cannot sidestep its fundamental obligation to uphold the right to life by going abroad to carry out targeted killings that would be impermissible within its borders under the same circumstances. Therefore, the International Court of Justice, the Human Rights Committee, and many others rightfully take the position that, at a minimum, states must respect human rights where they exercise power over individuals extraterritorially. This applies in particular to the right to life, as protected under customary international law and Article 6 of the ICCPR.[48] Applied to anti-piracy operations, this means that naval forces may therefore stop, board, and inspect

44. The United States and Israel still take this position, although the U.S. seems to have softened its stance under the Obama administration. See Fourth Periodic Report of the United States of America to the Human Rights Committee, U.N. Doc. CCPR/C/USA/4 (2012), para. 505; Israel Ministry of Foreign Affairs, On the Applicability of the ICCPR to the Current Situation in the West Bank and Gaza Strip (May 15, 1998), http://mfa.gov.il/MFA/AboutIsrael/State/Law/Pages/Legal%20Advisor%20of%20the%20Israel%20Ministry%20of%20Foreign%20Af.aspx.

45. Jordan J. Paust, Self-Defense Targeting of Non-State Actors and Permissibility of U.S. Use of Drones in Pakistan, Journal of Translational Law & Policy, vol. 19 (2010), 237–280, at p. 264. See also Bankovic et al. v. Belgium et al. [ECtHR Grand Chamber], Appl. No. 52207/99, Judgment of 12 December 2001, paras. 67–82. However, in more recent decisions, the European Court has gradually walked away from this principle by increasingly stretching the notion of what constitutes "effective control." See Jaloud v. The Netherlands, Appl. 47708/08, Judgment of 20 November 2014, paras. 149–153; al-Skeini et al. v. United Kingdom, Appl. No. 55721/07, Judgment of 7 July 2011, para. 149.

46. David Kretzmer, Targeted Killing of Suspected Terrorists: Extra-Judicial Executions or Legitimate Means of Defence?, European Journal of International Law, vol. 16 (2005), 171–212, at p. 184.

47. Schmahl, *supra* note 11, p. 243.

48. Armed Activities on the Territory of the Congo (Democratic Republic of the Congo v. Uganda I.C.J. Reports 2005, 168 (Dec. 19), at p. 243 [para. 216]; Human Rights Committee, General Comment 31: Nature of the General Legal Obligation on States Parties to the Covenant, U.N. Doc. CCPR/C/21/Rev.1/Add.13 (2004), para. 10; *id.*, Concluding Observations on the Report of the United States of America, U.N. Doc. CCPR/C/79/Add. 50 (1995), para. 19; Report of the Special Rapporteur on extrajudicial, summary or arbitrary executions, Christof Heyns, U.N. Doc. A/68/382 (2013), paras. 42–51; African Commission on Human and Peoples' Rights, General Comment on the Right to Life, *supra* note 11, para. 14; Alejandre et al. v. Cuba

a ship that is reasonably suspected to be a pirate ship. They may seize the ship and arrest the crew if the suspicion is confirmed.[49] If the pirates resist, the naval forces may use force, including deliberately lethal force where absolutely necessary to defend human life, such as that of their own crew or hostages onboard the pirate ship. However, the warship has no right to directly attack and sink a pirate ship as if it were a military target.[50] Similarly, deadly drone strikes outside armed conflict are only permissible where necessary to defend life against imminent threat. This means that they are generally impermissible unless they happen to target a person who is about to launch a deadly attack.[51]

C. "NAKED SELF-DEFENSE"—A CONFLATION OF PERSONAL AND INTERSTATE SELF-DEFENSE

In the debate about the permissibility of extraterritorial targeted killings through military drone strikes, some scholars have put forward the view that such killings can be justified directly under Article 51 of the U.N. Charter without the need to assess the killings separately against IHL or international human rights law.[52] Kenneth Anderson, one of the principal proponents, has called this suggested alternative justification "naked self-defense."[53] Although the U.S. government

[IACommHR], Case 11.589, Report No. 86/99, Report of 29 September 1999, para. 23; Theodor Meron, Extraterritoriality of Human Rights Treaties, American Journal of International Law, vol. 89 (1995), 78–82; Lubell, *supra* note 43, pp. 223–228; Francoise Hampson, The Relationship between International Humanitarian Law and Human Rights Law from the Perspective of a Human Rights Treaty Body, International Review of the Red Cross, vol. 90 (2008), 549–572, at p. 570; Nils Melzer, Targeted Killing in International Law, Oxford University Press: Oxford (2008), pp. 135–139, 189, 212; Schmahl; *supra* note 11, pp. 243–244; Wong, *supra* note 38, p. 159; Ramsden, *supra* note 38, p. 393; Guido den Dekker & Eric P.J. Myjer, The Right to Life and Self-Defence of Private Military and Security Contractors in Armed Conflict, in: Francesco Francioni and Natalino Ronzitti (eds.), War by Contract: Human Rights, Humanitarian Law and Private Contractors, Oxford University Press: Oxford (2011), 171–193, at p. 174.

49. Convention on the Law of the Sea, art. 105 & 110(1)(a).

50. See also Guilfoyle, *supra* note 37, pp. 10–11; Lubell, *supra* note 43, pp. 225–226. Mistaken therefore; Sandeeb Gopalan, Put Pirates to the Sword, Wall Street Journal, 10 January 2010, http://www.wsj.com/articles/SB10001424052748703652104574651962659622546 who argues that targeted killings of pirates setting out to sea are legal under international law.

51. See also U.N. Special Rapporteur on extrajudicial, summary or arbitrary executions, *supra* note 11, para. 33.

52. Kenneth Anderson, Targeted Killing in US Counterterrorism Strategy and Law, 2009, http://www.brookings.edu/papers/2009/0511_counterterrorism_anderson.aspx, at pp. 18 & 21; Paust, *supra* note 45, p. 260; Chris Downes, "Targeted Killings" in an Age of Terror: The Legality of the Yemen Strike, Journal of Conflict & Security Law, vol. 9 (2) (2004), 277–294, at pp. 286–287.

53. Kenneth Anderson, Targeted Killing and Drone Warfare: How We Came to Debate Whether There Is a "Legal Geography of War" (2011), http://media.hoover.org/sites/default/files/documents/FutureChallenges_Anderson.pdf, p. 8.

has yet to fully set out its views on the legality and criteria of extraterritorial drone killings, the "naked self-defense" view seems to underlie a 2016 presidential executive order and earlier pronouncements by senior U.S. officials, which all claim that such killings could be based on IHL or, alternatively, on self-defense.[54] Similarly, former British Prime Minister David Cameron has suggested that the targeted killing of two British "Islamic State" fighters through a British air strike could be legally justified with reference to interstate self-defense alone.[55]

In order to bring the "naked self-defense" approach into operation, Jordan Paust has suggested redefining the notions of necessity and proportionality under Article 51 of the U.N. Charter to be more or less congruent with IHL standards on necessity and proportionality.[56] For targeted killings that are actually carried out in armed conflict, the legal criteria would therefore remain unchanged. It would make no difference whether one adheres to "naked self-defense" or directly applies IHL norms to assess the legality of the killing. However, "naked self-defense" would radically transform the legal parameters for targeted killings executed without an armed conflict nexus. Under the "naked self-defense" approach, a targeted killing outside conflict would be legal even if it could not

54. See Presidential Executive Order—United States Policy on Pre- and Post-Strike Measures to Address Civilian Casualties in U.S. Operations Involving the Use of Force, 1 July 2016, https://www.whitehouse.gov/the-press-office/2016/07/01/executive-order-united-states-policy-pre-and-post-strike-measures; Legal Advisor to the U.S. Department of State Harold Koh, The Obama Administration and International Law, Speech to the American Society of International Law, 25 March 2010, http://www.state.gov/s/l/releases/remarks/139119.htm (emphasis added); *id.*, The Lawfulness of the U.S. Operation Against Osama bin Laden (2011), http://opiniojuris.org/2011/05/19/the-lawfulness-of-the-us-operation-against-osama-bin-laden/; Assistant to the President for Homeland Security and Counterrorism John O. Brennan, The Ethics and Efficacy of the President's Counterterrorism Strategy, Speech to the Wilson Center, 30 April 2012, http://www.wilsoncenter.org/event/the-efficacy-and-ethics-us-counterterrorism-strategy; U.S. Attorney General Eric Holder, Speech at Northwestern School of Law, 5 March 2012, http://www.justice.gov/iso/opa/ag/speeches/2012/ag-speech-1203051.html.

55. See David Cameron, Statement to the House of Commons on refugees from Syria and counter-terrorism, 7 September 2015, https://www.gov.uk/government/speeches/syria-refugees-and-counter-terrorism-prime-ministers-statement. For a critical analysis of the statement and the underlying legal views see U.K. House of Lords/House of Commons Joint Committee on Human Rights, *supra* note 43, para. 3.90, http://www.publications.parliament.uk/pa/jt201516/jtselect/jtrights/574/574.pdf; Robert McCorquodale, Human Rights and the Targeting by Drone, EJIL Talk, 18 September 2015, http://www.ejiltalk.org/human-rights-and-the-targeting-by-drone/.

56. Jordan J. Paust, Operationalizing Use of Drones against Non-State Terrorists under the International Law of Self-Defense, Albany Government Law Review, vol. 8 (2015), 166–203, at p. 172. See also Paust, *supra* note 45, p. 270. The U.K. government apparently follows the same approach. See U.K. House of Lords/House of Commons Joint Committee on Human Rights, *supra* note 43, para. 3.19. On the inappropriateness of directly applying Art. 51 criteria for necessity and proportionality to the assessment of specific operations, see Corn, *supra* note 9, pp. 66–72.

be shown that the target posed an imminent threat against life. Moreover, the foreseeable killing of innocent bystanders as collateral damage, a typical consequence of drone strikes but illegal in law enforcement operations, would also become permissible outside armed conflict. In other words, essential limitations on the use of lethal force outside armed conflict, which emerge from the limits on personal self-defense and the underlying human rights standards, would fall by the wayside.

The "naked self-defense" approach has rightfully met with overwhelming rejection by human rights bodies and scholars.[57] It neglects the fundamental distinction between the legality of going to war (*ius ad bellum*) and the legality of particular operations (*ius in bello*/IHL in armed conflict and "*ius in pace*"/international human rights law in times of peace).[58] At the root of this problem is an undue conflation of the right to interstate self-defense under Article 51 and the right to personal self-defense. Article 51 can only justify the infringement of another state's territorial integrity or sovereignty, but it has nothing to say about whether the killing itself is justified or not. The latter can only be determined, in armed conflict, on the basis of IHL, and, outside armed conflict, on the basis of the human rights standards applicable to the use of force and firearms.[59]

The International Law Commission had already made this point long before the "naked self-defense" approach was formulated: "As to obligations under international humanitarian law and in relation to non-derogable human rights provisions, [interstate] self-defense does not preclude the wrongfulness of conduct."[60] In the same vein, the Inter-American Court rejected the argument put forward by Ecuador in *Zambrano-Vélez* that the deprivation of life resulting

57. U.N. Special Rapporteur on extrajudicial, summary or arbitrary executions, *supra* note 11, paras. 42–44; ICRC Interpretive Guidance on Direct Participation in Hostilities, *supra* note 11, p. 61, note 158; Heller, *supra* note 14, p. 91; Corn, *supra* note 9, p. 60; Wong, *supra* note 38, pp. 133–134; Ramsden, *supra* note 38, pp. 392–393; Keiichiro Okimoto, The Cumulative Requirements of Jus ad Bellum and Jus in Bello in the Context of Self-Defense, Chinese Journal of International Law, vol. 11 (2012), 45–75, at p. 50; Melzer, *supra* note 48, pp. 51–52; Roland Otto, Targeted Killings and International Law, Springer: Berlin (2010), p. 539; Kinga Tibori-Szabó, Self-Defence and the United States Policy on Drone Strikes, Journal of Security & Conflict Law, vol. 20 (2015), 381–413, at p. 389; Ian Scobbie, Smoke, Mirrors and Killer Whales: The International Court's Opinion on the Israeli Barrier Wall, German Law Journal, vol. 5 (2004), http://www.germanlawjournal.com/print.php?id=495, 1107–1131, at p. 1130; Marko Milanovic, Drones and Targeted Killings: Can Self-Defense Preclude Their Wrongfulness?, 10 January 2011, http://www.ejiltalk.org/drones-and-targeted-killings-can-self-defense-preclude-their-wrongfulness.

58. See also Okimoto, *id.*, p. 50.

59. See also Heller, *supra* note 14, p. 91.

60. International Law Commission, Draft articles on Responsibility of States for Internationally Wrongful Acts, with commentaries, in: Report of the International Law Commission, Fifty-Third Session, U.N. Doc. A/56/10 (2001) pp. 59–365, at p. 178 [Art. 21, para. 3 of the commentary].

from a targeted killing could be justified under Article 51 of the U.N. Charter. The court held that Article 51 only provides an exception to the general prohibition of war but "would not apply, in any way, to the determination . . . of the international responsibility of the state under the American Convention for acts or omissions by state agents in a security operation."[61]

The "naked self-defense" approach is also irreconcilable with the established position under international criminal law that a military operation covered by Article 51 of the U.N. Charter does not in any way absolve the participants from criminal responsibility for unlawful killings. As underscored by the International Criminal Tribunal for the Former Yugoslavia, "military operations in [interstate] self-defense do not provide a justification for serious violations of international humanitarian law."[62] By the same token, Article 51 cannot provide a justification for deliberately depriving someone of his right to life. Outside the context of armed conflict, such deliberate killings can be justified only within the strict requirements of the right to personal self-defense.

D. CONCLUSION: EXCEPTIONAL RELEVANCE OF PERSONAL SELF-DEFENSE IN MILITARY-LED OPERATIONS

Even in military-led operations the right to personal self-defense becomes exceptionally relevant as a justification for the use of lethal force and resulting infringement of the right to life. In armed conflict hostilities, use of force by the military is regulated primarily by the rules of international humanitarian law, even though human rights continue to apply and have a certain impact on the interpretation of that law. However, there are a number of situations where the military is facing persons who are potentially violent but are still considered protected persons under international humanitarian law such as bandits, rioters, blockade runners, prisoners of war, and detained armed group fighters. When such persons use violence that remains below the threshold of direct participation in hostilities, the military may use force against them only within the confines of the law enforcement framework and the self-defense justification that it embodies.

Military forces must abide by the same strict standards when they are exceptionally tasked to carry out law enforcement functions in times of peace. In this regard, they must approach the situation with the training, equipment, and restricted mindset regarding the use of force that allows them to effectively carry out law enforcement functions.

61. Zambrano Vélez et al. v. Ecuador [IACtHR], *supra* note 33, para. 102.

62. Prosecutor v. Kordić & Čerkez [ICTY Trial Chamber], Case No. IT-95-14/2, Judgment of 26 February 2001, para. 452. See also Rome Statute, art. 31(1)(c), second sentence; United States v. Ohlendorf ["the "Einsatzgruppen Case" [Military Court No. 2], Trials of War Criminals before the Nurernberg Military Tribunals, vol. 4 (1949), 411, at p. 462.

In all cases, it must be carefully assessed whether a particular operation is carried out within an armed conflict or under a law enforcement framework. In extraterritorial operations, it is also imperative to distinguish between the distinct justificatory effects of the right to interstate self-defense under Article 51 of the U.N. Charter on the one hand and the right to personal self-defense on the other. Even accepting that Article 51 also applies to defense against attacks by nonstate actors operating from another state's territory, it can only justify the infringement of sovereignty of that other state. The legality of the impact on human rights of such use of force, including the killing of nonstate fighters or innocent bystanders, requires a separate analysis based on the rules of IHL and human rights law that jointly govern hostilities in armed conflict, or, where there is no conflict, the human rights–based law enforcement framework, which prohibits pre-emptive deliberate killings. Conflating the sovereignty and human rights issue in a single self-defense analysis, as the "naked self-defense" approach tries to do, is incompatible with international law and undermines the protection it offers to individuals.

6

Human Rights Standards for Self-Defense between Private Persons

On the night of May 10, 2008, Raúl Linares Amundaray from Caracas, Venezuela, shot dead Alejandro Buroz Morales, the 11-year-old son of a politically influential lawyer. According to the factual determinations of the U.N. Working Group on Arbitrary Detention, Buroz and three older boys had disabled the alarm system of Linares's private property and climbed on the balcony of the home where Linares, his wife, and his two young daughters were sleeping. After giving oral warning and firing a warning shot, Linares shot into the dark and killed the boy. He was detained and charged with murder. The Working Group found that Linares's human rights had been violated since he acted in legitimate self-defense under Venezuelan law and "the legislation of countries governed by the rule of law" and thus committed no criminal offense for which he should have been detained or prosecuted.[1]

While the human rights concern in the Linares affair relates to the undue denial of a self-defense plea, the shooting of 17-year old Trayvon Martin in the United States raised questions about self-defense going too far. On February 26, 2012, George Zimmerman, a member of a private neighborhood watch in Sanford, Florida, confronted Martin despite being advised by the emergency police operator not to do so. He wrongly considered the presence of the unarmed African-American teenager in the area to be suspicious and followed him. In an ensuing altercation, Zimmerman shot and killed Trayvon Martin. In July 2013, a jury accepted Zimmerman's self-defense plea and acquitted him of all charges for the killing. The affair did more than just spark a heated debate on racial justice in the United States. It also led several U.N. human rights mechanisms and the Inter-American Commission on Human Rights mechanisms to question the

1. José Daniel Ferrer García (on behalf of Raúl Linares Amundaray) v. Venezuela, Working Group on Arbitrary Detention, Opinion No. 28/2012, U.N. Doc. A/HRC/WGAD/2012/28 (2012), para. 28.

Human Rights and Personal Self-Defense in International Law. Jan Arno Hessbruegge

compatibility with human rights of the broad “stand your ground” self-defense laws existing in Florida and many other U.S. states.[2]

The two cases go to show that human rights have a bearing on self-defense between private persons. They also point to an inherent tension deriving from countervailing basic principles. On the one hand, human rights, seen in conjunction with the right to personal self-defense as a general principle of law, require that private individuals must be allowed to effectively defend themselves and others. On the other hand, international human rights law sets limits on the discretion of states to extend broad latitude to rights of self-defense between private persons.

A. APPLICABILITY OF HUMAN RIGHTS STANDARDS TO PRIVATE SELF-DEFENSE

It is now widely accepted that de facto authorities and armed groups exercising effective control over territory are bound by customary human rights law, including the rights to life and physical security.[3] Where they engage with civilians who are not directly participating in hostilities, they must therefore comply

2. Human Rights Committee, Concluding observations on the fourth periodic report of the United States of America, U.N. Doc. CCPR/C/USA/CO/4 (2014), para. 10; United Nations Working Group of Experts of People of African Descent & United Nations Special Rapporteur on Racism, Xenophobia and Related Forms of Intolerance, Trayvon Martin case: UN experts urge US to wrap up civil rights probe and examine discriminatory laws, 3 September 2013, http://www.ohchr.org/EN/NewsEvents/Pages/DisplayNews.aspx?NewsID=13675&LangID=E; Inter-American Commission on Human Rights, Report on the 150th Session of the Inter-American Commission on Human Rights (April 2014), http://www.oas.org/es/cidh/prensa/docs/report-150.pdf, at p. 14. This debate was fueled by the Trayvon Martin shooting, even though it was not clear whether Florida’s “stand your ground” law had a direct legal bearing on that case.

3. Christian Tomuschat, The Applicability of Human Rights Law to Insurgent Movements, in: Horst Fischer et al. (eds.), Crisis Management and Humanitarian Protection: Festschrift für Dieter Fleck, Berliner Wissenschafts-Verlag: Berlin (2004), 573–591, at pp. 577–588; Jean-Marie Henckaerts & Cornelius Wiesener, Human Rights Obligations of Non-state Armed Groups: A Possible Contribution from Customary International Law?, in: Robert Kolb and Gloria Gaggioli (eds.), Research Handbook On Human Rights And Humanitarian Law, Edward Elgar: Cheltenham (2013), 146–169, at pp. 154–158; Jan Arno Hessbruegge, Human Rights Violations Arising from Conduct of Non-State Actors, Buffalo Human Rights Law Review, vol. 11 (2005), 21–88, at pp. 39–41 (all with references to the relevant practice of U.N. human rights and political bodies). However, some still contest this view. See Lindsay Moir, The Law of Internal Armed Conflict, Cambridge University Press: Cambridge et al. (2004), p. 194.

There is also some authority suggesting that armed groups not controlling territory and other collective entities are at least bound by human rights obligations anchored in peremptory law (*ius cogens*). See Report of the independent international commission of inquiry on the Syrian Arab Republic, U.N. Doc. A/HRC/19/69 (2012), para. 106; Hessbruegge, *id.*, pp. 41–44 with further references.

with the human rights standards on the use of force in law enforcement.[4] This means notably that its members may use deliberately lethal force targeting such civilians only for purposes of self-defense or defense of others.

However, international human rights law does not directly bind ordinary private individuals unless they happen to exercise governmental functions.[5] This does not change when private individuals use force in self-defense. It has been argued that human rights obligations are directly applicable to self-defense since it is a public *acte de police*, where the private individual acts as a temporary defender of the legal order in the absence of regular law enforcement.[6] Yet, the proposition is wrong that self-defense by private persons amounts to a public act. At its heart, self-defense remains an act of private self-protection, even if it also happens to protect the state's legal order.[7] It constitutes an exception to the state's monopoly on the use of force, not its extension to private citizens.

Since self-defense is a private act and human rights obligations do not apply directly to private individuals, some authors have taken the position that human rights make no prescription on how the state ought to regulate self-defense between private individuals.[8] However, this position is no longer sustainable in light of the development of general human rights doctrine. It is now firmly

4. Cf. United Nations High Commissioner for Human Rights, Fourth periodic report on the human rights situation in the Occupied Palestinian Territory, U.N. Doc. A/HRC/19/20 (2011), paras. 10–14; Report of the United Nations High Commissioner for Human Rights on the situation of human rights in Mali, U.N. Doc. A/HRC/22/33 (2012) para. 27. On the standards for defensive force in law enforcement, see Fourth Chapter (pp. 91–216).

5. This can notably be the case regarding certain functions entrusted to private security companies. See this Sixth Chapter: C.V (pp. 270–274).

6. Klaus Marxen, Die "sozialethischen" Grenzen der Notwehr, Alfred Metzner Verlag: Frankfurt a.M. (1979), pp. 30ff. & 61. Cf. Mordechai Kremnitzer, Proportionality and the Psychotic Aggressor: Another View, Israeli Law Review, vol. 18 (1983), 178–214, at p. 190.

7. Helmut Frister, Zur Einschränkung des Notwehrrechts durch Art. 2 der Europäischen Menschenrechtskonvention, Goltdammer's Archiv für Strafrecht 1985, 553–565, at p. 554; Carl-Friedrich von Scherenberg, Die sozialethischen Einschränkungen der Notwehr, Peter Lang: Frankfurt a.M. (2009), 116; Onder Bakircioglu, The Right to Self-Defence in National and International Law: The Role of the Imminence Requirement, Indiana International & Comparative Law Review, vol. 19 (2009), 1–48, at p. 21.

8. Theoder Lenckner & Detlev Sternberg-Lieben, Notwehr und Notstand [§§ 32–35], in: Adolf Schönke, Horst Schröder et al. (eds.), Strafgesetzbuch: StGB, C.H. Beck: München (28th ed., 2010), p. 567 [Vorbem. §§ 32 ff., para. 24]; Paul Bockelmann, Menschenrechtskonvention und Notwehrrecht, in: Paul Bockelmann, Arthur Kaufmann & Ulrich Klug (eds.), Festschrift für Karl Engisch zum 70. Geburtstag, Vittorio Kostermann: Frankfurt am Main (1969), 456–467, at pp. 463–464; Ralf Krüger, Die Bedeutung der Menschenrechtskonvention für das deutsche Notwehrrecht, Neue Juristische Wochenschrift 1970, 1483–1485, at pp. 1484–1485; Felix Herzog, § 32, in: Urs Kindhäuser et al., Strafgesetzbuch: Band 1, Nomos: Baden-Baden (2nd ed., 2010), at p. 1173 [§ 32, para. 95]; Clemens Arzt, Europäische Menschenrechtskonvention und polizeilicher Todesschuss, Deutsche öffentliche Verwaltung (DöV) (2007), 230–237, at p. 234.

established that international human rights law has an indirect bearing on relations in the private sphere and thus also on self-defense between private persons.[9] This is the case because international human rights law imposes an obligation on states to protect with due diligence persons in their territory, or otherwise under their control, from violent criminal acts or other private conduct that would impair the enjoyment of their human rights. This due diligence obligation has been drawn from the law on diplomatic protection, where states' duty to protect foreigners with due diligence had already been set out by writers such as Grotius and Gentili in the 17th century.[10] Under contemporary international law, the obligation to exercise due diligence to protect human rights, in particular the rights to life and physical security, is embedded in universal and regional human rights treaties as well as customary human rights law. It requires state authorities to do their best to prevent violent crime by policing their jurisdiction and to deter future violence by identifying, prosecuting, and punishing the perpetrators of such criminal attacks.[11] However, the state cannot be expected to prevent

9. Human Rights Committee, Concluding observations on the fourth periodic report of the United States of America, *supra* note 2, para. 10; Andrew Ashworth, The Human Rights Act and the substantive criminal law: a non-minimalist view, Criminal Law Review 2000, 564–567, at p. 567; Walter Perron, 32 StGB, in: Schönke/Schröder (eds.), *id.*, p. 647 [§ 32, para. 62]; Jochen A. Frowein & Wolfgang Peukert, Europäische Menschenrechtskonvention: EMRK-Kommentar, N.P. Engel Verlag: Kehl (3d. ed., 2009), p. 37 [Art. 2, para. 12]; Boaz Sangero, Self-Defence in Criminal Law, Hart: Oxford (2006), pp. 111–112; Frister, *supra* note 7, p. 557; Heinz Koriath, Einschränkung des deutschen Notwehrrechts (§ 32 STGB) durch art 2 II a EMRK?, in: Filippo Ranieri (ed.), Europäisierung der Rechtswissenschaft, Nomos: Baden-Baden (2002), 47–60, at pp. 53–55; Nikolaos Bitzilekis, Die neue Tendenz zur Einschränkung des Notwehrrechts, Duncker & Humblot: Berlin (1984), p. 134; Fiona Leverick, Is English Self-Defence Law incompatible with art 2 of the ECHR?, Criminal Law Review (May 2002), 347–362, at p. 359; Claus Roxin, Strafrecht: Allgemeiner Teil, vol. I, Ch.Beck: Munich (4th ed., 2006), p. 698; Frank Zieschang, Tödliche Notwehr zur Verteidigung von Sachen und Art. 2 IIa EMRK, Goltdammer's Archiv für Strafrecht (GA) 2006, 415–419, at p. 419; von Scherenberg, *supra* note 7, pp. 118–119; Dirk Diehm, Die Menschenrechte der EMRK und ihr Einfluss auf das deutsche Strafgesetzbuch, Logos Verlag: Berlin (2006), p. 359; Rudolf Echterhölter, Die Europäische Menschenrechtskonvention in der juristischen Praxis, JuristenZeitung 1958, 142–148, p. 143; Anna Marie Smith, Deadly Force and Public Reason, Theory & Event vol. 15(3) (2012), http://muse.jhu.edu/journals/theory_and_event/v015/15.3.smith.html.

10. Jan Arno Hessbruegge, The Historical Development of the Doctrines of Attribution and Due Diligence in International Law, New York University Journal of International Law & Politics, vol. 36 (2004), 265– 306, at pp. 282–284.

11. Human Rights Committee, General Comment 6: Article 6 ICCPR (1982), para. 3, as restated in: U.N. Doc. HRI/GEN/1/Rev.1 at 6 (1994); *id.*, General Comment 31: Nature of the General Legal Obligation on States Parties to the Covenant, U.N. Doc. CCPR/C/21/Rev.1/Add.13 (2004), para. 8; Committee on the Elimination of Discrimination against Women, General Recommendation 19, Violence against women (Eleventh session, 1992), U.N. Doc. A/47/38 at 1 (1993), para. 9; Report of the Special Rapporteur on extrajudicial, summary or arbitrary executions, Philip Alston, U.N. Doc. E/CN.4/2006/53 (2006), para. 47; Report of the Special Rapporteur on violence against women, its causes and consequences, Ms. Yakin Ertürk: The Due Diligence Standard as a Tool for the Elimination of Violence against Women,

every such attack. As will be shown in the next section, it must therefore place citizens in a legal position that allows them to protect themselves where the state cannot provide protection—by recognizing their right to defend themselves and others against unlawful attack as a matter of law and practice.

B. DUTY TO RECOGNIZE A RIGHT TO SELF-DEFENSE BETWEEN PRIVATE PERSONS

As a matter of legal principle, every state in the world recognizes that private individuals may defend themselves against unlawful attacks.[12] This does not render moot the question of whether states have an international obligation to recognize the right to personal self-defense. States may occasionally seek to deny this right to specific groups of persons as a matter of law or legal practice.

Rules for disciplinary proceedings against prisoners in Indiana and other U.S. states, for instance, have denied prisoners the right to plead self-defense as a full defense against the imposition of disciplinary sanctions in cases of violence between inmates.[13] In the 1994 decision of *Rowe v DeBruyn*, the Seventh Circuit of the U.S. Court of Appeals upheld the constitutionality of Indiana's regulation. The court found that "a right that threatens to undermine prison discipline by encouraging inmates to combat violence with more violence subverts a core prison function of ensuring order and safety within the institution." The denial of self-defense served "legitimate penological interests" by "discouraging all physical violence amongst inmates" and acting "as a deterrent because a prisoner who is caught fighting cannot reliably exculpate himself later with a claim of self-defense."[14]

During her visit to Papua New Guinea, the U.N. Special Rapporteur on Violence against Women, Rashida Manjoo, found that judges showed little sympathy with evidence that women who killed abusive husbands or other aggressors had acted in self-defense. Apparently, the judges considered that the women

U.N. Doc. E/CN.4/2006/61 (2006), para. 29; Kilic v Turkey [ECtHR], Appl. No. 22492/93, Judgment of 28 March 2000, para. 62; Gonzales et al. v. Mexico (Cotton Field) [IACtHR], Series C No. 205, Judgment of 16 November 2009, para. 247; African Commission on Human and Peoples' Rights, General Comment No. 3 on the African Charter on Human and Peoples' Rights: The Right To Life (Art. 4), adopted at the 57th session (2015).

12. See Second Chapter: E (pp. 58–59).

13. In 1995, prison disciplinary regulations in six U.S. States treated self-defense solely as a mitigating factor in punishment. See James E. Robertson, "Fight or F . . ." And Constitutional Liberty: An Inmate's Right to Self-Defense when Targeted by Aggressors, Indiana Law Review, vol. 29 (1995), 339–363, at p. 354.

14. Rowe v. DeBruyn, 17 F3d 1047, 1052–1053 (7th Cir 1994), cert. denied, 115 S. Ct. 508 (1994). By refusing to hear a further appeal, the U.S. Supreme Court signaled that it did not fundamentally disagree with the decision. It is unclear, however, whether the Supreme Court would rule differently today, having recognized the constitutional pedigree of the right to self-defense in District of Columbia v. Heller, 128 S. Ct. 2783 (2008), at 2817.

needed to pay a price for taking life notwithstanding the circumstances surrounding their act.[15]

In both cases, members of populations particularly prone to suffer unlawful violent attacks were placed in a position where they had to choose between enduring the violence and facing sanctions for defending themselves. The imposition of this dilemma cannot be reconciled with basic precepts of justice or international law. Long before the advent of the modern human rights era, scholars such as Francisco Suarez and Immanuel Kant had already argued that state authorities must not deny human beings the right to self-defense, since this would amount to a denial of a higher natural right.[16] Their position continues to be valid. Contemporary international law would have to consider a total denial of the right to self-defense as a human rights violation, because human rights must be interpreted in light of the right to self-defense as a general principle of law. This becomes most obvious with regard to self-defense against lethal attacks, where the legal prohibition of self-defense would amount to a denial of the human right to life itself.[17]

International human rights mechanisms have sustained essentially the same conclusion, although they have generally approached the issue from the perspective of the human right to a fair trial.[18] In reviewing death penalty sentences, the U.N. Human Rights Committee has stressed that the right to a fair trial requires that self-defense pleas advanced by the defendant are duly considered and that

15. Report of the Special Rapporteur on violence against women, its causes and consequences, Rashida Manjoo: Mission to Papua New Guinea, U.N. Doc. A/HRC/23/49/Add.2 (2013), para. 42.

16. See Second Chapter: D.I.4&5 (p. 37 and p. 39).

17. S v Makwanyane [Constitutional Court of South Africa], 1995(3) SA 391 (CC), para. 138; Reinhard Merkel, Folter und Notwehr, in: Michael Pawlik / Rainer Zaczyk (eds.), Festschrift für Günther Jakobs zum 70. Geburtstag, C. Heymanns: Berlin (2007), 375–403, p. 386; B. A. Wortley, Some jurisprudential reflections on human rights and self-defense, in: Heinrich Kipp (ed.), Um Recht und Freiheit: Festschrift für Friedrich August Freiherr von der Heydte zur Vollendung des 70. Lebensjahres, Duncker and Humblot: Berlin (1977), 751–758, at p. 752; Volker Erb, Notwehr als Menschenrecht—Zugleich eine Kritik der Entscheidung des LG Frankfurt am Main im "Fall Daschner," Neue Zeitschrift für Strafrecht (NStZ) 2005, 593–602, at p. 594; Dale Stephens, Rules of Engagement and the Concept of Unit Self Defence, Naval Law Review, vol. 45 (1998), 126–151, at p. 147; Andrew J. Ashworth, Self-Defence and the Human Right to Life, Cambridge Law Journal, vol. 34 (1975), 282–307, at p. 283; David B. Kopel, Paul Gallant & Joanne D. Eisen, The Human Right of Self-Defense, BYU Journal of Public Law, vol. 22 (2008), 43–178, at p. 79 & 133; Don B. Kates, Genocide, Murder and the Fundamental Human Right to Defend One's Life, Journal of Law, Economics and Policy, vol. 2 (2006), 309–317, at p. 311; Michael Huemer, Is There a Right to Own a Gun?, Social Theory and Practice, vol. 29 (2003), 297–324, at p. 307; Catherine A. MacKinnon, Women's September 11th: Rethinking the International Law of Conflict, Harvard International Law Journal, vol. 47 (2006), 1–31, at p. 6 [n. 21]; Jens David Ohlin, The Doctrine of Legitimate Defense, International Law Studies vol. 91 (2015), 119–154, at p. 124.

18. For this approach also Prevention of human rights violations committed with small arms and light weapons: Final report submitted by Barbara Frey, Special Rapporteur in accordance with Sub-Commission resolution 2002/25, U.N. Doc. A/HRC/Sub.1/58/27 (2006), para. 24.

appropriate instructions are given to the jury.[19] The U.N. Special Rapporteur on the Human Rights Situation in Iran has observed that the failure of an Iranian court to take into account evidence indicating that a woman on trial for murder had killed her would-be rapist in self-defense "raises serious due process concerns."[20] In the *Linares Amundaray* opinion, summarized at the outset of this chapter, the U.N. Working Group on Arbitrary Detention considered that Venezuela's failure to consider self-defense as a waiver of criminal liability amounted to a breach of due process and fair trial rights under Articles 9 and 14 of the ICCPR.[21] In *Samokhalov*, the ECtHR found a violation of the right to a fair trial because the applicant was unfairly excluded from participating in the appeal hearing of his murder trial and therefore could not effectively argue for the existence of mitigating self-defense elements in his case.[22]

Cerone has called into question whether international law requires states to recognize the right to self-defense with the argument that it is left to every state to decide how best to protect the rights to life and physical security and that recognition of self-defense is only one way to do so.[23] This argument is not convincing. For one thing, it neglects that the right to self-defense amounts to a general

19. D. S. v. Jamaica, Comm. No. 234/1987, U.N. Doc. CCPR/C/41/D/234/1987 (1991).para. 5.2; Daniel Pinto v. Trinidad and Tobago, Comm. No. 232/1987, U. N. Doc. CCPR/C/39/D/232/1987 (1990), para. 12.3; Stephens v. Jamaica, Comm. No. 373/1989, U.N. Doc. CCPR/C/55/D/373/1989 (1995), para. 6.2; Tulyaganova v. Uzbekistan, Comm. 1041/2001, U.N. Doc. CCPR/C/90/D/1041/2001 (2007), para. 7.4. See also Jaime Carpo et al. v. Philippines, Communication No. 1077/2002, U.N. Doc. CCPR/C/77/D/1077/2002 (2002), Ind. Op. Nisuke Ando, Diss. Op. Maxwell Yalden & Abdallah Zakhia, Diss. Op. Lord Colville.

20. See UN Expert calls on Iran to halt execution of Iranian woman expected to take place tomorrow, 14 April 2015,http://www.ohchr.org/EN/NewsEvents/Pages/DisplayNews.aspx?NewsID=14509#sthash.f0YDm2Y2. See also Chair-Rapporteur of the Working Group on Arbitrary Detention; Special Rapporteur on the independence of judges and lawyers; Special Rapporteur on the situation of human rights in the Islamic Republic of Iran; Special Rapporteur on extrajudicial, summary or arbitrary executions; Special Rapporteur on torture and other cruel, inhuman or degrading treatment or punishment; and Special Rapporteur on violence against women, its causes and consequences, Urgent Appeal to Iran on Ms. Rayhaneh Jabbari, 14 April 2014, https://spdb.ohchr.org/hrdb/27th/public_-_UA_Iran_14.04.14_(6.2014).pdf.

While states may not prohibit women from exercising their right to defend themselves against sexual violence, they may not effectively require the exercise of self-defense by denying legal protection to women who do not physically defend themselves against sexual assault. For this reason, legal definitions of rape must not require that the victim offers physical resistance. See Tayag Vertido v. Philippines [CEDAW Cttee], Comm. 18/2010, U.N. Doc. CEDAW/C/46/D/18/2008 (2010); para. 8.5; R.P.B. v. Philippines, Comm. 34/2011, U.N. Doc. CEDAW/C/57/D/34/2011 (2014), para. 8.10.

21. José Daniel Ferrer García (on behalf of Raúl Linares Amundaray) v. Bolivarian Republic of Venezuela, *supra* note 1, paras. 28–29.

22. Samokhalov v. Russia, Appl. No. 3891/03, Judgment of 12 February 2009, paras. 52 & 54.

23. John Cerone, Is there a Human Right of Self-Defense?, Journal of Law, Economics and Policy, vol. 2 (2006), 319–329, at pp. 325–326.

principle of law recognized by nations, which must be considered in the interpretation of other norms of international law. Furthermore, states will never be in a position to exercise the level of surveillance and control of the private space necessary to effectively prevent any unlawful violent attack anywhere and at any time. An imaginary state that could achieve the objective of total security would have to be a totalitarian police state that systematically breaches human rights. Sir Edward Hall (1835–1894) already recognized (in relation to the state's duty to protect foreigners under classic international law) that states cannot be expected to protect foreigners against every possible violent crime, as this would require a "completely despotic government [that] can make its will felt immediately for any purpose."[24] International human rights law is the antithesis of totalitarianism and despotism. Therefore it does not require the state to successfully prevent all acts of private violence. Instead, the state must put in place a legal and institutional framework that prevents and deters violence as far as reasonably possible.[25] Part of this framework must consist in giving recognition to a reasonably broad right to self-defense as a matter of law and legal practice, so that individuals can duly protect themselves without running the risk of prosecution.

C. DUTY TO REGULATE AND REASONABLY CIRCUMSCRIBE SELF-DEFENSE BETWEEN PRIVATE PERSONS

The state has a duty to regulate by law the exercise of the right to self-defense by private persons. This follows from the principle of legality according to which no one shall be held guilty of any act that did not constitute a criminal offense at the time of commission.[26] Limits placed on the right to self-defense entail an extension of criminal responsibility. Therefore, these limits must be set forth by law, so as to provide legal certainty as to what defensive force is still justified and what is considered excessive and hence criminalized.[27] Furthermore, the duty to regulate self-defense finds a basis in the right to life, which has to be protected "by law" and is affected when private persons exercise lethal self-defense.[28]

24. William Edward Hall, A Treatise on International Law, Clarendon Press: Oxford (5th ed., 1904), p. 221. See also Karl Doehring, Zum "Recht auf Leben" aus nationaler und internationaler Sicht, in: Rudolf Bernhardt (ed.), Völkerrecht als Rechtsordnung, internationale Gerichtsbarkeit, Menschenrechte : Festschrift für Hermann Mosler, Springer: Berlin (1983), 145–157, at p. 151.

25. Kilic v. Turkey, *supra* note 11, para. 63; Montero-Aranguren et al. (Detention Center of Catia) v. Venezuela, Judgment of 5 July 2005, IACtHR Ser. C No. 150, para. 66.

26. See Art. 11(2) Universal Declaration, Art. 15 ICCPR.

27. See also Erb, *supra* note 17, p. 596; Sangero, *supra* note 9, p. 26.

28. See Art. 6(1) ICCPR, Art. 2(1) ECHR, Art. 4 ACHR, and Art. 5(2) Arab Charter on Human Rights. See also Robert Esser, EMRK; IPBPR, in: Erb, Volker et al. (eds.), Löwe-Rosenberg: Die Strafprozessordnung und das Gerichtsverfassungsgesetz: Grosskommentar, vol. 11, De Gruyter: Berlin (26th ed., 2012), pp. 117–118 [Art. 2 EMRK/Art 6 IPBPR, para. 42];

In establishing an effective legal framework, the state has to ensure that the right to self-defense of private persons is broad enough that they can effectively defend themselves. Yet, it cannot be so broad that the state fails to protect the right to life and physical security of aggressors or innocent bystanders against excessive self-defense or outright vengeance. It is generally agreed that international human rights law affects how states strike the compromise between allowing effective self-protection and outlawing over-aggressive self-assertion.[29] The question is whether the same human rights standards that govern the use of defensive force by law enforcement agents apply *mutatis mutandis* also to self-defense by private individuals. Some scholars are of this view, especially in relation to the standards emerging from Article 2(2) of the ECHR.[30] This approach is also followed by the Spanish Supreme Court, which has directly invoked Article 2(2)(a) of the ECHR to determine the scope of self-defense by private individuals in relation to property.[31]

According to the contrary view, the specific standards applicable to state agents do not apply to private self-defense. Instead, international human rights law allows states considerable discretion to regulate self-defense between private persons, as long as there is no obvious failure to adequately protect the rights of victims or aggressors.[32]

The present author takes an intermediate position that differentiates between law enforcement–specific human rights standards and standards that

African Commission on Human and Peoples' Rights, General Comment on the Right to Life, *supra* note 11, para. 10.

29. See the references *supra* note 9 and accompanying text.

30. Jacques Velu & Rusen Ergec, La Convention européenne des droits de l'homme, Brussels: Bruylant (2nd ed., 2014), para. 232; Frowein/Peukert, *supra* note 9, p. 37 [Art. 2, para. 12]; Ashworth, *supra* note 9, p. 567; Christoph Grabenwarter & Katharina Pabel, Europäische Menschenrechtskonvention, C.H.Beck: München (5th ed., 2012), p. 153; Marxen, *supra* note 6, p. 60. The debate has focused so far mainly on the standards established by Art. 2(2)(a) of the ECHR, especially on its prohibition of lethal force for the defense of property. However, the arguments raised in relation to Article 2 of the ECHR would generally also apply to the largely congruous standards imposed by the ICCPR, ACHR, and ACHPR.

31. Supreme Court of Spain [Penal Chamber], Case No. STS 7246/1986, Judgment of 20 December 1986; Case No. STS 2792/1988, Judgment of 19 April 1988; Case No. STS 8419/1989, Judgment of 17 June 1989; Case No. STS 8280/1990, Judgment of 15 November 1990; Case No. STS 8262/1990, Judgment of 15 November 1990; Case No. STS 2148/1995, Judgment of 11 April 1995; all available at: http://www.poderjudicial.es/search/.

32. Walter Gollwitzer, Menschenrechte im Strafverfahren: MRK und IPBPR, De Gruyter: Berlin (2005), p. 164 [Art. 6 IPBPR, para. 18–19]. Cf. Helmut Satzger, Internationales und Europäisches Strafrecht, Baden Baden: Nomos (4th ed., 2010), p. 200; Stefanie Schmahl, Targeted Killings—A Challenge for International Law?, in: Christian Tomuschat, Evelyne Lagrange & Stefan Oeter (eds.), The Right to Life, Brill: Leiden (2010), 233–266, at p. 241; Lindsey Cameron & Vincent Chetail, Privatizing War: Private Military and Security Companies under Public International Law, Cambridge University Press: Cambridge et al. (2013), p. 460.

incorporate general value decisions. Not all standards that apply to the state authorities as collective entities and bearers of public power are appropriate for private individuals. For instance, the requirement that law enforcements agents be provided with less lethal equipment so as to minimize the use of defensive force is appropriate for the state whose agents are regularly tasked to use force.[33] However, it would be too onerous for the average private citizen who is rarely placed in a situation of having to use defensive force. On the contrary, other human rights standards, such as the absolute prohibition of torture and inhuman treatment,[34] represent objective value decisions that should be upheld regardless of whether state officials or private persons employ defensive force.[35]

Laws on self-defense between private persons must be overall reasonable given the state's obligation to protect the life and physical security of victims, innocent bystanders, and even aggressors with due diligence. In devising reasonable self-defense laws, the state must take into account such factors as the structure of society, the type and prevalence of violent crime, the tendency of the state's citizens to resolve conflict through violence, their capacity to engage in serious violence (notably due to the prevalence of firearms), vulnerabilities of specific groups, and the state's own capacity to protect against private violence.[36] In light of these factors, reasonable self-defense rules may vary to some extent between countries. Measures to protect life and limb with due diligence may make sense in one social context but might be grossly inappropriate in another. However, central principles must at all times be respected.

I. Unlawful attack on a defensible interest

It is a universal feature of domestic laws on self-defense that they require an unlawful attack on a defensible interest.[37] International human rights law does not prescribe an exhaustive list of interests and rights that may be subject to self-defense. However, core rights such as life, physical security, physical freedom, property, and privacy must be defensible against imminent criminal attacks, subject to the requirements of necessity and proportionality. Beyond that, states enjoy a margin of regulatory discretion, provided that the defensible interests recognized are compatible with human rights values.

States also have a certain leeway on how to deal with cases of putative self-defense where an attack exists only in the mind of the defender, as long as their criminal law still provides reasonable protection of the right to life.

33. See Fourth Chapter: C.IV.2 and C.IV.3 (pp. 166–170).

34. See this Sixth Chapter: C.IV (pp. 268–270).

35. Cf. Bitzilekis, *supra* note 9, p. 145.

36. Cf. Ashworth, *supra* note 17, p. 291.

37. See Second Chapter: E.II.1 (pp. 63–64).

1. Gender-Discriminatory Definitions of Defensible Interests

In practice, concerns about states' definition of defensible interests arise mainly in connection with violence against women and the underlying gender discrimination that such abuses perpetuate.

In accordance with their obligation to protect physical security, states must criminalize and prosecute marital rape.[38] But marital rape is not yet a prosecutable offense in some fifty states of the world.[39] If such states consequently deny a woman the right to defend herself against being raped by her husband, they would violate the woman's right to physical security and also discriminate against her on the basis of gender. The same would apply if women were not allowed to defend themselves against other types of domestic violence.[40]

The attempt to perpetuate men's control over women's bodies and sexuality is often also at the root of the reverse scenario, where a domestic law recognizes too broad a range of defensible interests. In a number of countries, the perpetrators of so-called honor crimes can still expect to receive light or no punishment for murdering or committing other violence against female family members who assert their autonomy and defy gender-discriminatory social norms, for example, by having a romantic relationships without their family's approval. Legally, this is at times justified with reference to the right to self-defense by considering the woman's presumed moral transgression as an attack on the honor of other family members.[41] However, a "defense of honor" in such cases is not compatible with international human rights law,[42] because it is really a defense of gender discriminatory social norms.

By the same token, a man must not be allowed to claim defense of personal honor to justify physical violence against an adulterous wife. In Brazil, for instance, men

38. See United Nations General Assembly, Declaration on the Elimination of Violence against Women, U.N. Doc. A/RES/48/104 (1993), article 4(b) and (c) read in conjunction with article 2(2); In-depth study on all forms of violence against Women: Report of the Secretary-General, U.N. Doc. A/61/122/Add.1 (2006), para. 276; Human Rights Committee, Concluding Observations on Djibouti, U.N. Doc. CCPR/C/DJI/CO/1 (2013), para. 10; Committee on the Elimination of Discrimination against Women, Concluding Observations on the United Republic of Tanzania, U.N. Doc. CEDAW/C/TZA/CO/6 (2008), para. 23.

39. According to United Nations data from 2006, marital rape was not a prosecutable offence in at least 53 states. See U.N. in-depth study on all forms of violence against women, *id.*, para. 318 [Box 11].

40. Cf. Report of the Special Rapporteur on violence against women, its causes and consequences, Ms. Radhika Coomaraswamy, U.N. Doc. E/CN.4/1996/53 (1996), para. 130; MacKinnon, *supra* note 17, p. 6 [n.21].

41. On relevant jurisprudence in Pakistan, for instance, see Sohail Akbar Warraich, Honour killings and the law in Pakistan, in: Lynn Welchman & Sara Hossain (eds.), "Honour": Crimes, Paradigms and Violence against Women, Zed Books: London (2005), pp. 78–110.

42. See also Committee on the Elimination of Discrimination against Women, General Recommendation 19: Violence Against Women, U.N. Doc. A/47/38 at 1 (1993), para. 24(r)(ii).

who killed or otherwise assaulted their adulterous wives have often escaped punishment because courts justified the killings as legitimate defense of the perpetrators' personal honor. In 1991, the Superior Tribunal of Justice, Brazil's highest court of appeal in criminal and civil cases, passed a landmark judgment rejecting this jurisprudence. The court noted that "honor is a personal attribute which is the property of each spouse." What is really at stake in such cases, the Brazilian high court rightly observed, is "not honor but the pride of the lord who sees his wife as property."[43] The same consideration also holds true for international human rights law. The husband of an adulterous partner can respond by ending the relationship (or perhaps engaging in an adulterous "reprisal in kind"), but the state must not permit him to assault his wife under the guise of self-defense.[44]

In some regions of the world, women (and, to a lesser degree, men) also find themselves subject to accusations of causing harm through witchcraft. Those subjected to such accusations, which are often driven by ulterior motives, may be killed or driven by force from their communities. Where it is clearly established that the perpetrators of such violence were under the delusion that they were being attacked by witchcraft, pleas for mitigation or, in extreme cases, a full excuse of insanity can be exceptionally considered. However, violence based on an irrational belief in a supernatural attack must never be justified on the basis of the right to self-defense.[45]

2. Honest Belief in an Attack without Good Reason

Law enforcement agents who mistakenly believe it is necessary to use defensive force (putative self-defense) will avoid violating human rights only if their belief has a reasonable basis.[46] Some have argued that the "reasonable belief" standard

43. Decision of the Superior Tribunal of Justice of 11 March 1991, as translated in: Americas Watch/Human Rights Watch, Criminal Justice: Violence against Women in Brazil, Human Rights Watch: New York (1991), p. 23.

44. See also Committee on the Elimination of Discrimination against Women, Concluding Observations on Brazil, U.N. Doc. A/58/38 (Suppl.) (2003), para. 106 (expressing concern about lower Brazilian courts continuing to recognize defense of honor in cases of men assaulting or murdering women, notwithstanding the referenced 1991 decision of the Superior Tribunal of Justice); UN WOMEN, Supplement to the Handbook for Legislation on Violence against Women: "Harmful Practices" against Women, UN WOMEN: New York (2012), p. 19.

45. For relevant jurisprudence of courts from various African countries, see Olatokunbo John Bamgbose, Digest of Judgments of the Supreme Court of Nigeria: vol. 1 & 2, Safari Books: Ibadan (2013), p. 341; Onesimus K. Mutungi, Witchcraft and the Criminal Law in East Africa, Valparaiso University Law Review, vol. 5 (1971), 524–555, at pp. 159–162. Jennifer Dumin, Superstition-based Injustice in Africa and the United States: The Use of Provocation as a Defense for Killing Witches and Homosexuals, Wisconsin Women's Law Journal, vol. 21 (2006), 145–174, at pp. 533–538. Cf. the *King of Cats* judgment of the German Federal Supreme Court, Judgment of 15 September 1988, Case No. 4 StR 352/88, BGHSt 35, 347, also available at: http://www.servat.unibe.ch/dfr/bs035347.html.

46. See Fourth Chapter: C.I.6 (pp. 133–139) and C.III.1 (pp. 143–146).

also marks a minimum international standard for self-defense between private persons. Therefore, it is argued, international human rights law mandates legal reform in jurisdictions such as England and Wales where even an unreasonable but honest belief in a situation calling for self-defense constitutes a full defense against charges of murder or other intentional violent crime.[47] The point is made that killing without good reason cannot be necessary for self-defense.[48] Furthermore, a rule requiring good reasons for the mistaken belief would lead potential defenders to check more carefully whether they are really under attack before acting rashly in self-defense.[49]

However, this position is not convincing.[50] It neglects the difference between state responsibility for human rights violations and individual criminal responsibility. When it comes to the state, one can expect that its agents act reasonably. If they fail to do so, the state must compensate the victims and take measures to ensure that similar unreasonable mistakes will not occur again. However, it does not follow that private individuals should be convicted of an intentional crime if they honestly, though unreasonably, believed in circumstances that would have rendered their conduct lawful. Indeed, conviction for an intentional crime in such situations might be disproportional unless the punishment is then mitigated.

The state fulfils its obligation to protect the rights to life and physical security of potential victims of erroneous self-defense just as well by prosecuting individuals for crimes of negligence where they use unwarranted defensive force based on a particularly unreasonable mistaken belief in an attack. There is nothing to suggest that prosecuting for intentional crimes in such cases, rather than for crimes of negligence, would better protect the rights to life and physical security.[51]

II. Immediate defense: An exception for victims of intra-family violence?

Virtually everywhere, domestic criminal laws limit the right to self-defense to a defense against present or immediately antecedent attacks.[52] Some feminist

47. Andrew Ashworth, The European Convention and the Criminal Law, in: Jack Beatson & Tony Smith (eds.), The Human Rights Act and the Criminal Justice and Regulatory Process, Hart Publishing: Oxford (1999), 37–44, at p. 42; Leverick, *supra* note 9, p. 359.

48. Leverick, *id.*, p. 350.

49. *Id.*, p. 359.

50. David Ormerod, John Cyril Smith & Irian Hogan, Smith and Hogan's Criminal Law, Oxford University Press: Oxford (13th ed., 2010), p. 385. See also Fourth Chapter: E.III.1 (pp. 210–211) on whether law enforcement agents who use defensive force with an honest but unreasonable belief in an attack must be prosecuted.

51. See also Ormerod, Smith & Hogan, *id.*, 385.

52. See Second Chapter: E.II.2 (pp. 64–65).

scholars and children's rights activists have charged that this limitation is based on typical patterns of violence between men—such as a bar fight—where the violence takes the form of an unexpected single attack in the public sphere and the victim has at least a fighting chance (literally) to counter it in an open exchange.[53] Women's experience of violence is different. Rather than being a one-off unexpected experience, it often takes the shape of prolonged physical, sexual, and psychological abuse by a male intimate partner. Likewise, the most severe cases of violence against children typically occur within the family over a longer period of time. Since intra-family violence is recurrent, the victims can often anticipate violent episodes even if they are not immediately antecedent. Furthermore, women and children often lack the physical capacity and socialized mindset to effectively challenge their abusers in an open physical fight and have to wait for an opportune moment to overpower their abuser. Finally, the seemingly obvious solution of preventing future abuse by leaving the family or the abusive partner is not an option. Many countries still lack the legal and institutional framework to effectively protect women and children who flee abusive situations, and the victims are often so economically dependent on their abusers that leaving without external support is out of the question.[54] Psychologically, many victims of long-term abuse also suffer from battered person syndrome; they have become psychologically dependent on their abusers and a learned helplessness renders them unable to consider leaving as a viable option.[55]

In light of these peculiarities, the question arises whether victims of particularly egregious intra-family violence should be deemed to act in justified self-defense where they pre-emptively kill their abuser while he can still be overpowered and before he can commence a particularly vicious assault. The classical situation is that of the victim killing the habitual abuser in his sleep to prevent a life-threatening assault later.

Such cases have occupied the high courts of several countries and resulted in very different legal outcomes. The following three exemplary cases broadly reflect the spectrum of jurisprudential approaches.

In *State v Norman*, the Supreme Court of North Carolina upheld the voluntary man-slaughter conviction of Judy Norman, who had shot and killed her

53. See Julia Tolmie, Battered Defendants and the Criminal Defences to Murder—Lessons from Overseas, Waikato Law Review, vol. 10 (2002), 91–114, at pp. 93–95; Ian Leader-Elliot, Battered But Not Beaten: Women Who Kill in Self-Defence, Sydney Law Review, vol. 15 (1993), 403–460, at p. 404; Joelle Anne Moreno, Killing Daddy: Developing a Self-Defense Strategy for the Abused Child, University of Pennsylvania Law Review, vol. 137 (1989), 1281–1307, at p. 1283; Shana Wallace, Beyond Imminence: Evolving International Law and Battered Women's Right to Self-Defense, University of Chicago Law Review, vol. 71 (2004), 1749–1781, at p. 1753; MacKinnon, *supra* note 17, pp. 6–7.

54. See also Julie Stubbs & Julie Tolmie, Feminisms, Self-Defence, and Battered Women: A Response to Hubble's "Straw Feminist', Current Issues in Criminal Justice, vol. 10 (1998–1999), 73–84, at p. 78.

55. Wallace, *supra* note 53, p. 1755.

husband in his sleep. Despite Norman having suffered years of severe abuse at her husband's hands, the court ruled out self-defense due to the lack of an imminent threat. It advanced the following reasoning:

> The imminence requirement ensures that deadly force will be used only where it is necessary as a last resort in the exercise of the inherent right of self-preservation. It also ensures that before a homicide is justified and, as a result, not a legal wrong, it will be reliably determined that the defendant reasonably believed that absent the use of deadly force, not only would an unlawful attack have occurred, but also that the attack would have caused death or great bodily harm.[56]

Expanding the time window to allow for preventive defense, the court explained, would justify the taking of life based "upon purely subjective speculation that the decedent probably would present a threat to life at a future time and that the defendant would not be able to avoid the predicted threat."[57]

The Supreme Court of Canada took the opposite approach in *R v. Lavallee*, where it dispensed of the imminence requirement and could thus consider the preventive killing of an abusive partner to constitute self-defense.[58] In that case, Angelique Lavallee had shot and killed her habitually abusive partner as he was leaving the room. Just before that, the man had beaten her and made a credible threat to kill her later that day. The court accepted that battered wife syndrome could have prevented Lavallee from considering the option of fleeing before her partner returned. They key issue was therefore whether self-defense was precluded since Lavallee faced no imminent threat at the time of the killing. Justice Wilson, writing for the court, reasoned that in the typical case of an altercation between men the imminence requirement serves to ensure that the aggressor really threatened the life of the other who killed him in purported self-defense. Yet, this assumption does not necessarily hold in cases of battered women whose experience of long-term abuse have sensitized them to anticipate what will happen:

> [I]t may in fact be possible for a battered spouse to accurately predict the onset of violence before the first blow is struck, even if an outsider to the relationship cannot. Indeed, it has been suggested that a battered woman's knowledge of her partner's violence is so heightened that she is able to anticipate the nature and extent (though not the onset) of the violence by his conduct beforehand.[59]

56. North Carolina v. Norman, 324 N.C. 253 (N.C., 1989), 261.

57. *Id.*, at 264. The same approach was taken by the Supreme Court of Kansas in State v. Stewart, 763 P.2d 572 (Kan. 1988), at pp. 578–579.

58. R v. Lavallee [1990] 1 SCR 852. For cases from Australia following a comparable approach see Tolmie, *supra* note 53, 96–97.

59. *Id.*, pp. 880–881.

In response to the argument that the imminence requirement prevents victims from unreasonably assuming a deadly threat, Justice Wilson pointed to the difficulties that women face in defending themselves when already under attack:

> [D]ue to their size, strength, socialization and lack of training, women are typically no match for men in hand-to-hand combat. The requirement . . . that a battered woman wait until the physical assault is "underway" before her apprehensions can be validated in law would . . . be tantamount to sentencing her to `murder by instalment."[60]

A third approach that represents an intermediate position between the *Norman* and *Lavallee* approaches was taken by the Federal Supreme Court of Germany in the so-called *House Tyrant Case.* In that case, a woman had killed her sleeping husband, who had severely abused her and their daughters over a long period of time. The court accepted that the woman saw no other way to escape the husband's increasingly violent attacks but to shoot him dead while he slept. Nevertheless, the court did not make a finding of self-defense due to the lack of an imminent attack. However, it indicated that the case could be a case of excused necessity (*entschuldigender Notstand*), because the woman considered the killing to be the only way to protect herself and her daughters against a serious and constantly present threat. Accordingly, the woman would receive no punishment or a strongly mitigated punishment.[61]

The question is whether international human rights law prescribes or prohibits any of these three jurisprudential approaches or whether it leaves it entirely within the discretion of states to adopt one or the other approach. Yakin Erturk, U.N. Special Rapporteur on Violence against Women from 2003 to 2009, took the position that the intermediate approach taken also in *House Tyrant* should be followed. In relation to women victims of abuse who had killed their abusers in a premeditated manner, she observed:

> While recognizing the gravity of their crimes, women's criminality under situations of extreme abuse and violence needs to be treated with diligence, and their cases must be assessed in light of mitigating circumstances.[62]

60. *Id.*, p. 883.

61. German Federal Supreme Court, Case No. 1StR 274/03, Judgment of 25 March 2003, BGHSt 48, 155. For further examples from German jurisprudence, see Eduardo José Pintore, Das präventive Selbsverteidigungsrecht im Lichte allgemeiner Rechtsgrundsätze, Peter Lang: Frankfurt a.M (2011), pp. 217–223. Essentially the same approach was taken by the the South African Supreme Court of Appeal in Ferreira and others v. State, Case No. 245/03, Judgment of 1 April 2004, [2004] ZASCA 29 ; [2004] 4 All SA 373 (SCA), also available at: http://www.saflii.org/za/cases/ZASCA/2004/29.html.

62. Report of the Special Rapporteur on violence against women, its causes and consequences, Yakin Ertürk: Mission to Tajikistan Mission, U.N. Doc. A/HRC/11/6/Add.2 (2009), para. 37.

In recent communications to governments, several United Nations special rapporteurs seem to endorse a more radical view along the lines of the *Lavallee* approach, suggesting that international human rights law demands an expansion of the parameters of justified self-defense to include women survivors of long-term serious abuse who kill although they do not face an imminent attack. In 2014, several special rapporteurs sent an urgent appeal to Iran to prevent the execution of Razieh Ebrahimi, a 17-year-old Iranian woman who killed her husband in 2010. According to the information gathered by the special rapporteurs, Ebrahimi killed her husband while he was asleep after suffering years of physical and psychological abuse since marrying him when she was 14 years old. The special rapporteurs expressed concern that the

> alleged history of abuse suffered by Ms. Ebrahimi at the hands of her husband was reportedly not given due consideration during sentencing and that the legal system has allegedly failed to recognize persistent domestic violence as falling under the grounds of self-defense. This constitutes de facto discrimination. In domestic violence, the threat of violence by a persistently violent male partner has a cumulative impact as part of a pattern of behavior and *a woman's violent response should be interpreted as a defensive response to the cumulative acts of violence.*[63]

The same year several special rapporteurs also sent an urgent appeal to the United States of America, which reiterates essentially the same position:

> Concern is also expressed at the alleged failure of the legal system to recognize persistent domestic violence as falling under the grounds of self-defense, whereby according to the court, an individual must first suffer serious bodily injury in order to defend him/herself. This constitutes de facto discrimination. It has been argued that the prototype of male self-defense is the "bar-room brawl" in which the attack and the response are immediate. However, the prototype of domestic violence against women is persistent violence by the male against which the woman cannot immediately defend herself because of her lesser physical strength. In domestic violence, an additional threat of violence by a persistently violent male partner has cumulative impact as part of a pattern of behavior and a woman's violence

63. Chairperson-Rapporteur of the Working Group on the issue of discrimination against women in law and in practice, Special Rapporteur on the independence of judges and lawyers, Special Rapporteur on the situation of human rights in the Islamic Republic of Iran, Special Rapporteur on extrajudicial, summary or arbitrary executions, and Special Rapporteur on violence against women, its causes and consequences, Urgent Appeal to the Islamic Republic of Iran regarding the situation of Ms. Razieh Ebrahimi, 3 July 2014, https://spdb.ohchr.org/hrdb/28th/public_-_UA_Iran_03.07.14_(11.2014).pdf (emphasis added).

response should be interpreted as a defensive response to the cumulative acts of violence.[64]

The approach endorsed in these urgent appeals is problematic to the extent that it eclipses the requirement of imminence from self-defense as a full justification. In the present author's view, international human rights law calls for a more nuanced approach that takes into account the human rights of the abusive partner, no matter how heinous his own crimes, as well as wider concerns for the rule of law. This holds particularly true for pre-emptive killings. As observed by Judge Michael Kirby of the Australian High Court, "[n]o civilized society removes its protection to human life [from the habitual abuser] simply because of the existence of a history of long-term physical or psychological abuse."[65]

If the preventive killing of the habitual abuser could be considered justified and hence lawful, then the victim trying to prevent future severe abuse could even hire an assassin to carry out the defensive killing. Neither victim nor assassin could be punished, provided the latter also believed the killing to be the only viable option to prevent a future deadly attack.[66] Moreover, there is no justified self-defense against self-defense.[67] Thus, neither the abuser who is attacked in his sleep nor a third person, including police coming to the scene, would be allowed to resist the preventive killing.[68] Instead, such persons would probably have to be prosecuted if they use force against what would be considered the victim's lawful act.

There is also no need to go down the route of justification. As was done in the *House Tyrant* case and also called for by U.N. Special Rapporteur Erturk, a victim of severe abuse can be given no punishment or strongly mitigated punishment so as to duly take into account her situation, which limits her capacity to incur culpability. Some have argued that excuse-based approaches place

64. Chairperson-Rapporteur of the Working Group on the issue of discrimination against women in law and in practice; Special Rapporteur on contemporary forms of racism, racial discrimination, xenophobia and related intolerance; and Special Rapporteur on violence against women, its causes and consequences, Urgent Appeal to the United States of America concerning the conviction of Ms. Marissa Alexander, 6 May 2014, https://spdb.ohchr.org/hrdb/27th/public_-_AL_USA_06.05.14_(7.2014).pdf.

65. Osland v. The Queen [S.Ct. Australia, 1998] HCA 75, at 165 (Kirby, J.).

66. See also Eugene H. Milhizer, Group Status and Criminal Defenses: Logical Relationship or Marriage of Convenience?, Missouri Law Review, vol. 71 (2006), 547–635, at p. 588; Gail Hubble, Feminism and the Battered Woman: The Limits of Self-Defence in the Context of Domestic Violence, Current Issues in Criminal Justice, vol. 9 (1997–1998), 113–124, at p. 120.

67. See Weizsaecker et al. ["The Ministries Case"], Trials of War Criminals before the Nuernberg Military Tribunals, vol. XIV (1946–1949), 308, at p. 329; United States v. Ohlendorf, Trials of War Criminals before the Nurernberg Military Tribunals, vol. 4 (1949), 411, at p. 494.

68. See also Pintore, *supra* note 61, p. 341; Hubble, *supra* note 66, p. 120.

a label of irrationality on women survivors of violence,[69] thus "transforming an assertive act of self-defense into a manifestation of weakness and incapacity."[70] However, an element of irrationality is often present in such cases anyhow. In many situations, the self-defense account works only if one accepts that the psychological impact of sustained abuse made the victim psychologically unable to consider suitable alternatives to the killing, such as leaving the abusive partner and seeking the protection of the authorities.

Some proponents of awarding women survivors of intra-family violence a right to preventive self-defense seek to draw a parallel to extraterritorial targeted killings of suspected terrorists. If states are allowed to kill suspected dangerous terrorists to prevent future terrorist attacks, it is argued, women should be also allowed to kill an abusive partner while they can still stop him even if the assault will happen only at a later point in time.[71] This argument is buttressed with references to empirical research showing that victims of long-term abuse become hypersensitive to violence and can often accurately predict whether their partner will use life-threatening force in the near future.[72]

As noted above, however, international human rights law does not allow the preventive killing of terrorist suspects outside the specific context of an armed conflict.[73] Legal uncertainty would prevail in the absence of a palpable imminent threat. Genuine self-defense, used as a last resort, could no longer be distinguished from pure vengeance or extrajudicial punishment. The same concerns hold true with regard to preventive killings of abusive partners. In assessing the necessity of a preventive killing, the court would have to make a speculative determination whether the abusive partner would have really resorted in the future to violence so egregious as to justify killing him.[74] In jurisdictions that require only honest belief in a self-defense situation, such as England and Wales, the court would even have to acquit unless the prosecution could show that the woman did not act in the honest belief that it was necessary to kill her abuser to prevent serious violence at some point in the future. Given that the burden of proof is on the state, there is a real risk that the doctrine of preventive self-defense would be abused to gain acquittals for vengeance killings.[75] This concern

69. Jane Campbell Moriarty, While Dangers Gather: The Bush Pre-emption Doctrine, Battered Women, Imminence, and Anticipatory Self-Defense, New York University Review of Law and Social Change, vol.30 (2005), 1–33, at pp. 28–29. See also Ormerod, Smith & Hogan, *supra* note 50, p. 507.

70. Leader-Elliot, *supra* note 53, p. 411.

71. Campbell Moriarty, *supra* note 69, pp. 16 & 32; Wallace, *supra* note 53, p. 1766.

72. See Wallace, *id.*, p. 1772.

73. See Fourth Chapter: C.II.2 (pp. 140–143).

74. See also Bakircioglu, *supra* note 7, p. 25.

75. See also Whitley R. F. Kaufman, Self-Defense, Imminence, and the Battered Woman, New Criminal Law Review, vol. 10 (2007), 342–369, at pp. 365–367, Bakircioglu, *supra* note 7, p. 27; Hubble, *supra* note 66, pp. 116–117 & 120.

applies especially to jury-based systems where an experienced trial lawyer might sway the jurors with emotionally charged arguments that killing the abuser was the deserved punishment for past abuse.

The requirement of imminence in self-defense laws establishes a bright line to uphold the state's monopoly on the use of force and prevent vigilante justice or vengeance.[76] Once one departs from this bright line and allows preventive self-defense against intra-family violence, the same legal principle would also have to be considered for other cases where persons face life-threatening violence at an unspecified point in the future but are not in a position to seek the protection of the authorities and so proceed to help themselves by killing the author of the threat. For instance, an undocumented migrant might argue that he took it into his hands to kill a person who might otherwise have killed him in the future because he feared he would be deported if he turned to the police for help. Members of minorities subject to discrimination might justify preventive lethal self-defense against extremists threatening their life by arguing they could not rely on the authorities to effectively protect them.[77] Even organized criminals settling scores with other criminals could argue that they had to kill their rivals to pre-empt being killed first, as they could not have turned to the police for protection without revealing the reason for the threat and thus incriminating themselves. Expanding self-defense options for victims of intra-family violence creates a slippery slope toward inviting vigilante violence and this poses a serious risk for the rule of law.

A focus on expanding self-help options by victims of intra-family family also detracts attention from the real solutions to the root causes of the problem. Preventive killings of abusive partners are rare cases. Most victims of intra-family violence will find themselves psychologically unable to kill their intimate partners or parents no matter how violent they may be, and would thus not benefit from more permissive self-defense rules. Rather than signaling to victims that they have to resolve their own problems through preventive killing, the state's focus should be on empowering victims of intra-family abuse to leave such situations, providing those that do leave with effective protection and ensuring that potential perpetrators of intra-family violence are deterred by effective prosecutions and appropriate criminal sanctions.[78] In those cases where a victim who is not facing imminent attack nevertheless kills a habitually abusive partner, appropriate solutions can be found when considering culpability so as to ensure that the victim receives no punishment or only mitigated punishment. However, international human rights law should not be deemed to allow, let alone require, states to legalize preventive killings.

76. See also Kaufman, *id.*, pp. 354 & 363–364.

77. Bakircioglu, *supra* note 7, *id.*, p. 30.

78. See also Bakircioglu, *id.*, p. 48; Kaufman, *supra* note 75, p. 363.

III. Necessity and proportionality

International human rights law requires states to respect the basic requirements of necessity and proportionality when regulating self-defense between private persons.[79] Laws on self-defense must only allow the use of force to the extent necessary to effectively and safely ward off an unlawful attack. In addition, they must not authorize force that is out of proportion to the interests protected.

In applying these general principles, similar questions arise regarding the use of defensive force by law enforcement agents: whether lethal force may be used to protect property; whether there is a duty to retreat to avoid lethal force; and whether private "torture" can be justified to defend lives. However, the responses are not always the same given that self-defense by private persons and defensive force by law enforcement agents are somewhat different in nature.

1. Restrictions on the Use of Lethal Force to Defend Property

Law enforcement agents may not use lethal force for the sole purpose of defending property.[80] It is highly contested, though, whether international human rights law imposes the same restriction for self-defense by private persons so that private individuals must be prohibited from shooting at a fleeing non-violent thief in order to recover their property.

a) European Convention on Human Rights

The ECtHR has not yet ruled on this question and jurisprudence across Europe varies.[81] For instance, the German Federal Supreme Court allows lethal force in defense of property of significant value[82] and a part of the academic literature

79. U.N. Human Rights Committee, Concluding observations on the fourth periodic report of the United States of America, *supra* note 2, para. 10; Committee on the Elimination of Racial Discrimination, Concluding observations on the combined seventh to ninth report of the United States of America, U.N. Doc. CERD/C/USA/CO/7-9 (2014), para. 16; Report of the Special Rapporteur on extrajudicial, summary or arbitrary executions on the right to life and the use of force by private security providers in law enforcement contexts, U.N. Doc. A/HRC/32/39 (2016), para. 75; U.N. Special Rapporteur on Small Arms, Barbara Frey, Final Report, *supra* note 18, para. 26. See also Erb, *supra* note 17, p. 593; Cameron & Chetail, *supra* note 32, p. 460; Smith, *supra* note 9; Sophie Miller, "Grossly Disproportionate": Home Owners' Legal License to Kill, The Journal of Criminal Law, vol. 77 (2013) 299–309, at p. 308; Ashworth, *supra* note 17, p. 297.

80. See Fourth Chapter: C.V.2 (pp. 174–180).

81. For a summary of the prevailing views in different countries, see Frank Wittemann, Grundlinien und Grenzen der Notwehr in Europa, Peter Lang: Frankfurt a.M. (1997), pp. 240–241.

82. See German Federal Supreme Court, Judgment of 12 February 2003, Case No. BGH 1 StR 403/02, BGHSt 48, 207,: http://www.hrr-strafrecht.de/hrr/1/02/1-403-02.php3.

takes the view that such an approach is in line with the ECHR.[83] Conversely, the Supreme Court of Spain and an increasing number of scholars, including the present author, take the position that Article 2(2)(a) of the ECHR allows lethal force only "in defense of any person from unlawful violence" and thus prohibits private killings in defense of property.[84]

Against the proposition that Article 2(2)(a) of the ECHR limits self-defense by private persons, it has been argued that the provision demands that a deprivation of life be "inflicted" (or "*infligée*" in the equally authoritative French version). This is said to point to state conduct only.[85] However, private persons can also inflict harm, so the term is thus broad enough to also address private conduct.[86]

Equally unpersuasive is the argument that the drafters of the ECHR had no intention to impose restrictions on national laws regulating self-defense by private persons but only sought to curb the power of the state and its law enforcement agents.[87] Firstly, the *travaux préparatoires* do not provide clear support for this view.[88] Secondly, the ECHR is a living instrument with an evolving interpretation.[89] Therefore, any intentions the ECHR's drafters may have had when they prepared the Convention in 1950 are of limited value today.

More merit lies in the contextual argument that the exceptions in Article 2(2) (b) and (c) of the ECHR, which refer to deprivation of life when carrying out arrests, preventing escapes, and quelling riots or insurrections; these clearly

83. Hans-Ullrich Paeffgen, Art. 2 EMRK, in: Jürgen Wolter (ed.), SK-StPO: Systematischer Kommentar zur Strafprozessordnung, Band X: EMRK, Carl Heymanns: Köln (4th ed., 2012), p. 391 [art. 2, para. 62]; Doehring, *supra* note 24, p. 150; Herzog, *supra* note 8, p. 1173 [§ 32, para. 95]; Wittemann, *supra* note 81, p. 27; Ormerod, Smith & Hogan, *supra* note 50, pp. 387–388.

Roxin, *supra* note 9, pp. 698–699 and Zieschang, *supra* note 9, p. 419 consider that the ECHR allows private killings in defense of property, where the perpetrator acts with no more than *dolus eventualis*.

84. For the decisions of the Supreme Court of Spain, see *supra* note 31. See also Ashworth, *supra* note 47, p. 42; George P. Fletcher & Jens David Ohlin, Defending Humanity: When Force is Justified and Why, Oxford University Press: New York (2008), p. 121; Frister, *supra* note 7, p. 463; Perron, *supra* note 9, pp. 647–648 [§ 32, para 62]; Fiona Leverick, Killing in Self-Defence, Oxford University Press: Oxford (2006), p. 192; Velu/Ergec, *supra* note 30, para. 232; Gollwitzer, *supra* note 32, p. 164 [MRK art. 2, paras. 18–19]; Frowein & Peukert, *supra* note 9, p. 37 [Art. 2, para. 12]; Grabenwarter/Pabel, *supra* note 30, p. 153; Diehm, *supra* note 9, p. 386; Sangero, *supra* note 9, p. 182.

85. Herzog, *supra* note 8, p. 1173 [§ 32, para. 95]; Bockelmann, *supra* note 8, pp. 463–464.

86. Frister, *supra* note 7, p. 559.

87. But see Herzog, *supra* note 8, p. 1173 [§ 32, para. 95]; Bockelmann, *supra* note 8, p. 464.

88. Frister, *supra* note 7, pp. 557–559.

89. See Tyrer v. United Kingdom, Appl. No. 5856/72, Judgment of 25 April 1978, para. 31.

address the state only. This may suggest that Article 2(2)(a) was also meant to relate to state action only.[90] However, this argument is not determinative. It could also be that Article 2(2)(a) has a wider reach that also extends to the private sphere.[91] Article 2 would not mark an exception in including both state-specific and generally applicable norms under the same article. The prohibition of slavery, servitude, and forced labor in Article 4(1) and (2) of the ECHR, for instance, undoubtedly imposes a duty on the state to protect against such abuses at the hands of private individuals. This holds true, even though Article 4(3) sets out a number of exceptions that are specifically referring to state-imposed forced labor.

The object and purpose of Article 2(2)(a) provides the decisive argument for its extension into the private sphere, because the provision incorporates an objective value decision that property may not be protected at the expense of human life. This value decision can be effective only if it also limits the scope of self-defense by private persons. Otherwise, private citizens could, for example, contract private security companies to use violence that the state's law enforcement agents may not use.[92] In line with their obligation to protect life, state parties to the ECHR must therefore prohibit the private use of lethal force in defense of property.

b) ICCPR, African, and American conventions

In light of the U.N. Basic Principles on the Use of Force by Law Enforcement Officials, these human rights provisions must be interpreted as prohibiting the state's law enforcement agents from using lethal force for defending property.[93] However, as their name indicates, the Basic Principles provide only guidance on the use of force by law enforcement agents and do not define how far self-defense in the private sphere may extend.

The U.N. Special Rapporteur on Extrajudicial Executions now takes the view that the right to life requires states to prohibit private actors from using deliberately or potentially lethal force to defend property.[94] However, the other United Nations, American, and African human rights mechanisms have not yet adopted this position.

90. Kristian Kühl, Der Einfluss der Menschenrechte und Grundfreiheiten der Europäischen Menschenrechtskonvention auf das deutsche und europäische Strafrecht, in: Heinz Müller-Dietz (ed.), Festschrift für Heike Jung, Nomos: Baden-Baden (2007), 433–443, at p. 440.

91. Koriath, *supra* note 9, p. 55, Frister, *supra* note 7, p. 559.

92. Cf. Bockelmann, *supra* note 8, p. 466.

93. See Fourth Chapter: C.V.2.b (p. 178).

94. U.N. Special Rapporteur on extrajudicial, summary or arbitrary executions, *supra* note 79, paras. 89–90. See also Cameron & Chetail, *supra* note 32, p. 487. But see Doehring, *supra* note 24, p. 154.

Extending a general prohibition of lethal force in defense of property beyond the European level might not lead to appropriate results in light of the different social contexts. In considerable parts of the world, states have failed to develop their police's capacity to effectively protect private property against theft or to recover stolen property. States cannot rely on their own organizational failures in policing to claim more expansive rights of defensive force for its law enforcement agents. The case is different for private citizens in such places. Through no fault of their own, they must depend on themselves to protect their belongings and it would be unfair to categorically prohibit them from using lethal force to defend property that has particular value to them. It must be borne in mind that for many people, theft of their most valuable property, such as the farming tools of subsistence farmers or the cattle of nomadic groups, carries with it an existential threat to the survival of entire families and communities. International human rights law therefore does not require states to impose a blanket prohibition on any lethal force in defense of property. However, in accordance with their duty to protect life, states must still ensure that lethal force is allowed only in the most exceptional circumstances, as a last resort to protect property of particularly high or existential value.

2. "Stand Your Ground" Laws Abolishing the Duty to Retreat

Law enforcement agents do not have to retreat from a confrontation. In line with their duty to uphold law and order, they may stand their ground and use force against anyone who challenges their authority.[95] Yet the same consideration does not apply to private individuals. Instead, one must pose the question whether human rights impose a duty on private citizens to retreat safely if they can thereby avoid having to use force, in particular lethal defensive force, in self-defense.

The common law has traditionally imposed a duty to pursue available and safe options to retreat and withdraw from a violent confrontation. An exception applied only where one was being attacked in one's own home, pursuant to the old English adage that "a man's home is his castle." In the 19th-century United States, however, the duty to retreat from confrontations in the public sphere was often perceived as a sign of cowardice, so that courts in various U.S. states adopted broader self-defense rights.[96] In the 21st century, this thinking has been revived, notably due to a campaign driven by the National Rifle Association (NRA) and affiliated lobbying groups. They seek to abolish the duty to retreat and replace it with a right to always stand one's ground against an aggressor. In 2005, Florida was the first state to adopt a "stand your ground" law at the initiative of

95. See Fourth Chapter: C.III.2.b (pp. 148–149).

96. Jason W. Bobo, Following the Trend: Alabama Abandons the Duty to Retreat and Encourages Citizens to Stand Their Ground, Cumberland Law Review vol. 38 (2007–2008), 339–369, at pp. 343–346; Jennifer Randolph, How to Get Away with Murder: Criminal and Civil Immunity Provisions in "Stand your Ground" Legislation, Seton Hall Law Review, vol. 44 (2014), 599–630, at p. 606.

state Representative Marion Hammer, a former NRA president. Under Florida's amended law, a person who is lawfully present in a place may use force for purposes of self-defense, including lethal force, even if that person could have safely retreated to withdraw from the deadly confrontation. As of 2014, an additional 21 U.S. states had adopted similar "stand your ground" laws.[97]

In response to the killing of Trayvon Martin (see beginning of this chapter), the "stand your ground" principle has been at the center of a political controversy in the United States that has also attracted considerable international attention. In 2013, the U.S. government's Civil Rights Commission opened an inquiry into whether "stand your ground" laws imply a racial bias. In 2015, the American Bar Association passed a resolution calling for their repeal.[98]

Critics often portray "stand your ground" laws as an example of American exceptionalism. However, similar principles exist in the laws of other countries. Under German law, as currently interpreted by the German Federal Supreme Court, persons facing attack an unprovoked attack by a culpable aggressor in a public space have no duty to retreat to avoid having to defend themselves with lethal means.[99] The Austrian Supreme Court recognizes the "stand your ground" principle as well.[100] Even in common law jurisdictions such as the United Kingdom, Australia, and New Zealand, where the duty to retreat was once a firmly established principle of the law, a failure to exercise safe retreat is no longer determinative. It will be considered by the court as only one factor in the assessment of the reasonableness of a self-defense plea.[101]

97. Ahmad Abuznaid et al., "Stand your Ground" Laws: International Human Rights Law Implications, University of Miami Law Review vol. 68 (2013–2014), 1129–1170, at p. 1132. Including states that had not imposed a duty to retreat under their common law already, a total of 33 U.S. states now apply the "stand your ground" principle. See American Bar Association, National Task Force on Stand your Ground Laws: Final Report and Recommendations, September 2015, p. 10, http://www.americanbar.org/content/dam/aba/images/diversity/SYG_Report_Book.pdf.

For a detailed state-by-state overview that includes legislation up to 2012 see Association of Prosecuting Attorneys, Castle Doctrine Expansion Chart, https://prosecutingattorneys.org/wp-content/uploads/Castle-Doctrine-Expansion-Chart-10.20121.pdf

98. American Bar Association, Stand your Ground Resolution (112), February 2015, http://www.americanbar.org/content/dam/aba/images/abanews/2015mm_hodres/112.pdf.

99. German Federal Supreme Court, Judgment of 24 July 1979, Case No. 1 StR 249/79, BGH NJW 1980, 2263, also available at: https://www.jurion.de/Urteile/BGH/1979-07-24/1-StR-249_79; *id.*, Decision of 8 March 2000, Case No. 3 StR 67/00, NStZ 2000, 365, also available at: http://www.hrr-strafrecht.de/hrr/3/00/3-67-00.php3. See also Erb, *supra* note 17, p. 593.

100. See Supreme Court of Austria, Judgment of 18 April 1989, Case No. 150s27/89, JBl. 1990, p. 388, also available at: https://www.ris.bka.gv.at/Dokument.wxe?Abfrage=Justiz&Dokumentnummer=JJT_19890418_OGH0002_0150OS00027_8900000_000.

101. See the United Kingdom`s Criminal Justice and Immigration Act, section 76 (6A) as amended in 2012. See also Miller, *supra* note 79, p. 300. On the law of Australia and New Zealand, see Leader-Elliot, *supra* note 53, p. 450.

However, the human rights impact of the "stand your ground" principle is particularly profound in the United States due to the exceptionally high number of firearms in private hands. The proliferation of guns places more people in the position of having to assume they face a lethal threat from another private person. Furthermore, more people have themselves the lethal means at hand to kill the aggressor if they accept the confrontation rather than using an available safe opportunity to retreat.

In their respective reviews of the human rights record of the United States, the U.N. Human Rights Committee and the Committee on the Elimination of All Forms of Racial Discrimination both took the position that "stand your ground" laws "circumvent the limits of legitimate self-defense in violation of the state party's duty to protect life" and called on the United States to review such laws so as to "ensure strict adherence to the principles of necessity and proportionality when using deadly force in self-defense."[102]

There are good reasons for taking the position that international human rights law requires the imposition of a duty to pursue an available and safe retreat option at least to the extent that this avoids having to use lethal force in self-defense.[103] "Stand your ground" laws serve no legitimate purpose that is important enough to justify their negative impact on the right to life.

Supporters of the "stand your ground" principle argue that it protects victims from the humiliation of having to flee from a confrontation.[104] This argument harkens back to 19th century U.S. jurisprudence, according to which a "true man, who is without fault, is not obligated to fly from an assailant."[105] Yet the disproportionality of protecting honor at the expense of a human life ought to be obvious. It is for this very reason that modern legal orders no longer allow the arrangements of deadly duels to settle slights of honor. Furthermore, any negative psychological impact caused by having had to withdraw from a confrontation will be outweighed by not having to live with the responsibility of having killed another human being. More than a century ago, Harvard Law Professor Joseph H. Beale eloquently summarized the folly of the honor argument:

> A really honorable man, a man of truly refined and elevated feeling, would perhaps always regret the apparent cowardice of a retreat, but he would regret

102. Human Rights Committee, Concluding observations on the fourth periodic report of the United States of America, *supra* note 2, para. 10; Committee on the Elimination of Racial Discrimination, *supra* note 79, para. 16.

103. Abuznaid, *supra* note 97, pp. 1159–1163; Ashworth, *supra* note 17, p. 289; Smith, *supra* note 9. See also U.N. Special Rapporteur on Small Arms, Barbara Frey, Final Report, *supra* note 18, para. 33 [fn. 36]; Cameron & Chetail, *supra* note 32, p. 478; U.N. Special Rapporteur on extrajudicial, summary or arbitrary executions, *supra* note 79, para. 92.

104. Christine Catalfamo, Stand your Ground: Florida's Castle Doctrine for the Twenty-First Century, Rutgers Journal of Law & Public Policy, vol. 4 (2007), 504–545, at p. 534; Madison Fair, Dare Defend: Standing for Stand your Ground, Law and Psychology Review, vol. 38 (2014), 153–176, at p. 161.

105. Erwin v. State [Ohio Supreme Court] 29 Ohio St. 186 (1876), at p. 199. For a similar sentiment, see also German Federal Supreme Court, Judgment of 24 July 1979, *supra* note 99.

ten times more, after the excitement of the contest was passed, the thought that he had the blood of a fellow-being on his hands.[106]

There is more moral and legal merit to the argument that, in the absence of a "stand your ground" principle, criminals could intimidate law-abiding citizens because the latter would always be forced to retreat and could not defend their right to be present in a particular space.[107] The principle could thus be understood as protecting the human right to freedom of movement.[108] This may be a valid reason to uphold a "stand your ground" principle in relation to non-lethal self-defense. However, defending freedom of movement into a particular space at the price of taking life is grossly disproportional, in particular since immediate self-defense is not the only means to maintain access to public spaces. Such access, especially if denied on a recurrent basis, can also be ensured by enlisting the support of the police.

According to another proclaimed benefit of the "stand your ground" principle, it reassures victims that the law stands behind them when they have to use deadly force and, by the same token, also deters potential aggressors.[109] But nothing is really gained from the introduction of this principle, because the law provides enough reassurance and deterrence even without the principle. According to the traditional understanding of the duty to retreat, victims of aggression must retreat only where this can be safely done without having to risk their physical security or property.[110] If not, they are entitled to stand their ground and defend themselves—where necessary, even with lethal force.

"Stand your ground" laws also clash with the inherent moral justification of the right to self-defense, which serves to resolve a forced choice between the rights of the aggressor and those of the victim that is created by the aggressor's unlawful conduct. Such a forced choice is not really at issue where safe withdrawal from the confrontation is an alternative.[111]

Empirical research on the impact of "stand your ground laws" across the United States show that they do not have a deterrent effect on would-be aggressors, but exacerbate killings, including killings of innocent persons who are not actually aggressors.[112] Several reasons could account for this effect. Firstly,

106. Joseph H. Beale, Retreat from a Murderous Assault, Harvard Law Review, vol. 16 (1903), 567–582, at p. 581.

107. Erb, *supra* note 17, p. 597.

108. Art. 12 ICCPR; Art. 13(1) Universal Declaration.

109. Fair, *supra* note 104, p. 163.

110. See also Tamara Rice Lave, Shoot to Kill: A Critical Look at Stand Your Ground Laws, University of Miami Law Review, vol. 67 (2013), 827–860, at p. 846.

111. See also Second Chapter: D.II.10 (p. 57).

112. Cheng and Hoekstra compared states that have introduced the "stand your ground" doctrine (and related expansions of the right to self-defense) with states that have not done

abolishing the duty to avoid lethal confrontations increases the likelihood of shoot-outs in public spaces, with serious risks not only for the participants but also for innocent bystanders.[113] Secondly, "stand your ground" laws also increase the potential for deadly errors that could lead to the avoidable death of innocent people.[114] In conjunction with the "reasonable grounds to belief in an attack" standard that prevails in U.S. self-defense law, the "stand your ground" principle allows persons to shoot first if they can reasonably fear that their adversary is about to draw a gun on them (often a reasonable fear given the prevalence of concealed firearms). Safe and viable options to retreat from the (assumed) deadly confrontation no longer have to be considered.

Racial prejudices, whether explicit or subconscious, further compound the negative impact of the "stand your ground" principle. As the principle makes it easier to justify lethal force based on assumptions of danger, because the availability of a safe retreat option no longer has to be considered, they have a particularly negative impact on minorities who are stigmatized as dangerous. Even people who are not overtly racist may come to rely on stereotypes resulting from subconscious bias when making a quick judgment in a potential self-defense situation and thus wrongly perceive an individual as dangerous. Imposing a duty to retreat can help guard against the tragic outcomes that may follow from misperceptions, by reducing the likelihood of confrontation generally and also forcing individuals to think before acting on their first instincts.[115]

There is also reason to believe that the "stand your ground" principle reinforces the impact of overt or subconscious racial biases that may be held by police, judges, or jurors who assess self-defense claims, because the principle

so. They found that these expansions did not deter burglary, robbery, or aggravated assault. However, such laws did coincide with an increase of 8% in reported murders and non-negligent manslaughters. See Cheng Cheng & Mark Hoekstra, Does Strengthening Self-Defense Law Deter Crime or Escalate Violence?: Evidence from Expansions to Castle Doctrine, Journal of Human Resources, vol. 48 (2013), 821–854.

McClellan and Tekin, following a broadly similar methodology, estimate that 4.4 to 7.4 more white males are killed each month in the United States as a result of the introduction of "stand your ground" laws. Their findings also indicate that the increase is unlikely to be driven entirely by increased killings of assailants. See Chandler B. McClellan & Erdal Tekin, Stand your Ground Laws and Homicides, June 2012, http://www.flgov.com/wp-content/uploads/citsafety/20120913_secondchance1.pdf.

113. Steven Jansen & M. Elaine Nugent-Bokakove, Expansions to the Castle Doctrine: Implications for Policy and Practice, National District Attorneys Association: Alexandria, Virginia (2007), p. 7.

114. See also L. Song Richardson & Phillip Atiba Goff, Self-Defense and the Suspicion Heuristic, Iowa Law Review vol. 98 (2012–2013), 293–336, at pp. 331–334; Abuznaid, *supra* note 97, pp. 1159–1160.

115. Richardson & Atiba Goff, *id.*, p. 332; Rice Lave, *supra* note 110, pp. 850–854; Tamara F. Lawson, A Fresh Cut in an Old Wound—A Critical Analysis of the Trayvon Martin Killing: The Public Outcry, the Prosecutors' Discretion, and the Stand your Ground Law, University of Florida Journal of Law & Public Policy, vol. 23 (2012), 271–310, at p. 301.

removes a key objective factor—the option to retreat—from the consideration of whether self-defense was reasonable. All that remains to be assessed is whether the target of self-defense reasonably looked like an aggressor to the defender. Research based on U.S. data found in this respect that white-on-black homicides are already 250 percent more likely to be found justified than white-on-white homicides in U.S. states that do not have "stand your ground" laws. This disparity increases further to 354 percent in those U.S. states where "stand your ground" laws are in place.[116]

The "stand your ground" principle also makes it easier for persons who enter a confrontation with the intent to kill to mask their action as self-defense, because charges against them can no longer be upheld based on their failure to retreat.[117] Legal professionals in the United States have expressed concern that habitual criminal offenders are exploiting "stand your ground" laws to avoid liability for violent crime.[118] For instance, two armed rival gang members who have an altercation and end up shooting at each other could both claim self-defense based on a reasonable fear that the other was about to shoot first. No such defense would work if they were both under a duty to retreat before the confrontation escalates and avoid the need for lethal force.[119]

Perhaps most importantly, "stand your ground" laws have an overall pernicious psychological effect on respect for the right to life because of the subliminal messages they convey to citizens.[120] Rather than encouraging the nonviolent resolution of confrontations, the legislation sends the signal that it is right "to shoot first and ask questions later." Individuals are invited to see a confrontation through, like the archaic "true man," rather than walking away from it. A tacit

116. Abuznaid, *supra* note 97, pp. 1154–1155. Coming to similar results John K. Roman, Race, Justifiable Homicide, and Stand Your Ground Laws: Analysis of FBI Supplementary Homicide Report Data, Urban Institute (2013), p. 7, http://www.urban.org/sites/default/files/alfresco/publication-pdfs/412873-Race-Justifiable-Homicide-and-Stand-Your-Ground-Laws.PDF.

Another review of cases from Florida found that a defendant who asserted a stand your ground" defense was successful in 73% of cases if the victim was black, compared to only 59% if the victim was white. See Susan Taylor Martin, Kris Hundley & Connie Humburg, Race plays complex role in Florida's "stand your ground" law, Tampa Bay Times, 2 June 2012, http://www.tampabay.com/news/courts/criminal/race-plays-complex-role-in-floridas-stand-your-ground-law/1233152.

117. Lawson, *supra* note 115, p. 302. On the burden of proof for self-defense claims, see this Sixth Chapter: D.II (pp. 276–278).

118. American Bar Association, *supra* note 97, p. 19; Jansen & Nugent-Borakove, *supra* note 113, p. 6.

119. See Elizabeth B. Megale, Deadly Combinations: How Self-Defense Laws Pairing Immunity with a Presumption of Fear Allow Criminals to "Get Away with Murder," American Journal of Trial Advocacy, vol. 34 (2010), 105–134, at pp. 115–116.

120. Louis N. Schulze Jr., Of Trayvon Martin, George Zimmerman, and Legal Expressivism: Why Massachusetts Should Stand its Ground on "Stand Your Ground,", New England Law Review on Remand, vol. 47 (2012), 34–42, at pp. 37–41; Megale, *id.*, 129.

endorsement of private vigilante justice and punishment in an ever more threatening world also reverberates in the "stand your ground" principle.[121]

3. "Make My Day" and "Castle Doctrine" Laws Permitting Disproportional Force

Serious human rights concerns are also raised by laws that allow for the use of deadly force in self-defense, even where such force is disproportional because the victim faces no actual threat of death or serious bodily harm.

An example is the Home Owner Protection Act, adopted by the U.S. State of Colorado in 1985. It has become commonly known as the "make my day" law (based on an iconic quote from the Clint Eastwood character "Dirty Harry" warning an armed criminal that he would shoot him dead in self-defense). Under that Colorado law, the occupant of a home may use deadly force against a burglar or other unlawful home intruder "when the occupant reasonably believes that such other person might use any physical force, *no matter how slight*, against any occupant."[122] Thus, the law allows the killing of trespassers even if the homeowner knows that they do not pose any serious threat to his health. In 2012, for instance, Colorado home owner Timothy Justice shot and seriously injured Zoey Ripple, a 29-year-old unarmed woman. Ripple had accidentally wandered into his home through an open door and did not heed his warning to leave because she was extremely drunk and confused. In application of the "make my day" law, the prosecution declined to press any charges against Justice.[123] On New Year's Day 2014, Joe Hoskins and Randy Cook, of Grand Junction, Colorado commenced a drunken fistfight that subsequently moved into Hoskins's home. Once in the house, Hoskins shot Cook dead. Because Cook had entered Hoskins's home uninvited and used physical force against Hoskins, the responsible prosecutor had to determine that the "make my day" law rendered Hoskins immune from prosecution. The prosecutor felt compelled to add his personal assessment that he was "very sorry Colorado's criminal justice system does not have an adequate way to address this tragic travesty of a situation."[124]

In tandem with its efforts to entrench the "stand your ground" principle across the United States, the NRA has pushed for the adoption of a second generation

121. See, e.g., Catalfamo, *supra* note 104, p. 543, arguing that shooting dead would-be robbers and rapists, in reliance on the "stand your ground" doctrine, serves and protects the wider community.

122. Colo. Rev. Stat. § 18-1-704.5 (emphasis added).

123. See David Olinger, Colorado gun laws afford rights to those shooting in self-defense, The Denver Post, 30 July 2013, http://www.denverpost.com/ci_23756639/colorado-gun-laws-afford-rights-those-shooting-self.

124. District Attorney Pete Hautzinger, Letter of 10 June 2014 to Sheriff Stan Hilkey on the January 1, 2014, shooting incident at 2846 Unaweep Avenue, http://sheriff.mesacounty.us/search/Default.aspx?q=%22joe+hoskins%22.

of "make my day" laws. Rebranded as "castle doctrine" laws (after the adage that a man's home is his castle), the new generation of laws introduces legal presumptions considering reasonable and lawful any level of force against persons unlawfully intruding into a home or motor vehicle.[125] In 2005, for instance, Florida created an effectively irrebuttable presumption that a person who faces another person unlawfully trying to enter his home or motor vehicle has a "reasonable fear of imminent peril of death or great bodily harm" and may therefore shoot the intruder dead.[126] States such as Texas have adopted similar legal presumption, and they have extended its reach beyond homes and motor vehicles to cover even cases of unlawful intrusion into business premises. Unlike in Florida, however, a Texas prosecutor can rebut the presumption of lawful lethal self-defense with evidence showing that the fear of imminent peril of death or great bodily harm was unreasonable under the specific circumstances.[127]

The United States of America is not the only place where broader self-defense rights can be asserted against home intruders. Costa Rican law, for instance, also establishes a presumption that any level of defensive force used against home intruders, including deadly force, is lawful.[128] French, Belgian, and Honduran law establish the same presumption provided the home invasion occurred at night.[129] The United Kingdom has followed another legislative approach to produce a similar outcome: departing from the traditional common law approach that outlaws disproportionate self-defense, amendments to the Criminal Justice and Immigration Act were adopted in 2013 that stipulate only "grossly disproportionate" defensive force against a person unlawfully entering a private home is prohibited, which implies that a degree of disproportionate force against such intruders is justified.[130]

The recognition of broader self-defense rights against unlawful home invasions has a very long tradition. Ancient Jewish and Chinese laws both precluded

125. For an overview of U.S. states that have adopted such presumptions, see Association of Prosecuting Attorneys, *supra* note 97. A nuanced typology of different types of presumptions has been developed by Stuart P. Green, Castles and Carjackers: Proportionality and the Use of Deadly Force in Defence of Dwellings and Vehicles, University of Illinois Law Review (1999), 1–41, at pp. 11–18.

126. Fla. Stat. § 776.013(1) (2005). See also F. Patrick Hubbard, The Value of Life: Constitutional Limits on Citizens' Use of Deadly Force, George Mason Law Review (2014), vol. 21, 623–655, at p. 647; Megale, *supra* note 119, p. 129; Denise M. Drake, The Castle Doctrine: An Expanding Right to Stand your Ground, St. Mary's Law Journal vol. 39 (2008), 573–613, at pp. 590–591.

127. Drake, *id.*, pp. 590–591.

128. Código Penal [Costa Rica], Ley No. 4573, art. 28.

129. Code pénal [France], s. 122 (6); Code pénal [Belgium], article 417. Código Penal [Honduras], Decreto No. 144-83, art. 24(1). See also Bernard Bouloc, Droit pénal général, Dalloz: Paris (21st ed., 2009), pp. 347-348 [para. 399].

130. Criminal Justice and Immigration Act 2008 (as amended by the Crime and Courts Act 2013), section 76(5A).

the punishment of homeowners killing thieves who broke into their homes during the night.[131] In the present-day popular discourse, expansive self-defense rights are often justified with the need to stop home intruders who have entered with the intent to rape, rob, or otherwise violently attack the tenants.[132] In reality, however, most home intruders are actually nonviolent, unarmed thieves.[133] Nevertheless, the fact remains that for most people the idea of facing an intruder in one's own home (especially at night) is particularly frightening, not least since the intruders' true intentions will generally not be known. Furthermore, even though home intruders typically have no violent intentions, they do not merely pose a threat to the property they have come to steal or vandalize. Their invasion into the sanctity of a private home has a profound impact on the enjoyment of the human rights to privacy and family life.[134] Therefore, it does seem reasonable that states recognize more permissive self-defense rights to ward off a private home invasion; for instance, most domestic legal systems have traditionally not required a duty to retreat from one's home.[135]

However, legislation must still give consideration to the intruders' human rights, in particular their right to life, even if one takes into account that they put themselves in the situation where they may face defensive force. While international human rights law gives states a measure of discretion in striking the balance between the victim and aggressor's rights, this balance has to be reasonable. Where current United Kingdom legislation allows for use of disproportionate force against home intruders, this exceeds the bounds of reasonableness.[136] This is especially so because the law could be interpreted as authorizing homeowners to kill fleeing nonviolent thieves for the sole purpose of defending their property, which cannot be reconciled with Article 2(2)(a) of the ECHR.[137]

131. See Second Chapter: D.I.2 (pp. 31–32) and D.I.8 (p. 44).

132. Justifying castle doctrine laws, former National Rifle Association President Marion Hammer has argued that they would allow her "to use deadly force against an intruder without having to ask, 'Are you here to rape me and kill me, or are you just here to beat me and steal my jewellery?" See Drake, *supra* note 126, p. 575.

133. Green, *supra* note 125, p. 29; Miller, *supra* note 79, p. 306.

134. See also Sangero, *supra* note 9, p. 266; Renée Lettow Lerner, The Worldwide Popular Revolt against Proportionality in Self-Defense Law, Journal of Law, Economics and Policy, vol. 2 (2006), 331–364, at p. 360.

135. Cf. Hubbard, *supra* note 126, pp. 644–645; Erb, *supra* note 17, p. 597.

136. Cf. also Catherine Elliott, Interpreting the Contours of Self-Defence within the Boundaries of the Rule of Law, the Common Law and Human Rights, The Journal of Criminal Law, vol. 79 (2015), 330–343. But see Collins v. Secretary of State for Justice, [2016] EWHC 33 (Admin), paras. 63 & 70; https://www.judiciary.gov.uk/wp-content/uploads/2016/01/collins-v-sos-for-justice-householder-defence.pdf (considering English law to be compatible with the European Convention on Human Rights even though it only outlaws grossly disproportionate force).

137. See Miller, *supra* note 79, p. 308. See also this Sixth Chapter: C.III.1 (pp. 255–257).

Laws that establish a non-rebuttable presumption equating any unlawful home invasions with a deadly threat cannot be reconciled with international human rights law either. There will be cases of unlawful trespassing into a home for relatively harmless purposes. If the prosecution can show that the home occupant recognized such a relatively harmless invasion for what it was, the irrebuttable presumption that deadly force was reasonable would nevertheless stand. The law would therefore effectively provide a license to kill those who illegally trespass on private territory. This is grossly unreasonable and fails to assign due value to the right to life.[138] On 16 March 1997, for instance, two boys, aged 10 and 14 years, unlawfully entered a private property in Florida filled with seemingly abandoned junk, including caravan trailers, to find plywood to build a shack in a nearby forest. When the 14-year-old entered one of the caravan trailers, the owner shot and killed him. While the owner was convicted for manslaughter under Florida law as it then stood, it is doubtful whether the same result would obtain under Florida's present "castle doctrine" legislation.[139]

Even where the presumption that deadly force was reasonable can be technically rebutted, it is very hard to overcome and therefore has a chilling effect on police and prosecutors to press charges in cases involving dubious self-defense claims.[140] Early in the morning of September 4, 2007, for instance, Texas musician Carter Albrecht, extremely drunk at the time, banged on his sleeping neighbors' door and tried to get in. After shouting at Albrecht to go away, the homeowner fired at the closed door, hitting Albrecht in the head and killing him. Police refused to arrest or charge the shooter for the killing, which occurred only three days after legislation entered into force that further toughened Texas's "castle doctrine" law.[141]

Especially problematic from a human rights perspective is the extension of "make my day" and "castle doctrine" laws beyond the realm of the private home. As noted, a home invasion entails an assault on privacy and family life and is therefore of an inherent gravity. These values are not touched in the same way by illegal entries into business premises and motor vehicles. They do not establish a private retreat, but remain situated in the public realm.[142] The law therefore invites tragic errors, where it presumptively equates any unlawful entry into such places—for instance, a beggar extending his arm into a car window or a petty thief trying to snatch a cell phone from a car—with a deadly threat.

In the worst case, such laws may allow people to get away with killing an unarmed person who does not pose a serious threat, just because the altercation

138. See also Hubbard, *supra* note 126, p. 645.

139. Jansen & Nugent-Borakove, *supra* note 113, p. 11 referring to the facts underlying the decision of the Florida Court of Appeals in Quaggin v. State, 752 So. 2d 19 (Fla. App. 2000).

140. See also Jansen & Nugent-Borakove, *id.*, p. 6.

141. Gretel C. Kovac, Musician Is Killed for Banging on a Door, New York Times, 5 September 2007, http://www.nytimes.com/2007/09/05/us/05dallas.html?_r=0 .

142. See also Megale, *supra* note 119, p. 117.

plays out in or around a motor vehicle or business. Some examples follow. For instance, on July 21, 2007, Jimmy Hair and Charles Harper had a confrontation outside a nightclub in Florida. Harper, not armed at the time, entered the vehicle in which Hair was sitting and began to tussle with him. Although a third person was already trying to pull Harper away, Hair shot him dead. The Florida Court of Appeals held that the presumption of reasonable fear of death that attached to Harper's unlawful entry into the motor vehicle justified the killing as self-defense under Florida's law and hence rendered Hair immune from prosecution.[143] On October 9, 2011, in Dayton, Ohio, a verbal altercation ensued in Dayton, Ohio, between Robert Travis Miller and alleged drug dealer Tyler Hamilton, who happened to be sitting in his car. When the unarmed Miller tried to somehow attack Hamilton, the latter drew his gun, shot Miller dead, and fled the scene. The prosecutor refused to charge Hamilton in the killing, arguing that "[u]nder Ohio's Castle Doctrine, one is permitted to use whatever force necessary, if you're in your home, or if you're in a private vehicle, to defend yourself."[144]

These cases not only demonstrate that such laws, in their current form, represent a failure to protect the human right to life with due diligence against disproportional defensive force. They also bear out the concern voiced by the Association of Prosecuting Attorneys, a U.S.-based professional organization, that the adoption of such laws has "unintended consequences and inhibits the ability of law enforcement and prosecutors to fully hold violent criminals accountable for their acts."[145]

IV. Absolute prohibition of inhuman treatment

Law enforcement agents are absolutely prohibited from using torture and inhuman treatment, even for the purpose of defending life.[146] While torture, as defined in international human rights law, can only be committed on behalf of the state (see Article 1(1) of the CAT), it is contested to what extent international human rights law obligates the state to ban private individuals from using inhuman treatment to defend life. A slight alteration of the facts faced by the ECtHR in the *Gäfgen* child kidnapping case[147] illustrates the dilemma: May a state allow

143. Hair v State, 17 So. 3d 804 (Fla. Dist. Ct. App. 2009). See also Megale, *supra* note 119, pp. 105–106.

144. See Kelli Wynn, Murder charge denied due to self-defense law, prosecutors say, Dayton Daily News, 27 October 2011, http://www.daytondailynews.com/news/news/local/murder-charge-denied-due-to-self-defense-law-prose/nMwqL/ .

145. Association of Prosecuting Attorneys, Statement of Principles regarding Expansions to the Castle Doctrine (2012), https://prosecutingattorneys.org/wp-content/uploads/APA-Castle-Doctrine-Principles1.pdf.

146. See Fourth Chapter: C.VI (pp. 189–197).

147. In that case, police officers threatened to torture a child kidnapper to force him to reveal the child's location and save its life. See Gäfgen v. Germany, Appl. No. 22978/05, Judgment of 1 June 2010.

a father to torment the kidnapper of his son in order to give up the location of the child and safe his life?

Some authors are of the view that only the state is absolutely prohibited from using torture and inhuman treatment. If necessary to defend the life of others, private individuals are therefore not prohibited from causing severe pain to criminal suspects in order to force them to give up life-saving information about their victims.[148] It is argued that private "torture" is not the same as state-sponsored torture because it does not call the moral dignity of the state into question and does not have the same devastating symbolic effect.[149] Moreover, the threat emanating from the occasional case of private persons causing pain to get information is not nearly as grave as when the state uses its entire police machinery, backed up by the law, for purposes of torture and the victim has basically no chance to escape.[150]

According to the more persuasive contrary position, the state must prohibit private persons from engaging in inhuman treatment, even if it is meant to save life, because the state also has to protect persons from inhuman treatment by other private individuals.[151] The absolute prohibition of inhuman treatment embodies an objective value decision that also radiates into the private sphere. State tolerance for inhuman treatment in the private sphere also reflects back on the state itself and tarnishes it. Even if the state's own officials do not commit the acts, the symbolism of the state laws allowing inhuman treatment remains devastating. This is compounded by the fact that the state would have to set and enforce rules on how far private "torture" could go, signaling its moral approval of the general principle.

One must also imagine what it would mean in practical terms if self-defense could justify private "torture." Relatives of kidnapping victims could hire private security companies to capture suspected kidnappers and subject them to pain until they give up the location of the victim.[152] Police officers who found a suspect being mistreated would have no right to stop the torture, especially if they can offer no alternative means to obtain the lifesaving information. They would have to stand by and let the relatives or hired private security agent proceed.[153]

148. Eric Hilgendorf, Folter im Rechtsstaat?, JuristenZeitung 2004, 331–339, p. 335; Christian Fahl, Neue „sozialethische Einschränkung" der Notwehr: „Folter", Jura 2007, 743–750, at p. 748, Christian Jäger, Folter und Flugzeugabschuss—rechtsstaatliche Tabubrüche oder rechtsguterhaltende Notwendigkeiten?, Juristische Ausbildung (JA) 2008, 678–684, at p. 681; Merkel, *supra* note 17, p. 384.

149. Walter Perron, Foltern in Notwehr?, in: Bernd Heinrich et al. (eds.), Festschrift für Ulrich Weber zum 70. Geburtstag, Verlag Ernst und Werner Gieseking: Bielefeld (2004), 143–154, at p. 152; Jäger, *id.*, p. 681.

150. Perron, *id.*, pp. 151–152.

151. Perron, *id.*, p. 152; von Scherenberg, *supra* note 7, p. 256; Diehm, *supra* note 9, p. 370.

152. Perron, *id.*, 152; Scherenberg, *id.*, p. 256

153. Noting this problem, Jäger, *supra* note 148, pp. 681 implausibly argues that a private right to "torture" would cease to exist once police officers who represent the "neutral state" come to the scene—even though the officers could not engage in defensive torture themselves.

Legalized private "torture" would be even harder to control than state-inflicted torture.[154] There is a serious risk that desperate relatives of victims would end up tormenting innocent persons, driven by the faint hope of saving their loved one's life.[155]

A loophole for private "torture" also invites abuse by the state. Although police officers would remain formally prohibited from becoming complicit to torture, they might be tempted to clandestinely hand over suspects to private individuals to let them do what they are themselves prohibited from doing.[156] Especially in countries where serious human rights violations are regularly "outsourced" to seemingly private groups, such as death squads or "patriotic volunteers," permitting private "torture" might be easily provide states with a way to circumvent the absolute prohibition on torture and inhuman treatment.

The duty to prohibit private persons from using inhuman treatment does not mean that this must always result in criminal sanctions for desperate family members who torment a suspect in a genuine attempt to save the life of a loved one. In such cases, the relatives will find themselves in a dilemma: either respect the legal order, or follow their instinct to save the life of a loved one. These situations can therefore be appropriately resolved by applying criminal law provisions that excuse the concerned relatives from criminal responsibility without justifying their behavior, such as duress provisions.[157] Such excuses would be available only to close relatives. Private security agents, who lack emotional ties to the victim, could not rely on them if they made a business out of offering private "torture" services. By maintaining that the conduct remains illegal, the state still signals its disapproval of all forms of inhuman treatment. An excuse solution ensures also that police officers coming to the scene would retain the right, and even the duty, to intervene and protect the suspect from unlawful private inhuman treatment.

V. Special requirements regarding private security companies

Demand for private security is growing due to a combination of many states failing to provide adequate public security or taking deliberate policy decisions to outsource certain security-related functions that were previously assumed by the state. According to one estimate, global demand for private contract security services has been increasing by 7.4 percent per year and industry turnover will amount to USD $244 billion in 2016.[158] Against this backdrop, specialized

154. Perron, *supra* note 149, p. 152; von Scherenberg, *supra* note 7, p. 256.

155. Perron, *id.*, p. 152; Diehm, *supra* note 9, p. 372.

156. Perron, *id.*, p. 152; von Scherenberg, *supra* note 7, p. 257.

157. Perron, *id.*, p. 152; Diehm, *supra* note 9, pp. 373–374.

158. Freedonia, World Security Services (2013), http://www.freedoniagroup.com/industry-study/2978/world-security-services.htm.

international regulations on the private security sector have been developed in recent years. They include notably the Montreux Document and the related International Code of Conduct for Private Security Service Providers, which both focus on companies operating in armed conflict and similar complex environments.[159] In 2015, the International Standards Organization (ISO) adopted ISO 18778 on a Management System for Private Security Operations. While these are all nonbinding as a matter of international law, legally binding requirements relating to private companies flow from the general norms of international human rights law.

The conduct of private security companies is attributable to the state to the extent that state law empowers them to exercise elements of governmental authority.[160] To that extent, their activities would be have to be considered state activities and the human rights obligations on use of defensive force by state agents (elaborated in the Fourth Chapter) apply in full.[161] States that entrust governmental authority to private security companies are responsible for any violations the companies commit in exercise of such authority.

In light of this implication, it is contested to what extent the activities of private security companies involve elements of governmental authority. De Schutter contends that the acts of private companies that bear arms and use them in self-defense or defense of property or to arrest individuals and bring them to the police should be attributable in full to the state.[162] Similarly, Kontos argues that private security companies' conduct is attributable to the state even where they exercise no more powers than ordinary citizens, because they exercise such powers as an occupational activity with the potential to infringe seriously on civil liberties.[163] However, such an expansive approach to attribution would imply that the state would be responsible for any criminal activity of a professional armed

159. See Montreux Document: On pertinent international legal obligations and good practices for states related to operations of private military and security companies during armed conflict (2008), https://www.eda.admin.ch/content/dam/eda/en/documents/aussenpolitik/voelkerrecht/Montreux-Broschuere_en.pdf; International Code of Conduct for Private Security Service Providers (2010), http://icoca.ch/en/the_icoc.

160. See Art. 5 of the ILC Draft Articles on Responsibility for Internationally Wrongful Acts, as contained in Ch. IV.E.1 of the Report of the International Law Commission, U.N. Doc. A/56/10.

161. Cameron & Chetail, *supra* note 32, p. 263; Montreux Document, *supra* note, 159, Part One : para. 7.

162. Olivier De Schutter, The Responsibility of States, in: Simon Chesterman & Angelina Fisher (eds.), Private Security, Public Order: The Outsourcing of Public Services and Its Limits, Oxford University Press: Oxford/New York (2009), 25–45, at p. 31.

163. Alexis P. Kontos, "Private" security guards: Privatized force and State responsibility under international human rights law, Non-State Actors and International Law, vol. 4 (2004), 199–238, at p. 237.

private security guard, even if the person is contracted by a private actor to guard private interests with no involvement whatsoever of the state.[164]

According to the more convincing view, private security company conduct is attributable to the state, and hence directly subject to human rights obligations, only to the extent that the company is hired to assume intrinsic state functions.[165] Examples include private security companies administering places of detention or carrying out immigration control functions.[166] Private security companies also assume governmental authority if they are tasked to guard persons or objects that embody intrinsic state functions, for example, where private contractors are hired to protect diplomats or military bases.

Conversely, other types of guarding and security functions remain private in nature even if they involve elements of patrolling and surveillance.[167] Private security guards do not engage in law enforcement and have no law enforcement powers. Instead, they exercise a form of institutionalized self-defense, as their powers to use force emerge chiefly from their right to defend themselves, others, and their property (coupled with limited "citizen's arrest" powers where available under domestic law).[168] For this reason, their use of force is subsidiary to that of state law enforcement and may be exercised only to the extent that help from state security forces cannot be obtained in time.[169]

164. Cameron & Chetail, *supra* note 32, p. 171.

165. Corinna Seiberth, Private Military and Security Companies in International Law, Intersentia: Cambridge/Antwerp/Portland (2014), p. 85. See also U.N. Special Rapporteur on extrajudicial, summary or arbitrary executions, *supra* note 79, para. 73.

166. International Law Commission, Draft articles on Responsibility of States for Internationally Wrongful Acts, with commentaries, in: Report of the International Law Commission, Fifty-Third Session, U.N. Doc. A/56/10 (2001) pp. 59–365, at p. 93 [art. 5, para. 2 of the commentaries]; Human Rights Committee, Concluding Observations on the United Kingdom, CCPR/C/79/Add. 55 (1995), para. 16; Seiberth, *supra* note 165, pp. 85–86; Cameron & Chetail, *supra* note 32, pp. 200–201.

167. Cameron & Chetail, *supra* note 32, pp. 202–203.

168. Cameron & Chetail, *supra* note 32, p. 170; Seiberth, *supra* note 165, p. 171. Highly problematic therefore the suggestion of the International Code of Conduct for Private Security Providers, *supra* note 159, para. 31, that private security companies may use firearms not only for purposes of self-defense and defense of others, but also "to prevent the perpetration of a particularly serious crime involving grave threat to life." This phrase is borrowed from the Basic Principles on the Use of Force and Firearms by Law Enforcement Officials, adopted at the Eighth United Nations Congress on the Prevention of Crime and the Treatment of Offenders, Havana, 27 August to 7 September 1990, U.N. Doc. A/CONF.144/28/Rev.1 at 112 (1990), para. 9. Its inclusion fails to recognize that private companies are not law enforcement agents. See also Seiberth, *supra* note 165, p. 172.

169. See Human Rights Committee, Concluding Observations on Guatemala, U.N. Doc. CCPR/C/GTM/CO/3 (2012), para. 16; U.N. Special Rapporteur on extrajudicial, summary or arbitrary executions, *supra* note 79, para. 84. See also Seiberth, *supra* note 165, p. 173;

Although the power to use force granted to private security companies does not extend further than that of ordinary citizens, states have to impose more comprehensive requirements on them in order to discharge their obligation to protect human rights of life and physical security with due diligence against the excesses of private security guards. Such private security companies and their staff have a higher capacity to use force than the average private citizen, are trained to use force, work as an organized collective, and are usually armed. Furthermore, they are regularly placed in situations where their employees have to use defensive force, so that a higher degree of preparedness can be expected of them.

U.N. human rights mechanisms demand that states impose comprehensive regulation on private security companies.[170] The Inter-American Commission takes the view that the "domestic legal system must regulate the functions that private security services can perform; the types of weapons and materials they are authorized to use; the proper mechanisms to oversee their activities; introduction of licensing, and a system whereby these private security firms are required to report their contracts on a regular basis, detailing the typing [sic] of activities they perform."[171] In addition to requirements for mandatory training of staff, the state has to impose vetting requirements concerning the initial selection of staff to ensure that persons with a past record of serious human rights abuses or other relevant violent crime are not hired.[172]

The extent and type of regulation requirements will depend on the role particular private security companies may play.[173] In many cases, states will have to

Guido den Dekker & Eric P.J. Myjer, The Right to Life and Self-Defence of Private Military and Security Contractors in Armed Conflict, in: Francesco Francioni and Natalino Ronzitti (eds.), War by Contract: Human Rights, Humanitarian Law and Private Contractors, Oxford University Press: Oxford (2011), 171–193, at p. 182.

170. Human Rights Committee, Concluding Observations on Guatemala, *id.*, para. 16; Committee against Torture, Concluding Observations on Guatemala, U.N.Doc. CAT/C/GTM/CO5-6 (2013), para. 16; U.N. Special Rapporteur on extrajudicial, summary or arbitrary executions, *supra* note 79, para. 120; Working Group on the use of mercenaries as a means of violating human rights and impeding the exercise of the right of people to self-determination, Report to the General Assembly, U.N. Doc. A/68/339 (2013), para. 56; *id.*, Report on the Mission to Honduras, U.N. Doc. A/HRC/24/45/Add.1 (2013), para. 55 (a); *id.*, Report on the Mission to Peru, U.N. Doc. A/HRC/7/7/Add. 2 (2008), para. 75(c); *id.*, Report on the Mission to Somalia, U.N. Doc. A/HRC/24/45/Add.2 (2013), para. 78. See also Cameron & Chetail, *supra* note 32, p. 253.

171. Inter-American Commission on Human Rights, Report on Citizen Security and Human Rights, OEA/Ser.L/V/II.Doc. 57 (2009), para. 73. See also African Commission on Human and Peoples' Rights, Principles and Guidelines on Human and Peoples' Rights while Countering Terrorism in Africa, adopted by its 56th Ordinary Session (2015), p. 32 [para. 8:A].

172. See Inter-American Commission on Human Rights, *id.*, para. 74. See also African Commission on Human and Peoples' Rights, *id.*; U.N. Working Group on the use of mercenaries, Mission to Honduras, *supra* note 170, para. 55(a); U.N. Special Rapporteur on extrajudicial, summary or arbitrary executions, *supra* note 79, paras. 80 & 126(b).

173. See also Kontos, *supra* note 163, p. 236.

impose regulatory requirements similar to the organizational and precautionary requirements applicable to law enforcement agencies.[174] For instance, if private security guards can be expected to have to deal with potentially violent crowds, such as when guarding industrial premises with striking workers or angry demonstrators present, states would have to require the companies to equip their staff with less lethal weapons to defend themselves and their clients' property against crowd violence with minimal force until the police arrives to deal with the situation.

States have to enforce their regulation through effective preventive registration and oversight mechanisms,[175] including mandatory reporting requirements where private companies' use of force may have failed to respect human rights.[176] Where subsequent state investigations find that security guards use excessive force beyond the limits of self-defense, the state has to ensure that the employing companies are investigated and held responsible based on the principle of vicarious liability. States must impose administrative fines and corporate criminal sanctions where the latter are available, and must also ensure that victims have effective remedies allowing them to obtain compensation from the company concerned.[177]

Individual security guards who, intentionally or out of gross negligence, use excessive force resulting in death or serious injury must be held criminally accountable, in accordance with the general principles discussed in the following section.

D. DUTY TO INVESTIGATE AND PROSECUTE EXCESSIVE OR UNWARRANTED SELF-DEFENSE

In exercising its duty to protect the rights to life and physical security, the state must not only investigate serious acts of violence by its own agents but also by private individuals. Private individuals who commit unlawful violence resulting in death or serious injury must be prosecuted and appropriately punished so as

174. See also U.N. Special Rapporteur on extrajudicial, summary or arbitrary executions, *supra* note 79, para. 76. On the content of these organizational requirements see Fourth Chapter: C.IV (pp. 164–170).

175. See also U.N. Working Group on the use of mercenaries, Mission to Honduras, *supra* note 170, para. 55(c); Cameron & Chetail, *supra* note 32, p. 261. Overly permissive Seiberth, *supra* note 165, p. 138, who takes the view that a "rudimentary system of licensing" for private security companies would probably be sufficient to fulfil the state obligation to protect human rights with due diligence.

176. African Commission on Human and Peoples' Rights, Principles and Guidelines on Human and Peoples' Rights while Countering Terrorism in Africa, *supra* note 171, p. 32 [para. 8:A].

177. See also Working Group on the use of mercenaries as a means of violating human rights and impeding the exercise of the right of people to self-determination, Report on the Mission to Afghanistan, U.N. Doc. A/HRC/15/25/Add.4 (2010), para. 79; African Commission on

to deter future abuses.[178] In exercising this duty, states have to uphold the due process and fair trial rights of the person concerned.

These principles also apply to cases of excessive or unwarranted self-defense. In practice, two issues have been identified as raising serious human rights concerns: immunities from prosecution for self-defense claimants and full reversals of the burden of proof at the accused person's expense. Both types of measures fail in their own way to strike a reasonable balance between the duty to deter the exercise of unwarranted violence in purported self-defense and the duty to uphold the right to a fair trial.

I. Immunities from prosecution

The legislative amendments through which many U.S. states introduced the above mentioned "stand your ground" and "castle doctrine" expansions of the right to self-defense also included far-reaching immunities from civil and criminal action. These immunities are said be necessary to protect those who resort to self-defense from having to go to court and incur costly legal fees.[179] Previously, killings that involved a claim of self-defense would usually be brought before a grand jury or a judge. Under the amended laws, the police and prosecutor can bring the case to court only if they can affirmatively demonstrate that self-defense was unlawful. In some states, immunities even preclude the police from arresting a person who killed in purported self-defense until they can show probable cause that the claim of self-defense is not justified.[180]

The U.N. Human Rights Committee has taken issue with these far-reaching immunity provisions and recommended that the relevant U.S. states repeal them.[181] This view deserves support. While international human rights law does not require that investigations into unlawful killings and other serious violence

Human and Peoples' Rights, General Comment on the Right to Life, *supra* note 11, para. 18; Montreux Document, *supra* note, 159, Part One: para. 4. The U.N. Special Rapporteur on extrajudicial, summary or arbitrary executions (see *supra* note 79, para. 126(g)) calls for a strict vicarious liability standard that would preclude private security companies from exculpating themselves for excessive force used by their employees.

178. Ergi v. Turkey [ECtHR], Appl. No. 23818/94, Judgment of 28 July 1998, para. 82; Velasquez Rodriguez v. Honduras [IACtHR], Judgment of 29 July 1988, Ser. C No. 4, para 177; Committee on the Elimination of Discrimination against Women, A.T. v. Hungary, Comm. No. 2/2003, Views of 26 January 2005, para. 9.2; U.N. Special Rapporteur on extrajudicial, summary or arbitrary executions, *supra* note 79, para. 75; African Commission on Human and Peoples' Rights, General Comment on the Right to Life, *supra* note 11, para. 9.

179. Hubbard, *supra* note 126, pp. 646–647.

180. See Randolph, *supra* note 96, pp. 617–622; Lawson, *supra* note 115, p. 288 Megale, *supra* note 119, pp. 119–120.

181. Human Rights Committee, Concluding observations on the fourth periodic report of the United States of America, *supra* note 2, para. 10. See also American Bar Association, *supra* note 97, pp. 2-3;Abuznaid, *supra* note 97, pp. 1165–1166.

must be carried out by way of judicial proceedings, stricter scrutiny is warranted where only executive authorities are involved.[182] At all times, the investigation has to be effective, transparent, and conducted with adequate participation by the victim or victim's family.[183] Immunity provisions call these requirements into doubt, because they create serious practical obstacles to the effective investigation of cases.[184] It appears arbitrary that only self-defense should be exempt from the type of close judicial scrutiny that U.S. law provides for other types of affirmative criminal defenses. By design, immunities have a chilling effect on police and prosecutors and deter them from effectively investigating claims of self-defense and prosecuting excesses. This undermines the state's capacity to protect the rights to life and physical security with due diligence.

II. Burden of proof

States take different approaches in assigning the burden of proof, where a defendant claims to have killed or otherwise used force in self-defense. In Germany and Italy, for instance, the burden is entirely on the state to prove beyond reasonable doubt that the defendant did not act in justified self-defense.[185] In common law jurisdictions such as England and Wales, India, or Nigeria, self-defense must be explicitly pleaded by the defendant. Furthermore, the law places the evidential burden on the defendant to adduce enough evidence to establish a reasonable doubt as to whether his actions might not have been justified by self-defense. If the defendant manages to discharge this relatively light burden, the prosecution must show beyond reasonable doubt that the defendant did not act in self-defense.[186]

The same approach is also followed in almost all states of the United States. Ohio marks an exception, as it still follows a 19th century common law approach, according to which the defendant bears the full burden of proof, based on the preponderance of evidence, to show that he acted in self-defense.[187] In France

182. See Finogenov et al. v. Russia [ECtHR], Appl. No. 18299/03 & 27311/03, Judgment of 20 December 2011, para. 240.

183. See Fourth Chapter: E.II (pp. 204–209).

184. Cf. Randolph, *supra* note 96, pp. 617–619.

185. John R. Spencer, Evidence, in: Mireille Delmas-Marty & John R. Spencer (eds.), European Criminal Procedures, Cambridge University Press: Cambridge (2002), 591–650, at p. 598.

186. Andrew Ashworth, Four Threats to the Presumption of Innocence, South African Law Journal, vol. 123 (2006), 63-97, at pp. 88–89; R.D. Yadav, Law of Crime and Self-Defence, Mittal Publications: New Delhi (1993), pp. 343–346; Bamgbose, *supra* note 45, p. 340.

187. Eugene Volokh, Burden and Quantum of Proof as to Self-Defense. The Volokh Conspiracy, 14 July 2013, http://volokh.com/2013/07/14/burden-and-quantum-of-proof-on-self-defense. Some courts in Louisiana still follow this approach as well.

and Iceland, the view also prevails that it is on the defendant to prove the conditions for self-defense.[188]

Shifting the burden of proof to the defendant raises concerns in light of the human right to be presumed innocent until proved guilty according to law; see, for example, Article 14(2) of the ICCPR). In principle, this human right imposes the burden of proving the charge on the prosecuting state.[189] However, this allocation of the burden of proof is not absolute. States may establish reasonable presumptions of fact or law that the defendant has to overcome. The ECtHR requires in this respect that burdens of proof placed on the defendant stay within reasonable limits, taking into account the importance of what is at stake and maintaining the rights of the defense.[190] Similarly, the Human Rights Committee infers from the presumption of innocence only that legal presumptions may not place a "disproportionate burden of proof" on a criminal defendant, not that the burden of proof must fall entirely on the state.[191]

International human rights mechanisms have not yet ruled on how these principles apply to evidentiary rules on self-defense. However, it would appear that the prevailing approach in many common law countries, which requires the defendant to provide a limited amount of evidence that makes a claim of self-defense at least plausible, is still reasonable and not contrary to the presumption of innocence, even though it forces the defendant to actively contribute to the criminal proceedings.[192] If the state can show beyond a reasonable doubt that the defendant killed a person, then a factual presumption that the killing was

188. Eiríkur Tómasson, Presumed Innocent until Proven Guilty: The Principle of Article 6, Paragraph 2 of the European Convention on Human Rights and Article 70, Paragraph 2 of the Constitution of Iceland that the Burden of Proof Rests with the Prosecution, Scandinavian Studies in Law, vol. 51 (2007), 505-531, at pp. 524–525; Bernard Bouloc, *supra* note 129, pp. 346–347 [para. 397]; Walter Perron, Rechtsvergleichende Betrachtungen zur Notwehr, in: Jörg Arnold et al. (eds.), Menschengerechtes Strafrecht: Festschrift für Albin Eser zum 70. Geburtstag, C.H. Beck: München 2005), 1019–1039, at p. 1033. In French judicial practice, the courts will often expect the prosecution to react and adduce evidence of its own if the defendant makes out at least a prima facie case for self-defense. See Frédéric Desportes & Francis Le Gunehec, Droit Pénal Général, Economica: Paris (15th ed., 2008), p. 698 [para. 739].

189. Human Rights Committee, General Comment No. 32, Article 14: Right to equality before courts and tribunals and to a fair trial, U.N. Doc. CCPR/C/GC/32 (2007), para 30; Lopez Mendoza v Venzuela [IACtHR], Judgment of 1 September 2011, Ser. C No. 233, para 128.

190. Salabiaku v. France, Appl. No. 10519/83, Judgment of 7 October 1988, para. 28.

191. Mr. J. O. v. France, Comm. No. 1620/2007, U.N. Doc. CCPR/C/101/D/1620/2007/Rev.2 (2011), para. 9.6.

192. Ashworth, *supra* note 186, p. 89; Paul Roberts & Adrian Zuckerman, Criminal Evidence, Oxford University Press: Oxford (2nd ed., 2010), p. 229; Sangero, *supra* note 9, p. 281 [fn. 1097]. Ormerod, Smith & Hogan, *supra* note 50, p. 29. See also Prosecutor v. Fernandes, Court of Appeal of East Timor, File No. 7 of 2001, Ruling (Jun. 29, 2001), para. 11, also available at: http://www.worldcourts.com/un_etta/eng/decisions/2001.06.29_Prosecutor_v_Fernandes1.pdf#search=%22self-defence%22.

unlawful is not unreasonable. Furthermore, it does not require much from the defendant to meet the evidential burden of reasonable doubt as to whether he might have acted in self-defense after all. Conversely, it could impose an undue burden on the prosecution to proactively adduce evidence ruling out self-defense, along with any other possible defense, in every single case.

Far more troublesome is a full reversal of the burden of proof. While international human rights mechanisms have not yet considered the question, some national courts consider it compatible with the right to be presumed innocent until proven guilty. The Supreme Court of Iceland has ruled that the presumption of innocence under Article 6(2) of the ECHR does not preclude Icelandic law from requiring the defendant to prove self-defense, because the prosecution has only to prove the defendant's guilt and does not have to disprove the defendant's allegations of facts that could provide him with impunity.[193] Similarly, the U.S. Supreme Court has ruled—by five to four, the narrowest majority—that the State of Ohio's approach of requiring the defendant to prove a claim of self-defense can be reconciled with the presumption of innocence under the U.S. Constitution because the state still has to prove beyond reasonable doubt the elements of the offense itself.[194]

The present author considers that these rulings cannot be reconciled with international human rights law. In many self-defense cases, it is undisputed that the defendant committed the killing or other act of violence in question. The entire case therefore turns on whether there were circumstances establishing self-defense. If the defendant has to prove such circumstances based on a preponderance of evidence standard, there is hardly anything left of the presumption of innocence. The defendant could be convicted even if the court maintained reasonable doubts whether he actually acted unlawfully rather than in justified self-defense. A full reversal of the burden of proof to the disadvantage of the defendant is therefore unreasonable and violates the presumption of innocence under international human rights law.[195]

E. NO GENERAL RIGHT TO POSSESS FIREARMS AND OTHER MEANS OF SELF-DEFENSE

In the heated debate on gun rights and gun violence in the United States, pro-gun activists put forward the argument that the right to self-defense entails a right

193. Supreme Court of Iceland, Case. No. 248/2000, Judgment of 2 November 2000, http://www.haestirettur.is/domar?nr=972. English translation of the relevant passage of the judgment in Tómasson, *supra* note 188, p. 525.

194. Martin v Ohio, 480 US 228, 232 (1987). See also White v. Arn [U.S. Federal Court of Appeals] 788 F2d 338 (6th Cir. 1986). Supporting a reversal of the burden of proof *de lege ferenda*, also Joseph Kennedy, Why It Was Too Easy for George Zimmerman to Get Off for Self-Defense, Slate, 16 July 2013, http://www.slate.com/articles/news_and_politics/jurisprudence/2013/07/george_zimmerman_and_self_defense_why_it_was_too_easy_for_him_to_get_off.html .

195. See also Perron *supra* note 188, p. 1037.

to possess effective means of self-defense, namely firearms. In turn, attempts to restrict private gun ownership are often branded as denials of a "human right to self-defense."[196]

Arguments that seek to link self-defense and the private possession of arms are not new. An advisory opinion prepared for the court of the Chinese Emperor Han Wudi (156–87 BCE) opposed limitations on private possession of bows and crossbows with the argument that this would deny law-abiding people the possibility of defending themselves against criminals.[197] The Roman orator and jurist Cicero reversed the argument when he rhetorically asked why Romans have a right to own swords if they should be prohibited from using them in self-defense.[198] More recently, the U.S. Supreme Court took the position that an individual right to keep and bear firearms under the Second Amendment of the U.S. Constitution was underpinned by the right to self-defense.[199]

According to international human rights law, however, there is no general right to possess weapons as a means of self-defense. No international human rights mechanism has lent support to such a claim. To the contrary, international human rights bodies have emphasized that the duty of states to protect the human rights to life and physical security against private attacks obligates them to regulate and reasonably restrict private gun ownership.[200] The U.N. Human Rights Committee indicated in this context that states are required to protect their

196. See, e.g., Jessica Parks, Gun-rights activist sparks ire with Rosa Parks comparison, The Inquirer, 14 March 2015, http://articles.philly.com/2015-03-14/news/60090407_1_rosa-parks-gun-owners-gun-rights; Richard Feldman, Bernie Goetz "The Subway Gunman" 30 Years Later, Huffington Post, 23 December 2014, http://www.huffingtonpost.com/richard-feldman/bernie-goetz-the-subway-g_b_6369128.html. On the subject why there is no human right to self-defense, see Third Chapter (pp. 75–90).

197. See Charles Sanft, Bow Control in Han China: Yuqiu Shouwang on Self-Defense, Journal of Asian History, vol. 42 (2008), 143–164, at p. 158.

198. Marcus Tullius Cicero, For T.A. Milo, in: C.D. Yonge (trans.), The Orations of Marcus Tullius Cicero, vol. 3, Henry G. Bohn: London (1852), 390–437, at p. 394 [Mil. IV].

199. See District of Columbia v. Heller, *supra* note 14, p. 2817.

200. Human Rights Council, Resolution 29/10. Human rights and the regulation of civilian acquisition, possession and use of firearms, U.N. Doc. A/HRC/RES/29/10 (2015); U.N. Special Rapporteur on Small Arms, Barbara Frey, Final Report, *supra* note 18, paras. 16, 19 & 44; U.N. Human Rights Committee, Concluding observations on the fourth periodic report of the United States of America, *supra* note 2, para. 10; *id.*, Concluding Observations on Honduras, U.N. Doc. A/HRC/24/45/Add.1 (2013), para. 55 (d); Committee on the Elimination of Discrimination against Women, Concluding observations on the fourth periodic report of Pakistan, U.N. Doc. CEDAW/C/PAK/CO/4 (2013), para. 14(d); Committee on the Rights of the Child, Concluding Observations: El Salvador, U.N. Doc. CRC/C/SLV/C O/3-4 (2010), para. 32(d); Report of the Special Rapporteur on violence against women, its causes and consequences, Ms. Rashida Manjoo: Mission to the United States of America, U.N. Doc. A/HRC/17/26 (2011), para. 115(g); Inter-American Commission on Human Rights, *supra* note 171, para. 60. See also Cerone, *supra* note 23, pp. 323 [n.8] & 329.

population against the "risks of excessive availability of firearms."[201] Expressing concern about the indiscriminate issuing of firearms licenses, the Committee against Torture has recommended strengthening administrative measures to control the issuance of firearms licenses.[202] Emphasizing the human rights obligation of states to protect the rights to life and physical security with due diligence, the U.N. High Commissioner for Human Rights has called on states to regulate private access to firearms through criteria-based firearms licensing, registration, monitoring, auditing, and training requirements.[203]

Notwithstanding the clear position in international jurisprudence, proponents of the thesis that a right to self-defense entails a right to own and bear arms, either generally[204] or at least under certain circumstances,[205] advance several substantive arguments in support of their position. None of them is persuasive, as the remainder of the section will show.

I. Negative impact of gun proliferation on the protection of life and physical security

The first, most basic contention is that even the most diligent state cannot protect citizens from all crime and that armed citizens can better defend themselves against residual risks of criminal attacks, especially armed attacks.[206] A denial of the right to own and bear a gun as a means of self-defense, it is claimed, would amount to a denial of the right to self-defense itself where guns are needed to effectively defend oneself.[207]

The very factual premise of the argument—that gun owners are safer than people without arms—has been contested. For one, it is unclear how often guns are actually used for purposes of lawful self-defense. Estimates put forward by U.S. gun rights advocates on very high numbers of defensive uses of firearms are based on highly questionable methodology that extrapolates from a small

201. Human Rights Committee, General Comment No. 35: Article 9 (Liberty and security of person, U.N. Doc. CCPR/C/GC/35 (2014), para. 9.

202. Committee against Torture, Concluding Observations on Guyana, U.N. Doc. CAT/C/GUY/CO/1 (2006), para. 7.

203. United Nations High Commissioner for Human Rights, Human Rights and the regulation of civilian acquisition, possession and use of firearms, U.N. Doc. A/HRC/32/21 (2016), paras. 53–54.

204. Christopher Schmidt, An International Human Right to Keep and Bear Arms, William & Mary Bill of Rights Journal, vol. 15 (2007), 983–1017, at p. 998; Huemer, *supra* note 17, p. 323; Kates, *supra* note 17, p. 314.

205. Kopel, Gallant & Eisen, *supra* note 17, p. 175; Dekker/Myjer, *supra* note 169, pp. 187–188.

206. Kopel, Gallant & Eisen, *id.*, pp. 171–172; Huemer, *supra* note 17, p. 306; Schmidt, *supra* note 204, p. 1014.

207. Huemer, *id.*, p. 306 Kates, *supra* note 17, p. 314.

survey of self-reported incidents.[208] U.S. Federal Bureau of Investigation (FBI) data for 2012 show that there were only 259 justifiable homicides using a firearm all across the United States. Meanwhile, guns were used in 8,342 criminal homicides; that is, it is 32 times more likely that a criminal uses a gun to kill than that an innocent person uses a gun to kill in self-defense.[209]

Furthermore, the possible negative psychological effects of carrying and/or owning a gun must be considered. In particular, guns may provide their bearers with a false sense of security, causing them to instigate or exacerbate confrontations that might otherwise be resolved peacefully or with less violence. Armed resistance to crime may also invite stronger counterforce, and in some cases arms-bearing victims have had their own guns turned on them. One study conducted in Philadelphia, for instance, indicates that individuals in possession of a gun were 4.46 more likely to be shot in an assault than those who did not have a gun.[210] A broader study, based on several years of data from U.S. National Crime Victimization Surveys, showed that the percentage of victims who were injured after using a gun in self-defense during a crime was roughly the same as the percentage of victims injured after using other protective measures.[211] Several studies have also shown that living in a home where guns are kept is actually less safe than living in a gun-free home, because the gun-owning residents face a higher risk of homicide (notably at the hands of other family members), completed suicide, or deadly accidents.[212]

208. Pro-gun activists frequently cite an estimate of 2.5 million defensive gun uses per year that derives from extrapolations based on a telephone survey. See Gary Kleck & Marc Gertz, Armed resistance to crime: The prevalence and nature of self-defense with a gun, Journal of Criminal Law and Criminology, vol. 86 (1995),150–187. However, serious flaws in the study's methodology suggest that this figure is a gross overestimate. See David Hemenway, The Myth of Millions of Annual Self-Defense Gun Uses: A Case Study of Survey Overestimates of Rare Events, Chance [American Statistical Association), vol. 10 (1997), 6–10; Daniel Webster & Jens Ludwig, Myths about Defensive Gun Use and Permissive Gun Carry Laws, Berkeley Media Studies Group (2000), http://www.bmsg.org/pdfs/myths.pdf.

Another study, using data from the National Crime Victimization Survey, estimated the annual number of defensive gun uses in the United States to be as low as 108,000. See Philip J. Cook et al., The Gun Debate's New Mythical Number: How Many Defensive Uses per Year?, Journal of Policy Analysis and Management (1997), 463–469.

209. Violence Policy Center, Firearm Justifiable Homicides and Non-Fatal Self-Defense Gun Use, Violence Policy Center: Washington, D.C. (2015).

210. Charles C. Branas et al., Investigating the Link between Gun Possession and Gun Assault, American Journal of Public Health, vol. 99 (2009), 2034–2040.

211. David Hemenway & Sara J. Solnick, The epidemiology of self-defense gun use: evidence from the National Crime Victimization Surveys 2007–2011, Preventive Medicine, vol. 79 (October 2015), 22–27.

212. See David Hemenway, Risks and Benefits of a Gun in the Home, American Journal of Lifestyle Medicine, vol. 5 (6) (2011), 502–511; Linda L. Dahlberg et al., Guns in the Home and Risk of a Violent Death in the Home: Findings from a National Study, American Journal of Epidemiology, vol. 160 (2004), 929–936.

But even assuming that gun owners could more effectively protect themselves than the unarmed, this would not provide a conclusive argument for more permissive laws on keeping and bearing arms. As established in the Third Chapter, there is no "human right to self-defense" on which a human rights entitlement to bear firearms could be built. Instead, states' obligation to recognize the right to self-defense emerges from the state's duty to protect the rights to life and physical security, interpreted in line with the right to self-defense as a general principle of law. In exercising this duty to protect life and physical security though, states may and must also take into account the overall impact of the proliferation of private gun ownership.[213] Gun rights cannot be assessed based solely on their positive or negative impact on the right to self-defense, since no gun is inherently limited to defensive use. It may be used by its owner or a third party in an act of criminal aggression, used to commit suicide, or lead to an accidental shooting. In devising a policy, states must therefore have due regard to what impact the overall number of guns have on violence, in particular loss of life. In this regard, studies comparing the proliferation of private guns and the number of firearms-related deaths show that more guns result in more homicides and other firearms-related deaths.[214] There is also widespread agreement among researchers that assaults in which the assailant has a gun involve more violence

213. See also U.N. Special Rapporteur on Small Arms, Barbara Frey, Final Report, *supra* note 18, para. 33; Jeff McMahan, A Challenge to Gun Rights, Practical Ethics, 17 April 2015, http://blog.practicalethics.ox.ac.uk/2015/04/a-challenge-to-gun-rights/.

214. For comparisons between developed countries see Sripal Bangalore &Franz H. Messerli, Gun Ownership and Firearm-related Deaths, American Journal of Medicine, vol. 126 (2013), 873–876; David Hemenway & Matthew Miller, Firearm Availability and Homicide Rates across 26 High-Income Countries, Journal of Trauma, vol. 49 (2000), 985–988.

A major study comparing levels of household firearm ownership and firearm homicide levels across the fifty U.S. states over a 30-year period (1981–2010) found a robust correlation between higher levels of gun ownership and higher firearm homicide rates. The findings indicated that for each percentage point increase in gun ownership, the firearm homicide rate increased by 0.9%. See Michael Siegel, Craig S. Ross & Charles King III, The Relationship between Gun Ownership and Firearm Homicide Rates in the United States, 1981–2010, American Journal of Public Health, vol. 103 (2013), 2098–2105.

In Australia, tighter gun regulations coupled with a massive gun buyback programme have resulted in a drop of the firearm suicide rate by almost 80% and a drop in firearms homicides of similar magnitude. See Andrew Leigh & Christine Neill, Do Gun Buybacks Save Lives?: Evidence from Panel Data, American Law and Economics Review, vol. 12 (2010), 509–557.

Pro-gun authors in the United States often claim that an increase in private gun ownership has a deterrent effect that leads to an overall decrease in crime. They rely notably on John R. Lott Jr. & David B. Mustard, Crime, Deterrence, and Right-to-Carry Concealed Handguns, Journal of Legal Studies, vol. 26 (1997), 1–68. However, the methodology underlying the claims made by Lott & Mustard is flawed. See Webster & Ludwig, *supra* note 208; Jens Ludwig, Gun Self-Defense and Deterrence, Crime and Justice, vol. 27 (2000), 363–417, at pp. 407–408.

Recent research based on U.S. data suggests instead that more permissive gun laws coincide with increases in aggravated assaults with a gun. See Abhay Aneja, John J. Donohue III & Alexandria Zhang, The Impact of Right to Carry Laws and the NRC Report: The Latest (the "instrumentality effect"), so that limiting the availability of guns, in effect forcing criminals to use only knives or other weapons, will result in fewer and less severe injuries.[215]

All this indicates that states can protect people from violent death and injury by carefully devising regulations to regulate and restrict access to private firearms. Such restrictions may well mean that some individuals who are denied access to firearms might be less able to defend themselves. However, it is inherent in the exercise of the duty to protect with due diligence at the systemic level that the state crafts regulations with the overall impact in mind. Due diligence obligations are utilitarian in nature; they aim to protect the greatest possible number to the greatest extent possible. For instance, reasonable people would generally agree with laws that prohibit persons convicted of serious violent crimes from owning a gun. This is notwithstanding the fact that criminal offenders are on average more likely to become victims of violent attacks than are law-abiding citizens, because they tend to have more social interactions with fellow offenders and frequent the haunts of habitual criminals and high-crime areas.[216] Persons with a record of serious crime should therefore have a particularly strong claim to need a firearm for defensive purposes. Nevertheless, it is reasonable for states to bar them from gun ownership, based on the calculation that such a prohibition overall prevents more crimes than it facilitates, given the high risk of recidivist convicts abusing their firearms for criminal purposes.

In pursuing the overall aim to protect the rights to life and physical security, the state has a considerable margin of discretion to restrict access to firearms, as long as such regulation is not completely arbitrary or evidently discriminatory. This would be the case only in extreme scenarios—for instance, if only particular ethnic groups would be banned from owning guns, or if professionals in high-risk occupations that the state is unable to directly protect, such as persons who provide close protection to civilians in conflict situations,[217] cannot obtain a license to carry a gun despite otherwise having the necessary credentials and training.

Lessons for the Empirical Evaluation of Law and Policy, Stanford Law and Economics Olin Working Paper No. 461 (September 2014), http://papers.ssrn.com/sol3/papers.cfm?abstract_id=2443681; Eric W. Fleegler et al., Firearm Legislation and Firearm-Related Fatalities in the United States, JAMA Internal Medicine, vol. 173 (2013), 732–740.

215. Ludwig, *id.*, p. 364 ; Franklin Zimring, Firearms, Violence, and the Potential Impact of Firearms Control, Journal of Law, Medicine & Ethics, vol. 32 (2004), 34–37.

216. This well-documented phenomenon is known as the victim-offender overlap. See, e.g., Wesley G. Jennings, On the overlap between victimization and offending: A review of the literature, Aggression and Violent Behaviour, vol. 17 (2012), 16–26; Derek Deadman & Ziggy MacDonald, Offenders as Victims of Crime?: An Investigation into the Relationship between Criminal Behaviour and Victimization, Journal of the Royal Statistical Society. Series A (Statistics in Society), vol. 167, No. 1 (2004), pp. 53–67.

217. On that example, see also Dekker & Myjer, *supra* note 169, pp. 187–188 & 193.

II. No enhancement of women's right to self-defense

A second argument in favor of more permissive gun laws in the name of self-defense focuses on gender equality. Guns are presented as the "great equalizer" that allows women to effectively defend themselves against rape and other violent crime despite being on average physically weaker than men.[218] Thus, "procuring a gun and becoming proficient with it is, in fact, an act of 'physical feminism,' by way of which [a woman] asserts her human right to self-defense."[219]

Occasional cases of women successfully defending themselves with firearms against serious crimes are regularly promoted by pro-gun advocates. The reality, though, is that women suffer far more from the proliferation of guns than they benefit. For one thing, instances of women using guns to defend themselves successfully against sexual violence are statistically very rare.[220]

Furthermore, the vast majority or guns are bought, owned, and used by men.[221] This means that permissive gun laws and consequent proliferation of private gun ownership exacerbate the overall power differential between men and women.

The publicized cases of a woman successfully defending herself with a gun against a stranger defy the reality that women are far more likely to be victimized by their intimate partners and other family members. In domestic violence incidents, owning a gun is more likely to be a risk than a protection, since the gun can easily be turned against the victim and aggravate the violence. U.S. and international studies have shown that a gun in the home significantly increases the risk of a woman becoming a homicide victim, while access to a firearm by a woman victim of intra-family violence has no protective effect.[222] An international comparison between high-income countries show more women become

218. For the popular discourse see, e.g., Eric J. Reuter, The Great Equalizer: Women and the Right to Bear Arms, The Blaze, December 21 2012, http://www.theblaze.com/contributions/the-great-equalizer-women-and-the-right-to-bear-arms/. See also Mary Zeiss Stange, From Domestic Terrorism to Armed Revolution: Women's Right to Self-Defense as an Essential Human Right, Journal of Law of Economics and Policy, vol. 2 (2006), 385–411, at p. 385.

219. Zeiss Stange, *id.*, 397.

220. The U.S. National Crime Victimization Surveys for the years 2007 to 2011 do not indicate a single case in which a woman used a gun to defend herself against sexual assault. See Hemenway & Solnick, *supra* note 211.

221. See Small Arms Survey, Women and Gun Ownership (September 2014), http://www.smallarmssurvey.org/fileadmin/docs/H-Research_Notes/SAS-Research-Note-45.pdf (with further references).

222. Hemenway, *supra* note 212; Jacquelyn C. Campbell et al., Risk factors for femicide in abusive relationships: results from a multi-site case control study, American Journal of Public Health, vol. 93 (2003), 1089–1097; Susan B. Sorenson & Douglas J. Wiebe, Weapons in the lives of battered women, American Journal of Public Health, vol. 92 (2004),1412–1417; James E. Bailey et al., Risk factors for violent death of women in the Home, Archives of Interal Medicine, vol. 157 (1997), 777–782; Martin Killias, John van Kesteren & Martin Rindlisbacher, Guns, Violent Crime, and Suicide in 21 Countries, Canadian Journal of Criminology vol. 43 (2001), 429–448. See also U.N. Special Rapporteur on Small Arms, Barbara Frey, Final Report,

victims of firearms, where firearms are more readily available, with the highest homicide risk borne by women in the United States, the country with the highest level of small arms availability in the world.[223] Even where guns are not used to kill, they are often also used to intimidate women in domestic disputes, thus lessening the woman's ability to defend herself against sexual and other abuse. Rather than equalizing the sexes, the proliferation of private firearms widens the gap and decreases the overall ability of women to defend and protect themselves against violence, in particular domestic violence.

The findings of U.N. independent expert mechanisms on women's rights sustain this conclusion. In fact-finding missions to countries where gun ownership is common, successive U.N. Special Rapporteurs on violence against women have identified the possession of firearms as a factor contributing to gender-based violence and called for enhanced gun regulation.[224] The U.N. Committee on the Elimination of all Forms of Discrimination against Women noted that "especially small arms, including diverted arms from the legal trade, can have a direct or indirect effect on women as victims of conflict-related gender-based violence, as victims of domestic violence and also as protestors or actors in resistance movements."[225]

III. No effective means to pre-empt tyranny or atrocities

Another equality-based argument, which has prominently featured in the debate in the United States, concerns the relation between state and citizen. Gun ownership, it is claimed, puts private citizens in a position to defend themselves against the government in case the latter turns tyrannical.[226] Ronald Reagan notably claimed that the gun serves as a "great equalizer," because it "insures that the people are the equal of their government whenever that government forgets that

supra note 18, para. 36; U.N. Special Rapporteur on violence against women, its causes and consequences, Ms. Rashida Manjoo, *supra* note 200, para. 10.

223. David Hemenway, Tomoko Shinoda-Tagawa & Matthew Miller, Firearm Availability and Female Homicide Victimization Rates Among 25 Populous High-Income Countries, Journal of the American Medical Women's Association, vol. 57 (2002), 100–104.

224. Special Rapporteur on violence against women, its causes and consequences, Yakin Ertürk, Mission to El Salvador, U.N. Doc. E/CN.4/2005/72/Add.2 (2004), paras. 10 & 80; *id.*, Mission to Guatemala, U.N. E/CN.4/2005/72/Add.3 (2005), para. 10; id., Mission to Turkey, A/HRC/4/34/Add.2 (2007), para. 77; Special Rapporteur on violence against women, its causes and consequences, Ms. Rashida Manjoo, Mission to the United States of America, A/HRC/17/26, paras. 10 & 115(A)(g); *id.*, Mission to Honduras, A/HRC/29/27/Add.1 (2015), para. 30.

225. Committee on the Elimination of Discrimination against Women, General recommendation No. 30 on women in conflict prevention, conflict and post-conflict situations, U.N. Doc. CEDAW/C/GC/30 (2013), para. 32.

226. See, e.g., Schmidt, *supra* note 204, pp. 1012–1013; Lily Tang Williams, Guns against Tyranny, National Review, 7 September 2013,: http://www.nationalreview.com/article/357877/guns-against-tyranny-lily-tang-williams. For a critical review of the historical and

it is servant and not master of the governed."[227] This discourse continues to hold considerable sway in the U.S. public discourse. A 2013 opinion poll found that almost two-thirds (65 percent) of all Americans think that purpose of the right to keep and bear arms under the U.S. Constitution is to make sure that people are able to protect themselves from tyranny.[228]

Despite its popular appeal in the United States, the argument is based on a hypothesis of questionable validity. Research does not establish a clear correlation between private gun ownership levels and the relative political freedom of a particular country.[229] Thus, Latin American countries that had historically very permissive gun laws, such as Brazil, were not shielded from military dictatorships ousting democratic governments. They also did not see their newly found democratic orders undermined when they tightened gun laws. Conversely, Western European countries have proven overall very stable even though most have espoused rather restrictive gun legislation. This indicates that durable institutional protection of both civil and political rights and sound policies to uphold economic and social rights are far more relevant to stabilizing democracies and preventing tyranny than the distant prospect of citizens having to employ their handguns and hunting rifles to fight the military machinery of the state. Empirical studies into the reasons for military coups support these points, as they have identified as key factors for the likelihood of coups the quality of governance, economic performance, poverty and the standard of living and, respect for human rights, rather than the proliferation of private gun ownership.[230]

political underpinnings of this argument, see Joshua Horwitz & Casey Anderson, Guns, Democracy and the Insurrectionist Idea, University of Michigan Press: Ann Arbor (2009).

227. See Justen Charters, 13 Commanders-in-Chief and Where They Stood on Gun Rights, IJReview, August 2014, http://www.ijreview.com/2014/08/172102-u-s-presidents-throughout-history-2nd-amendment-supporters-gun-control-cheerleaders/.

228. Rasmussen Reports, 65% See Gun Rights As Protection Against Tyranny, 18 January 2013, http://www.rasmussenreports.com/public_content/politics/current_events/gun_control/65_see_gun_rights_as_protection_against_tyranny

229. See Casey Michel, Owning Guns Doesn't Preserve Freedom, The Atlantic, 25 April 2013, http://www.theatlantic.com/international/archive/2013/04/owning-guns-doesnt-preserve-freedom/275287/ (citing statistical analysis carried out by Dr. Justin Silver of Rice University, which finds only a minor correlation between private gun ownership figures and the Freedom House's freedom ranking of different countries). Another study, while finding a statistically significant relationship between gun ownership levels and levels of economic freedom, economic success, and corruption, apparently found no equivalent statistically significant correlation for gun ownership levels and political freedoms as measured by Freedom House. See David B. Kopel, Carlisle Moody & Howard Nemerov, Is There a Relationship between Guns and Freedom? Comparative Results from 59 Nations, Texas Review of Law & Politics, vol. 13 (2008), 1–41, at p. 21.A gun rights index from 2014 lists Yemen, Timor Leste, the United States, Bulgaria, Israel, Madagascar, and Saudi Arabia as the most permissive countries on gun rights. See Free Existence Gun Rights Index, http://www.freeexistence.org/gunindex.html.

230. See Habiba Ben Barka & Mthuli Ncube, Political Fragility in Africa: Are Military Coups d'Etat a Never-Ending Phenomenon?, African Development Bank: Abidjan (2012), at p. 15,

A variation of the argument for allowing guns as a prophylactic means of defense against oppression poses the question whether people should not have a right to possess arms for resisting genocide, at least "in nations, which have many of the immediate precursors of genocide—such as undemocratic rule, suppression of the free press, and active incitement to genocide."[231] A corresponding state duty to permit private gun ownership is notably supposed to be grounded in a state's duty to prevent genocide under Article 1 of the 1948 Convention on the Prevention and Punishment of the Crime Genocide.[232]

The idea that arming the civilian population in volatile regions with small arms is the best way to protect civilian populations against atrocities is simplistic and dangerous.[233] It is contradicted by a body of research and field experience showing that small arms proliferation is a major risk factor for the commission of mass atrocities.[234] For one thing, small arms proliferation aggravates the intensity and lethality of interethnic clashes and cycles of retributive atrocities. In many countries with a high risk of atrocities, small arms also come to be concentrated in the hands of nonstate armed groups that often end up being the major perpetrators. This is not least since they have the outside support or sources of income,

http://www.afdb.org/en/documents/document/economic-brief-political-fragility-in-africa-are-military-coups-detat-a-never-ending-phenomenon-29430/; Thomas Johnson, Robert O. Slater & Pat McGowan, Explaining African Military Coups d'état, 1960–1982, American Political Science Review, vol. 78 (1984), 622–640; Alberto Alesina et al., Political instability and economic growth. Journal of Economic Growth, vol. 1(2) (1996), 189–211; John B. Londregan & Keith T. Poole, Poverty, the Coup Trap, and the Seizure of Executive Power, World Politics, vol. 42 (1990), 151–183.

231. David B. Kopel, Paul Gallant & Joanne D. Eisen, Is Resisting Genocide a Human Right?, Notre Dame Law Review, vol. 81(4) (2006), 1275–1346, at p. 1279. The authors (*id.*, p. 1341) also indicate that foreign governments should consider supplying small arms to ordinary citizens at risk of genocide.

232. *Id.*, pp. 1277–1278.

233. See also Frédèric Mégret, Beyond the "Salvation" Paradigm: Responsibility To Protect (Others) vs. the Power of Protecting Oneself, Security Dialogue, vol. 40 (2009), 575–595, at p. 585.

234. See, e.g., International Committee of the Red Cross, Arms availability and the situation of civilians in armed conflict (1999), https://www.icrc.org/eng/assets/files/other/icrc_002_0734_arms_availability.pdf; Report of the Secretary-General on the Protection of Civilians in Armed Conflict, U.N. Doc. S/2016/447 (2016), para. 17; Human Rights Watch, Small Arms and Human Rights: The Need for Global Action (2003), http://www.hrw.org/legacy/backgrounder/arms/small-arms-full-070703.pdf; Committee on the Elimination of Discrimination against Women, General recommendation No. 30 on women in conflict prevention, conflict and post-conflict situations, U.N. Doc. CEDAW/C/GC/30 (2013), para. 32; United Nations Secretary-General, Fulfilling our collective responsibility: international assistance and the responsibility to protect, U.N. Doc. A/68/947-S/2014/449 (2014), para. 60; Edward Mogire, The Humanitarian Impact of Small Arms and Light Weapons and the Threat to Security, Paper presented at the 15th International Amaldi Conference (2004), http://www.lincei.it/rapporti/amaldi/papers/XV-Mogire.pdf; Rachel Stohl & EJ Hogendoorn, Stopping the Destructive Spread of Small Arms, Center for American Progress: Washington D.C. (2010), pp. 14–22.

possibly illicit, to pay for them. In volatile environments, weapons can also easily be diverted to such groups due to lack of state controls of weapons, unauthorized retransfer, thefts from stockpiles and handing out weapons to nonstate groups.[235] The influx of small arms therefore typically increases the potential for atrocities and leaves the civilian population at an even greater disadvantage to defend itself.

Only in rare cases would it appear reasonable to allow arms to flow to the legitimate representatives of particular population groups subjected to an ongoing genocide or other mass atrocities.[236] For instance, it is often considered that the arms embargo on former Yugoslavia under Security Council Resolution 713 (1991) weakened the capacity of Bosnia and Herzegovina to defend the Muslim population against genocide and other mass atrocities perpetrated by the Serb militia and thus was not in line with the duty to prevent genocide.[237] Allowing the Bosnian side to arm itself might have limited the level of atrocities. However, such cases are the exception, not the rule. As a matter of general principle, preventing genocide and other mass atrocities will typically require not an influx of more arms, but sustained efforts to counter the proliferation of small arms. Weapons embargoes, firearms restrictions, and disarmament will often form part of the solution.

Where such small arms control programs are put in place, they must be carried out even-handedly and without discrimination. In particular, if one ethnic group is being disarmed while a rival group is not, the first group may be placed at risk because they can no longer defend themselves against attacks from those who maintain their arms.[238] The duty to protect life without discrimination, considered in conjunction with the right to self-defense as a general principle of law, would therefore require a non-discriminatory approach to disarmament so as to avoid dangerous power imbalances between rival groups.

IV. The right to self-defense of unarmed citizens

The argument that a right to self-defense must entail a right to firearms fails to consider entirely what this would mean for the right to self-defense of those

235. Small arms and light weapons: Report of the Secretary-General, U.N. Doc. S/2015/289 (2015), paras. 9–10.

236. In their final conclusion, Kopel, Gallant & Eisen, *supra* note 231, p. 1344, also restrict their argument to international law only forbidding the denial of arms to people currently suffering from genocide.

237. See Application of the Genocide Convention (Bosnia and Herzegovina v. Serbia and Montenegro) [Further Provisional Measures], ICJ Rep. 1993, 325 (Sept. 13), sep. op. Judge Lauterpacht, 407, at p. 441 [para. 103]. See also Seventh Chapter: E.IV (pp. 340–341).

238. See, e.g., Human Rights Watch, Return to Tajikistan: Continued Regional and Ethnic Tensions (May 1995), http://www.hrw.org/reports/1995/Tajik.htm (recognizing that discriminatory disarmament in the context of ethnic tensions can contribute to instability and violence); Sudan Tribune, South Sudan calls for discipline during Jonglei disarmament, 28 February 2012, http://www.sudantribune.com/spip.php?article41734 (expressing concerns that some disarmament programmes in South Sudan were discriminatory and thus put certain ethnic groups at risk).

who are not armed. Many people make a conscious decision not to have a gun. Some cannot reconcile gun ownership with their religious or moral convictions. Indeed, according to international human rights law, they are entitled to refuse to have a gun, considering that human rights law also protects conscientious objection to military service.[239] Others feel physically or psychologically unable to handle guns. Yet others might lack the means to buy a gun or may simply choose to spend their money on more pressing needs.

The debate on gun rights and self-defense routinely neglects to consider how more permissive gun laws would undermine the capacity of these individuals to effectively exercise their right to self-defense. More permissive gun laws increase overall levels of gun ownership, especially since it sets in motion a circular effect known as the security dilemma. Unarmed persons feel generally less secure when more people around them purchase guns.[240] So to assuage this insecurity, more people buy arms, further aggravating the security dilemma. People who choose not to have a gun or are unable to have one will see their capacity to effectively implement their right to self-defense diminished, because any aggressors they face are more likely to be armed. As highlighted in the previous section, the impact may be particularly grave for populations at greater risk of becoming targets of violence, such as women or marginalized minorities.

Those who proclaim a right to firearms as a means of self-defense fail to see how such a right diminishes the right to personal self-defense of those who also insist on their right not to own a gun. This is of particular concern since unarmed citizens represent the majority everywhere. Even in countries with high rates of gun ownership, such as the United States, private gun owners remain a minority of the population. Concern for the right to self-defense of the unarmed majority must therefore carry particular weight in the state's considerations on reasonable firearms regulation, and states are well within their margin of discretion if they privilege the right to self-defense of unarmed citizens and the overall protection of the right to life through restrictive firearms regulation.

F. CONCLUSION: HUMAN RIGHTS CIRCUMSCRIBE THE AMBIT OF PRIVATE SELF-DEFENSE

Even though human rights are directed at states, they still shape the permissible ambit of self-defense between private persons, because the state must also protect the human rights to life and physical security against private violence. At the most basic level, international human rights law, interpreted in light of the

239. For a summary of the jurisprudence on conscientious objection, see Office of the United Nations High Commissioner for Human Rights, Conscientious Objection to Military Service, OHCHR: Geneva (2012), pp. 7–19.

240. See David Hemenway, Sara J. Solnick & Deborah R. Azrael, Firearms and community feelings of safety. Journal of Criminal Law and Criminology, vol. 1995 (86), 121–132; David Hemenway, Community firearms and community fear, Epidemiology, vol. 11 (2000), 709–714.

right to self-defense as a general principle of law, prohibits the state from denying particular groups or individuals the right to defend themselves as a matter of law or practice.

However, this does not extend to a duty to recognize a right to particular means of self-defense, and in particular not to a right to firearms. In line with the obligation to protect the rights to life and physical security, states must instead regulate and restrict access to firearms. States enjoy considerable discretion in devising firearms restrictions that ensure the greatest possible protection for the greatest number of individuals, even if such restrictions limit the capacity of some individuals to defend themselves. Only restrictions that are evidently arbitrary or discriminatory are not permissible.

States have a duty to regulate by law self-defense between private persons. Human rights limit their discretion to shape their self-defense laws as they please. The law must strike a reasonable balance, taking into account the human rights of victims, aggressors, and innocent bystanders. Values and interests that are incompatible with international human rights standards, in particular defenses of "honor" that actually serve to perpetuate discrimination against women, may not be considered valid objectives of self-defense. Furthermore, human rights limit lawful self-defense to the exercise of immediate, necessary, and proportional force only. Some value decisions that international human rights law establishes in respect of defensive force by law enforcement agents also find application in the private sphere. In particular, the state may not legalize pre-emptive self-defense. At most, it may consider legal excuses or mitigated punishment for groups in a special situation, such as victims of serious intra-family violence who kill habitual abusers when they do not pose an imminent threat.

Inhuman treatment can never be justified on self-defense grounds, even to defend the life of another. Desperate family members who torment kidnappers or other criminal suspects in an attempt to save the lives of their loved ones can, at most, be excused from criminal responsibility. Under the European Convention on Human Rights, states are also prohibited from allowing private persons to use lethal force for the sole purpose of defending property. While no equivalent general prohibition exists in general human rights law, private killings in defense of property can be considered proportional and compatible with human rights only in exceptional circumstances.

In some respects, international human rights law establishes tighter limits on self-defense by private persons than those applicable to law enforcement agents. Whereas police officers may and must "stand their ground" in upholding law and order, states must impose a duty on private individuals to use safe retreat options from confrontations in the public space in order to avoid having to kill in self-defense. Laws allowing people to "stand your ground" in such situations will escalate deadly confrontations and often also result in the tragic death of innocent persons, in particular when combined with a proliferation of private firearms and racial prejudice. "Castle doctrine" laws that presume the lawfulness of lethal force against unlawful intruders into a home, motor vehicle, or business can also be highly problematic from a human rights perspective, as they may justify grossly disproportional force.

Unless they are exceptionally empowered to assume law enforcement functions, private security companies may use force only in exercise of the right to personal self-defense, until they can obtain the assistance of the authorities. In light of the organized and armed nature of such companies, states must impose organizational requirements regarding training, equipment and oversight on private security companies that are similar to those applicable to law enforcement authorities. The state must enforce its regulation through preventive licensing and oversight regimes as well as the imposition of vicarious liability on private companies for cases where employees use force that exceeds the legal limits of self-defense, defense of others, or defense of property.

In order to deter abuses of the right to self-defense generally, excessive defensive force, whether exercised by security guards or individual citizens, must also result in individual accountability. The state must investigate claims of self-defense with due diligence, especially where they involve killings or serious injuries. Individuals who resort to unwarranted or excessive force in self-defense with intent or out of gross negligence must be prosecuted if their actions result in death or serious injury. Such prosecutions must respect the required due process and fair trial rights. In this respect, the presumption of innocence prohibits placing the full burden of proof of self-defense on the defendants. At most, defendants can be required to provide the minimum of evidence necessary to make their self-defense claim plausible.

7

Self-Defense Against the State—Resistance Against Human Rights Violations

In 1991, the German Constitutional Court overturned the conviction of a man for assault and resistance against police officers. The police had stopped the man in front of his own house and asked him to present his driver's license. Although the man indicated that he could retrieve his papers from the house, the police officers threatened him with a gun and tried to handcuff him. When he tried to withdraw his hands, the officers set their police dog on him and he was bitten. Then they tried to overpower him. He fought back, injuring one of the officers. The German Constitutional Court found that the man's conviction by a lower court breached his fundamental rights, since the court of first instance had arbitrarily denied him recognition of his right to self-defense against the police.[1]

In another German case involving resistance against the police, a man tried to stop police officers from illegally entering his apartment and arresting him. In that case, however, the German Federal Supreme Court considered that the man exceeded the limits of legitimate self-defense because he had thrown an axe at the officers.[2]

Competing legitimate interests are at play where individuals claim self-defense against unlawful force by law enforcement agents. The state has an interest to preserve public order and its authority by requiring that any challenges against its actions are mounted exclusively through legal avenues and not by way of defensive violence. Individuals have an equally legitimate interest to be allowed to act on their natural instinct to defend themselves when they come under unlawful attack, regardless of the identity of the assailant. These interests are not easily reconcilable and must be carefully balanced, as these two cases illustrate.

1. Bundesverfassungsgericht, Decision of 29 April 1991, Case No. 1 BvR 7/90, Neue Juristische Wochenschrift (NJW) 1991, 3023.

2. Bundesgerichtshof, Judgment of 16 July 1980, Case No. 2 StR 127/80, JuristenZeitung (JZ) 1981, 35.

The complexity and political sensitivity of the issue increases where individuals organize to forcibly resist systematic state tyranny and oppression. The origins of the armed conflict in Syria illustrate the question. In 2011, the Syrian security forces responded to massive anti-government demonstrations by shooting and killing unarmed demonstrators. A number of Syrian soldiers and police officers defected, many because they did not want to take part in the killings. Faced with the prospect of serious reprisals against themselves and family members, they organized themselves into local resistance groups under the rubric of the "Free Syrian Army" with the stated aim of protecting themselves, their families, and their communities.[3] Could these defectors have been tried under Syrian law for acts of insurgency and rebellion? Or did international law grant them a right to defend themselves against serious human rights violations? The initial resistance spun out of control. New nonstate armed groups emerged that showed no respect for international humanitarian law or human rights ideals. The situation turned into one of the worst armed conflicts and humanitarian crises of our time. Should this knowledge in hindsight have a bearing on the assessment of the initial armed resistance?

This chapter will address the question whether international human rights law provides rights of resistance and self-defense against human rights violations of the state. After a brief review of different philosophical approaches to the legitimacy of resistance, the discussion will first consider individual acts of self-defense against law enforcement officers before discussing the lawfulness of collective resistance against oppressive states.

A. RESISTANCE AGAINST THE STATE: A HISTORY OF OPPOSING VIEWS

Self-defense against state authorities poses a greater challenge to the state than self-defense between private persons, because the state's monopoly on the use of force is not only temporarily ignored but actively fought. Even though the right to self-defense as a principle of law has been accepted across different times and cultures,[4] it comes as no surprise that opinions diverge much more when self-defense is directed against the state and its authorities. Especially when considering organized armed resistance against oppressive states, views often are colored by the authors' attitudes towards particular regimes or revolutions.

I. Resistance as a legitimate defense against abusive governments

On one end of the spectrum of opinion are philosophers and ideologies espousing broad rights to resist state oppression and human rights violations, based

3. See Report of the independent international commission of inquiry on the Syrian Arab Republic, U.N. Doc. A/HRC/S-17/2/Add.1 (2012), paras. 27–29.

4. See Second Chapter: D.I (pp. 30–47).

on the right of self-defense. John Locke is representative of this group. Laying out his thoughts around the time of the Glorious Revolution that deposed King James II (1688) and the subsequent adoption of the English Bill of Rights (1689), Locke took the view that citizens may resist any "unjust and unlawful force" committed by state authorities.[5] It is lawful in some cases to resist the king, as "every one has a right to defend himself, and to resist the aggressor."[6] Locke's German contemporary Samuel von Pufendorf shared this view. Against a ruler who is "utterly hostile towards his subjects, and openly seeks their destruction without the pretext of a cause which has at least the appearance of justice, his subjects can rightly employ against him also the means customarily used against an enemy, for the sake of defending their own welfare."[7] If the prince tries to destroy particular individuals, "it will be permissible for them to use the defense otherwise licit against an enemy."[8]

These thoughts were readily adopted during the U.S. American and French Revolutions and featured prominently in their ideological justification. The American Declaration of Independence of 1776 sets out a right of the people "to throw off" a government where its "train of abuses and usurpations . . . reduce them under absolute despotism."[9] The French *Déclaration des droits de l'homme et du citoyen* of 1789 recognizes "*la résistance à l'oppression*" as a natural and imprescriptible human right.[10] Even more imbued with the spirit of revolution, the namesake Declaration of 1793 elaborates that the citizens have the right to resist by force against any unlawful act and even recognizes a "*droit sacré*" to mount an insurgency against a government that violates the right of the people.[11]

These views are not peculiar to Western Enlightenment philosophy and the revolutions that have sprung from it. They have much older and diverse roots. In the famous Behistan Inscription (6th century BCE), the Persian King Darius justified his overthrow of the ruler Gaumata by claiming that Gautama had imposed tyranny on the people and unjustly taken their property.[12] Around the same time, Confucius' disciple Mencius argued that oppressed people, led by a virtuous leader, may revolt against rulers who abuse their mandate from

5. John Locke, Two treatises of government [1689], Whitmore, Fenn and C. Brown: London (1821), p. 364 [Bk. II, Ch. XVIII Sec. 204].

6. *Id.*, p. 388 [Ch. XVIII Sec. 232].

7. Samuel Pufendorf, Two Books of the Elements of Universal Jurisprudence [1660] (trans. William Abbott Oldfather; ed. Thomas Behme), Liberty Fund: Indianapolis (2009), p. 393 [Observation V, § 22].

8. *Id.*, p. 394 [Observation V, § 22].

9. U.S. Declaration of Independence (1776), para. 2.

10. Déclaration des droits de l'homme et du citoyen (1789), art. II

11. Déclaration des droits de l'homme et du citoyen (1793), art. 11 & art. 35.

12. Herbert Cushing Tolman (ed.), The Behistan Inscription of King Darius (trans.), Vanderbilt University: Nashville (1908), pp. 11–13 [translation of Column I, paras. 13-14].

heaven.[13] The ancient Greek philosophers Aristotle, Plato, and Socrates all agreed that it was permissible to kill a tyrant, as did Cicero, the staunch defender of the Roman Republic.[14] Claims to a right to resist oppressive rulers with force and rebellion can also be found in pre-colonial African customary law, Buddhist scripture and Islamic jurisprudence.[15] The Quran itself enjoins believers to fight in the cause of those who, being weak, are ill-treated, and to rescue them from their oppressors.[16]

The Germanic tribes also recognized a right to resistance.[17] This still resonated in the writings of medieval scholars. The English scholar John of Salisbury wrote in his *Policraticus* (1159) that it is "not merely lawful, but right and just" to kill a tyrant, because "[h]e that taketh the sword is worthy of perishing with the sword."[18] The *Sachsenspiegel* (1285), one of the early German legal codifications, stipulated that men have to forcible resist kings and judges who commit injustices.[19] More focused on self-defense against individual wrongs, the 14th century jurist Giovanni da Legnano took the view that it is lawful to use violence in defense against a superior or a judge if the authority's actions are clearly unlawful or irreparable harm is caused.[20]

13. Tom Ginsburg, Daniel Lansberg-Rodriguez & Mila Versteeg, When to Overthrow your Government: The Right to Resist in the World's Constitutions, UCLA Law Review, vol. 60 (2013), 1184–1260, at pp. 1197–1198; Frederick Tse-shyang Chen, The Confucian View of World Order, Indiana International and Comparative Law Review, vol. 1 (1991), 45–69, at p. 62.

14. Shannon K. Brincat, "Death to Tyrants": The political philosophy of tyrannicide—Part I, Journal of International Political Theory, vol. 4(2) (2008), 212–240, at pp. 217–218.

15. Abdul Ghafur Hamid & Khin Maung Sein, Islamic International Law and the Right of Self-Defense of States, Journal of East Asia and International Law, vol. 2 (2009), 67–101, at pp. 90–92; Ginsburg et al., *supra* note 13, p. 1199; Fatsah Ouguergouz, The African Charter on Human and Peoples' Rights, Martinus Nijhoff: The Hague/London/New York (2003), p. 262. For Buddhism, see the glorified account of the killing of the tyrannical King Langdarma referenced in the Second Chapter: D.I.10 (pp. 45–47). The Dalai Lama has indicated that violence against oppression may be justifiable (although not desirable), if it is used as a last resort and based on compassionate grounds. See Till Fänders, Der Dalai Lama im Interview, Frankfurter Allgemeine Zeitung, 31 May 2016, http://www.faz.net/aktuell/politik/dalai-lama-tenzin-gyatso-im-interview-zur-fluechtlingskrise-14260431.html.

16. The Holy Quran (trans. Abdullah Yusuf Ali), Islamic Book Trust: Kuala Lumpur (2007), at 4:75.

17. Fritz Bauer, Ungehorsam und Widerstand in Geschichte und Gegenwart, Vorgänge, vol. 8–9/1968, 286–292, at p. 289.

18. John of Salisbury, Politicratus [ca. 1159] (trans. Joseph B. Pike), Octagon Books: New York (1972), p. 232 [Bk. III, Ch. 15].

19. Sachsenspiegel oder Sächsisches Landrecht (German trans. Carl Robert Sachsse), Winter: Heidelberg (1848), p. 297 [Third Book, Art. 78.2]. See also Bauer, *supra* note 17, p. 288; Ginsburg et al., *supra* note 13, p. 1199.

20. Giovanni Da Legnano, De Bello, de Represaliis et de Duello (ed. Thomas Erskine Holland, trans. J.K. Brierly), Carnegie Institution: Washington D.C. (1917), p. 289.

II. Unassailable authority based on divine mandate or constitutional supremacy

Assertions of a right to resistance have been met with the counterclaim that the authority of the state and its rulers is unassailable. In a more distant past, this view was based on the idea that the legitimacy of the sovereign and his state does not derive from the people and may thus not be resisted by the people. Jesus' disciple Paul opines in one of his biblical epistles to the Romans that the "authorities that exist have been established by God" so that "whoever rebels against the authority is rebelling against what God has instituted."[21] Martin Luther invoked Paul when condemning the 16th century German Peasants' Revolts (*Bauernkriege*) against feudal oppression and exploitation, notwithstanding the fact that the Peasants' Revolts were inspired by Luther's own efforts to end abuses of power within the Catholic Church. The peasants deserved to be killed, Luther wrote, because they broke the Christian command of obedience to the rulers.[22] John Calvin, another protagonist of the Reformation, followed the same line: subjects have the duty to recognize their rulers' "delegated jurisdiction from God."[23] They must therefore not resist state oppression and tyranny, as "even the most iniquitous kings are appointed by the same [divine] decree which establishes all regal authority" and such kings are often raised by God to punish the people for their own wrongdoing.[24]

Not surprisingly, Jean Bodin (1530–1596) derived from his theory on the king's absolute sovereignty a firm rejection of the right of resistance. To Bodin, "the subject is never justified in any circumstances in attempting anything against his sovereign prince, however evil and tyrannical he may be," because the sovereign is "ordained and set over his subjects by God."[25]

The view that the state's authority is not at the disposition of its subjects and must therefore not be resisted also appears in a secular, positivist form. According to that approach, the state's authority must not be resisted because it is grounded

21. Romans 13:1–2.

22. Martin Luther, Against the Robbing and Murdering Hordes of Peasants [1525] (trans. Charles M. Jacobs), http://www.scrollpublishing.com/store/Luther-Peasants.html.

Luther's position on resistance against oppression fluctuated with the political circumstances and he was not always as intransigent. See Eric W. Gritsch, Martin Luther and Violence: A Reappraisal of a Neuralgic Theme, The Sixteenth Century Journal, vol. 3 (1972), 37–55; Cynthia Grant Shoenberger, Luther and the Justifiability of Resistance to Legitimate Authority, Journal of the History of Ideas, vol. 40 (1979), 3–20.

23. John Calvin, Institutes of the Christian Religion (trans. Henry Beveridge), Christian Classics Ethereal Library: Grand Rapids, MI (2002), p. 912 [Bk. IV, Ch. 22].

24. *Id.*, pp. 914–915 [Bk. IV, Ch. 27].

25. Jean Bodin, Six Books of the Commonwealth (trans. M.J. Tooley), Blackwell: Oxford (1955), p. 68 [Bk. II, Ch. 5]. Grounding their rejection of resistance on divine command, both Calvin and Bodin have to admit an exception to the prohibition of resistance, however,

in law and the constitutional order. Hobbes argued that the authority received by the state and its sovereign under the social contract is absolute so that nothing the sovereign does can wrong any of his subjects or cause them injustice.[26] Immanuel Kant—in this context beholden to the Prussian *Obrigkeitsstaat* (state of authority)—takes this thought to its logical conclusion. According to Kant, resistance of the people against the state can never be legitimate. People have the duty to bear any abuse of the supreme power even if they considered it unbearable.[27] Kant grounds his position on the argument that resistance can never be lawful, as no legal order could authorize the people to rise up against it without that legal order losing the supremacy from which it derives its force of law. Kant considered it a logical impossibility that citizens should be entitled to pass judgment on the constitutional order to which they are subject.[28] Kant therefore replaces divine authority with the positivist notion of constitutional supremacy as the value that precludes challenges against the ruling authorities regardless of their conduct.

The relegation of the right to resistance to the extra-legal sphere gained further currency with the rise of positivism in 19th century Europe, sustained also by a growing belief among scholars and decision makers that "no state of that enlightened age could reasonably be apprehended ever to give cause to an insurrection."[29] Fascist tyranny and the Holocaust exposed the hubris of this belief; theories based on natural law, and rights of resistance grounded therein, gained credence again after the Second World War. Commensurate with that was a shift away from a focus on the authority of the state to the perspective of the individual. Representative is Albert Camus, who observed in *L'homme revolté* (1951) that individuals who realize that their situation is intolerable may rebel to resolve the contradiction between their internal perception of justice and the actual nature of the world.[30]

III. Rebellion as a threat to order and stability

In the present era, a rejection of a right of self-defense against state violations can no longer be based on a mere appeal to an absolute mandate to rule, whether

where a person has received a divine command to rise up against the sovereign. See Bodin, *id.*; Calvin, *supra* note 23, p. 916 [Bk. IV, Ch. 30].

26. Thomas Hobbes, Leviathan [1651] (ed. J.C.A. Gaskin), Oxford University Press: Oxford/New York (1998), p. 117 [Ch. 18.6].

27. Immanuel Kant, The Science of Right (trans. W. Hastie), Digireads: Stilwell (2005), p. 60.

28. *Id.* Kant's formalistic approach has been rightfully criticized for confusing the enforcement power of the sovereign (might) with the moral imperative (right). See Brincat, *supra* note 14, p. 233.

29. Haim A. Cohn, The Right and Duty of Resistance, Human Rights Journal, vol. 1 (1968), 491–517, at p. 499. See also Michael Geistlinger, Revolution und Völkerrecht, Böhlau Verlag: Wien/Köln/Graz (1991), pp. 357–358.

30. Albert Camus, L'homme révolté, Gallimard: Paris (1951), 310–314.

of divine or constitutional origin. International human rights law, as reflected in the Universal Declaration of Human Rights and the ICCPR, makes the will of the people, expressed through democratic elections, the basis of the authority of government.[31] Moreover, the rise of international human rights law as a distinct legal order also dispenses with the argument made, for instance, by Kant, that it would be a logical impossibility for a legal order to legalize resistance aimed at overcoming the very legal order that authorizes it. A key function of international human rights law is to categorize conduct as lawful when domestic authorities illegitimately treat it as unlawful. Conceptually, international human rights law could therefore well be deemed to designate acts of resistance lawful, even though they may contradict and challenge the domestic legal order in question.

However, the opposition to a right to resistance has always rested also on another argument, which emphasizes the instability and chaos that violent resistance may bring about. In order to buttress his condemnation of the German Peasants' Revolts, Martin Luther argued that "rebellion brings with it a land full of murder and bloodshed, makes widows and orphans, and turns everything upside down, like the greatest disaster."[32] Similarly, Hobbes supported his rejection of rebellion against oppression with the argument that the effects of state oppression are nothing compared to "the miseries, and horrible calamities, that accompany a civil war."[33]

At the heart of the argument is the contention that even the most benevolent ends cannot justify violent means in light of the wider repercussions of violence. Mahatma Gandhi stressed this very point in making the case for a strictly nonviolent resistance to British colonial domination in India. He considered that "violent means will give violent *swaraj* [independence]."[34] Recent empirical studies supported this claim, as they showed that violent regime change will usually achieve less durable and internally peaceful democracies than nonviolent revolutions.[35]

IV. Balancing stability and vindication of the right to self-defense

The classical writers of international law sought to reconcile concerns about stability and state authority with the right to self-defense by drawing the right more

31. See Article 21(3) UDHR; Art. 25(b) ICCPR.

32. Luther, *supra* note 22.

33. Hobbes, *supra* note 26, p. 122 [Ch 18.20].

34. As cited by Anthony Parel, Gandhi, Freedom and Self-rule, Lexington Books: Lanham/Oxford (2000), p. 73.

35. Erica Chenoweth & Maria J. Stephan, Why Civil Resistance Works: The Strategic Logic of Nonviolent Conflict, Columbia University Press: New York (2011), at p. 10.

narrowly when exercised against state authorities. In the 16th century, Francisco de Suárez argued that private persons may not resist the king's unlawful attacks on their property, because the king "represents God in a certain special way" and because the king can later be "obliged by justice to restore or compensate for the things taken away."[36] However, they may defend their life against a sovereign, "even if the death of the prince do thence follow, because the right to protect life is the greatest."[37] Likewise, if a sovereign attacks an entire city "so as unjustly to ruin it and kill the citizens . . . it will be licit to resist the prince, even by killing him, if defense cannot be done in any other way."[38] However, as a matter of "charity for the fatherland and for the common good," one should not kill the sovereign, even at the risk of one's own death, if his death should necessarily throw the state into disarray.[39]

Writing his *De Jure Belli* (1625) against the backdrop of the anarchy and horrors of the Thirty Years' War (1618–1648), Hugo Grotius was reluctant to recognize a right of violent self-defense against sovereign rule. He considered that the law of nature generally does not provide for a right of resistance against the state. The state can limit the right of resistance in the interest of public peace and order, for if a "promiscuous right of resistance should be allowed, there would no longer [be] a state, but a multitude without union."[40] Only in cases of extreme and imminent peril, he argued, do people have the right to defend themselves against violent authorities.[41] And even in such extreme situations there is no right to resistance if it causes "great disturbance in the state, or prove the destruction of many innocents."[42] It is worth noting, however, that Grotius allows for wider rights of resistance against leaders with a mandate derived from the people rather than divine authority, as in the case of democratic governments. According to Grotius, such authorities can be resisted by force if they "transgress against the laws and the state."[43]

Emmer Vattel recognizes a right of "defense of the nation"—that is, organized armed resistance—against a ruler who becomes "the scourge of the nation."[44] But

36. Francisco de Suárez, Defense of the Catholic and Apostolic Faith against the Errors of Anglicanism (trans. Peter L.P. Simpson), http://www.aristotelophile.com/Books/Translations/Suarez%20Defense%20Whole.pdf, p. 945 [Bk. 6, Ch. 4.5].

37. *Id.*

38. *Id.*, p. 946 [Bk. 6, Ch. 4.6].

39. *Id.*, p. 945 [Bk. 6, Ch. 4.5].

40. Hugo Grotius, The Rights of War and Peace: Book I (trans. John Morrice, ed. Richard Tuck/Jean Barbeyrac), Liberty Fund: Indianapolis (2005), pp. 338–339 [Bk. I, Ch. 4.2.1]

41. *Id.* 356–357 [Bk. I, Ch. 4.7.1–4.7.2].

42. *Id.* 358 [Bk. I, Ch. 4.7.2].

43. *Id.*, at 372 [Bk. I, Ch. 4.8].

44. Emer de Vattel (Béla Kapossy & Richard Whatmore, trans. & eds.), The Law of Nations, Or, Principles of the Law of Nature, Applied to the Conduct and Affairs of Nations and

he also sees the need to limit resistance due to its repercussions for public order. As organized resistance to depose a tyrannical ruler cannot be done "without raising great disturbances in the state, and the most violent and dangerous commotions, it ought to be attempted only in cases of extremity, when the public miseries are raised to such a height . . . that it is better [for the people] to expose themselves to a civil war than to endure them."[45] In the same vain, Vattel carefully calibrates the right to resistance at an individual level. If the wrongs suffered by individuals at the hand of the authorities "are supportable, they ought to be sacrificed to the peace and safety of the state, on account of the great advantages obtained by living in society."[46] However, there is a right to resistance "when the injuries are manifest and atrocious," in particular "when a prince, without any apparent reason attempts to deprive us of life."[47]

As will be shown in the following section, international law has stayed close to the positions taken by its classical authorities when it comes to resistance against unlawful attacks by individual state agents. Human rights grant a right of self-defense against such attacks. In the interest of stability, the rule of law, and the human rights of others, however, the ambit of this right has been limited to exceptional circumstances, where there is a real risk of serious and irreparable harm. When it comes to a wider right of organized armed resistance against an oppressive state or ruler, international law, as practiced by states, is far more guarded, essentially limiting such a right to certain forcible denials of the right to self-determination.

B. PERSONAL SELF-DEFENSE AGAINST UNLAWFUL INDIVIDUAL ACTS OF LAW ENFORCEMENT OFFICIALS

Even among states with a shared history of democracy and respect for human rights, very different legal doctrines have been espoused regarding the right to forcibly resist human rights violations by state authorities, especially excessive force and unlawful arrest by the police. On one end of the spectrum is the traditional approach of French jurisprudence, endorsed by older decisions of its *Cour de Cassation*, according to which individuals have an absolute duty to submit to the police and have accordingly no right to resist unlawful arrest or other unlawful police action.[48] On the other end of the spectrum is older U.S. case law,

Sovereigns, with Three Early Essays on the Origin and Nature of Natural Law and on Luxury, Liberty Fund: Indianapolis (2008), p. 105 [Bk. I, Ch. 4 § 51].

45. *Id.*, at 108 [Bk. I, Ch. 4 § 51].

46. *Id.*, at 110–111 [Bk. I, Ch. 4 § 54].

47. *Id.*, at 111 [Bk. I, Ch. 4 § 54].

48. Cour de Cassation [Chambre Criminelle], Decision of 2 July 1987, Case No. 86-94.149, Bulletin No. 281, p. 760, also available at: http://legimobile.fr/fr/jp/j/c/crim/1987/7/2/86-94149/; Cour de Cassation, Decision of 8 February 1972, Case No. 71-91.349, Bulletin

which often endorsed very broad rights of self-defense against state authorities. In one judgment, the U.S. Supreme Court even suggested that an individual may kill a law enforcement agent to resist unlawful arrest.[49] Extensive rights to resist unlawful arrest were also upheld by the supreme courts of various U.S. states.[50]

Both France and the United States have moderated their diametrically opposed jurisprudence. In France, reforms of relevant sections of the Penal Code have been interpreted to imply that individuals no longer have any obligation to endure manifestly unlawful police violence such as arbitrary beatings for no reason (the infamous *passage à tabac*).[51] Meanwhile, in the United States, a trend emerged from the 1960s to curtail far-reaching rights to resist unlawful arrest, although self-defense can still be exercised against excessive police violence that threatens death or injury.[52] France and the United States thereby converge with the standards applicable in many other democratic countries. Notably, in Germany, Switzerland and Belgium, self-defense against law enforcement officers is permissible only where the actions of the police are manifestly unlawful, in particular where police officers engage in abusive physical violence.[53]

No. 54, p. 126, also available at: http://legimobile.fr/fr/jp/j/c/crim/1972/2/9/71-91349/. See also Bernard Bouloc, Droit pénal général, Dalloz: Paris (21st ed., 2009), pp. 343–344 [para 393]; Boaz Sangero, Self-Defence in Criminal Law, Hart: Oxford (2006), p. 135.

49. John Bad Elk v. United States, 177 U.S. 529 (1900), at 537–538. See also United States v Di Re, 332 U.S. 581 (1948), at 594.

50. State v. Mobley [S. Ct. North Carolina], 83 S.E.2d 100 (1954), at 102; State v. Bethune [S. Ct. South Carolina], 99 S.E. 753, 754 (1919); Plummer v. State [S. Ct. Indiana], 135 Ind. 308, 34 N.E. 968 (1893), at 970; Adams v. State, 121 Ga 163, 48 S.E. 910 (1904); Housh v. People, 75 Ill. Rep. 487, 491 (1874).

51. Bouloc, *supra* note 48, pp. 343–344 [para 393]; Frédéric Desportes & Francis Le Gunehec, Droit Pénal Général, Economica: Paris (15th ed., 2008), p. 692 [para. 729].

52. Darrell A. H. Miller, Retail Rebellion and the Second Amendment, Indiana Law Journal, vol. 86 (2011), 939–977, at pp. 953–954. It remains to be seen to what extent the U.S. Supreme Court's constitutional recognition of a right to self-defense in District of Columbia v. Heller, 554 U.S. 570 (2008), will lead to a shift back to more extensive self-defense rights against public authorities. See Miller, *id.*, 966–967; Kindaka Sanders, A Reason to Resist: The Use of Deadly Force in Aiding Victims of Unlawful Police Aggression, San Diego Law Review, vol. 52 (2015), 695–750.

53. German Constitutional Court, *supra* note 1; Bundesgerichtshof [Federal Supreme Court of Germany], Decision of 9 June 2015, Case No. StR 606/14, Neue Juristische Wochenschrift 2015, 3019; Volker Erb, Notwehr gegen rechtswidriges Verhalten von Amtsträgern, in: Dieter Dölling & Volker Erb (eds.), Festschrift für Karl Heinz Gössel zum 70. Geburtstag, C.F. Müller: Heidelberg (2002), 217 –233, pp. 230–231; Swiss Federal Court, Judgment of 11 February 1972, Entscheidungen des Schweizerischen Bundesgerichts (BGE) 98 IV 41, 45; Stefan Trechsel & Hans Vest, Vor Art. 285, in: Stefan Trechsel & Mark Pieth (eds.), Schweizerisches Strafgesetzbuch, Praxiskommentar, 2. Auflage, Dike Verlag: Zürich/St. Gallen (2nd ed., 2012), p. 1317 [Vor Art. 285, paras. 22–23]; Court of Cassation [Belgium], 24 May 1976, Pas., 1976, 1014 and decision, 1976, 1053, as cited in Committee against Torture, Initial Reports of State Parties due in 2000: Addendum – Belgium, U.N. Doc. CAT/C/52/Add.2 (2002), para. 41.

International human rights law does not require states to recognize broader resistance rights than that. It does not establish a right of forcible resistance against every type of unlawful action by law enforcement agents. As a last resort, however, resistance must be permitted against manifest human rights violations that pose a real risk of serious and irreparable harm. As a matter of international human rights law, individuals who use timely, necessary, and proportional force or measures to defend themselves or others from such harm at the hands of the state must not be prosecuted or otherwise sanctioned for their actions.

This limited right of resistance can be derived from the right to personal self-defense as a general principle of law recognized by nations.[54] This right also matters in the relationship between individuals and state authorities. Law enforcement officers can rely on the right to personal self-defense to defend themselves against accusations of human rights violations when they must use deliberately lethal force to protect their right to life or that of others against unlawful assault. But they must then also accept that the same principle can be invoked against them, if they lead the assault.

The right to exercise resistance against violations that threaten serious and irreparable harm also flows from the right to an effective remedy that is enjoyed by all victims of human rights.[55] If a human rights violation threatens to cause serious and irreparable harm, forcible resistance may be the only effective remedy available. State courts and other national authorities can give effect to this remedy by ensuring that no one involved in necessary and proportional resistance against the police will be prosecuted or otherwise sanctioned. In that sense, resistance remains a state-sponsored remedy.[56]

Finally, the existence of a right to resist violations causing serious and irreparable harm can be discerned from international humanitarian law. Civilians may exercise self-defense against war crimes and other atrocities outlawed by international law without losing their protected status under international

Similar standards exist also in some non-Western legal codes. According to Art. 628 of the Iranian Penal Code, for instance, defense against police officers is permissible only if the police go beyond their authority and there is a fear that their acts will cause death or injury or assault to someone's honor or property.

54. See also Karl Doehring, Die humanitäre Intervention: Überlegungen zu ihrer Rechtfertigung, in: Antônio Augusto Cancado Trindade (ed.), The Modern World of Human Rights: Essays in Honour of Thomas Buergenthal, Inter-American Institute of Human Rights: San Jose (1996), 549–565, at p. 563.

55. David B. Kopel, Paul Gallant & Joanne D. Eisen, The Human Right of Self-Defense, BYU Journal of Public Law, vol. 22 (2008), 43–178, at p. 134; Tony Honoré, The Right to Rebel, Oxford Journal of Legal Studies, vol. 8 (1988), 35–54, at p. 38.

56. While Art. 2(3)(a) of the ICCPR does not specifically require that the effective remedy has to be provided by the state, Art. 8 of the UDHR requires that it be provided by a court. This is arguably still the case where the courts shield the lawfully resisting citizen from legal consequences.

humanitarian law.[57] This self-defense privilege makes sense only if international law also requires the state to consider such a defense as justified and lawful under its domestic law. Otherwise, the state could capture, prosecute, and punish civilians for their defensive action and use force against them if they resist. If individuals may therefore lawfully defend themselves against the state in times of armed conflict, the right must also be granted to them in times of peace, where violent abuses by those entrusted with state power are even less worthy of being shielded against legitimate self-defense measures.

I. Resistance against extrajudicial killings, torture, and other police brutality

International human rights bodies have not yet developed a doctrine indicating to what extent individuals may defend themselves against human rights violations by law enforcement agents. The closest to taking a position on the issue has been the Inter-American Court's judgment in *Miguel Castro Prison*. In that case, state security officials launched an unprovoked assault with lethal force on a group of detainees affiliated with the *Sendero Luminoso* armed group. A number of inmates were killed. The inmates put up violent resistance, which the court qualified "as a normal reaction to the offensive of the police officials, as the result of a natural instinct of defense of their life and physical integrity."[58] The court thus seemed to imply that the inmates had a right to defend themselves against deliberate attacks on their rights to life and physical security.

The academic literature provides some support for the view that individuals are entitled under international law to defend themselves at least against extrajudicial killings and torture, including rape as sexual torture, at the hands of state authorities.[59] In addition to these serious violations, the present author considers

57. See Second Chapter: F.I (pp. 68–70).

58. Miguel Castro-Castro Prison v. Peru, Judgment of 25 November 2006, IACtHR Ser. C No. 160, para. 241.

59. Doehring, *supra* note 54, pp. 562–563; Christian Tomuschat, The Right of Resistance and Human Rights, in: UNESCO, Violations of Human Rights: Possible Rights of Recourse and Forms of Resistance, UNESCO: Paris (1984), 13–33, at p. 22; Kai Ambos, May a State Torture Suspects to Save the Life of Innocents?, Journal of International Criminal Justice, vol. 8 (2008), 261–287, at p. 278; Asbjørn Eide, Leif Barlaug & Chakufuwa Chinana, The right to oppose violations of human rights: basis, conditions and limitations, in: UNESCO, *id.*, 34–66, at p. 60; Ted Goertzel, The Ethics of Terrorism and Revolution, Terrorism, vol. 11 (1988), 1–12, at p. 10; Ben Saul, Defending "Terrorism": Justifications and Excuses for Terrorism in International Criminal Law, Australian Year Book of International Law, vol. 25 (2006), 177–226, at p. 204. See also Bodo Missling, Widerstand und Menschenrechte: Das völkerrecht begründete Individualwiderstandsrecht gegen Menschenrechtsverletzungen, Medien Verlag Köhler: Tübingen (1999), pp. 252 & 255. But cf. Antonio Cassese, The Various Aspects of the Right to Self-Defence, in: Graduate Institute of International Studies (Geneva), Small Arms Survey 2004: Rights at Risk, Oxford University Press: Oxford (2004), 181 (taking the view that individuals have no right under international law to defend themselves against serious

that inhuman treatment that falls short of the torture threshold but still causes serious and irreparable harm may also be resisted by force. The typical example would be that of a police officer severely beating a suspect even though the suspect offers initially no resistance. Instructive in this respect is the *Affanger* judgment of the Supreme Court of Israel, which related to private persons defending themselves against unlawful police conduct. The President of the Israeli Supreme Court, Justice Zussman, pointedly observed in that case that, in a state of law, no person is obliged to suffer blows just because the person who delivers them is a police officer; rather, an attack by a police officer on a citizen is many times more serious than an attack by an another person.[60]

II. No resistance against arbitrary arrest and detention if judicial remedies available

The case for allowing a right to self-defense against other types of unlawful law enforcement action is less clear-cut, because countervailing human rights considerations are in play. In particular, there are good reasons to consider that international human rights law does not establish a general right to resist arbitrary arrest and arbitrary detention, even though both amount to human rights violations. In the heat of the moment, police officers may misjudge a situation and arrest the wrong suspect or they may commit procedural errors, such as not promptly informing a suspect of the reasons for the arrest. If individuals had a right to resist arrest on such grounds alone, this would undermine the capacity of the police officers to take decisive action to contain crime, arrest the suspects, and thereby protect the rights to life and physical integrity of the general population.[61] In many situations, police officers also carry out arrests based on assessments made by others, namely the investigating prosecutor or the judge who issued the arrest warrant. They will therefore have no basis to assess whether they are arresting the right person and whether other authorities have complied with relevant procedural requirements.[62]

Recognition of a right of resistance against unlawful arrest may also invite a dangerous escalation of violence and corresponding risks for the right to life and physical security of suspects and police officers, because police officers who

human rights violations or even genocide); Rachael E. Schwartz, Chaos, Oppression and Rebellion: The Use of Self-Help to Secure Individual Rights under International Law, Boston University Journal of International Law, vol. 12 (1994), 255–320, at p. 319 (finding that international law does not provide any rights of self-help to secure human rights, even though the logical foundations for such rights are in place).

60. Supreme Court of Israel, CA 89/78. Affangar v the State of Israel, PD 33(3), 141, at 162–63, as cited and translated by Sangero, *supra* note 48, p. 134.

61. See also Erb, *supra* note 53, p. 221; Stephan Neuheuser, Die Duldungspflicht gegenüber rechtswidrigem staatlichen Handeln im Strafrecht, Shaker Verlag: Aachen (1996), p. 5.

62. Erb, *id.*, p. 222; German Federal Supreme Court, *supra* note 53.

(wrongly) consider that they are carrying out a lawful arrest will react to violent resistance with increased force of their own.[63] Most importantly, unlawful arrest will not cause significant, irreparable harm in a state of law. Habeas corpus and other due process rights ensure that persons unlawfully arrested will be able to challenge the legality of their detention without delay and regain their liberty.[64]

This consideration holds true, though, only in states that generally respect such due process rights. The situation is different in countries where the rule of law is manifestly absent, and people may be arbitrarily arrested and not given a fair chance to challenge the legality of their detention. The most pertinent example would be politically motivated arrests of dissidents, who are then held in prolonged incommunicado detention without a chance to challenge their detention.[65] Secret detention and other forms of enforced disappearances can also give rise to a right to forcible resistance, since the unacknowledged nature of such cases of arbitrary detention denies the victim or third parties the opportunity to pursue legal remedies. In such cases, the victims and others have the right to offer proportional resistance against the initial arrest or subsequent detention if escape is impossible without resort to violence and resistance against their captors is the only means of fending off serious and irreparable harm to their liberty. The case for a right to resistance against arrest becomes even more obvious where there is a real risk that the victim, once in detention, will be subjected to torture, inhuman treatment, or extrajudicial killing.[66]

Similar considerations also guide cases of wrongful imprisonment based on a judicial sentence. If a person is convicted of a crime and sentenced in fair trial, the subsequent imprisonment is lawful and there is no unlawful attack that could be made the subject of self-defense. Even if the person is actually innocent but could not achieve an acquittal despite using all available means of appeal, this does not give rise to a right of resistance. There is simply no other basis than a fair judicial process to determine the lawfulness of imprisonment and the innocent who nevertheless suffers a miscarriage of justice will have to endure the punishment, as harsh as this may be for the individual victim.[67]

But the case is once again different altogether if a person is convicted and sentenced to long imprisonment based on trumped-up charges in a judicial process that is manifestly unfair. In such cases, the convicted person is a victim of arbitrary detention and may resist imprisonment if there are no other nonviolent means, such as escape or recourse to international legal or diplomatic processes,

63. *Id.*, p. 222; Miller, *supra* note 52, p. 956. See also State v. Koonce [New Jersey Appellate Court], 214 A.2d 428 (1965), at 436.

64. See also Tomuschat, *supra* note 59, p. 19; Miller, *supra* note 52, p. 956; Eide, Barlaug & Chinana, *supra* note 59, p. 45; Neuheuser, *supra* note 61, p. 5.

65. See also Saul, *supra* note 59, p. 204.

66. See also Schwartz, *supra* note 59, 308–309.

67. See also Tomuschat, *id.*, p. 24.

to prevent serious and irreparable harm to his liberty. However, requirements of proportionality must be respected. In particular, ordinary prison guards who had no part in the unfair judicial process are typically only unwitting accomplices to the human rights violations. In line with general principles of self-defense, only a limited degree of force is proportional against such non-culpable aggressors,[68] and the guards may not be killed or seriously wounded.

III. Force to escape inhuman conditions of detention

There will be cases where there are lawful grounds of detention, such as an arrest warrant issued with due process or a criminal conviction after a fair trial, but the conditions of detention are so dismal that they amount to inhuman treatment or even threaten the detainees' very survival. Detainees finding themselves in such situations would have to seek all available legal remedies to challenge the conditions of detention, including available recourse to international human rights mechanisms. However, if such efforts prove unsuccessful, it could be argued that, as a last resort, the detainees have the right to break out of prison, if necessary by destroying state property or overpowering their guards in self-defense.

However, international human rights bodies have so far shied away from the conclusion that escape from inhuman prisons could be justified on self-defense or any other grounds. For instance, U.N. human rights mechanisms have repeatedly criticized inhuman conditions and deaths in detention in the Democratic Republic of the Congo, while at the same time decrying that a number of perpetrators of rape and other human rights abuses had managed to escape such inhuman prisons.[69] No suggestion was made that such breakouts could be justified in light of the prison conditions.

In *Montero Aranguren (Detention Center at Catia)*, the Inter-American Court had to assess whether Venezuelan security forces had lawfully killed prisoners in response to what Venezuela claimed was an attempted mass breakout. The court noted that at the root of the prisoners' uprising were longstanding problems of inhuman detention conditions, characterized by the death and disappearance of prisoners, severe overcrowding, frequent incidents of violence and maltreatment, malnutrition, poor sanitary conditions, inadequate health care, and outbreaks of serious disease.[70] Arguably, the prisoners therefore had good reason to attempt

68. Cf. Fourth Chapter: C.I.4 (pp. 129–131).

69. Office of the High Commissioner for Human Rights, The Human Rights Situation in the Democratic Republic of Congo (DRC) (27 September 2007), paras. 6, 92–97 & 119, http://www.ohchr.org/Documents/Countries/UNHROBiannualReport01to062007.pdf; Report of the Special Rapporteur on violence against women, its causes and consequences, Yakin Ertürk, Addendum: Mission to the Democratic Republic of the Congo, U.N. Doc. A/HRC/7/6/Add.4 (2008), paras. 80–85.

70. Montero-Aranguren et al. (Detention Center of Catia) v. Venezuela, Judgment of 5 July 2005, IACtHR Ser. C No. 150, paras. 60(8)–60(15).

to break out. However, the court gave no indication that the inmates' violent breakout attempt could have constituted an act of justified self-defense against the violations suffered at the hands of the prison authorities. To the contrary, the court acknowledged that the state had the right to use force to control the uprising and merely rebuked Venezuela for using a disproportionate level of force.[71]

At the national level, the issue has come before U.S. courts. The U.S. Supreme Court considered a case where several defendants tried to justify their (nonviolent) prison break with necessity and duress, because their security was threatened by beatings from guards and fellow inmates and the setting of fires within the prison. The Supreme Court refused to answer the question whether in principle their escape could be justified, holding that, even if it was, the defendants should have surrendered to the authorities once the threat passed.[72] In the case of *Lovercamp*, which concerned an escape of an inmate threatened with rape, the California Court of Appeals held that a prison break could be justified if prisoners faced a specific threat of death, forcible sexual attack, or substantial bodily injury in the immediate future. However, according to the court, force must not be used against the guards during such a prison break and the prisoners must report to the authorities as soon as they safely can.[73]

IV. General limits of the right to resist individual human rights violations

Regardless of the category of case, resistance against law enforcement agents can be justified only within the general limits of the right to personal self-defense as a general principle of law. Forcible resistance is justified only against a present or imminent attack that is unlawful under domestic or international law. Only necessary and proportional force to fend off that attack may be used.

1. Present or Imminent Unlawful Attack

Deliberate attacks justifying self-defense against law enforcement will usually entail active physical violence or violent restraint. In some circumstances, deliberate omissions can meet the definition of an unlawful attack, provided they have a direct impact on the life, physical liberty, or security of the targeted person. In 1961, for instance, a German higher court of appeal legally rehabilitated Charlotte Klaes, a Jewish woman who had been unjustly sentenced to death by a National Socialist special court in 1942 and subsequently executed. Klaes had stolen ration cards for food and clothes from a local authority and used them for herself and other Jews. In rehabilitating her, the German court considered that access to rations was essential for survival in the circumstances of World War II and the persecution of the Jews, and that the authorities had deliberately omitted

71. *Id.*, paras. 70–73.

72. United States v. Bailey, 444 U.S. 394, at 41--413 (1980).

73. People v. Lovercamp, 43 Cal. App. 3d 823, at 831 (1979).

to provide the Jewish population with ration cards. Accordingly, the court held that both self-defense as well as the defense of necessity justified stealing cards from the state.[74] International law would come to the same conclusion.[75]

Self-defense against the state can be invoked only against present or imminent attacks.[76] A continuous ongoing attack can also give rise to a right of self-defense, as in the Klaes case, which involved the continuous denial of basic survival necessities. However, lawful resistance cannot be exercised pre-emptively in anticipation of future attacks or in response to past attacks. The point was underscored by the Court of Appeals in Northern Ireland in *Devlin v. Armstrong*. The defendant in that case was convicted of riotous behavior and incitement to riotous behavior because she had exhorted people to use violence to keep the police out of a particular neighborhood and had also thrown a stone herself at the police. She claimed self-defense with the argument that the police would have physically abused residents if it had taken control of the neighborhood, as it had done on past occasions. The Court of Appeal rejected her claim with the argument that her interventions "were far too aggressive and *premature* to rank as justifiable efforts to prevent the *prospective* danger of the police getting out of hand and acting unlawfully."[77]

2. Necessity

No more force than necessary may be used to defend against human rights violations.[78] This means that legal avenues to challenge state action must be pursued as an alternative to resistance.[79] This is why only human rights violations threatening irreparable harm can make forcible resistance necessary. Furthermore, victims of police violence have to pursue safe retreat options to avoid violations. They must try to run from abusive police officers rather than fight them, unless there is a real risk that they may incur an even greater risk of harm—for example, if the police are likely to shoot at them when they run. This applies as well where the victims have a right to be in a particular space, such as when they are participating in a peaceful demonstration that is violently and unlawfully

74. Oberlandesgericht Bamberg, Judgment of 10 July 1961, Case No. Ws 29/61, Neue Juristische Wochenschrift (NJW) 1962, 457, at pp. 458–459. Although self-defense is not explicitly mentioned, similar reasoning underlies a decision of the German Federal Supreme Court, rehabilitating a man who was executed in 1943 for having provided medicine to Jews in the Ghetto of Kovno. The Federal Supreme Court held that this amounted to resistance comparable to active combat. See Bundesgerichtshof, Judgment of 24 November 1956, Case No. IV ZR 189/56, Neue Juristische Wochenschrift/Rechtsprechung zum Wiedergutmachungsrecht (RzW) 1957, 55, also available at: https://www.jurion.de/Urteile/BGH/1956-11-24/IV-ZR-189_56.

75. See also Schwartz, *supra* note 59, p. 315.

76. Saul, *supra* note 59, pp. 204–205.

77. Devlin v. Armstrong [1971] N.I. 13, at 33 (per Lord Macdermott C.J.) (emphasis added).

78. See also Schwartz, *supra* note 59, p. 307.

79. See also German Federal Supreme Court, *supra* note 53.

dispersed by the police. The demonstrators would have to pursue safe escape options and would have no right to fight the police. Human rights grant a right to resistance only against irreparable harm. Merely losing the opportunity to finish their demonstration does not meet this high threshold, since effective redress can subsequently be sought in the courts.[80]

There is only a limited right to self-defense against law enforcement agents if the victims' prior unlawful conduct unnecessarily provoked the human rights violation.[81] An example would be that of demonstrators unlawfully taunting police with serious insults to provoke a confrontation. While this does not justify the police beating them in self-defense,[82] it will limit the demonstrators' own claim to lawful resistance to more passive defensive action and does not give rise to a full-fledged right to fight back and further escalate the situation. What constitutes unlawful provocation must be assessed in light of human rights standards. Thus, demonstrators cannot be said to provoke police violence if they shout political slogans that ought to be considered lawful as a matter of international human rights law, even if they know that police are likely to brutally suppress such exercises of the freedom of expression.

Individuals may also exercise their right to freedom of movement, including their right to leave and return to their country, without this being considered a provocation to a state that suppresses freedom of movement. The issue arose in case before the German Federal Supreme Court concerning a man who had fled East Germany and sought political asylum in West Germany. He later tried to visit his family in West Berlin by crossing on land through East Germany rather than taking the plane. East German authorities arrested and detained him. Faced with the prospect of transfer to an East German prison known for inhuman conditions of detention and ill-treatment of detainees, he staged a prison break and killed a guard in the process. The Federal Supreme Court considered that the killing could not be justified either on the basis of self-defense or the defense of necessity. The court notably reasoned that his imprudent decision to travel through East Germany had provoked his arbitrary arrest.[83] However, the court's reasoning neglects that the man's travel through East Germany—imprudent as it may have been—constituted an exercise of freedom of movement (freedom of movement within the same country, according to the West German authorities' position that there was only one German State). Accordingly, such action should not have been deemed an act of provocation. A more convincing solution would

80. See also Saul, *supra* note 59, p. 204.

81. On the issue of provocation, cf. Fourth Chapter: C.III.2.a (pp. 146–148).

82. Cf. Fourth Chapter: C.I.1 (p. 125).

83. Bundesgerichtshof, Judgment of 29 October 1957, Case No. 5 StR 407/57, Recht in Ost und West (ROW), 1958, 33, at 34. In addition, the court (*id.*, at 34) held that self-defense was not applicable since the transfer to the inhumane prison was not imminent.

have been to call in question the proportionality of killing the guard, who was only a minor contributor to the human rights violations faced by the victim.[84]

3. Proportionality

Human rights limit self-defense by state agents to proportional force. By the same token, human rights provide a right to defend oneself against state agents only within the bounds of proportionality.[85] Two other German Federal Supreme Court judgments, each rejecting claims of self-defense against law enforcement agents, illustrate relevant considerations. The first decision, discussed at the beginning of this chapter, concerned an attempt by two police officers to enforce a warrant to appear in court against a man. Contrary to German law, the officers had tried to break into the man's apartment without first formally informing him about the reasons for the warrant. The man tried to keep them out by throwing an axe at one of the officers. The Federal Supreme Court rejected the man's self-defense plea, holding that the risk to life entailed in his throwing the axe was grossly out of proportion to the officers' unlawfully entering his apartment.[86] This decision is in accordance with human rights standards, given that the imminent violations of the man's human rights were relatively minor and the victim could have sought a remedy in court, so no irreparable harm would have been done. Moreover, the police officers were not aware their actions were unlawful. If resistance with potentially lethal force were legal in such a situation, it would encourage a dangerous escalation of violence, seriously putting at risk the right to life of the police officers and the target person. It makes therefore sense to restrict self-defense against law enforcement agents and allow it only in relation to human rights violations threatening serious and irreparable harm.

The second judgment concerns, once again, the killing of an East German law enforcement agent. Shortly after the construction of the Berlin Wall, the defendant had dug a tunnel to help his family escape from East Berlin. When an East German border guard confronted the family, the defendant shot and killed the guard to prevent his family's arrest. In its judgment, handed down in 2000, the Federal Supreme Court acknowledged that East Germany's closed-border regime violated human rights, but still considered that killing to secure one's escape was not justified by self-defense. The court took into account that the border guard had tried to enforce orders that were binding on him and had not posed a threat to the family's life.[87] This decision is more of a borderline case (no pun intended). On the one hand, self-defense was directed against significant human

84. See also this Seventh Chapter: B.III (pp. 307–308).

85. See also Saul, *supra* note 59, p. 204; Schwartz, *supra* note 59, p. 307.

86. Bundesgerichtshof, Judgment of 16 July 1980, Case No. 2 StR 127/80, JuristenZeitung (JZ) 1981, 35.

87. Bundesgerichtshof Judgment of 5 July 2000, Case. No. 5 StR 629/99, Neue Juristische Wochenschrift (NJW) 2000, 3079.

rights violations. An entire family was denied their human right to leave their own country, they were about to be arbitrarily arrested, and it was highly likely the adults would face lengthy prison terms. Under the political circumstances, the victims would have had no realistic chance to obtain an effective remedy in an East German court. On the other hand, the judgment rightfully considers that in a state characterized by systematic human rights violations, individual law enforcement agents are themselves not free to refuse orders, but are always to some extent non-culpable aggressors. Therefore, self-defense against them is subject to special proportionality considerations.[88] Killing the guard to preserve the family's liberty could therefore be deemed disproportional, especially since merely threatening the guard with the gun to secure the escape might have also been a viable cause of action, even though perhaps a more risky one.

C. COLLECTIVE SELF-DEFENSE BELOW THE THRESHOLD OF DIRECT PARTICIPATION IN ARMED CONFLICT

In the face of the sheer power of state authority, individuals will often not be able to effectively defend themselves against human rights violations on their own. In particular during times of armed conflict, individual self-defense against heavily armed soldiers will often be futile and effective resistance can only be exercised collectively. International humanitarian law recognizes to some extent that civilians may defend themselves collectively against state atrocities without losing their protected status. The Security Council's Committee of Experts on the former Yugoslavia, chaired by the late Professor Kalshoven, clarified that civilians who defended themselves and others against war crimes and crimes against humanity during the wars leading to the dissolution of Yugoslavia did not lose their civilian status "even if they joined hands to try to prevent the cataclysm."[89] In the same vein, the International Criminal Tribunal for the former Yugoslavia held in *Blaskic* that a group of 120 armed Muslims who were carrying out night watches during the Bosnian armed conflict remained a protected civil defense group and could not be regarded as combatants.[90] In *Bagosora*, the International Criminal Tribunal for Rwanda found that Tutsi civilians who had taken refuge in a church against *Interahamwe* militia could claim protected status, even though a group among them was using traditional weapons for purposes of self-defense.[91] The Nuremberg Judgment qualified the brutal suppression of the 1943 Uprising in the Warsaw Ghetto as an example of the "planned and systematic

88. Cf. Fourth Chapter: C.I.4 (pp. 129–131).

89. Final Report of the Commission of Experts Established Pursuant to Security Council Resolution 780 (1992), U.N. Doc. S/1994/674 (1994), para. 78.

90. Prosecutor v. Blaskic [ICTY Trial Chamber], Case No. IT-95-14-I-T, Judgment of 3 March 2000, para. 407.

91. Prosecutor v. Bagosora et al. [ICTR Trial Chamber], Case No. ICTR-98-41-T, Judgment of 18 December 2008, para. 2238.

character of the Jewish persecutions."[92] During the Uprising, several hundred Jews, armed mainly with handguns, had managed for several months to prevent German forces from taking control of the Warsaw Ghetto and deporting the entire population for extermination in concentration camps. In its assessment of the suppression of the resistance by German forces, the International Military Tribunal at Nuremberg did not differentiate between actions targeting armed and unarmed civilians, which suggests that even the armed civilians did not become lawful targets, although they offered improvised armed resistance against genocide.

In all of these cases, civilians were defending themselves against unlawful attacks threatening serious and irreparable harm in accordance with the right to personal self-defense as a general principle of law. Accordingly, they did not only have a claim to protected status under international humanitarian law, but their resistance was lawful as a matter of human rights law. Therefore, the state authorities were not allowed to subject them to prosecution or counterforce. If it were otherwise, the continuation of their protected status under international humanitarian law would be undermined and effectively worthless. Furthermore, there is every reason to contend that the right of civilians to defend themselves collectively is not specific to armed conflict, but also applies in times of peace. For instance, if the Rwandan Genocide had not been committed in the context of an armed conflict, victims could have still banded together and collectively tried to save their lives.

However, there are clear limits to the right to collective self-defense. These emerge from the right of self-defense itself and from the prohibition of direct participation in armed conflict that civilians have to obey to maintain their protected status under IHL.

I. Limits based on the right to self-defense

If civilian self-defense groups no longer respond to present or imminent violence, but preventively attack rogue military units known to be planning future unlawful attacks, this would not meet the requirement of imminence and could not qualify as self-defense.[93] The same applies where civilians use more violence

92. International Military Tribunal, Judgment of 1 October 1946, in: The Trial of German Major War Criminals. Proceedings of the International Military Tribunal sitting at Nuremberg, Germany, Part 22 (22nd August,1946 to 1st October, 1946), p. 465.

93. See also Lindsey Cameron & Vincent Chetail, Privatizing War: Private Military and Security Companies under Public International Law, Cambridge University Press: Cambridge et al. (2013), p. 478; Corinna Seiberth, Private Military and Security Companies in International Law, Intersentia: Cambridge/Antwerp/Portland (2014), p. 145. But see Michael N. Schmitt, Direct Participation in Hostilities and 21st Century Armed Conflict, in: Horst Fischer et al. (eds.), Crisis Management and Humanitarian Protection: Festschrift für Dieter Fleck, Berliner Wissenschafts-Verlag: Berlin (2004), 505–529, at p. 520.

than actually necessary to repel an unlawful attack,[94] for example, because they want to militarily weaken the attacking forces.

Any action taken also must be proportional to the defensive purpose. In particular, some acts are categorically outlawed under international law and thus per se disproportional. For instance, if a civilian self-defense group were to take civilian hostages, such as family members of security officials, this would be disproportional even if it served to achieve the release of their own people from arbitrary state detention and related torture or prevent their disappearance at the hand of the security forces.[95]

Civilians will also lose their protected status if their action serves to defend combatants or military objects. Under international humanitarian law this amounts to direct participation in hostilities.[96] Similarly, any action to defend combatants or military object exceeds the inherent limits of self-defense, since self-defense may be directed only against unlawful attacks. In armed conflict, combatants and military objects are lawful targets. For instance, civilian security guards who are defending a munitions depot against an enemy attack cannot claim to use force in exercise of their right to personal self-defense. The same applies if civilians and combatants are fighting side by side so that they are protecting each other. In both cases, the civilians are directly participating in hostilities and there are no lawful attacks that could give rise to a claim of self-defense.

II. Distinction between civilian defense groups and organized armed groups

There is an important distinction between armed civilian self-defense and organized defensive action of a military nature.[97] Civilians who resist cannot claim the self-defense exception to direct participation in hostilities if their degree of organization and capacity to engage in hostilities reaches a high enough level to actually qualify them as an organized armed group that would thus be considered a party to an armed conflict. At this stage, the hostilities paradigm of international humanitarian law and its distinction between combatants/fighters and protected civilians takes over, and it becomes irrelevant whether the armed group engages in defensive or offensive action.

94. Chia Lehnhardt, Private military companies, in: Nigel D. White & Christian Henderson (eds.), Research Handbook on International Conflict and Security Law (Cheltenham: Edward Elgar, 2013), 421–443, at p. 429.

95. See also Independent international commission of inquiry on the Syrian Arab Republic, *supra* note 3, paras. 106 & 117.

96. Lehnhardt, *supra* note 94, p. 429; Seiberth, *supra* note 93, p. 111; Cameron & Chetail, *supra* note 93, p. 464.

97. Final Report of the Commission of Experts Established Pursuant to Security Council Resolution 780 (1992), *supra* note 89, para. 78.

Establishing the character of a group requires a careful assessment. Civilians defending themselves collectively cannot be regarded as an organized armed group solely because they possess firearms and engage in planned and coordinated defensive activities such as carrying out patrols around their neighborhood or setting up night watches. This issue arose during the armed conflict in Darfur, where many rural villagers have long possessed firearms, including automatic assault rifles, to defend their land and cattle. The U.N. Commission of Inquiry on Human Rights Violations in Darfur, led by the late Professor Cassese, stressed that the mere presence of arms did not deprive the villagers of their protected status as civilians.[98]

The provenance of the arms held by a group is also immaterial. Even if a government or armed group provided the weapons to a civilian group, this does not exclude the group's protected civilian character as long as the weapons are used only for self-defense and the group does not support the military objectives of any of the parties to the armed conflict.[99]

A civilian self-defense group becomes an organized armed group once it develops and demonstrates the capacity to engage in actual military operations. Factors considered in making this determination include the existence of a hierarchical structure and chain of command within the group; its ability to plan and carry out operations of a military nature; its weapons, communications devices, uniforms, and other equipment; the issuing of internal regulations and external communications; the capacity to recruit, train, and equip members; and the extent, seriousness, and intensity of its involvement in the overall hostilities.[100] None of these factors is individually determinative, but the determination has to be made on a case-by-case basis by carefully weighing all factors.[101]

If a self-defense group meets the threshold of an organized armed group, its members become lawful targets during hostilities. The self-defense paradigm is no longer applicable and is replaced by the principle of distinction between combatants and other direct participants in hostilities on the one hand and protected persons on the other, which is characteristic of international humanitarian law. However, as will be explored in the remainder of the chapter, if people provide organized armed resistance against the state, the right to self-defense can still become relevant at the *ius ad bellum* level. In exceptional circumstances, international law grants armed groups the right to engage in an armed conflict against the government to defend the right to self-determination by way of organized

98. Report of the International Commission of Inquiry on Darfur to the United Nations Secretary-General (2004), http://www.un.org/news/dh/sudan/com_inq_darfur.pdf, para. 292.

99. See also Schmitt, *supra* note 93, p. 520.

100. Prosecutor v. Lubanga [ICC Trial Chamber I], Judgment of 14 March 2012, Case No. ICC-01/04-01/06, para. 537; Prosecutor v. Boskoski [ICTY Trial Chamber], Judgment of 10 July 2008, Case No. TC IT-04-82-T, paras. 195–203.

101. Prosecutor v. Lubanga, *id.*, para. 537; Prosecutor v. Boskoski, *id.*, para. 198.

armed resistance. This has also repercussions at the *ius in bello* level, as the resistance fighters enjoy the entitlements of lawful combatants.

D. ORGANIZED ARMED RESISTANCE AGAINST DENIALS OF THE RIGHT TO SELF-DETERMINATION

International law has traditionally been neutral on rebellions.[102] It does not prohibit the governed from waging an armed struggle against their government, even if that struggle becomes a revolution and overturns the government.[103] But neither does it prohibit the state from using force to quell the rebellion and from prosecuting the rebels as long as due process is respected.

There is one exception, still contested by some, where international law considers a rebellion against the government to be a lawful exercise of a right to resistance. Peoples and the national liberation movements representing them may engage in militarily organized armed resistance as a last resort, including a full-fledged war of national liberation, if their right to self-determination is forcibly denied due to colonial domination, unlawful alien occupation, or a racist regime.[104]

102. Hans Kelsen, General Theory of Law and State (trans. Anders Wedberg), Harvard University Press: Cambridge (1945), p 368; Peter Malanczuk, Akehurst's Introduction to International Law, Routledge: London/New York (7th ed., 1997), p. 336; Jean d'Aspremont, Le Tyrannicide en Droit International, in: Christian Tomuschat, Evelyne Lagrange & Stefan Oeter (eds.), The Right to Life, Brill: Leiden (2010), 287–313, at p. 310.

103. According to an emerging principle, however, states must not recognize governments that came to power as a result of coups d'etat against democratically elected governments. African states in particular have made requisite commitments. See Eki Yemisi Omorogbe, A Club of Incumbents?: The African Union and Coups d'État, Vanderbilt Journal of Transnational Law, vol. 44 (2011), 123–154.

104. Eide, Barlaug & Chinana, *supra* note 59, p. 59; Honoré, *supra* note 55, p. 44; Malanczuk, *supra* note 102, p. 336; Bertil Dunér, Rebellion: The Ultimate Human Right?, The International Journal of Human Rights, vol. 9 (2005), 247–269, at p. 250; Antonio Cassese, Terrorism and Human Rights, American University Law Review, vol. 31 (1982), 945–958, at p. 946; James Summers, People and International Law, Brill Nijhoff: Leiden, Boston (2nd ed., 2014), p. 458; Georges Abi Saab, Wars of National Liberation in the Geneva Conventions and Protocols, Recueil des cours de l'Academie de la Haye, vol. 165 (1979), 353–445, at pp. 371–372; Kjell Anderson, The Universality of War: Jus ad Bellum and the Right to Peace in Non-International Armed Conflicts, in: David Keane; Yvonne McDermott (eds.), The Challenge of Human Rights: Past, Present and Future, Edward Elgar: Cheltenham/Northampton (2012), 52–73, at p. 65; d'Aspremont, *supra* note 102, p. 309; Shannonbrooke Murphy, The right to resist reconsidered, in: David Keane & Yvonne McDermott (eds.), The Challenge of Human Rights: Past, Present and Future, Edward Elgar: Cheltenham/Northhampton (2012), 91–113, at p. 106; Thomas Keenan, The Libyan Uprising and the Right of Revolution in International Law, International and Comparative Law Review [Palacky University, Czech Republic], vol. 11(1) (2011), 5–29, at p. 17; Robert McCorquodale, Self-Determination: A Human Rights Approach, The International and Comparative

These three exceptions emerged against the backdrop of the movements against colonialism, the struggle against Apartheid, and Israel's occupation of Palestinian territories. The three categories are therefore narrowly defined so that the right to resist forcible denials of self-determination applies to few cases today. Colonial occupation only refers to the "saltwater colonialism" of Western states, where the colonized territory was geographically separated and distinct from the colonial power controlling it.[105] If states historically extended their territory by conquering and annexing adjacent territories this is not covered, even if the people living in the annexed territories remained ethnically, religiously, or culturally distinct and may feel colonized. The category of racist regimes was established with the institutionalized racism of the Apartheid regimes in South Africa and the former Rhodesia in mind. For a government to be qualified as a racist regime, it is therefore not enough that the authorities practice some racial discrimination, but the regime must be founded on racist criteria.[106] Alien occupation extends to cases where the occupied territory did not yet form part of a state at the time of occupation but was populated by a distinct group, such as the Palestinian people.[107]

Law Quarterly, vol. 43 (1994), 857–885, at p. 882; Saul, *supra* note 59, p. 184; Schwartz, *supra* note 59, p. 267; Missling, *supra* note 59, pp. 247–248. For a right to resist occupation specifically, Report of the United Nations Fact-Finding Mission on the Gaza Conflict, U.N. Doc. A/HRC/12/48 (2009), para. 1875: A/59/2005, para 91; Tomuschat, *supra* note 59, pp. 27–29; Christian Tomuschat, Gezielte Tötungen (Targeted Killings): Zugleich ein Kommentar zum Gutachten des Internationalen Gerichtshofs vom 9. Juli 2004, Vereinte Nationen, vol. 52 (2004), 136–140, at pp. 136 & 139.

For the contrary position B. A. Wortley, Some jurisprudential reflections on human rights and self-defense, in: Heinrich Kipp (ed.), Um Recht und Freiheit: Festschrift für Friedrich August Freiherr von der Heydte zur Vollendung des 70. Lebensjahres, Duncker and Humblot: Berlin (1977), 751–758, at p. 758; Nigel D. White, Defending Humanity: When Force is Justified and Why [Book Review], Melbourne Journal of International Law, vol. 10 (2009), 379–393, at p. 391; Christopher Greenwood, Terrorism and Humanitarian Law—The Debate Over Additional Protocol I, Israel Yearbook of Human Rights, vol. 19 (1989), 187–207, at p. 193.

105. See Declaration of Principles of International Law Concerning Friendly Relations and Co-operation Among States in Accordance with the Charter of the United Nations, G.A. Res. 2625 (XXV) of 24 October 1970; Principles which should guide members in determining whether or nor an obligation exists to transmit the information called for under Article 73e of the Charter, G.A. Res. 1541 (XV), U.N. Doc. A/RES/1541 (XV) (1960).

106. Greenwood, *supra* note 104, p. 194. Yves Sandoz, Christophe Swinarski & Bruno Zimmerman (eds.), Commentary on the Additional Protocols of 8 June 1977 to the Geneva Conventions of 12 August 1949, ICRC/Martinus Nijhoff: Dordrecht (1987), p. 54 [para. 112].

107. Greenwood, *supra* note 104, p. 194; ICRC, *id.*; Walter Kälin & Jörg Künzli, Article 1F(b): Freedom Fighters, Terrorists, and the Notion of Serious Non-Political Crimes, International Journal of Refugee Law, vol. 12 (2000) 46–78, at pp. 56–57; Antonio Cassese, Self-Determination of Peoples, Cambridge University Press: Cambridge (1995), at p. 61; Abi Saab, *supra* note 104, p. 395.

I. Legal basis for a right to organized armed resistance

Articles 1(2) and 55 of the U.N. Charter recognize the principle of self-determination, which "constitutes one of the essential principles of contemporary international law."[108] Building on these references, Common Article 1 of the ICCPR and ICESCR, Article 20 of the African Charter on Human and Peoples' Rights, and Article 2 of the Arab Charter on Human Rights recognize peoples' right to self-determination as a human right. Furthermore, the right to self-determination has also been recognized as a right under general international law.[109]

The two regional human rights charters both indicate that self-determination may be achieved through armed resistance. Article 20(2) of the ACHPR recognizes that all colonized or oppressed peoples have the right to free themselves from the bonds of domination. Article 2(4) of the Arab Charter on Human Rights recognizes a right to resist occupation. The same can be discerned from a series of U.N. Resolutions, which, although not legally binding, provide an authoritative interpretation of the right to self-determination under general international law. The General Assembly's Friendly Relations Declaration of 1970, adopted by consensus after several years of painstaking negotiations, indicates that states have a duty to refrain from any forcible action depriving peoples of their right to self-determination.[110] It further indicates that such peoples may seek and receive support in their resistance to forcible denials of self-determination, which implies that they also have a right to resistance.[111] The General Assembly's 1974 Definition of Aggression, also adopted by consensus, establishes that people forcible deprived of their right of self-determination have a "right to struggle" to achieve self-determination.[112] Other General Assembly resolutions, adopted by vote, refer even more clearly to "man's basic human right to fight for the self-determination of his people"[113] or to peoples' "inherent right to struggle *by all necessary means* at their disposal against colonial powers and alien domination in exercise of their right of self-determination"[114] ("all necessary means" being

108. East Timor (Portugal v. Australia), ICJ Rep. 1995, 90, at p. 102 [para. 29].

109. *Id.*

110. See *supra* note 105.

111. See also Honoré, *supra* note 55, pp. 43–44; Abi Saab, *supra* note 104, p. 372.

112. Definition of Aggression, G.A.Res. 3314 (XXIX), U.N. Doc. A/RES/3314 (XXIX) (1974), art. 7.

113. Importance of the Universal Realization of the Right of Peoples to Self-Determination and of the Speedy Granting of Independence to Colonial Countries and Peoples for the Effective Guarantee and Observance of Human Rights, G.A.Res. 2787 (XXVI), U.N. Doc. A/RES/2787 (XXXVI) (1971), para 2.

114. Basic Principles of the Legal Status of the Combatants Struggling against Colonial and Alien Domination and Racist Regimes, G.A. Res. 3103 (XXVIII), U.N. Doc. A/RES/3103 (XXVIII) (1973), preamble (emphasis added). See also Implementation of the Declaration on the Granting of Independence to Colonial Countries and Peoples, G.A.Res. 34/94,

the established U.N. diplomatic code for the use of armed force). The General Assembly expressly commended the "armed struggle" of the people of Namibia and South Africa against the Apartheid regime.[115] In the same vein, the Security Council recognized the legitimacy of the struggle for self-determination of the peoples of Southern Rhodesia (present-day Zimbabwe) and Namibia,[116] fully cognizant of the fact that national liberation movements were waging armed struggles in both places.

The existence of a right of national liberation movements to engage in armed resistance against denials of self-determination can also be inferred from the First Additional Protocol to the Geneva Conventions. According to Article 1(4) of the Protocol, "armed conflicts in which peoples are fighting against colonial domination and alien occupation and against racist regimes in the exercise of their right of self-determination" are subject to the same rules as classical international armed conflicts. This means that fighters for national liberation movements are lawful combatants and must not be punished for their participation in fighting for their right to self-determination. The First Additional Protocol thus implicitly recognizes the lawfulness of their resistance at the *ius ad bellum* level.[117] It is worth noting that at the 1977 diplomatic conference that adopted the First Geneva Protocol, only Israel voted against Article 1, although several Western states abstained.[118] Today, the Protocol has been ratified by 174 states.

U.N. Doc. A/RES/34/94 (1979), para. 4; Programme of Action for the Full Implementation of the Declaration on Granting of Independence to Colonial Countries and Peoples, G.A. Res. 2621 (XXV), U.N. Doc. A/RES/2621 (XXV) (1970), para. 2.

115. Question of Namibia, G.A. Res. 34/92, U.N.Doc. A/RES/34/92 (1979), section G; Question of Namibia. G.A.Res. 35/227, U.N. Doc. A/RES/35/227 (1981), preamble; Policies of Apartheid of the Government of South Africa, G.A.Res. 36/172, U.N. Doc. A/RES/36/172 (1981), sec. A, para. 13.

116. Security Council Resolution 269, U.N. Doc. S/RES/269 1969, para 4; Resolution 301, U.N. Doc. S/RES/301 (1971), preamble Resolution 403, U.N. Doc. S/RES/403 (1977), preamble; Resolution 445, U.N. Doc. S/RES/445 (1979), preamble; Resolution 448, U.N. Doc. S/RES/448 (1979), preamble,

117. But see Greenwood, *supra* note 104, who considers that the provision only affects the political legitimacy of national liberation movements.

For cases of resistance against belligerent occupation outside the decolonialization/national liberation context, the Geneva Conventions afford few protections. Notably, members of organized resistance movements operating in occupied territory can exceptionally claim prisoner of war status if they fulfil a number of (unrealistically onerous) conditions. See Geneva Convention (III) relative to the Treatment of Prisoners of War, art. 4(2). For a more detailed reflection, including the question of whether a population living under belligerent occupation may invoke a right to self-defense that trumps its traditional duty to obey the occupier, see Frédéric Mégret, Grandeur et déclin de l'idée de résistance à l'occupation: réflexions à propos de la légitimité des insurgés', Revue belge de droit international, vol. 41 (2008), 382–425.

118. Abi Saab, *supra* note 104, p. 392.

Doctrinally, it may seem like a jump to conclude a right to self-determination entails a right to armed resistance. The fact that people have a right does not necessarily mean that they may use force to realize it. However, the right to organized armed resistance against denials of self-determination can be seen as a case of self-defense. Some have argued in this respect that the right to resistance exercised by national liberation movements flows from Article 51 of the U.N. Charter.[119] Yet, as per its express wording, Article 51 relates only to self-defense exercised by states, whereas the people defending their self-determination typically do not represent a state yet.[120] For people defending their right to self-determination against colonial domination and alien occupation, it could at least be argued that they are defending a state *in nascendi*. However, racist regimes clearly are an internal threat from within the state and the struggle against them can hardly be framed as self-defense by a state. It would therefore appear that a right of resistance against denials of self-determination also relies on elements of the right to personal self-defense as a general principle of law, also considering that the peoples concerned are defending their human rights and not only the state-centric values of (future) independence and sovereignty.

II. Limits of the right to organized armed resistance

Being a subcategory of the right to self-defense, the right to organized armed resistance against forcible denials of self-determination is not an unfettered license for violence; rather, it is limited by the general requirements of self-defense. This means, for one thing, that it may be exercised only against ongoing *unlawful* denials of the right to self-determination. Colonial domination and racist oppression will always meet the standard. However, occupation may sometimes be lawful to the extent that it is authorized by the Security Council or amounts to a justified exercise of the right to self-defense under Article 51 of the U.N. Charter. To draw on an example outside the decolonialization context: The Allied occupation of Germany or Japan after World War II would also be lawful by today's standards, because that occupation marked a continuation of the exercise of interstate self-defense against Germany and Japan's prior acts of aggression. In the assessment of the Israeli-Palestinian conflict, the question who exercises self-defense against whom is the crux of the matter. Either Israel's occupation is still covered by a right of interstate self-defense against past aggression because Israel has not been provided with adequate subsequent assurances of its security, or the occupation has become an unlawful de facto annexation

119. Cassese, *supra* note 107, p. 198; Christopher C. Quaye, Liberation Struggles in International Law, Temple University Press: Philadelphia (1991), pp. 276–277; Anderson, *supra* note 104, p. 65. See also Saul, *supra* note 59, p. 189.

120. John Dugard, The Organization of African Unity and Colonialism: An Inquiry into the Plea of Self-Defense as a Justification for the Use of Force in Eradication of Colonialism, International and Comparative Law Quarterly, vol. 16 (1967), 157–190, p. 172.

that justifies the Palestinians' defense of their right to self-determination to the extent that force is a last resort, employed for purposes only of ending the occupation, and using only means of warfare permissible under international law.[121]

Armed force may be used for achieving self-determination only where force is necessary. This may seem self-evident, but has been contested at least at the level of political discourse. National liberation theorist Frantz Fanon notably contended that liberation from colonial rule should always be achieved through violence. He argued that violence has a detoxifying impact, cleansing the subjects of their inferiority complex and giving each individual a personal stake in the liberation achieved.[122] As doubtful as this proposition may already be on a psycho-sociological and moral level, it certainly finds no reflection in international law. Under the right of self-defense, violence can be justified only to the extent that there are no nonviolent means to end the denial of the right to self-determination, notably because the oppressor government is using force to maintain the status quo. A national liberation movement can therefore not move to an armed struggle without first making a good faith, serious attempt to negotiate a transition to self-determination and, if that fails, trying a campaign of nonviolent resistance.[123] Furthermore, it must restrict its objective to the achievement of self-determination and notably may not seek to eradicate the oppressing state.

In assessing proportionality of using armed force to protect the human right to self-determination, the struggle's impact on individual rights of the population must be taken into account. The very recognition of the right to armed struggle for self-determination indicates that the prospect of loss of lives does not render the struggle disproportional.[124] However, a national liberation movement still has to choose strategies of armed resistance that minimize the impact

121. For the opposing positions on this issue see Report of the United Nations Fact-Finding Mission on the Gaza Conflict, *supra* note 104, para. 1875; Richard Falk & Burns Weston, The relevance of international law to Palestinian rights in the West Bank and Gaza: in legal defense of the intifada, Harvard International Law Journal, vol. 32 (1991), 129–157, at pp. 155–156; Tomuschat, *supra* note 104, p. 139; Stephen M. Schwebel, What Weight to Conquest?, in: Stephen M. Schwebel (ed.), Justice in International Law, Cambridge University Press: Cambridge (1994), 521–525, at pp. 521–522; George P. Fletcher & Jens David Ohlin, Defending Humanity: When Force is Justified and Why, Oxford University Press: New York (2008), p. 40; Ariel Zemach, Can Occupation Resulting from a War of Self-Defense Become Illegal?, Minnesota Journal of International Law vol. 24 (2015), 313–350.

122. Frantz Fanon, Les damnés de la terre, La Découverte & Syros: Paris (2002), p. 90.

123. Eide, Barlaug & Chinana, *supra* note 59, p. 58; Tomuschat, *supra* note 59, p. 22; *id., supra* note 104, p. 139.

124. See also Karl Doehring, Zum, "Recht auf Leben" aus nationaler und internationaler Sicht, in: Rudolf Bernhardt (ed.), Vo̍lkerrecht als Rechtsordnung, internationale Gerichtsbarkeit, Menschenrechte: Festschrift fu̍r Hermann Mosler, Springer: Berlin (1983), 145–157, at p. 155. Conceptually, this is hard to square with the idea of the right to life being the supreme right, in which all others are rooted. Critical therefore Saul, *supra* note 59, p. 188.

on the civilian population. In this regard, it must seek the views of the civilian population concerned and not launch a full-fledged war of national liberation without the support of the people whose rights it purports to defend.

Given the power differential between oppressing state and national liberation movement typical of wars of national liberation, it has been tempting for national liberation movements to focus their limited military means on softer targets. However, some forms of violence are categorically outlawed under international law and therefore also per se disproportional. In particular, resistance against denials of self-determination cannot justify war crimes, crimes against humanity, acts of torture, enforced disappearances, and other violations of peremptory law (*ius cogens*).[125] Occasionally, supporters of national liberation struggles try to argue that resistance in the name of self-determination plays by different rules and can even justify attacks on civilians.[126] This neglects the fundamental distinction between the *ius ad bellum* that establishes the lawfulness of the armed conflict itself and the *ius in bello* defining the lawful means and targets in armed conflict. As underscored by the ICJ, the rules of international humanitarian law are intransgressible.[127]

III. Legal implications of the right to resistance

The recognition of the lawfulness of wars of national liberation has important legal implications. In accordance with the U.N. General Assembly's Friendly Relations Declaration,[128] every state must promote realization of the right to self-determination and must refrain from taking any forcible action to deny the exercise of self-determination. This means that third states may not provide any military, political, or other support to help states in their suppression of national liberation movements.[129]

The principle of non-intervention in the internal affairs of other states generally prohibits third states from providing military assistance to nonstate armed

125. In larger freedom: towards development, security and human rights for all: Report of the Secretary-General, U.N. Doc. A/59/2005, para 91; Independent international commission of inquiry on the Syrian Arab Republic, *supra* note 3, para. 106; Honoré, *supra* note 55, p. 39; Jordan J. Paust, The Human Right to Revolution, in: Richard Pierre Claude & Burns H. Weston (eds.), Human Rights in the World Community: Issues and Action, University of Pennsylvania Press: Philadelphia (3rd ed., 2006), 445-452, at p. 451; Eide, Barlaug & Chinana, *supra* note 59, p. 58; Tomuschat, *supra* note 59, p. 29.

126. See, e.g., Bassey E. Ate, Terrorism in the Context of Decolonization, in: Hans Köchler (ed.) Terrorism and National Liberation, Peter Lang: Frankfurt a.M./Bern/New York (1988), 79–93, at p. 83.

127. Legality of the Threat or Use of Nuclear Weapons (Advisory Opinion), ICJ Rep. 1996, 226, at p. 257 [para 79].

128. See *supra* note 105.

129. See also McCorquodale, *supra* note 104, p. 882; Cassese, *supra* note 107, p. 62; Malanczuk, *supra* note 102, p. 337.

groups involved in a non-international armed conflict with their government.[130] Many developing countries, and a number of academic writers, take the view that this restriction does not apply to wars of national liberation, so that third states can provide national liberation movements with arms and any other military assistance short of sending troops.[131] However, this has been challenged by a number of Western states, and it is uncertain whether a right to provide military support to national liberation movements represents customary international law.[132] The Friendly Relations Declaration is deliberately ambiguous on the question. It recognizes that national liberation movements have a right to "seek and receive support in accordance with the purposes and principles of the [U.N.] Charter." It is left open what assistance is referred to and what limits the U.N. Charter imposes on the provision of such assistance.

At the individual level, national liberation fighters are regarded as lawful combatants in an international armed conflict.[133] The lawfulness of their defensive cause does not protect them from being targeted and killed in hostilities in accordance with international humanitarian law. However, unlike other rebels, they enjoy the combatant's privilege, which means they must not be prosecuted for their mere participation in the conflict and enjoy prisoner of war status if captured. Where a state unlawfully prosecutes national liberation fighters for their mere participation in the struggle, third states must not support such prosecutions and must refuse to extradite suspects or provide judicial assistance.

IV. No right to rebel against undemocratic governments

The right to self-determination, viewed together with the human right to effectively participate in public affairs (see Article 21 of the UDHR and Article 25 of the ICCPR) also embodies the right to a democratically legitimated government.[134] After all, the right to self-determination, as laid down in Common

130. Military and Paramilitary Activities (Nicaragua v. U.S.) (Merits), I.C.J. Reports 1986, 14, at p. 108 [para. 205].

131. See also Cassese, *supra* note 107, p. 62; McCorquodale, *supra* note 104, p. 882; d'Aspremont, *supra* note 102, p. 310; Abi Saab, *supra* note 104, p. 372; Quaye, *supra* note 119, pp. 289 & 301.

132. Jochen A. Frowein, Self-Determination as a Limit to Obligations under International Law, in: Christian Tomuschat (ed.), Modern Law of Self-Determination, Martinus Nijhoff: Dordrecht/Boston/London (1993), 211–223, at p. 213; Summers, *supra* note 104, p. 460; Malanczuk, *supra* note 102, p. 337.

133. See Art. 1(4) First Geneva Protocol. See also U.N. G.A. Res. 3103 (XXVIII), *supra* note 114.

134. McCorquodale, *supra* note 104, p. 864; Manfred Nowak, UN Covenant on Civil and Political Rights: CCPR Commentary, N.P. Engel: Kehl/Strasbourg/Arlington (2nd ed., 2005), pp. 20 & 24 [Art. 1, paras. 28 & 34]; Frowein, *id.*, pp. 222–223. See also Human Rights Committee, General Comment 12: Article 1, para.6, in: Compilation of General Comments and General Recommendations Adopted by Human Rights Treaty Bodies, U.N. Doc. HRI/GEN/1/Rev.1 at 12 (1994). But cf. Jerzy Tyranowski, Der Grundsatz

Article 1 of the ICCPR and ICESCR, entitles peoples to "freely determine their political status."

It has been suggested that the right to self-determination therefore gives rise to a right to launch a violent rebellion against an undemocratic government that either denies the entire population democratic rights[135] or totally excludes particular groups from the political process.[136] However, positive international law has not endorsed this position yet,[137] except where the rebellion targets Apartheid-like regimes that base their undemocratic rule on institutionalized racism.[138] International law remains neutral on pro-democracy rebellions.

It would also be hard to square a right to violent revolution for democratic change with the limits of the right to right to self-defense. The proportionality of massive loss of life to achieve democratic governance is questionable already. In any case, the principle of necessity would usually not be fulfilled, since nonviolent resistance offers an alternative that causes less harm to the human rights of security forces and innocent bystanders and is actually more effective in securing the right to democratic self-determination. Empirical evidence indicates that undemocratic regimes can be more successfully challenged using non-violent resistance. One major study of 323 violent and nonviolent resistance campaigns that took place between 1900 and 2006 showed that nonviolent campaigns were nearly twice as likely as the violent ones to fully or partially achieve their political objective.[139] In particular, nonviolent campaigns aimed at regime change, a category that includes all democratization campaigns, had a success rate of almost 60 percent, while violent campaigns only achieved that objective in 27 percent of all cases.[140]

der souveränen Gleichheit der Staaten und der Grundsatz der Selbstbestimmung der Völker, in: Vorträge, Reden und Berichte aus dem Europa-Institut, vol. 234, Europa Institut: Saarbrücken (1991), at p. 10.

135. Paust, *supra* note 125, pp. 449–450; Cassese, *supra* note 104, p. 950.Cf. Shannonbrooke Murphy, Unique in international human rights law: Article 20(2) and the right to resist in the African Charter on Human and Peoples' Rights, African Human Rights Law Journal, vol. 11 (2011), 465–494, at p. 472; Nowak, *id.*, p. 24 [art. 1, para. 34]; Goertzel, *supra* note 59, p. 9. De lege ferenda, Frédéric Mégret, Le droit international peut-il être un droit de résistance? Dix conditions pour un renouveau de l'ambition normative internationale, Études internationales, vol. 39 (2008) 39–62, at p. 57.

136. Kälin & Künzli, *supra* note 107, p. 58; Paust, *supra* note 125, p. 449. See also Frowein, *supra* note 132, p. 214.

137. See this Seventh Chapter: E.I and the references below, p. 327, note 149.

138. See *supra* note 104 and accompanying text.

139. Chenoweth & Stephan, *supra* note 35, p. 7. Another empirical study that compared autonomy movement that existed in 87 states between 1945 and 2000 comes to similar results. See Renat Shaykhutdinov, Give peace a chance: Nonviolent protest and the creation of territorial autonomy arrangements, Journal of Peace Research, vol 47 (2010), 179–191.

140. Chenoweth & Stephan, *id.*, p. 9.

Nonviolent campaigns are more effective since the physical, moral, and informational barriers to participation are lower. They can therefore ensure mass participation on a scale that violent campaigns cannot. Mass participation in turn will cause a higher degree of disruption and also cause loyalty to shift among the security forces and other essential supporters of the regime. Furthermore, nonviolent campaigns are more likely to win crucial international support.[141] As noted above, nonviolent action will also achieve more durable and internally peaceful democracies than attempts than armed struggles.[142] This is true because nonviolent movements prepare the population for settling differences by political means. Conversely, violent resistance often empowers the most violent factions among regime opponents, which may also carry the seed of continued inter-factional fighting after regime change is achieved.

According to the position taken here, an undemocratic regime has to be challenged by means of peaceful protest and nonviolent resistance. However, the legal position may change if that regime seeks to suppress the pro-democracy movement by way of mass atrocities and an organized armed resistance movement then emerges to end the atrocities with military means. In that case, the violent suppression of democratic aspirations, rather than the democratic aspirations themselves, would become the subject of militarily organized armed resistance. As will be explored in the following section, a case can be made, at least *de lege ferenda,* that international law ought to recognize a right of organized armed resistance against mass atrocities amounting to genocide, crimes against humanity, or war crimes.

E. ORGANIZED ARMED RESISTANCE AGAINST MASS ATROCITIES

Between April and July 1994, perhaps as many as one million people were killed in the Rwandan Genocide. The international community failed to stage a meaningful intervention to stop the killings. The Rwandan Genocide came to an end only because the Rwandan Patriotic Front (RPF), then a rebel movement and now the ruling party in Rwanda, recommenced its armed campaign against the government once the Genocide started and ousted the genocidal government forces and government-sponsored *Interahamwe* militia. From a legal perspective, and without losing sight of serious concerns about the RPF's own human rights record, this raises the question whether an armed group like the RPF has a right under international law to engage in an armed conflict against the government to defend a population against mass atrocities and, if so, what legal implications such a right of military organized armed resistance would entail.

141. *Id.*, pp. 220–221.

142. *Id.*, p. 10.

I. No state recognition of a right of armed resistance against mass atrocities

Some writers take the view that international law establishes a right to organized armed resistance against governments that commit international crimes[143] or are oppressive and tyrannical in nature.[144] Others recognize such a right at least in response to resisting genocide.[145] The right would be underpinned by the rights to life and physical security, interpreted in light of the right to personal self-defense as a general principle of law.[146] In addition, it can be argued that it follows from the right to an effective remedy for human rights violations where organized armed resistance is the only remedy to end massive violations of the rights to life and physical security.[147] In the case of genocide, it can also be argued that it follows from every state's obligation under the 1948 Genocide Convention and customary international law to do what it can to prevent genocide, because the recognition of resistance as lawful can potentially help prevent or mitigate the commission of genocide.[148]

143. Tomuschat, *supra* note 59, p. 22; Frédéric Mégret, Response to Claus Kreß: Leveraging the privilege of belligerency in non-international armed conflict towards respect for the jus in bello, International Review of the Red Cross, vol. 96 (2014), 44–66, at p. 49; Wolfgang Graf Vitzthum, Stauffenberg—Zur Rechtfertigung von Eidbruch und Tyrannenmord, in: Holger P. Hestermeyer et al. (eds.), Coexistence, Cooperation and Solidarity: Liber Amicorum Rüdiger Wolfrum, vol. 1, Martinus Nijhoff: Leiden/Boston (2012), 2145–2164, at p. 2159; Shannon K. Brincat, "Death to Tyrants": Self-Defence, Human Rights and Tyrants—Part II, Journal of International Political Theory, vol. 5 (2009), 75–93, at p. 76; Ouguerguez, *supra* note 15, pp. 262–267; Kälin & Künzli, *supra* note 107, p. 52. De lege ferenda, Claus Kreß, The regulation of non-international armed conflicts: Can a privilege of belligerency be envisioned in the law of non-international armed conflicts?, International Review of the Red Cross, vol. 96 (2014), 29–44, at p. 40; Saul, *supra* note 59, p. 216; See also Missling, *supra* note 59, p. 255.

144. Jordan J. Paust, International Law, Dignity, Democracy, and the Arab Spring, Cornell International Law Journal, vol. 46 (2013), 1–19, at p. 19; Kopel, Gallant & Eisen, *supra* note 55, p. 131. Alan Rosas, Internal Self-Determination, in: Christian Tomuschat (ed.), Modern Law of Self-Determination, Martinus Nijhoff: Dordrecht/Boston/London (1993), 225–252, at p. 249; Cassese, *supra* note 104, pp. 946–947; Anderson, *supra* note 104, pp. 65–66; Hurst Hannum, Rethinking Self- Determination, Virginia Journal of International Law, vol. 34 (1993), 1–69, at p. 45; Syméon Karagiannis, Qu'est il, en droit international, le droit à la résistance devenu, Revue trimestrielle des droits de l'homme, vol. 76 (2008), 949–1005, at p. 1005; Ellery C. Stowell, Intervention in International Law, John Byrne: Washington D.C. (1921), p. 354.

145. Jens David Ohlin, The Doctrine of Legitimate Defense, International Law Studies vol. 91 (2015), 119–154, at p. 142; Quaye, *supra* note 119, p. 277; Goertzel, *supra* note 59, pp. 3 & 9; David B. Kopel, Paul Gallant & Joanne D. Eisen, Is Resisting Genocide a Human Right?, Notre Dame Law Review, vol. 81(4) (2006), 1275–1346, at p. 1277; Schwartz, *supra* note 59, p. 268.

146. Cf. Tomuschat, *supra* note 59, p. 29.

147. Kopel, Gallant & Eisen, *supra* note 145, pp. 1276–1277; Tomuschat, *supra* note 59, p. 20; Murphy, *supra* note 104, p. 110. See also Saul, *supra* note 59, p. 195.

148. Cf. Kopel, Gallant & Eisen, *id.*, p. 1277.

Yet, leaving aside the abovementioned peculiar case of self-determination, states have been loath to recognize any rights of organized armed resistance that could be invoked to threaten their authority. The prevailing view remains that even in cases of mass atrocities there is no right to resistance under positive international law.[149] Unsatisfactory as this may be (see the following section), this view accurately reflects international law as applied by states.

The Universal Declaration of Human Rights, although not binding as such as a General Assembly Resolution, is often cited as evidence of a right to organized armed resistance. Its preamble regards it "essential, if man is not to be compelled to have recourse, as a last resort, to rebellion against tyranny and oppression, that human rights should be protected by the rule of law." The clause can be given a normative meaning according to which it implicitly recognizes a right of rebellion against tyranny and oppression if all else fails.[150] However, a different reading is also possible. The rebellion clause could have a merely descriptive character, warning governments that tyranny and oppression may lead to (unlawful) rebellion.[151] The ambiguity of the wording is not a coincidence but reflects a diplomatic compromise. During the drafting of the Universal Declaration, pre-Castro Cuba had proposed inclusion of a "right to resist any form of oppression". A subsequent draft presented by René Cassin, the principal drafter of the Universal Declaration, set out a right to resist tyranny and oppression whenever a government seriously or systematically tramples human rights. However, a number of states involved in drafting the Universal Declaration opposed the inclusion of references to any right to resistance. In the end the clause was relegated to the preamble and any direct reference to a right of resistance was removed.[152] In light of this drafting history, the Universal Declaration provided, at best, a seed for the recognition of a right of resistance but did not establish such a right itself.

149. Olivier Corten, La rébellion et le droit international: le principe de neutralité en tension, Recueil des cours de l'Academie de la Haye, vol. 374 (2014), 53–312, at p. 231; Cassese, *supra* note 59, p. 181; Dunér, *supra* note 104, p. 248; Keenan, *supra* note 104, pp. 15–16 & 29; Yuval Shany, The Analogy's Limit: Defending the Rights of Peoples, Journal of International Criminal Justice, vol. 7 (2009), 541–553, at p. 549; Gerald Sumida, The Right of Revolution: Implications for International Law and Order, in: Charles A. Barker (ed.), Power and Law: American Dilemma in World, Johns Hopkins Press: Baltimore/London (1971), 130–167, at p. 132; d'Aspremont, *supra* note 102, pp. 310–311; Tyranowski, *supra* note 134, p. 16.

150. Karagiannis, *supra* note 144, pp. 957–966; Sumida, *id.*, p. 135; Cassese, *supra* note 104, p. 947; Kälin & Künzli, *supra* note 107, p. 51; Kopel, Gallant & Eisen, *supra* note 145, p. 1277; Paust, *supra* note 125, p. 448; Honoré, *supra* note 55, p. 43; d'Aspremont, *id.*, p. 310; Murphy, *supra* note 104, p. 96; Missling, *supra* note 59, p. 127.

151. Dunér, *supra* note 104, p. 253; Corten, *supra* note 149, p. 235; Geistlinger, *supra* note 29, p. 364; Keenan, *supra* note 104, p. 21; Saul, *supra* note 59, p. 192.

152. For details on the drafting history, see Johannes Morsink, The Universal Declaration of Human Rights: Origins, Drafting and Intent, University of Pennsylvania Press: Philadelphia (1999), pp. 300–312; Geistlinger, *supra* note 29, pp. 360–361.

Nor did any of the subsequently adopted universal human rights treaties set forth a right to resist mass atrocities.[153] At the regional level, the European Convention on Human Rights rather recognizes states' right to quell insurrections and take lives in the process (see Article 2(2)(c) of the ECHR), without any qualifier that some insurrections may be justified and must not be suppressed. Solely Article 20(2) of the ACHPR provides some support for a right to resistance. The provision recognizes that "oppressed peoples shall have the right to free themselves from the bonds of domination by resorting to any means recognized by the international community." While Apartheid in South Africa and Namibia may have been on the mind of the African states that adopted the treaty, the wording is broad enough to encompass other cases of oppression as well.[154] Even if one assumes that the African Charter recognizes a right to resistance against all forms of oppression, however, it is unclear whether such resistance may be take the form of violent resistance against oppressive regimes (other than racist regimes denying the right to self-determination). Article 20(2) of the ACHPR only endorses those means "recognized by the international community." The text could be read as excluding particular types of violence, namely attacks on civilians and other violations of international humanitarian law. The more probable reading is that it reverts the entire question on the legality of forcible resistance back to general international law.[155] Article 20(2) therefore does not provide an argument for or against a right to forcible resistance, but depends on customary international law for the answer.

Under customary international law, there is not enough state practice and requisite *opinio juris* to conclude that there is a right to resist mass atrocities. A few states recognize a fundamental right to use organized armed resistance against human rights violations. For example, Article 87 of the Constitution of El Salvador provides for a right to insurrection against grave human rights violations. Article 7 of the Portuguese Constitution recognizes the right of peoples to revolt against all forms of oppression. Other constitutions include a right of resistance against attempts to overturn the constitutional order, which would presumably also cover cases where a government forsakes constitutional rights and turns tyrannical. In total, there are some 27 states that recognize resistance

153. See also Corten, *supra* note 149, p. 236; Karagiannis, *supra* note 144, pp. 966–987.

154. Murphy, *supra* note 135, p. 483; Ouguerguez, *supra* note 15, p. 263; Paust, *supra* note 144, p. 18. The African Commission apparently endorses a wide reading of the term "oppressed," covering cases beyond the contexts of colonialism and Apartheid, given that it has considered Article 20(2) ACHPR in relation to allegations of central government oppression made by the people of Southern Cameroon. See Kevin Mgwanga Gunme et al. v. Cameroon, Case No. 266/03, Decision of 27 May 2009, para 197.

155. See also Murphy, *supra* note 104, p. 103. See also Corten, *supra* note 149, p. 249, who also argues that the opening of legal avenues to complaint about violations of Article 20 of the ACHPR to the ACommHR makes the assumption far-fetched that Article 20 entails a right to rebel.

rights.[156] This is only a small minority of the world's 193 states. Furthermore, there is no evidence that these 27 states adopted constitutional resistance provisions based on a legal conviction (*opinio juris*) that doing so is required under international law.[157] In many contexts, constitutional resistance clauses rather reflect the historical experience of a particular oppressive regime having ruled the country concerned.

Outside the context of self-determination, it is hard to find any intergovernmental resolutions that explicitly endorse organized armed resistance as legitimate and lawful. No General Assembly or Human Rights Council resolutions endorse a right to forcibly resist even the gravest human rights violations. To the contrary: when defining who is a human rights defender, the General Assembly took great care to ensure that only people committed to peaceful action would fall under the definition.[158]

In 2012, the Human Rights Council Advisory Committee, which is composed of independent experts not representing their governments, proposed that the Human Rights Council recognize a right to resist and oppose dictatorial domination and domestic oppression as well as a right to oppose genocide, war crimes, and crimes against humanity.[159] This proposal did not receive support from states in the subsequent intergovernmental negotiations. Instead, several states expressly opposed making any reference to a right to resistance, while others only agreed only to a reference to the right to resist occupation by force.[160]

The practice of the Security Council does not support a right to resist mass atrocities either. During the Rwandan Genocide, the Security Council repeatedly called on both the Rwandan government and the rebels of the Rwandese Patriotic Front to cease hostilities "for an end to the mindless violence and carnage which are engulfing Rwanda."[161] This approach was taken even though in the absence of international intervention, the RPF's military campaign was the only hope to end the Genocide and defend the lives of the remaining Tutsi population. In the case of Syria, the Security Council called on the government and all

156. See the listing of relevant constitutional provisions in the Third Chapter: B.II (p. 82).

157. Cassese, *supra* note 59, p. 181.

158. Declaration on the Right and Responsibility of Individuals, Groups and Organs of Society to Promote and Protect Universally Recognized Human Rights and Fundamental Freedoms Declarations on Human Rights Defenders, G.A. Res. 53/144, U.N. Doc. A/RES/53/94 (1999), articles 5, 12 & 13. Critical of this approach Murphy, *supra* note 104, p. 95.

159. Report of the Human Rights Council Advisory Committee on the right of peoples to peace, U.N. Doc. A/HRC/20/31 (2012), Annex: Draft declaration on the Right to Peace, art. 7.

160. Report of the Open-ended Inter-Governmental Working Group on the Draft United Nations Declaration on the Right to Peace, U.N. Doc. A/HRC/WG.13/1/2 (2013), para. 60.

161. Security Council Resolution 912, U.N. Doc. S/RES/912 (1994), para. 6; Security Council Resolution 918, U.N. Doc. S/RES/918 (1994), para. 1. See also Security Council Resolution 925, U.N., Doc. S/RES/925 (1994), preamble.

opposition groups "immediately to cease all armed violence in all its forms."[162] No concession was made for those along the spectrum of armed groups in Syria that were focused mainly on defending their communities against mass atrocities, at least in the initial stages of the crisis.

Security Council Resolutions 1970 and 1973 on Libya mark a notable exception, as they conspicuously fail to condemn the use of force by the Libyan rebels in the aftermath of the Gaddafi regime's brutal suppression of protests. However, any inferences that can be derived from these two resolutions are not enough to establish that the state community has made an about-face and now recognizes a right to resist mass atrocities.[163]

The strongest argument against the existence of a right to organized armed resistance against atrocities emanates from international humanitarian law. In adopting the Geneva Protocols, states took a deliberate decision to only grant privileged combatant status to members of national liberation movements fighting colonial domination, alien occupation, and racist regimes.[164] Rebels in nonstate international armed conflicts may be punished for their mere participation in the conflict, regardless of the motives for their rebellion.[165] This implies that they have no right to engage in organized armed resistance against mass atrocities.

In theory, it would be possible to reconcile international humanitarian law with a right to resist mass atrocities without requiring an amendment of the Geneva Conventions or Protocols. The law of armed conflict has always recognized the option of the territorial state or third states to recognize the belligerency of a nonstate armed group. Where belligerency has been recognized, the conflict is governed by the rules of international armed conflict,[166] meaning that the rebels participate as lawful combatants and may not be punished for their

162. Security Council Resolution 2042, U.N. Doc. S/RES/2042 (2012), para. 4; Resolution 2043, S/RES/2043 (2012), para. 3. See also Statement of the President of the Security Council, U.N. Doc. S/PRST/2011/16 (2011); Security Council Resolution 2139, U.N. Doc. S/RES/2139 (2014), para. 2, which "[d]emands that all parties immediately put an end to all forms of violence, irrespective of where it comes from."

163. See also Murphy, *supra* note 104, p. 107.

164. At the time, only Australia made a declaration that it considered the list in Art. 1(4) to be non-exhaustive so that other struggles for self-determination could also be considered privileged. See Antonio Cassese, Wars of national liberation and humanitarian law, in: Christophe Swinarski (ed.), Etudes et essais sur le droit international humanitaire et sur les principes de la Croix-Rouge—en honneur de Jean Pictet, Martinus Nijhoff Publishers: Leiden (1984), 313–324, at p. 318.

165. Cf. Art. 6 of the Second Geneva Protocol.

166. Sasha Radin, The Current Relevance of the Recognition of Belligerency, in: M. Matthee et al. (eds.), Armed Conflict and International Law: In Search of the Human Face, TMC Asser: The Hague (2013), 116–152, at p. 141; Yoram Dinstein, The International Law of Belligerent Occupation, Cambridge University Press: Cambridge (2009), p. 34 [para. 77]; Sumida, *supra* note 149, p. 154.

mere participation in the armed conflict. It is often suggested that recognition of belligerency requires four elements: (1) the existence of an armed conflict, (2) a rebel group that occupies a substantial portion of national territory, (3) organized conduct of hostilities by the rebels in accordance with the law of armed conflict and under responsible command, and (4) the existence of circumstances that require third states or the government to recognize the conflict.[167] Actual state practice has handled the recognition of belligerency much more flexibly, guided primarily by the fourth requirement, thus recognizing belligerency where their political, institutional or commercial interests made recognition necessary.[168] In light of this flexible approach, it could be argued that states are required to recognize the belligerency of nonstate armed groups that engage in necessary and proportional armed resistance measures against ongoing mass atrocities.[169] This requirement would derive from their obligation to respect the human rights to life and physical security, interpreted in light of the right to personal self-defense as a general principle of law. In the case of genocide, it could also stem from their obligation to do what they can to prevent genocide even if it does not occur on their own territory.[170]

State practice does not yet follow the proposed approach. In recent crises in Libya and Syria, some states have pursued a different path though to achieve a similar result: They recognized the political representation of rebel groups that they considered to have a just cause as the legitimate government.[171] Such recognition implied that the forces under the control of these new governments were considered government forces and thus lawful participants of the armed conflict. Though interesting, that approach has disadvantages compared to the idea proposed here. For one, early recognition is often premature, because the resistance movement does not yet have effective control of a majority of the territory. Furthermore, recognition of the political leadership of a resistance movement commits the recognizing third states to supporting regime change or secession, while mere recognition of belligerency would leave more space for negotiated solutions to end the crises and its atrocities. Finally, the indicated practice of political recognition is not based on clear normative principles that indicate when recognition will be afforded and is thus prone to reflect political considerations.

167. Hersch Lauterpacht, Recognition in International Law, Cambridge University Press: Cambridge (1947), p. 176; Sumida, *id.*, 153–154.

168. Sam Foster Halabi, Traditions of Belligerent Recognition: The Libyan Intervention in Historical and Theoretical Context, American University International Law Review, vol. 27 (2012), 321–390, at p. 326.

169. Mégret, *supra* note 143, p. 65, seems to contemplate an approach along these lines.

170. Application of the Genocide Convention (Bosnia and Herzegovina v. Serbia and Montenegro) [Merits], I.C.J. Reports 2007, 43 (26 February), at p. 120 [para. 187] and p. 221 [para. 430].

171. Cf. Corten, *supra* note 149, p. 248. However, a number of states only extended political recognition of the opposition representatives as the "legal representative of the people," without

II. The case for a right of armed struggle against mass atrocities

The prevailing state practice is deeply unsatisfactory. It abandons the victims of mass atrocities to their fate by denying them international legal recognition of the only action they can take to save themselves in extreme situations where nonviolent resistance leads to only more government atrocities and an international intervention is not forthcoming.

As it stands, the law is full of jarring contradictions. Cases that are morally distinct are subject to the same rules. As it stands, international law places a group that takes up arms to prevent a genocide on the same level as rebels that plunge the country into war for purposes of a naked power grab. Meanwhile, morally comparable cases are subject to different rules. A government that extends tyrannical oppression to all of its citizens may outlaw any organized armed resistance that forms in response and severely punish the resistance fighters. But if it limits its oppression to specific ethnic groups, using institutionalized racist criteria, the rebellion would be a lawful war of national liberation in the defense of the right to self-determination.[172]

There is also inconsistency with international criminal law. Under international criminal law, soldiers are under an obligation to disobey manifestly unlawful orders to commit mass atrocities involving international crimes.[173] But in the type of existential crisis where such crimes tend to occur, soldiers who disobey and refuse to carry out the orders may be summarily executed by their superiors. Desertion and taking refuge abroad might not be a viable option, also considering the potential of reprisals against the extended family. This leaves resistance as the only alternative to complicity to international crimes. But international law offers no legal protection to soldiers who take this option. It should be noted that the dilemma staked out here is not theoretical in nature. In the case of Syria, the armed resistance against the government was started by defecting soldiers, many of whom did not want to take part in the Syrian government's crimes against humanity but also were aware that refusal to partake would make them liable to be executed.[174]

legally recognizing them as the government. See Stefan Talmon, Recognition of Opposition Groups as the Legitimate Representative of a People, Chinese Journal of International Law, vol. 12 (2013), 219–253.

172. See also Keenan, *supra* note 104, p. 22; Dunér, *supra* note 104, p. 252; Mégret, *supra* note 135, p. 52.

173. Rome Statute of the International Criminal Court, art. 33; United States v. Wilhelm List et al., Reports of Trials of War Criminals, vol. XI (1950), p. 1236; United States v. Erhard Milch, Reports of Trials of War Criminals, vol. VII (1947), p. 42.

174. Cf. Independent international commission of inquiry on the Syrian Arab Republic, *supra* note 3, para. 17. Missling, *supra* note 59, pp. 259–260, sees therefore in the duty not to follow orders to commit international crimes an indication for the existence of a right of resistance against severe human rights violations under international law.

The non-recognition of a right to resist mass atrocities is also hard to square with the commitments on the responsibility to protect that were made by heads of state and governments gathered at the 2005 World Summit. Where a state subjects its population to genocide, ethnic cleansing, war crimes, or crimes against humanity, the international community has assumed a responsibility to protect that population, if necessary through military means as a last resort.[175] If the international community claims a right to use armed force to protect human rights in such extreme cases, one would expect that it affords the victims the right to protect themselves from the same type of atrocities.[176] After all, a crucial prong of human rights is empowering people to become actors in achieving those rights. Instead, the current state practice treats them as passive beneficiaries who can only be saved by international intervention. Tellingly, the option of providing assistance to resistance movements, nonviolent or armed, under the responsibility-to-protect framework has not yet been seriously contemplated in practice, even though it might be an effective element of an overall strategy to end a particular set of mass atrocities.[177] The unsatisfactory state of the law becomes painfully obvious where the international community fails to discharge its responsibility to protect, as was the case, for example, in Rwanda, but still does not recognize the lawfulness of organized armed resistance by the victims of the genocide or armed groups close to them.

In failing to recognize a right to resistance even in the gravest circumstances, international law divests itself of the cloak of moral legitimacy from which it ultimately derives its force. If one looks at the 1943 Uprising in the Warsaw Ghetto from the perspective of present international law and assumes that the Jewish resistance fighters had the weaponry and organization to be considered an organized armed group, can it really be said that the Jews had no right to resist, but had to submit to their deportation to the gas chambers? Could it seriously be claimed that those resistance fighters who were caught alive could have been lawfully convicted and sentenced to death for acts of rebellion? It appears that international law, as currently understood by states, and natural law are far apart in cases involving resistance to mass atrocities.

III. Limits of a right to resist mass atrocities

Skeptics of a right to resist mass atrocities argue that its legal recognition may invite abuse. Even the most unsavory rebel groups may style themselves as resistance fighters.[178] However, the current state of international law is worse, as it

175. World Summit Outcome, G.A. Res. 60/1, U.N. Doc. A/RES/60/1 (2005), paras. 138–139.

176. Keenan, *supra* note 104, p. 24; Mégret, *supra* note 135, p. 51. In light of this, Corten, *supra* note 149, p. 244 describes the responsibility to protect as "neo-paternalistic."

177. For a critical discussion of this shortcoming, see Frédèric Mégret, Beyond the "Salvation" Paradigm: Responsibility To Protect (Others) vs the Power of Protecting Oneself, Security Dialogue, vol. 40 (2009), 575–595.

178. Keenan, *supra* note 104, pp. 21 & 23; Dunér, *supra* note 104, p. 263.

makes no distinction whatsoever between the causes of different groups. It provides no legal guidance on what armed action is legitimate and what is not. It is left entirely to the political savvy of the conflict parties and their supporters whether a particular armed group is framed in the public perception as "freedom fighters" or "terrorist criminals." A clearly delineated right to resist mass atrocities could help in limiting violence to deserving cases and exposing undeserving claimants.[179] It would force opposition groups on the brink of launching an armed struggle to justify themselves based on legal criteria. Whereas some have expressed concern that a right to resistance would lead to more non-international armed conflict,[180] it could actually limit resort to violent rebellion to fewer cases where the rebels actually defend a just cause with necessary and proportional means.

The right to personal self-defense offers viable limiting criteria to determine when organized armed resistance against mass atrocities ought to be lawful.[181]

1. Present or Imminent Unlawful Attack

To invoke self-defense, there must be a present or imminent unlawful attack on human rights,[182] such as an ongoing or imminent state campaign of genocide, crimes against humanity, or widespread war crimes that posed a latent risk of individuals in the target group being subjected to particular atrocities. A mere fear of future atrocities or historical grievances could not justify taking up arms.[183]

As a safeguard against unmerited claims, a right to resistance could only be invoked on the basis of solid, objective, and up-to-date evidence establishing that the state commits human rights violations that amount to mass atrocities. Such evidence could notably consist of findings made by credible and independent international human rights mechanisms such as a U.N.-mandated independent commission of inquiry, a regional human rights court, or a field office of the U.N. High Commissioner for Human Rights.[184] Despite claims to the contrary, this would not overburden limited human rights monitoring resources.[185] Most crises involving potential mass atrocities are already subject to dedicated human rights monitoring and inquiry mechanisms, which have been set up by the United Nations or regional organizations and produce relevant and credible information. As an alternative, some scholars have contemplated to leave it up to the Security Council to determine that a situation involves violations of such gravity

179. Cf. Murphy, *supra* note 104, p. 109.

180. Dunér, *supra* note 104, p. 258; Keenan, *supra* note 104, p. 21.

181. See also Brincat, *supra* note 143, p. 77.

182. Brincat, *id.*, p. 86. See also Fourth Chapter: C.II (pp. 140–143).

183. Brincat, *id.*, p. 86.

184. See also Ouguerguez, *supra* note 15, p. 266.

185. But see Dunér, *supra* note 104, p. 264.

that a right to resistance ensues.[186] However, this would only further politicize the issue and would introduce the same problems of selectivity and inertia that plague the Security Council's application of the responsibility to protect.[187]

Resistance could be directed only against those persons or institutions that engage in the mass atrocities and not against all institutions of the state.[188] Thus, if only particular army and special security forces commit atrocities, an armed response must not be directed against the regular police and army, even if this may be a convenient way to acquire more weaponry. By the same token, criminal activities to acquire the finances necessary to wage the rebellion, such as drug trafficking or taking hostages for ransom, cannot be justified as a defensive measure under a right to resistance.

2. Necessity

In accordance with the requirement of necessity, and as also emphasized by the Universal Declaration's rebellion clause, armed force must be the last resort. Because the justification of the right to resistance is based on human rights, its exercise must not infringe on human rights more than necessary, even if those rights are those of the aggressors.[189] This means that to justify resort to resistance, no other effective remedy must be available to stop the atrocities. Thus, a right of armed resistance is out of the question where democratic processes are functioning and can be used to replace an oppressive government.[190] Other nonviolent means to end atrocities must have been exhausted as well. The resistance movement would have to show that it has made every effort to pursue political negotiations, public denunciation of the violation, and appeals to international human rights mechanisms, nonviolent resistance, and pleas to the international community to exercise its responsibility to protect.[191] Only if all these options have demonstrably failed, especially if they were brutally repressed, may armed resistance be considered. Incidentally, this approach also increases the overall chances of efforts to stand up to oppression, since nonviolent resistance measures can be taken before the state escalates its oppression to mass atrocities and a broader resistance movement hence becomes more difficult to organize.

186. Dunér, *id.* p. 263; Cohn, *supra* note 29, p. 513.

187. See also Dunér, *id.* p. 263.

188. Kälin & Künzli, *supra* note 107, p. 53; Tomuschat, *supra* note 59, p. 30; Saul, *supra* note 59, p. 204.

189. See also Missling, *supra* note 59, p. 249.

190. See also Goertzel, *supra* note 59, p. 9; Cassese, *supra* note 104, p. 950.

191. See also Kälin & Künzli, *supra* note 107, pp. 51–52; Cohn 511; Dunér, *supra* note 104, p. 260; Keenan, *supra* note 104, p. 28; Murphy, *supra* note 104, p. 110; Ouguerguez, *supra* note 15, p. 266; Susan H. Farbstein, Reflections on the Question of When, if Ever, Violence Is Justified in Struggles for Political or Social Change, Harvard Human Rights Law Journal, vol. 27 (2014), 1–5, at p. 2; Cassese, *supra* note 104, p. 947; Mégret, *supra* note 135, p. 57.

Even when nonviolent means have proven futile, only the minimum level of violence necessary to end the atrocities can be considered lawful.[192] A right to resistance does not necessarily extend to a right to revolution or regime change. At the same time, force directly targeting those who are ordering the mass atrocities, within the bounds of international humanitarian law, may be in some situations the measure of defense involving the least bloodshed.

An armed struggle would be illicit if it became necessary only because the resistance movement unlawfully provoked the mass atrocities, such as by consistently launching attacks from behind civilian shields or carrying out attacks specifically designed to result in atrocious state reprisals against the civilian population. However, activities that are lawful under international law, namely peaceful protests against authoritarian rule, cannot be considered undue provocation.

3. Proportionality

A right of resistance would have to be exercised in accordance with the principle of proportionality that generally limits the right to self-defense.[193] As it crosses the threshold into an armed conflict, organized armed resistance will almost certainly have severe repercussions for the civilian population. From the perspective of the right to self-defense, civilians are innocent bystanders. Any negative consequences they face are proportional only if the positive human rights impact of the resistance outweighs the negative impact on them.[194] For that reason, organized armed resistance can only be proportional in response to the worst atrocities, which, according to the proposal made here, would comprise genocide, crimes against humanity, and war crimes on a massive scale. These crimes are defined by the Rome Statute and an ever-growing body of jurisprudence under international criminal law, so that they are less prone to be wrongly claimed than are more amorphous concepts such as "oppression" or "tyranny." Restricting a right of armed resistance to these international crimes would also align its ambit with that of the international community's responsibility to protect.[195] This accords with the argument that people should be allowed to protect themselves where the international community fails to assume its own responsibility to protect.

192. See also Farbstein, *id.*, p. 4.

193. Tomuschat, *supra* note 59, p. 27; Eide, Barlaug & Chinana, *supra* note 59, p. 55; Cohn, *supra* note 29, p. 513; Murphy, *supra* note 104, p. 110; See also Paust, *supra* note 125, p. 451; Herbert Marcuse, Ethics and Revolution, in: Richard T. DeGeorge (ed.), Ethics and Society Anchor: New York (1966), 133–147, at p. 140; Brincat, *supra* note 143, p. 86; Missling, *supra* note 59, p. 251.

194. See also Fourth Chapter: C.V.3 (p. 180).

195. The responsibility to protect also relates to ethnic cleansing. Although not defined in international law, the term *ethnic cleansing* is generally used to apply to systematic and serious violations that would already be encapsulated under the category of crimes against humanity, so that legally the term does not expand the ambit of the Responsibility to Protect.

The proportionality analysis cannot stop there. Even in the face of mass atrocities, it has to be weighed whether the human rights impact of an armed conflict might yet still be worse than continued suffering of the atrocities.[196] However, armed resistance cannot be ruled out by the fact that a state already committing mass atrocities may react to armed resistance with yet more atrocities against innocent civilians. Otherwise the law would create a perverse incentive for tyrannical authorities to aggravate their repression when challenged, so as to render any resistance unlawful.

In making the proportionality assessment, the views of the general population are paramount, since civilians will face the brunt both of atrocities and repercussions of armed conflict. International law should therefore consider lawful only those armed resistance movements that represent the affected population and can credibly point to a popular mandate, for instance, because the armed resistance movement grew out of a broad nonviolent resistance movement. As already observed by Emmer de Vattel, the judgment on whether to launch an armed struggle against a tyrannical government "can only be passed by the nation, or by a body which represents it."[197]

The resistance movement has to be driven by the intent to defend the victims, end the mass atrocities and improve the human rights situation.[198] Armed groups that follow an agenda to establish a government as tyrannical as that of the government they are fighting could not claim a right to resistance.

In assessing proportionality, the chances of the armed struggle of successfully stopping or at least mitigating the mass atrocities must be taken into account.[199] Plunging the country into a fully-fledged armed conflict without a discernible chance of success would be disproportional. In such cases, the resistance would have to resign itself to sporadic shows of force that do not trigger large-scale civilian losses, but still keep the flame of resistance alive until a more opportune moment arises to launch a fully-fledged campaign. However, the immediate victims of mass atrocities should always have a right to use any level of organized force, where this is the last resort to save their lives, even if the chances of success are slim.

Means of violence outlawed under international law, in particular serious violations of international humanitarian law, are always disproportional in an

196. Cf. Missling, *supra* note 59, p. 261.

197. Vattel, The Law of Nations, *supra* note 44, p. 106 [Bk. I, Ch. 4 § 51]. See also Dunér, *supra* note 104, pp. 260–261.

198. Kälin & Künzli, *supra* note 107, p. 53; Dunér, *supra* note 104, p. 260; Keenan, *supra* note 104, p. 27.

199. Keenan, *id.*, p. 28; Goertzel, *supra* note 59, p. 9; Marcuse, *supra* note 191, p. 140. The German Federal Supreme Court made the same point in relation to the legitimacy of resistance under German law. See Bundesgerichtshof, Judgment of 21 November 1958, Case No. IV ZR/58, Juristenzeitung 1958, 770, at p. 771.

armed struggle against mass atrocities, because they negate the very ends for which the armed resistance is the means.[200] A resistance movement that incorporates such means into its strategy could therefore never be considered lawful, regardless of the merits of its cause. Insisting on this requirement also creates an incentive for compliance with international humanitarian law, which does not yet exist under the legal status quo according to which even rebels with a cause may be criminalized regardless of whether their campaign respects international humanitarian law at all times.

Seen together, the requirements emerging from a consistent application of the right to self-defense to the case of resistance are very onerous. Few, if any, contemporary rebel groups would live up to them. And herein lies exactly the value of a right to resistance that is properly defined: it will identify the rare cases in which armed resistance against mass atrocities is legitimate and hence lawful, while exposing the other cases as not deserving of international legal recognition. There will always be armed groups, and states friendly with them, that will seek to twist the facts to fit the indicated criteria of lawful resistance, just as almost any state involved in an international armed conflict will claim to be the one acting in self-defense. However, the present situation—where no legal criteria exist to assess the lawfulness of organized armed resistance and where legitimacy is entirely a matter of political argument—leaves even more room for undeserving pretenders to take up the mantel of legitimate resistance.

IV. Legal implications of a right to resist mass atrocities

The value of recognizing a right to organized armed resistance has been called into doubt because international law as it stands is already neutral on rebellions against autocratic governments and does not prohibit them.[201] Some have also questioned whether recognition of a right to resistance may raise false expectations among the victims, who will risk their lives in asserting a right that will not be respected.[202]

It is true that a government that callously subjects its own population to mass atrocities will not honor a right of resistance against these very atrocities and will continue to treat the resistance fighters as criminals. However, recognition of the lawfulness of armed struggle is still significant in a number of other respects.

First of all, international recognition of the legality of armed resistance sends an important political signal to the state, the resistance movement and its supporters, and the general population. Non-international armed conflicts are usually struggles for legitimacy, not least since military success for either

200. Marcuse, *supra* note 191, p. 141; Murphy, *supra* note 104, p. 110. Cf. *supra* note 125.

201. See also d'Aspremont, *supra* note 102, p. 310.

202. Cohn, *supra* note 29, p. 512; Tomuschat, *supra* note 59, p. 20.

side depends on winning the hearts and minds of the population. It is therefore important whether the international community and international law consider them legal or not.

Second, a significant value of the right to resistance also lies in it being available, as opposed to actually invoked. The authorities may think twice before engaging in mass atrocities if they know the international community will consider resistance to be lawful.[203] By the same token, opposition groups have an incentive not to launch an armed struggle that would not meet the criteria of lawful resistance which could therefore not claim the legitimacy provided by international law. Thus, a carefully delineated right to resistance can actually curb violence.

Third, the regime responsible for the atrocities may not be in power forever, because of internal political reforms, the death of the regime's leader, or the resistance movement's success in toppling it. In such cases, resistance fighters who were punished for their participation in the rebellion, or their surviving families, have a legitimate interest in their formal legal rehabilitation and related reparation for their wrongs. If their rebellion was lawful under international law, they would have a right to such treatment and the government could not merely provide them with an amnesty, in line with the hortatory Article 6(2) of the Second Geneva Protocol, or with no remedy at all.

Fourth, a right to resistance would entail important obligations for third states. They would not be allowed to cooperate in the prosecution and punishment of resistance fighters (unless they had committed international crimes) even if the prosecuting state were to guarantee fair trials and humane punishment. In particular, third states would not be allowed to extradite suspects. Most extradition treaties contain political offense exceptions, which allow the third state to deny extradition for offenses such as treason. However, states retain considerable discretion in defining what political offenses are not subject to extradition.[204] If there is a right to resistance, this would entail a firm legal duty not to extradite fighters and other supporters of a lawful resistance movement on charges related to mere participation in the resistance.[205]

Fifth, the right to resistance would have an impact on the granting of refugee status. Under Article 1F(b) of the 1951 Convention on the Status of Refugees, refugee status can be denied if the person has committed a serious non-political crime. People who merely participated in an armed struggle lawful under international law cannot be considered as having engaged in any crime. Thus, the receiving state cannot exclude them from refugee status on this ground, for instance, by categorizing their armed engagement as non-political domestic

203. See also Honoré, *supra* note 55, p. 39.

204. Cf. Kälin & Künzli, *supra* note 107, p. 65.

205. See also Schwartz, *supra* note 59, p. 260 & 306; Saul, *supra* note 59, p. 192. Historically, the political offense exception was often understood as an instrument to protect those who had resisted against oppressive regimes. See Missling, *supra* note 59, pp. 182–187 & 259.

terrorism.[206] However, resistance fighters could still be excluded under Article 1F(a) of the Refugee Convention if they committed war crimes or crimes against humanity.

Sixth, third states would be barred from providing other states with troops, weapons, intelligence information, or other support for fighting a group waging a lawful struggle against mass atrocities—in the same way that third states may not support the suppression of national liberation movements fighting for self-determination.[207] Under existing international law, states are already precluded from providing weapons for the purpose of committing mass atrocities.[208] However, weapons suppliers can still make a fine distinction between weapons used to carry out the actual atrocities and weapons used to fight the rebellion. If the resistance was lawful, there would no longer be room for this distinction.

Seventh, a right to resistance would affect international sanctions practices. Armed resistance movements that wage a lawful struggle against mass atrocities should not be subjected to travel bans and financial sanctions due to their engagement in the struggle. Sanctions could be imposed only if the group exceeded the bounds of lawful resistance, notably if it engaged in international crimes or resorted to activities recognized as criminal under international law, such as drug or human trafficking, to finance themselves.

The issue of the lawfulness of sanctions in a mass atrocity context arose before the ICJ when it had to consider provisional measures in the *Bosnian Genocide* case. The question was whether the Security Council was under an obligation to amend the weapons embargo that it had imposed on all of Yugoslavia, given that the embargo prevented the Bosnians from arming themselves to resist Serb atrocities, while the Serbs had access to ample weapons from Yugoslav army stocks. While the court declined to address the issue, given that it had jurisdiction only to consider provisional measures against Serbia,[209] the issue was taken up by Judge Lauterpacht in a separate opinion. Lauterpacht held that the embargo violated an *ius cogens* obligation to prevent genocide:

> [T]he inability of Bosnia-Herzegovina sufficiently strongly to fight back against the Serbs and effectively to prevent the implementation of the Serbian policy of ethnic cleansing is at least in part directly attributable to the fact that Bosnia-Herzegovina's access to weapons and equipment has been severely limited by the embargo. Viewed in this light, the Security Council resolution

206. See also Kälin & Künzli, *id.*, p. 77.

207. Cf. *supra* note 129.

208. Application of the Genocide Convention (Bosnia and Herzegovina v. Serbia and Montenegro) [Merits], *supra* note 170, at p. 223 [para. 432]; Andrew Clapham, Weapons and Armed Non-State Actors, Stuart Casey-Maslen (ed.), Weapons under International Human Rights Law, Cambridge University Press: Cambridge (2014), 163–196, at p. 164.

209. See Application of the Genocide Convention (Bosnia and Herzegovina v. Serbia and Montenegro) [Further Provisional Measures] ICJ Rep. 1993, 325 (Sept. 13), at p. 345 [para. 41].

> can be seen as having in effect called on Members of the United Nations, albeit unknowingly and assuredly unwillingly, to become in some degree supporters of the genocidal activity of the Serbs and in this manner and to that extent to act contrary to a rule of jus cogens.[210]

Lauterpacht invokes the inability of the state of Bosnia and Herzegovina to defend its Muslim citizens against atrocities carried out by ethnic Serb citizens. However, the case against the weapons embargo is similar to that for the period before the Bosnian forces were representing a recognized state, if one assumes that they had a right to "fight back" against ethnic cleansing and genocide in accordance with a right to resist mass atrocities.[211]

V. No justification of unilateral humanitarian interventions

Some have claimed that a right to armed resistance would also justify unilateral military interventions to stop the atrocities, that is, so-called humanitarian interventions. If people have a right to defend themselves against atrocities, the argument goes, then others, namely third states, have such a right as well.[212] Others cite this claimed consequence as an argument against recognizing a right to resist mass atrocities in light of the risk for the prohibition on the use of force under Article 2(4) of the U.N. Charter that any right of unilateral intervention would entail.[213]

However, both camps fail to take into account the crucial distinction between state and personal self-defense. The right to resist mass atrocities is grounded in the right to personal self-defense, because it seeks to defend individual rights. It can therefore justify infringing on the human rights of others, namely of the security forces and, to some degree, of innocent bystanders. However, unlike the right to interstate self-defense under Article 51 of the U.N. Charter, it could not

210. *Id.*, Sep. Op. Lauterpacht, at p. 441 [para. 103].

211. Arguing that embargoes denying weapons to genocide victims are unlawful, Kopel, Gallant & Eisen, *supra* note 145, pp. 1345–1346. See also Remarks by Claus Kreß, Proceedings of the Annual Meeting (American Society of International Law), vol. 108 (April 2014), pp. 326–331, at p. 329, arguing that international law permits the provision of arms to a rebel movement which was formed in defense of a civilian population under lethal attack by its government, and which enjoys wide international recognition as being representative of this civilian population. For the contrary position, see Remarks by Sean Murphy, *id.*, 331–333; Remarks by Christine Chinkin, *id.*, pp. 333–336. In the present author's view weapons embargoes are not a clear-cut case, comparable to other sanctions, given that the unilateral provision of weapons by third states, raises the question of intervention discussed in this Seventh Chapter: E.V (pp. 341–343).

212. Ohlin, *supra* note 145, p. 143; Doehring, *supra* note 54, p. 563. See also Kreß, *supra* note 143, p. 41.

213. Dunér, *supra* note 104, pp. 258–259; Shany, *supra* note 149, p. 549; Frowein, *supra* note 132, p. 214.

justify the infringement of sovereignty caused by a military intervention of third states.[214] Personal and interstate self-defense cannot simply be equated to justify unilateral humanitarian intervention, not least since the benefits of unilateral intervention may be outweighed by the risks for global peace and international security that is created by the military involvement of third states.[215] In the contemporary international legal order, the Security Council is mandated to calibrate such benefits and risks.[216] In the case of humanitarian interventions, only a Security Council mandate, issued in application of the responsibility to protect, can therefore authorize infringement of state sovereignty.[217]

The right to defend against mass atrocities still has normative value vis-à-vis outside interventions in mass atrocities—but only in relation to multilateral, U.N.-approved interventions. It justifies why and to what extent a multilateral intervention that is duly authorized by the Security Council may take lives to defend lives and it provides criteria for the use of force for that purpose. It therefore informs the content of the emerging doctrine of the "responsibility while protecting," which seeks to establish how the responsibility to protect can be implemented with the least negative impact to human rights and the international legal order.[218] Furthermore, if the responsibility to protect is ever invoked to justify the provision of assistance to resistance movements, the right to defend against mass atrocities will provide normative criteria on what type of assistance should be provided to whom.[219]

214. Tomuschat warns in this respect that one cannot transpose conclusions from self-defense at the interpersonal level to the interstate level, not least since foreign unilateral intervention poses risks.

215. Christian Tomuschat, Humanitäre Intervention—Ein Trojanisches Pferd?, in: Herfried Münkler & Karsten Malowitz (eds.), Humanitäre Intervention: Ein Instrument außenpolitischer Konfliktbearbeitung, Verlag für Sozialwissenschaften: Wiesbaden (2008), 65–88, at p. 82.

216. *Id.*

217. See also World Summit Outcome, *supra* note 175, para. 139; United Kingdom Foreign Office, Policy Document No. 148, British Yearbook of International Law, vol. 57 (1986), 614–620, at p. 619; Bruno Simma, NATO, the UN and the Use of Force: Legal Aspects, European Journal of International Law, vol. 10 (1999), 1–22, at p. 5; Ryan Goodman, Humanitarian Intervention and Pretexts for War, American Journal of International Law, vol. 100 (2006), 107–141, at pp. 108–109.

218. On the responsibility while protecting, see Letter from the Permanent Representative of Brazil to the United Nations addressed to the Secretary-General, U.N. Doc. A/66/551-S/2011/701 (2011), annex.

219. For instance, assistance to armed resistance movements would not live up to the criterion of necessity if there are non-violent resistance movements whose campaigns can remain effective with international support. Armed resistance movements whose strategy relies on violations of international humanitarian law would be automatically be disqualified from assistance, as resistance of that kind is per se disproportional. For further discussion of relevant considerations, see also Mégret, *supra* note 177, 589–591.

The position taken here is not at odds with has been said about outside intervention in wars of national liberation against denials of self-determinations.[220] In the case of self-determination, a number of states are willing to concede only a right to provide military assistance to national liberation movements, but not a right to intervene with their own military forces. And even this guarded legal position is heavily contested by a number of other states. Furthermore, wars of national liberation are special in that they very often involve peoples who represent states *in nascendi*. They therefore combine elements of both interstate and personal self-defense.[221] Therefore the right to resist denials of self-determination can more readily explain infringements of sovereignty by third states than a right to resist mass atrocities could, as the latter is based solely on personal self-defense.

Ohlin has argued that at least the case of genocide is similar to that of self-determination, since in both cases there is a collective right of a whole people at stake; in the case of genocide, the right of a people to exist. He contends that humanitarian intervention by third states to stop genocide ought to be regarded as a case of Article 51 of the U.N. Charter since that provision is really grounded in a right of defense of nations or peoples, which was then transposed to the states representing such nations.[222] However, even if one were to concede the transposition theory, the fact remains that the prohibition of genocide protects not only a people representing an entire nation but any distinctive national, ethnic, racial, or religious group.[223] Indeed, in the history of the 20th Century, genocides have generally targeted minority groups within a state, rather than peoples representing an entire nation. Even with a very generous reading of Article 51, minority groups cannot be equated with nations and hence with states. Therefore, no justification of unilateral humanitarian intervention can be derived from a right to defend others, even in the case of genocide.

F. CONCLUSION: A RIGHT TO RESISTANCE ONLY IN EXCEPTIONAL CIRCUMSTANCES

Rights of resistance find their roots in the victims' human rights, interpreted in accordance with the right to personal self-defense as a general principle of law. Forcible resistance can also be understood as an exercise of the right to an effective remedy for human rights violations where no effective remedy can be directly obtained from the state authorities. However, international law recognizes a right to resist state authorities only in exceptional circumstances, because states have a legitimate interest to preserve their authority and monopoly on the

220. See this Seventh Chapter: D.III (p. 323).

221. See this Seventh Chapter: D.I (p. 320).

222. Ohlin, *supra* note 145, p. 142.

223. See Convention on the Prevention and Punishment of the Crime of Genocide, art. 2.

use of force, as this forms the basis for the rule of law and effective protection of human rights.

At the individual level, human rights entitle persons to use necessary and proportional force against present or imminent human rights violations by the state that pose a real risk of serious and irreparable harm. In particular, resistance is lawful against extrajudicial killings, torture, and inhuman treatment. Conversely, there is no right to resist arbitrary arrest and detention in states where the rule of law and related due process rights are otherwise upheld. Victims of such violations have to assert their rights through the appropriate judicial processes.

In times of armed conflict, civilians may collectively defend themselves against war crimes and other international crimes without losing their protected status under international humanitarian law. They must not be prosecuted or otherwise punished for exercising such collective self-defense, nor may they be targeted as if they were combatants. However, collective self-defense has limits that emerge from the general requirement of self-defense and international humanitarian law. In particular, civilian defense groups must not directly participate in the hostilities. This would notably be the case if they defended combatants or military objectives from attack. They also lose their protected status where they achieve such a degree of military organization and capacity that they must be considered an organized armed group participating in the conflict.

At the level of military organized armed resistance, it is widely considered that international law recognizes a right of peoples to wage an armed struggle to defend against forcible denial of their right to self-determination through colonial domination, unlawful alien occupation, and racist regimes. However, force must be used only as a last resort within the bounds of necessity, proportionality, and international humanitarian law.

There would be good reasons to recognize a right of militarily organized armed resistance against the mass atrocities of genocides, crimes against humanity, and widespread war crimes. Through the rigorous application of self-defense requirements, this right could be reasonably framed to distinguish legitimate uprisings from illegitimate rebellions through the use of international law. However, state practice does not yet recognize such a right. Instead, international law is neutral on rebellions against oppressive states, neither prohibiting nor allowing them.

8

The Right to Personal Self-Defense in a *Rechtsstaat*—Final Reflections

The state's monopoly on the use of force, the rule of law, and respect for human rights form the pillars underpinning what German legal philosophy calls the *Rechtsstaat,* that is, a state where law and justice reign supreme.[1] The right to personal self-defense has an ambivalent relationship with all three pillars of that edifice. On the one hand, self-defense forms the capstone that makes realization of these values possible. Individuals will accept the state monopoly on the use of force only if they maintain the right to defend themselves where the state cannot do so. The right to personal self-defense also helps to uphold the rule of law and protect human rights in those situations where state authorities and the legal process cannot offer protection. Because of these central functions, it is a shared feature of various natural law traditions and the major domestic legal systems of the world. In international law, it finds recognition as a general principle of law recognized by nations and amounts to an individual right sui generis.

On the other hand, assertions of self-defense can pose a threat to the foundations of the *Rechtsstaat*. Excessive self-help can unravel the rule of law, negate the state's claim to a monopoly on power and violate the right to life, the most fundamental of all human rights. The challenge therefore lies in calibrating the right so as to maximize its positive impact, while limiting its disruptive impact. More than a century ago, the famous British jurist A.V. Dicey (1835–1922) summed up the challenge as follows:

> [T]he rule which fixes the limit to the right of [self-defense] must, from the nature of things, be a compromise between the necessity, on the one hand, of allowing every citizen to maintain his rights against wrongdoers, and the necessity, on the other hand, of suppressing private warfare. Discourage

1. The term *Rechtsstaat* does not have an exact translation in the English language. Often equated with the English "rule of law," it represents broader ideals. It not only refers to the supremacy of the law but also encapsulates values of substantive justice and gives greater emphasis to the state as the guarantor of law and justice.

Human Rights and Personal Self-Defense in International Law. Jan Arno Hessbruegge

> self-help, and loyal subjects become the slaves of ruffians. Over-stimulate self-assertion, and for the arbitrament of the Courts you substitute the decision of the sword or the revolver.[2]

Today, international human rights law plays a vital role in fixing the rules on personal self-defense, not least since it recognizes that Dicey's "ruffians" who abuse the rights of loyal subjects may also wear state uniforms. For this reason, human rights law entitles citizens to defend themselves against human rights violations at the hands of state agents, where such violations pose a real risk of serious and irreparable harm. To curb state abuses of power, human rights law also places a number of procedural and substantive requirements on the right of law enforcement agents to defend themselves and others. These requirements have to be strict, given that the right to personal self-defense is the sole ground recognized under international human rights law that allows police to shoot to kill or to use other types of deliberately lethal force.

Reaching into the private sphere, international human rights law also establishes minimum standards to keep domestic laws governing self-defense between private persons within reasonable bounds that respect the human rights of victims, perpetrators and innocent bystanders, while preserving the rule of law and the state's monopoly on the use of force. This dimension will only gain in significance as power is shifting from the state to the private sphere. To some extent, this power shift is driven by the weakness of state institutions. Also in play are market-oriented philosophies, which claim that the private sector will be more efficient in covering many traditionally public functions. This power shift can also be observed in the security sector, where the role and influence of private security companies has grown steadily. The privatization of security marks a serious problem for the poor who cannot afford to pay for their own security, adding yet another layer to the discrimination that has made many among them poor in the first place. Furthermore, the rise of private security companies erodes the state's monopoly on the use of force because they are armed, organized, and trained to use force. Since private security companies usually do not assume law enforcement functions, but rely chiefly on the right to self-defense to justify use of force, it becomes even more relevant from a human rights perspective to ensure that self-defense in the private sphere is appropriately regulated and that excesses result in accountability.

The basic criteria of self-defense are the same whether self-defense is exercised by state authorities against private persons, by private persons against state authorities, or between private persons. Necessary and proportional force may be used to defend against an ongoing or imminent unlawful attack. Notable similarities extend across very different contexts; for instance, preemptive killings cannot be justified as self-defense in light of international human rights law,

2. Albert V. Dicey, Introduction to the Study of the Law of the Constitution, MacMillan and Co.: London/New York (3rd ed., 1889), p. 406 [Appendix Note III].

regardless of whether they involve law enforcement agents pre-emptively killing dangerous criminals or victims of intra-family violence preemptively killing their habitual abusers before they can strike again.

Any violations of *ius cogens* are per se disproportional and hence not justifiable as self-defense. The state cannot invoke defense of life as a justification to torture suspected kidnappers in the hope of forcing them to reveal life-saving information. By the same token, national liberation movements cannot justify taking hostages or violating other intransgressible principles of international humanitarian law as a means to defend their people's right to self-determination against oppressive states.

However, there are also significant differences across contexts, depending on whether self-defense is exercised by state agents or by private persons. These differences are linked to the monopoly on the use of force. For instance, state agents have no duty to retreat to avoid using force in self-defense, because they represent the state and its monopoly on the use of force. Conversely, human rights prohibit legalizing lethal self-defense by private persons who could instead safely retreat from the threat. Due to the state's monopoly on the use of force, law enforcement can also be expected to have better means and situational sensitivity than private persons to handle security threats. This is why they have to take much more precautions than the average private person to minimize the use of defensive force, for instance, by employing less lethal weapons and de-escalation strategies.

The right to personal self-defense, if framed in accordance with international human rights law, thus plays a significant role in regulating violence and power relations in a *Rechtsstaat*, where law and justice reign supreme. By contrast, international law, as it stands, fails to give due recognition to the right to self-defense vis-à-vis an *Unrechtsstaat*, where serious injustice prevails. Even where such a state subjects its population to mass atrocities amounting to genocide, crimes against humanity, or war crimes, the victims have, at present, no right under international law to engage in militarily organized armed resistance, even though this is where such a right is most necessary. Self-defense by affected citizens as the remedy of last resort against the concentrated power of the state machinery committing such atrocities can often be effective only if it takes the form of organized armed resistance. Yet positive international law, as practiced by states, does not recognize a right of organized armed resistance even in such extreme cases. Instead, the prevailing view in international law recognizes a right to resistance (as a last resort and using only lawful means of force) only in the exceedingly rare cases of colonial domination, unlawful occupation, or racist regimes forcibly denying a people their human right to self-determination. By not recognizing a narrowly tailored right of last resort to resist mass atrocities, international law misses an opportunity to construct a *ius ad bellum* for non-international armed conflict that gives legal recognition to legitimate uprisings and at the same time forms a *ius contra bellum* that delegitimizes rebels without a cause.

Among the latter group of illegitimate insurgents are all groups that resort to terrorist tactics. Since these means are categorically outlawed under international law, their users automatically disqualify themselves from advancing any claim of legitimate self-defense—regardless of the merits of the cause they claim to espouse. At the same time, the absolute illegitimacy of terrorism does not give states a *carte blanche* to abandon fundamental human rights principles in its counterterrorism efforts. In particular, the right to personal self-defense cannot be invoked to trump peremptory human rights law. A claim that lives may be at stake cannot justify the torture of suspected terrorists even if it could (theoretically) prevent a deadly attack. Nor can a claim to defend life against future attacks justify the preemptive targeted killing of suspected terrorists outside the context of armed conflict. States increasingly evade the latter restriction by framing counterterrorism efforts as pertaining to an open-ended armed conflict. In light of the worsening scale and nature of the terrorist threat, the proposition that fighting terrorism often crosses the threshold into non-international armed conflict cannot be dismissed. However, it carries significant risks. In order to protect the *Rechtsstaat*, which guarantees the very way of life attacked by terrorism, in such never-ending wars, some moderating features of the law enforcement paradigm—for instance, the requirement to use only the minimal force necessary to neutralize a threat—should be incorporated into the international humanitarian law applicable to non-international conflicts. Such progressive development of international law would not only be sensible, but also further increase the practical significance of the jurisprudence on the right to personal self-defense and its limits of necessity and proportionality.

Bibliography

Abi Saab, Georges, Wars of National Liberation in the Geneva Conventions and Protocols, Recueil descours de l'Academie de la Haye, vol. 165 (1979), 353–445

Abuznaid, Ahmad et al., "Stand Your Ground" Laws: International Human Rights Law Implications, University of Miami Law Review, vol. 68 (2013–2014), 1129–1170

Akehurst, Michael, Equity and General Principles of Law, The International and Comparative Law Quarterly, vol. 25 (1976), 801–825

Alesina, Alberto et al., Political instability and economic growth, Journal of Economic Growth, vol. 1(2) (1996), 189–211

Ambos, Kai, Defenses in international criminal law, in: Bretram S. Brown (ed.), Research handbook on international criminal law, Elgar: Cheltenham et al. (2011), 299–329

———, May a State Torture Suspects to Save the Life of Innocents?, Journal of International Criminal Justice, vol. 8 (2008), 261–287

———, Other Grounds for Excluding Criminal Responsibility, in: Antonio Cassese, Paola Gaeta & John R.W.D. Jones (eds.), The Rome Statute of the International Criminal Court: A Commentary, vol. I, Oxford University Press: Oxford (2002), 984–1029

American Bar Association, National Task Force on Stand your Ground Laws: Final Report and Recommendations, September 2015, http://www.americanbar.org/content/dam/aba/images/diversity/SYG_Report_Book.pdf

———, Stand your Ground Resolution (112), February 2015, http://www.americanbar.org/content/dam/aba/images/abanews/2015mm_hodres/112.pdf

Amnesty International, Policing Demonstrations in the European Union, October 2012, http://www.amnesty.org.uk/sites/default/files/eu-police.pdf

———, Report 2014/15: United States of America, https://www.amnesty.org/en/countries/americas/united-states-of-america/report-united-states-of-america/

———, Use of Force: Guidelines for the Implementation of the UN Basic Principles on the Use of Force of Force and Firearms by Law Enforcement Officials, Amnesty International Dutch Section: Amsterdam (2015)

Human Rights and Personal Self-Defense in International Law. Jan Arno Hessbruegge

——, You killed my son: Homicides by military police in the city of Rio de Janeiro, 3 August 2015, https://www.amnesty.org/en/documents/amr19/2068/2015/en/

Amore, Christopher D., Rules of Engagement: Balancing the (Inherent) Right and Obligation of Self-Defense with the Prevention of Civilian Casualties, National Security Law Journal, vol. 1 (2013), 39–76

Anderson, Kenneth, Targeted Killing and Drone Warfare: How We Came to Debate Whether There Is a "Legal Geography of War," 2011, http://media.hoover.org/sites/default/files/documents/FutureChallenges_Anderson.pdf

——, Targeted Killing in US Counterterrorism Strategy and Law, 2009, http://www.brookings.edu/papers/2009/0511_counterterrorism_anderson.aspx

Anderson, Kjell, The Universality of War: Jus ad Bellum and the Right to Peace in Non-International Armed Conflicts, in: David Keane & Yvonne McDermott (eds.), The Challenge of Human Rights: Past, Present and Future, Edward Elgar: Cheltenham/Northampton (2012), 52–73

Aneja, Abhay; Donohue, John J. III & Zhang, Alexandria, The Impact of Right to Carry Laws and the NRC Report: The Latest Lessons for the Empirical Evaluation of Law and Policy, Stanford Law and Economics Olin Working Paper No. 461, September 2014, http://papers.ssrn.com/sol3/papers.cfm?abstract_id=2443681

Aquinas, Thomas, Summa theologiae, vol. II (transl. by fathers of the English Dominican Province), Benziger Bros: New York (1947)

Arbour, J.-Maurice & Parent, Geneviève, Droit International Public, Editions Yvons Blais: Montreal (6th ed., 2012)

Aristotle, Rhetoric (ed. W.D. Ross, transl. W. Rhys Roberts), Cosimo: New York (2010)

Arzt, Clemens, Europäische Menschenrechtskonvention und polizeilicher Todesschuss, Deutsche öffentliche Verwaltung (DöV) (2007), 230–237

Ashworth, Andrew, Four Threats to the Presumption of Innocence, South African Law Journal, vol. 123 (2006), 63–97

——, Self-Defence and the Human Right to Life, Cambridge Law Journal, vol. 34 (1975), 282–307

——, The European Convention and the Criminal Law, in: Jack Beatson & Tony Smith (eds.), The Human Rights Act and the Criminal Justice and Regulatory Process, Hart Publishing: Oxford (1999), 37–44

——, The Human Rights Act and the substantive criminal law: a non-minimalist view, Criminal Law Review 2000, 564–567

Association of Prosecuting Attorneys, Castle Doctrine Expansion Chart, 2012, https://prosecutingattorneys.org/wp-content/uploads/Castle-Doctrine-Expansion-Chart-10.20121.pdf

——, Statement of Principles regarding Expansions to the Castle Doctrine, 2012, https://prosecutingattorneys.org/wp-content/uploads/APA-Castle-Doctrine-Principles1.pdf

Ate, Bassey E., Terrorism in the Context of Decolonization, in: Hans Köchler (ed.) Terrorism and National Liberation, Peter Lang: Frankfurt a.M./Bern/New York (1988), 79–93

Augustine, On Free Choice of the Will (trans. Thomas Williams), Hackett: Indianapolis (1993)

Bailey, James E. et al., Risk factors for violent death of women in the Home, Archives of Internal Medicine, vol. 157 (1997), 777–782

Bakircioglu, Onder, The Right to Self-Defense in National and International Law: The Role of the Imminence Requirement, Indiana International & Comparative Law Review, vol. 19 (2009), 1–48

Bamgbose, Olatokunbo John, Digest of Judgments of the Supreme Court of Nigeria: vol. 1 & 2, Safari Books: Ibadan (2013)

Bangalore, Sripal & Messerli, Franz H., Gun Ownership and Firearm-related Deaths, American Journal of Medicine, vol. 126 (2013), 873–876

Bantekas, Ilias & Oette, Lutz, International Human Rights Law and Practice, Cambridge University Press: Cambridge (2013)

Barney, Stephen A. et al. (eds.), The Etymologies of Isidore of Seville, Cambridge University Press: New York (2006)

Bauer, Fritz, Ungehorsam und Widerstand in Geschichte und Gegenwart, Vorgänge, vol. 8–9/1968, 286–292

Bayani, Chaloka, Reconstituting the universal: human rights as a regional idea, in: Conor Gearty & Costas Douzinas (eds.), The Cambridge Companion to Human Rights Law Cambridge University Press: Cambridge (2012), 173–190

Beale, Joseph H., Retreat from a Murderous Assault, Harvard Law Review, vol. 16 (1903), 567–582

Beaumont, John S., Self-Defence as a Justification for Disregarding Diplomatic Immunity, Canadian Yearbook of International Law, vol. 29 (1991), 391–402

Bellamy, Alex J., No Pain, No Gain? Torture and. Ethics in the War on Terror, International Affairs, vol. 82 (2006), 121–148

Ben Barka, Habiba & Ncube, Mthuli, Political Fragility in Africa: Are Military Coups d'Etat a Never-Ending Phenomenon?, African Development Bank: Abidjan (2012)

Bentham, Jeremy, Theory of Legislation, Vol. II, (ed. Richard Hildreth), Weeks, Jordan & Company: Boston (1840)

Berner, Albrecht Friedrich, Die Notwehrtheorie, Archiv des Criminalrechts, vol. 29 (1848), 547–598

Bin Cheng, General Principles of Law as Applied by International Courts and Tribunals, Cambridge University Press: Cambridge (1953)

Biot, Edouard, Le Tcheou-Li ou Rites des Tchéou, vol. 2, Imprimerie nationale: Paris (1851)

Bitzilekis, Nikolaos, Die neue Tendenz zur Einschränkung des Notwehrrechts, Duncker & Humblot: Berlin (1984)

Blackstone, William, Commentaries on the Laws of England, vol. 3, Clarendon Press: Oxford (1769)

———, Commentaries on the Laws of England, vol. 4, Clarendon Press: Oxford (1769)

Blain, Peter, Scientific and medical assessment of new weapons for law enforcement: Issues that would be raised by "incapacitating chemical agents", in: ICRC,

Expert Meeting: "Incapacitating Chemical Agents"—Law Enforcement, Human Rights Law and Policy, ICRC: Geneva (2013), 30–33

Blank, Laurie R., The use of force against pirates, in: Michael P. Scharf, Michael A. Newton & Milena Sterio (eds.), Prosecuting Maritime Piracy: Domestic Solutions to International Crimes, Cambridge University Press: New York (2015), 103–118

Bobo, Jason W., Following the Trend: Alabama Abandons the Duty to Retreat and Encourages Citizens to Stand their Ground, Cumberland Law Review vol. 38 (2007–2008), 339–369

Bockelmann, Paul, Menschenrechtskonvention und Notwehrrecht, in: Paul Bockelmann, Arthur Kaufmann & Ulrich Klug (eds.), Festschrift für Karl Engisch zum 70. Geburtstag, Vittorio Kostermann: Frankfurt am Main (1969), 456–467

Boddens Hosang, J.F.R., Self-Defense in Military Operations: The Interaction between the Legal Bases for Military Self-Defense and Rules of Engagement, The Military Law and the Law of War Review, vol. 47 (2008), 25–96

Bodin, Jean, Six Books of the Commonwealth (trans. M.J. Tooley), Blackwell: Oxford (1955)

Bodnar, Adam & Pacho, Irmina, Targeted Killings (Drone Strikes) and the European Convention on Human Rights, Polish Yearbook of International Law, vol. 32 (2012), 189–208

Bouloc, Bernard, Droit pénal général, Dalloz: Paris (21st ed., 2009)

Boyle, C.K., The concept of arbitrary deprivation of life, in: Bertrand Ramcharan (ed.), The Right to Life in International Law, Martinus Nijhoff: Dordrecht (1985), 221–244

Branas, Charles C. et al., Investigating the Link between Gun Possession and Gun Assault, American Journal of Public Health, vol. 99 (2009), 2034–2040

Brietzke, Paul, Murder and Manslaughter in Malawi's Traditional Courts, Journal of African Law, vol. 18(1) (1974), 37–56

Brincat, Shannon K., "Death to Tyrants": The political philosophy of tyrannicide—Part I, Journal of International Political Theory, vol. 4(2) (2008), 212–240

Bruce, David, Beyond Section 49: Control of the use of lethal force, South African Crime Quarterly, vol. 36 (2011), 3–12

Brugger, Winfried, Vom unbedingten Verbot der Folter zum bedingten Recht auf Folter?, JuristenZeitung 2000, 165–173

Bühler, Georg (ed.), The Laws of Manu, Library of Alexandria: Los Angeles (1964)

Burlamaqui, Jean Jacques, Principes du droit naturel et politique, vol.1, Barrillot: Geneva (1747)

———, Principes du Droit politique: ou second volume du droit naturel, Geneva (1754) [no identified publisher]

Busch, Werner, Die Entstehung der kritischen Rechtsphilosophie Kants, De Gruyter: Berlin/New York (1979)

Buxton, Richard, The Human Rights Act and the Substantive Criminal Law, Criminal Law Review 2000, 331–340

Calvin, John, Institutes of the Christian Religion (trans. Henry Beveridge), Christian Classics Ethereal Library: Grand Rapids, MI (2002)

Cameron, Lindsey & Chetail, Vincent, Privatizing War: Private Military and Security Companies under Public International Law, Cambridge University Press: Cambridge et al. (2013)

Campbell, Jacquelyn C. et al., Risk factors for femicide in abusive relationships: results from a multi-site case control study, American Journal of Public Health, vol. 93 (2003), 1089–1097

Campbell Moriarty, Jane, While Dangers Gather: The Bush Pre-emption Doctrine, Battered Women, Imminence, and Anticipatory Self-Defense, New York University Review of Law and Social Change, vol. 30 (2005), 1–33

Camus, Albert, L'homme révolté, Gallimard: Paris (1951)

Canosa Usera, Raúl; Fix Zamudio, Héctor & Corzo Sosa, Edgar, El Derecho a la Integridad Personal, in: Javier García Roca et al. (eds.), El Diálogo entre los sistemas Europeo y Americano de Derechos Humanos, Civitas/Thomson Reuters: Cizur Menor (2012), 138–185

Casey-Maslen, Stuart, Crowd management, crowd control, and riot control, in: Stuart Casey-Maslen (ed.), Weapons under International Human Rights Law Cambridge University Press: Cambridge (2014), 53–70

———, The use of weapons in armed conflict, in: Stuart Casey-Maslen (ed.), Weapons under International Human Rights Law Cambridge University Press: Cambridge (2014), 240–281

———, The use of weapons in law enforcement, in: Stuart Casey-Maslen (ed.), Weapons under International Human Rights Law Cambridge University Press: Cambridge (2014), 3–31

Cassese, Antonio, Self-Determination of Peoples, Cambridge University Press (1995)

———, Terrorism and Human Rights, American University Law Review, vol. 31 (1982), 945–958

———, The Statute of the International Criminal Court: Some Preliminary Reflections, European Journal of International Law vol. 10 (1999), 144–171

———, The Various Aspects of the Right to Self-Defence, in: Graduate Institute of International Studies (Geneva), Small Arms Survey 2004: Rights at Risk, Oxford University Press: Oxford (2004), 181

———, Under What Conditions May Belligerents Be Acquitted of the Crime of Attacking an Ambulance?, Journal of International Criminal Justice, vol. 6 (2) (2008), 385–397

———, Wars of national liberation and humanitarian law, in: Christophe Swinarski (ed.), Etudes et essais sur le droit international humanitaire et sur les principes de la Croix-Rouge—en honneur de Jean Pictet, Martinus Nijhoff Publishers: Leiden (1984), 313–324

Cassese, Antonio et al., International Criminal Law: Cases and Commentary, Oxford University Press: Oxford (2011)

Catalfamo, Christine, Stand your Ground: Florida's Castle Doctrine for the Twenty-First Century, Rutgers Journal of Law & Public Policy, vol. 4 (2007), 504–545

Cathcart, Blaise, Application of Force and Rules of Engagement in Self-Defence Operations, in: Terry D. Gill & Dieter Fleck (eds.), Handbook of International Law of Military Operations, Oxford University Press: New York (2010), 201–210

Catholic Church, Catechism of the Catholic Church; Burns & Oates: London (2nd ed., 2002)

Cerone, John, Is there a Human Right of Self-Defense?, Journal of Law, Economics and Policy, vol. 2 (2006), 319–329

Chanock, Martin, Law Custom and Social Order: The Colonial Experience in Malawi and Zambia, Cambridge University Press: Cambridge (1985)

Charters, Justen, 13 Commanders-in-Chief and Where They Stood on Gun Rights, IJReview, August 2014, http://www.ijreview.com/2014/08/172102-u-s-presidents-throughout-history-2nd-amendment-supporters-gun-control-cheerleaders

Chen, Frederick Tse-shyang, The Confucian View of World Order, Indiana International and Comparative Law Review, vol. 1 (1991), 45–69

Cheng, Cheng & Hoekstra, Mark, Does Strengthening Self-Defense Law Deter Crime or Escalate Violence?: Evidence from Expansions to Castle Doctrine, Journal of Human Resources, vol. 48 (2013), 821–854

Chenoweth, Erica & Stephan, Maria J., Why Civil Resistance Works: The Strategic Logic of Non-Violent Conflict, Columbia University Press: New York (2011)

Childers, Andrew & Lamut, Anna, Legal Foundations for "Making Amends" to Civilians Harmed by Armed Conflict, International Human Rights Clinic, Harvard Law School, February 2012, http://hrp.law.harvard.edu/wp-content/uploads/2012/02/making-amends-foundations-paper-feb-2012-final.pdf

Cicero, Marcus Tullius, For T.A. Milo, in: C.D. Yonge (trans.), The Orations of Marcus Tullius Cicero, vol. 3, Henry G. Bohn: London (1852), 390–437

———, The Republic and The Laws (trans. C.D. Yonge), Digireads: Lawrence (2009)

Clapham, Andrew, Weapons and Armed Non-State Actors, in: Stuart Casey-Maslen (ed.), Weapons under International Human Rights Law, Cambridge University Press: Cambridge (2014), 163–196

Cleary, Thomas (ed.), Classics of Buddhism and Zen, vol. 5, Shambhala Publications: Boston (2002)

Cohn, Haim A., The Right and Duty of Resistance, Human Rights Journal, vol. 1 (1968), 491–517

Cook, Philip J. et al., The Gun Debate's New Mythical Number: How Many Defensive Uses per Year?, Journal of Policy Analysis and Management (1997), 463–469

Corn, Geoffrey S., Self-Defense Targeting: Blurring the line between the Jus ad Bellum and the Ius in Bello, in: Kenneth Watkin and Andrew J. Norris (eds.), Non-International Armed Conflict in the Twenty-First Century, Naval War College: Newport, Rhode Island (2012), 53–92

Cox, Katherine E., Beyond Self-Defense: United Nations Peacekeeping Operations & The Use of Force, Denver Journal of International Law and Policy, vol. 27 (1999), 239–273

Crawford, James, Brownlie's Principles of Public International Law, Oxford University Press: Oxford (8th ed., 2012)

Crawshaw, Ralph; Cullen, Stuart & Williamson, Tom, Human Rights and Policing, Martinus Nijhoff: Leiden/Boston (2nd ed., 2007)

d'Aspremont, Jean, Le Tyrannicide en Droit International, in: Christian Tomuschat, Evelyne Lagrange & Stefan Oeter (eds.), The Right to Life, Brill: Leiden (2010), 287–313

Da Legnano, Giovanni, De Bello, de Represaliis et de Duello (ed. Thomas Erskine Holland, trans. J.K. Brierly) Carnegie Institute: Washington D.C. (1917)

Dahlberg, Linda L. et al., Guns in the Home and Risk of a Violent Death in the Home: Findings from a National Study, American Journal of Epidemiology, vol. 160 (2004), 929–936

David, Eric, Self-Defence and State of Necessity in the Statute of the ICC, in: José Doria, Hans-Peter Gasser & M. Cherif Bassiouni (eds.), The Legal Regime of the International Criminal Court, Martinus Nijhoff : Leiden/Boston (2009), 757–777

de Hert, Paul et al., Code of International Criminal Law and Procedure, Larcier: Brussels (2013)

de Rover, Cees & Bienert, Anja, To Serve and to Protect: Human Rights and Humanitarian Law for Police and Security Forces, ICRC: Geneva (2nd ed., 2014)

De Sanctis, Francisco, What duties do states have with regard to the rules of engagement and the training of security forces under article 2 of the European Convention on Human Rights?, International Journal of Human Rights, vol. 10 (2006), 31–44

De Schutter, Olivier, International Human Rights Law: Cases, Materials, Commentary, Cambridge University Press: Cambridge (2014)

——, The Responsibility of States, in: Simon Chesterman & Angelina Fisher (ed.s), Private Security, Public Order: The Outsourcing of Public Services and Its Limits, Oxford University Press: Oxford/New York (2009), 25–45

De Vitoria, Francisco, On the Law of War, in: Anthony Pagdan & Jeremy Lawrance (eds.), Vitoria: Political Writings, Cambridge University Press: Cambridge (1991)

Deadman, Derek & MacDonald, Ziggy, Offenders as Victims of Crime?: An Investigation into the Relationship between Criminal Behaviour and Victimization, Journal of the Royal Statistical Society. Series A (Statistics in Society), vol. 167, No. 1 (2004), 53–67

Delannay, Axel, Les homicides et lésions corporelles volontaires, in: Henri-D. Bosly & Christian De Valkeneer (eds.), Les Infractions, Larcier: Bruxelles (2007), vol. 2, 85–420

Delmas-Marty, Mireille, The Contribution of Comparative Law to a Pluralist Conception of International Criminal Law, Journal of International Criminal Justice, vol. 1(1) (2003), 13–25

Demosthenes, Oratio 23 against Aristocrates, in: James Herbert Vince (trans.), Demosthenes against Meidias, Androtion, Aristocrates, Timocrates, Aristogeiton, Harvard University Press: Cambridge (1935), 212–367

Den Dekker, Guido & Myjer, Eric P.J., The Right to Life and Self-Defence of Private Military and Security Contractors in Armed Conflict, in: Francesco Francioni and Natalino Ronzitti (eds.), War by Contract: Human Rights, Humanitarian Law and Private Contractors, Oxford University Press: Oxford (2011), 171–193

Denza, Eilleen, Diplomatic Law, Oxford University Press: Oxford (3rd ed. 2008)

Dershowitz, Alan, Israel obeyed international law: Legally, the Gaza flotilla conflict is an open-and-shut case, 1 June 2010, http://www.nydailynews.com/opinion/israel-obeyed-international-law-legally-gaza-flotilla-conflict-open-and-shut-case-article-1.180324

——, Why Terrorism Works, Yale University Press: New Haven (2002)

Desportes, Frédéric & Le Gunehec, Francis, Droit pénal général. Economica: Paris (15th ed., 2008)

Dicey, Albert Venn, Introduction to the Study of the Law of the Constitution, MacMillan and Co.: London/New York (3rd ed., 1889)

Diehm, Dirk, Die Menschenrechte der EMRK und ihr Einfluss auf das deutsche Strafgesetzbuch, Logos Verlag: Berlin (2006)

Dinstein, Yoram, The International Law of Belligerent Occupation. Cambridge University Press: Cambridge (2009)

——, War, Aggression and Self-Defence, Cambridge University Press: New York (5th ed., 2011)

Doehring, Karl, Die humanitäre Intervention: Überlegungen zu ihrer Rechtfertigung, in: Antônio Augusto Cancado Trindade (ed.), In The Modern World of Human Rights: Essays in Honour of Thomas Buergenthal, Inter-American Institute of Human Rights: San Jose (1996), 549–565

——, Zum "Recht auf Leben" aus nationaler und internationaler Sicht, in: Rudolf Bernhardt (ed.), Völkerrecht als Rechtsordnung, internationale Gerichtsbarkeit, Menschenrechte: Festschrift für Hermann Mosler, Springer: Berlin (1983), 145–157.

Doswald-Beck, Louise, Assessing "incapacitating chemical agents" under human rights law, in: ICRC, Expert Meeting: "Incapacitating Chemical Agents"—Law Enforcement, Human Rights Law and Policy, ICRC: Geneva (2013), 39–45

——, The right to life in armed conflict: Does international humanitarian law provide all the answers?, International Review of the Red Cross, vol. 88 (2006), 881–904

Downes, Chris, "Targeted Killings" in an Age of Terror: The Legality of the Yemen Strike, Journal of Conflict & Security Law, vol. 9(2) (2004), 277–294

Drake, Denise M., The Castle Doctrine: An Expanding Right to Stand Your Ground, Saint Mary's Law Journal, vol. 39 (2008), 573–613

Dreier, Horst, Grenzen des Tötungsverbots—Teil 1, Juristen Zeitung (JZ), vol. 62 (2007), 261–270

Dugard, John, The Organization of African Unity and Colonialism: An Inquiry into the Plea of Self-Defence as a Justification for the Use of Force in Eradication of Colonialism, International and Comparative Law Quarterly, vol. 16 (1967), 157–190

Dumin, Jennifer, Superstitition-based Injustice in Africa and the United States: The Use of Provocation as a Defense for Killing Witches and Homosexuals, Wisconsin Women's Law Journal, vol. 21 (2006), 145–174

Dunér, Bertil, Rebellion: The Ultimate Human Right?, The International Journal of Human Rights, vol. 9 (2005), 247–269

Durand, Claude, Les Anciennes Coutumes Penales Du Tchad, Harnattan: Paris/Budapest/Turin (2002)

Dymond-Bass, Abi & Corney, Neil, The use of "less lethal" weapons in law enforcement, in: Stuart Casey-Maslen (ed.), Weapons under International Human Rights Law, Cambridge University Press: Cambridge (2014), 32–52

Echterhölter, Rudolf, Die Europäische Menschenrechtskonvention in der juristischen Praxis, JuristenZeitung 1958, 142–148

Eide, Asbjorn; Barlaug, Leif & Chinana, Chakufuwa, The right to oppose violations of human rights: basis, conditions and limitations, in: UNESCO, Violations of Human Rights: Possible Rights of Recourse and Forms of Resistance, UNESCO: Paris 1984, 34–66

Elias, Taslim Olawale, The Nature of African Customary Law, Manchester University Press: Manchester (1972)

Ellis, Jaye, General Principles and Comparative Law, European Journal of International Law, vol. 22(4) (2011), 949–971

Epstein, A.L., Injury and Liability in African Customary Law in Zambia, in: Max Gluckman (ed.), Ideas and Procedures in African Customary Law, Oxford University Press: London (1969), 292–304

Erb, Volker, Notwehr als Menschenrecht—Zugleich eine Kritik der Entscheidung des LG Frankfurt am Main im "Fall Daschner", Neue Zeitschrift für Strafrecht (NStZ) 2005, 593–602

———, Notwehr gegen rechtswidriges Verhalten von Amtsträgern, in: Dieter Dölling & Volker Erb (eds.), Festschrift für Karl Heinz Gössel zum 70. Geburtstag, C.F. Müller: Heidelberg (2002), 217–233

Erb, Volker et al. (eds.), Löwe-Rosenberg: Die Strafprozessordnung und das Gerichtsverfassungsgesetz: Grosskommentar, vol. 11, De Gruyter: Berlin (26th ed., 2010)

Eser, Albin (ed.), Schönke/Schröder Strafgesetzbuch: Kommentar, München: C.H.Beck (28th ed., 2010)

———, Article 31: Grounds for Excluding Criminal Responsibility, in: Triffterer, Otto (ed.), Commentary on the Rome Statute of the International Criminal Court, C.H.Beck-Hart-Nomos: München/Oxford/Baden-Baden (2nd ed., 2008), 863–893

Eyffinger, Arthur, Self-Defence or the Meanderings of a Protean Principle, in: Arthur Eyffinger, Alan Stephens & Sam Muller (eds.), Self-Defence as a Fundamental Principle, T.M.C. Asser Press: The Hague (2009), 103–138

Fadlalla, Mohammed Hassan, Customary Laws in Southern Sudan: Customary Laws of Dinka and Nuer, iUniverse: Bloomington (2009)

Fahl, Christian, Neue "sozialethische Einschränkung" der Notwehr: "Folter", Jura 2007, 743–750

Fair, Madison, Dare Defend: Standing for Stand Your Ground, Law and Psychology Review, vol. 38 (2014), 153–176

Falk, Richard & Weston, Burns, The relevance of international law to Palestinian rights in the West Bank and Gaza: in legal defense of the intifada, Harvard International Law Journal, vol. 32 (1991), 129–157

Fanon, Frantz, Les damnés de la terre, La Découverte & Syros: Paris (2002)

Farbstein, Susan H., Reflections on the Question of When, if Ever, Violence Is Justified in Struggles for Political or Social Change, Harvard Human Rights Law Journal, vol. 27 (2014), 1–5

Farrant, James, The Gaza Flotilla Incident and the Modern Law of Blockade, Naval War College Review, vol. 66 (2013), 81–98

Fassbender, Bardo, Der Gesetzesvorbehalt in europäischen und internationalen Menschenrechtsverträgen in: Eckart Klein (ed.), Gewaltenteilung und Menschenrechte, Berliner Wissenschaftsverlag: Berlin (2nd ed., 2010), 83–137

Faure, Bernard, Buddhism and Symbolic Violence, in: Andrew R. Murphy (ed.), The Blackwell Companion to Religion and Violence, Blackwell Publishing: Chichester (2011), 211–226

Feldman, Richard, Bernie Goetz "The Subway Gunman" 30 Years Later, Huffington Post, 23 December 2014, http://www.huffingtonpost.com/richard-feldman/bernie-goetz-the-subway-g_b_6369128.html

Fernandez, Julian & Pacreau, Xavier, Statut de Rome de la Cour pénale international: Commentaire article par article, vol.1, Pedone: Paris (2012)

Finkelstein, Claire O., Self-Defense as a Rational Excuse, University of Pittsburgh Law Review, vol. 57 (1996), 621–649

Fleck, Dieter, Law Enforcement and the Conduct of Hostilities: Two Supplementing or Mutually Excluding Legal Paradigms?, in: Andreas Fischer-Lescano et al. (eds.), Frieden in Freiheit. Peace in Liberty. Paix En Liberté. Festschrift für Michael Bothe zum 70 Geburtstag, Nomos/DIKE: Baden-Baden/Zürich (2008), 391–407

Fleegler, Eric W. et al., Firearm Legislation and Firearm-Related Fatalities in the United States, JAMA Internal Medicine, vol. 173 (2013), 732–740

Fletcher, George P., A Crime of Self-Defense: Bernhard Goetz and the Law on Trial, Free Press: New York (1988)

———, Proportionality and the Psychotic Aggressor, A Vignette in Comparative Criminal Theory, Israel Law Review, vol. 8 (1973), 367–390

———, Punishment and Self Defense, Law and Philosophy, vol. 8 (1989), 201–215

———, The Right and the Reasonable, Harvard Law Review, vol. 98 (1985) 949–982

Fletcher, George P. & Ohlin, Jens David, Defending Humanity: When Force is Justified and Why, Oxford University Press: New York (2008)

Forteau, Mathias, Reparation in the Event of a Circumstance Precluding Wrongfulness, in: James Crawford et al. (eds.), The Law of International Responsibility, Oxford University Press: Oxford (2010), 887–893

Foster Halabi, Sam, Traditions of Belligerent Recognition: The Libyan Intervention in Historical and Theoretical Context, American University International Law Review, vol. 27 (2012), 321–390

Friedmann, Wolfgang, The Uses of "General Principles" in the Development of International Law, American Journal of International Law, vol. 57(2) (1963), 279–299

Frister, Helmut, Zur Einschränkung des Notwehrrechts durch Art. 2 der Europäischen Menschenrechtskonvention, Goltdammer's Archiv für Strafrecht 1985, 553–565

Frowein, Jochen, Der europäische Grundrechtsschutz und die nationale Gerichtsbarkeit, De Gruyter: Berlin/New York (1983)

———, Self-Determination as a Limit to Obligations under International Law, in: Christian Tomuschat (ed.), Modern Law of Self-Determination, Martinus Nijhoff: Dordrecht/Boston/London (1993), 211–223

Frowein, Jochen & Peukert, Wolfgang, Europäische Menschenrechtskonvention: EMRK-Kommentar, N.P. Engel Verlag: Kehl (3rd ed., 2009)

Gaeta, Paola, May Necessity Be Available as a Defense for Torture in the Interrogation of Suspected Terrorists?, Journal of International Criminal Justice, vol. 2 (2004), 785–794

Gagarin, Michael, Self-defense in Athenian Homicide Law, Greek, Roman, and Byzantine Studies, vol. 19 (1978), 111–120

Gaggioli, Gloria, The Relevance of International Criminal Law for Interpreting and Applying Human Rights Treaties: A Study of the Case Law of the European Court of Human Rights, in: Robert Kolb & Damian Scalia (eds), Droit international penal: Précis, Helbing: Lichtenhahn (2nd ed., 2012), 397–422

———, Expert Meeting of the International Committee of the Red Cross on the use of force in armed conflict: Interplay between the conduct of hostilities and law enforcement paradigms, ICRC: Geneva (2013)

Gaja, Giorgio, General Principles of Law, in: Rüdiger Wolfrum (ed.), Max Planck Encyclopedia of Public International Law (online ed., updated May 2013), http://opil.ouplaw.com/home/EPIL

Garcia Roca, Javier, El Diálogo entre el Tribunal Europea de Derechos Humanos y los Tribunales Constitutionales en la Construcción de un Orden Público Europea, Teoría y Realidad Constitucional, vol. 30 (2012), 183–224

Geistlinger, Michael, Revolution und Völkerrecht, Böhlau Verlag: Wien/Köln/Graz (1991)

Gentili, Alberico, De Iure Belli Tres Libri, Vol. II: The Translation of the Edition of 1612 (John C. Rolfe, trans.) Oxford: Clarendon Press (1933)

Ghafur Hamid, Abdul & Maung Sein, Khin, Islamic International Law and the Right of Self-Defence of States, Journal of East Asia and International Law, vol. 2 (2009), 67–101

Ginsburg, Tom; Lansberg-Rodriguez, Daniel & Versteeg, Mila, When to Overthrow Your Government: The Right to Resist in the World's Constitutions, UCLA Law Review, vol. 60 (2013), 1184–1260

Goertzel, Ted, The Ethics of Terrorism and Revolution, Terrorism, vol. 11 (1988), 1–12

Gollwitzer, Walter, Menschenrechte im Strafverfahren: MRK und IPBPR, De Gruyter: Berlin (2005)

Goodman, Ryan, Humanitarian Intervention and Pretexts for War, American Journal of International Law, vol. 100 (2006), 107–141

Gopalan, Sandeeb, Put Pirates to the Sword, Wall Street Journal, 10 January 2010, http://www.wsj.com/articles/SB10001424052748703652104574651962659622546

Gorr, Michael, Private Defense, Law and Philosophy, vol. 9 (1990), 241–268

Grabenwarter, Christoph & Pabel, Katharina, Europäische Menschenrechtskonvention, C.H.Beck: München (5th ed., 2012)

Graf Vitzthum, Wolfgang, Stauffenberg—Zur Rechtfertigung von Eidbruch und Tyrannenmord, in: Holger P. Hestermeyer et al. (eds.), Coexistence, Cooperation and Solidarity: Liber Amicorum Rüdiger Wolfrum, vol. 1, Martinus Nijhoff: Leiden/Boston (2012), 2145–2164

Grant Shoenberger, Cynthia, Luther and the Justifiability of Resistance to Legitimate Authority, Journal of the History of Ideas, vol. 40 (1979), 3–20

Gratian, The Treatise on Laws (Decretum DD. 1–20) (trans. Augustine Thompson), Catholic University of America Press: USA (1993)

Green, Stuart P., Castles and Carjackers: Proportionality and the Use of Deadly Force in Defense of Dwellings and Vehicles, University of Illinois Law Review (1999), 1–41

Greenwood, Christopher, Terrorism and Humanitarian Law—The Debate Over Additional Protocol I, Israel Yearbook of Human Rights, vol. 19 (1989), 187–207

Greer, Steven, Should Police Threats to Torture Suspects Always Be Severely Punished?: Reflections on the Gäfgen Case, Human Rights Law Review, vol. 11(1) (2011), 67–89

Gritsch, Eric W., Martin Luther and Violence: A Reappraisal of a Neuralgic Theme, The Sixteenth Century Journal, vol. 3 (1972), 37–55

Grotius, Hugo, The Rights of War and Peace: Book I (trans. John Morrice, ed. Richard Tuck/Jean Barbeyrac), Liberty Fund: Indianapolis (2005)

———, The Rights of War and Peace [1625], Book II (ed. Richard Tuck/Jean Barbeyrac, trans. John Morrice), Liberty Fund: Indianapolis (2005)

Guggenheim, Paul, Contribution à l'histoire des sources du droit des gens, Collected Courses of the Hague Academy of International Law, vol. 94 (1958), 1–84

Guilfoyle, Douglas, International Criminal Law, Oxford University Press: Oxford (2016)

———, The Laws of War and the Fight against Somali Piracy: Combatants or Criminals?, Melbourne Journal of International Law, vol. 11 (2010), 1–13

———, The *Mavi Marmara Incident* and Blockade in Armed Conflict, British Yearbook of International Law, vol. 81 (2011), 171–223

Haggenmacher, Peter, Self-defence as a general principle of law and its relation to war, in: Arthur Eyffinger; Alan Stephens; Sam Muller (eds.), Self-Defence as a Fundamental Principle, T.M.C. Asser Press: The Hague (2009), 3–38

Hall, Stephen, The Persistent Spectre: Natural Law, International Order and the Limits of Legal Positivism, European Journal of International Law, vol. 12(2) (2001), 269–307

Hall, William Edward, A Treatise on International Law, Clarendon Press: Oxford (5th ed., 1904)

Hampson, Francoise, The Relationship between International Humanitarian Law and Human Rights Law from the Perspective of a Human Rights Treaty Body, International Review of the Red Cross, vol. 90 (2008), 549–572

Hannum, Hurst, Rethinking Self- Determination, Virginia Journal of International Law, vol. 34 (1993), 1–69

Happold, Matthew, International humanitarian law and human rights law, in: Nigel White & Christian Henderson (ed.), Research Handbook on International Conflict and Security Law, Elgar: Cheltenham (2013), 444–466

Harris, D.J. et al., Law of the European Convention on Human Rights, Oxford University Press: Oxford (3rd ed., 2014)

Hart, H.L.A., Are There Any Natural Rights?, The Philosophical Review vol. 64.2 (1955), 175–191

Hays Parks, W., Part IX of the ICRC's "Direct Participation in Hostilities" Study: No Mandate, No Expertise, and Legally Incorrect, New York University Journal of International Law and Politics, vol. 42 (2010), 767–830

Hedayati-Kakhiki, Mohammad M., Islamic Law, in: Alan Reed & Michael Bohlander (eds.), General Defenses in Criminal Law: Domestic and Comparative Perspectives, Ashgate: Dorchester (2014), 241–254

Hegedüs, Zoltan & Bumgardner, Sherrod Lewis (eds.), NATO Legal Deskbook, NATO Office of the Legal Advisor: Mons/Norfolk (2nd ed., 2010)

Heintschel von Heinegg, Wolff, Die weiteren Quellen des Völkerrechts, in: Knut Ipsen (ed.),Völkerrecht, C.H.Beck: München (6th ed., 2014), 470–510

———, Repressing Piracy and Armed Robbery at Sea—Towards a New Legal Regime?, Israel Yearbook of International Law, vol. 40 (2010), 219–241

Heller, Kevin Jon, "One Hell of a Killing Machine": Signature Strikes and International Law, Journal of International Criminal Justice, vol. 11 (2013), 89–119

Hemenway, David, Community Firearms and Community fear, Epidemiology, vol. 11 (2000), 709–714

———, Risks and Benefits of a Gun in the Home, American Journal of Lifestyle Medicine, vol. 5(6) (2011), 502–511

———, The Myth of Millions of Annual Self-Defense Gun Uses: A Case Study of Survey Overestimates of Rare Events, Chance [American Statistical Association), vol. 10 (1997), 6–10

Hemenway, David & Miller, Matthew, Firearm Availability and Homicide Rates across 26 High-Income Countries, Journal of Trauma, vol. 49 (2000), 985–988

Hemenway, David & Solnick, Sara J., The epidemiology of self-defense gun use: evidence from the National Crime Victimization Surveys 2007–2011, Preventive Medicine, vol. 79 (October 2015), 22–27

Hemenway, David; Solnick, Sara J. & Azrael, Deborah R., Firearms and community feelings of safety, Journal of Criminal Law and Criminology, vol. 1(86) (1995), 121–132

Hemenway, David; Tomoko Shinoda-Tagawa & Miller, Matthew, Firearm Availability and Female Homicide Victimization Rates Among 25 Populous High-Income Countries, Journal of the American Medical Women's Association, vol. 57 (2002), 100–104

Henckaerts, Jean-Marie & Doswald-Beck, Louise, Customary International Humanitarian Law, vol. I: Rules, International Committee of the Red Cross and Cambridge University Press: Cambridge (2005)

Henckaerts, Jean-Marie & Wiesener, Cornelius, Human Rights Obligations of Non-state Armed Groups: A Possible Contribution from Customary International Law?, in: Robert Kolb and Gloria Gaggioli (eds.), Research Handbook On Human Rights And Humanitarian Law, Edward Elgar: Cheltenham (2013), 146–169

Henkin, Louis, International law: politics, values and functions, Recueil des Cours de l'Académie de la Haye, vol. 216 (1989), 9–400

Herzberg, Rolf Dietrich, Folter und Menschenwürde, Juristen Zeitung 2005, 321–328

Herzog, Felix,§ 32: Notwehr, in: Urs Kindhäuser et al., Strafgesetzbuch: Band 1, Nomos: Baden-Baden (4th ed., 2014), 1490–1533

Hessbruegge, Jan Arno, ECtHR Armani Da Silva v. UK: Unreasonable on Police Killings in Putative Self-Defence?, EJIL Talk, 14 April 2016, http://www.ejiltalk.org/ecthr-armani-da-silva-v-uk-unreasonable-police-killings-in-putative-self-defence/

———, Human Rights Violations Arising from Conduct of Non-State Actors, Buffalo Human Rights Law Review, vol. 11, (2005), 21–88

———, The Historical Development of the Doctrines of Attribution and Due Diligence in International Law, New York University Journal of International Law & Politics, vol. 36 (2004), 265–306

Hilgendorf, Eric, Folter im Rechtsstaat?, Juristen Zeitung 2004, 331–339

Hobbes, Thomas, Leviathan (1651) (ed. J.C.A. Gaskin), Oxford University Press: Oxford/New York (1998)

Hohfeld, Wesley Newcomb, Some Fundamental Legal Conceptions as Applied in Judicial Reasoning, Yale Law Journal, vol. 23 (1913) 16–59

Honoré, Tony, The Right to Rebel, Oxford Journal of Legal Studies, vol. 8 (1988), 35–54

Hörnle, Tatjana, Shooting Down a Hijacked Plane—The German Discussion and Beyond, Criminal Law and Philosophy, vol. 3 (2009), 111–131

Horwitz, Joshua & Anderson, Casey, Guns, Democracy and the Insurrectionist Idea, University of Michigan Press: Ann Arbor (2009)

Hubbard, F. Patrick, The Value of Life: Constitutional Limits on Citizens' Use of Deadly Force, George Mason Law Review (2014), vol. 21, 623–655

Hubble, Gail, Feminism and the Battered Woman: The Limits of Self-Defence in the Context of Domestic Violence, Current Issues in Criminal Justice, vol. 9 (1997–1998), 113–124

Huemer, Michael, Is There a Right to Own a Gun?, Social Theory and Practice, vol. 29 (2003), 297–324

Human Rights Watch, Mexico: Police Killings in Michoacán, 28 October 2015, https://www.hrw.org/news/2015/10/28/mexico-police-killings-michoacan

———, Return to Tajikistan: Continued Regional and Ethnic Tensions (May 1995), http://www.hrw.org/reports/1995/Tajik.htm

———, Small Arms and Human Rights: The Need for Global Action (2003), http://www.hrw.org/legacy/backgrounder/arms/small-arms-full-070703.pdf

Institut de Droit International, Annuaire de l'Institut, Vol. 14 : 1895-1896 (session de Cambridge—août 1895), A. Pedone: Paris (1895), http://gallica.bnf.fr/ark:/12148/bpt6k5721782t/f223.image

International Association of Police Chiefs, Model Policy on the Use of Force, IACP: Alexandria (2006)

Jäger, Christian, Folter und Flugzeugabschuss—rechtsstaatliche Tabubrüche oder rechtsguterhaltende Notwendigkeiten?, Juristische Ausbildung (JA) 2008, 678–684

Jansen, Steven & Nugent-Bokakove, M. Elaine, Expansions to the Castle Doctrine: Implications for Policy and Practice, National District Attorneys Association: Alexandria, Virginia (2007)

Javed, Azhar, Intoxication & Self-Fefence: A Comparative Study of Principles of English Law and Shari'ah, (2004), http://etheses.whiterose.ac.uk/526/1/uk_bl_ethos_416550.pdf

Jennings, Wesley G., On the overlap between victimization and offending: A review of the literature, Aggression and Violent Behaviour, vol. 17 (2012), 16–26

Jerouschek, Günter & Kölbel, Ralf, Folter von Staats wegen?, Juristen Zeitung 2003, 613–620

Jerrold, Blanchard (ed.), The Wit and Opinions of Douglas Jerrold, W. Kent: London (1859)

Jerryson, Michael, Buddhist Traditions and Violence, in: Mark Juergensmeyer, Marco Kitts & Michael Jerryson (eds.), Oxford Handbook of Religion and Violence, Oxford University Press: New York (2013), 41–66

Jessberger, Florian, Bad Torture—Good Torture?: What International Criminal Lawyers May Learn from the Recent Trial of Police Officers in Germany, Journal of International Criminal Justice, vol. 3 (2005), 1059–1073

Johnson, Thomas; Slater, Robert O. & McGowan, Pat, Explaining African Military Coups d'état, 1960–1982, American Political Science Review, vol. 78 (1984), 622–640

Johnson, Wallace (ed.), The T'Ang Code, Volume II: Specific Articles, Princeton University Press: Princeton (2012)

Joseph, Sarah, Denouement of the Deaths on the Rock: The Right to Life of Terrorists, Netherlands Quarterly of Human Rights, vol. 14 (1996), 5–23

Joyner, Charles & Basile, Chad, Dynamic Resistance Response Model: A Modern Approach to the Use of Force, FBI Law Enforcement Bulletin, vol. 76 (9) (2007), 15–20

Kadish, Sanford H., Respect for Life and Regard for Rights in Criminal Law, California Law Review, vol. 64 (1976), 871–901

Kälin, Walter & Künzli, Jörg, Article 1F(b): Freedom Fighters, Terrorists, and the Notion of Serious Non-Political Crimes, International Journal of Refugee Law, vol. 12 (2000) 46–78

——, The Law of International Human Rights Protection, Oxford University Press: Oxford (2009)

Kant, Immanuel, Metaphysik der Sitten (1797), in: Immanuel Kant, Gesammelte Schriften, vol. VI, Preußische Akademie: Berlin (1907/1914)

——, The Science of Right (trans. W. Hastie), Digireads: Stilwell (2005)

Kapossy, Béla & Whatmore, Richard (eds.), Emer de Vattel: The Law of Nations, Or, Principles of the Law of Nature, Applied to the Conduct and Affairs of Nations and Sovereigns, with Three Early Essays on the Origin and Nature of Natural Law and on Luxury, Liberty Fund: Indianapolis (2008), 747–771

Kasenene, Peter, Religious Ethics in Africa, Fountain: Kampala (1998)

Kates, Don B., Genocide, Murder and the Fundamental Human Right to Defend One's Life, Journal of Law, Economics and Policy, vol. 2 (2006), 309–317.

Kaufman, Whitley, Is there a "right" to self-defence?, Criminal Justice Ethics, vol. 23(1) (2004), 20–32

——, Self-Defense, Imminence, and the Battered Woman, New Criminal Law Review, vol. 10 (2007), 342–369

Keenan, Thomas, The Libyan Uprising and the Right of Revolution in International Law, International and Comparative Law Review [Palacky University, Czech Republic], vol. 11(1) (2011), 5–29

Kelsen, Hans, General Theory of Law and State (trans. Anders Wedberg), Harvard University Press: Cambridge (1945)

——, The Natural Law Doctrine before the Tribunal of Science, Western Political Quarterly, vol. 2(4) (1949), 481–513

Kennedy, Joseph, Why It Was Too Easy for George Zimmerman to Get Off for Self-Defense, Slate, 16 July 2013, http://www.slate.com/articles/news_and_politics/jurisprudence/2013/07/george_zimmerman_and_self_defense_why_it_was_too_easy_for_him_to_get_off.html

Kessler Ferzan, Kimberly, Self-Defense and the State, Ohio State Journal of Criminal Law, vol. 5 (2007-2008), 449–478

Killander, Magnus, Interpreting Regional Human Rights Treaties, Sur-International Journal on Human Rights, vol. 13 (2000), 145–170

Kleck, Gary & Gertz, Marc, Armed resistance to crime: The prevalence and nature of self-defense with a gun, Journal of Criminal Law and Criminology, vol. 86 (1995),150–187

Knoops, Geert-Jan, Defenses in Contemporary International Criminal Law, Transnational Publishers: Ardsley, New York (2nd ed., 2008)

Kokott, Julia, The Burden of Proof in Comparative and International Human Rights Law, Kluwer Law International: The Hague (1998)

Kontos, Alexis P., "Private" security guards: Privatized force and State responsibility under international human rights law, Non-State Actors and International Law, vol. 4 (2004), 199–238

Kopel, David B., Self-Defense in Asian Religions, Liberty University Law Review, vol. 2 (2007), 79–164

Kopel, David B.; Gallant, Paul & Eisen, Joanne D., Is Resisting Genocide a Human Right?, Notre Dame Law Review, vol. 81(4) (2006), 1275–1346

——, The Human Right of Self-Defense, BYU Journal of Public Law, vol. 22 (2008), 43–178

Koriath, Heinz, Einschränkung des deutschen Notwehrrechts (§ 32 STGB) durch art 2 II a EMRK?, in: Filippo Ranieri (ed.), Europäisierung der Rechtswissenschaft, Nomos: Baden-Baden (2002), 47–60

Kovac, Gretel C., Musician Is Killed for Banging on a Door, New York Times, 5 September 2007, http://www.nytimes.com/2007/09/05/us/05dallas.html?_r=0

Kremnitzer, Mordechai, Präventives Töten, in: Dieter Fleck (ed.), Rechtsfragen der Terrorismusbekämpfung durch Streitkräfte, Nomos: Baden-Baden (2004), 201–222

——, Proportionality and the Psychotic Aggressor: Another View, Israeli Law Review, vol. 18 (1983), 178–214

Kreß, Claus, The regulation of non-international armed conflicts: Can a privilege of belligerency be envisioned in the law of non-international armed conflicts?, International Review of the Red Cross, vol. 96 (2014), 29–44

Kretzmer, David, Targeted Killing of Suspected Terrorists: Extra-Judicial Executions or Legitimate Means of Defense?, European Journal of International Law, vol. 16 (2005), 171–212

Krey, Volker, Deutsches Strafrecht Allgemeiner Teil, vol. 1, Kohlhammer Verlag: Stuttgart (2008)

Krüger, Ralf, Die Bedeutung der Menschenrechtskonvention für das deutsche Notwehrrecht, Neue Juristische Wochenschrift 1970, 1483–1485

Kühl, Kristian, Der Einfluss der Menschenrechte und Grundfreiheiten der Europäischen Menschenrechtskonvention auf das deutsche und europäische Strafrecht, in: Heinz Müller-Dietz (ed.), Festschrift für Heike Jung, Nomos: Baden-Baden (2007), 433–443

Ladiges, Manuel, Die notstandsbedingte Tötung von Unbeteiligten im Fall des § 14 Abs. 3 LuftSiG—ein Plädoyer für die Rechtfertigungslösung, Zeitschrift für internationale Strafrechtsdogmatik, vol. 3 (2008), 129–140

Laly-Chevalier, Caroline, Lutte contre la piraterie maritime et droits de l'homme, Revue Belge de Droit International 2009, 5–51

Lao Tse, Tao Te Ching (trans. James Legge), Arc Manor: Rockville, Maryland (2008)

Laufhütte, Heinrich Wilhelm; Rissing-van Saan, Ruth & Tiedemann, Klaus (eds.), Strafgesetzbuch. Leipziger Kommentar, vol. 2: §§ 32–55, Berlin: De Gruyter (12th ed., 2010)

Lauterpacht, Hersch, An International Bill of Rights of Man, Columbia University Press: New York (1945)

——, The Function of Law in the International Community, Oxford University Press: Oxford (2011)

Lawson, Tamara F., A Fresh Cut in an Old Wound—A Critical Analysis of the Trayvon Martin Killing: The Public Outcry, the Prosecutors' Discretion, and the Stand Your Ground Law, University of Florida Journal of Law & Public Policy, vol. 23 (2012), 271–310

Leader-Elliot, Ian, Battered But Not Beaten: Women Who Kill in Self-Defence, Sydney Law Review, vol. 15 (1993), 403–460

Legge, James (ed.), The Chinese Classics, Vol. 1: Confucian analects, the Great Learning and the Doctrine of the Mean, Trübner & Co.: London (1861)

Lehnhardt, Chia, Private military companies, in: Nigel D. White & Christian Henderson (eds.), Research Handbook on International Conflict and Security Law (Cheltenham: Edward Elgar, 2013), 421–443

Leigh, Andrew & Neill, Christine, Do Gun Buybacks Save Lives?: Evidence from Panel Data, American Law and Economics Review, vol. 12 (2010), 509–557

Lettow Lerner, Renée, The Worldwide Popular Revolt against Proportionality in Self-Defense Law, Journal of Law, Economics and Policy, vol. 2 (2006), 331–364

Leverick, Fiona, Defending Self-Defence, Oxford Journal of Legal Studies, vol. 27(3) (2007), 563–579

———, Is English Self-Defence Law incompatible with art 2 of the ECHR, Criminal Law Review (May 2002), 347–362

———, Killing in Self-Defence, Oxford University Press: Oxford (2006)

———, The use of force in public or private defense and Article 2: A reply to Professor Sir John Smith, Criminal Law Review 2002, 963–967

Lippman, Matthew, McConville, Sean & Yerushalmi, Mordechai, Islamic Criminal Law and Procedure: An Introduction, Praeger: New York (1988)

Locke, John, Two treatises of government [1689], Whitmore, Fenn and C. Brown: London (1821)

Londregan, John B. & Poole, Keith T., Poverty, the Coup Trap, and the Seizure of Executive Power, World Politics, vol. 42 (1990), 151–183

Lott, John R. Jr. & Mustard, David B., Crime, Deterrence, and Right-to-Carry Concealed Handguns, Journal of Legal Studies, vol. 26 (1997), 1–68

Löwenstein, Stefan, Zur Durchsetzung des Auftrags, Frankfurter Allgemeine Blog, 27 July 2009, http://blogs.faz.net/sicherheit/2009/07/27/auftrag-39/

Lubell, Noam, Extraterritorial Use of Force against Non-State Actors, Oxford University Press: Oxford (2010)

Ludwig, Jens, Gun Self-Defense and Deterrence, Crime and Justice, vol. 27 (2000), 363–417

Luther, Martin, Against the Robbing and Murdering Hordes of Peasants [1525] (trans. Charles M. Jacobs), http://www.scrollpublishing.com/store/Luther-Peasants.html

MacKinnon, Catherine A., Women's September 11th: Rethinking the International Law of Conflict, Harvard International Law Journal, vol. 47 (2006), 1–31

Maihold, Harald, Folterknechte im Dienste des Rechtsstaats?—Zur Strafbarkeit der "Gefahrenabwehrfolter" nach schweizerischem und deutschem Recht, in: Martino Mona & Kurt Seelmann (eds.), Grenzen des rechtfertigenden Notstands, Schulthess: Zurich (2006), 117–142

Malanczuk, Peter, Akehurst's Introduction to International Law, Routledge: London/New York (7th ed., 1997)

Mamdani, Mahmood, Citizen and Subject, Princeton University Press: Princeton (1996)

Marcuse, Herbert, Ethics and Revolution, in: Richard T. DeGeorge (ed.), Ethics and Society Anchor: New York (1966), 133–147

Marin, André, "In the line of duty": Investigation into operational stress injuries affecting police officers, Ombudsman of Ontario: Ottawa (2012)

Marxen, Klaus, Die "sozialethischen" Grenzen der Notwehr, Alfred Metzner Verlag: Frankfurt a.M. (1979)

Maxwell, Mark David, Individual Self-Defense and the Rules of Engagement: Are the Two Mutually Exclusive?, The Military Law and the Law of War Review, vol. 41(1–2) 2002, 39–53

Mayerfeld, Jamie, In Defense of the Absolute Prohibition of Torture, Public Affairs Quarterly, vol. 22 (2008), 109–128

McClellan, Chandler B. & Tekin, Erdal, Stand Your Ground Laws and Homicides, June 2012, http://www.flgov.com/wp-content/uploads/citsafety/20120913_secondchance1.pdf

McCormack, Wayne, Targeted Killing at a Distance: Robotics and Self-Defense, Pacific McGeorge Global Business & Development Journal, vol. 25 (2012), 361–379

McCorquodale, Robert, Human Rights and the Targeting by Drone, EJIL Talk, 18 September 2015, http://www.ejiltalk.org/human-rights-and-the-targeting-by-drone/

———, Self-Determination: A Human Rights Approach, The International and Comparative Law Quarterly, vol. 43 (1994), 857–885

McLaughlin, Rob, The Legal Regime Applicable to Use of Lethal Force When Operating under a United Nations Security Council Chapter VII Mandate Authorising 'All Necessary Means' Journal of Conflict & Security Law, vol. 12 (2007), 389–417

McMahan, Jeff, A Challenge to Gun Rights, Practical Ethics, 17 April 2015, http://blog.practicalethics.ox.ac.uk/2015/04/a-challenge-to-gun-rights/

———, Self-Defense and the Problem of the Innocent Attacker, Ethics, vol. 104 (1994), 252–290

Megale, Elizabeth B., Deadly Combinations: How Self-Defense Laws Pairing Immunity with a Presumption of Fear Allow Criminals to "Get Away with Murder", American Journal of Trial Advocacy, vol. 34 (2010), 105–134

Mégret, Frédéric, Grandeur et déclin de l'idée de résistance à l'occupation: réflexions à propos de la légitimité des insurgés, Revue belge de droit international, vol. 41 (2008), 382–425

———, Le droit international peut-il être un droit de résistance? Dix conditions pour un renouveau de l'ambition normative internationale, Études internationales, vol. 39 (2008) 39–62

———, Response to Claus Kreß: Leveraging the privilege of belligerency in non-international armed conflict towards respect for the jus in bello, International Review of the Red Cross, vol. 96 (2014), 44–66

Melzer, Nils, Interpretative Guidance on the Notion of Direct Participation in Hostilities under International Humanitarian Law, ICRC: Geneva (2009)

——, Targeted Killing in International Law, Oxford University Press: Oxford (2008)

Merkel, Reinhard, Gründe für den Ausschluss der Strafbarkeit im Völkerrecht, Zeitschrift für die gesamte Strafrechtswissenschaft (2002), 437–454

——, Folter und Notwehr, in: Michael Pawlik & Rainer Zaczyk (eds.), Festschrift für Günther Jakobs zum 70. Geburtstag, C. Heymanns: Berlin (2007), 375–403

Meron, Theodor, Extraterritoriality of Human Rights Treaties, American Journal of International Law, vol. 89 (1995), 78–82

Meyer-Ladewig, Jens, EMRK : Europäische Menschenrechtskonvention, Nomos: Baden-Baden (3rd ed., 2011)

Michel, Casey, Owning Guns Doesn't Preserve Freedom, The Atlantic, 25 April 2013, http://www.theatlantic.com/international/archive/2013/04/owning-guns-doesnt-preserve-freedom/275287/

Milanovic, Marko, Drones and Targeted Killings: Can Self-Defence Preclude Their Wrongfulness?, 10 January 2011, http://www.ejiltalk.org/drones-and-targeted-killings-can-self-defence-preclude-their-wrongfulness

Milanovic, Marko & Hadzi-Vidanovic, Vidan, A taxonomy of armed conflict, in: Nigel White & Christian Henderson (ed.), Research Handbook on International Conflict and Security Law, Elgar: Cheltenham (2013), 256–314

Milhizer, Eugene H., Group Status and Criminal Defenses: Logical Relationship or Marriage ofConvenience?, Missouri Law Review, vol. 71 (2006), 547–635

Miller, Darrell A. H., Retail Rebellion and the Second Amendment, Indiana Law Journal, vol. 86 (2011), 939–977

Miller, Sophie, 'Grossly Disproportionate': Home Owners' Legal License to Kill, The Journal of Criminal Law, vol. 77 (2013) 299–309

Missling, Bodo, Widerstand und Menschenrechte: Das völkerrecht begründete Individualwiderstandsrecht gegen Menschenrechtsverletzungen, Medien Verlag Köhler: Tübingen (1999)

Mogire, Edward, The Humanitarian Impact of Small Arms and Light Weapons and the Threat to Security, Paper presented at the 15th International Amaldi Conference (2004), http://www.lincei.it/rapporti/amaldi/papers/XV-Mogire.pdf

Moir, Lindsay, The Law of Internal Armed Conflict, Cambridge University Press: Cambridge et al. (2004)

Monro, Charles Henry (ed.), The Digest of Justinian, vol. 1, Cambridge University Press: Cambridge (1904)

——, The Digest of Justinian, vol. 2, Cambridge University Press: Cambridge (1909)

Montague, Philip, Self-Defense and Choosing among Lives, Philosophical Studies, vol. 40 (1981), 207–219

Montesquieu, Baron de, Spirit of the Laws, vol. 1 (ed. or trans. not identified), Ebenezer Wilson Bookfeller in Dumfries: Edinburgh (3rd ed., 1762)

Moreno, Joelle Anne, Killing Daddy: Developing a Self-Defense Strategy for the Abused Child, University of Pennsylvania Law Review, vol. 137 (1989), 1281–1307

Morsink, Johannes, The Universal Declaration of Human Rights: Origins, Drafting and Intent, University of Pennsylvania Press: Philadelphia (1999)

Murdoch, Andrew, Recent Legal Issues and Problems Relating to Acts of Piracy off Somalia, in: Clive R. Symmons (ed.), Selected Contemporary Issues in the Law of the Sea, Martinus Nijhoff: Leiden (2011)

Murphy, Shannonbrooke, The right to resist reconsidered, in: David Keane & Yvonne McDermott (eds.), The Challenge of Human Rights: Past, Present and Future, Edward Elgar: Cheltenham & Northampton (2012), 91–113

——, Unique in international human rights law: Article 20(2) and the right to resist in the African Charter on Human and Peoples' Rights, African Human Rights Law Journal, vol. 11 (2011), 465–494

Mutungi, Onesimus K., Witchcraft and the Criminal Law in East Africa, Valparaiso University Law Review, vol. 5 (1971), 524–555

Neff, Stephen C., War and the Law of Nations: A General History, Cambridge University Press: Cambridge (2005)

Neuheuser, Stephan, Die Duldungspflicht gegenüber rechtswidrigem staatlichen Handeln im Strafrecht, Shaker Verlag: Aachen (1996)

Neuman, Gerald L., Import, Export, and Regional Consent in the Inter-American Court of Human Rights, European Journal of International Law, vol. 19 (2008), 101–123

Nolte, Georg, Preventive Use of Force and Preventive Killings: Moves into a Different Legal Order, Theoretical Inquiries in Law, vol. 5 (2004) 111–129

——, The *Bundesverfassungsgericht* on the German Aerial Security Law: A *Sonderweg* from the perspective of international law?, in: Christian Tomuschat, Evelyne Lagrange & Stefan Oeter (eds.), The Right to Life, Brill: Leiden (2010), 83–94

Nowak, Manfred, Article 6: The Right to Life, Survival and Development, Martinus Nijhoff: Leiden/Boston (2005)

——, UN Covenant on Civil and Political Rights: CCPR Commentary, N.P. Engel: Kehl/Strasbourg/Arlington (2nd ed., 2005)

Nsereko, Daniel D., Arbitrary Deprivation of Life: Controls on Permissible Deprivations, in: Bertrand Ramcharan (ed.), The Right to Life in International Law, Martinus Nijhoff: Dordrecht (1985)

O'Boyle, Michael & Michelle Lafferty, Michelle, General Principles and Constitutions as Sources of Human Rights Law, in: Dinah Shelton (ed.), Oxford Handbook for International Law, Oxford University Press: Oxford (2013), 194–221

Ohlin, Jens David, The Doctrine of Legitimate Defense, International Law Studies, vol. 91 (2015), 119–154

Okimoto, Keiichiro, The Cumulative Requirements of Jus ad Bellum and Jus in Bello in the Context of Self-Defence, Chinese Journal of International Law, vol. 11 (2012), 45–75

Olinger, David, Colorado gun laws afford rights to those shooting in self-defense, The Denver Post, 30 July 2013, http://www.denverpost.com/ci_23756639/colorado-gun-laws-afford-rights-those-shooting-self

Omorogbe, Eki Yemisi, A Club of Incumbents?: The African Union and Coups d'État, Vanderbilt Journal of Transnational Law, vol. 44 (2011), 123–154

Orakhelashvili, Alexander, Natural Law and Customary Law, Zeitschrift für ausländisches öffentliches Recht und Völkerrecht, vol. 68 (2008), 69–110

Ormerod, David, Smith, John Cyril & Hogan, Irian, Smith and Hogan's Criminal Law, Oxford University Press: Oxford (13th ed., 2010)

Otsuka, Michael, Killing the Innocent in Self-Defense, Philosophy & Public Affairs, vol. 23 (1994), 74–94

Otto, Roland, Targeted Killings and International Law, Springer: Berlin (2010)

Ouguergouz, Fatsah, The African Charter on Human and Peoples' Rights, Martinus Nijhoff: The Hague/London/New York (2003)

Paparinskis, Martins, Investment Treaty Arbitration and the (New) Law of State Responsibility, European Journal of International Law, vol. 24(2) (2013), 617–647

Parel, Anthony, Gandhi, Freedom and Self-rule, Lexington Books: Lanham/Oxford (2000)

Parks, Jessica, Gun-rights activist sparks ire with Rosa Parks comparison, The Inquirer, 14 March 2015, http://articles.philly.com/2015-03-14/news/60090407_1_rosa-parks-gun-owners-gun-rights

Paust, Jordan J., International Law, Dignity, Democracy, and the Arab Spring, Cornell International Law Journal, vol. 46 (2013), 1–19

———, Operationalizing Use of Drones against Non-State Terrorists under the International Law of Self-Defense, Albany Government Law Review, vol. 8 (2015), 166–203

———, Self-Defense Targeting of Non-State Actors and Permissibility of U.S. Use of Drones in Pakistan, Journal of Translational Law & Policy, vol. 19 (2010), 237–280

———, The Absolute Prohibition of Torture and Necessary and Appropriate Sanctions, Valparaiso University Law Review, vol. 43 (2009), 1535–1575

———, The Human Right to Revolution, in: Richard Pierre Claude & Burns H. Weston (eds.), Human Rights in the World Community: Issues and Action, University of Pennsylvania Press: Philadelphia (3rd ed., 2006), 445–452

Perron, Walter, Foltern in Notwehr?, in: Bernd Heinrich et al. (eds.), Festschrift für Ulrich Weber zum 70. Geburtstag, Verlag Ernst und Werner Gieseking: Bielefeld (2004), 143–154

———, Rechtsvergleichende Betrachtungen zur Notwehr, in: Jörg Arnold et al. (eds.), Menschengerechtes Strafrecht: Festschrift für Albin Eser zum 70. Geburtstag, C.H. Beck: München 2005), 1019–1039

Peters, Rudolph, Crime and Punishment in Islamic Law, Cambridge University Press: Cambridge (2005)

Pintore, Eduardo José, Das präventive Selbsverteidigungsrecht im Lichte allgemeiner Rechtsgrundsätze, Peter Lang: Frankfurt a.M. (2011)

Pradel, Jean, Droit Pénal Comparé, Dalloz: Paris (3rd ed., 2008)

Priddy, Alice, The use of weapons in counterpiracy operations, in: Stuart Casey-Maslen (ed.), Weapons under International Human Rights Law Cambridge University Press: Cambridge (2014), 122–160

von Pufendorf, Samuel, The Whole Duty of Man According to the Law of Nature (trans. Andrew Tooke, ed. Ian Hunter/David Saunders), Liberty Fund: Indianapolis (2003)

———, Two Books of the Elements of Universal Jurisprudence [1660] (trans. William Abbott Oldfather; ed. Thomas Behme), Liberty Fund: Indianapolis (2009)

Quaye, Christopher C., Liberation Struggles in International Law, Temple University Press: Philadelphia (1991)

Raday, Frances, Privatising Human Rights and the Abuse of Power, Canadian Journal of Law and Jurisprudence, vol. 13 (2000), 103–134

Radin, Sasha, The Current Relevance of the Recognition of Belligerency, in: Marielle Matthee et al. (eds.), Armed Conflict and International Law: In Search of the Human Face, TMC Asser: The Hague (2013)

Ramsden, Michael, Targeted Killings and International Human Rights Law: The Case of Anwar Al-Awlaki, Journal of Conflict & Security Law, vol. 16 (2011), 385–406

Randolph, Jennifer, How to Get Away with Murder: Criminal and Civil Immunity Provisions in "Stand Your Ground" Legislation, Seton Hall Law Review, vol. 44 (2014), 599–630

Rasmussen Reports, 65% See Gun Rights As Protection Against Tyranny, 18 January 2013, http://www.rasmussenreports.com/public_content/politics/current_events/gun_control/65_see_gun_rights_as_protection_against_tyranny

Redelbach, A., Protection of the Right to Life by Law and by Other Means, in: Bertrand Ramcharan (ed.), The Right to Life in International Law, Martinus Nijhoff: Dordrecht (1985), 182–221

Regan, Donald H., Rewriting Roe v. Wade, Michigan Law Review, vol. 77 (1979), 1569–1646

Rejali, Darius, Torture and Democracy, Princeton University Press: Princeton (2009)

Reuter, Eric J., The Great Equalizer: Women and the Right to Bear Arms, The Blaze, December 21 2012, http://www.theblaze.com/contributions/the-great-equalizer-women-and-the-right-to-bear-arms/.

Rice Lave, Tamara, Shoot to Kill: A Critical Look at Stand Your Ground Laws, University of Miami Law Review, vol. 67 (2013), 827–860

Roberts, Paul & Zuckerman, Adrian, Criminal Evidence, Oxford University Press: Oxford (2nd ed., 2010)

Robertson, David, A Dictionary of Human Rights, Europa Publications: London/New York (2nd ed., 2004)

Robertson, James E., "Fight or F . . ." and Constitutional Liberty: An Inmate's Right to Self-Defense when Targeted by Aggressors, Indiana Law Review, vol. 29 (1995), 339–363

Rodley, Nigel & Pollard, Matt, The Treatment of Prisoners under International Law, Oxford University Press: Oxford (3rd ed., 2009)

Roman, John K., Race, Justifiable Homicide, and Stand Your Ground Laws: Analysis of FBI Supplementary Homicide Report Data, Urban Institute

(2013), p. 7, http://www.urban.org/sites/default/files/alfresco/publication-pdfs/412873-Race-Justifiable-Homicide-and-Stand-Your-Ground-Laws.PDF

Ronzitti, Natalino, The Expanding Law of Self-Defence, Journal of Conflict & Security Law, vol. 11:3 (2006), 343–359

Rosen, Carthryn Jo, The Excuse of Self-Defense: Correcting a Historical Accident on Behalf of Battered Women Who Kill, American University Law Review, vol. 36 (1986) 11–56

Rosenne, Shabtai, Self-Defence and the Non-use of Force: Some Random Thoughts, in: Arthur Eyffinger; Alan Stephens; Sam Muller (eds.), Self-Defence as a Fundamental Principle, T.M.C. Asser Press: The Hague (2009), 49–65

Rousseau, Jean Jacques, What is the origin of inequality among men? And is it authorized by natural law? [1754], in: Jean Jacques Rousseau, The Social Contract and Discourses (trans. G.D.H.Cole), J.M. Dent: London/Toronto (1923)

Roxin, Claus, Der Abschuss gekaperter Flugzeuge zur Rettung von Menschenleben, Zeitschrift für internationale Strafrechtsdogmatik, vol. 6 (2011), 552–563

———, Kann staatliche Folter in Ausnahmefällen zulässig oder wenigstens straflos sein?, in: Jörg Arnold et al. (eds.), Menschengerechtes Strafrecht: Festschrift für Albin Eser zum 70. Geburtstag, C.H. Beck: München 2005), 461–471

———, Strafrecht: Allgemeiner Teil, vol. I, Ch.Beck: Munich (4th ed, 2006)

Ruys, Tom, 'Armed Attack' and Article 51 of the UN Charter, Cambridge University Press: Cambridge (2010)

Salisbury, John, Politicratus [ca. 1159] (trans. Joseph B. Pike), Octagon Books: New York (1972)

Salmon, Jean, Manuel de Droit Diplomatique, Bruylant: Brussels (1994)

Sanders, Kindaka, A Reason to Resist: The Use of Deadly Force in Aiding Victims of Unlawful Police Aggression, San Diego Law Review, vol.52 (2015), 695–750

Sandoz, Yves; Swinarski, Christophe & Zimmerman, Bruno (eds.), Commentary on the Additional Protocols of 8 June to the Geneva Conventions of 12 August 1949, International Committee of the Red Cross/Martinus Nijhoff: Geneva (1987)

Sanft, Charles, Bow Control in Han China: Yuqiu Shouwang on Self-Defense, Journal of Asian History, vol. 42 (2008), 143–164

Sangero, Boaz, Self-Defence in Criminal Law, Hart: Oxford (2006)

Sassoli, Marco & Olson, Laura M., The Relationship between international humanitarian and human rights law where it matters: admissible killing and internment of fighters in non-international armed conflicts, International Review of the Red Cross, vol. 90 (2008), 599–627

Satzger, Helmut, Internationales und Europäisches Strafrecht, Baden Baden: Nomos (4th ed., 2010)

Saul, Ben, Defending "Terrorism": Justifications and Excuses for Terrorism in International Criminal Law, Australian Year Book of International Law, vol. 25 (2006), 177–226

Scalliotti, Massimo, Defenses before the international criminal court: Substantive grounds for excluding criminal responsibility—Part 1, International Criminal Law Review, vol. 1 (2001), 111–172

Schabas, William, The European Convention on Human Rights: A Commentary, Oxford University Press: Oxford (2015)

Schlieter, Jens, Compassionate Killing or Conflict Resolution? The Murder of King Langdarma according to Tibetan Buddhist Sources, in: Michael Zimmermann (ed.), Buddhism and Violence, Lumbini International Research Institute: Bhairahawa, Nepal (2006), 131–158

Schmahl, Stefanie, Targeted Killings—A Challenge for International Law?. in: Christian Tomuschat, Evelyne Lagrange & Stefan Oeter (eds.), The Right to Life, Brill: Leiden (2010), 233–266

Schmidt, Christopher, An International Human Right to Keep and Bear Arms, William & Mary Bill of Rights Journal, vol. 15 (2007), 983–1017

Schmidt, Eberhard, Einführung in die Geschichte der deutschen Strafrechtspflege, Vandenhoek & Ruprecht: Göttingen (3rd ed., 1995)

Schmithausen, Lambert, Aspects of the Buddhist Attitude Towards War, in: Jan E.M. Houben & Karel R. Van Kooij (eds.) Violence Denied: Violence, Non-Violence and the Rationalization of Violence in South Asian Cultural History, Brill: Boston (1999), 45–68

Schmitt, Michael N., Counter-Terrorism and the Use of Force in International Law, Israel Yearbook of Human Rights, vol. 32 (2002), 53–116

———, Direct Participation in Hostilities and 21st Century, Armed Conflict, in: Horst Fischer et al. (eds.), Crisis Management and Humanitarian Protection: Festschrift für Dieter Fleck, Berlinre Wissenschafts-Verlag: Berlin (2004), 505–529

———, The Interpretive Guidance on the Notion of Direct Participation in Hostilities: a Critical Analysis, Harvard National Security Journal, vol. 1 (2010), 5–55

Schopp, Robert F., Self-Defense, in: Jules L. Coleman & Allen Buchanan (eds.), In Harm's Way: Essays in Honor of Joel Feinberg, Cambridge University Press: New York (1994), 255–290

Schroeder, Friedrich-Christian, Die Notwehr als Indikator politischer Grundanschauungen in: Friedrich-Christian Schroeder & Heinz Zipf (eds.), Festschrift für Reinhart Maurach zum 70. Geburtstag, C.F. Müller: Karlsruhe (1972), 127–142

Schübel-Pfister, Isabel, Art. 2 EMRK, in: Ulrich Karpenstein & Franz Maye, EMRK: Konvention zum Schutz der Menschenrechte und Grundfreiheiten, C.H.Beck: München (2012)

Schulze, Louis N. Jr., Of Trayvon Martin, George Zimmerman, and Legal Expressivism: Why Massachusetts Should Stand its Ground on "Stand Your Ground", New England Law Review on Remand, vol. 47 (2012), 34–42

Schwartz, Rachael E., Chaos, Oppression and Rebellion: The Use of Self-Help to Secure Individual Rights under International Law, Boston University Journal of International Law, vol. 12 (1994), 255–320

Schwebel, Stephen M., What Weight to Conquest?, in: Stephen M. Schwebel (ed.), Justice in International Law, Cambridge University Press: Cambridge (1994), 521–525

Scobbie, Ian, Smoke, Mirrors and Killer Whales: The International Court's Opinion on the Israeli Barrier Wall, German Law Journal, vol. 5 (2004), http://www.germanlawjournal.com/print.php?id=495, 1107–1131

Seiberth, Corinna, Private Military and Security Companies in International Law, Intersentia: Cambridge/Antwerp/Portland (2014)

Shany, Yuval, The Analogy's Limit: Defending the Rights of Peoples, Journal of International Criminal Justice, vol. 7 (2009), 541–553

———, The Prohibition against Torture and Cruel, Inhuman, and Degrading Treatment and Punishment: Can the Absolute be Relativized under Existing International Law?, Catholic University Law Review, vol. 56 (2007), 837–869

Shaykhutdinov, Renat, Give peace a chance: Nonviolent protest and the creation of territorial autonomy arrangements, Journal of Peace Research, vol. 47 (2010), 179–191

Siegel, Michael; Ross, Craig S. & King, Charles III, The Relationship between Gun Ownership and Firearm Homicide Rates in the United States, 1981–2010, American Journal of Public Health, vol. 103 (2013), 2098–2105

Simma, Bruno & Alston, Philip, The Sources of Human Rights Law: Custom, Jus Cogens and General Principles, Australian Yearbook of International Law, vol. 12 (1988–1989), 82–108

Simma, Bruno, NATO, the UN and the Use of Force: Legal Aspects, European Journal of International Law, vol. 10 (1999), 1–22

Skinner, Stephen, Populist politics and shooting burglars: comparative comments on the Lega Nord's proposal to reform Italian self-defence law, Criminal Law Review 2005, 275–284

———, The Right to Life, Democracy and State Responsibility in 'Urban Guerrilla" Conflict: The European Court of Human Rights Grand Chamber Judgment in Giuliani and Gaggio v. Italy, Human Rights Law Review, vol. 11(3) (2011), 567–577

Small Arms Survey, Women and Gun Ownership, September 2014, http://www.smallarmssurvey.org/fileadmin/docs/H-Research_Notes/SAS-Research-Note-45.pdf

Smith, Anna Marie, Deadly Force and Public Reason, Theory & Event vol. 15(3) (2012), http://muse.jhu.edu/journals/theory_and_event/v015/15.3.smith.html

Smith, John C., The use of force in public or private defence and Article 2 ECHR, Criminal Law Review 2002, 958–962

Song Richardson, L. & Atiba Goff, Phillip, Self-Defense and the Suspicion Heuristic, Iowa Law Review, vol. 98 (2012–2013), 293–336

Sorenson, Susan B. & Wiebe, Douglas J., Weapons in the lives of battered women, American Journal of Public Health, vol. 92 (2004), 1412–1417

Spencer, John R., Evidence, in: Mireille Delmas-Marty & John R. Spencer (eds.), European Criminal Procedures, Cambridge University Press: Cambridge (2002), 591–650

Spiropoulous, Ioannes, Die allgemeinen Rechtsgrundsätze im Völkerrecht, Verlag des Instituts für Internationales Recht an der Universität Kiel: Kiel (1928)

Sprick, Daniel, Die Grenzen der Notwehr im Strafrecht der Volksrepublik China, Nomos: Baden-Baden (2015)

Steinhoff, Uwe, Defusing the Ticking Social Bomb Argument: The Right to Self-Defensive Torture, Global Dialogue, vol. 12 (1) (2000), http://www.worlddialogue.org/print.php?id=457

Stephens, Dale, Rules of Engagement and the Concept of Unit Self Defense, Naval Law Review, vol. 45 (1998), 126–151

Stohl, Rachel & Hogendoorn, EJ, Stopping the Destructive Spread of Small Arms, Center for American Progress: Washington D.C. (2010)

Stott, Clifford; Scothern, Martin & Gorringe, Hugo, Advances in Liaison Based Public Order Policing in England: Human Rights and Negotiating the Management of Protest?, Policing, vol. 7 (2) (2013), 212–226

Stowell, Ellery C., Intervention in International Law, John Byrne: Washington, D.C. (1921)

Stubbs, Julie & Tolmie, Julia, Feminisms, Self-Defence, and Battered Women: A Response to Hubble's "Straw Feminist", Current Issues in Criminal Justice, vol. 10 (1998-1999), 73–84

Suárez, Francisco, A Treatise on Laws and God the Lawgiver, in: Gwladys L. Williams et al. (eds.), Selections from Three Works of Francisco Suárez, S. J., Clarendon Press: Oxford (1944)

——, Defense of the Catholic and Apostolic Faith against the Errors of Anglicanism (trans. Peter L.P. Simpson), http://www.aristotelophile.com/Books/Translations/Suarez%20Defense%20Whole.pdf

Sudan Tribune, South Sudan calls for discipline during Jonglei disarmament, 28 February 2012, http://www.sudantribune.com/spip.php?article41734

Sumida, Gerald, The Right of Revolution: Implications for International Law and Order, in: Charles A. Barker (ed.), Power and Law: American Dilemma in World Affairs, Johns Hopkins Press: Baltimore/London (1971), 130–167

Summers, James, People and International Law, Brill Nijhoff: Leiden, Boston (2nd ed., 2014)

Sumner, L. W., Abortion and Moral Theory, Princeton University Press: Princeton (1981)

Talmon, Stefan, Recognition of Opposition Groups as the Legitimate Representative of a People, Chinese Journal of International Law, vol. 12 (2013), 219–253

Tavernier, Paul, Le recours à la force par la police, in: Christian Tomuschat, Evelyne Lagrange & Stefan Oeter (eds.), The Right to Life, Brill: Leiden (2010), 41–64

Taylor Martin, Susan; Hundley, Kris & Humburg, Connie, Race plays complex role in Florida's "Stand Your Ground" law, Tampa Bay Times, 2 June 2012, http://www.tampabay.com/news/courts/criminal/race-plays-complex-role-in-floridas-stand-your-ground-law/1233152

Thanissaro Bhikkhu, The Buddhist Monastic Code I: The Pattimokkha Rules, The Metta Forest Monastery: Valley Center, California (3rd ed., 2013)

The Holy Quran (trans. Abdullah Yusuf Ali), Islamic Book Trust: Kuala Lumpur (2007)

Thiele, Carmen, Fragmentierung des Völkerrechts als Herausforderung für die Staatengemeinschaft, Archiv des Völkerrechts, vol. 46 (2008), 1–41

Thiravilluvar, Tirrikular (trans. G.U. Pope et al.), Project Madurai: Lausanne (2002)

Thomson, Judith Jarvis, Self-Defense, Philosophy and Public Affairs, vol. 20 (1991), 283–310

Thouvenin, Jean-Marc, Circumstances Precluding Wrongfulness in the ILC Articles on State Responsibility: Self-Defence, in: James Crawford et al. (eds.), The Law of International Responsibility, Oxford University Press: Oxford (2010), 455–467

Thürer, Daniel, Religion and International Humanitarian Law: Support and Tension, Recueil des cours de l'Academie de la Haye, vol. 338 (2008), 165–195

Tibori-Szabó, Kinga, Self-Defense and the United States Policy on Drone Strikes, Journal of Security & Conflict Law, vol. 20 (2015), 381–413

Tolman, Herbert Cushing (ed.), The Behistan Inscription of King Darius, Vanderbilt University: Nashville (1908)

Tolmie, Julia, Battered Defendants and the Criminal Defenses to Murder—Lessons from Overseas, Waikato Law Review, vol. 10 (2002), 91–114

Tómasson, Eiríkur, Presumed Innocent until Proven Guilty: The Principle of Article 6, Paragraph 2 of the European Convention on Human Rights and Article 70, Paragraph 2 of the Constitution of Iceland that the Burden of Proof Rests with the Prosecution, Scandinavian Studies in Law, vol. 51 (2007), 505–531

Tomuschat, Christian, Gezielte Tötungen (Targeted Killings): Zugleich ein Kommentar zum Gutachten des Internationalen Gerichtshofs vom 9. Juli 2004, Vereinte Nationen, vol. 52 (2004), 136–140

———, Humanitäre Intervention—Ein Trojanisches Pferd?, in: Herfried Münkler & Karsten Malowitz (eds.), Humanitäre Intervention: Ein Instrument außenpolitischer Konfliktbearbeitung, Verlag für Sozialwissenschaften: Wiesbaden (2008)

———, The Applicability of Human Rights Law to Insurgent Movements, in: Horst Fischer et al. (eds.), Crisis Management and Humanitarian Protection: Festschrift für Dieter Fleck, Berliner Wissenschafts-Verlag: Berlin (2004), 573–591

———, The Right of Resistance and Human Rights, in: UNESCO, Violations of Human Rights: Possible Rights of Recourse and Forms of Resistance, UNESCO: Paris (1984), 13–33

Tonkin, Hannah, Defensive Force under the Rome Statute, Melbourne Journal of International Law, vol. 6 (2005), 86–117

Trechsel, Stefan & Pieth, Mark (eds.), Schweizerisches Strafgesetzbuch, Praxiskommentar, 2. Auflage, Dike Verlag: Zürich/St. Gallen (2nd ed., 2012)

Trumbull, Charles P., The Basis of Unit Self-Defense and Implications for the Use of Force, Duke Journal of Comparative and International Law, vol. 23 (2012) 121–148

Turner, Ian, Human Rights and Antiterrorism: A Positive Legal Duty to Infringe Freedom From Torture?, Studies in Conflict & Terrorism, vol. 35 (11) (2012), 760–778

Twinning, W.L. & P.E., Bentham on Torture, Northern Ireland Law Quarterly, vol. 24 (1973), 305–356

Tyranowski, Jerzy, Der Grundsatz der souveränen Gleichheit der Staaten und der Grundsatz der Selbstbestimmung der Völker, in: Vorträge, Reden und Berichte aus dem Europa-Institut, vol. 234, Europa Institut: Saarbrücken (1991)

Uniacke, Suzanne, Self-Defense and Natural Law, American Journal of Jurisprudence, vol. 36 (1991), 73–101

van Dijk, Pieter et al., Theory and Practice of the European Convention on Human Rights, Intersentia: Antwerpen (4th ed., 2006)

Velu, Jacques & Ergec, Rusen, La Convention européenne des droits de I 'homme, Bruylant : Brussels (1990)

Villamur, Roger & Delafosse, Maurice, Les Coutumnes Agni, rédigées et codifies d'après les documents officiels les plus récents, Challamel: Paris (1904)

Violence Policy Center, Firearm Justifiable Homicides and Non-Fatal Self-Defense Gun Use, Violence Policy Center: Washington, D.C. (2015)

Vitoria, Francisco, De Indis et de Ivre Belli Reflectiones (Ernest Nys., ed.; John Pawley Bate, transl.), Carnegie Institution: Washington, D.C. (1917)

Volokh, Eugene, Burden and Quantum of Proof as to Self-Defense (2013), http://volokh.com/2013/07/14/burden-and-quantum-of-proof-on-self-defense

———, Medical Self-Defense: Prohibited Experimental Therapies and Payment for Organs, Harvard Law Review, vol. 120 (2007), 1813–1846

von Scherenberg, Carl-Friedrich, Die sozialethischen Einschränkungen der Notwehr, Peter Lang: Frankfurt a.M. (2009)

Wallace, Shana, Beyond Imminence: Evolving International Law and Battered Women's Right to Self-Defense, University of Chicago Law Review, vol. 71, 1749–1781 (2004)

Wallerstein, Shlomit, Justifying Self-Defense: A Theory of Forced Consequences, Virginia Law Review, vol. 91 (2005), 999–1035

Warraich, Sohail Akbar, Honour killings and the law in Pakistan, in: Lynn Welchman & Sara Hossain (eds.), "Honour": Crimes, Paradigms and Violence against Women, Zed Books: London (2005)

Wasserman, David, Justifying Self-Defense, Philosophy & Public Affairs, vol. 16 (1987), 356–378

Webster, Daniel & Ludwig, Jens, Myths about Defensive Gun Use and Permissive Gun Carry Laws, Berkeley Media Studies Group (2000), http://www.bmsg.org/pdfs/myths.pdf

Weigend, Thomas, Notwehr im Völkerstrafrecht, in: Ulrich Sieber et al. (eds.), Strafrecht und Wirtschaftsstrafrecht—Dogmatik, Rechtsvergleich, Rechtstatsachen: Festschrift für Klaus Tiedemann zum 70. Geburtstag (2008), 1439–1451

Wen-Tzu, Understanding the Mysteries, No. 80 (trans. Thomas Cleary), in: Thomas Cleary (ed.), The Taoist Classics, Shambhala Publications: Boston (1999)

Werle, Georg, Principles of International Criminal Law, TMC Asser Press: The Hague (2nd ed., 2009)

White, Nigel D., Defending Humanity: When Force is Justified and Why [Book Review], Melbourne Journal of International Law, vol. 10 (2009), 379–393

Williams, Lily Tang, Guns against Tyranny, National Review, 7 September 2013, http://www.nationalreview.com/article/357877/guns-against-tyranny-lily-tang-william

Wittemann, Frank, Grundlinien und Grenzen der Notwehr in Europa, Peter Lang: Frankfurt a.M. (1997)

Wittreck, Fabian, Menschenwürde und Folterverbot, Die öffentliche Verwaltung (DöV) 2003, 873–882

Wolfe, George W., The Spiritual Power of Nonviolence, JOMAR Press: Austin (2012)

Wolter, Jürgen (ed.), SK-StPO: Systematischer Kommentar zur Strafprozessordnung, Band X: EMRK, Carl Heymanns: Köln (4th ed., 2012)

Wong, Meagan S., Targeted Killings and the International Legal Framework: With Particular Reference to the US Operation against Osama Bin Laden, Chinese Journal of International Law, vol. 11(1) (2012), 127–163

Wortley, B. A., Some jurisprudential reflections on human rights and self-defence, in: Heinrich Kipp (ed.), Um Recht und Freiheit: Festschrift für Friedrich August Freiherr von der Heydte zur Vollendung des 70. Lebensjahres, Duncker and Humblot: Berlin (1977), 751–758

Wynn, Kelli, Murder charge denied due to self-defense law, prosecutors say, Dayton Daily News, 27 October 2011, http://www.daytondailynews.com/news/news/local/murder-charge-denied-due-to-self-defense-law-prose/nMwqL

Yadav, R.D., Law of Crime and Self-Defence, Mittal Publications: New Delhi (1993)

Yeo, Stanley, Anglo-African Perspectives on Self-Defence, African Journal of International and Comparative Law, vol. 17 (2009), 118–135

Zahar, Alexander & Sluiter, Göran, International Criminal Law: A Critical Introduction, Oxford University Press: Oxford (2008)

Zeiss Stange, Mary, From Domestic Terrorism to Armed Revolution: Women's Right to Self-Defense as an Essential Human Right, Journal of Law of Economics and Policy, vol. 2 (2006), 385–411

Zemach, Ariel, Can Occupation Resulting from a War of Self-Defense Become Illegal?, Minnesota Journal of International Law, vol. 24 (2015), 313–350

Zieschang, Frank, Tödliche Notwehr zur Verteidigung von Sachen und Art. 2 IIa EMRK, Goltdammer's Archiv für Strafrecht 2006, 415–419

Zimring, Franklin, Firearms, Violence, and the Potential Impact of Firearms Control, Journal of Law, Medicine & Ethics, vol. 32 (2004), 34–37

Zipes, Douglas P., Sudden Cardiac Arrest and Death Associated with Application of Shocks from a TASER Electronic Control Device, Circulation [American Heart Association], vol. 125 (2012), 2417–2422

Index

www.ingramcontent.com/pod-product-compliance
Ingram Content Group UK Ltd.
Pitfield, Milton Keynes, MK11 3LW, UK
UKHW041434160926
475595UK00019B/18

9 780190 655020